HISTORICAL DICTIONARY

The historical dictionaries present essential information on a broad range of subjects, including American and world history, art, business, cities, countries, cultures, customs, film, global conflicts, international relations, literature, music, philosophy, religion, sports, and theater. Written by experts, all contain highly informative introductory essays on the topic and detailed chronologies that, in some cases, cover vast historical time periods but still manage to heavily feature more recent events.

Brief A–Z entries describe the main people, events, politics, social issues, institutions, and policies that make the topic unique, and entries are cross-referenced for ease of browsing. Extensive bibliographies are divided into several general subject areas, providing excellent access points for students, researchers, and anyone wanting to know more. Additionally, maps, photographs, and appendixes of supplemental information aid high school and college students doing term papers or introductory research projects. In short, the historical dictionaries are the perfect starting point for anyone looking to research in these fields.

HISTORICAL DICTIONARIES OF PROFESSIONS AND INDUSTRIES

Jon Woronoff, Series Editor

Journalism, by Ross Eaman, 2009.
U.S. Maritime Industry, by Kenneth J. Blume, 2012.
Librarianship, by Mary Ellen Quinn, 2014.
Japanese Business, Second Edition, by Stuart D. B. Picken, 2016.
Fashion Industry, Second Edition, by Francesca Sterlacci and Joanne Arbuckle, 2017.
Petroleum Industry, Second Edition, by Marius S. Vassiliou, 2018.
American Music Industry, by Keith Hatschek and Veronica A. Wells, 2018.
American Criminal Justice, by Matthew J. Sheridan, Raymond R. Rainville, Anna King, Brian Royster, and Giuseppe M. Fazari, 2019.

Historical Dictionary of American Criminal Justice

Matthew J. Sheridan, Raymond R. Rainville, Anna King,
Brian Royster, and Giuseppe M. Fazari

ROWMAN & LITTLEFIELD
Lanham • Boulder • New York • London

Published by Rowman & Littlefield
A wholly owned subsidiary of The Rowman & Littlefield Publishing Group, Inc.
4501 Forbes Boulevard, Suite 200, Lanham, Maryland 20706
www.rowman.com

6 Tinworth Street, London SE11 5AL

British Library Cataloguing in Publication Information Available

Library of Congress Cataloging-in-Publication Data

Names: Sheridan, Matthew J., 1948–, editor. | Rainville, Raymond R., 1943–, editor. | King, Anna, 1970–, editor. | Royster, Brian (Brian Lee), editor. | Fazari, Giuseppe (Giuseppe M.), editor.
Title: Historical dictionary of American criminal justice / Matthew J. Sheridan, Raymond R. Rainville, Anna King, Brian Royster, Giuseppe M. Fazari.
Description: Lanham : Rowman & Littlefield, [2019] | Series: Historical dictionaries of professions and industries | Includes bibliographical references.
Identifiers: LCCN 2018040420 (print) | LCCN 2018053011 (ebook) | ISBN 9781538111413 (Electronic) | ISBN 9781538111406 (cloth : alk. paper)
Subjects: LCSH: Criminal justice, Administration of—United States—History—Dictionaries. | Criminal law—United States—History—Dictionaries.
Classification: LCC HV7411 (ebook) | LCC HV7411 .H57 2019 (print) | DDC 363.97303—dc23
LC record available at https://lccn.loc.gov/2018040420

∞ ™ The paper used in this publication meets the minimum requirements of American National Standard for Information Sciences Permanence of Paper for Printed Library Materials, ANSI/NISO Z39.48-1992.

Printed in the United States of America.

To Raymond R. Rainville, Ph.D. (Feb. 21, 1943–Nov. 16, 2018), our coauthor, friend, colleague, and at time conscience, who could always be counted on to redefine what goodness should be in life. You will be missed, and your contributions never forgotten. We love you.—Matt, Anna, Brian, & Joe

* * *

To my wife, Lynda, daughter, McKenzie, sister, Catherine, and brothers, Edward and Paul: a family who understands the importance of history.—MJS

For Pat, my wife, life support, and friend. Always there when I needed you.—RRR

For Kyle and Maylth, and to the keepers of history, the time you devote to the past colors our future in so many ways.—AKD

To the memory of my mother, Edith R. Royster (1937–2012).—BLR

For my parents, Michael and Antonietta, who defined for me the most important of words: love and support.—GMF

Contents

Editor's Foreword

American criminal justice, starting from a rudimentary state three centuries ago, has developed into one of the most complete and sophisticated systems in the world and has become a model for many other countries. It is more responsive to change than is taught in schools, to say nothing of its portrayal in popular literature, television, and cinema. But not everything we know—or think we know—about American criminal justice is correct. This historical dictionary, therefore, should be of interest to a broad array of readers. The evolution of criminal justice is presented in the chronology and then more fully explained in the introduction. The dictionary section explains in detail the various aspects of the American criminal justice system. Not everyone will need more information, but if you do, the extensive bibliography provides a great number of additional sources.

Historical Dictionary of American Criminal Justice was written by five specialists on the topic with a broad range of specializations and an impressive number of achievements. Matthew J. Sheridan, who led the team, is a convict criminologist on the faculty of Georgian Court University. Raymond R. Rainville is a specialist in corrections, teaching at Saint Peter's University, and past president of the New Jersey Association of Criminal Justice Educators. Brian L. Royster spent 25 years with the New Jersey State Police and is a professional mediator, certified crisis negotiator, and longtime member of Saint Peter's College. Anna King deals with female criminology and corrections and is an associate professor and chair at Georgian Court University. Giuseppe M. Fazari, a trial court administrator, is on the faculty of the National Center for State Courts and is past president of the New Jersey Association of Criminal Justice Educators. More information can be found in the "About the Authors" section at the end of the book.

Jon Woronoff
Series Editor

Preface

> I have striven not to laugh at human actions, not to weep at them, not to hate them, but to understand them.
> —Baruch Spinoza, *Tractatus Politicus*, 1676

This text centers on the American experience of criminal justice, particularly during the last 50 years as criminal justice has developed as an independent academic discipline and area of study. Criminal justice is an inherently multidisciplinary endeavor, emerging across time and place through the fields of philosophy, law, biology, anthropology, and sociology. Criminal justice professionals likewise represent a broad area of specialized knowledge and expertise across legal, criminological, psychological, sociological, and administrative fields. As such, the people who inhabit the discipline, like the fields of study from which American criminal justice materialized, inevitably take residence in unique perspectives that are a reflection of the knowledge, experiences, and normative judgments associated with their respective areas of expertise. Where we have been aware of how these subjectivities might create biases and/or blind spots, we have tried to compensate.

Criminal justice is not only interdisciplinary; it is also dynamic. Developments in criminal justice happen quickly and regularly, the meanings of which are deeply embedded, not only in a historical context but in complicated social, economic, and political circumstances as well. Accordingly, some terms covered will be reflective of the period out of which we are writing, while others are more immutable.

We have aimed to provide readers with an unrestricted, easily accessible, historical overview of the field in a climate where the general public and specialists alike are increasingly hungry for broader and more in-depth information about criminal justice and its relationship to freedom, liberty, and the pursuit of happiness in modern American life. Our long-term intention is to provide readers with a fuller story of criminal justice that is critical to the development of informed opinions and rational decision making. In the short term, our objective is less abstract: to give clarity to the multiplicity of professional jargon that composes the multilayered criminal justice system. Below we expand upon the reasons for writing such a book and clarify some of our fundamental assumptions about the nature of history as it applies to the realm of criminal justice.

There has perhaps never been a more important time for those involved in criminal justice policy, operations, and civil service to know their history. Criminal justice is a field particularly vulnerable to the exploitations of power—being as closely aligned with the forces of social control as it is. Power exists where people believe it exists, and the backstory to knowledge, so integral to its substance, can easily be manipulated for the benefit of those in power. The terms selected for inclusion in this text, and our interpretation of their significance, have heightened our awareness of the mediated and political nature of historical knowledge. Combined with the volatility of global and domestic politics today, questions about the value of truth and the nature of reality press upon our collective conscience in more concrete ways than they ever have before; the mere intellectual titillations of postmodern discourse have seemingly manifested into the everyday existence of modern life. For many, this is an undesirable state of affairs; for others, the notion of multiple, equally credible perspectives is liberating. We take a position somewhere in the middle, that perhaps in especially divisive political environments, generally agreed upon facts that help to develop a common narrative about our past serve constructive purposes.

Recalling events of the recent past can help identify levels of credibility in different perspectives. For instance, under the Donald Trump administration, a motion was put forth to cease the practice of federal consent decrees. The discontinuance of a policy that allows for federal oversight of state and local law enforcement and criminal justice operations might be appealing absent a memory of not-so-distant occurrences. For instance, in 2001, the Los Angeles Police Department, long marred by allegations of police misconduct (e.g., the Rodney King beating in 1991 and the 1992 Los Angeles riots) was finally put under a federal decree that lasted more than a decade. The policy of federal decree once applied to the LAPD brought about impressive reform in the department. Likewise, in the Northeast, following the deaths of four African American motorists during a traffic stop, the New Jersey State Police came under federal decree. After a decade of forced oversight, allegations of racial profiling and other forms of inequitable policing decreased, and state police training improved. Assessments of criminal justice policy need not be guided by the achievements and failures of the past but must be considered if one is to engage in a process of informed decision making. A judgment regarding the policy of federal decree that does not take into account past events can easily result in a belief that federal decree is reducible to the power needs of big government. This is a more challenging position to hold in light of the positive, practical impacts that the practice has evidenced throughout history.

Knowledge of the broader context of the historical trends within which the American criminal justice system has developed serves a similar function. Organizations that have arisen to combat racial conflict in the United States (e.g., the Anti-Defamation League and American Civil Liberties Union) and the frequency with which so many otherwise reputable figures from the past have been involved in one form of prejudicial action or another (e.g., Barnes) remind us of the importance of checks and balances. A civic atmosphere that allows for the emergence of organizations such as these is easy to take for granted in our modern American justice system—a system that in a global context is and always has been oriented toward due process.

Reader's Notes

There is extensive cross-referencing to enhance the usefulness of the dictionary as a reference tool. Some terms have no description, just a "*See*" reference to direct the reader to another associated term. The same is true for "*See also*" references, which appear at the end of terms. These direct the reader to related terms and therefore a more complete description. We hope these tools will contribute to your appreciation of the underlying history of American criminal justice.

An in-depth chronology and array of appendixes provide an abridged, albeit thorough, account of the most relevant considerations in American criminal justice. The appendixes include abbreviated lists of the most noteworthy Supreme Court decisions, including death penalty cases and the U.S. Constitution's Bill of Rights (the hallmark document of American criminal justice). Finally, readers will find a wide-ranging bibliography that provides sources from which the dictionary is largely comprised, as well as a broad list of literature for those interested in further investigation.

Acronyms and Abbreviations

AA	Alcoholics Anonymous
AAFS	American Academy of Forensic Sciences
ABA	American Bar Association
ABC	American Board of Criminalistics
ABF	American Bar Foundation
ABFO	American Board of Forensic Odontology
ACA	American Correctional Association
ACJS	Academy of Criminal Justice Sciences
ACLU	American Civil Liberties Union
ADAM	Arrestee Drug Abuse Monitoring
Add Health	National Longitudinal Study of Adolescent to Adult Health
ADHD	attention deficit/hyperactivity disorder
ADL	Anti-Defamation League
ADR	alternative dispute resolution
AFIS	Automated Fingerprint Identification System for the Classification of Fingerprints
AIC	Australian Institute of Criminology
AIM	American Indian Movement
AJA	American Jail Association
ALI	American Law Institute
ALKN	Almighty Latin King Nation
ALKQN	Almighty Latin King and Queen Nation
AMA	American Medical Association
AMBER	America's Missing: Broadcast Emergency Response Alert
AMW	*America's Most Wanted*
ANZSOC	Australian and New Zealand Society of Criminology

AOD	alcohol and other drugs
APB	all-points bulletin
APPA	American Probation and Parole Association
APW	all-ports warning
ARIMA	autoregressive integrated moving average
ASC	American Society of Criminology
ASIS	American Society for Industrial Security
ASV	American Society of Victimology
ATF	Bureau of Alcohol, Tobacco, and Firearms
BARJ	balanced and restorative justice
BAU	behavioral analysis unit
BJS	Bureau of Justice Statistics
BOLO	be on the lookout
BOP	(Federal) Bureau of Prisons
BSISU	Behavioral Science Investigative Support Unit
BSU	Behavioral Science Unit
BTK	bind, torture, kill
BWS	battered woman syndrome
CALEA	Commission on Accreditation of Law Enforcement Agencies
CASA	court-appointed special advocate
CBT	cognitive behavioral therapy
CCA	Correctional Corporation of America
CCH	Computerized Criminal History
CCJA	Canadian Criminal Justice Association
CDC	Center for Disease Control and Prevention
CDS	controlled dangerous substance
CFAA	Computer Fraud and Abuse Act
CHINS	child in need of supervision
CIA	Central Intelligence Agency
CICJ	Center for International Criminal Justice
CJ	criminal justice

CNU	Crisis Negotiation Unit
CODIS	Combined DNA Index System
COINTELPRO	Counter Intelligence Program
COPS	Office of Community Oriented Policing Services
CPTED	crime prevention through environmental design
CRIPA	Civil Rights of Institutionalized Persons Act
CSA	Covenant, Sword, and Arm of the Lord
CSAP	Center for Substance Abuse Prevention
CSAT	Center for Substance Abuse Treatment
CSFS	Chartered Society of Forensic Sciences
CSG	Council of State Governments
CSI	Crime Scene Investigation
CSPV	Center for the Study and Prevention of Violence
DARE	Drug Abuse Resistance Education
DEA	Drug Enforcement Agency
DMC	disproportionate minority confinement
DNA	deoxyribonucleic acid
DSM	*Diagnostic and Statistical Manual of Mental Disorders*
DUI	driving under the influence
DWB	driving while black
ECPA	Electronic Communications Privacy Act
FBI	Federal Bureau of Investigation
FCI	federal correctional institution
FCPA	Foreign Corrupt Practices Act
FDA	Food and Drug Administration
FEMA	Federal Emergency Management System
FFT	functional family therapy
FLETC	Federal Law Enforcement Training Center
FOIA	Freedom of Information Act
FOP	Fraternal Order of Police
FPC	federal prison camp
FSAB	Forensic Specialties Accreditation Board

FTIR	Fourier Transform Infrared Spectroscopy
GPS	Global Positioning System
GREAT	Gang Resistance Education and Training
GST	general strain theory
IACP	International Association of Chiefs of Police
IAFIS	Integrated Automated Fingerprint Identification System for the Classification of Fingerprints
IAPP	International Association of Police Professors
ICCA	International Community Corrections Association
ICD	International Classification of Diseases
ICVS	International Crime Victim Survey
IED	improvised explosive device
INS	Immigration and Naturalization Service
INTERPOL	International Criminal Police Organization
IRS	Internal Revenue Service
ISIL	Islamic State in Iraq and the Levant
ISIS	Islamic State in Iraq and Syria
ISP	Intensive Supervision Program (Parole and Probation)
ISU	Investigative Support Unit
JDAI	Juvenile Detention Alternative Initiative
JINS	juvenile in need of supervision
K & A	knock and announce
KGB	Komitet Gosudarstvennoy Bezopasnosti
KKK	Ku Klux Klan
LEAA	Law Enforcement Assistance Administration
LEOSA	Law Enforcement Officers Safety Act
LKN	Latin King Nation
LSA	Law and Society Association
LSD	lysergic acid diethylamide
MADD	Mothers against Drunk Driving
MAGLOCLEN	Middle Atlantic Great Lakes Organized Crime Law Enforcement Network
MDB	minimal brain dysfunction

MDPV	methylenedioxypyrovalerone
MLI	McDonald Laurier Institute
MO	modus operandi
MPC	Model Penal Code
MPD	multiple personality disorder
MRI	magnetic resonance imaging
MST	multisystemic therapy
N.A.	Narcotics Anonymous
NACDL	National Association of Criminal Defense Lawyers
NACJD	National Archive of Criminal Justice Data
NACPTO	National Association of College Police Training Officials
NamUs	National Missing and Unidentified Persons Systems
NAPO	National Association of Police Organizations
NAS	National Academy of Sciences
NCAVC	National Center for the Analysis of Violent Crime
NCCD	National Council on Crime and Delinquency
NCETR	National Center for Explosives Training and Research
NCHIP	National Criminal History Record Improvement Program
NCHS	National Center for Health Statistics
NCIC	National Crime Information Center
NCJA	National Criminal Justice Association
NCJFCJ	National Council of Juvenile and Family Court Judges
NCJJ	National Center for Juvenile Justice
NCJRS	National Criminal Justice Reference Service
NCOVR	National Consortium on Violence Research
NCPC	National Crime Prevention Council
NCRS	National Crime Recording Standard
NCVC	National Center for Victims of Crime
NCVS	National Crime Victimization Survey
NDAA	National District Attorneys Association
NGC	National Gang Center

NIBRS	National Incident-Based Reporting System
NIC	National Institute of Corrections
NIDA	National Institute on Drug Abuse
NIJ	National Institute of Justice
NIMBY	"Not in My Back Yard"
NOBLE	National Organization of Black Law Enforcement Executives
NORC	National Opinion Research Center
NORML	National Organization for the Reform of Marijuana Laws
NOVA	National Organization for Victim Assistance
NRA	National Rifle Association
NSA	National Security Agency
NSA	National Sheriffs Association
NSF	National Science Foundation
NVDRS	National Violent Death Reporting System
NYPD	New York City Police Department
OBTS	Offender Based Transaction Statistics
OJJDP	Office of Juvenile Justice and Delinquency Prevention
OJP	Office of Justice Programs
OMVI	Operating a Motor Vehicle under the Influence
ONDCP	Office of National Drug Control Policy
OR	own recognizance
OVC	Office for Victims of Crime
OVW	Office on Violence against Women
PBA	Patrolmen's (Policemen's) Benevolent Associations
PC	protective custody
PCL-R	Psychopathy Check List–Revised
PCR	polymerase chain reaction
PERF	Police Executive Research Forum
PHDCN	Project on Human Development in Chicago Neighborhoods
PIC	promotions in custody

PINS	person in need of supervision
PIS	post-incarceration supervision
PLO	Palestinian Liberation Organization
POMC	Parents of Murdered Children
PREA	Prison Rape Elimination Act
PROMIS	Prosecutor's Management Information System
PTC	Police Training Commission
PTI	pretrial intervention
PTSD	posttraumatic stress disorder
PSI	presentence investigation
RCMP	Royal Canadian Mounted Police
RDCJN	Racial Democracy, Crime and Justice Network
RFLP	restriction fragment length polymorphism
RICO	Racketeer Influenced Corrupt Organization
RISS	Regional Information Sharing System
RLUIPA	Religious Land Use and Institutionalized Persons Act
ROR	release on own recognizance
ROTC	Reserve Army Officer Training Corps
SAC	statistical analysis center
SACB	Subversive Activities Control Board
SAFE	sexual assault forensic examination
SAMHSA	Substance Abuse and Mental Health Services Administration
SANE	sexual assault nurse examiner
SHR	supplementary homicide reports
SJI	State Justice Institute
SLA	Symbionese Liberation Army
SLAM	Society for Laws against Molesters
SMART	Office of Sex Offender Sentencing, Monitoring, Apprehending, Registering, and Tracking
SORNA	Sex Offender Registration and Notification Act
SPLC	Southern Poverty Law Center
SSA	Social Security Act

STOP	Stop Turning Out Prisoners
SWAT	Special Weapons and Tactics
TASC	Treatment Alternatives to Street Crime
TSC	Terrorist Screening Center
UCMJ	Uniform Code of Military Justice
UCR	Uniform Crime Report
UNODC	United Nations Office on Drugs and Crime
USCIS	United States Citizenship and Immigration Services
USDB	United States Disciplinary Barracks
USP	United States Penitentiary
VAWA	Violence against Women Act
VCIT	Violent Crime Impact Team
VICAP	Violent Criminal Apprehension Program
VORP	Violent Offender Reconciliation Program
VWPA	Victim and Witness Protection Act
WAR	White Aryan Resistance
WITSEC	Witness Security Program
WMD	weapon of mass destruction
WSV	World Society of Victimology
WUO	Weather Underground Organization

Chronology

Approximately 430,000 B.C. Spain: In 2015, archeologists uncovered a skull in Spain. The skull was in 52 pieces, and after reconstruction it was determined that there were two blunt force-trauma-injuries around the eyes. The type of injuries has led the prehistoric man to be called "The First Murder."

Prior to 3500 B.C. Middle East: Precivilization farming communities slowly develop in the Middle East. As individuals and groups began living and working in closer proximity to one another, the potential for land disputes and the general occurrence of crime increased and, in some instances, endured into blood feuds.

3500 B.C. Sumer: The first known civilization, Sumer, is established as the first city-state model of government to settle disputes.

2050 B.C. Mesopotamia: The earliest known legal code, Ur-Nammu's Code, is established.

1754 B.C. Babylonia: The Code of King Hammurabi of Babylonia, ancient Mesopotamia, is known to be the oldest written collection of laws.

621 B.C. Greece: Draco's Law, the first documented laws of Greece, is written by a Greek citizen for Athens and introduces the concept of the state's exclusive role in administering punishment to those convicted of crimes.

509 B.C. Roman Empire: During the reign of the Roman Empire, its military served as the governing body's law enforcement.

428–347 B.C. Greece: The Greek philosopher Plato, a student of Socrates, introduced the concept that humans are inherently good, which would come to influence views of crime and punishment.

399 B.C. Greece: The trial of Socrates occurred, and he was convicted and sentenced to death for corrupting the youth and not believing in the gods.

384–327 B.C. Greece: The Greek philosopher Aristotle, a student of Plato and a tutor to Alexander the Great, expounded upon the study of science and scientific observation, which would later influence forensics and crime investigations.

44 B.C. Roman Empire: The first recorded autopsy is performed on Julius Caesar following his assassination.

50–70 Greece: The Greek physician Pedanius Dioscorides categorizes various plants, their medicinal effects, and symptoms of poisoning. The work *De Materia Medica* is considered as the foundation of forensic toxicology.

500–1000 The decline of the Roman Empire leads to destabilization in the Western world and a return to kin policing, in which clans police themselves and mete out punishment on their own terms.

1215 England: The Magna Carta charter is agreed to by King John of England at Runnymede to make peace with a group of rebel barons.

1265–1274 Saint Thomas Aquinas composes the *Summa Theologica*, in which he espoused the notion of the natural law, building on Plato's philosophy, and suggested that crime was an affront to God and that, since people are inherently good, crime damaged not only the victim but the criminal as well.

1300–1600 The Renaissance period influenced attitudes toward government, crime, and punishment.

1447 France: The missing teeth of the French Duke of Burgundy were used to identify remains in what was the first use of dentistry to solve a crime.

1514 England: Blood spatter evidence is used for the first time in London during the trial of Richard Hunne.

1608 Virginia: The first colonial government to perform an execution (George Kendal) for spying on Spain.

1635 Boston, Massachusetts: The first system of law enforcement in the 13 colonies. The system was referred to as the "night watch," and officers were appointed on a part-time basis and without pay.

1650 The pistol is developed.

1692 Massachusetts: The Salem witch trials are held in Salem, Massachusetts, where more than 300 people are accused of practicing witchcraft and 20 are eventually executed.

1751 Philadelphia: The first police department in the United States is established.

1764 Italy: The Italian lawyer and philosopher Cesare Beccaria publishes his best-known work, *On Crimes and Punishments*, calling for a fixed scale in which the severity of the punishment would increase with the severity of the crime.

1787 Pennsylvania: The Constitution of the United States of America is signed in Philadelphia, and the original seven articles formed the basis of the first republican government.

1789 Washington, D.C.: The U.S. Supreme Court is created, becoming the highest appellate court of the United States. The U.S. Congress creates the first federal law enforcement officer position, the U.S. marshal—13 of whom were appointed by President George Washington.

1790 Philadelphia, Pennsylvania: The Walnut Street Jail begins the penitentiary experiment in the United States.

1791 Washington, D.C.: The Bill of Rights is added to the U.S. Constitution. **New York:** Sheriff Cornelius Hogeboom of Hudson is shot while serving a writ of ejectment, becoming the first law enforcement officer in the United States to be killed in the line of duty.

1803 Washington, D.C.: The U.S. Supreme Court ruling in *Marbury v. Madison*, 5 U.S. 137 (1803), upholds the supremacy of the U.S. Constitution and maintains its power to strike down any action by a federal or state legislative body in contravention of the Constitution.

1810 France: The Napoleonic Code is established.

1827 Belgium: Adolphe Quetelet, a Belgian statistician, reviewed the national crime statistics from France and identified correlations between crime and demographics, which included age, gender, education, and socioeconomic status.

1829 England: The Metropolitan Police Service was established in London, marking the first full-time, uniformed, and professional police force. Sir Robert Peel's nine principles of policing were issued to every officer.

1829 Philadelphia: Eastern State Penitentiary is built; this marks the birth of the modern prison.

1835 Texas: The Texas Rangers are created to be the first statewide law enforcement agency in the United States.

1840 England: Alexander Maconochie, a naval captain, institutes a primitive form of parole at Norfolk Island.

1841 Boston, Massachusetts: John Augustus, "Father of Probation," convinces a judge to turn over custody of a convicted offender.

1847 Michigan: The first government in the English-speaking world to abolish the death penalty. They retained capital punishment for treason. **Massachusetts:** Miller Lyman School for Boys established as the state reform school.

1850 Chicago, Illinois: The Pinkerton National Detective Agency becomes the first detective agency. It is founded by Allan Pinkerton, who received national recognition after uncovering a plot to assassinate Abraham Lincoln in 1861. He would later become the chief of the federal secret service during the Civil War. **California:** The first state prison opens in California on a ship named *Waban* to house the criminal element that had come to the state as a part of the gold rush.

1852 Rhode Island: The first state to ban the death penalty for all crimes.

1859 Italy: The psychiatrist and criminologist Cesare Lombroso founds the Positivist School of Criminology and suggests psychological and biological links to criminal behavior.

1861 New York: The first parole system was created by Zebulon Brockway, who devised the "indeterminate sentencing" concept while serving as the warden for the Detroit House of Corrections.

1865 Washington, D.C.: President Abraham Lincoln approves the formation of the U.S. Secret Service. Lincoln is assassinated by John Wilkes Booth.

1865–1891 West Virginia and Kentucky: The active period of the Hatfield and McCoy feud.

1866 United Kingdom: The Howard League for Penal Reform, a nonprofit organization, is established.

1871 Fairfax, Virginia: The National Rifle Association (NRA) is a nonprofit organization founded by William C. Church and George W. Wingate.

1876 New York: Zebulon Brockway, "Father of American Parole," institutes parole at Elmira Reformatory. The first reformatory is established at Elmira.

1880 United Kingdom: Henry Faulds and William Herschel publish a study in *Nature* demonstrating that fingerprints were unique to individuals.

1881 Tombstone, Arizona: The Wild West's most famous gunfight, at the O.K. Corral, is won by Wyatt Earp and other lawmen.

1882 Saint Joseph, Missouri: Jesse James is killed by another fugitive in his own gang.

1884 United States: The Pullman Strike developed into full-scale riots with armed police intervention.

1887 United Kingdom: Arthur Conan Doyle publishes his first Sherlock Holmes story.

1888 New York: Doctor Julius Myer Blount proposed lethal injection and claimed it to be cheaper than hanging. George Eastman's revolutionary Kodak camera became widely available and used to photograph and document crime scenes.

1890 New York: William Kemmler becomes the first person executed by electrocution on 6 August 1890 at Auburn Correctional Facility.

1891 Washington, D.C.: Three Prisons Act of 1891 is established.

1892 Argentina: The first fingerprint classification system is created by Juan Vucetich while working for the Central Police Department in La Plata, Argentina. The system was referred to as the "comparative dactyloscopy" and was used to identify the bloody fingerprint at the scene of a double homicide.

1893 United States: The National Chiefs of Police Union, later renamed as the International Association of Chiefs of Police, is formed.

1895 Kansas: The first federal prison, USP Leavenworth, is opened.

1899 Chicago, Illinois: The United States' first juvenile court for youth under the age of 16 is established to provide rehabilitation in lieu of punishment.

1901 Chicago, Illinois: A method for using hydrogen peroxide to detect traces of blood through oxidation is discovered.

1902 United States: Fingerprinting is first used by law enforcement.

1905 Pennsylvania: The first state police agency is created as recommended by Theodore Roosevelt's Anthracite Strike Commission and Governor Samuel Pennypacker. The department became a model for other state police agencies throughout the nation.

1908 Washington, D.C.: An act of Congress created the Bureau of Investigators, the antecedent organization to the FBI, employing 25 investigators. The organization was created after Charles Bonaparte lobbied Congress in 1906 for a team of investigators who could pursue specific types of crimes. **Oregon:** The first U.S. paid policewoman, Lola Baldwin, is officially sworn in as a part of a program to protect visitors, particularly unsuspecting women, during the Lewis and Clark Exposition fair in Portland.

1910 France: The father of crime scene investigation, Dr. Edmond Locard, establishes the first crime lab in two attic rooms at the Lyon, France, police department. **Washington, D.C.:** The Mann Act, which is also referred to as the White-Slave Traffic Act, is established.

1911 France: Vincenzo Peruggia, an employee of the Louvre museum in Paris, steals the *Mona Lisa* to bring the painting back to its place of origin in Florence, Italy.

1919 Washington, D.C.: Congress passes the National Motor Vehicle Theft Act, also known as the Dyer Act, which authorizes the FBI to investigate auto thefts that cross state lines.

1920 New York: The American Civil Liberties Union (ACLU) is formed. The nonprofit, nonpartisan organization was founded by Roger Nash Baldwin, Crystal Eastman, and Walter Nelles in response to the Palmer Raids in which thousands of antiwar protestors were arrested for the purposes of identifying suspected anarchists and radicals as they were referenced by Attorney General A. Mitchell Palmer.

1921 California: John Larson, a University of California medical student, invents the polygraph, the modern lie detector.

1923 Austria: The president of the Vienna, Austria, police force, Johannes Schober, creates the International Criminal Police Commission, a collaboration among Czechoslovakia, Poland, Austria, Belgium, China, Egypt, France, Germany, Greece, Hungary, Italy, the Netherlands, Romania, Sweden, Switzerland and Yugoslavia. The international police organization, now known as Interpol, is created. **California:** The Los Angeles Police Department establishes the first police department crime laboratory in the United States.

1924 Alderson, West Virginia: First women's prison is established. **Carson City, Nevada:** The gas chamber is used for execution for the first time. The first person executed in the gas chamber was Gee Jon.

1929 Alexandria, Virginia: The Uniform Crime Report (UCR) is created by the International Chiefs of Police, and the FBI is tasked with gathering statistics a year later. **Colorado:** Eight correctional officers are killed at the Colorado State Penitentiary, which was the deadliest incident at a correctional institution up to that time.

1932 New Jersey: The 20-month-old son of the famous aviator Charles Lindbergh Jr. is kidnapped and murdered. Forensic evidence led investigators to Bruno Hauptmann, who was later convicted and executed.

1934 California: Alcatraz becomes the prototype for the "supermax" prison. **France:** Dr. Edmond Locard publishes his exchange principle, a belief that a perpetrator of a crime will bring something to a crime scene and likewise leave with something from that scene, both of which can be used as forensic evidence. **Chicago:** The most notorious of gangsters during the Depression era, John Dillinger, is shot and killed by the FBI.

1934 Texas: Bonnie and Clyde are shot and killed by four Texas officers. **Washington, D.C.:** The Securities Exchange Act and the National Firearms Act are passed.

1936 Philippines: The first fingerprint technician is purported to be Agustin C. Patricio.

1945–1946 Germany: The Nuremberg war crimes trials are held in Nuremberg, where a panel of eight judges from the United States, the United Kingdom, France, and the Soviet Union tried Nazi officers for crimes against peace and humanity and for war crimes committed during World War II.

1947 Washington, D.C.: The CIA is created with the signing of the National Security Act.

1950 Washington, D.C.: The FBI director, J. Edgar Hoover, implements the FBI's "Ten Most Wanted Fugitives" program.

1957 Washington, D.C.: The U.S. Congress passes the Civil Rights Act, the first act of civil rights legislation since Reconstruction in America.

1962 Washington, D.C.: The Model Penal Code is formulated.

1963 Texas: Lee Harvey Oswald assassinates President John F. Kennedy. **Washington, D.C.:** The U.S. Supreme Court rules in *Gideon v. Wainwright*, 372 U.S. 335 (1963), that the Sixth Amendment guarantees a right to counsel in all criminal cases where defendants are charged with a serious offense, even if they cannot afford one themselves.

1966 Washington, D.C.: Juveniles are afforded due process rights following the *Kent v. United States*, 383 U.S. 541 (1966), ruling. The Supreme Court rules in *Miranda v. Arizona*, 384 U.S. 436 (1966), that all persons accused of a crime must be informed of their constitutional rights, including the right against self-incrimination and the right to an attorney.

1967 Texas: AT&T announces that the company will establish a special number, 911, for emergency calls to the police, fire, and other emergency services.

1968 Nashville, Tennessee: James Earl Ray assassinates Dr. Martin Luther King. **Washington, D.C.:** The Omnibus Crime Control and Safe Streets Act is passed.

1970 Washington, D.C.: The Racketeer Influenced and Corrupt Organization (RICO) Act is passed as part of the Organized Crime Control Act of 1970. The legislation was drafted by G. Robert Blakey and was originally written so that law enforcement could more effectively pursue the American Mafia, but it has since expanded to other realms of criminal activity.

1971 New York: Seven correctional officers are killed during riots at the Attica State Prison. **California:** The trial of Charles Manson is concluded, and Manson is sentenced to death. The death sentence was vacated by the U.S. Supreme Court's declaration of the penalty's unconstitutionality in 1972.

1972 Washington, D.C.: The National Institute of Justice initiates a project that leads to the development of body armor made from Kevlar, a fabric originally developed to replace steel belting for radial tires. The U.S. Supreme Court rules that Georgia's death penalty statute could be interpreted as cruel and unusual punishment.

1974 Washington, D.C.: The Office of Juvenile Justice and Delinquency Prevention (OJJDP) is signed into law.

1976 Washington, D.C.: The death penalty is reinstated in the United States in the Supreme Court ruling of *Gregg v. Georgia*, 428 U.S. 153 (1976).

1977 New York: New York City experiences a 25-hour blackout that results in massive looting and arson. The Son of Sam killer, later found to be David Berkowitz, sends perverse letters to the police and to the *New York Daily News* columnist Jimmy Breslin. **Washington, D.C.:** The Foreign Corrupt Practices Act is passed to address accounting transparency.

1978 Utah: Gary Gilmore is the first person to be executed following the reinstatement of the death penalty. The execution was by firing squad.

1981 Washington, D.C.: Sandra Day O'Connor becomes the first woman appointed to the U.S. Supreme Court.

1982 December 7 Texas: The first state to use lethal injection.

1984 Washington, D.C.: The Comprehensive Crime Control Act of 1984 is passed. DNA is first used for biological identification after a geneticist at the University of Leicester, Alec Jeffreys, discovers biological material on a slide that was left from his assistant. Dr. Jeffreys initially uses the discovery to solve an immigration issue that reunited an African boy with his family residing in England. He later used DNA to assist in the arrest and conviction of a suspect charged with the rape and murder of two girls. The events occurred three years apart. Digital and computer forensics are first developed by the FBI to examine computer evidence of a crime.

1986 Washington, D.C.: The U.S. Computer Fraud and Abuse Act is passed.

1987 Florida: DNA evidence is used for the first time in criminal court. Tommie Lee Andrews becomes the first person to be convicted using DNA analysis.

1988 New York: The earliest cyberattack is carried out by Robert Morris in 1988 with his "Morris worm," a malware computer program that slowed computers.

1989 Florida: The first drug court is established in Miami-Dade County. **Washington, D.C.:** Fawaz Younis becomes the first foreign terrorist sentenced by a U.S. district court for a crime against Americans on foreign soil. **Arlington, VA:** David Vasquez is the first person exonerated by DNA. **New Zealand:** The Family Group Conference concept is created.

1991 Portage, Wisconsin: The notorious serial killer Jeffrey Dahmer is arrested, and his subsequent insanity defense fails. **Washington, D.C.:** The National Law Enforcement Officers Memorial is dedicated.

1993 Washington, D.C.: Janet Reno becomes the first woman appointed as the U.S. attorney general. The Brady Handgun Violence Prevention Act is passed. **Waco, Texas:** Four U.S. Bureau of Alcohol, Tobacco, and Firearms (ATF) special agents are killed while attempting to execute a search warrant at a Branch Davidian compound.

1994 New Jersey: The New Jersey legislature enacts Megan's Law, which requires community notification when a sex offender is scheduled to be released, following the sexual assault and murder of Megan Kanka by a neighbor who, unknown to the victim's family, had been previously convicted of sex offenses against children.

1995 Oklahoma City, Oklahoma: The deadliest act of domestic terrorism on record is committed by Timothy McVeigh when he detonates a truck bomb that destroys the Alfred P. Murrah Federal Building. The explosion kills 168 and injures more than 600 people. **California:** O. J. Simpson is acquitted of the murders of Nicole Brown and Ronald Goldman.

1996 Lincoln, Montana: The FBI apprehends the Unabomber, Ted Kaczynski.

2001 New York: On 11 September, terrorist attacks occur on the World Trade Center and the Pentagon, and there is a related plane crash in Pennsylvania. **Washington, D.C.:** The U.S. Patriot Act is enacted—a controversial antiterrorism law that allows law enforcement to employ a series of tactics to secure the nation's borders and target international money laundering. **Washington:** The Green River serial killer, Gary Ridgway, pleads guilty to 48 murders after new DNA techniques are used to incriminate him of the killings committed decades earlier.

2002 Washington, D.C.: The Department of Homeland Security is formed to lead the unified national effort to secure America.

2004 Washington, D.C.: President George W. Bush signs the Justice for All Act, which significantly enhanced funding and guidelines for the use of DNA technology in the judicial process.

2010 Iran: First government-sanctioned use of sustained cyberwarfare called Stuxnet is used in targeting five of Iran's nuclear facilities, having been designed to destroy centrifuges used to enrich uranium. The United States purportedly collaborated with Israel on the attack to develop and launch the computer worm that spread through the Iranian facilities for a year before it was discovered.

2011 Pakistan: Osama bin Laden is killed by a team of U.S. Navy SEALs in his compound in Pakistan.

2012 The year of the greatest number of deaths by mass shootings up to that time. The shootings included Sandy Hook Elementary School with 20 children, aged six and seven, and seven adults.

2013 Boston, Massachusetts: On 15 April, brothers Dzhokhar and Tamerlan Tsarnaev set off two homemade bombs at the Boston Marathon, killing three and injuring approximately 260 more. Tamerlan was killed by police, and Dzhokhar was captured, tried, and is awaiting execution for the terrorist attack.

2015 Homicide increases 10 percent from previous year, and violent crime increases 4 percent.

2016 Violent crime in the United States increases for second year in a row.

2017 Las Vegas, Nevada: Worst mass shooting in U.S. history. Stephen Paddock on 1 October kills 58 and wounds 600 more. Devin Kelly, in a Baptist church (Sutherland Springs, Texas), on 5 November commits the deadliest shooting in Texas history, killing 26 and injuring 20 more. These and other shootings added to the debate over the purchase and possession of weapons.

Introduction

The United States is a federal republic, a representative democracy grounded in the U.S. Constitution that is populated with more than 310 million people living in 54 jurisdictions. Since the arrival of the first European settlers in the early 15th century, criminal justice has been a cornerstone to the foundation of American society. Crime in the early 21st century bears little resemblance to the legal structure and judicial practices that were in use during the founding of the colonies and the establishment of the republic. Indeed, the system of justice and the processes with which we attempt to understand and control criminal behavior have undergone a series of changes since those early years of the nation.

Urbanization, industrialization, westward migration, population growth, and the metamorphosis of crime, including the increasing prevalence of terrorism, have not changed the need to continually address the crime problem. What has changed, however, is how society has come to view and understand crime—that is, how we have come to define it—and how American civilization has attempted to develop strategies to prevent or otherwise address its effect on the population. The means by which crime is prevented, prosecuted, and penalized have undergone substantial change. In addition, the protections of individual rights have been subject to a more stringent review by the legislature and the judiciary to ensure a balanced system of justice. At times, the criminal justice system has also been affected by criminological research, which offers evidence to support needed or desired change. However, new legislative statutes are influenced by politicized constructs (such as the War on Drugs, the shift to a crime control model, or public reactions to terrorism and recent school shootings), which are not necessarily empirically grounded.

More fundamental are the profound shifts in attitude toward what leads to crime and what should be done to control it—the systemic responses to criminal events. From an early emphasis on "degenerate and immoral" individuals, views regarding the causes of crime have increasingly focused on social and psychological factors as well as the biological and neurological effects that contribute to criminality.

THE FOUNDATION OF CRIMINAL JUSTICE

The originators of the U.S. Constitution struggled with the existing British legal system that they inherited and the colonies largely adopted. The result of the new federal constitution was a complex, highly individualized and multilayered system of checks and balances from which legal statutes were developed at both the national and local levels. Legislators at both the national and local level have been responsive to specific, timely contexts that reflect the changing philosophical, social, and cultural influences affecting the public. The American criminal justice system, as a theoretical concept and an applied practice, has a rich history of blending new and old, indeed even ancient, ideas with which to promote social control and achieve (maintain) a just society.

The term *criminal justice*, particularly as it has developed in the United States, is worthy of both definition and explanation. The effort to define criminal justice—the rule of law, the nature of crime, the institutional actors and their roles, the prospect of social control and justice, and reform efforts—has been and remains an ongoing process. There have been shifts in laws, policies, and procedures which at first included some propositions that were later disallowed, only to have those laws/policies/operations reinstated. Any understanding of the current complexities of criminal justice and its applications must include an understanding of the administrative components (as they exist in law enforcement, the courts, and corrections), the key theoretical concepts and empirical data, and the men and women (the pioneers and the notorious) who are responsible for shaping it.

A discussion of present law must at minimum consider a brief history of the rule of law vis-à-vis the rule of man. Criminal law in the United States undergoes perpetual change (often in unpredictable ways), some of which is—as argued by pundits—contrary to the original intentions of the Founding Fathers. This is observed in the current debate regarding the right to bear arms addressed in the Second Amendment.

Historically, crime has been understood as, among other things, a social problem, an individual problem, a political problem, a spiritual problem, and an economic problem. These diverse perspectives can be seen as representing different theoretical frameworks, each of which informs public policy in ways that often seem contradictory. The current consensus, however, is that public policy on the subject of crime must acknowledge the complexities of the problem. This includes an understanding of types of crime, criminals (those who are formally charged within the context of criminal justice administration), and the criminal code/law. The dynamic interplay between the loosely coupled organizations charged with enforcing the law (law enforcement, the courts, corrections, and the legislature) and the multiple interdependent functions and responsibilities of each are collectively referred to as the "criminal justice system." Together, this system seeks to achieve social control, deter crime, intervene in criminal activity, sanction those who violate the law, and attempt to reorient offenders toward law-abiding behavior.

LAW FOR A NEW COUNTRY

In the United States, those suspected of having committed criminal offenses have their circumstances addressed through a legal system that guarantees specific rights enumerated in the Constitution to ensure protection from the unfair or excessive use of government power, including those exercised by law enforcement. The writers of the U.S. Constitution faced the daunting task of determining the legal structure for the new country and ultimately settled on a federalist system. While the U.S. Constitution is often referred to as the overarching law of the land, it refers to federal law and not necessarily the legislative mandate within the individual states, which was intended as the primary instrument in ensuring states' rights. States' rights are proposed to ensure not the sovereignty of a state but rather its existence as an independent legal entity (within the federal structure) capable of self-governance, with its own constitution, laws, and government. To that end, it is not an exceptional circumstance for states to have internal operations that are distinct from the general tenets of federal law. That prohibitions still exist against marijuana at the federal level while some states have decriminalized it is an example of this.

Still, the U.S. Supreme Court has the role of affirming constitutional uniformity between state and federal law. The Court in its holdings interprets the meaning and intended purpose of the Constitution, sets precedents, and, to the extent possible, ensures the applicability of those mandates to current circumstances. For instance, in the case of *Gideon v. Wainwright*, 372 U.S. 335 (1963), regarding the Court's role, Robert F. Kennedy stated,

> If an obscure Florida convict named Clarence Earl Gideon had not sat down in his prison cell . . . to write a letter to the Supreme Court . . . the vast machinery of American law would have gone on functioning undisturbed. But Gideon did write that letter, the Court did look into his case . . . and the whole course of American legal history has been changed.[1]

Clarence Earl Gideon also remarked on the timeliness of the Court's decision in his letter to his attorney, Abe Fortas: "Each era finds an improvement in law for the benefit of mankind."

This dictionary does not propose to explore all aspects of criminal law. It does propose, however, to attempt to address the complexity, purpose, and applicability of law through the appropriate U.S. Supreme Court cases that have historical significance in addressing current circumstances vis-à-vis its application to the U.S. Constitution. Thus, the Constitution is an evolving document subject to U.S. Supreme Court justices' interpretations, which account for contemporary realities and ultimately affirm existing law or establish new precedents for future legislative action.

TYPES OF CRIME AND CRIME CREATION

Crimes are generally referred to as felonies or misdemeanors. Common discussions of serious crime are described as felonies, which are penalized by confinement or execution. Less serious offenses are described as misdemeanors wherein individuals are reprimanded by confinement or fines. Legal terminology describes crime as *malum in se* (a crime that is wrong in and of itself) or as *malum prohibitum* (a crime that is wrong because it is prohibited by legislative action). *Malum in se* crimes are inherently wrong, such as murder, while *malum prohibitum* crimes are denoted as fitting the situated definition of what is immoral or depraved. *Malum prohibitum* crimes are specified by legislation and include prostitution, gambling, loitering, and trespassing.

Much crime is not of the *mala in se* or natural crime variety (e.g., murder, rape) but is more difficult to define. *Mala prohibita* are acts criminalized by statute, the legality of which can be inconsistent across both time and place. Legislation that criminalized an act during a given period may be changed by statute later to decriminalize the very same action (e.g., prohibition of alcohol mandated by the Eighteenth Amendment to the Constitution and later repealed by the Twenty-First Amendment). Social and moral values prompt changes in legislation and can redefine the nature and extent of what constitutes crime. For instance, during the 1960s there was a declaration of a *War on Crime* that was followed by a *War on Drugs*. Both initiatives have been challenged and reconsidered in subsequent decades with statutes that have modified criminal justice processes intended to accomplish the objectives of those mandates. Statements such as these inter alia have advanced a paradigm shift in the administration of justice from a *due process model* to a *crime control model*.

The *law and order* politics and the rhetoric that surrounded it impacted the development of "new" crimes. Each year the proverbial net widened—behaviors once disregarded by the criminal justice system or oftentimes managed without legal formality were suddenly brought within its formal purview to more fully enforce and prosecute. With crime as its unifying principle, the organization and respective functions of the criminal justice system have expanded greatly in the United States since the 1960s, particularly in the realm of corrections. The correctional population in the United States mushroomed from a quarter of a million in the mid-1970s to almost 2.5 million today. The legislation, policies, and operational mandates that affected corrections resulted in the United States accruing the largest-known prison population in the developed world.

CRIMINOLOGICAL THEORY AND CRIMINAL JUSTICE

Criminal justice and criminology are distinct from one another but are frequently used synonymously. At the same time, it is difficult to discuss one without including the other. Criminal justice consists of practitioners and procedures regarding criminal events that comprise investigation, apprehension, prosecution, determination of guilt, and (if appropriate) sentencing. Criminal justice procedures are reviewed by the courts to ensure that individual rights, protected by the Constitution, are preserved. Criminology, on the other hand, is the scientific review and analysis of crime and offenders and explores, among other things, the nature of crime, causation, outcome variance, offender behavior, victim correlations, prevention, and social, political, and economic causes and effects.

Criminology is the older academic discipline, rooted in the teachings of St. Augustine of the 5th century, the Code of Hammurabi of the 18th century B.C., Cesare Beccaria of the 18th century, Jeremy Bentham of the 19th century, and George H. Mead of the 20th century. Their considerations of what constituted crime, the role of government, and what is required for institutional intervention have influenced the development of criminal justice into the 21st century.

Criminal justice, as an academic discipline, is still in its infancy stage, being less than 100 years old. The work of August Vollmer, considered by many to be a key pioneer of the discipline, sought to professionalize policing in the United States during the 1920s. His efforts to develop the practice into a disciplinary study were bolstered in 1932 when the University of California appointed him professor of police administration. College and university criminal justice programs began a gradual expansion after 1950 under a variety of program designations, including criminology, criminal justice, and police science. Following the 1965 publication of *The Challenge of Crime in a Free Society*, which provided recommendations in response to the perceived increase in the crime rate, civil rights challenges, and issues involving the rights of convicts, the discipline burgeoned. Colleges and universities responded to the increased demand by offering new courses in the study of corrections, victimology, juvenile justice, criminal justice statistics, and policing. New disciplines in the field of criminal justice emerged that were separate and distinct from the disciplines of sociology, psychology, and philosophy, among others, wherein criminal justice was sometimes housed. Today, criminal justice programs continue their expanded reach by drawing on the latest concepts, such as forensic science, cybersecurity, and homeland security—each of which is a response to contemporary forms of the criminal enterprise that pose a threat to a free society. Academic programs are also developed with a renewed emphasis on higher educational standards for police officers, corrections personnel, and judiciary staff.

Many researchers and scholars today seek to apply their research to real-world circumstances, which in turn influences the development of modern procedures and spurs reforms of existing operational structures. The push to grow the academic discipline of criminal justice into a distinct social science field of study is ongoing and continued throughout the latter part of the last century. This distinction has led to novel approaches in studying subjects that were previously not as cultivated, such as serial killers, terrorism, and capital punishment. The pursuit of evidence-based practices has also come to the forefront of the field—much of which is promulgated to influence legislation and the allocation of state funds that are directed toward programs, prevention, and intervention efforts.

The varied contributions to the knowledge base of criminological theory and practice have demonstrated that those efforts can have significant implications. For instance, prisons that were originally intended for offender accountability, reformation of wrongdoers, and the protection of society have fallen short of those stated objectives. Research findings have instead demonstrated that the instrumental goal of incarceration—recidivism reduction—often does not occur but rather incarceration increases the likelihood of recidivism.

The most notable impacts on the criminal justice system have been shown to be the result of allocating resources in a manner that couples research findings and practitioner application. Policy and practice that are implemented on this basis have validated an understanding of "what works."[2] The system of corrections in modern America, for instance, has been especially vulnerable to a wide-scale misapprehension by the public. This ultimately resulted in substantial changes to policy and practice that culminated in massive rates of incarceration—the consequences of which have affected every segment in modern America.[3] More recent studies now question the underpinnings of the accepted policy and recommend that decision makers revisit guidelines. The failure of the corrections system to fulfill public expectations is now used to cultivate legislative reform to slow the growth of the prison population apart from the fiscal demands it imposes on states' limited resources.

THE LANGUAGE OF CRIMINAL JUSTICE

Criminal justice terminology provides language that is specific to describe the structures, operations, persons, and concepts of the field. Criminal justice language is also a diverse amalgamation of words that incorporates jargon and legal and technological terms that can sometimes be redefined or supplanted over time. Depending on the area of criminal justice in which one serves (e.g., law enforcement, courts, corrections, policy and research), there exists a unique professional jargon that one will become familiar with and eventually apply in daily practice. For instance, criminal justice professionals from two areas will use different terms to describe the same object. Historically, a law enforcement officer might have referred to being locked up as being in the "slammer," whereas a prison guard or keeper (now, "correctional officer") might use "cell," or an inmate (or convict)[4] will refer to it as being in the "clink." To laypeople outside of these systems, the overlapping terminology can be confusing and sometimes misleading. The terms in this dictionary are defined in the context of their historical significance. Terms are empirically based and denoted so that clarity is achieved. The *Historical Dictionary of American Criminal Justice* provides definitions and descriptions for fundamental terms, names, U.S. Supreme Court cases, and other concepts, as well as circumstances that explain the complex historical and legal proceedings and critical developments of criminal justice in the United States. We included select terms from other times and places due to the relative impact those matters had on the development of American criminal justice.

The dictionary includes information about the three major components of criminal justice and includes notable persons—namely those who violate the law (criminals), craft the legislation (politicians), interpret the law (jurists), enforce the law (law enforcement), and conduct research in the criminal justice field (scholars/theorists). For instance, Clarence Earl Gideon (a convict) was represented by Abe Fortas (later to become a Supreme Court justice) before the U.S. Supreme Court. The result was the landmark decision *Gideon v. Wainwright*, 372 U.S. 335 (1963), which held that all persons in criminal matters are entitled to attorney representation. In another landmark decision, *Miranda v. Arizona*, 384 U.S. 436 (1966), involving Ernesto Miranda, another convict, the Court held that persons taken into custody must be read a Miranda warning—a criminal procedure that is administered by law enforcement to ensure that the individual's Fifth Amendment right against self-incrimination is not violated. J. Edgar Hoover, the director of the FBI, led the agency for nearly half a century and put into effect several institutional changes that cultivated the bureau to become the premier law enforcement agency in the United States. Donald Cressey, a sociologist, provided theories to explain the occurrence of crime, and Francis Galton, an English scientist of the Victorian era, promoted the use of examining fingerprints because of their unique characteristics to identify individuals—a procedure that continues to be presently followed with each arrest. Individuals noted in the dictionary are persons who, through their actions, have left an indelible mark in the study and practice of criminal justice in the United States by affirming the legitimacy and need for the profession, by reframing or reorganizing its structure to better address the needs and demands of the public, or by impacting the accepted practices and perspectives of the field to the extent that it required the system to redress aspects of itself to ensure social justice.

LEGAL FOUNDATIONS OF CONTEMPORARY CRIMINAL JUSTICE

While the public and those in the criminal justice professions are generally familiar with the documents that serve as the basis for American governance (the U.S. Constitution, the Bill of Rights, and rights afforded by due process that are intended to guarantee individual safety and fair treatment), there are fewer who recognize the origins of these hallmark texts. The Magna Carta, for instance, which attempted to regulate medieval conduct, was modified as the English Bill of Rights of 1689. This particular document is indispensable to American criminal justice history due to its influence on the development of colonial law in the United States. Ultimately the early settlers would amalgamate old and new philosophical thought about justice, which resulted in a constitution tailored to meet the needs and demands of the New World. The U.S. government of the late 18th century, structured around three branches of government, would have the duty to ensure and maintain the adequacy of law for the social order. The purpose of three distinct but equal branches of government was to ensure balance and a separation of powers, which would prevent any one party (or unit of government) from attaining too much power.

The U.S. Constitution has been celebrated as the hallmark document in American society. At the time of its ratification, however, it was noted that the document conspicuously lacked a bill of rights. Thomas Jefferson, one of its writers, remarked in 1787, "A bill of rights is what the people are entitled to against every government on earth, general or particular, and what no just government should refuse, or rest on inference."[5]

The new Constitution did specify what the government was allowed to do and, in its nomenclature, did make known the apprehension and distrust that the founders held against too powerful a government. Jefferson and others recognized the need to specify the limits of government authority. An incentive for that specification was the English Stamp Act of 1765 and the "writs of assistance" that were issued for its enforcement. Those writs permitted warrantless searches of homes irrespective of the evidence and provisions pursuant to the Stamp Act (these were later reviewed and generally disallowed by the U.S. Supreme Court). James Madison authored the first 10 amendments in 1791. Unfortunately, those rights (purported as unalienable or natural rights) were not guaranteed for all members of society. Women, slaves, and Native Americans in particular were denied the rights afforded to free white men for 130 years following the ratification of the Constitution.

The U.S. Supreme Court was slow in establishing itself as the guardian of rights espoused in the Constitution. Its role in interpreting the Constitution and solidifying itself as a coequal branch of government was likewise protracted relative to the other two branches. Two Supreme Court cases help illustrate the perceived role of the Court during the early days of the country and the apprehension it had regarding the impact of its decisions on the executive and legislative branches. In *Marbury v. Madison*, 5 U.S. (1 Cranch) 137 (1803), for instance, the Court affirmed that it had judicial review but did not act to have Marbury appointed as a judge. The Court recognized that the failure to appoint Marbury was illegal but did not mandate action despite finding the Judicial Act of 1789 unconstitutional. In *Pervear v. Massachusetts*, 72 U.S. (5 Wall.) 475 (1866), the Court had an even more puzzling holding along a three-prong basis. The Court held that it could not rule because, first, corrections were within the purview of the executive branch and thus out if its jurisdiction; second, they lacked the requisite experience with corrections; and third, a ruling by the Court might unduly interfere with discipline in the prison. The historical significance of the *Pervear* case precipitated a period of more than 100 years wherein convicted felons were civilly invalidated (in essence convicts were afforded few to no rights). Since that 1866 ruling, the Court has ruled in matters that include executive branch functions, and it gradually applied articles specific to the Bill of Rights in decisions involving the rights of convicts.

Although the *Marbury* holding demonstrated the capacity of the Court's power for judicial review, the Court cannot act on its own—there must be an appeal to the Court for review. The Court over time has established itself to be the contemporary guide in assuring that the U.S. Constitution is appropriately applied to present circumstances indicative of the social and political climate. This specific function of the Court was emphasized over the course of the 20th century as American society grappled with a variety of issues including racial segregation, sexual discrimination, police corruption, and government operations and procedures involving the inmate population. The Bill of Rights existed as it always did during the onset of the 20th century but was not applied as liberally in safeguarding the rights of all persons equally. During the formative years of the 20th century, the American Civil Liberties Union (ACLU), among other interest groups, and Supreme Court jurists, such as Felix Frankfurter, acknowledged the abject failure that the government was perpetuating by not safeguarding the rights of the most vulnerable people in society.

Despite the renewed focused given to the Bill of Rights, there was little done to immediately ensure its application toward protected classes. The change, however intended, was unsurprisingly protracted. The Constitution, for instance, served as the foundation of the newly formed nation for almost eight decades following ratification, yet slavery and racial discrimination were accepted norms throughout that period. For example, there was the *Dred Scott* (a slave who sued for his freedom) decision by Chief Justice Taney, who opined in 1857 that "Blacks had no rights which the white man was bound to respect." Eight years later, in 1865, slavery would be abolished despite the forgoing decision with the ratification of the Thirteenth Amendment. The amendment, however, did not guarantee rights—instead, that would take more than another century and the passage of the Civil Rights Acts of 1964 and 1991.

A sociopolitical change in criminal justice that began in the mid-1970s perpetuated a shift from a due process model to a crime control model of justice. The emerging change centered on efficiently determining guilt and the swift and certain imposition of harsher punishments. Jury trials diminished as the system transitioned and became more focused on plea bargain and resembled more of an assembly line in processing cases from arrest to disposition. For instance, by 2015 the *New York Times* reported that jury trials in the federal courts had declined to 1,650 jury convictions out of 81,000 defendants.[6]

CONTEMPORARY ISSUES

The contention and debate regarding rights and entitlements is ever present in the criminal justice landscape. Terroristic attacks on U.S. soil from domestic and foreign entities during the latter part of the 20th century and early part of the 21st century have resulted in government actions that many believe to be essential in safeguarding American freedoms. Others, however, purport that these measures curtail and are an infringement on the very same rights that they are purported to. For instance, the use of torture, a violation of the Eighth Amendment as cruel and unusual punishment, was approved for the interrogation of enemy combatants by President George H. W. Bush during the late 1980s and early 1990s. Whether torture and deprivation of the enemy is constitutionally acceptable remains an unresolved debate in the public forum.

The tragic events of 11 September 2001 introduced American society to terrorism on a scale that was previously inconceivable by many. Even though this international act occurred just six years after the Oklahoma City bombing, the worst domestic act of terrorism in modern history, the concern for balancing public safety and individual liberties took on a new emphasis. The tragic and extraordinary events of 11 September 2001 brought to bear the swift and unanimous action of the U.S. Congress to draft and pass the Uniting and Strengthening America by Providing Appropriate Tools Required to Intercept and Obstruct Terrorism Act of 2001 (commonly referred to as the Patriot Act). The Patriot Act, deemed critical at the time to safeguard public safety from a terroristic attack as well as to preclude future acts from occurring, was perhaps one of the most transformative pieces of legislation since the writing of the U.S. Constitution. The Patriot Act affected each aspect of criminal justice. It redefined the agencies charged with providing protection by expanding law enforcement authority and influencing the policies and procedures by which those organizations function and operate. Law enforcement powers were significantly expanded in ways previously considered to be constitutional violations. For instance, actions that previously required a warrant, such as allowing wiretaps and other unwarranted searches, including those of library records and the internet, were permitted within specifically constructed parameters.

Disapproval and condemnation of the legislation materialized from watchdog groups. The ACLU, in particular, expressed concern that the act allowed far too much latitude in the issuance of subpoenas with little to no evidence of criminal activity or wrongdoing. They wrote, "The USA PATRIOT Act gives the Attorney General and federal law enforcement unnecessary and permanent new powers to violate civil liberties that go far beyond the stated goal of fighting international terrorism." The concerns went further by probing whether the Central Intelligence Agency (CIA) could now spy on citizens—a governmental operation that was unprecedented. The contention by the ACLU, among other interest groups, that claim the Patriot Act has infringed on the public's civil liberties remains controversial.

LAW ENFORCEMENT

There are more than 750,000 sworn law enforcement officers in the United States, who are assisted by more than 325,000 nonsworn or civilian staff who operate out of more than 18,000 agencies. The steady progression in law enforcement since the settlement of North America has been heavily influenced by Gabriel Nicolas de la Reynie of Paris during the 17th century and Robert Peel of London during the 19th century. In both cases, the intention was to have an organized police force to prevent crime and civil disturbances, investigate offenses, and maintain the public peace. These objectives are not unlike the primary functions of today's modern policing.

Colonial American policing consisted of "the watch," an informal community-based force akin to the English watch that required an assembly of volunteers who would come together for mutual protection. Among the earliest in America was in 1636 in Boston and in 1700 in Philadelphia, who were referred to as "the watch." The watchmen performed both a night watch and day watch; however, historically neither was regarded as performing a significant police function. Another effort to establish an ad hoc police presence during the same time period was a "for profit" force where the watchmen's salary was compensated by an unpopular imposed tax. The paid policemen would perform the same tasks as the volunteer watchmen and at times became monitors of the volunteer watch. Whether paid or not, the watch would respond to threats and other problems with shouts or the shaking of a wooden rattle to alert citizens.

In 1634, William Stone became the first appointed sheriff in the colonies in Accomack County, Virginia. Stone's appointment was the start of what has been an extensive history of the sheriff's office in the United States. An interesting departure from other colonies was that in 1651 the sheriff would become an elected position in Virginia—a change that did not occur in colonial America until after the establishment of the United States in 1776. Law enforcement in the United States would begin to assume its own unique and varied structure following the signing of the Declaration of Independence. The 1789 Judiciary Act provided for U.S. marshals, and the first 13 marshals—one for each federal district—would be appointed on 22 October 1791 by President Washington.

Cities expanded through the 1800s, and disorder in the form of violence and "moral offenses" such as drunkenness and prostitution accompanied that growth. In 1833, Philadelphia created the first 24-hour police department that was compensated with designated staffed stations throughout the city. Other cities would soon follow, including Boston in 1838, New York City in 1845, and Baltimore in 1857. By the end of the 1800s almost all cities had an established police force.

The motivations for establishing a police force were different in the South as they sought to preserve slavery. Police forces in the South were instituted primarily to capture absconding slaves and to suppress potential revolts. During the Civil War, the military assumed many of these police duties. Following the war, the sheriff was charged with enforcing segregation and ensuring that freed slaves were precluded from engaging in standard activities of citizenship. The subjugation of those emancipated by the war would persist through the 19th and into the 20th century.

The political organizations that developed throughout the country would later come to influence the formation and responsibilities assigned to police forces. Police would generally be expected to fight crime, but methods varied, shaped by the political, social, and criminal organizations indigenous to those cities and regions. In the late 1800s, widespread corruption would be supported by New York City's Tammany Hall. Graft, bribery, voter fraud, extortion, gambling, and police brutality were rampant. One police lieutenant, Alexander "Clubber" Williams (also described as the Czar of the Tenderloin), would declare, "There is more law in the end of a policeman's nightstick than in a decision of the Supreme Court." Williams was charged with offenses at least 18 times and each time was acquitted.[7] Various commissions including the Lexow Committee[8] would be impaneled to investigate corruption, institute reform efforts, and realign police practices toward an actual profession.

The westward development of the United States brought with it new forms of lawlessness that were often coupled with a great deal of controversy. The expansion of the United States fostered the emergence of new models of law enforcement, such as the Texas Rangers in 1823 (sometimes functioning as what was analogous to a military) who would protect families seeking to settle in the new frontier of Texas from Native Americans among other threats. Texas Rangers were the first law enforcement agency in the United States to have statewide law enforcement powers. The size of the ranger force would increase in subsequent decades, and their duties would expand to include investigations into cattle rustling and horse theft. These crimes along with other lesser infractions were enforced and penalized harshly at the time. In some instances, offenses were handled informally by a lynch mob, and in more formal instances, with a court-sanctioned hanging. In 1901, the Rangers would come to resemble a less militarized force with similar duties to police officers.

The states in the western frontier generally employed town sheriffs for the purposes of law enforcement. During the mid-1800s, assignments that were too burdensome for town sheriffs to address were handled by marshals. Public opinion of sheriffs, marshals, and other figures during this period in American history were mixed. Judge Roy Bean, the self-proclaimed "law west of the Pecos," was referred to as the hanging judge because he would order the closing of the saloon, impanel its patrons as jurors, hold court, and render a judgment. Wyatt Earp, the deputy marshal of Tombstone in the Arizona Territory, is recognized for the shootout at the O.K. Corral and for deputizing a force of men in locating and capturing lawless "cowboys." Both Roy Bean and Wyatt Earp, however, had their own encounters with law enforcement before assuming their "law-abiding" duties.

Each of the other states would follow the precedent set by Texas and create an agency with statewide policing authority, with the exception of Hawaii. These police agencies, however would not be established without controversy. The first of which occurred in 1905 in Pennsylvania, which was quietly created because of fear they would be "strike-breaking police." New York followed in 1917 amid similar concerns. The New Jersey State Police would be established with fewer factions disputing its existence. The southern states that initially sought to form a police force experienced a binary burden. The federal government feared that an agency with statewide authority would be used against African Americans to infringe upon their civil rights. At the same time local sheriffs were apprehensive about how the overarching force would curtail their power and authority, particularly with respect to motor vehicle enforcement. These concerns among others resulted in statewide agencies being formed, with diverse names such as highway patrol, state troopers, and state highway patrol, despite their enforcement powers having little to no difference from a state police model. The other states were eventually formalized as state police agencies, apart from California, which maintains its agency name as the California Highway Patrol.

FEDERAL LAW ENFORCEMENT

The federal government singularly employs the greatest number of law enforcement officers, totaling approximately 100,000 along a very diverse spectrum operating out of more than 100 federal agencies. Some agencies such as the Library of Congress employ as few as two law enforcement officers, while the U.S. Customs and Border Protection employs almost 40,000 armed officers who hold the power to arrest.[9] Federal agencies were created as specific needs arose. Each agency employs its own law enforcement agents, some of which have broad areas of responsibility, such as the FBI, while others are guided by more restrictive obligations. A few examples help to illustrate the rationale for the creation of some federal law enforcement agencies, the diversity of their roles, and the implications posed in their interface with other agencies and organizations.

The first federal agency, the Postal Inspection Service, created in 1772, preceded the creation of the United States and would later be retained by federal government. The first federal law enforcement agency was the U.S. Marshals Service (USMS), created in 1789 to support the federal courts in their issuance of warrants. Eventually the role of the USMS would include the protection of federal courts, its officers, and government property; the management of fugitive operations; and the performance of other specified law enforcement functions.

The U.S. Secret Service was established on 5 July 1865 (originally as a branch of the U.S. Treasury) and became the fourth federal law enforcement agency responsible to protect the U.S. economy by investigating and preventing the circulation of counterfeit monies. The limited personnel of the other agencies compelled the Secret Service to expand its functions into investigating other federal offenses, including bank robbery, gambling, and murder. In 1901, the Secret Service assumed the task for which the agency has come to be known as its core mission—the guarding of the president—following the 1901 assassination of President McKinley. Today, the Secret Service is also responsible for the protection of visiting foreign dignitaries as well as for having oversight of special events held in the nation's interest.

The Department of Justice (DOJ) was established on 1 July 1870 and is the designated agency charged with enforcing federal law. The DOJ represents the U.S. government and defends legal issues before the U.S. Supreme Court. One of the department's earliest investigations involved prosecuting the activities of the Ku Klux Klan. Other agencies within the purview of the DOJ include the FBI, the DEA, and the Bureau of Prisons.

The Federal Bureau of Investigation (FBI) was formed in 1896 as the National Bureau of Criminal Identification (NBCI), which was later changed to the FBI on 28 July 1908. The initial tasks of the NBCI were the identification of criminals. The FBI was formed at first to enforce the Mann Act. The FBI would undergo considerable change when J. Edgar Hoover became its director in 1924. One of the key changes instituted by Hoover included expanding its authority beyond that which was exercised by local police by utilizing the UCR to expand its scope of operations. More recent areas of responsibility include the investigation of suspected terrorists, cybercrimes, public corruption, transnational crime, white-collar offenses, and violent crime.

The Bureau of Alcohol, Tobacco, and Firearms (ATF) was formed on 1 July 1972 under the auspices of the DOJ to investigate and prevent the illegal use, sale, and possession of firearms, explosives, alcohol, and tobacco and to ensure that interstate transfers of such products were within the legal limits. The ATF also regulates explosives and investigates arson, violent crimes, and other criminal threats within the United States.

The U.S. Drug Enforcement Administration (DEA) was formed on 1 July 1973 by President Nixon to fortify through the establishment of one cohesive agency the government's initiative of the "War on Drugs." The War on Drugs was initially spearheaded by the 1914 Harrison Narcotics Tax Act. The DEA was charged with operating at the national and international levels to investigate violations of drug laws and to gather evidence for the prosecution of offenders engaged in the illegal drug trade.

The Central Intelligence Agency (CIA) was established on 18 September 1947 in response to the absence of intelligence gathering that could have been used to prepare or otherwise prevent the attack on Pearl Harbor by Japan during World War II. Although the CIA serves no law enforcement function, it is an intelligence-gathering agency charged with conducting covert operations on foreign soil to protect American interests. Among other tasks, those secret operations may include paramilitary functions. Prior to the attacks of 11 September 2001, the CIA was precluded from conducting operations on U.S. soil, but it has since been authorized to partake in and share information with other intelligence organizations to protect America's welfare.

The Department of Homeland Security (DHS), the largest law enforcement agency in the nation, was created on 25 November 2002 pursuant to the passage of the Homeland Security Act. The formation of the DHS was prompted by the attacks of 11 September 2001 and mandated the reorganization of many federal law enforcement agencies including the Coast Guard, the Transportation Security Administration, and Customs and Border Protection to better coordinate the efforts of various agencies with the goal of preventing terroristic attacks on American soil. In theory, the DHS would provide the needed leadership and authority to clarify points of conflict and jurisdictional control that previously created an inefficiency of response.[10] The events of 9/11 illustrated the fragmentation of federal agency authority and the complacency that can sometimes occur in large government bureaucracies. Subsequent reports showed that agencies did not share respective information in a manner that was well coordinated and timely.

CURRENT TRENDS IN THE CRIMINAL JUSTICE LANDSCAPE

All societies during the course of their history seek to address and resolve the crime problem specific to that place and time. The United States is no exception in this endeavor and has demonstrated this by developing a myriad of practices, systems, and agencies while committing countless resources to addressing crime throughout its own history. Much crime is a manufactured event that is constructed by law and social conventions, which can change over time. Most recently, during the early 1990s, the United States experienced a significant drop in both violent and nonviolent crime. This has continued through the early part of the current century. Property and violent crime rates in 2002 were the lowest recorded since the inception of the National Crime Victims Survey (NCVS) in 1973. The causes for the fluctuation in crime continue to be debated. Some criminologists and practitioners believed that tougher sentencing laws, such as California's "three strikes" policy, have been critical to crime reduction, while other experts believe that changing demographics, such as the aging population, and the robust economy during the 1990s had the most impact on reducing crime rates.

Georgette Bennett, in her book *Crimewarps: The Future of Crime in America*, found that crime in America is undergoing a shift in its pattern. *Crimewarps* refers to the significant changes or complete reversal in the geography, type, and offender characteristics of crime. Some of the emerging patterns include the decline of street crime and a corresponding rise in occupational crime, an increasing rate of female and elderly offenders, and a shift in high crime rates from the northern to the southern part of the country. She also noted decreasing crime rates in urban areas while rural crime rates are showing an uptick, as well as the rise of technology-based offenses.

Crime and the manner in which the nation addresses the problem are not static. Changes in society and culture influence the public's perspective and understanding of crime and in turn compel the government to respond using varied means. Recent events involving school and other mass shootings, for instance, are prompting a review and debate on the Second Amendment, which may culminate in tougher gun laws. The definition of criminal justice constructs will continue to evolve as scholars and practitioners address the changing landscape of crime, juxtaposing it against the underlying causes and those who commit it. As criminal justice changes unfold, new or perhaps modified definitions will be warranted to reflect the emerging realities.

NOTES

1. Lewis, Anthony, *Gideon's Trumpet: How One Man, a Poor Prisoner, Took His Case to the Supreme Court, and Changed the Law of the United States* (New York: Random House, 1964).
2. Martinson, Robert, "What Works: Questions and Answers about Prison Reform," *Public Interest* 35 (1974): 22–54.
3. Clear, Todd R., and Natasha A. Frost, *The Punishment Imperative: The Rise and Failure of Mass Incarceration in America* (New York: New York University Press, 2015).
4. Ross, Jeffrey, and Stephen Richards, *Convict Criminology* (Belmont, California: Wadsworth, 2003).
5. Letter of Thomas Jefferson to James Madison, 20 December 1787, https://founders.archives.gov/documents/Jefferson/01-12-02-0454.

6. https://www.nytimes.com/2016/08/08/nyregion/jury-trials-vanish-and-justice-is-served-behind-closed-doors.html accessed 2/10/18.

7. Asbury, Herbert, *The Gangs of New York: An Informal History of the New York Underworld* (New York: Knopf, 1928).

8. Savell, Isabelle, *Politics in the Gilded Age in New York and Rockland County: A Biography of Senator Clarence Lexow* (New York: Historical Society of Rockland County, 1985).

9. Federal Law Enforcement Officers, 2008, https://www.bjs.gov/content/pub/pdf/fleo08.pdf obtained 1 March, 2018.

10. Carter, M., "Law Enforcement and Federalism: Bordering on Trouble," *Policy Studies Journal* 7 (1978): 423–18.

A

ABBOTT, JACK HENRY (1944–2002). Jack Henry Abbott wrote *In the Belly of the Beast* (1981) detailing his life under state correctional supervision in the United States. A child of a soldier and a prostitute, Abbott was raised in foster care, then in **juvenile detention** centers, and eventually spent his adult life in and out of **prison**. In 1977, from prison, he learned of Norman Mailer's intention to write about **Gary Gilmore**. Abbott intervened and convinced Mailer that he could write a more honest account of life on the inside. Mailer agreed and eventually was instrumental in getting Abbott out on **parole**. Less than two months into his parole, at the age of 37, Abbott killed a 22-year-old waiter, Richard Adan, with whom he had gotten into an argument over the restroom. A positive *New York Times* book review came out the very next day. Abbott wrote one other book, *My Return* (1987), which revolved largely around the court case for Adan's **murder**, before he committed suicide in a prison cell in 2002. Abbott never received any royalties from either book; all proceeds went to Adan's widow. *See also* REENTRY.

ABOLITIONISM. The history of the abolition of slavery has its origins in Western Europe and the Americas from the late 1700s to the late 1800s. Slavery had all but disappeared following the Roman period in the 5th century, but when new colonies formed in the 15th century (the Americas and West Indies), interest in labor to work plantations grew. It is estimated that between the 16th and 19th centuries, 12 million people from Africa were **kidnapped** and forcibly taken to these colonies as forced laborers/slaves. In modern times, the term is used to describe the fight to abolish the use of **mass incarceration** and **capital punishment**. Many see these modern criminal sanctions as euphemisms for and/or extensions of slavery (i.e., Michelle Alexander).

ABORTION. The act of willfully terminating a human pregnancy. The criminalization of the act has varied. Some primitive peoples criminalized the act under conditions usually related to the husband's will (see Code of Assura, 11th century B.C.), while others did not. In Greek and Roman times, methods of abortion became more advanced but were not criminalized. In modern times, there remains much variation in attitudes and laws regarding the termination of a pregnancy. The criminalization of abortion in England occurred in the 1803 Malicious Shooting or Stabbing Act. This made it illegal to perform or cause an abortion. Antiabortion statutes began to appear in the United States from the 1820s. The Comstock Law of 1873 widened the net of antiabortion law and was largely due to the efforts of (male-majority) legislators, doctors, and the American Medical Association (AMA). Popular feminist writers of the time such as Elizabeth Cady Stanton and Susan B. Anthony also opposed the practice. They argued that the root cause of abortion was gender inequality and that abortion was the equivalent of a choice under duress, a choice that women would not make in a world where their rights were equal to those of men (Mohr 1978). While movements to legalize abortion began in the United Kingdom and in Russia in the 1920s, America did not experience this shift until the 1960s. In 1963, grassroots organizations formed to help women find information on getting abortions. Women who died of illegal abortions gained more attention in the media (e.g., Gerri Santoro), and the legalization movement picked up momentum. In 1967, members of the clergy announced their support of **decriminalization**, and that same year Colorado became the first state to begin to make abortions legal. This movement culminated in the **U.S. Supreme Court** case *Roe v. Wade*, 410 U.S. 113 (1973), which held that it was unconstitutional to deny a woman the right to an abortion. Since that time, there has been a slow but steady effort at the state level in the United States to recriminalize abortion.

ACADEMY OF CRIMINAL JUSTICE SCIENCES (ACJS). The ACJS was founded in 1963 as the International Association of **Police** Professors (IAPP), an alternative to the **American Society of Criminology (ASC)** founded in 1941, for criminal justice academics who saw police science as more central to the discipline than did the ASC. Following the 1960 ASC annual conference in San Francisco, many of these former officers turned scholars ("police professors") felt that the original intent of August Vollmer was to create an organization that would promote the professionalization of police which had been abandoned by ASC. *See also* ALPHA PHI SIGMA.

ACCOMPLICE. An accomplice is generally present during a criminal offense and thus is viewed as assisting in the crime. Terms similar to *accomplice* that are often used synonymously, albeit incorrectly, are *accessory* and *abettor*. *Abettor* is not often used in the United States. *Accomplice* is the more accepted term. An accessory is also viewed as assisting in the crime, although they may not be present during the crime. An accomplice may or may not be viewed the same as the party who commits the crime. In criminal law the principal is the person who authorizes the crime. The accomplice may be charged the same as the principal and receive a similar penalty. Often the accomplice is less culpable and will receive a reduced penalty. Whether the accomplice is as guilty as the principal has been subject to debate, especially in cases where the defendant is charged with a **capital offense**. There are several points to the debate. The major point is the culpability of the accomplice. This is more contentious when the principal dies at the crime scene and thus cannot be prosecuted. The question is whether the accomplice should be sentenced the same as the principal. The seriousness of the debate has consequences. For example, the **hanging** of an accomplice in England led to the abolition of **capital punishment** in that country. That case is more complicated because the accomplice was mentally challenged, the victim was a constable, and the principal was 16 years old and could not be tried as an adult. He was released after serving 10 years. The accomplice, Bently, was pardoned 45 years after his hanging. The United States has had similar debates with less response to the debates. *See also* AIDING AND ABETTING; PARDON.

***ACTUS REUS*.** A Latin term meaning "guilty act." The term developed as applied to English **common law** as part of legal proceedings in the mid-15th century, most notably in the work of Edward Coke. It refers to an act that produces criminal liability when combined with **mens rea** (guilty mind); the act can consist of voluntary or involuntary "bodily movement" or to the omission of an act where statute or duty specifies that a criminal act has occurred when there has been a failure to act to prevent injury or harm.

***ADAMSON V. CALIFORNIA*, 332 U.S. 46 (1947).** Adamson, charged with first-degree **murder**, chose not to take the stand in his own defense. This action was viewed by the prosecution as an admission of guilt, citing California statutes that allowed the **jury** to regard it as such. The **U.S. Supreme Court** held that if it were a federal case then his rights would have been violated. However, those rights did not extend to state courts, and his right against **self-incrimination** was not violated in that circumstance. The first eight amendments had not yet been incorporated at that point as noted in the dissenting argument, which also suggested that they should be incorporated. Refer to appendix 1, "The Bill of Rights." *See also* DUE PROCESS; FIFTH AMENDMENT; FOURTEENTH AMENDMENT; *GIDEON V. WAINWRIGHT*, 372 U.S. 335 (1963).

ADDICTION. A term used to describe a state of physiological, behavioral, and or cognitive dependence on some substance (or behavior) that alters one's state; cessation/withdrawal from use causes the addict suffering. Addiction to illegal substances has not typically, or directly, been criminalized throughout history, but possession and distribution of illegal substances has been criminalized. The connection between alcohol and drug addiction to deviance, crime, and **violence** is consistently high. In the United States, one of the earliest publications (Benezet 1774) argued that what we now call alcoholism (referred to then as drunkenness) should be considered a disease. In 1849, a Swedish doctor coined the term *alcoholism*. Through the 1800s in the United States, there were calls for the creation of what we would today call rehabilitation centers, then called sober houses or **inebriate asylums**. In 1939, *The Big Book* is published by Alcoholics Anonymous (AA). Somewhere between 1947 and 1953, meetings for other substances, such as **Narcotics** Anonymous (NA), began. In 1952, the American Medical Association (AMA) defined *alcoholism*. Shortly thereafter, in conjunction with the **American Bar Association (ABA)**, they issued a joint report, *Drug Addiction: Crime or Disease?* (1961), calling for community-based treatment. During President Ford's administration, a contested white paper was released in 1975 calling for expanded federal support of addiction treatment. Three years later the First Lady, Betty Ford, began a campaign against addiction. In 1984, First Lady Nancy Reagan began a "Just Say No" campaign. During this period, mandatory sentencing for drug-related crimes in the United States caused an explosion in the incarcerated population that persists today (White 1998).

ADJUDICATION. A form of *adjudicate* (verb), which is from the Latin *adjudicare*, meaning to award something to someone. The exact meaning of the term has changed throughout history. In France, in the late 14th century, the meaning was altered to clarify the act of making a judicial decision or to pass judgment on. Today, *adjudication* refers to the legal process of having arguments and **evidence** evaluated by formally sanctioned decision maker(s) (e.g., a judge, an arbiter, a **jury**) who resolves the dispute with a legally binding decision. Juvenile defendants, for example, do not have a **trial** and a jury; the judge adjudicates the case. For criminal charges, a determination of guilt or innocence is made.

ADLER, FREDA (1934–). Freda Adler is an American criminologist who is best known for having developed feminist theory in **criminology** through her well-known and controversial *Sisters in Crime: The Rise of the New Female Criminal* (1975). Her thesis proposes that increases and changes in female criminality during this period were not due to political backlash against gains made in women's rights but to the erosion of sex roles and to women taking on more "masculine" aspirations, and it is often regarded as antifeminist. Adler is known as one of the first female criminologists to impact the field.

She has served as a consultant to the United Nations and as president of the **American Society of Criminology**. She is emeritus professor at Rutgers University in New Jersey.

ADMAX. *See* SUPERMAX PRISON.

ADONIS, JOE (1902–1971). An American **Mafia** crime **syndicate** boss who operated through the 1920 and 1930s in New York and New Jersey. His crimes included assassination, rape, trafficking in **prostitution**, running **gambling** operations, **bootlegging** alcohol (then prohibited), **kidnapping**, extortion, **assault**, and other illicit endeavors. Born "Giuseppe Antonio Doto" in Italy, 22 November 1902, he married an American woman and had four children. Shortly thereafter, he was deported to Italy, without his family, but able to take his illicit gains. Following the assassination of an Italian prosecutor, the Italian **police** cracked down on **organized crime**. Adonis was relocated within Italy, and following a subsequent **interrogation**, he suffered a fatal heart attack in 1971. His body was brought back to the United States, and he was buried in Fort Lee cemetery in New Jersey. The nickname "Adonis" either came from a former girlfriend or as a comment on his vanity. He has been portrayed in several films, including *Bugsy* (1991) and ***Gangster** Wars* (1984). *See also* PROHIBITION.

ADVERSARIAL JUSTICE. The origins of this feature of **common law** systems, whereby the accused is pitted against the prosecution to resolve disputes and arrive at legal guilt or innocence, is often traced back to **trial** by combat (e.g., a duel). Trial by combat is a procedure of Germanic law used as early as 803 A.D. under tribal law. Those accused were allowed champions to defend them in physical combat, the rules of which varied. The practice continued, largely in Europe, until the 16th century. However, sometime in the 15th century, lawyers began to take control of **evidence** by sending written pleadings, and the judge or magistrate's role in the proceedings became more of a referee than a decision maker. Prior to the solidification of lawyers' primacy in the **adjudication** process and the adversarial system that it created in the 18th and 19th centuries, a man accused of robbery would have his case heard by a magistrate and perhaps a **jury** of local landowners, and little emphasis if any was given to **due process** rights. Refer to appendix 1, "The Bill of Rights." *See also* DUELING.

AGGRAVATING CIRCUMSTANCES. Judges consider aggravating and mitigating circumstances prior to sentencing a defendant. Aggravating circumstances are presented by the prosecutor and represent conditions, actions, incidents, and other contextual factors that influence or have impacted upon the gravity of the crime. These are generally special since they go beyond the typical or customary situations of a crime. Aggravating circumstances may include elements of cruelty or ruthlessness, which may be crimes themselves. When aggravating circumstances are present and are viewed to outweigh mitigating circumstances, more severe sentencing may be handed down by a judge. Examples of aggravating circumstances that may make a crime more serious include **arson**, alteration of or disposal of **evidence**, **premeditation**, **torture**, and prior history of similar or other serious offenses. *See also* AIDING AND ABETTING.

AGING OUT. An expression initiated after cohort study research done by **Dr. Marvin Wolfgang** which provided data suggesting that many offenders age out of committing crime around their mid- to late 20s. Aging out is often discussed in the context of the age-crime curve, a predictable relationship in the distribution between age and crime.

AGNEW, ROBERT (1953–). American sociologist/criminologist well known for his **general strain theory** (GST). The theory originally emerged from **anomie theory** and the work of **Durkheim** (1897/1951), **Merton** (1938), and later Cohen (1955) and Cloward and **Ohlin** (1960). During the late 1960s, the theoretical perspective had begun to decline in favor of other theories. It was often criticized because it was difficult to empirically test and perhaps due to an increasingly contentious political mood at the time that pitted individual responsibility against structural inequities. Agnew's revisions (1985) successfully addressed these criticisms by extending the theory to include individual-level variables, such as an individual's class, future expectations, and peer group relationships (Agnew et al. 1996). In 2015, he received the **American Society of Criminology** lifetime achievement award for his work on GST. Agnew was born in Atlantic City, New Jersey. He has been a professor at Emory University in Atlanta, Georgia, since 1980.

AIDING AND ABETTING. The United States first passed a statute in 1790 and expanded it in 1870 specifying criminal liability for assistance in all felonies. Once more in 1948, the language was clarified so that a person who aids and abets during the commission of a felony is regarded as a principal in the criminal event, thus qualifying him or her for the same penalties as the person who committed the actual offense. *See also* ACCOMPLICE.

AKERS, RONALD L. (1939–). An American criminologist who developed differential reinforcement theory in a paper published in *Social Problems* in 1966 (the same year he completed his Ph.D.) with coauthor Ronald Burgess. The theory belongs to the social learning perspective, which argues that criminality is learned through imitation and modeling. The theory builds on early work by **Edwin Sutherland** (sometimes called the father of **criminology**), who developed **differential association** theory in a social context. Differential reinforcement theory argues that learning crime happens in nonsocial ways as well social. Structures and patterns of reinforcement also shape behavior. Two widely known texts on criminological theory, *Deviant Behavior* and *Criminological Theories*, were written by Akers. He is emeritus professor at the University of Florida.

***AKE V. OKLAHOMA*, 470 U.S. 68 (1985).** A **murder** case in which the **U.S. Supreme Court** held that indigent defendants should be provided a psychiatric evaluation if needed. In this case, the defendant's bizarre behavior prior to **trial** resulted in his being held in a state hospital but found to be competent to stand trial. He was ultimately convicted and sentenced to **execution**, but at no point was a psychiatric evaluation (requested by the defense attorney before trial) conducted. *See also* DUE PROCESS; DURHAM RULE.

ALCATRAZ ISLAND PRISON (1934–1963). The **prison** was described by **James Bennet** (1894–1978), the second director of the **Federal Bureau of Prisons (BOP)**, as the "darkest day in American prison history." Alcatraz, loosely translated as the Island of Pelicans, has had several uses, including the property of Native Americans, military forts, and as the most maximum-security prison of its day. The prison has held such infamous persons as **Al Capone**, **John Dillinger**, and **Robert Stroud**, better known as the "Birdman of Alcatraz." Alcatraz has been described as the prototype for the modern **supermax prison**. Alcatraz had one of the more extreme guard-to-prisoner ratios under its first warden, James Aloysius Johnston (approximately 1:3).

ALDERSON PRISON, FPC. The first federal **prison** for women, opened in 1928. Alderson is also referred to as "Camp Cupcake" and confined such personalities as Martha Stewart and Billie Holiday. Prior to its opening, women were either housed in male prisons or given other sentences that did not require incarceration. A minimum-security prison houses person for lower-level offenses such as insider trading, for which Martha Stewart was convicted and sentenced to prison. Other well-known persons who served time at Alderson Prison include Lolita Lebrón (member of a group of Puerto Rican nationalists who attacked the U.S. Congress); Lynette "Squeaky" Fromme (a follower of **Charles Manson** who attempted to assassinate President Gerald Ford); and Elizabeth Gurley Flynn, cofounder of the **American Civil Liberties Union**. *See also* FEDERAL BUREAU OF PRISONS (BOP).

ALFORD PLEA. This unusual type of plea is given when a defendant asserts his or her innocence and at the same time acknowledges that the prosecution has sufficient **evidence** to convict. The term comes from a 1970 **U.S. Supreme Court** case, *North Caroline v. Alford*, 400 U.S. 25 (1970). At the time in North Carolina, by pleading "not guilty" and losing, a defendant could be subject to the **death penalty**. When Alford was indicted in 1963, he argued that the only reason he was pleading guilty was to avoid the death penalty. After several appeals at the state and regional levels, the case went to the U.S. Supreme Court. U.S. Supreme Court justice Byron White wrote the decision for the majority. Alford died in **prison** five years after the decision.

ALLOCUTION. In the criminal procedure of most **common law** systems, this is a phase right before sentencing where the defendant is given the opportunity to speak on his or her behalf directly to the judge (e.g., for mercy, to consider additional information, etc.). The right initially applied only in capital cases in the late 1700s and early 1800s in England and could result in the entire case being thrown out (see Thomas 2007). It has since evolved in an American context as part of possible sentence mitigation.

ALL-POINTS BULLETIN (APB). A term used since approximately 1960 by U.S. law enforcement to describe internal broadcasts to other law enforcement agencies that are critical in locating a suspect or missing person. Some speculate that the term originated in the American noir genre. In Australia, law enforcement uses the phrase "keep a look out for" or "KLO4." In the U.K., law enforcement refers critical information to ports where suspects might escape, issuing "all-ports warnings" or "APWs."

ALPHA PHI SIGMA. The national honors society for criminal justice students, which was initially intended to award high-performing students in **police** science. It was established in 1942 by Dr. V. A. Leonard of the Department of Police Science at Washington State University. Leonard was instrumental in founding what is now the **Academy of Criminal Justice Sciences (ACJS)**. In 1976, ACJS formally became the supporting organization for Alpha Phi Sigma, recognizing high-performing students across criminal justice.

AL-QAEDA. Al-Qaeda is best known for planning the 11 September 2001 attacks in the United States. It is an Islamic (radical Sunni) organization formed around the Soviet-Afghan War in approximately 1988 by **Osama bin Laden**. In English, the term literally means "the base." The group ideology supports militant and terrorist strategies and opposes the United States and the Western world, along with corrupt leaders in the Muslim world. Initially allied with the Taliban in Afghanistan, the group was influenced by Wahhabism (an extreme practice of Islam rejected by most Muslims). Following a U.S.-led invasion of Afghanistan in response to the 2001 attacks, Al-Qaeda evolved from being a hierarchically structured group with key leaders to a ground-up network structure that spread jihad throughout the world. In 2011, bin Laden was killed in Pakistan by the U.S. military. *See also* TERRORISM; WORLD TRADE CENTER (WTC) BOMBINGS.

AL-SHABAAB. Islamic (Salafist fundamentalist) organization formed as a militia after the collapse of the government in Somalia in 1991. The collapse gave rise to the Islamic Courts Union (sharia courts) during this period; from 2004, Al-Shabaab was its armed force. In English, it literally means "Movement of Striving Youth." Al-Shabaab revolted against the federal government in 2006. In 2012, the group was briefly aligned with **Al-Qaeda** and called for single females to be sent to Al-Shabaab to "fight alongside the militants." Bin Laden would criticize their leader, Godane, for being too brutal in his practice of sharia. Al-Shabaab was responsible for the 2013 terror attack at the Westgate Mall in Kenya that left 67 dead and for the 2015 Garissa University College attack, where militants from Al-Shabaab went through the college campus killing students believed to be Christians. *See also* TERRORISM.

ALTERNATIVE SENTENCING. Alternative sentencing is also referred to as "noncustodial penalties." The phrase used to refer to sentences (criminal sanctions) that do not rely on incarceration. It was not until the early 1600s that incarceration began to be used more regularly and for more than just debtors or short-term detention. By the 1800s, it was the primary mode of correctional intervention. Through the 1900s, reformers were beginning to examine criminogenic effects of imprisonment and a lack of intended impact on **recidivism** rates. At the same time, alternatives to incarceration began to emerge. For example, conditional suspension of **punishment** was first enacted in France in 1891 and then spread throughout Europe. Judicial reprieve, recognizance, and benefit of clergy were all noted as precursors to what is typically called "**probation**" today. Other alternative punishments have included **fines**, forced work, and home detention (now with **electronic monitoring**).

AMERICAN BAR ASSOCIATION (ABA). An association of lawyers established in 1878 in Saratoga Springs, New York. The group sets ethical codes of conduct for lawyers in the United States and curriculum standards for American law programs. Lawyers and law students also rely on the almost half-a-million-member group to discuss issues of law and legal practice. Even though the association cites the elimination of bias and the enhancement of diversity as one of its three goals, as with most groups in the United States throughout this period, the inclusion of women and minorities came late; women were not allowed membership until 1918, and African Americans not until 1943. Other goals of the association include serving members, improving professional standards, and advancing the rule of law. *See also* AMERICAN BAR FOUNDATION, THE (ABF).

AMERICAN BAR FOUNDATION, THE (ABF). A research institute that supports empirical, multidisciplinary research into law and legal institutions. The foundation was established in 1952 on the University of Chicago campus. In 1976, the ABF established its flagship peer-reviewed journal, *Law and Social Inquiry*.

AMERICAN CIVIL LIBERTIES UNION (ACLU). An organization founded in 1920 by civil liberties activists Roger Baldwin, Crystal Eastman, and Albert DeSilver to protect the rights of American citizens that are endowed to them in the **Bill of Rights**. Its aim was to bring the knowledge and benefit of these rights to marginalized populations (African Americans; lesbian, gay, bisexual, and transgender (LGBT) people; and women). One of their first cases involved protecting the free speech rights of immigrants to protest deportation. They later helped to legalize unions in 1939. Three years later, they were the sole arbiter condemning the internment of Japanese Americans. The organization now has more than one million members nationally. Using the court and political systems in their defense of civil liberties, the organization files cases in both state and federal courts and is second only to the Department of Justice in frequency of appearances in front of the **U.S. Supreme Court**. They employ numerous lobbyists across the legislative branches of state and federal government as well. Refer to appendix 1, "The Bill of Rights." *See also* DUE PROCESS.

AMERICAN CORRECTIONAL ASSOCIATION (ACA). The ACA began as the National **Prison** Association and later adopted the name the American Prison Association. In 1954, the association assumed its current name, the American Correctional Association. The stated mission of the ACA is to provide "a professional organization for all individuals and groups, both public and private that share a common goal of improving the justice system." It has the distinction of **Rutherford B. Hayes** as its first president. The ACA is an organization for correctional practitioners that conducts conferences and trainings.

AMERICAN SOCIETY OF CRIMINOLOGY (ASC). The ASC is the world's largest professional criminological society. Founded in 1941 as the National Association of College **Police** Training Officials (NACPTO) by practitioner-academic August Vollmer (Vollmer was chief of police and a University of California, Berkeley, professor). In 1957 the international organization took on its current name. Members include mostly scholars and students and a smaller portion of practitioners. The organization publishes two peer-reviewed journals, ***Criminology*** (1963–) and *Criminology & Public Policy* (2001–). *Criminology* is consistently ranked as the top journal out of all peer-reviewed criminal justice journals. The offices of ASC have been on the campus of Ohio State University since the mid-1960s.

AMERICA'S MISSING: BROADCAST EMERGENCY RESPONSE (AMBER) ALERT. This is a community mobilization notification system. The program relies on various partnerships between law enforcement and modern wireless technology to instantly notify communities of suspected child abductions in almost real time. The Amber Alert Program was named after nine-year-old Amber Hagerman, who was **kidnapped** in 1996 in Texas while riding her bicycle. Her lifeless body, throat slit, was found shortly after, floating in a nearby creek. The idea for the program came from Diane Simone, a Texas citizen, who suggested the idea on a local radio call-in show the day Amber's body was found. The program began in 1997 in Texas and now is coordinated by the U.S. Department of Justice and used in all 50 states, the District of Colombia, Puerto Rico, and the U.S. Virgin Islands. In 2015, social media groups like Facebook joined radio, television, and cell phone providers in adding Amber Alerts to their newsfeeds. Since its inception, the alert has been credited with rescuing 794 missing children. *See also AMERICA'S MOST WANTED (AMW)*; CODE ADAM; WALSH, ADAM (1974–1981).

***AMERICA'S MOST WANTED* (*AMW*).** A popular American television show that dramatized unsolved crimes and solicited information from the public to close cases. The show was created by Fox News in 1988 but in 2011 was sold to the Lifetime network, which canceled the show in 2013. After a very brief (one and a half months) and dramatic cancellation in 1996 (due to high production costs), the show was renamed *America's Most Wanted: America Fights Back*. Upon learning of the show's cancellation, public response was so intense, including almost 40 U.S. governors' protests, that the show was quickly reinstated. The format of the show was not new; in the 1950s, the American network CBS briefly ran a similar show called *Wanted*, and the current British **true crime** program *Crimewatch* began in 1984. The show's host, Joe Walsh, was selected in 1988 after he had successfully fought for stronger legislation to protect children from crime following the abduction and brutal **murder** of his six-year-old son in 1981. The show was created by Michael Lander and Steven Chao. *See also* LIST, JOHN (1925–2008); MEGAN'S LAW.

AMICUS CURIAE. Also referred to as an amicus curiae brief, a Latin phrase meaning "friend of the court." This is a party who acts to assist the court by offering case-relevant information but who is not directly or indirectly involved in the case (e.g., not working for either side). The origin is Roman law, which was followed by **common law** systems and then **civil law** systems. In addition to its application in American law, it is used by several international bodies such as the European Court of **Human Rights** and the Court of Justice of the European Union.

ANASTASIA, ALBERT (1902–1957). An infamous **Mafia** boss born Umberto Anastasio. His organization would later become the **Gambino** crime family and would be the founder of **Murder Inc.** His specialty was assassination, earning him the nicknames "the Mad Hatter" and "Lord High Executioner." He was born in Calabria, Italy, and his family immigrated to New York when Anastasia was 17. He and his brothers quickly made a name for themselves working on the Brooklyn docks. Just two years into his life in America, he was convicted of murder and sentenced to death. However, witnesses in the case vanished, and Anastasia was released the following year in 1922. Anastasia was ultimately the victim of what would become a well-known assassination and part of American popular culture. He was assassinated while getting a haircut in Manhattan, ambushed by two gunmen. *See also* LANSKY, MEYER (1902–1983).

ANDERSON, ELIJAH. American urban ethnographer, sociologist, and cultural theorist who is best known for *Code of the Street: Decency, Violence, and the Moral Life of the Inner City* (Anderson 1999). The **ethnography** argued that much of the **violence** found in inner cities was the result of informal rules that governed interactions through a subcultural language of respect. Prior to this, while a professor at the University of Pennsylvania, Anderson detailed the nuances of African American life in the inner city in *Streetwise: Race, Class, and Change in an Urban Community* (Anderson 1990). Anderson was a student of **Howard S. Becker** at Northwestern University, where he received his doctorate. He currently holds the William K. Lanman Jr. Professorship in Sociology at Yale University. *See also* AUTO-ETHNOGRAPHY.

ANGEL OF DEATH/MERCY. A type of **serial killer** who utilizes medical training to contribute to the death of those under their care. Typically angels of death allege that they are advocates of **euthanasia** regarding their acts as **mercy killing**. Some examples include Jane Toppan, a nurse, who in the early 1900s used injections of morphine to kill approximately 33 patients; Harold Shipman, a British doctor, who was found guilty of killing 15 patients in 2000 but has been implicated in about 200 **murders**; and John Adkins, a British doctor, implicated in the deaths of 163 patients and found not guilty when tried. The list of mercy killers also includes nurses Beverly Allit, Richard Angelo, and Kristin Gilbert; orderly **Donald Harvey**; and doctor **Michael Swango**. *See also* KEVORKIAN, JACK (1928–2011).

ANGER MANAGEMENT. A popular group therapy or class applied in different types of criminal cases (e.g., **domestic violence**, drunk driving) in and outside of correctional settings to teach offenders how to control and prevent outbursts of anger. The desire to develop skills to make one able to successfully negotiate anger has been present since ancient philosophers such as Seneca, who discussed ways of avoiding rage in 4 B.C. (Reynolds, Griffin, and Fantham 2012). Its use in modern criminal justice systems stemmed from research by psychologists in the 1970s, which resulted in **cognitive behavioral therapy (CBT)**. In particular, anger management classes as developed by Meichebaum (1975) and Navaco (1975) focused on stress and anxiety involved in anger. *See also* VIOLENCE.

ANOMIE THEORY. Anomie theories derive from the work of French sociologist **Émile Durkheim**. In 1897, he published his foundational study of suicide, examining rates of variation through the lens of macro-level societal forces that function either to support a constructive set of means, expectations, and norms regulating human behavior or that fail to. Anomie describes the state of societal-level forces not satisfactorily coming together to create a cohesive set of norms. Causes of this state of normlessness are things such as dramatic shifts in economics (i.e., industrialization, depression) or rapid population change (e.g., immigration). In 1938, **Robert Merton** used anomie to explain crime as the product of an inconsistency between agreed-upon goals and access to achieving those goals. The theory was popularized further in the 1990s by American sociologists Messner and Rosenfeld (2013) in their *Crime and the American Dream*. Empirical tests of anomie were complicated, but more recent evolutions of anomie found in **strain theory**, which incorporates a more micro-level analysis, have been promising.

ANTI-DEFAMATION LEAGUE (ADL). A nonprofit, Jewish American–based organization founded in 1913 by Sigmund Livingston, a lawyer from Chicago. Livingston set out to defend the rights of Jewish people and all people who were the target of defamation and hatred. Around the same time, a Jewish man who had recently moved to the South was killed by a mob when Georgia's governor pardoned him for a sentence that was delivered at an overtly anti-Semitic **trial**. At the time, stereotypes about Jews appeared openly in the press (and in at least one U.S. Army training manual), and discriminatory practices such as barring those with Jewish-sounding names from certain resorts were commonplace. In 1947, the ADL filed an **amicus curiae** brief in *Shelley v. Kraemer*, 334 U.S. 1 (1948), successfully arguing that restrictive housing covenants are unconstitutional. In the 1950s, the organization was instrumental in *Brown v. Board of Education*, 347 U.S. 483 (1954); in criticizing Senator Joseph McCarthy; and in passing the anti-mask legislation that made it illegal for members of the **Ku Klux Klan** to demonstrate anonymously. In the 1960s, the organization made a lasting impact on Catholic-Jewish relations by working with the Catholic Church to craft a statement (*Nostra aetate*) rejecting Jewish responsibility in the death of Jesus. These early years characterize the continued mission of the organization in modern times. The ADL now has almost 30 regional offices throughout the United States and a national headquarters. ADL professionals include researchers, legal scholars, and experts in education and intergroup and interfaith understanding. *See also* HATE CRIME; PARDON.

***APPRENDI V. NEW JERSEY*, 530 U.S. 466 (2000).** A landmark **U.S. Supreme Court** case which determined that a sentence that exceeds a statutory maximum length must be determined by a **jury**. Apprendi was assigned a greater sentence (12 years, which exceeded the maximum by two years) because of **aggravating circumstances**.

***ARGERSINGER V. HAMLIN*, 407 U.S. 25 (1972).** Argersinger was caught with a concealed weapon and imprisoned without representation from an attorney. The **U.S. Supreme Court** held that a defendant must have attorney representation for sentences that include jail time. *See also GIDEON V. WAINWRIGHT*, 372 U.S. 335 (1963).

ARGOT. A secret language or slang utilized in a criminal justice context by **gangs**, subcultures, convicts, or any group wishing to keep communications private. In fact, the first known appearance of the term in 1628 was in relation to a group of thieves called the "les argotiers." The term appears in

Victor Hugo's *Les Misérables* and is referred to frequently in discussions of Anthony Burgess's "nadsat," an argot used by the group of criminals called "droogs" who appear in his *A Clockwork Orange* (1962).

ARPAIO, JOE (1932–). American **sheriff** of Maricopa County, Arizona, who came to national attention in the late 1990s and through the 2000s for his "name-and-shame" approaches to criminal justice. Arpaio was first elected sheriff in 1993 and served through 2016; he was previously a **police** officer. Notable strategies imposed by him included the development of a "tent city" for **inmates** as an ancillary to the Maricopa county jail, which he referred to as a "concentration camp"; making inmates wear pink underwear; and implementing work on volunteer chain gangs. He has operated the only female chain gang. In 2005, his aggressive and possibly unconstitutional style of immigration enforcement landed him in court. The list of controversies surrounding his terms as sheriff included unconstitutional jail conditions, improper clearance of cases, failure to investigate sex crimes, feuds with judges and county supervisors, misuse of funds, **racial profiling** (and a related class action lawsuit), contempt of court, and election law violations. In 2016, he finally lost his bid for reelection to Democrat Paul Penzone.

ARRESTEE DRUG ABUSE MONITORING (ADAM). ADAM began as the **Drug Use Forecasting** program in 1987. The aim was to **drug test** and interview adult arrestees in major metropolitan areas (approximately 30 areas, four times annually) to assess the prevalence of alcohol and drug use among arrestees. Juvenile arrestees began being tested in some sites in 1991. The program was expanded in 1996 to include rural and suburban areas under the Clinton administration. Up until 2000, all subjects were voluntarily and confidentially tested at random; after 2000, males were tested at random and female subjects were chosen where available.

ARSON. Human beings have set fire to others' property for thousands of years. In England, arson first surfaced as land ownership did around 1750. Resources on these lands were once common; but now private, they became blocked, and non-landowners burned the lands and resources in protest. Up until 1837, property arson in England was a **capital offense** punishable by death. In the United States, arson is prosecuted to the extent that it coincides with other offenses (e.g., someone is injured or dies in the fire, first degree; significant property losses are sustained, second degree). Prosecution of arson varies by state. It is typically prosecuted as a felony but can also be charged as a misdemeanor (e.g., criminal mischief). Arson is one of the crimes followed closely by the **Federal Bureau of Investigation**'s (FBI's) **Uniform Crime Reports** issued annually. *See also* PANZRAM, CARL (1891–1930); PYROMANIA.

ARYAN BROTHERHOOD. A white supremacist group that originated in the early 1960s in American **prisons**. Most note its origin in **San Quentin**, a California state prison. Initially the group was a response to desegregation in American prisons but had evolved sometime in the 1990s outside of prisons into organized criminal activities. The Order of the Blood is one notable crime organization operating out of the American Midwest under Aryan Brotherhood authority. In the 1970s the group was briefly associated with **Charles Manson** and the Family. Throughout the 1980s and early 1990s, the group was involved in several prison riots that resulted in the deaths of **inmates** and correctional officers. Attempts were made in the 2000s to prosecute several members using federal **Racketeer Influenced Corrupt Organizations (RICO)** laws. About 30 members were successfully prosecuted, but prosecutors had sought the **death penalty** for members at the top of the hierarchy, which were not granted. *See also* GANG; WHITE SUPREMACY.

ASHURST-SUMNERS ACT (1935). An American law that makes it illegal to knowingly transport commerce goods made by convict labor. There are several exceptions to this law, including agricultural products, farm machinery, anything made in a federal **prison** (or in a state prison that the federal government uses) or the District of Columbia, or anything made by nonprofit organizations subcontracted by a prison. Penalties for failing to abide by this legislation are a **fine**, incarceration for less than two years, or both. In 1979, an additional "exception" was granted by Congress. The Prison Industry Enhancement Certification Program made it possible for state and local facilities to sell commodities made in prisons across state lines and mandated that **inmates** work while incarcerated—seemingly reversing Ashurst-Sumners. All individuals confined to prison in the United States today work in "self-sustaining" facilitates where inmates work in cooking, cleaning, and washing laundry, but a percentage are also contracted by private industries from within the prison. Companies such as IBM, Boeing, Motorola, Microsoft, AT&T Wireless, Texas Instruments, Dell, Compaq, Honeywell, Hewlett-Packard, Nortel, Lucent Technologies, 3Com, Intel, Northern Telecom, TWA, Nordstrom's, Revlon, Macy's, Pierre Cardin, and Target all contract with prisons for prison labor in 37 states (Peláez 2016). Prison labor is paid at a rate well under minimum wage.

ASSAULT. The illegal intention or threat to use **violence** against another person—though some definitions include the actual violence ("assault and battery"). Specific definitions vary across place and time. Typically, assault is further defined by its seriousness (e.g., simple assault does not include the use of weapons, aggravated assault does). Unlawful threats of violence and violence itself are human behaviors that have been present since the beginning of law. Its first known use is from the 13th-century Middle English *assaut*.

ASSEMBLY LINE JUSTICE. A pejorative term coined by **Herbert Packer**, Stanford law professor, to describe the nature of 15 phases of criminal justice discretion that determine whether a citizen gets processed further down the line. For instance, Packer identifies the initial contact, then the investigation phase when officers must decide to pursue a case or to terminate it, the **bail** stage, through to post-release. Packer highlights that each decision point is critical to the defendant, the justice system, and society. *See also* PLEA BARGAIN.

ASSET FORFEITURE. The confiscation by the government of individual assets thought to have been acquired directly or indirectly through criminal activity. In the United States, the practice has grown since the 1970s. The passage of **Racketeer Influenced Corrupt Organizations (RICO)** laws and then the **Patriot Act** in 2001 helped to strengthen the government's authority to seize property and funds to disrupt criminal, organized, and terrorist enterprises. Since 2010, asset forfeiture as it is practiced particularly with those in lower socioeconomic classes has come under increased scrutiny (see Hudetz 2015).

ASYLUMS. Institutions which have also been called lunatic asylums, mental institutions, and psychiatric hospitals. Places such as these have housed the insane since medieval times, e.g., Egypt, Germany, Spain, England, and Iran (Persia). The word *bedlam* came from an actual English asylum, the Priory of Saint Mary of Bethlehem, which was founded between 1247 and 1400. Gradually, housing the insane made its way into the private sphere of charitable organizations, which usually ran them, and, with the birth of psychiatry, eventually became public in the 19th century. This change was prompted by calls for more humanitarian treatment of residents in these places, where they were often found to be living in filth and in chains. In the United Kingdom, the County Asylums Act was passed in 1808. New York was the first state to pass a law for public asylums in 1842. By the end of the 19th century, most asylums throughout the world were public and regulated. The number of people housed in asylums, however, rose steadily and drastically throughout this period, often causing overcrowding and thwarting effective treatment. The reason for this increase is that asylums received those who had previously been in poorhouses. The conditions in public asylums soon became just as inhumane as they had been in privately run asylums, and reformers responded. At the same time, through the first half of the 20th century, radical treatments such as shock therapy and lobotomies began. By 1960, deinstitutionalization of the mentally ill in the United States had begun. *See also* INEBRIATE; INSTITUTIONALIZATION.

ATAVISM. Atavism is also referred to as atavistic stigmata, the idea that criminal behavior is a type of evolutionary throwback to more primitive states of being and that criminals are born deviant. The term originated with Darwin's *Origin of Species* (1859) and was adopted in the study of crime by the father of **criminology**, **Cesare Lombroso** (1835–1909), who was heavily influenced by positivistic philosophy and his training in medicine and surgery. He is said to have developed the theory after performing an autopsy on an infamous criminal of the time (ca. 1871). He noted that the man had features, including an indentation at the back of his skull, similar to that of apes. From this he wrote, "At the sight of that skull, I seemed to see all of a sudden, lighted up as a vast plain under a flaming sky, the problem of the nature of the criminal—an atavistic being who reproduces in his person the ferocious instincts of primitive humanity and the inferior animals" (Lombroso 1876). The idea that atavism could be recognized by external features or stigmata followed: "Thus were explained anatomically the enormous jaws, high cheek bones, prominent superciliary arches, solitary lines in the palms, extreme size of the orbits, handle shaped or sessile ears found in criminals, savages and apes, insensibility to pain, extremely acute sight, tattooing, excessive idleness, love of orgies and the irresistible craving for evil for its own sake, the desire not only to extinguish life in the victim, but to mutilate the corpse, tear its flesh, and drink its blood" (ibid.). Atavism was an early form of psychological pathology and is an antecedent of current biological (e.g., traumatic brain injury) theories of crime. *See also* CLASSICAL SCHOOL OF CRIMINOLOGY.

***ATKINS V. VIRGINIA*, 536 U.S. 304 (2002).** A **U.S. Supreme Court** decision on **capital punishment** in which the court ruled six to three that a death sentence for intellectually disabled persons violated **Eighth Amendment** rights against **cruel and unusual punishment**. States were granted broad discretion as to the meaning of intellectual disability (narrowed in *Hall v. Florida*, 572 U.S. ___ (2014), but in practice it was generally defined by an intelligence quotient scored below 70. The decision was based on the case of Daryl Atkins, who was 18 years old, high, and drunk when in 1996 he and an

accomplice murdered Eric Nesbitt, a member of the U.S. Air Force, during a robbery. During the original **trial**, it was found that Atkins was mildly retarded with an IQ of 59. Ironically, in 2005, Atkins was found to have an elevated IQ of 70 (attributed to his years of working with lawyers) and found fit for **execution**. The execution was stayed and commuted to a life sentence in 2008, which was later appealed by prosecutors and overturned by the Virginia Supreme Court in 2009. *See also* DEATH PENALTY; MURDER.

ATTACHMENT THEORY. A theory that proposed instability was caused by inadequate attachment between an infant and the primary caregiver and/or that prolonged separation causes insecurity, depression, anxiety, aggression, and delinquency. The effects last through the life course and cause the perception that people are unavailable or hostile. The theory was initially developed by psychologist John Bowlby (1944). Criminologists such as **Travis Hirschi** (**social control theory**), Hirschi and Gottfredson (a general theory of crime), and Sampson and Laub (age-graded **life course theory**) built on the research findings generated from attachment theory.

ATTENTION DEFICIT/HYPERACTIVITY DISORDER (ADHD). A condition usually diagnosed in children who display an inability to control impulses, an inability to focus, and hyperactivity. The condition seems to have been identified in 1902 by a British pediatrician, Sir George Still. He observed a level of impulsivity in some children that fell outside of the norm but did not correlate to lower intelligence. Originally called "hyperkinetic impulse disorder," it first appeared in the American Psychiatric Association's (APA's) *Diagnostic and Statistical Manual* (*DSM-II*) in 1968. The contemporary concept of ADHD is defined in the *DSM-IV-TR* (2000).

ATTICA CORRECTIONAL FACILITY AND RIOTS. A maximum-security **prison** in Attica, New York, built in the 1930s and the site of the infamous Attica prison riot of 9–11 September 1971. The riots were the result of prison overcrowding, the prisoner rights movement that was part of the climate of social protest of the 1960s and 1970s, and the death of George Jackson, a prominent figure in the Black Panther Party, who was killed by guards in the **San Quentin** State Prison riots two weeks earlier. Initially, **state police** came in and regained control of three prison areas without incident. Later, however, when a group of **inmates** with 42 hostages occupied D-Yard, Prison Superintendent Russell G. Oswald made the decision with Governor Rockefeller (who refused to come to the prison to negotiate) to have state police take back control of the prison by force. Thirty-three inmates and nine correctional officers were killed when they did so. One correctional officer had been killed by inmates at the outset of the rioting.

Rockefeller attributed the deaths to the inmates, but medical reports later showed that they died from gunfire, not knives, which were the only weapon inmates had. In 2000, inmates and inmates' families settled out of court with New York State for $8 million. Five years later, the state of New York settled with correctional officers injured and the families of those slain for $12 million.

ATTORNEY CLIENT PRIVILEGE. A client's right when working with an attorney to have all communications between the two kept confidential. The right was established in the case of *Berd v. Lovelace* (1577) Cary 62. It originated in the **common law** system as a way of ensuring that a client, unversed in the law, could disclose all details of their case to their attorney without fear. Without the expert opinion of an attorney, whether a client's fears were warranted or not, it would be impossible to determine the accuracy of details without knowing all the facts.

ATTORNEY GENERAL. In **common law** systems, an attorney who advises the state or the government on legal issues. The attorney general may also provide legal guidance for law enforcement and or prosecutorial offices. This is also the case in **civil law** systems, but in some places these attorneys are referred to under different titles such as "procurators," "advocates general," or "public attorneys." The earliest known appearance of the term comes from 1292. The term is French in origin; therefore, the adjective *general* comes after and not before attorney, which is common in French compounds. Today, most attorneys general are permanently appointed.

AUBURN PRISON. The **penitentiary** was built in 1818 for $40,000 and represented many shifts from the original plans and intentions begun at **Eastern State Penitentiary**. The first was a change in architectural style. Eastern was a radial design. Auburn would be the first warehouse design, which would become a widely replicated style. The cellblocks would be inside a hollow building with cells back to back and five tiers high. The change was instituted for economic reasons. The change in operational style fostered several deviations from the Eastern model. The **prison** is referred to as the congregate style and included the introduction of the lockstep. This change came about because **solitary confinement** in the Eastern design drove men mad. The congregate style allowed prisoners to leave their cells to eat in a mess hall and to work in shops. The lockstep was a means of controlling when convicts would leave their cells and consisted of having the convicts walk in step with one hand on the shoulder of the convict in front of them. The guards could more clearly observe whether someone was speaking or simply out of line. The **congregate system** maintained the **rule of silence**, which was an integral feature of the Eastern Penitentiary. Auburn was the first prison to use the profit from convict work to support the prison. The changes in philosophy are highlighted by the change from a penitentiary to a prison that would utilize work to defray costs. Work was substituted for the prayer that was emphasized in the Eastern system, silence would be a control mechanism as opposed to its use for self-reflection, and **corporal punishment** was used to maintain discipline. Auburn devised several punishments. The stocks and **whippings** with the cat-'o-nine-tails were approved by the New York legislature. In 1839, a convict died from excessive **flogging**. The shower bath (which may be the origin of waterboarding) placed a convict bound hand and foot in a barrel and set under a stream of freezing water. The yoke was a metal bar placed across the shoulders, and the arms were tied to it. The convict was forced to stand with the yoke in place. Auburn construction included a hidden passageway behind the congregate work areas for visitors and staff to observe the convicts. Visitors were charged a fee of 12 and a half cents and could purchase a souvenir book for a nickel. Eventually the cost of a visit was raised to discourage visitors from coming to the prison. Women were housed at Eastern and were kept in the attic to ensure separation from the male convicts. Other firsts at Auburn included the first **electric chair** and its use for **execution**, a three-tiered **classification** system, striped clothing, and shaved heads. *See also* DEATH PENALTY.

AUGUSTUS, JOHN (1785–1859). The founding father of **probation**, Augustus was a cobbler by trade living in Boston who had interest in criminal law and often visited the criminal courts. Augustus became especially moved by defendants arrested for violations of public drunkenness laws. He soon began paying their **bail** and helping them to give up alcohol. Once Augustus could demonstrate to the judges that several of his wards had become sober, the charges were dismissed. Eventually the procedure became regular. Augustus began collecting donations for bail, and by the time he passed away at 74 he is said to have rehabilitated at least 2,000 people. In 1878, those who supported his efforts were successful in getting the city of Boston to assign a permanent professional "probation" officer, and by 1891 the practice was codified into Massachusetts state law. *See also* BROCKWAY, ZEBULON (1827–1920); PAROLE.

***AUSTIN V. U.S.*, 509 U.S. 390 (1993).** A **U.S. Supreme Court** decision on civil **forfeiture** cases. The court held that the seizure of property is a monetary **punishment** subject to the excessive **fines** clause of the **Eighth Amendment** protecting against **cruel and unusual punishment**. The ruling was based on the case of Richard Lyle Austin, a South Dakota drug dealer serving seven years for distribution. He filed his argument when the U.S. government went to seize his mobile home and auto-body shop as property involved in his crimes. He successfully argued that this violated his Eighth Amendment right against excessive fines. *See also* CIVIL RIGHTS.

AUTOEROTIC FATALITY. An accidental death occurring during masturbatory sexual activity. The overwhelming majority of these cases are the result of accidental asphyxia that are the result of **hanging** or some kind of suffocation (e.g., chemicals, plastic bag). Autoerotic asphyxiation has been around since at least the 1600s. Historians interpret its appearance as related to the practice of hanging as a public sanction, whereby the death of male criminals was accompanied by an erection. Medical science has since determined that the erection (and sometimes ejaculation) witnessed is a part of automatic muscle death and not signs of sexual stimulation (Ehrlich and Sheleg 2006). Still, the practice persists. Other methods of documented autoerotic fatality have included electrocution (Klintschar, Grabuschnigg, and Beham 1998), power hydraulics (O'Halloran and Dietz 1993), and hemorrhage caused by insertion of objects such as a pencil or shoehorn (Byard, Eitzen, and James 2000). The incidence of autoerotic fatality is incredibly rare, with studies estimating that it is generally between 0.2 and 0.5 cases per million people (Sauvageau and Geberth 1983).

AUTO-ETHNOGRAPHY. A method of scientific inquiry advocated by qualitative researchers and social interactionist theorists in criminological research. It involves a conscious reflexive effort by the writer/researcher to identify and question meanings as they are situated in the self, culture, and political realities. One of the first auto-ethnographies in criminal justice was Clifford Shaw's *The Jack Roller* (1930). A growing body of work in **convict criminology** uses this genre. *See also* ETHNOGRAPHY.

AVERSION THERAPY. A therapeutic practice used in the elimination of undesirable behaviors such as drug and alcohol abuse, nail biting, and aggression. The therapy links the target behavior with unpleasant stimuli through principles of conditioning used in behavioral psychology. The adverse stimuli are typically a chemical (i.e., in alcohol abuse treatment, Antabuse that triggers immediate hangover effects when consuming alcohol), electric shock, and more recently negative imagery. Aversion therapy was famously dramatized in Anthony Burgess's *A Clockwork Orange* as the "Ludovico treatment."

B

BABY FACE NELSON (1908–1934). *See* GILLIS, LESTER JOSEPH (1908–1934); HOOVER, J. EDGAR (1895–1972); PURVIS, MELVIN (1903–1960).

BACKGROUND CHECK. In the field of criminal justice in the United States, the most common use of the phrase applies to potential gun buyers. The National Instant Criminal Background Check System (NICS) was established in 1998 by the **FBI** as mandated under the 1993 Brady **Handgun** Violence Prevention Act. The desire to conduct background checks for those seeking to buy firearms has been a part of the national conversation in the United States since the 1930s (Carroll 2002). However, no formal action was taken until the **Gun Control** Act of 1968 (GCA) mandated federal firearms dealers to ask a series of background questions (i.e., Are you a fugitive from justice?) but were not required to verify answers. *See also* BRADY CENTER TO PREVENT GUN VIOLENCE; VIOLENCE.

BAD SEED HYPOTHESIS. The belief that deviance and aggression are biological, genetic traits determined from birth. The exact phrase for what is essentially the nature part of the **"nature-nurture" debate** regained popularity in the United States during the 1950s when **juvenile delinquency** was becoming a national issue. In 1954, a provocative novel by American writer William March, *The Bad Seed*, and later a movie (LeRoy 1956) and Broadway play by the same name, became very popular. The story revolves around a prepubescent girl who is outwardly the picture of perfection, but who also has no conscience and **murders** friends. The story was based on real-life **serial killer** Belle Gunness (1859–1908), a Norwegian American female serial killer. Robert D. Hare, who is best known for his extensive work into psychopathy, or the personality disorder characterized by narcissism, antisocial behavior, and a complete lack of empathy, references the work in his own *Without Conscience* (1993) as an accurate portrayal of psychopathy (also often referred to as sociopathy). *See also* PROFILING; RESSLER, ROBERT (1937–2013).

BAD TENDENCY TEST. *See BRANDENBURG V. OHIO*, 395 U.S. 444 (1969); FIRST AMENDMENT.

BAD TIME, DISCIPLINARY TIME. Time that is accumulated incidents of misconduct or bad behavior while in **prison**. Many states added considerations of "bad time" as part of **truth in sentencing** legislation in the late 1990s. Disciplinary time is not a formal part of sentencing but is usually required to be taken into **parole** board decisions.

BAIL. *See* EIGHTH AMENDMENT.

BAILEY, F. LEE (1933–). A high-profile criminal defense attorney known for his defense of **Albert DeSalvo**, **Patty Hearst**, Captain Ernest Medina from the Vietnam My Lai massacre, **Dr. Sam Sheppard**, **O. J. Simpson**, and others. He has been disbarred from both Florida (2001) and Massachusetts (2003) for mishandling the stocks of a client valued at up to $20 million. For the same event, Bailey was held in contempt of court and spent six weeks confined and was released upon surrendering the stock. He coauthored the popular book *The Defense Never Rests*.

BAIT AND SWITCH. Technique of grifters and con artists where a target is promised one thing, usually of high quality or monetary value, but upon delivery receives an inferior product. The term is commonly applied to crimes of fraud. The origin of the phrase comes from unethical advertising practices. "Bait and switch" occurs when retailers advertise a product for a low price (the bait), but when a customer goes to make the purchase he or she is told that the product is no longer available, but another, more expensive product is available (the switch). The practice is legal in the United States but can put companies at risk of a lawsuit. The practice has been criminalized in other Western countries such as Canada (Competition Act, 2002) and England and Wales.

BALANCED AND RESTORATIVE JUSTICE (BARJ). *See* BAZEMORE, GORDON; PEACEMAKING CRIMINOLOGY; RESTORATIVE JUSTICE.

BALANCING TEST AND BRIGHT LINE RULE. The balancing test and the bright line rule are at opposite ends of standard decision-making practice in a legal context. Balancing tests refer to considering or "balancing" competing interests to decide which interest prevails and whether that interest is more subjective, while bright line rules refer to a more objective process of decision making where definite rules are set out a priori and simply adhered to. Legal scholars are divided as to which approach is best. For instance, in the United States, former **U.S. Supreme Court** justice Antonin Scalia supported the bright line rule, whereas Justice Stephen Breyer is an advocate for the balancing test. Some have noted a trend over the last three decades toward the latter.

BALLISTICS. The science of projectiles and firearms developed in the 1880s. Historically, guns first appeared around 1300, with the first known image of what we now call a "gun" in 1326; they were earlier referred to as "hand cannons." Large cannons first appeared in England in 1346 at the Battle of Crecy. In the 1800s, in the United States, John Hall created the use of assembly lines for manufacturing, which standardized the gun industry. Calvin Goddard conducted the first forensic analysis of bullets in 1927 as part of a **murder** investigation. *See also* HANDGUN.

BANISHMENT. *See* PENAL COLONY; TRANSPORTATION.

BARBIE, KLAUS (1913–1991). Infamous Nazi SS officer who was stationed in Lyon, France, during World War II. The extreme **torture** that he inflicted on adults and children committed from his base (a hotel in Lyon) earned him the nickname the "Butcher of Lyon." He is said to have skinned victims alive, sexually abused them (with animals), and committed other horrors. He is suspected of being responsible for the deaths of at least 15,000 people. Following the war, he fled to Bolivia, where he worked for various foreign intelligence services as a spy. For instance, the United States and West Germany recruited him. In 1967, he allegedly helped the CIA capture Argentine revolutionary Che Guevara. When the Bolivian government fell in 1983 he was finally extradited to France. He was convicted of his horrific **crimes against humanity** and died just eight years later, of cancer, in **prison**. *See also* EXTRADITION; WAR CRIMES.

BARKER-KARPIS GANG (1931–1935). A Depression-era **gang** of approximately 25 members best known for the idea that Fred Barker's mother, Kate (aka "Ma Barker"), ran the gang (whether she was even involved in the gang's criminal activities was doubted). Fred Barker and **Alvin Karpis** met in **prison** and upon release began robbing banks and killed a **sheriff** in Missouri. Arthur "Doc" Barker, Fred's brother, joined the gang in 1932 when he was paroled from the Oklahoma State **Penitentiary**, where he was serving a life sentence for **murder**. In 1933, the gang switched **modus operandi** from bank robbery to **kidnapping**, which had just become a federal crime in 1932 following the **Lindbergh** baby kidnapping. Following the death of **Lester "Baby Face Nelson" Gillis**, Karpis became **Public Enemy** No. 1 on the **Federal Bureau of Investigation**'s (FBI's) Most Wanted List. Shortly thereafter, Fred and Kate Barker were killed in a shootout on 16 January 1935. Throughout that year, most gang members were arrested and sent to **Alcatraz**. Doc Barker was killed while attempting an escape, but Karpis was paroled in 1969. He moved to Spain in 1973 after publishing *The Alvin Karpis Story* (1971). He died in 1979, the same year that his second book, *On the Rock*, was released. *See also* PAROLE.

BARNES, HARRY ELMER (1889–1968). An American **prison** historian who around the late 1930s began to publish works that would characterize him as the main force behind Holocaust denial (Lipstadt 1994). He taught at Columbia University from 1918 to 1929 and had been one of the most successful and prolific historians of his day. By the end of the 1950s, however, his reputation had become irrevocably tarnished by his contributions to the development of the Holocaust denial movement.

BARROW, CLYDE (1909–1934). The other half of the infamous and now legendary "Bonnie and Clyde" criminal couple. Barrow was born in a poor area of Texas, the fifth of seven children, and was involved in crime and delinquency from an early age. He dropped out of school at 16, and at age 21 he met **Bonnie Parker**, aged 20. From 1930 to 1932 the couple and affiliated gang members engaged in bank robbing, which was prevalent during the Great Depression period in American history. They also were involved in several **murders**, which led to a **police** ambush in Louisiana where they were both gunned down by law enforcement officials on 23 May 1934. *See also* FEDERAL BUREAU OF INVESTIGATION (FBI); HOOVER, J. EDGAR (1895–1972); PURVIS, MELVIN (1903–1960).

***BATSON V. KENTUCKY*, 476 U.S. 79 (1986).** The **U.S. Supreme Court** held that jurors may not be dismissed solely because of race as a peremptory challenge and that this was a violation of the **Fourteenth Amendment**'s equal protection clause. It also held that a defendant was not entitled to a **jury** comprised solely of members of his/her own race. The defendant, Batson, was tried and convicted of burglary by an all-white jury and sentenced to 20 years. Batson was African American. He first appealed his case to the Kentucky Supreme Court, which upheld the conviction. Batson chose a **plea bargain** rather than be retried and was resentenced to five years. *See also* JURY SELECTION.

BATTERED WOMAN SYNDROME (BWS). The psychological syndrome formally outlined by psychologist Lenore Walker in her book *The Battered Woman* (1979) was based on research with battered women. Walker found a predictable psychological pattern to battering relationships that contained a repeated cycle of **violence** occurring in three phases: (1) emotional, verbal, and/or sexual humiliation and **torture** that builds tension; (2) the physical incident of violence; and (3) batterer guilt and repentance (a phrase that eventually disappears). Walker found that battered women stay initially due to phase three; thereafter, they stay due to a combination of fear and learned helplessness (comparable to the dynamics found in **Stockholm syndrome**). Walker's discussion of learned helplessness was based on earlier work by Martin Seligman, who demonstrated in experimental studies with dogs that this type of cycle of abuse produces deep, visceral defeat on the part of the abused. The belief system of battered women is eventually so decimated that they are cognitively incapable of perceiving alternatives. Walker's study was published just two years after the infamous case of **Francine Hughes**, a 29-year-old housewife charged with the first-degree **murder** of her abusive husband and acquitted under the temporary **insanity defense**. While Walker's study has been criticized for perpetuating certain myths about **domestic violence** (e.g., that victims suffer low self-esteem, etc.), it eventually became the basis for the battered woman's defense (BWD). The BWD argues that women who kill their batterers are not temporarily insane but are acting (even when the threat is not physically imminent) rationally in self-defense to an irrational situation and that their actions are consistent with a legal reasonable standard. Australia, Canada, New Zealand, the United Kingdom, and United States have used BWS as a mitigating factor in similar cases, but the Hughes decision and the proliferation of BWS research have not impacted case decisions as predicted. Women charged with killing their abusers rarely avoid conviction. In 1997, the U.S. Congress issued a report rejecting "all terminology related to the battered woman syndrome . . . noting that these terms were 'no longer useful or appropriate'" (Rothenberg 2003, 784). BWS is classified internationally in the World Health Organization's International Classification of Diseases (ICD) as ICD-9 code 995.81, battered person syndrome. In the United States, BWS can be classified under the *Diagnostic and Statistical Manual* as a type of posttraumatic stress disorder and or depression.

BAZEMORE, GORDON. An American criminologist known for his contributions to **restorative justice** in the United States. He has written several books and multiple journal articles on this topic and on juvenile justice, youth policy, corrections, and victims' issues. His work has been funded by George Soros's Open Society Institute, the Florida Department of Health and Rehabilitative Services, the Annie E. Casey Foundation, and the U.S. Department of Justice. Dr. Bazemore has spent most of his career at Florida Atlantic University in Boca Raton. *See also* BALANCED AND RESTORATIVE JUSTICE (BARJ).

***BAZE V. REES*, 553 U.S. 35 (2008).** A **U.S. Supreme Court capital punishment** case that upheld Kentucky's three-drug **lethal injection** protocol. The Court did not find that lethal injection was an **Eighth Amendment** violation because the first drug rendered the sentenced convict unconscious and thus did not inflict unnecessary pain. The appellant Baze had been convicted of a double **murder**. *See also* CRUEL AND UNUSUAL PUNISHMENT; DEATH PENALTY.

BEAN, JUDGE ROY (1825–1903). He was self-described as the "Law West of the Pecos" and after his death was referred to as the "**Hanging** Judge." He is reported to have killed a Mexican, in 1848, who made a threat to kill a "gringo." He escaped prosecution by fleeing to Sonora and later moved to California. In 1852 he fought a duel and was charged with attempted **murder** and later escaped jail. In 1854, he fought a second duel and escaped an attempted **lynching** when a woman cut him down. He left California for New Mexico where his troubles continued, including cutting the timber of a neighbor, watering down milk, and rustling. In 1882, Bean moved to Vinegaroon, Texas. There he became the justice of the peace for Precinct No. 6, for which he had no legal training. His courtroom was a store and saloon named after Lily Langtree. The courtroom contained a pet bear and was the scene of prizefights. How much justice was dispensed is as much myth as fact. While many hangings are attributed to him, only one seems to be verified. Known for his strange rulings, the most bizarre was perhaps to declare that there was a law that governed the killing of a man but no law for killing a Chinaman. He would rap his **pistol** on the bar, and the case was dismissed. He died in bed after a drinking binge. *See also* DUELING.

BEASTIALITY. *See* ZOOPHILIA.

BECCARIA, CESARE (BONESANA) (1738–1794). Often referred to as the "father of **criminology**," he was more specifically the founding father of classical criminal theory. His best-known publication is *On Crimes and **Punishments*** (1764). The text served as a foundation for penology and had a profound influence on American jurisprudence. In the text, Beccaria opposes the use of **torture** and **capital punishment**, advocating a fair and just deterrent-based criminal justice system centered on the principles of celerity, certainty, and severity of punishments. Beccaria was born in Milan, Italy, and educated in the Jesuit tradition. He graduated in law from the University of Pavia in 1758. His early interests included mathematics and economics. In his 20s, Beccaria was affiliated with a small group of affluent students who called themselves "L'Accademia dei pugni" (the Academy of Fists). The group discussed politics, often critiquing the Italian criminal justice system, and read the work of many great philosophers of the day, such as Hobbes, Diderot, Helvétius, Montesquieu, and Hume (Tibbetts and Hemmens 2009).

BECKER, HOWARD S. (1928–). American sociologist educated in the University of Chicago's "**Chicago School**." Best known for bringing a social interactionist perspective (Mead 1934) to mainstream **criminology** in the form of **labeling theory**. His 1963 qualitative analysis of subcultures, *The Outsiders*, established labeling theory in criminology. A decade later, Becker added a final chapter to the book clarifying that labeling theory intends only to explain secondary deviance and challenges to desistance, not initial deviance (based on **Edward Lemert**'s 1951 work). Becker's *Tricks of the Trade* (1998) is an equally well-known text on conducting systematic data collection and rigorous analysis as part of qualitative research. Becker taught at Northwestern University for 25 years before retiring. *See also* DESISTANCE FROM CRIME.

BEDAU, HUGO ADAM (1926–2012). An American philosopher best known for his many contributions to the anti–**death penalty** movement. He completed his undergraduate education at the University of Redlands in California (1949) before moving to the East Coast where he remained throughout his life. He earned his graduate degrees from Boston University (M.A., 1951) and Harvard (Ph.D., 1961) and spent most of his career at Tufts University from 1966 to 1999. While there he published *Courts, the Constitution and* ***Capital Punishment*** (1977), *Death Is Different* (1987), *Current Issues and Enduring Questions* (1996), and *The Death Penalty in America* (1997). He served on the boards of reformist organizations (e.g., the National Coalition to Abolish the Death Penalty), wrote numerous op-eds on the topic, and testified frequently on the subject before legislative committees.

BEHAVIORAL ANALYSIS UNIT (BAU). A special branch of the **FBI** that grew up around the psychological profiling work of special agents **Robert Ressler**, **Robert Roy Hazelwood**, and John Douglas throughout the 1990s, investigating cases of **serial killing** and rape. The unit was initially created in 1974 under the FBI training division to aid in such investigations and consisted of just 11 agents. A decade later, a faction of the BAU split off as the Behavioral Science Investigative Support Unit (BSISU). The Behavioral Science Unit (BSU) maintained its role under the training division, and the BSISU took over active investigation of cases. In 1994, the BSISU was further integrated with FBI crisis management and critical response group tactics and became the Investigative Support Unit (ISU). By 1997, the name had changed slightly again to the current BAU. Following the 9/11 attacks, the unit was expanded and divided into four subgroups: counterterrorism and **threat assessment** (e.g., threats, **arson**, bombings, stalking, cyber-related violations, and anticipated or active crisis situations); crimes against adults (e.g., serial, spree, and **mass murder**; sexual **assault**; **kidnapping**; and missing person cases, while also assisting in **white-collar crime**, public corruption, **organized crime**, and **civil rights**–related cases); crimes against children (e.g., child abductions, **homicides**, and sexual victimization); and the **Violent Criminal Apprehension Program (ViCAP)**. The unit has been the subject of various products of American modern popular culture, including, but not limited to, CBS's hit show *Criminal Minds* (2005–current) and the very successful novel by Thomas Harris, and later films about fictional forensic psychiatrist and **serial killer** Hannibal Lecter: *Red Dragon* (novel, 1981), *Manhunter* (film, 1986), *The Silence of the Lambs* (novel, 1988; film, 1991), and *Hannibal* (novel, 1999; film, 2001).

BEHAVIOR MODIFICATION. Behavior modification is the alteration of behavioral patterns through the use of positive and/or negative reinforcement. The intention is to extinguish or modify undesirable behaviors in favor of encouraging desired patterns of behavior. Among the earliest discussions of behavior modification was by Edward Thorndike in 1911. The employment of techniques of behavior modification was greatly increased following the work of B. F. Skinner in the 1960s and 1970s, which utilized his principle of reinforcement. Skinner's work led to the more accepted term "applied behavioral analysis" in the 1990s. Applications of behavior modification have been used to treat **addictions** and convicts returning home from **prison** and in residential treatment settings.

BELTWAY SNIPER. *See* MALVO, LEE (1985–); MUHAMMAD, JOHN ALLEN (1960–2009); SERIAL KILLER.

BENCH WARRANT. *See* WARRANT.

BENNET, JAMES V. (1894–1978). Second director of the **Federal Bureau of Prisons (BOP)** from 1937 to 1964. Bennet was a World War I veteran who was appointed at age 25 to the U.S. Bureau of Efficiency. He wrote *The Federal Penal and Correctional Problem* (1928), which helped to set the arguments for centralizing federal **prisons** resulting in the BOP. Bennet was a penal reformer who advocated education and **work release** for prison populations. He has the distinction of both opening and closing **Alcatraz**. He described Alcatraz as "the darkest day in American prison history." *See also* PENAL REFORM.

BENTHAM, JEREMY (1748–1832). A 19th-century British philosopher whose ideas became foundations across several areas of the criminal justice system, including law, ethics, and **prison** architecture (Bentham 1789). Bentham was born in London to affluent parents and had one brother, Samuel, to whom he was close throughout his life. He completed his undergraduate education at Oxford University at the age of 15 and his master's degree at 18. A decade later when the United States became a country and the Declaration of Independence was published, Bentham published a vicious critique of the contents, a position he never parted from (Armitage 2007). Bentham was a proponent of Utilitarianism, which defines what is good as that which results in the greatest happiness for the most people; his most famous student was John Stuart Mill. He advocated for a prison design, the **panopticon**, which maximizes supervisory and disciplinary vision. The idea is attributed to Bentham's brother, who while working in Russia became familiar with the idea of a process of central inspection that Bentham developed into an inspection house—an immense circular structure that positioned the guard in the center, from where he could peer into all prisoners' cells, and in which no prisoner could easily communicate with the prisoner next to him. Part of Bentham's reasoning was that the confined would eventually internalize the gaze of the inspector and behave (even when they might not actually be watched). There were two attempts to adopt the panopticon to meet needs in the United States. The first was what would eventually become **Western Penitentiary**, and the second was Statesville. Modern reformers came to view his design as draconian and Orwellian (Foucault 1971).

***BENTON V. MARYLAND*, 395 U.S. 784 (1969).** *See PALKO V. CONNECTICUT*, 302 U.S. 319 (1937).

BERKOWITZ, DAVID (1953–). *See* SON OF SAM.

BERTILLION, ALPHONSE (1853–1914). A French innovator in **forensics** and a Parisian **police** officer working in the classical tradition who developed anthropometrics and standardized the process of photographing arrested persons in the late 1800s (aka, the **mug shot**). Borrowing also from anthropology as **Lombroso** did, anthropometrics intended to identify criminals quantitatively based on their physical measurements. Bertillion was born to a statistician father but was expelled from the university. He was drafted into the French military at 22 years of age and served approximately four years before his father got him a clerical job with the Paris police. During those years, he developed this system, as well as biometric processes related to footprints, **ballistics**, and force. He published a paper in 1912 on the process of fingerprinting, which was later shown to involve data fraud (Miller 2013). Bertillion's work helped provide the foundation for what has become modern American **forensic** science. *See also* FINGERPRINT.

BEST PRATICE. *See* EVIDENCE-BASED PRACTICES.

***BETTS V. BRADY*, 316 U.S. 455 (1942).** A landmark **U.S. Supreme Court** case which held that **indigent** defendants were not entitled to an attorney. Following his charging for robbery, Betts had to defend himself and was convicted and sentenced to **prison**. The issue of representation had also been argued in the case of the **Scottsboro Boys** and notably in ***Gideon v. Wainwright*, 372 U.S. 335 (1963)**, which reversed the Court's holding in Betts. The dissenting opinion in Betts noted the unfairness of failure to have representation, noting the greater likelihood of conviction. It was also noted in the dissenting opinion that those untrained in law suffered a disadvantage in court. *See also* DUE PROCESS; FOURTEENTH AMENDMENT; *POWELL V. ALABAMA*, 287 U.S. 45 (1932).

BEYOND A REASONABLE DOUBT. The phrase describes the standard by which juries are told to make their determination of guilt. If they can judge the defendant to be guilty beyond a reasonable doubt, they must return a guilty verdict. Its first appearance in written American jurisprudence is in 1880, **U.S. Supreme Court** case *Miles v. United States*, 103 U.S. 304 (1880). In 1970, the standard was applied to juvenile justice in U.S. Supreme Court case, ***In re Winship*, 397 U.S. 358 (1970)**. *See also* JURY.

BIANCHI, KENNETH (1951–). He is otherwise known as the **Hillside Strangler** due to the location of his victims' bodies on the hillsides of an area in California known as Glendale Highland Park. Bianchi **kidnapped**, raped, **tortured** (e.g., injecting them with household chemicals, electric shock), and **murdered** 12 women between 1977 and 1978 with his cousin Angelo Buono. Bianchi was originally from New York and moved to California in 1975, moving in with Buono, who resided there. The men allegedly soon got involved in pimping prostitutes, and once violent with them, moved on to upper- and middle-class women by posing as **police** officers. They killed both women and girls ranging in age from 12 to 28. Bianchi was born in New York to an alcoholic mother who was a prostitute and gave up Bianchi a few weeks after his birth. His adoptive mother reported that Bianchi had several issues since he was an infant, including chronic bedwetting, and petit mal seizures, pathological lying, and he was diagnosed at age 10 with passive-aggressive personality disorder. Following his convictions, he was also diagnosed with antisocial personality disorder and sexual sadism. Bianchi posed as a police officer in the commission of his crimes. This was something that he had professional interest in: he had worked as a security guard in New York, applied to the Los Angeles Police Department (LAPD), and did several ride-alongs with the LAPD even during the period in which the majority of his murders were committed. Bianchi had also posed as a psychologist. In 1979, Bianchi was given six life sentences for his crimes, which he is serving in Washington State, where he committed his last two known murders. His cousin, Buono, died in **prison** in 2002. Bianchi has one child with a previous girlfriend, Kelli Boyd. *See also* PROSTITUTION; SERIAL KILLER.

BIAS/HATE CRIME. The development of legal provisions to protect against crimes motivated strictly by hate and prejudice based on one's classification into a group (e.g., race, religion, or national origin) began early in the United States with the **Civil Rights** Act of 1871. After the Civil War, bias crimes toward African Americans were on the rise, especially with the growth of the **Ku Klux Klan**. In 1968, federal statute 18 U.S. 245, part of the Civil Rights Act of 1968 (aka, the Fair Housing Act), broadened the scope of previous legislation to include discriminatory housing practices (devastating and rampant especially through the 1950s; see Glotzer 2015) based on race, religion, or national origin. The **Violent Crime** Control and Law Enforcement Act (1994) increased the sanctions for those convicted of **hate crimes** at the federal level. At the state level, in 1978, California was the first to pass their own hate crime legislation, and many states followed. Alaska was the first to add sexual orientation as a protected group. At the state level, criminal actions taken against people based on their gender (28 states), age (13 states), ancestry, marital status, ethnicity, disabilities (32 states), military status, activist status (e.g., member of a civil rights organization), sexual orientation (31 states), political affiliation, and most recently homelessness (3 states) have all been included under the definitions of these crimes. In 1987, California allowed that all crimes could be driven by group hatred. In 2009, following the heinous and well-known **murder** of a young **homosexual** man, **Matthew Shepard**, perceived gender, gender identity, sexual orientation, and disability were added to the federal law. As of 2007, all but five states—Arkansas, Georgia, Indiana, South Carolina, and Wyoming—have bias/hate crime laws. The U.S. Congress passed the Matthew Shepard and James Byrd, Jr., Hate Crimes Prevention Act (2009), which was signed into law by President Obama. More than half of the states are required to collect hate crime statistics and allow for civil suits. The federal government and all campus security authorities are required to collect hate crime statistics. At the federal level, crimes committed based on race, religion, ethnicity, nationality, gender, sexual orientation, gender identity, and disability are considered bias crimes.

BIFURCATED PROCESS. This phrase refers to the dual nature of some **trial** processes, especially in the U.S. court system. The first phase involves the determination of guilt, and the second, deliberations over sentencing. The aim is to create a separation between the deliberations made for each phase. For instance, one will argue that guilt is to be determined by proof of the allegations, not on the basis of the subsequent **punishments**.

BILL OF RIGHTS. The first 10 amendments to the U.S. Constitution. These amendments were introduced in the wake of deliberations over the U.S. Constitution. A group of founders including Patrick Henry and Samuel Adams, who came to be known as the Anti-Federalists, raised objections and demanded that additional assurances of specific personal liberties be codified, that the balance between state and federal authority be more clearly articulated, and that government authority be more generally limited. These ideas built upon earlier state legislation such as the Virginia Declaration of Rights and on English law found in the English Bill of Rights (1689) and the **Magna Carta** (1215). Refer to appendix 1, "The Bill of Rights."

BIN LADEN, OSAMA (1957–2011). A Saudi Arabian man best known for founding the Islamic terrorist group **Al-Qaeda**, the group responsible for orchestrating three coordinated attacks on America on 11 September 2001. The attacks were on the World Trade Center (United Airlines Flights 11 and 175 crashed into the buildings in downtown Manhattan), the United States Pentagon (American Airlines Flight 77), and a failed attack on the White House (United Airlines Flight 93). The plane crashed instead into a nearby field. The total number of deaths was 2,996 people, and injuries totaled twice that number. The death toll has continued to rise to this day as emergency responders in New York City develop various forms of cancer due to the inhalation of hazardous building materials that day at ground zero. Bin Laden was born to the 10th wife of Mohammed bin Awad bin Laden, the wealthiest nonroyal Saudi in the country. His Syrian mother, Alia Ghanem, was dismissed from Mohammed bin Laden's harem and passed on to one of his business associates, Mohammed al-Attas, for marriage. The couple went on to have four children, and bin Laden was raised a devout Sunni Muslim with his half-siblings. At the age of 18, bin Laden married his first cousin, Najwa Ghanem, who was 14 years old at the time. Through his life he went on to take at least four or five additional wives (reports vary) resulting in his fathering at least 20 to 26 children. He attended the prestigious, secular King Abdulaziz University in Saudi Arabia, studying business and economics. Five years after his first marriage, bin Laden joined Abdullah Azzam via Pakistan. Azzam had issued a fatwa requiring all Muslims to fight with the Mujahideen in their war against the Soviet Union in Afghanistan. The United

States had also joined the Pakistani army in this fight, albeit for very different reasons, namely to combat communism. Like the United States, who funneled money and arms for the war, bin Laden used his substantial inheritance (reported to be upward of $30 million) and other business connections to develop a global network of militants to fight the Soviets. Bin Laden was also charged by the Pakistani government during this period to suppress a possible Shia uprising. The subsequent action taken is now referred to as the 1988 Giglia massacre in which 400 to 700 Shias were slaughtered in an ambush of burnings, **lynchings**, and rapes. It was during this period that bin Laden gained a reputation as a leader and fighter. Al-Qaeda was formed that same year, reportedly in an informal meeting between bin Laden, Azzam, and leaders within the Egyptian Islamic Jihad (Wright 2006). The idea was to sustain the connections made in the fight against the Soviets so that the arm of jihad could go wherever needed. When the Soviets withdrew from Afghanistan the following year, bin Laden was credited with the success, and his power grew. Bin Laden quickly went on to exploit the global infrastructure that he had formed, especially with Azzam. They developed training camps, marketing strategies for their ideology, and a belief system that explicitly condoned a merciless jihad that considered even innocents such as children as viable targets. The group grew as a series of cells. Bin Laden was finally brought to justice by the U.S. military under the Obama administration in Pakistan on 2 May 2011 after years of successfully eluding detection, most likely under the protection of the Pakistani government (Ross 2011). *See also* WORLD TRADE CENTER (WTC) BOMBINGS.

BIOLOGICAL CRIMINOLOGY. Biological theories of crime are based on the idea that people who engage in crime are physiologically different from birth from individuals who do not offend. This theoretical approach is part of the positivist tradition and began to be applied to the study of crime with the work of **Cesare Lombroso** in the 19th century. Initially, differences in physical appearance and structure were targeted as the causal mechanisms of criminality. The physical manifestations were thought to be indications of an inferiority that was the cause of crime. Early methods included physiognomy, **phrenology**, and somatology. While biological **criminology** was the first theory of criminality to bring science to bear on the question, which up until that point had been a matter for philosophers from the classical school, the process of measuring a person's facial features or expression (physiognomy), skull dimensions (phrenology), and body types (somatology) failed to produce valid results. The logical implications for managing crime from this point of view (e.g., isolating, treating, separating, sterilizing, or killing) present ethical challenges. The school has since evolved into what many refer to as contemporary trait theory. This modern version of biological criminology seeks to identify various individual chemical and genetic variations as the source of criminality, first through heredity studies and now primarily through new scientific technologies such as magnetic resonance imaging (MRI). Other variables studied as possible causes of criminality include things like IQ and hormones (e.g., testosterone). *See also* ATAVISM.

BIOLOGICAL DETERMINISM. *See* BIOSOCIAL CRIMINOLOGY.

BIOSOCIAL CRIMINOLOGY. Biosocial theories of crime combine fundamental assumptions of both biological criminology and a more external/sociological approach to understanding criminality. The field originated with biological **criminology** but suggests a softer form of determinism, as criminality is not predestined but rather is the result of a complex interplay between nature (i.e., one's biology, neurology, physiology, genetics, and evolutionary pressures) and nurture (i.e., the social and physical environment). Biosocial criminology importantly does not include judgments that qualify differences as defects or abnormalities. From this point of view, crime control can logically intervene with social programs and rehabilitative efforts. Biosocial theories have enjoyed a reemergence in mainstream criminology in the late 20th century. *See also* NATURE-NURTURE DEBATE.

BIOTERRORISM. The deliberate use of biological material (e.g., viruses, bacteria, toxins, chemicals) as weapons of death, illness, and fear. Biological weapons were used in warfare prior to their use by terrorists. During World War I, Germany is reported to have sent soldiers to infect the U.S. Army's horses that were used to transport supplies and arms to troops. Examples of bioterrorism in modern America began in the 1970s when a small terrorist group called RISE attempted to infiltrate the Chicago public water supply with typhoid (Carus 2000). The first of two and the largest successful bioterrorist attacks in the United States occurred in 1984 in the state of Oregon (the second being the 2001 anthrax attacks). A cultlike group led by Bhagwan Shree Rajneesh poisoned 751 people by contaminating various public places (e.g., restaurants, salad bars, doorknobs, countertops) with salmonella. Seven hundred fifty-one got serious food poisoning, 45 were hospitalized, and there were no fatalities. The group's aim was to incapacitate voters so that the group could elect their candidates during a local election. In 2001, the week after the attacks on America, several letters admonishing America and praising Allah, laced with deadly anthrax, were received by news media offices and the U.S. Congress; five people died as a result, and 17 were hospitalized. **Bruce Edwards Ivins**, a U.S. government scientist, was convicted posthumously of the crimes (he committed suicide as a suspect in the case), but there remains doubt as to the veracity of the **Federal Bureau of Investigation**'s (FBI's) finding. *See also* TERRORISM.

BIRMINGHAM CHURCH BOMBING. On Sunday, 15 September 1963, during Sunday school, right before the 11 a.m. service at the 16th Street Baptist Church in Birmingham, Alabama, white supremacist terrorists set off at least 15 sticks of dynamite under the front steps of the church (where many **civil rights** protests of the time began). The bombing took the lives of four children attending Sunday school, all girls. Many others were injured. The church was located in what had become one of the most racially charged cities in the United States. The governor, George Wallace, was outwardly unsupportive of desegregation, and the city was known to have one of the most violent **Ku Klux Klan (KKK)** chapters in the country. The congregation of the church was primarily black, and civil rights activists and leaders congregated there. It took almost 40 years for all of the perpetrators and all members of the KKK to be brought to justice. Much of this had to do with **discrimination**, not just at the state and local levels but at the federal level as well. **J. Edgar Hoover**, then **FBI** director, allegedly ignored **evidence** in the case and was known to disapprove of civil rights generally. Alabama state **attorney general** Bob Baxley reopened the case and brought KKK leader Robert E. Chambliss to account for his crime. He was convicted in 1977 and died in **prison** in 1985. There were three other known perpetrators. Thomas Blanton and Bobby Frank Cherry, KKK members, were not convicted until 2001 and 2002, almost 40 years after murdering the children. The last suspect, KKK member Herman Frank Cash, died before he could account for his crimes. *See also* WHITE SUPREMACY.

BLACK CODES. A continuation of former "slave codes" passed after the end of the Civil War (1865–1866) that applied only to Americans of African descent. Under the slave codes, blacks were not allowed to vote, bear arms, or be educated (anything that might undermine the mechanism that kept slavery in place). The black codes had the same intent and effect of destroying African American freedom: blacks could not testify against whites in court, could not serve on juries or in state militias, could not vote, and could not take a job without permission from the former employer (in other words, they were still slaves). White legislatures had a vested interest in controlling black labor at this time to guarantee a low-wage workforce. Black codes created a **vagrancy** law that effectively criminalized minor infractions. Blacks who were deemed to have violated these vagrancy laws could then be committed to involuntary labor (this was the precursor to the **convict lease**

system). The codes were repealed in 1888 but reappeared later that century and remained in place under the provisions of Jim Crow laws until the **civil rights** movement of the 1960s.

***BLAKELY V. WASHINGTON*, 542 U.S. 296 (2004).** Blakely was charged with first-degree **kidnapping** for kidnapping his wife after she filed for divorce. He pled guilty to second-degree kidnapping. The judge's sentence exceeded the **sentencing guidelines** because of what he called "deliberate cruelty." The **U.S. Supreme Court** in a landmark decision held that the judge violated the Sixth Amendment and that enhanced sentences could only be done by a **jury**. *See also* DETERMINATE SENTENCING; DUE PROCESS; UNITED STATES SENTENCING COMMISSION.

BLENDED SENTENCING. The blending of adult and juvenile sentencing provisions. Many American states adopted these laws at the beginning of what many call "the punitive turn" in American sentencing and corrections which began about 1985. By the end of 1995, 16 states had blended-sentencing statutes in place and at least 26 more by the end of 2004. The states that allow the **juvenile court** to draw upon adult sentencing options make up 60 percent of the nation's juvenile population between the ages of 10 and 17 (U.S. Census 2000).

BLOOD FEUDS. These are lengthy, violent conflicts usually between families and spanning several generations. Historically, these feuds appear most often in areas and in times that the authority of the law (e.g., government, **police**) is secondary to family authority, loyalty, and association. In ancient Greek and Hebraic law, avenging one's family or kin was a right and part of good justice. Today, the right to vengeance appears in sacred law systems (i.e., sharia). Well-known feuds between families have persisted throughout human history across almost all cultures. In the United States, well-known blood feuds have found their way here from Sicily, Italy (dramatized and popularized in the *Godfather* films), and the **Hatfield and McCoy feud**. *See also* FEUDING.

BOESKY, IVAN (1937–). A stock trader who along with Michael Milken became infamous for insider trading. Investigations into his trading activity began in 1987 because of trades that occurred just before the takeover of companies. This was one of the few times that insider trading was aggressively prosecuted, and it set the stage for similar actions in the future. Boesky plea-bargained and received a three-and-a-half-year sentence and a $1 million **fine**. Part of the plea required his cooperation and the subsequent incrimination of Michael Milken for similar activities. Boesky's illegal activities have been detailed in *Den of Thieves* (Stewart 1991). Milken received a 10-year sentence, which was reduced to two years, and he served 10 months; however, he also paid approximately $1.1 billion to settle fines and lawsuits. Unlike Boesky, who struggled to recover after **prison**, Milken has become a renowned philanthropist. Milken was diagnosed and treated for prostate cancer, which led to the founding of the Prostate Cancer Foundation. *See also* PLEA BARGAIN.

BONANNO, JOE (1905–2002). He was the head of the Bonanno crime family at age 26, and his criminal history began at about 20 years of age. Bonanno served time in state and federal penitentiaries, although he was never convicted of a major crime. He retired from mob activities (which were reputed to include **murder**, **gang** wars, and **money laundering**) following a heart attack in 1968 and never broke his "blood" oath. *See also* CASTELLAMARESE WARS.

BOOKIE. A professional bettor who analyzes, determines, or simply posts the betting odds in games, especially horse racing and team sports; receives and records wagers from a number of people on a regular basis; collects from losers; and pays off winners. Bookmaking started around 1780 at horse auctions. The name Tattersall is immortalized at English racetracks today by bookmakers who set up their stands at the "Tattersall Enclosure." The term *bookie* originated with the activity of "making book" or keeping a notebook of wagers. In the early days, bookmakers were involved in handicapping. However, chaos prevailed both at the track and in betting shops throughout London until the tradition of the "honest bookmaker." A bookie's reputation of honesty was and is very important for the success of the business and apparently originated with the reputations of two famous bookmakers, Fred Swindell and Leviathan Davies. Around 1850, Davies also created "lists of odds" that were posted throughout London, which made offtrack betting possible. In 1866, the first American bookmaking business was established in Philadelphia, Pennsylvania.

BOOT CAMP. Correctional boot camps are modeled after military recruit training programs and are often considered to be shock incarceration. The first boot camps appeared in Georgia and Oklahoma in 1983. Youth and young adults assigned to boot camps are predominantly first-time and nonviolent offenders. The duration is intended to be shorter than **prison** and usually lasts less than six months. Boot camps have varied in operational style. One type relies primarily on a military-style regimen, another on educational programs combined with military structure, and the third incorporates the characteristics of the second style combined with aftercare. Boot camps began to fall out of favor when statistics revealed little change from traditional **recidivism** rates; however, the third style consistently demonstrates the most success. Improper personnel training and supervision became manifest in the abusive deaths of some boot camp participants and the trauma experienced by some youths who attended the camps. *See also* PRISON REFORM.

BOOTHE, MAUDE BALLINGTON (1865–1948). An American social reformer and advocate for **prison reform** with a concentration on **prisons** and their failures with convicts. She developed her interest in social issues while affiliated with the Salvation Army's Paris branch and went on to co-found Volunteers of America, which continues her work operating halfway houses and other programs for ex-offenders. While she published several books, the one that described her work with convicts was *After Prison—What?* (1905).

BOOTLEGGING. Bootlegging is most commonly associated with the illegal transportation of alcohol (whiskey, rum, etc.) when it is prohibited (see the Eighteenth Amendment of 1920 and the Twenty-First Amendment of 1933, which repealed **Prohibition**) or to avoid taxation. One derivation for the term is that early automobiles were built with a "boot" for storage. A container of alcohol would be kept in the boot to dispense to buyers. Some examples include rumrunners smuggling rum to Florida and Canadian whiskey across the Canadian border into the United States during Prohibition. Prohibition also encouraged other illegal activity, such as the illegal operation of stills (in the South referred to as "moonshine" and in cities to keep up with the demand for alcohol and for "speakeasies," which also operated illegally). Bootlegging in modern times is sometimes used to describe the smuggling of goods both real and counterfeit. *See also* CAPONE, ALPHONSE (1899–1947); COUNTERFEITING.

BORDEN, LIZZIE (1860–1927). The primary suspect in the unsolved 1892 **murder** case of her father and stepmother. She was charged with the murders, tried, and acquitted. No one else has ever been charged. She was held in **prison** for the duration of her **trial**. The crime is infamously remembered because of a rhyme that depicts the gruesome nature of the offense—multiple axe blows, a total of 81. In reality, there were either 29 or 30 wounds.

BORDER PATROL. *See* CUSTOMS AND BORDER PROTECTION, UNITED STATES.

BOSTON MARATHON BOMBINGS. *See* TSARNAEV BROTHERS (DZHOKAR, 1993–, AND TAMERLAN, 1986–2013).

BOSTON STRANGLER. *See* DESALVO, ALBERT (1930–1973).

BOUNTY. A fee for the return/apprehension of someone who escapes from custody, does not appear, or avoids the judicial process. *See also* BAIL; BOUNTY HUNTER.

BOUNTY HUNTER. Also referred to as a **bail** bond recovery agent, bail enforcement agent, or fugitive recovery agent who earns a living by retrieving and bringing (rearresting) defendants who have absconded from **trial** ("fugitives of the law") to the proper authorities for a monetary reward ("**bounty**"). Bail bond agents are considered part of the criminal justice system per the **U.S. Supreme Court** ruling in *Taylor v. Taintor*, 83 U.S. 366, 21 l.ed. 287 (1872). In the Unites States, most bail bond agents work under bail agents for a commission (similar to a bounty or reward). The extent of their authority varies by state. For instance, in some states bail bond agents are legally able to enter a defendant's premises without a **warrant**.

BOW STREET RUNNERS. The Bow Street Runners (a nickname given to them by the London public) were the United Kingdom's first professional **police** force, established by Henry Fielding in London in 1749. The Bow Street Runners would operate until 1839, when they were officially replaced by the Metropolitan Police, which were established in 1829. Many of the principles and practices of the Bow Street Runners, such as conducting investigations, would be incorporated into early American colonial towns and retained in modern law enforcement practices. *See also* DETECTIVE; PEEL, SIR ROBERT (1788–1850).

BRADY CENTER TO PREVENT GUN VIOLENCE. The central theme for the center is its Brady Campaign (founded in 1974), which is opposed to gun **violence** and consequently promotes **gun control**. During the 1981 attempted **assassination** of President Ronald Reagan by **John Hinckley**, James Brady was disabled, and he and his wife initiated the center and would be its supporters. The campaign gained support following the 1980 **murder** of John Lennon, which influenced the Million Mom March in 1981. Attempts to strengthen the effort were increased with the passage of the Brady Act (also referred to as the Brady Bill, named for James Brady) in 1993. The Brady Act and the Brady Campaign in general were opposed by the National Rifle Association (NRA), which attempted to have the act declared unconstitutional by the **U.S. Supreme Court**. The Court, in *Printz v. United States*, 521 U.S. 898 (1997), did not do so except to recognize that the imposition of a mandate for local law enforcement to conduct **background checks** for purchases was a Tenth Amendment violation and thus unconstitutional. The system of background checks not blocked by the Court has resulted in over 200 million such checks and more than one million being prohibited from purchases. The primary reason for denial to purchase a weapon is a previous felony conviction; however, prosecutions for violating the Brady Act are infrequent. *See also* COLUMBINE MASSACRE; MASS MURDER; OMNIBUS CRIME CONTROL AND SAFE STREETS ACT OF 1968, PUB. L. NO. 90-351, 82 STAT. 197; SANDY HOOK MASSACRE.

***BRADY V. MARYLAND*, 373 U.S. 83 (1963).** A landmark **U.S. Supreme Court** case which held that **exculpatory evidence** capable of exonerating the defendant must be provided to the defendant/defense attorney. Brady admitted his involvement in the **murder** but not the actual killing. The failure to produce that **evidence** by the prosecutor denied Brady **due process** and his **Fourteenth Amendment** protections. This resulted in what is known as the Brady rule, also referred to as disclosure of material. In a related situation, law enforcement officers who do not submit evidence that might clear a defendant are referred to as Brady cops. This evidence often is that obtained from an informant or someone who is paid to be a **witness**. *See also* EXONERATION.

BRANCH DAVIDIANS. A Seventh-Day Adventist sect founded in 1955 by Victor Houteff and later led by David Koresh, they were served in 1993 with a **search warrant** from the Bureau of Alcohol, Tobacco, and Firearms (ATF) because of a suspicion of illegal weapons, explosive materials, and other offenses. This resulted in what has come to be called the **Waco siege**. A compound belonging to the Branch Davidians engaged in a standoff that lasted 51 days with federal and state law enforcement as well as the U.S. military, resulting in a gun battle that took the lives of four government agents and six members of the sect. An **assault** on the compound with tear gas and a fire of disputed origin culminated in a total of 76 dying, including Koresh and British nationals, from a potential mass suicide involving cyanide poisoning. The Waco siege raised a number of questions about the appropriateness of actions on both sides. In addition to the weapons suspicion, there were allegations of sexual misconduct and possibly the operation of a methamphetamine laboratory, as well as questions whether someone in the compound fired the initial shot. The federal side faced questions of who was in charge, whether **warrants** were appropriate, on-site procedures, training for the confrontation, the use of incendiary devices (including the existence of and use of a flamethrower), where firing was launched at the compound (i.e., at exits, preventing escape by Branch Davidians), whether the federal authorities were aggressive and reckless, and more. There was enough gunfire exchanged that federal authorities ran low on ammunition.

Criminal prosecutions after the incident led to 12 Branch Davidian survivors being charged with **aiding and abetting** in the **murder** of federal authorities and weapons charges. They were acquitted on the murder charges and convicted of voluntary **manslaughter**, weapons use, and resisting arrest. The sentences ranged up to 40 years. Appeals followed, including with the **U.S. Supreme Court**, and defendants were engaged in a variety of legal actions, including the vacating of sentences, being resentenced, and then having sentences reduced by 25 years. All defendants have been released from **prison** as of 2007. **Timothy McVeigh** wrote that the Waco siege was the motivation for the **Oklahoma City bombing**. Former U.S. **attorney general** Ramsey Clark, acting as a civil attorney, referred to the Waco Incident as "the greatest domestic law enforcement tragedy in the history of the United States."

***BRANDENBURG V. OHIO*, 395 U.S. 444 (1969).** A series of **U.S. Supreme Court** holdings led up to *Brandenburg*, beginning with *Whitney v. California*, 249 U.S. 47 (1927). Brandenburg was a member of the **Ku Klux Klan** and had made inflammatory racist speeches for which he was convicted and sentenced to 10 years in **prison**. The Court holding avoided the clear and present danger test and substituted the idea of imminent lawless action for determining seditious speech. The Court overturned the conviction as a violation of Brandenburg's **First** and **Fourteenth Amendment** protections and created what is referred to as the Brandenburg test, which is the current standard for inflammatory speech. *See also* FREEDOM OF SPEECH.

BRANDING. A design either burned into the skin or applied with a frozen iron which would produce a permanent scar. The brand itself was a form of **punishment** because of the degree of pain during application. The brand either indicated reduced status, such as for a slave, or was used for punishment. The French used different brands to signify different types of punishment, such as indicating life on a galley, forced labor, or a fleur-de-lis specific to certain offenses. Depending on the degree of notoriety or humiliation desired, the brand could be applied in different places, such as between the eyes or on a hand or wrist. Puritan brandings during colonial times, made infamous by Nathaniel Hawthorne's *Scarlet Letter*, applied letters such as *A* for adultery or *B* for blasphemy, which signified the offense to those who encountered the offender. Brandings as punishment are now considered a violation of the **Eighth Amendment** and constitute **cruel and unusual punishment**. *See also* CORPORAL PUNISHMENT.

***BRAZENBURG V. HAYES*, 408 U.S. 665 (1972).** A landmark **U.S. Supreme Court** case which held that the **First Amendment** did not disallow members of the press from testifying before grand juries. A reporter (Brazenburg) witnessed the making and use of hashish and in his article noted that his sources were users of hashish. He was subpoenaed and refused to testify, resulting in a contempt of court citation. The arguments included that any necessity for reporters to testify would affect news making. The Court disagreed, denying privilege to reporters. There has been interpretation to suggest that the Brazenburg case is a specific case and that the holding does not necessarily apply in all cases of reporters being obligated to testify because of knowledge and should be determined on a case-by-case basis. *See also* CIVIL RIGHTS; WITNESS.

BRIBERY. Money or items of value used in an exchange (intended to influence) to receive a favorable response that might not otherwise occur. Bribery can take many forms, including gifts, promises of payments, refunds, goods provided for free, and more. The legal response to accepting a bribe may range from unethical conduct to criminal conduct because it creates a circumstance of favoritism rather than fair play. History has many examples of scandals that have resulted from bribes, including Pope Alexander VI (a member of the Borgia family), President Grant (1869–1877), **William "Boss" Tweed** of New York City, and more recently Halliburton, which, in 2009, paid Nigerian officials about $180 million in bribes. *See also* POLICE CORRUPTION.

BRIDEWELL. Bridewell, from St. Bridget's Well, was an early form of **prison**, which had originally been a palace and later an orphanage before being utilized as a **debtor's prison** beginning in 1553. It was also used for homeless children and unruly women, that is, women who violated female gender roles or engaged in behaviors such as drinking alcohol, disobeying husbands/fathers, and having romantic relations out of wedlock. The prison was known for corruption, its reliance on **solitary confinement**, the **whipping** of women (in the presence of governors and interested observers), and other abuses, as well as for being a generally unhealthy environment as repeatedly pointed out by reformers. The term spread to other countries and has been used in the United States, with one jail in Chicago being given the name. Bridewell was closed in the mid-1800s. *See also* CRUEL AND UNUSUAL PUNISHMENT.

BRINK'S ROBBERY. A 1981 armed robbery that was jointly carried out by the Black Liberation Army and the **Weather Underground Organization** (which later became the May 19th Communist Organization), during which $1.6 million were stolen and two **police** officers were killed. The defendants represented themselves during the **trial**, claiming they did not recognize the authority of the U.S. government. The first three to go to trial were found guilty of **murder** and three counts of armed robbery, for which they received a 25-to-life **prison** sentence. One died of AIDS in 1986, and another has been granted clemency by Governor Andrew Cuomo for his conduct in prison. Two others were also convicted, one receiving a 75-to-life sentence. Kathy Boudin is perhaps the best known of those involved. She **plea-bargained** for a 20-year sentence and was released from Bedford Hills prison at age 60 in 2003. She is currently an adjunct professor at Columbia University. *See also* SYMBIONESE LIBERATION ARMY; TERRORISM.

BROCKWAY, ZEBULON (1827–1920). *See* CROFTON, SIR WALTER (1815–1897); ELMIRA REFORMATORY; MACONOCHIE, CAPTAIN ALEXANDER (1787–1860); PAROLE; PRISON REFORM.

BROKEN WINDOWS THEORY. *See* ORDER MAINTENANCE POLICING; WILSON, JAMES QUINN (1931–2012).

***BROWN V. MISSISSIPPI*, 297 U.S. 278 (1936).** A **U.S. Supreme Court** case which held that confessions obtained involuntarily and as a result of **police** violence violated the **Fourteenth Amendment due process** clause and may not be considered as **evidence**. Three black men were arrested for **murder**, beaten, and abused by police officers and then confessed. This was the only evidence entered into the **trial**. They were sentenced to death by **hanging**. While the Mississippi Supreme Court affirmed the conviction, the U.S. Supreme Court reversed it, citing the due process clause. The defendants, rather than risk retrial, would plead nolo contendere or no defense to **manslaughter** and would be sentenced to terms of seven and a half years, two and a half years, and six months in **prison**. *See also MIRANDA V. ARIZONA*, 384 U.S. 436 (1966); SCOTTSBORO BOYS; THIRD DEGREE; VIOLENCE.

BTK KILLER. *See* RADER, DENNIS (1945–).

BUGGERY. An English term derived from the **common law** Buggery Act 1533 that criminalized sodomy and bestiality. Buggery is often used interchangeably with the term sodomy to mean anal sex. In 1861, Section 61 of the Offences against the Person Act from the British Parliament made sodomy and bestiality the offense defined as "the abominable crime of buggery," but no longer punishable by death but by life in **prison**. The act was defined by case precedent, which at the time meant that buggery was specifically defined as anal intercourse or oral intercourse by a man with a man or woman or vaginal intercourse by either a man or a woman with an animal. In 1817, "oral" was dropped. Engaging in sexual relations with nonconsenting animals remains criminalized in many jurisdictions, but most common law jurisdictions, such as the United States, no longer criminalize the behavior between human beings who are able to give consent.

BULGER, JAMES (1929–2018). An **organized crime** figure of Boston, Massachusetts, who also went by the nickname Whitey. Bulger was implicated in as many as 11 **murders** and been convicted of racketeering and other offenses. An arrest and conviction in 1956 for bank robbery resulted in his being sentenced to **prison** and then transferred to **Alcatraz** in 1959 (released in 1962) when he was suspected of planning an escape. Following his release, he gradually resumed his **gang** activities, eventually becoming the head of the Winter Hill Gang. However, he also became an informant for the **FBI** and used that position to remove rival gang members, solidifying the status of the Winter Hill Gang. Just before the FBI was to act on sealed indictments in 1994, Bulger fled with a new identity and was placed on the FBI's Most Wanted List. He spent 16 years as a fugitive before being arrested in California at age 81. He was tried and convicted of 31 counts, including racketeering, extortion, and weapons charges. He received two consecutive life sentences plus five years and was incarcerated at the U.S. **Penitentiary**, Sumterville, in Florida until his death. *See also* FEDERAL BUREAU OF PRISONS (BOP); RACKETEER INFLUENCED CORRUPT ORGANIZATION (RICO).

BULLYING. The physical, sexual, verbal, or emotional victimization of another, now including **cyber-bullying**. Among the causes of bullying are gender inequality, social practices, and bias. The effects of victimization include depression, stress, and self-harm, which may be accompanied by suicide. School shootings (e.g., the **Columbine massacre**) have also been associated with bullying. Legislation was slow to develop, and while it does not specifically prevent bullying, it does increase awareness about bullying, as seen in recent litigation where the bully and/or a school have been sued. The final state to adopt antibullying legislation was Montana in 2015. *See also* SHEPARD, MATTHEW (1976–1998).

BUNDY, THEODORE (1946–1989). A **serial killer** who confessed to 30 murders committed in multiple states during the mid- to late 1970s. He is suspected of committing many others. He was particularly heinous in the commission of his crimes, raping and mutilating the bodies by decapitation and committing sexual acts with the corpses. He escaped twice from confinement and continued his spree of **murder**. He was sentenced to death and was executed at Raiford **Prison**, Florida, in the **electric chair**. A biography of

Bundy's troubled parentage and life has been documented in Ann Rule's *The Stranger beside Me* (2009). *See also* CAPITAL PUNISHMENT; DEATH PENALTY; EXECUTION.

BURDEN OF PROOF. The burden of proof is what must be produced in several different ways during a **trial**. The burden is that the charging party must prove what is alleged against the other party. However, once the charging party has demonstrated that onus, then the other side must similarly confront what has been presented and successfully refute it. The complications with understanding the burden of proof are reflected in the **U.S. Supreme Court** cases that have addressed the language surrounding burden of proof. They include preponderance of the **evidence** (*Dixon v. United States*, 548 U.S. 1 [2006]); reasonable indications and reasonable suspicions (*United States v. Montoya De Hernandez*, 473 U.S. 531 [1985]; ***Terry v. Ohio*** **, 392 U.S. 1 [1968]**; and *Arizona v. Gant*, 556 U.S. 332 [2009]); **probable cause** (*United States v. Sokolow*, 490 U.S. 1 [1989]); credible evidence (*Valmonte v. Bane*, 18 F.3d 992 [2nd Cir. 1994]); substantial evidence (*United States v. Williams*, 504 U.S. 36 [1992]); clear and convincing evidence (*Addington v. Texas*, 441 U.S. 418 [1979]); **beyond a reasonable doubt** (*Victor v. Nebraska*, 511 U.S. 1 [1994]); and circumstantial evidence (*Holland v. United States*, 348 U.S. 121 [1954]). *See also* CIVIL RIGHTS; DUE PROCESS.

BUREAU OF JUSTICE STATISTICS (BJS). Located within the **Office of Justice Programs** in the U.S. Department of Justice, the BJS was created in the 1979 Justice Improvement Act. The BJS gathers data on crime in the United States from more than 50,000 criminal justice agencies, conducts analyses, and publishes the data collected in print and online at https://www.bjs.gov.

BUREAU OF PRISONS (BOP). *See* FEDERAL BUREAU OF PRISONS (BOP).

C

CADAVER. The cadaver, also referred to as a body or a corpse, has a long history with grave robbing and body snatching. Grave robbing was the disinterment of a corpse to steal any jewelry left on the deceased. Body snatching was the disinterment of the cadaver for anatomical examination. At times this was done by physicians and at others by grave robbers who would sell the cadaver to schools. In the 1800s, London anatomy schools hired body snatchers to dig up graves for the cadavers. Grave robbing was deterred by the United Kingdom's Anatomy Act of 1832 and the Pennsylvania Anatomy Act of 1863. These acts were preceded by the Massachusetts Act of 1784, which permitted dissection of those who had been executed or had been shot during a duel. *See also* DUELING; EXECUTION.

***CALDER V. BULL*, 3 DALL. (3 U.S.) 386 (1798).** A **U.S. Supreme Court** case that focused on the U.S. Constitution's **ex post facto** clause. The significance of the holding was that ex post facto laws are unconstitutional only in criminal cases, not civil cases. That is, in criminal cases, laws changed after an action that now make the action a criminal offense are more likely to get a conviction when prosecuted. Passing laws after an offense has occurred is generally but not always found to be unconstitutional. For example, the **Adam Walsh** Child Protection and Safety Act of 2006 has been found to be constitutional because the intent is not to punish but to protect. *See also* CIVIL COMMITMENT.

CALI CARTEL. A multibillion-dollar **drug cartel** named after the city of Cali, Colombia, in South America. The founding members, once part of the **Medellín Cartel**, formed their cartel in mid-1980 and went on to dominate the worldwide marketing of cocaine. The United States was one of the markets for the cartel's distribution. The cartel was maintained by **murder** and **kidnapping** for **ransom** (which helped finance the cartel's initial drug enterprises). The Cali Cartel operated with the strategy that independent drug distribution cells would be more immune to the efforts of law enforcement to shut them down. *See also* DRUG ENFORCEMENT AGENCY (DEA); DRUG TRAFFICKING.

CAMBRIDGE-SOMERVILLE YOUTH STUDY. The 1939 study was conducted by Edwin Powers and Helen Witmer to investigate the reduction of delinquency rates resulting from various programs. Despite the use of tutoring, camping programs, and psychiatric care, after a 10-year follow-up and again at 30 years (by Joan McCord), there were no significant differences in arrest rates. McCord's hypotheses were that the exposure to middle-class values failed for the sample of youth from lower socioeconomic status; support from counselors was no longer available when the program concluded; there was a labeling effect; and the youths' loss of aspirations was caused by a failure to maintain contact with program staff following the conclusion of the program. Nevertheless, the study guided future delinquency studies. *See also* JUVENILE DELINQUENCY.

CAMORRA. An Italian crime **syndicate** and secret society dating to the 16th century in Campania and Naples. The camorra lacked a central leadership, which resulted in constant infighting among the various individual bands that had developed to protect their territory. **Police** records from 1820 indicate that written regulations existed detailing its organization, initiation rituals, and money for camorra families when someone was placed in **prison**. Under pressure from Italian police, many camorra relocated and established themselves in California, New York, and Massachusetts beginning in the 1950s and engaged in criminal activities such as **counterfeiting**, extortion, **kidnapping**, **money laundering**, and political corruption. The camorra smuggling operation was converted into **drug trafficking**. They cooperate with other **organized crime** groups and as of 2012 are considered a transnational organized crime group. *See also* TRANSNATIONAL CRIME.

CAMPBELL COLLABORATION. This group aims to promote "what works" in social and criminal justice policy by basing interventions on research rather than ideology or unsystematic research. The group began in 2000 as the result of an exploratory meeting at the University of London the year prior. The group is international, with researchers from at least 13 countries participating, and is named after a psychologist, Donald Campbell, who passed away not long before the group's emergence. *See also* EVIDENCE-BASED PRACTICES.

CANING. A form of **corporal punishment** in which a criminal offender is struck with a cane or similar object. This form of **punishment** can be either an official state sanction or a tool of discipline in private contexts. It has grown less common (legally and in practice) since its emergence in the 19th century. It is now illegal in the United States; however, it remains legal in some countries, such as Singapore. *See also* CRUEL AND UNUSUAL PUNISHMENT.

CAPITAL JURY PROJECT. This was research on jurors' determinations to sentence someone to death and whether the concept of arbitrary application of death sentences held to be unconstitutional by the **U.S. Supreme Court** has been corrected. The project, begun in 1991, interviewed 1,198 jurors from 14 states who had participated in 353 capital **murder trials**. The project, under the direction of principal investigator William Bowers, sought to determine the arbitrariness of discretion by jurors, the extent of arbitrariness, and an assessment of the effectiveness of the involved states to control arbitrariness through their legislation. *See also* BIFURCATED PROCESS; CAPITAL OFFENSE; CAPITAL PUNISHMENT; DEATH PENALTY; *FURMAN V. GEORGIA*, 408 U.S. 238 (1972).

CAPITAL OFFENSE. Capital offenses are eligible for judicial **death sentences**, called **capital punishment**. Capital offenses have evolved since the first federal statute, the Crimes Act of 1790, which specified the offenses of **treason**, **counterfeiting**, **piracy** and other felonies on the high seas, and assisting in the escape of a prisoner under a capital sentence. All **death penalty** statutes were invalidated by the **U.S. Supreme Court** in ***Furman v. Georgia*, 408 U.S. 238 (1972)**. Capital **punishment** was again allowed following *Gregg v. Georgia*, 428 U.S. 153 (1976). The states were the swiftest to restore capital punishment. The federal government initially restored the death penalty with the 1988 Anti-Drug Abuse Act for drug offenses and **murder**. The death penalty was again expanded in 1994 with the **Violent Crime** Control and Law Enforcement Act (which also specifies the procedures for carrying out the death penalty) and in 1996 with the Antiterrorism and Effective Death Penalty Act. There are currently 41 federal statutes that permit capital punishment for 60 crimes. *See also* EXECUTION.

CAPITAL PUNISHMENT. *See* CAPITAL OFFENSE; CAPITAL JURY PROJECT; DEATH PENALTY; EXECUTION.

CAPO DI TUTTI CAPI. The title given to the most influential/powerful **Mafia** boss which became popularly known through the 1950 Kefauver Commission hearings on **organized crime**. However, the title probably originated during the early 1900s as different Mafia bosses attempted to consolidate all organized crime under a centralized leadership. The **murder** of boss Salvatore Maranzano in 1931 created the opportunity for **Charles "Lucky" Luciano** to establish the original crime commission, which evolved into the **National Crime Syndicate**. The syndication of organized crime resulted in the most powerful Mafia boss assuming this role with the title. The Genovese crime family boss Vincent Giganti (1992–1997) was the last to hold the title. *See also* GOTTI, JOHN (1940–2002); KEFAUVER COMMITTEE.

CAPONE, ALPHONSE (1899–1947). The crime boss of Chicago during the **Prohibition** era. He was called **Public Enemy** No. 1 following the **Saint Valentine's Day massacre**. Starting in 1931, he served eight years of an 11-year federal **prison** sentence for **tax evasion** (a crime that was little used with **Mafia gangsters**), which was begun at USP Atlanta and completed at **Alcatraz** Island. Capone's transfer to Alcatraz was because of the **Federal Bureau of Prisons**' concern that he would receive favorable treatment from guards and other convicts. He also served time at **Eastern State Penitentiary** for possession of a weapon. Capone's death was from cardiac arrest that followed a stroke. He also suffered from syphilitic dementia and gonorrhea.

CAR BOMB. A car bomb is an explosive device created to be hidden within a car or truck for the purpose of **murder**, **assassination**, or **terrorism**. The device is made from materials that can be combined to create the bomb. In Iraq, they have been made from unexploded shells. In the first **World Trade Center bombing** (2007) attack, the device was contained in a truck and left in the parking garage. The **Oklahoma City bomb** (1995) was made of fertilizer. The forerunner of the car bomb was the placement of explosive devices in horse-drawn carriages.

CARDOZO, BENJAMIN NATHAN (1870–1938). A **U.S. Supreme Court** justice appointed in 1932 by President Hoover to succeed Oliver Wendell Holmes. He was a critic of the **exclusionary rule**. While he was influential in many landmark cases, his opinion in ***Palko v. Connecticut*, 302 U.S. 319 (1937)**, resulted in the incorporation of the **Fifth Amendment**, which guaranteed protection against **double jeopardy**.

CARJACKING. A crime that involves the theft of a motor vehicle. The earliest use of the term appears in Detroit in 1991. The U.S. Congress passed the Federal Anti Car Theft Act of 1992, 18 U.S.C. § 2119, which did not meet federal standards for prosecution, and cases were handed down to state courts. The **Violent Crime** Control and Law Enforcement Act of 1994 made it a federal **capital offense** when the carjacking involved the killing of a victim.

***CARROLL V. UNITED STATES*, 267 U.S. 132 (1925).** This case (also referred to as the *Carroll* decision or *Carroll* doctrine) produced what has come to be known as the "automobile exception" because the court upheld **warrantless searches** of automobiles. The decision was based on the National **Prohibition** Act of 1919 (also referred to as the **Volstead Act**), which authorized warrantless searches of vehicles by federal Prohibition officers to search for illegal alcohol to enforce the Eighteenth Amendment. *United States v. Di Re*, 332 U.S. 581, 68 S. Ct. 222, 92 L. Ed. 210 (1948), was a **U.S. Supreme Court** decision that declined to allow an extension of Carroll to include passengers in a car. Finally, *Cooper v. California*, 386 U.S. 58, 87 S. Ct. 788, 17 L.Ed.2d 730 (1967), distinguished the reasonableness of a search of a vehicle as opposed to a search of a house.

CASTELLAMARESE WARS. The Castellamarese Wars was a struggle for leadership of the Italian American **Mafia** and predated the creation of the commission under **Lucky Luciano**. The 1920 wars were between adherents of two Mafia families under the leadership of Joe Masaria and Salvatore Maranzano. The Maranzano faction came out on top, and it was shortly after that Maranzano was murdered and Luciano became the "**capo di tutti capi**" or boss of bosses. The Castellamarese Wars were the beginning of shifts in leadership in the Mafia during the 1930s highlighted by the murders of those believed to be threats (primarily old-style mafiosi in favor of younger up-and-coming Mafia members) until Luciano consolidated the leadership under himself. *See also* MURDER.

CHEMICAL CASTRATION. The use of drugs for treatment, control, and **punishment** of sex offenders, especially those convicted of rape or pedophilia. The earliest uses of chemical castration date from the mid-1960s for nonoffenders and later with offenders. Not all states have utilized chemical castration. California in 1996 and Florida in 1997 were the first states with statutes to apply the concept to offenders. In some cases, the incentive has been for a reduced sentence, although the application has never been sanctioned by the Federal Drug Administration for sex offenders. Chemical castration has its detractors. The arguments include that the **Fourteenth Amendment** provision of equal protection is violated because chemical castration is disproportionately applied to males. The **American Civil Liberties Union** asserts that it also violates the **Eighth Amendment**. *See also* CRUEL AND UNUSUAL PUNISHMENT.

CHESSMAN, CARYL (1921–EXECUTED 1960). Chessman has the distinction of having been, at that time, the American to be the longest on **death row** prior to **execution** and the first to be executed for a **kidnapping** which did not also include a **murder**. His execution resulted in controversy surrounding the law of execution for kidnapping that did not include murder. Chessman had been involved in criminal activity (a car theft) since he was 16 years of age. This act led to a series of convictions and incarcerations, which would culminate with his 1948 charging for a series of sex offenses and identification as the "Red Light Bandit." During his almost 12 years on California's **San Quentin** Prison death row, Chessman acted as his own attorney, filing a great number of appeals (challenging the so-called Little Lindbergh Law) and stirred up public and international sentiment through his publication of four books, one of which (*Cell 2455, Death Row*) was made into a feature film. *See also* LINDBERGH KIDNAPPING, "THE CRIME OF THE CENTURY".

CHICAGO SCHOOL. *See* McKAY, HENRY D. (1899–1980); ZONE THEORY.

CHILD SAVERS. A 19th-century juvenile justice initiative that sought to intervene with youth, predominantly the poor and immigrants, believed to potentially be at risk with the criminal justice system. This was a movement influenced greatly by women and helped to establish the first **juvenile court** in Cook County, Chicago, in 1899, which through the principle of ***parens patriae*** sought to be a parental, albeit guiding, force in the child's life as opposed to criminalizing them. Among the progressive influences for the movement was Jane Addams, who founded Hull House in 1879 for European immigrants. *See also* JUVENILE OFFENDER.

***CHIMEL V. CALIFORNIA*, 395 U.S. 752 (1969).** A **U.S. Supreme Court** case that further defined the parameters of **search and seizure** (a **Fourth Amendment** protection) by **police**. The holding specified that an arrest of a person did not also allow an extensive search of a home by law enforcement. However, it was deemed reasonable that a search of an area around the person was practical. The intention of the holding was to ensure that a **warrant** is essential and protected against abuse by the government. The opinion in this matter was delivered by Justice Stewart, and such searches are now commonly referred to under the Chimel rule. *See also* WARRANTLESS SEARCHES.

***CITY OF CHICAGO V. MORALES*, 527 U.S. 41 (1999).** The **U.S. Supreme Court** case which held that laws that are unclear or ambiguous and thus unable to be understood by someone of ordinary intelligence violate the **Fourteenth Amendment**, specifically the **due process** clause. More explicitly, such laws may not allow for arbitrary enforcement that would violate personal liberties. *See also* CIVIL RIGHTS; FREEDOM OF ASSEMBLY.

CIVIL COMMITMENT. The court determination that to release someone would pose a threat to the community, and thus they are subject to confinement following a **prison** sentence. This legal process is most often used with violent sex offenders. The **U.S. Supreme Court** case ***Kansas v. Hendricks*, 521 U.S. 346 (1997)**, holding was that this process is constitutional and that the offender is to be held at a medical facility. Additional clarification was given in *Kansas v. Crane*, 534 U.S. 407 (2002), which held that the offender had to have shown a lack of ability to control aberrant behavior. Finally, in *United States v. Comstock*, 560 U.S. 126 (2010), the U.S. Supreme Court held that Congress could pass laws that apply to federal prisoners.

CIVIL DEATH. A reference to the loss of **civil rights**. This is an old concept dating back to the middle ages in which a convicted felon would lose all civil rights. This idea was incorporated into the U.S. system of justice and is often referred to as disenfranchisement. ***Pervear v. Massachusetts*, 72 U.S. 475 (5 Wall.) 475 (1866)**, affirmed that convicts have no rights, and this included **Eighth Amendment** rights. *Ruffin v. Commonwealth*, 62 Va. 790 (Va. Ct. App. 1871), referred to the convict as a slave of the state. This would essentially remain the circumstance until the 1960s, when courts began to consider which were fundamentally legal and **human rights** to be afforded convicted persons. *See also* COLLATERAL CONSEQUENCES.

CIVIL DISOBEDIENCE. The active rejection of law and the power of government over citizens. The idea of civil disobedience in one context is viewed as nonviolent action, while in other contexts as anarchy or the encouragement to reject lawful authority. Since the 1850s a wide range of activities of civil disobedience have been witnessed to expose or draw attention to ethnic, racial, or religious inequalities. For example, Dr. Martin Luther King Jr. was arrested and placed in jail for his participation in protests. Other examples include sit-ins and the many recent examples labeled as Occupy Wall Street.

CIVILIAN REVIEW BOARD. Oversight of **police** by independent citizens or civilian boards with the intention to provide unbiased investigation and accountability of civilian complaints and allegations of misconduct. Since the early 1900s, citizen review boards were controversial. The **Wickersham Commission** in 1931 made the recommendation for the creation of an agency, independent of the police force, and it was rejected. The first review board appeared in 1948 in Washington, D.C. However, it handled few complaints. Citizens' complaints, combined with the **civil rights** movement of the 1960s, brought about the first significant movement in creating the review boards led by New York City in 1966. However, the effort to expand such boards was not successful, but they would get new life in the 1970s in Kansas City, Missouri, and Berkeley, California, in 1973. From this point forward, civilian review boards would grow, and there were about 100 by the year 2000. This would be followed by the creation of professional associations that would help ensure their permanence despite opposition by police unions. *See also* POLICE CORRUPTION; POLICE MISCONDUCT; SERPICO, FRANK (1936–).

CIVIL LAW. This refers primarily to a country's reliance on written code in making legal decisions. Civil law derived from Roman law in the 3rd century and canon law, which applied to most of continental Europe until the 11th century. The primary source of civil law is codification (the law is derived from what is written). Legislation/substantive law is generally considered more specific, and trials are conducted in an inquisitorial nature, where the procedures are those of a continuing investigation. For instance, an admission of guilt in a **common law** system like the United States would end the need for a **trial**; in a civil law system such as France, the admission would just be another piece of **evidence**.

CIVIL RIGHTS. The first Civil Rights Act was passed by the U.S. Congress in 1866. Congress revised the act several times, and the last revision was in 1991. Civil Rights are those governmental guarantees to citizens of protection from **discrimination** by government, other organizations, and private persons. Such civil rights protections include age, disability, ethnicity, gender, race, religion, and sexual orientation. Refer to appendix 1, "The Bill of Rights."

CIVIL RIGHTS OF INSTITUTIONALIZED PERSONS ACT (CRIPA). A 1980 federal law to protect the federal rights of those confined to state facilities including **prisons** and juvenile institutions. The law permits the **Civil Rights** Division of the U.S. Department of Justice to investigate complaints. The identification of patterns of abuse may lead to prosecution and result in the imposition of federal **consent decrees**, which will remain in effect until such time as the identified unconstitutional practices have ended or other solutions have been enacted. New York State **Prison**, **Attica**, was investigated after the riot, and convicts are now guaranteed protection of their civil rights. Refer to appendix 1, "The Bill of Rights."

CLASSICAL SCHOOL OF CRIMINOLOGY. The classical school of criminology was formed in the 18th century and was heavily influenced by theorists such as **Cesare Beccaria**, **Jeremy Bentham**, John Locke, and Thomas Hobbes. Their ideas and others of that time have had a significant impact on **criminology** and the response to crime. Among the advances were that man has free will and thus calculates his actions. In addition, they believed that **punishment** was a **deterrence** and that it should fit the crime (**proportionality**). While they believed that punishment should be swift and felt by the offender, they also believed that many punishments such as the **death penalty** were excessive or extreme for many crimes due to improper training of judges. While the importance of the classical school declined with the advent of other schools of thought, it has seen a revival in recent times.

CLASSIFICATION. *See* INMATE CLASSIFICATION.

COCHRAN, JOHNNIE (1937–2005). The lead attorney in the 1995 **O. J. Simpson trial** and other celebrity criminal cases including those of Sean "Puffy" Combs, Michael Jackson, and Tupac Shakur. He achieved prominence for his advocacy of victims of **police** brutality. O. J. Simpson was on trial for the **murder** of his wife and Ron Goldman and was acquitted. The case is an example of defendants having attorneys who match the skills and the resources of prosecutors. His skillful comment, "If the glove don't fit, you must acquit," enhanced his popularity.

CODE ADAM. A protocol named in memory of six-year-old **Adam Walsh** who was abducted in Florida at a department store in 1981; his decapitated head was found two weeks after his disappearance. The protocol was initiated by the retailer Walmart in 1994 and is now used by participating businesses across the United States and Canada. When missing children are reported, to employees issue the Code Adam, including a detailed description of the child. Designated employees stop work, monitor entrances and exits, and look for the child. If the child is not found within 10 minutes, law enforcement is called. If the child is found with someone other than his or her guardian, employees are to make reasonable efforts to delay that person and inform law enforcement of their presence. Code Adam is canceled when law enforcement arrives or when the child is found. *See also* AMERICA'S MISSING: BROADCAST EMERGENCY RESPONSE (AMBER) ALERT.

CODE OF HAMMURABI. One of the oldest compilations of law (from approximately 1754 B.C.) to guide a society. The code consisted of 282 laws and graded **punishments** to fit the crime, including the often-quoted "eye for an eye." The code was unknown until its discovery in 1901 and has influenced many criminal justice venues, illustrating what is common practice in the creation of criminal justice law such as that promulgated at the highest levels of government. *See also* COMMON LAW; PENAL CODE; PENAL PHILOSOPHY; SENTENCING GUIDELINES.

COGNITIVE BEHAVIORAL THERAPY (CBT). A now common and effective strategy in many rehabilitative therapies across the criminal justice system (correctional populations, victim services, drug abuse, and especially the treatment of sexual offenders). Rooted in philosophical stoicism, the basic premise of this therapy is that logic can solve most emotional disturbances. CBT came to criminal justice via psychology's behavior theory and later cognitive theory (Milkman and Wanberg 2007). Psychologists such as Albert Ellis and Aaron Temkin Beck were pioneers in the practice of identifying distorted or false beliefs and interrupting them before they create attitudes and emotions that lead to destructive behaviors. Notable scholars in CBT and criminal justice include Mark Lispey and Donald Andrews (see, e.g., Lipsey, Chapman, and Landenberger 2001). *See also* ANGER MANAGEMENT; EVIDENCE-BASED PRACTICES.

***COKER V. GEORGIA*, 433 U.S. 584 (1977).** The **U.S. Supreme Court** decision that made rape nonpunishable by the **death penalty** on the basis of the **Eighth Amendment** protection against **cruel and unusual punishment**; death was ruled as a disproportionate **punishment** for rape. Ehrlich Anthony Coker was a convicted felon who escaped **prison** and broke into a Georgia home, using a gun to rob Allen and Elnita Carver and raping Elnita. He was sentenced to death in 1974 on the basis of **aggravating factors**, which included his previous record and the armed robbery. The court noted that only a few states had statutes for such penalties and that there had been a progression of court decisions holding individual state statutes for death penalties as unconstitutional. *See also* PROPORTIONALITY.

COLLATERAL CONSEQUENCES. These are civil penalties, legislated by individual states and varying from state to state, which are not part of the criminal conviction and the sentence prescribed by the judge but do become a consequence. Collateral consequences represent some type of loss such as the right to own or possess firearms, to vote or serve on juries, to obtain student loans, to public housing and welfare benefits, or to professional licenses. These consequences extend beyond the length of a judicial sanction.

A controversial feature is that if innocence is established, collateral consequences remain active. Sixth and **Eighth Amendment** Supreme Court challenges have included arguments that they constitute **cruel and unusual punishment** because they exceed the limits of the sentence and that failure to consider them by the defense represents ineffective counsel. A National Inventory of Collateral Consequences was created in 2009 by the **American Bar Association**. This database allows interested persons to search for collateral consequences in their states.

COLUMBINE MASSACRE. An extreme school shooting by **Eric Harris** and **Dylan Klebold** (high school seniors) on 20 April 1999 at Columbine (Colorado) High School, with 12 students and 1 teacher killed and 21 injured and 3 others injured as they attempted to escape. The shooters committed suicide before they could be captured. Harris often wrote in a journal about the killings in the **Oklahoma City bombing**, the **Waco siege**, and the Vietnam War. The Columbine High School shootings caused national consciousness of such events to skyrocket. On one level, schools increased security and taught students and teachers how to respond when such events occur. On another level, states passed legislation and other official acts to increase the involvement of law enforcement and to take preventive action. An example was the 1988 New Jersey Uniform Memorandum of Agreement between Education and Law Enforcement Officials, which allowed law enforcement to examine school records upon request and with suspicion that a crime may be imminent.

COMMON LAW. The legal system of England in the 12th century. The U.S. legal system is based on common law. The sources of this law are decisions made in preceding, similar cases or stare decisis. Precedent is not binding but is used as part of judicial arguments. Substantive law in this system is not declared from above but is intended to be open to revision on the basis of argument and changing **mores**. Trials are adversarial and emerged historically from the resolution of disputes via "**trial** by ordeal" (e.g., sword fight, gun duel). The last adversary standing, essentially, is the innocent. *See also* CODE OF HAMMURABI; DUELING; PENAL CODE.

COMMUNITY CORRECTIONS. Community corrections supervises more than five million offenders in the community as opposed to in **prison** or other forms of confinement. Community corrections encompasses more than **probation** (**John Augustus**) and **parole** (**Zebulon Brockway**); it seeks to enhance the treatment of offenders or to aid in the transition from prison back into the community. Community corrections programs often rely on risk-needs assessment and other **evidence-based practices** from which modalities can be applied that directly enhance the offenders' likelihood for success. *See also* DAY REPORTING CENTER; HALFWAY HOUSE.

COMMUNITY COURT. Community courts began with the 1993 Mid-Town Community Court in New York City. The intention of the court was to be a **problem-solving court** (which is also referred to as a special court) for the local community. The model of the court followed that of the **drug court** initiated in 1989 in Miami-Dade County, Florida.

COMMUNITY JUSTICE. The community justice model represents a shift in **punishment** philosophy during the mid-1990s from an effort to resolve a specific problem to emphasizing problem solving and involving the community. This model intends to focus on such community issues as drugs, **prostitution**, and disorderly conduct. Recognition of the value of this approach to solving crime can be found in such earlier works as Kelling's **broken windows theory**.

COMMUNITY-ORIENTED POLICING. A partnership between law enforcement, community organizations, and individuals to focus on pressing concerns related to crime and conditions causing social unrest. The partnerships are a problem-solving approach designed to create strategies that will solve problems and increase trust in law enforcement. The roots of community-oriented policing can be traced to the earliest efforts to control crime and provide community safety. Such efforts include those of the pledge system of England in the 9th century. This became an organized effort under **Sir Robert Peel**. In the United States, the community-oriented policing model re-emerged in the 1990s.

COMPARATIVE CRIMINOLOGY. Comparative criminology is the inquiry into crime and criminal control and currently includes delinquent behavior across national boundaries and schools of thought. Early criminologists such as **Cesare Lombroso** and Enrico Ferri substantially contributed to it by exploring whether criminal behavior was the product of nature or nurture. There were criticisms of those early efforts, and some of it was considered incorrect. Their work, however, was not referred to as comparative **criminology**. The emergence of this term occurred in the late 1800s, specifically with the publication of *Comparative Criminology* (1866) by **Gabriel Tarde**. The comparative study of delinquency appears in 1955 at the United Nations First Congress on the Prevention of Crime and Treatment of Delinquents, which encouraged research on the impact of programs in other countries. *See also* NATURE-NURTURE DEBATE.

COMPREHENSIVE CRIME CONTROL ACT OF 1984. President Reagan signed the act in 1984. The act contained the greatest number of revisions and at the same time repealed many prior acts of the U.S. Criminal Code, some of which dated back to the early 1900s. Among the new revisions were the following: Title II, Sentencing Reform; Title III, **Forfeiture**; Title IV, Offenders with Mental Disease or Defect; Title V, Drug Enforcement Amendments; Title VI, Justice Assistance; Title VII, Surplus Federal Property Amendments; Title VIII, Labor Racketeering Amendments; Title IX, Currency and Foreign Transactions Reporting Act Amendments; Title X, Miscellaneous **Violent Crime** Amendments; Title XI, Serious Nonviolent Offenses; and Title XII, Procedural Amendments. The repealed acts included Title I, **Bail**. Some specific changes were to reinstall the **death penalty** for specified federal offenses and increase federal jurisdiction of the Secret Service to include credit card and computer fraud.

CONGREGATE SYSTEM. A system (also called the **silent system**) that was implemented in **Auburn Penitentiary** in 1876 to ensure control over convicts. The congregate system utilized features of the **separate system** of **Eastern State Penitentiary**, which had relied upon silence and **solitary confinement**. The congregate system, however, relied on mass movements, eating in a mess hall, and work in shops, which would be conducted in silence. **Prisons** maintain congregate movement for many activities such as eating and recreation for prison efficiency and supervision.

CONJUGAL VISIT. A period during which a convict may spend time in a specially designated space with a spouse, which is believed to help maintain family ties for improved success upon release from **prison**. A second argument supporting conjugal visits is that they help to maintain order by encouraging good behavior. These are not authorized in all states or by the **Federal Bureau of Prisons**. Parchman **Penitentiary**, Mississippi, was the first to utilize some form of conjugal visits with black convicts (often using prostitutes) under the belief that this would reduce aggression while increasing the work of harvesting cotton. More conventional conjugal visits began with white convicts in the 1940s, and then with females in 1972. Mississippi and New Mexico discontinued the visits in 2014. Other states have maintained their programs. A U.S. district court has held that there is no constitutional right to such visits. Currently, only four states still allow conjugal visits. *See also* PRISON REFORM; PROSTITUTION.

CONSENT DECREE. A judicial decree instrumental in correcting unconstitutional situations in the criminal justice system. A federal judge will hand down the decree and upon acceptance by the state will then appoint a federal master to oversee actions taken to ensure that constitutional compliance is achieved. Upon determination that constitutional compliance has been achieved, the decree will then be lifted by the federal judge. Notable examples of consent decrees include Kentucky's Juvenile Justice system (facilities failed to comply with the **Civil Rights of Institutionalized Persons Act**) in 1995, which ended in 2001, and the New Jersey **State Police** (for **racial profiling**), which ended in 2009 after more than 10 years.

CONSUMER PROTECTION FROM UNFAIR TRADING REGULATIONS, 2008. *See* BAIT AND SWITCH.

CONTAINMENT THEORY. *See* CONTROL THEORY.

CONTRACT KILLINGS. Contract killing is also called **murder** for hire. It is a legally nonbinding and unenforceable contract accepted by one person to kill another person for payment or other benefit. Contract killing is associated with **organized crime** and was made famous by **Murder Inc.**, a tool of the **National Crime Syndicate** in the 1930s. It is not uncommon for private citizens to utilize contract killing to eliminate a spouse, business partner, or other person for whom the contracting party has no further use.

CONTROL THEORY. Walter Reckless in 1973 originated the concept of control theory. He took the position that individuals do what they want and are not influenced by other motivations. However, he also postulated that when social systems lack dominant norms (social bonds), then more deviant behavior will result. That is to say, when social controls are weak, deviance becomes more attractive, and when **mores** are strong there is a reduced tendency to be deviant. According to **Travis Hirschi** (1969), the social bonds components that most strongly influence deviance are attachment, belief, commitment, and involvement.

CONVICT CRIMINOLOGY. More formally referred to as the New School of Convict Criminology, an informal organization with ex-convicts and nonconvicts (referred to as enlightened practitioners) with terminal degrees and others who seek humane practices helpful to those in **prison** and in contributing to society through successful **reentry**. The idea emerged at the 1997 **American Society of Criminology** (ASC) conference and was formalized through the publication of *Convict Criminology* (2001). Convict Criminology is a subset of the ASC's **Critical Criminology** division. *See also* RICHARDS, DR. STEPHEN.

CONVICT LEASE SYSTEM. Following the Civil War, convicts, many of whom were former slaves, were utilized as the new labor force for business and farms. The system benefited both the farmers now denied slaves and the **prison** system because they did not have to house or provide for the convicts and received a monetary return on the lease. Convicts at this time were considered civilly dead, meaning they had no rights, and the Thirteenth Amendment permitted this despite abolishing slavery. Alabama was the last state to abolish the practice in 1928. *See also PERVEAR V. MASSACHUSETTS*, 72 U.S. (5 WALL) 475 (1866); SELLIN, THORSTEN (1896–1994).

COP-KILLER BULLETS. Traditional lead bullets lack the lethality and the ability to penetrate dense material. Experiments during the 1960s produced Teflon-covered bullets made of hardened brass with a steel core, and manufacture took place in the 1980s. The Teflon was added to prevent wear on the interior of the barrel of the gun. While they were designed for law enforcement personnel, a controversy arose about others using the ammunition because of its ability to effectively penetrate vests, thus leading to the term "cop-killer bullets." This argument, however, has been proven to be false.

COPYRIGHT INFRINGEMENT. Copyrights protect created work from distribution, copying, reproduction, **counterfeiting**, and unauthorized use of the material. Protected material includes print, music, and broadcast. Copyright infringement is often referred to as **piracy**, or theft, and is done for profit. The earliest protection may be found in the 1897 U.S. Copyright Law. Copyright infringement for commercial purposes may be a criminal offense; however, when not for commercial purposes, it may not be an offense at all or at worst a misdemeanor. *See also* PAYOLA; VINTAGE FRAUD.

CORONER. A coroner is responsible for establishing the cause of death, how, and when it occurred. The authority of the office varies from state to state, from taking charge of the office to taking charge of the investigation. The position of coroner dates to the 11th century and was included in the **Magna Carta**. When the "hue and cry" would go out, the coroner was also notified. There is a distinction between the office of coroner and **medical examiner**. Generally, a coroner is a political office, while the medical examiner must be a physician, possibly with a specialty such as **forensic pathologist**.

CORPORAL PUNISHMENT. In corporal punishment, physical pain is inflicted on the body. This has been used throughout history, mostly on children, slaves, prisoners, criminal suspects, and other oppressed groups (e.g., women). The purposes are multiple and include judicial purposes, education, **deterrence**, and to solicit information. Corporal punishments have been traced back as far as the 1st century to ancient Egypt and the Roman Empire. In modern America, corporal punishments were most common prior to the creation of the **prison** in the early 1880s; however, they were used in the prison for violations of prison rules. The argument of whether **punishment** was for **retribution** or for reformation gradually had an impact on the use of corporal punishment. In 1870, the courts began to rule that husbands could no longer inflict pain on their wives. The use of corporal punishment in prisons and as a sentence outside of prisons has been recognized as a violation of the **Eighth Amendment** prohibition against **cruel and unusual punishment**. For example, **whipping** was prohibited in 1948. Many Western countries still allow forms of educational corporal punishment in schools (e.g., several American states). Some Asian countries utilize forms of judicial corporal punishment today (e.g., Singapore, Malaysia) and in many areas where Islamic law is making a resurgence (e.g., United Arab Emirates, Nigeria, Malaysia, Iran, Saudi Arabia) and interpretations of sharia dictate its use. *See also* CANING.

COSA NOSTRA. *See* LA COSA NOSTRA; MAFIA; ORGANIZED CRIME.

***COUNSELMAN V. HITCHCOCK*, 142 U.S. 547 (1982).** The **U.S. Supreme Court** made a distinction in its holding that the **Fifth Amendment** guarantee against **self-incrimination** was not met with testimony that was compelled. This was the impetus for the "Transactional Immunity" statute, which provides the **witness** with total immunity from prosecution due to **evidence** revealed through compelled testimony. Refer to appendix 1, "The Bill of Rights." *See also* BILL OF RIGHTS; DUE PROCESS.

COUNTERFEITING. The U.S. Secret Service was created in 1865 with the responsibility to combat counterfeit currency, which was widespread during the Civil War and comprised about one-third of the available currency in the United States. Modern counterfeiters are adept at using both household goods such as degreasers to wash the ink off existing bills and technology such as a laser printer to create new bills of higher denomination. While U.S. currency is a frequent target of counterfeiters, currency from other countries is also vulnerable.

COURT-APPOINTED ATTORNEY. The court-appointed attorney is also referred to as a public defender and represents **indigent** offenders. The idea of a court-appointed attorney, clearly stated as a right in the Sixth Amendment, has been available throughout most of U.S. history; however, this was not extended to the states. The **U.S. Supreme Court** case ***Gideon v . Wainwright***, 372 U.S. 335 (1963), held that persons charged with criminal offenses at the state level who could not afford an attorney should have one appointed by the court, a Sixth Amendment right. Refer to appendix 1, "The Bill of Rights." *See also* BILL OF RIGHTS; DUE PROCESS.

CRESSEY, DONALD (1919–1987). An American sociologist who made significant contributions to the study of **organized crime**, **prisons**, and **white-collar crime**. He served between 1966 and 1967 on the **President's Commission on Law Enforcement and Administration of Justice**. His theory of the "fraud triangle" included the elements of perceived need or pressure, opportunity, and rationalization, which remain in use to explain **occupational crime**.

CRIME MAPPING. Adriano Balbi (an Italian geographer) and André Michel Guerry (a French lawyer) created crime maps of France in 1829 that detailed the correlation between education levels, **violence**, and property crime. That effort led to mapping with more extensive crime features within geographic areas. The **Chicago School** mapping of the early 1900s, especially the work of Clifford Shaw and **Henry McKay**, focused on the locations of juveniles involved in delinquency. Mapping indicates the location of crimes and has been used to argue that crime is an outcome of community characteristics, including illness, mortality, poverty rates, and mental illness. Crime mapping techniques assist **police** by identifying crime "hot spots" and assist in the formulation of strategies for problem-oriented and community policing. There has been some reduction in the use of crime mapping since the mid-1980s. The arguments include the need to upgrade equipment, the ability to gain technical assistance for analysis, and training.

CRIME NOVEL. The crime novel has both literary and pulp appeal as **detective** stories, private eyes, mystery (such as the "whodunit"), suspense, **police** drama (Alex Cross), legal thrillers, science fiction, historical fiction, and more well-developed characters (Sherlock Holmes, Hercule Poirot, Miss Marple), written by authors (too numerous to mention all) such as Wilkie Collins (1844–1899), Arthur Conan Doyle (1859–1930), Agatha Christie (1890–1976), and James Patterson (1947–), who developed fame. The stories are set in time, can be upscale or with back-alley settings, and are located in famous cities and across international boundaries. Many of the original works of the genre began as serialized stories in newspapers and popular magazines, later to be reprinted as books as interest in crime and their popularity grew. *See also* NOIR CRIME NOVEL; TRUE CRIME.

CRIME PATTERN THEORY. *See* ROUTINE ACTIVITY THEORIES.

CRIMES AGAINST HUMANITY. The aggressive, deliberate, methodical, and violent **assault** upon some group of a civilian population during either war or peace. Such crimes include **murder**, **kidnapping**, extermination, **genocide**, slavery, rape, **torture**, and more and are carried out by official forces. Some of the more infamous examples include the Holocaust of World War II, Apartheid in South Africa, and the Rwandan genocide. The Nuremburg **trials** that followed World War II set a precedent to achieve justice against those who would commit crimes against humanity. At the time of the Nuremberg trials, there was no international accord among nations for guidance. The Nuremberg Accords were a consequence of the trials and defined actions of international crimes against persons. Actions that define and attempt to achieve justice have been steady since Nuremburg. Of note, it has been the United Nations that has been the principal agency that has sought prosecution. However, since the mid-1990s some aggressive actions include the 1996 United Nations definition of crime against humanity in a draft code. The International Criminal Court established in the Netherlands in 2002 has jurisdiction over such crimes. The types of offenses that fall under the heading of crimes against humanity were expanded in the 2008 United Nations Resolution 1820 to include rape and sexual violence. *See also* VIOLENCE.

CRIMINAL ANTHROPOLOGY. The study of humans and criminal offenders had an early influence from **Cesare Lombroso**, Enrico Ferri, and **Raffaele Garofalo** in the late 19th century. The argument centered on whether the criminal was born (nature) or criminality was learned (nurture). Their work gave rise to ideas such as **atavism**, the utilization of physiognomy, and later the XYY proposition. These early ideas and the later suggestion of the contribution of the **XYY chromosome** have been discredited. However, there is continued discussion of the effect of mental and physical characteristics on criminality. *See also* CLASSICAL SCHOOL OF CRIMINOLOGY; NATURE-NURTURE DEBATE.

CRIMINAL CAREER. The concept began with studies by **Sheldon and Eleanor Glueck** and was reported in their seminal work *500 Criminal Careers* (1936). The Gluecks view the criminal career as a longitudinal progression of criminal behavior that extends from childhood through adulthood. Longitudinal studies are seldom used (thus data is lacking) in **criminology**, making concise definitions of criminal careers difficult. This has frequently been studied, most notably by Blumenthal et al. who through **meta-analyses** identified four key variables: participation/prevalence, frequency/incidence, seriousness, and career length. Furthermore, they determined that between 25 to 40 percent of offenders might qualify as career criminals. The percentage is affected by the definition of the variable participation.

CRIMINOGENIC FACTORS. These are also referred to as criminogenic needs, which are broken down into two classifications called static and dynamic. Criminogenic factors are those elements of a person's life that may or may not influence a person's disposition to commit crime and reoffend. Static factors do not change, whereas dynamic factors may be overcome. Much of the identification of criminogenic factors was a result of **meta-analyses** (a method of reviewing and classifying research) that were begun in the late 1970s and early 1980s by criminologists such as **Robert Martinson**, Paul Gendreau, Don Andrews, and Edward Latessa. The research into criminogenic factors contributed to the development of what has been referred to as the "literature of what works" or programs that are **evidence** based as they influence the propensity to commit a crime. That research also directly influenced the creation of "**risk assessment**" instruments, such as the Level of Service Inventory–Revised or LSI-R (developed in 1994), which are used to identify criminogenic risk/needs factors. *See also* EVIDENCE-BASED PRACTICES.

CRIMINOLOGY. The study of the nature and causes of crime. Advances in criminology now include theories of crime prevention and control. Initially, criminal acts began to be thought of as works and influences of the devil or Satan. Crimes were equated with sin. Criminology draws heavily on the academic disciplines of sociology, psychology, and other social sciences, as well as biology. The earliest reference to the term is by **Raffaele Garofalo** in 1855. Early philosophers such as Garofalo and **Cesare Lombroso** represent what has been referred to as the **classical school of criminology**. Advancements in thought, especially the contributions of science, saw shifts in criminological theories, and new schools of thought arose, such as the positivists and the **Chicago School** of the mid-20th century. Modern criminology continues to evolve and now includes strains of thought with influences that are reflected in their names, such as **convict criminology**, **critical criminology**, **Marxist criminology**, and **feminist criminology**.

CRIPS. Stanley Williams and Raymond Washington organized the Crips in Los Angeles in 1969. Los Angeles **gang** history dates to the 1920s, with organizations named the Kelleys, the Magnificents, and the Blodgets. The 1950s gangs often centered around cars and had names such as Low Riders, Huns, and Boozies. The Crips were more violent, better organized, more prone to use automatic weapons, and engaged in the drug trade. They spread nationally and operate individually. They are identified by clothing, beads, bandanas, and other paraphernalia in the color blue. Law enforcement views the Crips as a violent street gang that commits **murder**, the sale of drugs, robbery, and **assault** and as rivals of the Bloods, another street gang. Membership in the Crips has steadily increased, and currently they have more than 30,000 members.

CRITICAL CRIMINOLOGY. A branch of **criminology** that is comprised of conflict theories such as **convict criminology**, **Marxist criminology**, and **feminist criminology**. These approaches to criminology challenge traditional perspectives while proposing alternative theories to dispel myths and other misunderstandings about crime and the criminal justice systems as they are related to class and social inequality. Critical Criminology and Social Justice is a division of the **American Society of Criminology** founded in 1990.

CROFTON, SIR WALTER (1815–1897). Crofton followed in the footsteps of **Alexander Maconochie** by developing the **Irish system** or marks system for promoting the good behavior of convicts, which would lead to their gradual and conditional release from **prison**. This system was one of the forerunners of modern **parole**. Crofton wrote about his system, and it was adopted by **Zebulon Brockway** at the **Elmira Reformatory** in New York State in the mid-1800s. *See also* TICKET OF LEAVE.

CRUEL AND UNUSUAL PUNISHMENT. *See* EIGHTH AMENDMENT.

***CSI* EFFECT.** The *CSI* effect refers to the televised dramatization of crime scene investigations and the utilization of forensic science to solve crimes. The dramatizations expand the normal scope of law enforcement forensic investigations and include raids, pursuit of offenders, capture, and arrest, as well as other avenues of investigation typical of **detective** work. An early use of the expression was in a 2004 article in *USA Today* titled, "CSI Effect Has Juries Wanting More **Evidence**." Empirical research has demonstrated that *CSI* has also affected crimes by influencing the offender to clean up the crime scene and encouraging the victim to leave evidence at the crime scene. Tens of millions of people watch these television shows, and research indicates that they are heavily influenced by them as to be misinformed about forensic science, its use in investigations, and the real work of law enforcement, judges, and juries. In addition, the popularity of the show(s) has resulted in colleges and universities offering courses and degrees in forensic science.

CUNANAN, ANDREW (1969–1997). A **serial killer** known to have murdered at least five persons, including the fashion designer Gianni Versace. Cunanan committed suicide prior to his capture. His killing spree occurred during a three-month period. In 1997, Cunanan was the 449th fugitive to be placed on the **FBI**'s Most Wanted List. *See also* MURDER.

CURFEW. A curfew in the United States is generally governed by local ordinances and specifies which regulations are to be applied. Curfews when applied to juveniles attempt to control or be a **deterrence** to crime and disorderly conduct. For example, malls often have curfews that prohibit minors from entering or remaining in the mall after a specified time unless accompanied by a parent or guardian. When curfews are applied to adults, the rationale is to protect persons and property during a time of emergency such as severe storms or in areas that have experienced damage from other environmental circumstances such as flooding. The earliest curfews originated in the 11th century and were enacted to control fires by having citizens extinguish the fire. Curfews also existed during World War II on the West Coast and for African Americans through the Jim Crow laws. In 2005, the city of Baltimore enforced curfews from 10:00 p.m. to 5:00 a.m. for five days while protests were occurring.

CUSTODIAL SENTENCE. Also referred to as a judicial sentence or just sentence. A custodial sentence is imposed by a judge upon a finding of guilt or an admission of guilt for the commission of a felony, that is, a violation of criminal law. A custodial sentence is fulfilled in a jail, **prison**, **reformatory**, or other setting in which the offender is secured. Custodial sentences were uncommon until the creation of the prison in the early 1800s as an alternative to death sentences and **corporal punishment**.

CUSTOMS AND BORDER PROTECTION, UNITED STATES. Its origins date to 1904, when mounted **patrols** were utilized by the U.S. Immigration Services to block illegal entry into the United States from Mexico. The U.S. Border Patrol was officially named in 1924 and has been responsible for patrolling more than 8,000 miles of borders with approximately 21,000 agents. Attention to borders increased during the period of **Prohibition**, and responsibility for monitoring coastlines was added in 1925. Illegal immigrants became subject to arrest in 1952, and authority was expanded to board and search all transportation. In 2003, the U.S. Border Patrol became part of the newly established U.S. Customs and Border Protection agency, a component of the Department of Homeland Security.

***CUTTER V. WILKINSON*, 544 U.S. 709 (2005).** A **First Amendment** issue before the **U.S. Supreme Court** in which it held that institutions that receive federal funds cannot deny convicts from exercising their religious beliefs and practices. The Court in doing so considered the Religious Land Use and Institutionalized Persons Act (RLUIPA) of 2002. Specific to this case were convicts who practiced nonmainstream religions. The Court's holding also specified that correctional administrators should consider potential threats to the security of the **prison** and could deny religious practice if such practice represented a threat to the prison. *See also* CIVIL RIGHTS.

CYBERATTACK. An attack that damages or attempts to damage, destroy, engage in theft from, or alter personal, corporate, or governmental computers, systems, networks, or infrastructures. The Department of Homeland Security, the **FBI**, and the Department of Defense are lead agencies in the protection against cyber-attacks. The earliest cyber-attack was carried out by Robert Morris in 1988 with his "Morris worm," a malware computer program that slowed computers. Morris also became the first person tried and convicted under the 1986 Computer Fraud and Abuse Act. *See also* CYBERCRIME.

CYBER-BULLYING. *See* CYBERSTALKING.

CYBERCRIME. The use of computers and the internet in the commission of a crime. The estimated cost of these crimes is greater than $2 billion. In 2015, President Obama signed Pub. L. 114-113, Cybersecurity Act of 2015, into law to increase surveillance and penalties that address cybercrime. *See also* CYBERATTACK; CYBERSECURITY; CYBERSTALKING.

CYBERSECURITY. The protection of information technology or computer systems from harm and theft as well as safeguarding them from damage. The emphasis on cybersecurity has increased with the development of Bluetooth, Wi-Fi, and wireless networks. The Computer Fraud and Abuse Act 1986, 18 U.S.C. § 1030, has attempted to legislate protections against unauthorized access and damage. The **FBI** and the Department of Homeland Security prioritized the protection of U.S. assets from cyber-attacks, which resulted in President Obama signing Executive Order 13636, Improving Critical Infrastructure Cybersecurity, in 2013.

CYBERSTALKING. The use of any electronic apparatus such as the internet to stalk individuals or groups. Cyberstalking is threatening and can be harassment or also include stalking offline. The 2000 **Violence against Women Act**, 47 U.S.C. § 223, made cyberstalking a federal offense. The initial cyberstalking law was California **Penal Code** § 646.9, Cyberstalking. Laws that have followed specify imprisonment or **fines** or both. An example is the case of Dharun Ravi, a Rutgers University student, who filmed his roommate's affair. The roommate committed suicide, and Ravi was sentenced in 2012 to 30 days in jail and $11,000 in **restitution** with three years' **probation**.

D

DACTYLOGRAPHY. A type of analysis that compares **fingerprint** impressions that are left on an exterior surface. These are the ridges of a fingertip. Dactylography was refined in the late 19th and early 20th centuries by Juan Vucetich and is deemed to be dependable for the identification of persons. *See also* BERTILLION, ALPHONSE (1853–1914).

DAHMER, JEFFREY (1959–1994). A **serial killer** and sex offender sentenced to 15 life terms in Wisconsin and one life term in Ohio. His offenses began in 1978 and ended with his arrest in 1991. The details of his actions include **murder**, cannibalism, dismemberment of bodies, and rape. He was beaten to death in **prison** by Christopher Scarver, another convict.

DANBURY, FCI. The Federal Correctional Institution, Danbury, was opened in August 1940. Originally it was to confine males and females convicted of federal offenses. During World War II, Danbury housed political prisoners, including those charged with **treason**. In 1993, it was converted exclusively for female prisoners. In 2013, overcrowding caused its conversion back to all male prisoners. A satellite unit houses female offenders. Among the better-known convicts have been Leona Helmsley and Sun Myung Moon.

DARK FIGURE OF CRIME. A term describing what is referred to as **hidden crime**. Official crime statistics are unreliable because of **unreported crime**, which is greatest for lower-level crime. Victim studies, self-report studies, and other types of surveys such as the **Uniform Crime Report (UCR)** and the **National Crime Victimization Survey** provide information about the gaps in unreported crime. While unreported crime was examined in the 19th century, sociologist **Edwin Sutherland** may have been the first to use the term "dark figure of crime" in 1947.

DATE RAPE. Date rape is often referred to as acquaintance **rape**; however, it is not the same. Date rape involves romantic attachment, whereas acquaintance rape implies a more casual relationship such as between neighbors or coworkers. These are nonconsensual sexual encounters. The notion of date rape originates in the United States, where it is most prevalent, and where most research has been conducted. In 1975, Susan Brownmiller wrote about it in her book, *Against Our Will: Men, Women, and Rape*. However, Mary Koss is acknowledged as coining the term from her study in 1987 of 7,000 students at 25 schools. Date rape is frequently associated with alcohol and drugs (also called predator drugs), such as Rohypnol in conjunction with alcohol.

DAUBERT RULE. Also referred to as the Daubert standard, it is an **evidence** rule regarding expert testimony during federal proceedings. The Daubert rule is primarily based on the 1923 Frye test and the 1975 Federal Rules of Evidence. The Frye test affirmed that in cases in which expert testimony depends upon scientific evidence, the science must have acceptance from the scientific field to which it corresponds. Rule 702 of the Federal Rules of Evidence specifies that **expert witnesses** must possess knowledge as a consequence of education and knowledge, skill or training, and experience. Part of the intention of the Daubert rule is to ensure that pseudoscience is not a standard of proof. *See also* FORENSICS.

DAVIS, RICHARD ALLEN "RICK" (1954–). Davis was convicted of the 1993 California **murder** of 12-year-old **Polly Klaas** and sentenced to death. The prior criminal record of Davis coupled with the circumstances of the Klaas murder resulted in California passing its 1994 "**three strikes** and you're out" act for the commission of three violent offenses. Many other states passed similar legislation following California. Georgia went one step further and passed a **two-strikes law** in 1997.

DAY REPORTING CENTER. Day reporting centers were first utilized in the United Kingdom in the 1970s. They were slow to start in the United States, with about 13 by 1990. However, they have since increased in popularity and are now utilized in almost every state by **probation** and **parole** offices, private nonprofit agencies, and private corporations such as GEO and CEC. Day reporting centers are a subset of **community corrections** and serve a variety of purposes including **diversion** and **reentry** to provide accountability and prevent rearrest. The services rendered include education, job skills readiness, counseling, housing attainment, and employment.

DEADLY FORCE. The consideration in law and by law enforcement that the degree of force used was intended to cause death or did result in death. Civilian use of deadly force is only justified if it is used when there is no other option available with which to provide personal defense. The use of deadly force by law enforcement is only acceptable in the absence of accessible means of preventing personal harm or harm to others; that is, there is no other choice and less deadly means have been employed, if available. The use of deadly force by law enforcement has been upheld and defined by the **U.S. Supreme Court** in ***Tennessee v. Garner*, 471 U.S. 1 (1985)** and *Graham v. Connor*, 490 U.S. 386 (1989). *See also* USE OF FORCE.

DEAD MAN WALKING. The phrase "dead man walking" was used by guards as they escorted a condemned man to the death house for **execution**. The phrase became popularized by the book (1993) and movie (1995) of the same title. Sister Helen Prejean, a longtime advocate for the abolition of **capital punishment**, who ministered for many years to convicts on Louisiana's death row at Angola **Prison**, wrote the book and was featured in the movie.

DEATHBED CONFESSION. Also called a dying declaration, it is the revelation at the time of impending death of a secret or a crime that someone has been keeping hidden during their life. If the confession is about a crime the dying person has committed, it cannot be prosecuted once the person is deceased. However, if the crime is about knowledge the dying person has of a crime, it may be admissible in court. The confession is generally not considered to be **hearsay** and thus is admissible in court. The confession may be considered as **evidence** to pursue an active case or a cold case, a case that has not been solved for a long period of time. This is especially permissible in **murder** cases for which there is no statute of limitations. The longest-standing cold case to be solved by a deathbed confession was the murder of seven-year-old Maria Ridulph of Sycamore, Illinois, December 1957.

DEATH BY COP. Another expression for the term is **suicide by cop**. There are three groupings of individuals who act in such a way as to be killed by law enforcement. The first is when an individual who is suicidal provokes a law enforcement officer to a point where they have no choice but to respond with **deadly force**. The second is when an individual has committed a crime with the intention of being fatally shot by a **police** officer. Third is when an individual has committed a crime and has the perception that arrest and incarceration are worse alternatives than to be killed. The foundation is that law enforcement is trained to respond when required with deadly force. An example is the 1966 Texas Tower shooter, **Charles Joseph Whitman**, who it has been suggested was waiting for the police, leaving them no choice but to shoot and kill him. Suicide by cop was first described in news accounts in 1981 and scientific journals in 1985. It became common in the early 2000s. It has also become an accepted cause of death. London **coroner** Dr. William Dolman used the term between 1993 and 2007. Police training programs have been adjusted to sensitize law enforcement. *See also* USE OF FORCE.

DEATH PENALTY. *See* CAPITAL PUNISHMENT.

DEATH PENALTY INFORMATION CENTER. The center was founded in 1990 as a nonprofit organization that serves as a depository for a wide variety of **death penalty** information and as such is the most comprehensive resource. While the Death Penalty Information Center does not take an official position on the death penalty, its presentation emphasizes an anti–death penalty stance.

DEATH-QUALIFIED JURY. A selection of jurors who are (1) not opposed to the **death penalty** and (2) do not believe that the death penalty is applicable in all cases of **murder** and agree that a sentence of life in **prison** is an alternate sentence. A death-qualified **jury** is not a violation of the Sixth Amendment and has been upheld in ***Lockhart v. McCree*, 476 U.S. 162 (1986)** and ***Witherspoon v. Illinois*, 391 U.S. 510 (1968)**. The *Witherspoon* holding has resulted in such determinations being referred to as *Witherspooning* the jury. *See also* JURY DUTY; JURY INSTRUCTIONS; JURY SELECTION.

DEATH SQUAD. Death squads perform unlawful killing common during times of political upheaval or as acts of **terrorism**. The death squads generally operate in secrecy, such as secret **police** supported by government, as vigilantes, or as a function of **organized crime**. While death squads have not been common in the United States, some examples include the funding by and the authorization of California between 1850 and 1852 and again between 1854 and 1859 to eliminate Native Americans. Another infamous example is 1865 to 1877, the Reconstruction era, during which the **Ku Klux Klan** lynched African Americans. The Klan additionally lynched those referred to as scalawags and carpetbaggers who supported Reconstruction. *See also* EXTRAJUDICIAL KILLING; LYNCHING; VIGILANTISM.

DEATH WARRANT. A death **warrant** (which may also be referred to as an **execution warrant** or black warrant) is the court order that sanctions the execution of a person convicted of a capital crime. Death warrants are usually completed within a limited time frame of about 60 days. The **Federal**

Bureau of Prisons or state departments of correction carry out the orders in **prisons** with a death house created for this purpose. For example, USP Terre Haute is the federal prison designated to carry out federal death sentences. No death warrants were issued between 1972 and 1978. In 1972, the **U.S. Supreme Court** decision in *Furman v. Georgia*, 408 U.S. 238 (1972), held the death penalty to be arbitrary and unconstitutional under the Eighth and Fourteenth Amendments. In 1976, the U.S. Supreme Court in ***Gregg v. Georgia*, 428 U.S. 153 (1976)**, held that executions could be completed with new criminal procedures. Under the new guidelines, an execution warrant was issued for **Gary Gilmore**, and in 1977 he became the first person to be executed (by **firing squad**) in the United States under the new guidelines.

DEBTOR'S PRISON. The **debtor's prison** (pre-dates the modern **prison** as **punishment**) was a European innovation of the 18th century to confine persons until such time as they paid their debt. The U.S. colonies similarly adopted the debtor's prison for unpaid debts. There is carryover of the concept into the present time since individuals who are **indigent** or who fail to pay their debt can be confined to prison for unpaid debts. For example, failure to pay child support payments, back taxes, and **fines** may be considered as contempt of court, for which a judge will sentence or remand the offender to jail. *See also* BRIDEWELL.

DECARCERATION. Decarceration is the response to the **mass incarceration** movement in the United States that began in the late 1970s. Decarceration, which seeks to challenge the punitive nature of incarceration, opts instead for smarter productive solutions to offending and offenders. Decarceration is a proposed solution to mass incarceration that began in the late 1990s. *See also* MARTINSON, ROBERT (1927–1979).

DECRIMINALIZATION. Decriminalization is the reduction or elimination of criminal sanctions. **Drug possession** and use currently carry criminal sanctions. Recently there have been efforts to amend or eliminate sanctions such as the New York **Rockefeller drug laws**. For example, personal possession of and consumption of **marijuana** has been legalized in some jurisdictions. *See also* MASS INCARCERATION.

DENIAL OF COUNSEL. *See GIDEON V. WAINWRIGHT*, 372 U.S. 335 (1963).

DEPRIVATION MODEL. A theory advanced to explain the **prison** culture. The theory suggests that convicts are deprived of autonomy, goods, sexual relationships, liberty, and security, which results in a culture that is different from that of normal society. The model was conceived during the 1950s and 1960s by Sykes (1958) and Goffman (1961). They suggest that convicts in the **total institution** suffer losses that are degrading and that result in stigma from the experience. The importation model was developed in contrast to the deprivation model and suggests that convicts bring the culture into prison and that it is comprised of characteristics that are similar to those found in normal society. *See also* PRISONIZATION.

DESALVO, ALBERT (1930–1973). Albert DeSalvo is the self-identified "Boston Strangler." He is believed to have **murdered** at least 13 women between 1962 and 1964. DeSalvo was convicted of the rapes but not of the murders. There is controversy about which of the crimes he may or may not have committed. DeSalvo received a life sentence, and while at Walpole State **Prison** in Massachusetts he was purportedly stabbed to death by Robert Wilson of the Winter Hill **Gang**. Wilson was tried and found not guilty. The murder of DeSalvo remains unsolved. DeSalvo's attorney was **F. Lee Bailey**. *See also* SERIAL KILLER.

DESERTS. Deserts is more commonly referred to as "**just deserts**." Deserts refers to the offender receiving a **punishment** that is deserved for committing a crime. This means that the punishment should fit or be commensurate with the crime. There is the implication that "just deserts" should serve as an example for others, such as the 1599 quote from an anonymous play, *Warning Faire Women* (which may be the earliest derivation of the phrase), "Upon a pillory—that all the world may see, A just desert for such impiety."

DESIGNER DRUGS. A term that refers to both synthetic and nonsynthetic drugs for recreational drug use. Following a 1925 ban on morphine by the International Opium Convention, **heroin** and other derivatives of morphine were manufactured and sold, including ether as a substitute for alcohol during **Prohibition**. The 1960s saw the introduction of synthetic hallucinogens. There was little prosecution during this time. The 1980s added synthetic opioids, what was called **ecstasy** (several different drugs), methamphetamine, and fentanyl. Fentanyl refers to several different drugs with adverse effects similar to Parkinson's disease, brain damage, and overdoses. The **Drug Enforcement Agency (DEA)** used emergency scheduling of these drugs to facilitate prosecution as controlled dangerous substances (CDS). From 1990 to the present, more recreational drugs became available on the streets and through the internet. This was in addition to an increase in the availability and demand for steroids and human growth hormone for athletes and others. A variety of legislative actions have been enacted in an attempt to curtail both the manufacture and use of recreational drugs. The 1970 Controlled Substances Act amended by the 1986 Controlled Substances Analogue Enforcement Act made the sale, possession, or manufacture of such drugs illegal. Many other countries have adopted similar legislation.

DESISTANCE FROM CRIME. A central concept of **life course theory**. Desistance from crime may be viewed as the termination of criminal offending. Criminological research by Sampson and Laub in 1993 and 2003 suggests that the definition is more process oriented to also include deescalation from crime.

DETECTIVE. This refers to either a member of law enforcement or individuals who operate privately. The role of detective developed with the creation and professionalization of municipal **police** departments such as the **Bow Street Runners** of England in 1749. Boston established the first detectives in 1846. The first private detective agencies appeared in Paris in 1833 headed by Eugene Vidocq. The first private detective agency in the United States was the Pinkerton Agency, founded in 1850. Private detectives often did the work of police when no formal police agency existed. Law enforcement detectives often begin as uniformed police officers. Demonstrated ability or in some cases passing tests is deemed to illustrate the aptitude of police officers to be detectives and establish their eligibility for promotion. Detectives examine crime scenes, secure **evidence**, make arrests, and do criminal **background checks**. In larger police departments, there is greater specialization of detective work; for example they may be assigned to **homicide**, juvenile, vice, or sexual assault, or they may be designated as a major crimes unit. Private detectives perform similar tasks and sometimes have served as private guards for businesses. Ironically, Vidocq began the processes of investigative record keeping and **ballistics**. Paradoxically, Vidocq and other early private detectives were unscrupulous, at times criminal, and violated the law. Private detectives are now required to be licensed. *See also* CRIME NOVEL; FORENSICS; NOIR CRIME NOVEL; PRIVATE SECURITY; TRUE CRIME; VIDOCQ SOCIETY.

DETERMINATE SENTENCING. A judicial sentence with a specified duration that may not be altered by a paroling authority. The determinate sentence may be affected by statutory conditions such as commutation (good) time or work time earned by the offender, which provides some relief from the full length of the sentence. The earliest penal sentences were determinate sentences. Concepts such as conditional release and **parole** of the mid-1800s saw sentencing changes to allow offenders to earn their way back into society. Post–World War II reforms to **prison** practices introduced sentencing structures which during the mid-1970s and later were viewed as failing to have a deterrent effect on crime. The "**tough on crime**" agenda initiated in the late 1970s and early 1980s saw changes back to determinate sentencing patterns, which included such language as life without parole, mandatory minimums, and **two-** and **three-strikes laws**. In addition, determinate sentencing received a new twist with legislated mandatory sentencing and **sentencing guidelines**. Under these conditions, **judicial discretion** was severely limited. In the first instance, the sentence was specified, and judges were given no choice. In the second instance, guidelines dictated the range within which the judge must sentence an offender.

DETERRENCE. Deterrence is a goal of sentencing and **punishment**. The sentence reflects the need for the punishment based on the severity of the crime. There are two types of deterrence. **General deterrence** refers to the sentence as an example to society. General deterrence is associated with the philosophical treatise of **Cesare Beccaria**, *On Crimes and Punishment* (1764), which states that this is the primary rationale for punishment. The other form of deterrence is **specific deterrence**, which emphasizes that the punishment intends to deter the offender from committing future crimes. The punishment should be commensurate with the degree of harm caused by the crime. The need for deterrence has been an argument for harsher sentencing. *See also* RETRIBUTION.

DEVELOPMENTAL CRIMINOLOGY. The origins of developmental **criminology** lie with Cyril Burt and his research into adolescent offending during the 1920s. His research focused on **life course** developments and the effects on individuals. Among the specific interests are when (at what age) **desistance from crime** initiates and how behavior and other changes develop. Experiences (whether sexual abuse or positive occurrences) during the life course affect future development and life choices, for example, rejection of criminal ideation or involvement in criminal behavior. Research since the 1990s has contributed to understanding both risk and protective factors of crime involvement and healthier choices. This approach has contributed to the idea that crime is a **rational choice (theory)** because of earlier life course events.

***DICKERSON V. U.S.*, 530 U.S. 428 (2000).** The **Omnibus Crime Control and Safe Streets Act of 1968** was passed two years after the ***Miranda v. Arizona*, 384 U.S. 436 (1966),** ruling by the **U.S. Supreme Court**. This act became the rationale for congressional legislation that overruled *Miranda*. *Dickerson v. U.S.*, 530 U.S. 428 (2000), later upheld the earlier ruling affirming that suspects be read the Miranda warning.

DIFFERENTIAL ASSOCIATION. Edwin Sutherland introduced the theory of differential association in 1947. He stressed nine points that help to explain why crime is committed. He emphasized that crime is learned through association with others, specifically values, attitudes, techniques, and motives. In addition, he theorized that the early influence of someone of a higher status increases the likelihood that an individual will follow the example that has been set. Furthermore, there is an expectation of criminal behavior when reasons for engaging in criminal behavior exceed those for remaining in adherence of the law.

DILLINGER, JOHN (1903–1934). A Depression-era **gangster** infamous for bank robbing. Dillinger fancied himself a modern-day Robin Hood who exclaimed that he robbed banks because that was where the money was. His bank-robbing career (allegedly 24 banks) was short and began in 1933 after his release from Indiana State **Prison** (1924–1933) and ended in 1934 after he was fatally shot by agents of the **FBI** led by Agent **Melvin Purvis**. **J. Edgar Hoover**, director of the FBI, used Dillinger as an example of **organized crime** and labeled him as the first gangster to be called **Public Enemy** No. 1. In large part this enabled Hoover to reorganize the FBI into a cutting-edge crime-fighting agency.

DIMINISHED CAPACITY. Diminished capacity is also referred to as diminished responsibility. Diminished capacity is a defense argument suggesting that while the defendant violated the law, their liability is moderated because their mental capacity has been compromised, and this should be considered throughout **adjudication** and sentencing. *People v. Gorshen*, 51 Cal.2d 716 (1959), challenged the intention of the defendant to commit a crime. *People v. Wells*, 8 Cal. 4th 1078, 136 p.3D 810, 45 Cal. RPTR. 3D 8 (2006), began a court process that would lead to the acceptance of a diminished capacity defense. In this case, a defendant was stopped because of an anonymous tip called in to the **police**. The defendant was determined to be under the influence. However, in 1978, Dan White murdered the mayor of San Francisco, and the defense argued that his intake of junk foods affected his mental state. Coincidentally, this became known as a "Twinkie defense," named after the sugary cake. California abolished the defense of diminished capacity in 1982, in part because of the negative publicity from the White **murder trial**, for which White received a seven-year sentence and served five years in **prison**.

DIPLOMATIC IMMUNITY. Diplomatic immunity is protection for foreign diplomats against lawsuits and prosecution for crime committed in the United States. The protection of diplomatic immunity was created by the

1961 Vienna Convention on Diplomatic Relations. However, the immunity does not protect the diplomat from host country expulsion or the commission of crime in the host country. Should the host country waive immunity, then the diplomat may be prosecuted by the host country.

DISCHARGE RESIDUE. **Forensics** uses gunshot residue, which is comprised of burnt and unburnt substances from the primer and the propellant, and may be on either or both the victim and the shooter, to determine the distance from the victim of the shooter. Gunshot residue may be found on hands and clothing, Gunshot residue has a spread of about three to five feet after leaving the muzzle of a gun. The use of gunshot residue by forensics experts began with the 1971 analysis by John Boehm who found residue in gunshot wounds. This was followed by the development of gunshot residue classification, which detailed four potential arrangements of components. Additional analysis in 1984 has increased the number of elements in the composition of gunshot residue. *See also* DETECTIVE.

DISCOVERY. Discovery is also called disclosure. The prosecution is constitutionally required to hand over to the defense all **exculpatory evidence**, including recordings of interviews and **interrogations**, photographs, and other information obtained, whether it favors the defense or the prosecution. ***Brady v. Maryland*, 373 U.S. 83 (1963)**, a **U.S. Supreme Court** landmark case, held that it is a violation of **due process**, a **Fourteenth Amendment** guarantee, for the prosecution to suppress **evidence** requested by the defense. In this case, the prosecution withheld a document in which the codefendant had admitted to the killing.

DISCRETIONARY RELEASE. *See* PAROLE.

DISCRIMINATION. Discrimination refers to prejudice and the treatment of individuals and groups based on their ethnicity, race, or other characteristics. Treatment refers to such actions as favoring one over another, restricting, or denying opportunities. On the one hand, counter actions to discrimination have resulted in what has come to be known as reverse discrimination and affirmative action. In law enforcement, a form of discrimination has been **racial profiling**. In law, the passage of some laws emerging from the **War on Drugs** declared in the 1960s, such as those that penalize crack cocaine differently from cocaine, are said to be discriminatory.

DISMISSAL. Dismissal refers to charges being dropped after they have been filed. Dismissal occurs after a determination that there is insufficient **evidence** to continue a case. New evidence, such as **DNA**, may be obtained to refute the original conviction. Other determinations about the admissibility of evidence include a request from the victim and violations of constitutional rights of the defendants. Dismissed charges are not the same as being found not guilty. They do not affirm an individual's innocence and can be refiled after obtaining new evidence. Dismissals also remain on an individual's criminal record. *See also* EXONERATION; INNOCENCE PROJECT.

DISORGANIZED OFFENDER. The disorganized offender is another description for a **serial killer** and was originally distinguished from an **organized offender** by **FBI** profiler **Robert Hazelwood** in 1986. Hazelwood believed the disorganized offender to be of below-average intelligence, with poor work habits and a sporadic work history, a loner with poor social skills who is brutal, sadistic, and violent in and after the commission of the **murder**. *See also* FEDERAL BUREAU OF INVESTIGATION (FBI); PROFILING.

DISPARITY. Disparity has multiple references in the criminal justice system, including **sentencing disparity** and **racial disparity** in which one group is maligned more than another. That is, race becomes an issue in responses from the criminal justice system. What is referred to as **disproportionate minority confinement (DMC)** argues that more minorities receive sentences of confinement than nonminorities. In other instances, such as **racial profiling**, a minority is more likely to be a suspect than a nonminority, even though there has been no action on the part of the minority to suggest a need for criminal justice intervention. Finally, there have been instances of hiring and promotional disparity because of someone's race.

DISPROPORTIONATE MINORITY CONFINEMENT (DMC). The disproportionate representation of minority youth and adults in the juvenile and adult justice systems. The concept of DMC was introduced in 1988 to Congress by the Coalition for Juvenile Justice. The outcome was increased funding for the states to address DMC. It has been a central theme of the **Office of Juvenile Justice and Delinquency Prevention (OJJDP)**. Since 2002, states that neglect to do anything to reduce DMC for juveniles may have their grants reduced by as much as 20 percent.

DISTRICT ATTORNEY. The title *district attorney* was never an officially designated title at either the federal or state level, although it has long been a practiced usage to describe a prosecutor of criminal offenses who operates within a specified geographical location and is generally considered to be the chief law enforcement officer for that location. For example, the Judiciary Act of 1789 provided a person to prosecute crimes within a specific district, and in 1948 they became referred to in the judicial code as **United States attorneys**. The use of the title *district attorney* is related to a person assigned to be the prosecutor in a specific district.

***DISTRICT OF COLUMBIA V. HELLER*, 554 U.S. 570 (2008).** The first **U.S. Supreme Court** holding to clarify that an individual possessed the right to possess firearms for self-defense as specified in the Second Amendment and which at the same time struck down conditions of the 1975 Firearms Control Regulations Act, such as requiring a trigger lock. The holding of the Court was that Heller would be allowed to register his firearm, license it, and possess it in his home for personal protection, family, and property. The decision noted that it hinged on Heller's not failing to qualify for possession of a weapon. Refer to appendix 1, "The Bill of Rights." *See also* BILL OF RIGHTS.

DIVERSION. Diversion programs date back to 1967 and the **President's Commission on Law Enforcement and the Administration of Justice** report, which recommended the creation of programs that would service juveniles in the community. The programs are alternatives to traditional approaches for the courts and corrections, which generally require incarceration. There is recognition that traditional responses to crime, including incarceration, do not deter offenders from committing crime and at the same time that offenders may be harmed by incarceration. Participants are deemed to be nonviolent and of little threat to the community, and through services to be deterred from future offending while giving back to the community and paying **restitution**. Beginning in the early 1990s, the Annie E. Casey Foundation funded the **Juvenile Detention** Alternative Initiative (JDAI), which in some cases dramatically reduced the number of youth held in correctional facilities. *See also* PRETRIAL DIVERSION.

DNA (DEOXYRIBONUCLEIC ACID). DNA is a molecule that possesses the unique characteristics of an individual. The isolation of DNA began in 1869 by Friedrich Miescher. In the 1980s, DNA became recognized for its accuracy in determining paternity. Its first use in a criminal justice matter was in 1986 when it was used to determine if a 17-year-old male suspect committed two rape-murders. The importance of DNA testing, in this seminal use, was incontrovertible, as DNA proved the suspect did not commit the crime and at the same time led to the arrest and conviction of the actual offender. The initial use of DNA in the United States was in Florida in 1987, where it became the critical **evidence** used in the conviction of Tommy Andrews. As DNA evidence became more widespread, challenges and appeals to its authenticity surfaced in the courts. West Virginia in 1989 was the first appellate court to respond to a legal challenge upholding the validity of DNA as evidence. Other challenges during the 1980s and 1990s included the acquisition of the evidence, the scientific process used for establishing DNA comparisons, the background of the scientists who did the testing, the creation of DNA databases, and more. The 1994 **Violent Crime** Control and Law Enforcement Act espoused the need for uniform standards. By 2000, all states had developed DNA databases, which resulted in an increase in arrests and convictions for previously unsolved crimes. *See also* FORENSICS.

DOMESTIC TERRORISM. Domestic terrorism is defined in the **Patriot Act** (Public Law 107-56-26 [October 2001]) as any act of **assassination**, **kidnapping**, or mass destruction that is dangerous to human life, violates U.S. federal and state criminal laws, or affects governmental policy. The acts are committed within the borders of the United States. An example of domestic **terrorism** was the 19 April 1995 bombing of the Alfred P. Murrah federal building in Oklahoma City, Oklahoma. *See also* McVEIGH, TIMOTHY (1968–2001); WORLD TRADE CENTER (WTC) BOMBINGS.

DOMESTIC VIOLENCE. Domestic violence is comprised of **assaults** (physical or sexual), threats, domination, intimidation, and other forms of maltreatment that would place a victim at risk. The victims are predominantly women, although men and children, as well as domestic partners (also referred to as intimate partner **violence**), have been included. Historically, before the mid-1800s, women and children received few legal protections from beatings or death from husbands and fathers. An initial effort to control violence by husbands was the "rule of thumb." That is, the wife could not be beaten with an object thicker than a thumb. In 1641, the Body of Liberties of the Massachusetts Bay colonists declared that beating could not leave marks on the woman. The beating of women was first outlawed in Tennessee in 1850. Late 1800s courts barred claims by husbands that they had a right to beat their wives. The phrase *domestic violence* appears to have its first use in British Parliament in 1973 by Jack Ashley. In 1993, the Declaration on the Elimination of Domestic Violence against Women provided a definition that incorporated many forms of domestic abuse against women. **Police** generally avoided or were uncertain how to respond to domestic violence until the latter half of the 20th century. Police and other training specifically addressing domestic violence, legislated changes such as the Protection of Women from Domestic Violence (2005), advocacy groups, and the creation of **domestic violence court** have all contributed to a more comprehensive and effective response. *See also* BATTERED WOMAN SYNDROME (BWS).

DOMESTIC VIOLENCE COURT. Domestic violence court emerged nationally as a special, community, or **problem-solving court** (modeled after **drug courts**) in the 1980s as a more effective response to offenders and for victims in an effort to prevent ongoing **assaults**. Judges, prosecutors, and staff are specially trained to participate in, monitor, and provide victim assistance. *See also* DOMESTIC VIOLENCE; VIOLENCE.

DOUBLE JEOPARDY. The double jeopardy clause of the **Fifth Amendment** prohibits retrial for the same or similar charges after an acquittal, conviction, specific mistrials, or different **punishments** for the same indictment. However, if new **evidence** is presented, then a retrial is permitted. Several **U.S. Supreme Court** cases, including *Brown v. Ohio*, 432 U.S. 161 (1977), have refined the meaning of double jeopardy. In the case of *Brown*, the defendant was charged with two crimes (joyriding and auto theft), which were essentially the same crime and thus constituted double jeopardy. *See also PALKO V. CONNECTICUT*, 302 U.S. 319 (1937); TRIAL.

DRIVE-BY SHOOTING. A shooting (also referred to as a drive-by) that is generally associated with **gang** violence and involves the firing of a weapon from a vehicle at a suspecting or unsuspecting victim, often in urban areas. The motives include **assassination**, intimidation, and **terrorism**. Drive-by shootings were utilized during the 1920s by **gangsters** attempting to control territory during **Prohibition**. They were also used during the 1970s and 1980s in Florida as the cocaine trade began, and more recently during hip-hop disputes and by militants in the Iraq conflict. *See also* VIOLENCE.

DRIVING WHILE BLACK (DWB). The expression implies **racial profiling** because of the suggestion that black drivers are more likely to be targeted by law enforcement for questioning, personal search, or search of a vehicle, and to be suspected of being in possession of or under the influence of illicit substances. As early as 1985, Florida issued examples for law enforcement to aid in the identification of "drug couriers," which included a statement about ethnic groups. The **Kerner Commission**, or the National Advisory Commission on Civil Disorders hearing of 1967, listed complaints of African Americans "being detained by law enforcement without substantive cause or reasonable suspicion," a violation of the **Fourth Amendment**. Significantly, law enforcement began training officers with regard to racial profiling. A federal **consent decree** was filed against the New Jersey **state police** in 1999 requiring that state police be retrained to avoid profiling. The consent decree ended in 2009.

DRUG ABUSE RESISTANCE EDUCATION (DARE). A nationwide drug prevention program started in the city of Los Angeles in 1983. DARE also diverts youth from **gang** membership and involvement in **violence**. **Police** officers speak to students and youth in schools and other organizations of the dangers of drugs and gangs and have them sign pledges promising that they will avoid such involvement. Earlier efforts include Nancy Reagan beginning the "Just Say No" campaign in 1987, which continued into the 1990s in an attempt to divert schoolchildren and others from drug abuse. The United Kingdom began a similar program in 1995.

DRUG CARTELS. A criminal enterprise engaged in **drug trafficking**. While drug trafficking is an old enterprise, the formation of the modern well-organized drug cartel is relatively recent, with roots in the 1970s. The cartels of Colombia, Mexico, and a few other countries were organized to produce, transport, and distribute drugs. Cocaine was the most popular drug of the cartel and initially the most profitable. The coordinated efforts of law enforcement began during the Reagan presidency when it was likened to the threat of a world war. While drug trafficking still exists, the cartel in terms of its size, power, and influence has generally ceased to exist. The U.S. government has prosecuted drug traffickers under **Racketeer Influenced Corrupt Organization (RICO)** statutes. Among the more notorious persons involved in the trafficking of tons of cocaine each month into the United States was Pablo Escobar. Escobar amassed great wealth, becoming one of the richest men in the world from his criminal enterprise. Pressure from the United States resulted in Colombian authorities pursuing him, and he was killed in a shootout on 2 December 1993. *See also* CALI CARTEL; MEDELLÍN CARTEL.

DRUG COURT. The origin of drug court was in 1989 in Miami-Dade County, Florida. The creation of the court was a response to a large number of individuals ineffectively being managed by the criminal justice system, especially in **prisons**, for their substance abuse. The court is referred to as **community court**, special court, **problem-solving court**, and the new court. The drug court is recognized as the modern beginning of the new community courts. The drug court differentiates from traditional courts in several ways. Primary to the process is that defendants volunteer to be participants, the court only addresses offenders who are drug involved, and the judge is specially trained about drug offenders. In addition, the judge follows the defendant's process and maintains a hands-on approach with all who interface with the defendant, including **probation** officers, parents, spouses, children, and agencies who are identified to service the needs of defendants. Drug courts have withstood the scrutiny of researchers with findings that they are much more effective than traditional courts and drug treatment programs. In addition, they are more cost effective than traditional ways of managing offenders through probation and incarceration. The original courts in the United States, in the colonies, were community courts.

DRUG CZAR. The unofficial title for the director of the White House Office of National Drug Control Policy created under the administration of President Reagan in the Anti-Drug Abuse Act of 1988. The earliest use of the term was by Senator Joe Biden in 1988. The position of drug czar has traditionally been held by someone with political, law enforcement, or military experience. Michael Botticelli currently holds the position and has the distinction of being a person in substance abuse recovery. The drug czar guides the creation of policy to address the work of law enforcement, public health officials, and others to curtail the use, sale, and treatment of drugs. The office also advises and supports efforts to curb **drug trafficking**. *See also* DRUG ENFORCEMENT AGENCY (DEA).

DRUG ENFORCEMENT AGENCY (DEA). The DEA was created in 1973 and combined several federal offices as well as the Bureau of **Narcotics** and Dangerous Drugs and the Office of Drug Abuse Law Enforcement to form the DEA under the U.S. Department of Justice. The DEA operated out of Washington, D.C., until 1989 when it was relocated to Arlington, Virginia.

DRUGFIRE PROGRAM. The Drugfire Program enhanced firearms identification through bullet and cartridge casing imaging. The imaging process allows comparisons with such items recovered from crime scenes. The Drugfire Program was begun by the **FBI** in 1993 and was replaced by the Alcohol, Tobacco, and Firearm's National Integrated Ballistic and Identification Network in 1999. The use of the system has become a worldwide standard. *See also* BALLISTICS; FORENSICS.

DRUG LEGALIZATION. Also referred to as drug **decriminalization**, it is the social and legal attempt to eliminate the harsh sentencing prescribed by drug laws or to alter laws that prevent **drug possession** and use. The **War on Drugs** declared by President Nixon in 1971 resulted in ill-founded and failed policy and legislation. The consequences were **mass incarceration** due to increased crime, which was unequaled in any other country; the creation of **drug cartels**, which profited from providing illegal drugs to American citizens; governmental interference in the lives of citizens; and tax revenue lost from drugs that could be legalized. A central theme of drug decriminalization is reduction in the harm that originates from criminal records and the **collat-**

eral consequences associated with such criminal records. Several countries, including Portugal, Italy, Spain, and the Netherlands, have decriminalized the use of drugs with positive results. Harm reduction through decriminalization allows for more effective treatment and prevention of drug abuse while at the same time minimizing disruption of lives because of criminal convictions. *See also* DRUG USE FORECASTING; HARM PRINCIPLE.

DRUG POSSESSION. The possession of drugs designated as illegal, whether for distribution, personal use, or sale. Penalties for drug possession range from very small **fines** to **probation** or imprisonment. What constitutes possession and applicable penalties varies from state to state and with the federal government. Increasingly harsher penalties for possession began after President Nixon's declaration of a national **War on Drugs**. New York implemented the **Rockefeller drug laws** in 1973, which contained provisions for mandatory minimum **prison** sentences. The appeal of that law led to drug laws being passed throughout the United States. Laws for possession of drugs were instrumental for fueling the **mass incarceration** binge of the past 40 years. *See also* DRUG CZAR.

DRUG TEST. An analysis of urine, hair, blood, or other biological sample to ascertain whether prohibited or legal drugs are present and the quantity in a person or body. Drug testing has become standardized screening for pre-employment, athletes, drug offenders, and others. Executive Order 12564, Drug-Free Federal Workplace (1986), issued by President Reagan required mandatory drug testing for federal employees. The **U.S. Supreme Court** in 1988 upheld federal workplace drug testing and later extended it to the states. Some jurisdictions, including federal **probation** and supervised release, mandate that offenders serving probation and **parole** test for drug use. Some professional sports also regularly test athletes for drug use, and if tested positive the offender may be suspended or terminated from sporting participation. Drug testing has been fundamental to the operation of **drug courts** since their inception in 1989. *See also* FORENSICS.

DRUG TRAFFICKING. The national and international manufacture, distribution, and sale of illegal drugs. Prohibitions against the use of drugs began in early 1700 in China. The transportation of drugs and specifically opium became an illegal enterprise in China in the 19th century. The attempt to control the drug trade began in the United Kingdom with the 1868 Pharmacy Act. The United States has experienced increased drug trafficking from South America, Latin America, and Mexico since the 1960s, beginning with **marijuana** followed by cocaine and **heroin**. The United States enacted the 1914 Harrison Act to control drug trafficking. South American and Mexican

drug cartels were responsible for importing more than 50 percent and up to 90 percent of the cocaine entering the United States. The 2008 Merida Initiative provided about $1.5 billion to increase security in Mexico to combat the cartels. The defeat of the cartels, which included the death (Pablo Escobar) and imprisonment of cartel drug kingpins in the mid-1990s saw a reduction in drugs trafficked into the United States. It is suggested that the increase in drug users combined with strong economies is now stimulating a debate to legalize drugs and the **decriminalization** of drug use. *See also* CALI CARTEL; MEDELLÍN CARTEL.

DRUG USE FORECASTING. Drug Use Forecasting began in 1987 when the U.S. Department of Justice administered the **Arrestee Drug Abuse Monitoring (ADAM)** survey to adult arrestees who are randomly selected because of their drug involvement with cocaine, **marijuana**, methamphetamine, opiates, and phencyclidine (PCP). Data was obtained from juvenile arrestees beginning in 1991. The program was discontinued in 2004 because of lack of funding.

DRY LABBING. Dry labbing refers to the falsification of **evidence**, which may result from improper evidence handling, the failure to perform or properly perform or the faking of tests on evidence, deliberately contaminating evidence, forging signatures of others on evidence, and/or false testimony in court about evidence and its tests. Dry labbing generally occurs in the context of forensic analysis of crime scene evidence, such as **DNA** evidence. *See also* FORENSICS.

DUELING. A combat engagement between two individuals with rules and corresponding weapons. Duels date back to medieval times and occurred because of some disagreement or some insult or other offense. The rules of engagement evolved over time, and in the 18th century in the United States there were as many as 25 controlling conditions. Legislation outlawing dueling began in Europe in the 13th century. While duels declined because of unfavorable public opinion, federal legislation outlawing duels did not occur until 1839 following the death of Congressman Jonathan Cilley by fellow congressman William Graves. U.S. states soon followed with similar legislation banning duels. *See also* ADVERSARIAL JUSTICE; HAIR TRIGGER.

DUE PROCESS. Due process protects the individual from harm (unfairness or physical abuse) by the government. A due process section is included in both the **Fifth** and **Fourteenth Amendments**, which protect against governmental denial of life, liberty, and property without appropriate legal actions, referred to as the rule of law. One of the earliest efforts to provide due process protections can be found in the **Magna Carta** of 1215. Refer to appendix 1, "The Bill of Rights." *See also* BILL OF RIGHTS; DUE PROCESS MODEL.

DUE PROCESS MODEL. One of two models (the other is the crime control model) described by **Herbert Packer** in his book *The Limits of the Criminal Sanction* (1968), which emphasizes philosophical approaches to criminal justice management. The **due process** model emphasizes that in order for fairness to prevail, the elements of due process must prevail; that defendants' rights are stipulated in the **Bill of Rights**; that the persecution of the defendant by officials is prohibited, and thus the powers of law enforcement are restricted; that agents of criminal justice must adhere to constitutional rights, including rules and other guidelines that ensure fairness; that barriers which exist in the criminal justice system are necessary to ensure safeguards for individuals who may be convicted as guilty and for those who are innocent; and that criminal justice procedures must be followed in addition to establishing guilt based on factual **evidence**. The due process model has come under criticism since the mid-1970s when fear of crime, based upon the perceived failure of the criminal justice system, resulted in calls for law and order supported by more severe legislation and a reduction in rights. While the due process model appears to have been weakened over the past four decades, due process rights remain available for challenge by defendants in the appellate courts. Refer to appendix 1, "The Bill of Rights." *See also* CIVIL RIGHTS.

***DUNCAN V. LOUISIANA*, 391 U.S. 145 (1968).** Duncan was charged with a misdemeanor and received a 60-day sentence. The **U.S. Supreme Court** held that Louisiana law which governed misdemeanor offenses was unconstitutional and atypical when compared with the standards of the other 49 states. The Court held that request for a **trial** by **jury** in a criminal case was a constitutional guarantee of the Sixth and **Fourteenth Amendments** (**due process**) and that the states must abide by it. However, no trial by jury is required for crimes that are petty, with penalties of less than a $500 **fine** and six months of incarceration.

DURESS DEFENSE. Duress is also referred to as coercion. The use of it, as *defense* implies, is for people who have acted other than the way they normally would as the result of some unlawful threat. In the defense, there is acknowledgment by defendants that they committed the act; however, the defendants claim that it occurred because of an unlawful strain. The act of omission is similar to pleading guilty if the duress defense is rejected. *See also* DURHAM RULE; ENTRAPMENT; STAND YOUR GROUND LAW.

DURHAM RULE. The Durham rule provides the foundation for the **insanity defense**. The 1954 U.S. court of appeals held that mental illness frees the individual of criminal responsibility. However, *United States v. Brawner*, 471 F.2d 969 (1972), resulted in the abandonment of the rule, finding that it was ambiguous and placed too much reliance on **expert witnesses**—that is, psychologists and psychiatrists—for a **jury** to interpret.

DURKHEIM, ÉMILE (1858–1917). Durkheim is recognized as the father of sociology. In 1897, he published his case study, *Suicide*, through which he is credited with developing quantitative **criminology**. He argued that crime was influenced by the breakdown of society and introduced **anomie theory**. *See also* MERTON, ROBERT (1910–2003).

DYE PACK. The dye pack was patented in 1993 and is used in about 75 percent of all banks as a device to frustrate bank robberies. The radio-controlled device is placed inside a hollowed-out stack of bills and ignites within 10 seconds of the robbers taking the stolen money through the doorway. The signal causes an explosion, ruining the money and staining the thief, and is **evidence** that may be used in the investigation and conviction of guilty persons. The dye pack is a frequent convention used in movies and TV.

E

EASTERN STATE PENITENTIARY (PENNSYLVANIA). The first modern **prison** (built on Cherry Hill Farm on the outskirts of Philadelphia), which operated from 1829 to 1971 and became the model for most prison systems worldwide. The system utilized at Eastern State Penitentiary has been referred to as the "separate system" or the "**Pennsylvania system**." As the separate system, it emphasized reform and not **punishment** by keeping convicts separate from each other and society. A "code of silence" was enforced to enable the convict to focus on his misdeeds and seek redemption. The prison was designed by architect **John Haviland** and included running water, a flush toilet, and a central heating system. It would be the most expensive public building in the United States. The original Pennsylvania system would be a single-level hub-and-spoke design that housed 450 convicts. It would not be replicated in other parts of the United States, which found the operational style ineffective and problematic. Other state prison systems would attempt different architectural styles and methods of operation. In 1965, Eastern State Penitentiary became a National Historic Landmark and today operates as a museum. Among its more famous convicts were **Alphonse Capone** and **Willie Sutton**. *See also* SILENT SYSTEM; SOLITARY CONFINEMENT.

ECOLOGICAL CRIMINOLOGY. Ecological **criminology**, sometimes referred to as urban sociology, applies **ethnography** to theory and emphasizes the impact of bad environments on crime. This study takes into account the imbalance of economic factors in the community, such as population density, aptitude, illiteracy, and other variables, as they influence criminality. For example, when schooling is diminished, the decision to commit crime increases. This concept was developed at the **Chicago School** in the 1920s and 1930s. George L. Kelling proposed in the mid-1990s what has popularly been called the **broken windows theory**. This theory has been summarized into concepts such as "if a window remains unbroken, then there is encouragement to do more damage." Ecological theory has had an influence on the development of **community-oriented policing** and the intentions of its operations.

ECONOMIC ESPIONAGE. Economic espionage, also referred to as corporate **espionage** or spying, is the actions of an agent of government or of a corporation to acquire information about manufacturing or to obtain other knowledge of a corporation to gain an advantage. Economic espionage is the acquisition of information about new products, contracts, or technology to gain a strategic advantage or to undermine the efforts of a competitor. In 1712, the Chinese produced porcelain, and the West sent agents to steal the process. In the 20th century, the former Soviet Union attempted to acquire the technology behind CPU chips made in the United States. The Economic Espionage Act of 1996 was passed to address a wider range of economic espionage issues, including the theft of or misappropriation of trade secrets.

ECOTERRORISM. Ecoterrorism came to prominence in the 1960s to draw attention to government and corporate actions that defile or degrade environments. The movement is rooted in the principles of biocentrism, which assert that man is a part of the environment and equally shares it with the remainder of the environment, which also deserves to have its rights recognized and protected. Ecoterrorists commit acts of **violence** (sometimes symbolic) against property and persons or objects as support for their cause. Examples of ecoterrorism include tree spiking, **arson**, and bombings. **Ted Kaczynski** (confined in ADX Florence) committed acts of ecoterrorism between 1978 and 1995. The intentions of ecoterrorists vary depending on specific organizational goals, such as restoring an environment to a natural state. Most U.S. states have passed ecoterrorism legislation in an attempt to control and prevent it. *See also* ADMAX; TERRORISM.

ECSTASY. Ecstasy is the recreational drug methylenedioxymethamphetamine (MDMA), which was first created in 1912, started being used in psychotherapy during the 1970s, and became a street drug in the 1980s. The drug causes heightened sensations similar to those achieved with adrenaline or ephedrine, described as a stimulant. Ecstasy is popular in the rave culture and with party groups because of its sensory intensification related to music. The drug has been known to cause higher temperatures and dehydration leading to death. Ecstasy is a Schedule 1 drug of the 1970 Controlled Substances Act with criminal penalties for possession, use, and sales.

EIGHTH AMENDMENT. The Eighth Amendment was based on the Virginia **Bill of Rights** of 1776 and adopted in 1791. The amendment prohibits **cruel and unusual punishment**, excessive **fines**, and excessive **bail**. The amendment has roots in English case law of the 17th century, when extreme and disproportionate sentences were imposed, and influenced a similar action in the English Bill of Rights of 1689 but did allow **judicial discretion**. The **U.S. Supreme Court** has held that the Eighth Amendment forbids some **punishments** entirely such as **torture**, burning, and drawing and quartering. The Eighth Amendment has been frequently cited in U.S. Supreme Court cases that have centered on the **death penalty**, corporal punishment and torture, fines, and property seizure. *See also FURMAN V. GEORGIA*, 408 U.S. 238 (1972), which describes the four conditions for determining CRUEL AND UNUSUAL PUNISHMENT; PROPORTIONALITY.

ELECTRIC CHAIR. *See* AUBURN PRISON; CAPITAL PUNISHMENT; EXECUTION.

ELECTRONIC MONITORING. Electronic monitoring was developed in the 1960s by twin brothers (Robert and Kirk Gable) at Harvard University. The original use was to monitor **juvenile offenders** and provide rewards such as free pizza when they complied with the assigned conditions. Electronic monitoring has been expanded from its original intentions to include use with parolees and probationers and to provide tracking for sex, DUI, and violent offenders. It has been used with high-profile offenders such as Martha Stewart and Paris Hilton. One of the more popular devices is an ankle bracelet. Among the arguments for implementing the devices is cost saving because it frees up jail and **prison** space and allows an offender to work, support a family, and pay taxes. More advanced devices include Global Positioning Systems (GPS), which utilize cell towers for location and monitors for blood alcohol levels. Some studies have reported successful reductions in repeat offenses by more than 30 percent. An interesting note is the criticism of one of the inventors, who states that current use is for **punishment** as opposed to recognition for acknowledging changed behavior through positive reinforcement. *See also* PAROLE.

ELMIRA REFORMATORY. Zebulon Brockway established Elmira Reformatory in 1876 with a pathological treatment model that focused on convict reform. First Maconochie at Norfolk Island and later **Walter Crofton's Irish system** influenced the Elmira model. Elmira Reformatory was innovative in the diversity of its education programs introduced to criminals, and it expanded **prison** recreation programs by having organized sports for the men, which were intended to provide them with activities they could engage in after prison as an alternative to criminal behavior. Brockway's success with his model resulted in 12 states constructing 25 more reformatories in the next quarter century. Unfortunately, the success led to overcrowding the reformatory. The strain on resources resulted in a collapse of the programs and greater reliance on **corporal punishment** and standard correctional practices to maintain discipline. Elmira Reformatory would be converted to a maximum-security prison. Brockway resigned. However, correctional practices would derive two central themes from Elmira Reformatory. The first was the separation of **youthful offenders** from adults, and the second was the possibility of rehabilitation, themes that dominate criminological discussion. *See also* MACONOCHIE, CAPTAIN ALEXANDER (1787–1860); PAROLE.

EMPLOYEE THEFT. The categories of employee theft include money, supplies, property, time, and information. The employee has no permission to take or remove any of the items listed above for personal use or to surrender them or information to someone else. Oftentimes, items removed for personal use are viewed by the offender as being of little or no consequence and include items such as pens or paper. These are assets of a company with tangible value. Research indicates that as many as half of all employees steal at least once. Managers or supervisors represent the cohort most likely to steal, and the areas of greatest concern to companies include time and expense accounts. Employee theft is currently responsible for business losses of more than $50 billion annually and for about one-third of business failures. The reasons for employee theft are somewhat vague, but **Donald Cressey**'s "fraud triangle" theory, proposed in 1950, suggests the combination of opportunity at the business, a need of the employee, and rationalization for committing the theft. Recent research (Kennedy 2016) has suggested that such thefts occur over time with an average cash theft of $20,000 from small businesses.

ENHANCED INTERROGATION TECHNIQUES. Enhanced interrogation techniques is synonymous with the application of systematic **torture** (utilizing sleep deprivation, beatings, hoodings, waterboarding, and more) of political prisoners by the **Central Intelligence Agency (CIA)**, other governmental agents, and **police** to intimidate and obtain intelligence and **evidence**. The use of these methods has been controversial, and debate was intensified following reports that emerged from Abu Ghraib in 2003, **Guantanamo Bay** in the same time period, and other **military prisons**. The derivation of the term is unknown. The methodologies employed were primarily developed around 2002 by psychologists James Mitchell and Bruce Jessen, who were hired by the CIA. *See also* EIGHTH AMENDMENT; INTERROGATION.

***ENMUND V. FLORIDA*, 458 U.S. 782 (1982).** A **U.S. Supreme Court** case of **proportionality** in which the driver of a car during a **murder** was sentenced to death. The **death penalty** was set aside by the court for the driver of the car. The determination was based on **Eighth Amendment** interpretations that a driver of a car during a murder was not the same as actually committing the murder inasmuch as the driver was not shown to have intended to commit murder. *See also* ACCOMPLICE; AIDING AND ABETTING; PUNISHMENT.

ENRON SCANDAL. In 2001, the Enron Corporation became known as the biggest audit fraud because it persuaded the auditors of Arthur Andersen, a Chicago accounting firm, to overlook questionable practices. This strategy kept the board of directors in the dark and led to the bankruptcy of Enron, the greatest bankruptcy reorganization in history. Several executives of Enron were indicted along with the auditor Arthur Andersen. The charges included fraud, wire fraud, **money laundering**, insider trading, conspiracy, securities fraud, and **obstruction of justice**. Sixteen Enron executives and employees pleaded guilty along with four Merrill Lynch employees. The share price of Enron stock dropped from more than $90 a share to less than $1 a share. The scandal resulted in the passage of the Sarbanes-Oxley Act (2002) and new regulations being promulgated for the energy industry to prevent similar occurrences.

ENTRAPMENT. The act by law enforcement to prompt someone to commit a crime that might not otherwise have been committed. This happens in "sting" operations. Entrapment is controversial and has raised ethical questions in both state and federal courts beginning in the New York Supreme Court in 1864 (*Board of Commissioners v. Backus*, 29 How. Pr. 33, 42). The federal courts have acknowledged that entrapment was a legitimate defense in 1915 (*Woo Wai v. United States*, 223 F.1d 412). Among the questions the courts have addressed is whether the individual, if misled, should be considered guilty of criminality for committing a crime; whether guilt may be established; whether someone is predisposed to commit a crime; whether entrapment represents a defense against criminal responsibility, and whether the government's act caused the crime. The following cases argued these questions and illustrate the extensive consideration given to entrapment by the courts:

Jacobson v. United States, 503 U.S. 540 (1992)
Raley v. Ohio, 360 U.S. 423 (1959)
Sherman v. United States, 356 U.S. 369, 375 (1958)
Sorrells v. United States, 287 U.S. 435, 451 (1932)
United States v. Howell, 37 F.3d 1197, 1204 (7th Cir. 1994)

United States v. Russell, 411 U.S. 423 (1973)

ENVIRONMENTAL CRIME. An act that damages the environment and includes the illegal trade (transportation) of endangered species and plants and illegal hunting and fishing. The 1899 Rivers and Harbor Act was of little use since it addressed waterways, and dumping was classified as a misdemeanor. The earliest dedicated effort on environmental crime was the 1982 creation of the Office of Criminal Enforcement in the Environmental Protection Agency (EPA), which focuses on violations of laws passed during the 1970s to address pollution. Legislation since the 1970s classifies environmental crimes as felonies. *See also* ECOTERRORISM; ENVIRONMENTAL CRIMINOLOGY.

ENVIRONMENTAL CRIMINOLOGY. In the 1980s, Paul and Patricia Brantingham discussed the relationships among five factors that represent a criminal incident: space, time, law, offender, and victim. Environmental **criminology** has origins in the **Chicago School** of the 1920s and 1930s and in the concentric **zone theory** of Parks and Burgess, which led to such tools as **crime mapping** to study **juvenile delinquency**. Understanding the relationship between environmental variables may result in the reduction of criminal activity in specific areas. However, environmental criminology has done little to deter dumping of hazardous materials since the **fines** are less than the cost of legal dumping. A recent example is the 2015 case in which subsidiaries of the Duke Energy Corporation were prosecuted for violations of the 1972 Clean Water Act. The corporation was fined $69 million and would pay $34 million for environmental projects. *See also* ENVIRONMENTAL CRIME.

EQUITY FUNDING SCANDAL. In the 1960s and 1970s, the Equity Funding Corporation of America scandal was the center of the greatest fraud (over $2 billion) in U.S. history until the **Bernie Madoff** Ponzi scheme was prosecuted in 2009. The investigation was the first time a computer was audited. The IBM computer in question was the excuse for not producing the annual report and kept shareholders from understanding the swindle. The Equity Funding Corporation of America had been called the fastest-growing financial company in the United States. *See also* ENRON SCANDAL.

ESCOBEDO V. ILLINOIS*, 378 U.S. 478 (1964).** The **U.S. Supreme Court** determined that the Sixth Amendment afforded suspects a right to counsel during **interrogation**. Escobedo had been held for 14 hours of interrogation, repeatedly requesting an attorney. His attorney did go to the **police** station and was denied access to his client. This holding extended the determination in ***Gideon v. Wainwright **, 372 U.S. 335 (1963)** that **indigents** must be provided with counsel. *See also* DENIAL OF COUNSEL.

ESPIONAGE. Espionage, also referred to as spying, is the act of obtaining information that is secret or confidential. Espionage is part of what is known as intelligence gathering. It is common to most cultures and governments and is found in biblical references, the writings of Sun Tzu, and the acts of the Roman and Egyptian empires. Modern espionage seeks information about **drug cartels, terrorism**, and the potentially dangerous activities of foreign governments. Espionage is a federal crime (Espionage Act of 1917) and carries serious consequences, such as the **execution** of **Julius and Ethel Rosenberg** in **Sing Sing Prison** in 1953. The Rosenbergs provided secrets to the USSR considered to be a threat, whereas Jonathan Pollard, during his employment with the Naval Intelligence Support Center, provided secrets for ideological reasons to an ally (Israel). Pollard served almost 30 years in **prison** and was released in 2016. *See also* ECONOMIC ESPIONAGE; TREASON.

ETHNOGRAPHY. A method of criminological inquiry that studies subcultures and the inhabitants. The method came to **criminology** via anthropology and the sociology of deviance. **Sutherland** (1938) and **Clemmer** (1940/1950) were two of the first sociologists to research criminality and penal institutional settings using ethnographic methods, such as Sykes and Messinger. Many early and well-known studies came out of the **Chicago School** (i.e., **Anderson**, Thrasher, Landesco, Thomas, and Whyte). Contemporary ethnographies in crime include Cohen's ***Folk Devils*** *and* ***Moral Panics*** (1972), Anderson's *Code of the Street* (1999), and Venkatesh's ***Gang*** *Leader for a Day* (2008). **Convict criminology** considers ethnography (convict writings) essential to understanding and reforming **prisons. [AU: ADD ENTRIES TO BIB FOR SYKES & MESSINGER, ANDERSON, LANDESCO, THOMAS, AND WHYTE]**

EUTHANASIA. *See* KEVORKIAN, JACK (1928–2011); MERCY KILLING.

EVERS, MEDGAR (1925–1963). An African American activist in the **civil rights** movement who challenged segregation at the University of Mississippi. He was **assassinated** in 1963 by Byron De La Beckwith. De La Beckwith was tried twice by an all-white **jury** (blacks were excluded from juries) who failed to reach a verdict. He was again prosecuted in 1994 and was convicted with new **evidence**. Beckwith died in **prison** in 1992. *See also* JURY SELECTION.

EVIDENCE. Evidence is any material gathered by law enforcement, prosecution, or the defense that would prove the guilt or innocence of a suspect. The issues with evidence are numerous and range from what may or may not be acceptable based upon how it was obtained or maintained, who establishes that it is acceptable evidence, and what that evidence actually determines. Edmond Locard, who helped establish **forensic science**, remarked that "every contact leaves its trace." There have been many challenges to evidence in the **U.S. Supreme Court**. Among the more frequent appeals concern **due process** issues such as **warrantless searches**, the **exclusionary rule**, and withholding evidence, which have been addressed through interpretations of the **Fourth**, **Fifth**, Sixth, and **Fourteenth Amendments**. The court also is concerned with the destruction of evidence, the falsification of evidence (such as **dry labbing**), and tampering with evidence, which constitute **obstruction of justice**. The value of evidence has changed over time. Where **eyewitness testimony** was once considered invaluable for the prosecution, the **Innocence Project** has demonstrated that eyewitnesses are questionable and often faulty. The following U.S. Supreme Court case holdings provide a sample of the evidence issues.

Boyd v. United States, 116 U.S. 616 (1886): The issue was a warrantless search objected to but ignored, thus a violation and application of the exclusionary rule.

***Brady v. Maryland*, 373 U.S. 83 (1963)**: A Fourteenth Amendment violation because the prosecution withheld evidence.

***Horton v. California*, 496 U.S. 128 (1990)**: The application of the **Fourth Amendment** and the **plain view doctrine** upholding the seizure of evidence that is in plain view. A similar holding was made in ***Nix v. Williams*, 467 U.S. 431 (1984)**.

***Mallory v. U.S.*, 354 U.S. 449 (1957)**: The holding is that confessions (evidence) are inadmissible following an unreasonable long time spent in detention without a court appearance. This has become known as the McNabb-Mallory rule. A similar holding was made in ***McNabb v. U.S.*, 318 U.S. 332 (1943)**.

***Pointer v. Texas*, 380 U.S. 400 (1965)**. The holding was that a defendant, in an examining **trial**, during which evidence is presented to determine whether charges should be filed, should be represented by an attorney and has the right to confront an accuser as a Sixth Amendment guarantee.

See also DAUBERT RULE; EXCULPATORY EVIDENCE; EXTRA Y CHROMOSOME; FINGERNAIL SCRAPINGS; FIRE DEBRIS ANALYSIS; IMPRESSION EVIDENCE; INCRIMINATING EVIDENCE; INDICTABLE OFFENSE; LOCARD'S EXCHANGE PRINCIPLE; SYNANON; TRACE EVIDENCE; TYLENOL MURDERS.

EVIDENCE-BASED PRACTICES. Evidence-based practices are those modalities verified by empirical research to be the most effective means of responding to the risk of reoffending and the needs of offenders, which if obtained might prevent reoffending. Evidence-based practices emerged in large part from the **meta-analyses** performed by researchers such as **Robert Martinson**, Douglas Lipton, and Judith Wilkes in the 1970s and Paul Gendreau and others in the 1980s, followed by Dr. Edward Latessa in the 1990s. Large-scale applications of evidence-based practices began in the early 1990s and remain the foundation for treating offenders in **prison** and in **community corrections** programs. *See also* NOTHING WORKS.

EVIDENCE TAMPERING. Evidence tampering is the alteration, destruction, concealment, or falsification of evidence that hinders or obstructs an investigation conducted by an official agency. It is a criminal offense. Evidence tampering was suggested in the investigation of the Kennedy **assassination** of 1963. That accusation has been proven false. More recent examples involve several instances in the 1994 **O. J. Simpson** case including missing evidence (a vial of blood) and the failure to obtain **search warrants** or to follow protocols (securing evidence), and the controversial 2007 case of **Amanda Knox** in which neither gloves nor protective headgear were worn. Both cases resulted in the defendants being found not guilty, Simpson by jurors and Knox by the Italian appellate court. *See also* FORENSICS; WARRANTLESS SEARCHES.

***EWING V. CALIFORNIA*, 538 U.S. 11 (2003).** The **U.S. Supreme Court** upheld California's **three-strikes law**, determining that it did not represent disproportionality to the crime committed even though it was a noncapital offense. Ewing's offense was relatively minor (the theft of three golf clubs), although he was charged with felony grand theft. Ewing's past criminal history was warranted severe, including that he had been paroled only 10 months earlier and thus justified the application of the three-strikes law. The holding also concluded that the **Eighth Amendment** did not include a standard for **proportionality** and thus did not apply. Three-strikes laws and other more severe sentencing standards were a response to the failure to successfully reduce **recidivism** rates. These efforts have also failed to affect crime rates. *See also* CAPITAL OFFENSE; CRUEL AND UNUSUAL PUNISHMENT; PAROLE; SENTENCING PROJECT, THE; TWO-STRIKES LAW.

EXCESSIVE FORCE. The application of physical and verbal attacks as well as intimidation by law enforcement when confronting civilians for such activities as **interrogation**. Excessive force, or what had earlier been referred to as **police brutality**, has been recognized since the 1800s, including the 1877 Great Railroad Strike and in the 1900s the 1919 steel strike. Excessive force became more controversial following the **civil rights** movement of the 1960s and maintained front-page prominence in the 1991 Rodney King beating by the Los Angeles **Police** Department. The **Bureau of Justice Statistics** has documented 4,813 deaths between 2003 and 2009. Incidents videotaped by civilians and other documentation have led to calls for civilian oversight of police and additional training. *See also* POLICE MISCONDUCT; USE OF FORCE.

EXCLUSIONARY RULE. The **U.S. Supreme Court** in ***Mapp v. Ohio*, 367 U.S. 643 (1961)**, held that all **evidence** obtained through a violation of a defendant's constitutional rights was inadmissible. Such evidence would be considered "**fruit of the poisonous tree**." In the case of Mapp, **police** officers entered a premise without a **warrant**. U.S. Supreme Court holdings begin as early as *Boyd v. United States*, 116 U.S. 616 (1886), which specifically addressed unwarranted **search and seizure**. In Boyd, papers were seized without a warrant over the objection of the holder. Thus, evidence acquired without a warrant is a violation, and the exclusionary rule applies. *See also* FIFTH AMENDMENT; FOURTH AMENDMENT; WARRANTLESS SEARCHES.

EXCULPATORY EVIDENCE. Exculpatory **evidence** may prove nonguilt or exonerate the defendant from the criminal charges. Prosecutors are required by statute to provide the defense with any exculpatory evidence that they have acquired before the defendant makes a plea. The **U.S. Supreme Court** in ***Brady v. Maryland*, 373 U.S. 83 (1963),** determined it was a **due process** violation for the prosecution which withheld evidence and thus was unconstitutional. *See also* CIVIL RIGHTS.

EXECUTION. Executions are also referred to as the **death penalty** or **capital punishment**. Executions are federal or state sanctions handed down by a judge following a guilty verdict for a crime. Eighteenth-century England listed as many as 200 crimes punishable by execution. Some ancient systems prescribed cruel methods of death such as by strangulation or "death by

1,000 cuts." In U.S. state systems, an execution may only occur for the crime of **murder**. The federal court system may authorize an execution for federal murder, **treason**, **terrorism**, **espionage**, **drug trafficking**, and attempting to kill a **witness**, juror, or court officer. Almost all cultures have used executions as a method of crime control, **deterrence**, and political control, such as the Stalinist Great Terror, during which approximately one million citizens were executed between 1937 and 1938. Executions are controversial, and as early as 1764 **Cesare Beccaria** called for their abolition. Challenges for violations of the **Eighth Amendment**, other constitutional issues, uncertainty of proof of guilt, inhumanity, and more have led to the abolition or abandonment of the use of the death penalty. *See also* CRUEL AND UNUSUAL PUNISHMENT; INNOCENCE PROJECT; PROPORTIONALITY.

EXECUTIONER. The executioner is the person assigned by the state to carry out an order of **capital punishment**. In some countries the profession of executioner was held by a family. France, Germany, and England provide examples of its being handed down from generation to generation. The Sanson family of France held the position from 1688 to 1847. In the United States the identity of executioners (and often others who assist in the **execution**) is generally kept confidential. Missouri, Oklahoma, and Texas have laws to ensure the secrecy of the executioner(s). *See also* DEATH PENALTY.

EXECUTION WARRANT. The execution **warrant** is also referred to as a **death warrant**. A death warrant empowers the appointed official to carry out the judicial order for **execution**. A condemned person may experience several warrants before an execution is carried out. The execution can only occur after all appeals have been exhausted or the condemned person does not elect to allow the appeal process to move forward. Execution warrants typically establish a time limit within which the execution must occur. If for any reason the execution warrant cannot be fulfilled within the specified time, the condemned person must wait until another death warrant with a new date is issued. A death warrant may be stayed by the order of an appeals court, the **U.S. Supreme Court**, or a governor. An early and unusual death warrant was the one that specified the execution of King Charles I in 1625. There were 59 signers of the warrant, the most infamous being Oliver Cromwell. In this circumstance, the signers were referred to as regicides and were later put to death themselves for signing the death warrant. *See also* GILMORE, GARY (1940–1977).

EXIT WOUND. The exit wound is a site of forensic examination. The wound is caused by some object (usually a bullet or a knife) that has entered and then exited the body. In the case of a bullet, the exit wound may be larger than the entrance wound because the projectile has slowed and then explodes, causing the exit area to have more bleeding than the entrance wound. The examination helps to determine the type of weapon used, the caliber of the bullet, the pattern, and whether there were multiple exits. An exit wound does not occur in all cases. *See also* FORENSICS.

EXONERATION. Exoneration is the reversal of a conviction. Innocence has been established by the introduction of new **evidence**. The **Innocence Project**, created after the **O. J. Simpson murder** case, has exonerated more than 350 wrongfully convicted persons since 1992. **DNA** has been critical to proving innocence. David Vasquez was the first person exonerated by DNA in 1989.

EX PARTE. A legal expression which means that all parties are not or do not have to be present for the proceedings to move forward. Ex parte proceedings have been conducted since the early 1800s in the United States.

EXPERT WITNESS. An individual who possesses the skills, experience, training, or education or who is reinforced with certifications that are relevant to the specific subject matter before the court and may provide testimony in support of contentions made by either the prosecution or the defense. Areas of expertise may include but are not limited to **fingerprint** analysis, **DNA**, other forensic matters, and medical and automotive information. The earliest use of expert witnesses dates to the late 1700s. *See also* FORENSICS.

EX POST FACTO. Ex post facto refers to legislation that changes consequences, such as crimes that may be categorized as more or less severe, **punishments** that will now be either more or less harsh, or rules of **evidence** that occurred before such legislation was enacted. The **Adam Walsh** Child Protection and Safety Act of 2006, 42 U.S.C. 16901, serves as an example because it requires those convicted of sexual offenses after and before the passage of the act to be placed on the National Registry. In 2010, the **U.S. Supreme Court** in *Carr v. United States*, No. 08-1301 98 U.S. 433 (1878), allowed the retroactive (ex post facto) condition contained in the legislation.

EXPRESSIVE CRIME. Rational choice theory (conceived of during the 1970s) suggests that expressive crime contains no rational thought. This type of crime happens without **premeditation** because it occurs during some incident that was not planned or anticipated. Distinguishing between expressive crime and instrumental crime is important for **punishment** considerations and the value of the goal of **deterrence** as proposed by **Cesare Beccaria** and **Jeremy Bentham**. Since there was no planning to commit the crime, punishment has less value for deterrence than instrumental crime.

EXPUNGEMENT. Expungement is provided through a court order and effectively "seals" a criminal conviction or arrest. However, expungement does not mean that arrests or conviction reports are unavailable or kept secret from all parties. Governmental agencies generally retain the ability to review such records. Crimes that may be expunged vary from state to state. New York State does not allow expungement of criminal records. Other states specify by legislation which crimes may be expunged and which may not. For example, **murder** and motor vehicle offenses are often not eligible, while disorderly persons and other nonviolent offenses are eligible. The legislation also provides a waiting period for expungement, generally based on the severity of the offense. *See also* INNOCENCE PROJECT; PARDON.

EXTRADITION. The process of transferring a suspect or convicted person from one state to another or from one country to another. Among the earliest examples of an extradition agreement (the modern expression would be treaty because it is between two sovereign nations) was when an Egyptian pharaoh in the 13th century B.C. made an arrangement with a Hittite king to turn over an individual who had fled Egypt. Extradition is initiated from the state or the country that claims jurisdiction over the suspected or convicted person. Extradition is not compulsory, and the laws of a state or another country govern the manner in which extradition may be granted or denied. Such individuals may request that they not be extradited. An example is the state of New Jersey, in the Robert Burns case (*I Am a Fugitive from a Georgia Chain Gang*, 1932), which refused extradition to Georgia. Another is the Soviet Union, in the 2013 Snowden case (violations of the **Espionage** Act of 1917), which denied extradition to the U.S. government. Edward Snowden continues to live in Moscow and is seeking asylum in other countries.

EXTRAJUDICIAL KILLING. Extrajudicial killings are not a sanction of the criminal justice system. These types of killings are sanctioned by governments. They occur outside the scope of war or protective **police** action. Sanctioned killings do not afford **due process** protections and are unethical. Examples of extrajudicial killings would include dissidents, union executives, political figures, and others who have some influence over a sphere of activity. Protection against such acts is codified in the **Torture** Victim Protection Act of 1991. *See also* DEATH SQUAD.

EXTRALEGAL FACTORS. Extralegal factors are issues or circumstances that are discriminatory and may not be considered in criminal justice decision making and that are not specified by law. The race of someone is one of those factors and may not be an influential determinant for an arrest or decision by a **jury** or judge. Research conducted since 1970 has provided significant data to suggest that extralegal (discriminatory) factors have influenced behavior and decision making by members of the criminal justice community when interacting with offenders.

EXTRA Y CHROMOSOME. The extra Y chromosome, or **XYY chromosome** as it is referred to, was discovered in 1956, and those who possessed this chromosome were mischaracterized in 1965 and 1966 to be violent and aggressive or otherwise likely to be criminal. The error was in the research conducted on institutionalized males and supported by the false report that **Richard Speck** (convicted of **mass murder**) was XYY, who then used the argument for an appeal. Ironically, some have described such persons as super males, and this led to additional stigmatizing of those with XYY. The XYY myth has been additionally supported in novels (*The XYY Man*, 1970), television dramas (*Doomwatch*, *Law and Order*, and *CSI–Miami*), and horror films (*The Cat o'Nine Tails* and *Alien 3*). Subsequent research on the theory of the extra Y chromosome or XYY has failed to produce any compelling **evidence** of its causality in criminal behavior. *See also* MURDER.

EYEWITNESS ERROR. Eyewitness testimony had been distrusted since the early 1900s and has since been proved to be unreliable. More than 70 percent of **wrongful convictions** are the result of eyewitness error. *See also* INNOCENCE PROJECT.

EYEWITNESS TESTIMONY. Testimony in a courtroom by a **witness** or a victim of a crime or an event about which they have personal knowledge. The information provided is evaluated by a judge or **jury** for its truth and accuracy. Previously, this has been a valuable courtroom tool. As early as 1908, it came under attack, notably in *On the Witness Stand* (1917) by Hugo Munsterberg. Since then, psychologists and others have come to understand that memory recall, vision, and other senses are influenced by perceptions and other occurrences that happen in close proximity which may and do influence what the witness "believes" they have experienced. In addition, the element of time also distorts beliefs. The **Innocence Project** since its founding in 1992 has successfully used **DNA evidence** to overturn criminal convictions by refuting eyewitness testimony. *See also* EXONERATION; EYEWITNESS ERROR.

F

FACIAL COMPOSITE SKETCH. A hand-sketched (by a composite artist) or computer-generated image of an eyewitness and/or victim's memory of an individual's face. **Scotland Yard**, in 1881, was among the earliest of law enforcement agencies to utilize a composite sketch to solve a **murder**. The **FBI** utilized composite sketches to arrest a suspect believed to be involved in the 1920 bombing of a Wall Street office. A database consisting of individualized facial characteristics (eyes, nose, mouth, facial hair, and other features) were developed and then laid one at a time onto a blank face to develop a composite likeness. This system (first called the *portrait parte*) was originated in the 1880s by **Alphonse Bertillion**, who is often referred to as the "father of scientific detection." *See also* FACIAL RECOGNITION SYSTEM.

FACIAL RECOGNITION SYSTEM. A computer system that is used to identify facial characteristics of individuals from digital images or videos. The system measures distances within a facial structure, which includes the nose, eyes, mouth, and edges of the jawline. The first documented use of this technology was recorded in the 1960s, but its development wasn't widely publicized. The technique has been enhanced since 1993, and the occurrences of false positives have significantly decreased. Facial recognition systems have come under attack by the **American Civil Liberties Union** and other groups for their potential to be an invasion of privacy and for violations of civil liberties. Criticism of such usage has included the stalking of women. *See also* FACIAL COMPOSITE SKETCH; FACIAL RECONSTRUCTION.

FACIAL RECONSTRUCTION. The process of creating a facsimile of the facial characteristics of an individual's skeletal remains to determine its identity. Hermann Welker created the first reproduction in 1883, but the foremost expert is believed to be Wilhelm His Sr., who created his version in 1895. Techniques of facial reconstruction are frequently employed in dramatic film portrayals such as *Bones* and *CSI*. *See also* FACIAL COMPOSITE SKETCH; FACIAL RECOGNITION SYSTEM; FORENSICS.

FAITH-BASED PROGRAM. Programs founded in a particular religion or ideology, which assist criminal justice programs to provide support for offenders and ex-offenders. The federal government provides financial support to assist specific programs in providing its mandated social services. President George W. Bush issued an executive order in 2001 supporting these programs, which expanded the "Charitable Choice" provision under President Bill Clinton's 1996 Welfare Reform bill.

FALCON AND THE SNOWMAN. A 1979 book and movie. The book is based on the life of a former Catholic seminary student, Christopher Boyce, and a drug dealer, Andrew Daulton Lee, who sold confidential documents to the Soviet Union in the mid-1970s. Boyce was convicted of **espionage** and other offenses and served time in **USP Leavenworth** and ADX Florence. He was released after serving 25 years. Lee was convicted of espionage and received a 40-year sentence, which he served in federal **prisons** in Lompoc and Terre Haute. He was released in 1998.

FALN. Fuerzas Armadas de Liberación Nacional, or FALN, is a separatist organization founded around 1974, but it had been active since the 1930s under the auspices of Pedro Albizu Campos, leader of the Nationalist Party. Their violent campaign is for the independence of Puerto Rico from the United States. FALN claimed responsibility for setting bombs off in Manhattan, which killed four people and injured more than 50 others. They are also responsible for bombings in Puerto Rico; Washington, D.C.; and Chicago. In 1980, 11 FALN members were sentenced to extended **prison** terms. *See also* TERRORISM.

FALSE ADVERTISING. A false statement or false account by an advertiser intended to mislead a consumer to purchase a product. An early attempt at creating standards for the industry came in 1911, which made it a misdemeanor crime in 44 states. Today's regulations are outlined in the Lanham Act of 1946, which govern trademark laws in the United States.

FAMILY COURT. A court with specific limits that presides over cases involving child custody, divorce, and domestic abuse matters. The concept of a family court was initiated in the 19th century in Rhode Island, Indiana, Massachusetts, and Chicago to have a separate court for children and was officially established in the 1960s. *See also* JUVENILE COURT.

FAMILY VIOLENCE. *See* DOMESTIC VIOLENCE.

FANTASY. A word often used in the psychology field, which involves an individual's imagination and can be co-opted to control thoughts and dreams. Several books about fantasy were written in the 1700s. Fantasy has also been explored in sexual offending and prompted an adjoining defense in criminal matters. In 1999, attorney Donald B. Marks proposed the fantasy defense for his client, Walt Disney executive Patrick J. Naughton, which sought to explain his role in illegal sexual activities via the internet.

***FAY V. NEW YORK*, 332 U.S. 261 (1947).** A New York State Supreme Court case that found defendants Bove and Fay guilty of conspiracy to extort and of extortion. The defendants challenged the makeup of the "blue ribbon" **jury** based on the **jury selection**, **due process**, and the **Fourteenth Amendment**. In this case, in a 5–4 decision, the Court held that the defendants' rights were not violated and that they had received a fair **trial**. *See also* CIVIL RIGHTS.

***FAY V. NOIA*, 372 U.S. 391 (1963).** The issue before the court was the coerced **confessions** of two defendants found guilty of **murder** during the commission of a robbery. One of the defendants appealed the verdict and lost because of a failure to appear. The **U.S. Supreme Court**, in a 6–3 decision, held that the defendant, while failing to exhaust all state remedies, wasn't prevented from being granted a federal **writ of habeas corpus**. The judicial matter being addressed was the **due process** clause of the **Fourteenth Amendment**.

FEDERAL BUREAU OF INVESTIGATION (FBI). The nation's premier law enforcement agency was founded in 1908 as the Bureau of Investigation. The name changed to the Federal Bureau of Investigation in 1935. The FBI's primary functions are to protect the United States of America from foreign terrorist attacks, **espionage**, and **cyberattacks** and investigate violations of federal laws. The director of the FBI is appointed by the president of the United States and confirmed by the Senate to a 10-year term. The FBI employs more than 10,000 men and women in an array of positions who are assigned to the more than 50 field offices located in the main cities across the United States and the Commonwealth of Puerto Rico. The FBI's headquarters is situated in Washington, D.C., and is named after its former director, **J. Edgar Hoover**. *See also* HAZELWOOD, ROBERT ROY (1938–2016); PISTONE, JOE (1939–); PURVIS, MELVIN (1903–1960); RESSLER, ROBERT (1937–2013).

FEDERAL BUREAU OF PRISONS (BOP). The BOP was created in 1930 by Public Law No. 71-218, 46 Stat. 325. The regulation would cover an existing 11 **prisons**. The law specified that the Department of Justice would oversee the "management and regulation of all Federal penal and correctional institutions." The Three Prisons Act of 1891 authorized the construction of the first three federal prisons. Federal prisons would house offenders convicted of federal crimes such as federal **income tax evasion**. The creation of the federal prison system halted the practice of placing federal prisoners in state prisons. **USP Leavenworth** was the first federal prison, established in 1895. More than 208,000 convicts are housed in 121 federal facilities. The BOP is managed through six regional offices, a central office, and another 26 residential **reentry** facilities. There are four levels of supervision (high, medium, minimum, and low) in federal facilities to which convicts are assigned according to security needs. Levels are identified by their security features, including perimeter security (such as fences, **patrol** officers, and towers), level of staffing, internal controls for **inmate** movement and accountability, and type of living quarters (for example, cells or open dormitories). In addition, the BOP operates pretrial detention and medical referral centers that are classified as levels 1–4 based on types of medical services available. They have specialized missions and respond to offenders at all security levels. *See also* ADMAX; ALCATRAZ ISLAND PRISON (1934–1963); ALDERSON PRISON, FPC; BENNET, JAMES V. (1894–1978).

FEDERAL EMERGENCY MANAGEMENT AGENCY (FEMA). An agency created by President Jimmy Carter in 1979, via an executive order, to coordinate the federal response in preparing for and mitigating the effects of natural and man-made disasters. The concept was first established in New Hampshire following a large-scale fire and subsequent Congressional Act of 1803, which provided assistance to survivors.

FEDERAL LAW ENFORCEMENT TRAINING CENTER (FLETC). An interagency law enforcement facility that trains 91 separate federal agencies in Glynn County, Georgia. FLETC also manages programs in international academies in Botswana, Thailand, Hungary, and El Salvador. It was initiated in 1970 as a bureau within the Department of Treasury and operated in Washington, D.C. FLETC officially came under the Department of Homeland Security in 2003, which oversees its financial and administrative duties.

FEDERAL WITNESS PROTECTION PROGRAM OR WITNESS SECURITY PROGRAM (WITSEC). A program instituted by the **U.S. Department of Justice** that protects federal witnesses who have been threatened. The U.S. **Marshals** Service oversees the program, which extends through all phases of a **trial** and afterward. In 1970, the program, which was formerly called the WITSEC, was incorporated under Title V of the **Organized Crime** Control Act. *See also* RACKETEER INFLUENCED CORRUPT ORGANIZATION (RICO); WITNESS PROTECTION PROGRAM.

***FEINER V. NEW YORK*, 340 U.S. 315 (1915).** A **U.S. Supreme Court** case that addresses public disturbance as a **First Amendment** right. In 1949, defendant Irving Feiner delivered a provocative speech about President Harry S. Truman and other politicians before a crowd in Syracuse, New York. After being asked to refrain from continuing by the **police**, he was subsequently arrested for violating New York **Penal Code**, Section 722. Feiner's appeal to the U.S. Supreme Court was upheld and found that his rights had not been violated because his speech created an imminent threat. *See also* CIVIL RIGHTS.

FELONY DISENFRANCHISEMENT. The restriction placed on individuals who have been convicted of a felony, which excludes them from voting in public elections. Disenfranchisement laws have been in existence since the founding of the United States and were expanded upon in 1870, particularly in southern states. The U.S. Constitution allows states to deny felons the right to vote under amendments made to the **Fourteenth Amendment**. The most controversial example of voting as felony disenfranchisement came in Florida's 2000 presidential election. *See also* COLLATERAL CONSEQUENCES.

FELONY MURDER DOCTRINE. A principle of a criminal statute which states that any death that happens during the commission of a crime is to be considered first-degree **murder**. Also, anyone involved in the commission of a crime and a murder, even if accidental, can be charged and convicted of murder as well. One of the earliest states to have a felony murder statute adopted into law was Illinois in 1827.

FEMINIST CRIMINOLOGY. A theoretical perspective in **criminology** that emerged in the 1960s and centered on the general disregard of the study of women in the study of crime. A core principle of feminist criminology is to include the feminist perspective in all practice and research. Feminist criminologists seek to insert gender into the discourse of criminological theory and address its limitations vis-à-vis the criminal justice system. The primary concerns are victimization of women, female delinquency, **prostitution**, and gender inequality.

***FERGUSON V. CITY OF CHARLESTON*, 532 U.S. 356 (2001).** A **U.S. Supreme Court** case that looked at whether or not the government had a right to require pregnant women to submit to involuntary testing to ascertain if they had been under the influence of drugs, and if so, they were to be arrested. The impetus for this case was a 1989 policy authored by the Medical University of South Carolina that administered a urine **drug test** to women who met certain criteria that suggested drug usage. The court found that the actions of the hospital, under a special non–law enforcement need, violated the women's **Fourth Amendment** rights because the women had not consented to be drug screened. *See also* SEARCH AND SEIZURE.

FERRACUTI, FRANCO (1927–1992). An Italian criminologist whose work explored subcultures and **violence**. He cowrote the book *The Subculture of Violence: Towards an Integrated Theory in* ***Criminology*** (1967) with **Dr. Marvin E. Wolfgang**, who influenced the development of criminology in the United States.

FEUDING. The continuous and oftentimes contentious arguing between friends, families, or others. One of the most infamous feuds was between the Hatfields of West Virginia and the McCoys of Kentucky, which began in 1865 after the killing of Asa Harmon McCoy by a group of Hatfields over a disagreement about the Civil War. The families intermarried over the years, and loyalties varied. In 1888, the feuding culminated with the life imprisonment of seven Hatfields and the **hanging** of another. The families agreed to stop fighting in 1891. In the end, four supporters, seven McCoys, and four Hatfields were killed as a result of the feud. *See also* HATFIELD AND MCCOY FEUD.

FIFTH AMENDMENT. An amendment to the U.S. Constitution that guarantees **due process**, protects against **self-incrimination**, protects against government seizing of private property for public use without fair compensation, provides protection against **double jeopardy**, and allows for grand **jury** procedures for significant offenses. Refer to appendix 1, "The Bill of Rights."

FINE. The amount of money paid to a lead authority by someone who has committed a violation of a statute, ordinance, or law. The courts levy the amount of penalty based on the infraction or required **restitution**. The U.S. Congress codified the sanctioning of penalties in the 1984 **Comprehensive Crime Control Act**.

FINGERNAIL SCRAPINGS. The residual material underneath a person's fingernails that is scraped for collection and can be used as **evidence** in an investigation. The **U.S. Supreme Court** in *Cupp v. Murphy*, 412 U.S. 291 (1973), upheld a **murder** conviction based on a sample of the defendant's fingernail scrapings, which contained dry skin and blood cells from the victim. *See also* FORENSICS.

FINGERPRINT. The unique pattern of skin on the tips of a person's finger that is used to identify someone unambiguously. An impression is left after the fingertip touches something. Between 1000 and 2000 B.C. in ancient Babylon, fingerprints were used on clay tablets to distinguish business transactions. In later years, **Alphonse Bertillon**, a French **police** officer and researcher developed the anthropological technique of anthropometry to identify the physical measurements of suspects. In 1902, Henry P. DeForest, M.D., of the New York civil service was the first to use fingerprints in the United States. The **FBI** maintains a searchable database that contains almost all fingerprints ever taken and from almost all sources. While fingerprints are now taken digitally, the fingerprint card developed in 1908 is still used to record fingerprints. The uniqueness of the fingerprint is described in three patterns (loops, arches, and **whorls**) first discovered in 1686. *See also* DACTYLOGRAPHY.

FIREARMS EXAMINATION. A skilled examiner identifies the characteristics of a gun or bullets from a crime scene in an attempt to ascertain if the gun and bullets can be linked to a suspect. Harold Peterson (1961) reported that, between the years 1493 and 1508, Emperor Maximilian was documented as being one of the first to hire gunsmiths to examine a weapon through a process called rifling, the pattern left on the bullet after being fired. *See also* FORENSICS.

FIREARMS TRAFFICKING. A crime committed by someone who legally obtains or steals any quantity of weapons and then sells them illegally for profit. In the 16th century, European traders trafficked arms in America, Africa, and to a limited extent in Asia. Between 1985 and 1987, U.S. Marine Corps colonel Oliver North was alleged to have trafficked arms from the United States to Iran, with the funds going to the Nicaraguan Contras and to arrange the release of American **hostages**. He was convicted, but the charges were later dismissed.

FIRE DEBRIS ANALYSIS. The process of examining materials left at the scene of a fire to determine if there is a presence or absence of ignitable liquids. The material undergoes a three-step process, which is then analyzed to ascertain if the fire had been committed by **arson** or was accidental. The first attempts at analyzing fire debris began in the 1930s identifying that a liquid accelerant was used. *See also* EVIDENCE; FORENSICS.

FIRE SETTER. Someone who intentionally or accidentally starts a fire—an arsonist. Intentional fire setting is not always a criminal act. It becomes a crime when the person starts the fire willfully or maliciously to destroy a structure, dwelling, or someone's property. Some fire setters are known to engage in **homicide**, cruelty to animals, and setting multiple fires. A psychiatric diagnosis for the behavior of a person involved in illegally starting fires, aka pyromania, was first used in 1833 by French physician Charles Marc. **David Berkowitz**, an American **serial killer**, was also an arsonist. *See also* ARSON; PYROMANIA.

FIRING SQUAD. A method that was utilized by the military or law enforcement to **execute** a person who had been sentenced to die by the courts. In 1977, following the reinstatement of the **death penalty**, the first person killed by firing squad was **Gary Gilmore** in the state of Utah. **Ronnie Lee Gardner**, a convicted murderer, was the last person to be executed by firing squad, also in the state of Utah. The process of **execution** by firing squad is only allowed in two states, Oklahoma and Utah, but only as a secondary method if **lethal injection** drugs aren't available. *See also* CAPITAL OFFENSE; CAPITAL PUNISHMENT; MURDER.

FIRST AMENDMENT. The First Amendment to the U.S. Constitution was adopted in December 1791 and established the protections for American citizens emphasizing freedom of religion, free speech, the right to assemble peacefully, freedom of the press, and protection for citizens seeking redress from the government. Refer to appendix 1, "The Bill of Rights."

FIRST OFFENDER. Someone who has been charged and convicted of a crime for the first time. The U.S. Congress promoted the first-offender philosophy in the Sentencing Reform Act of 1984. The first-offender emphasis was an effort at **diversion** that would provide reduced **punishment** for first offenders with less serious offenses.

FIXED SENTENCE. A sentence of imprisonment for a period specified by statute that cannot be adjusted. A fixed sentence, also referred to as **determinate sentencing**, became widely used in the 1970s and 1980s as part of the "tough on crime" criminal justice system, which led to the infamous "**three**

strikes and you're out" law of the 1990s. The rationale for such stringent **punishment** was to incapacitate repeat offenders as a deterrent from committing future crimes. *See also* DETERRENCE.

FLASH BANG. A device used by the military or elite law enforcement personnel in **hostage** rescue and tactical situations to create a diversion or produce momentary confusion of a suspect's or combatant's senses. It discharges a loud noise and bright light, which disorients its targeted adversary. A flash bang is not designed to cause any physical injury; rather, it makes the recipient briefly lose their vision and produces a ringing in the ears, which mimics a concussed sensation. Flash bangs were used during the 1970s by the Israeli military to effectuate rescues.

FLEEING FELON DOCTRINE. The legal use of any force by a law enforcement officer, victim, or bystander toward a suspected felon who has attempted to escape. This law was overturned by the **U.S. Supreme Court** in ***Tennessee v. Garner*, 471 U.S. 1 (1985)**. *See also* DEADLY FORCE; USE OF FORCE.

FLEISS, HEIDI (1965–). An American criminal, referred to as the **Hollywood Madam**, who in 1990 started her high-class **prostitution** business that catered to wealthy clients. The state of California charged her with five counts of pandering, and she was convicted on three of the counts in 1993. **Fleiss** was sentenced to three years of incarceration but appealed and had her conviction overturned in 1996 due to juror misconduct. Later, she served 37 months in the Federal Correctional Institution, California, on a conviction for **tax evasion** and **money laundering**. Her **trials** garnered considerable media coverage due to the notion that she would expose the names of some of her former clients. *See also* JURY TAMPERING.

FLOGGING. The intentional beating of someone's back with an instrument such as a cane, stick, or whip to punish. In some instances, the floggings killed the person. Flogging was continued as a practice to punish slaves. It has also been utilized as a way of conserving discipline within a **prison** system, school environment, or military forces. In 1820, Representative Samuel Foot was the first to propose legislation to the U.S. Congress to abolish flogging. *See also* EIGHTH AMENDMENT; PUNISHMENT.

FLOODGATE THEORY. The premise that if a certain practice, demographic, or idea is allowed to be accepted, then more of the same will be forthcoming. This theory on occasion has been applied by judges to diminish the rights of litigants to pursue claims, lest it encourage others to pursue similar claims. *Victorian Railways Commissioners vs. Coultas*, 13 App. Cas. 222 (1888), is the court case that originated this sentiment.

***FLORIDA V. HARRIS*, 568 U.S. __ (2013).** A **U.S. Supreme Court** case that confronted the dependability of whether a trained or certified **narcotics** sniffing dog's detection of drugs is enough to establish **probable cause**. Based on the dog's established record of certification, the courts found probable cause had been established and overruled a lower court's judgment. *See also* EVIDENCE; *FLORIDA V. JARDINES*, 569 U.S. __ (2013).

***FLORIDA V. JARDINES*, 569 U.S. __ (2013).** A **Fourth Amendment U.S. Supreme Court** case that challenged, based on an anonymous tip, whether a drug detection sniffing dog deployed to the front entrance of a private residence where **marijuana** had been grown was deemed a violation of the U.S. Constitution. In this case, a 5–4 decision held that there was a violation of the Fourth Amendment and a **warrant** was needed. *See also* EVIDENCE; *FLORIDA V. HARRIS*, 568 U.S. __ (2013).

FOCAL CONCERNS THEORY. The theory hypothesized that members of juvenile groups who congregate on street corners in underprivileged neighborhoods present six identifiable concerns: toughness, trouble, smartness, excitement, fate, and autonomy because they are devoid of traditional values. Walter B. Miller, an American anthropologist and former director of the Boston Roxbury **Gang** Delinquency Research Project, developed this theory in 1962. *See also* JUVENILE DELINQUENCY.

FOLK DEVILS. Individuals who have been depicted in mainstream media or folktales as being deviant and outcast and are accused of an array of crimes that are problematic for society. At times, folk devils were targeted for persecution. Stanley Cohen, a criminologist and sociologist, used the term in his work ***Folk Devils** and **Moral Panics*** (1972) to describe the eccentric behavior of certain individuals in the United Kingdom. Historically, the consequence of such labeling or symbolism has been a **moral panic** followed by events such as witch hunts, persecutions, and the blaming of groups such as immigrants. The consequences can be severe as illustrated in the **Columbine massacre**, the **Jim Jones** mass suicide and murder, and the Hitler concentration camps and attempted extermination.

FOLK NATION. An association of several street gangs that were formed in the Department of Correction in Illinois in 1978. Also referred to as Folk, they originated in Chicago but have spread their sphere of influence across the United States with a directed emphasis on the Midwest. To distinguish themselves from their rival, **People Nation**, they utilize identifiers and wear clothes, caps, and bandanas to the right to highlight right-handedness. *See also* CRIPS; GANG.

FOLKWAYS. The standard actions of a group of individuals or a community who, without any guided directions, act in concert to provide rules for the collective sum. These activities range from how to greet one another to how to eat with utensils and are handed down via generations. William G. Sumner, social scientist, coined the term *folkways* in 1906.

FOOD AND DRUG ADMINISTRATION (FDA). A federal executive department within the U.S. Department of Public Health and Human Services responsible for providing food- and health-related services. The FDA's regulatory functions were created under the 1906 Food and Drug Act, which President Theodore Roosevelt signed into law. The driving force behind the FDA was Harvey Washington Wiley, who at the time was the chief chemist of the Bureau of Chemistry. The predecessor to the FDA was the Department of Agriculture, directed by a chemist, Charles M. Wetherill, who was appointed by President Abraham Lincoln in 1862.

FORD PINTO CASE. A civil and criminal case that involved the Ford Motor Company's 1970 introduction of a subcompact car, the Ford Pinto, which caused the death of motorists due to the rear-positioned fuel system, which ruptured and leaked when struck from the rear. A civil case brought by the family of Matthew Grimshaw in 1972 against the Ford Motor Company was awarded $2.5 million in compensatory damages, along with $125 million in punitive damages. This was later reduced to $3.5 million. In the criminal case, three young women were burned to death when their 1973 Ford Pinto was struck from the rear and burst into flames. A grand **jury** charged the Ford Motor Company with criminal **homicide**, which was the first to occur against an American corporation. However, after a 10-week **trial**, the Ford Motor Company was exonerated.

***FORD V. WAINWRIGHT*, 477 U.S. 399 (1986).** A **U.S. Supreme Court** case that questioned whether the defendant, Alvin Bernard Ford, convicted of **murder** in 1974 and waiting to be executed, was competent to be executed. The primary issue was whether the state of Florida violated Ford's **Eighth Amendment** rights, which prohibited executing individuals who are insane. Ford sued **Louie L. Wainwright**, the secretary of the Florida Department of Corrections and won his suit after being reevaluated. He was found to be **incompetent** and transferred to a Florida hospital for mental health treatment. A subsequent federal **trial** found that Ford was indeed sane. Ford appealed and later died of natural causes at age 37 while his appeal was pending. *See also* CAPITAL PUNISHMENT; EXECUTION.

FOREIGN CORRUPT PRACTICES ACT (FCPA). A 1977 federal anti-corruption law that addressed accounting transparency via the Securities Exchange Act of 1934 and the **bribery** of officials from foreign countries. The FCPA has been amended on two separate occasions, 1988 and 1998 respectively, and is still a concern for members of Congress.

FORENSIC ANTHROPOLOGY. A unique subfield in anthropology that applies the analysis of skeletal and archaeological techniques to solve criminal cases. It was developed as early as 1918 within the field of physical anthropology. Thomas Dwight (1843–1911) is recognized as being the first to publish articles concerning forensic anthropology. In the United States, he is renowned for being the father of forensic anthropology. *See also* FORENSICS.

FORENSIC DENTISTRY. Forensic dentistry is also known as forensic odontology. It is a scientific way of identifying an unknown subject by their teeth or bite-mark indentations. A forensic dentist can assist law enforcement in determining the age, social economic status, and race of an unknown subject. The findings from a thorough examination can then be used in a court proceeding and presented as valid **evidence**. In 1775, Paul Revere became the first American forensic dentist when he identified the remains of a body by a bridge he constructed for the victim. The first documented case of a forensic dentist being used as an **expert witness** came in 1814 in Scotland.

FORENSIC PATHOLOGIST. A medical doctor, trained in anatomical pathology, who specializes in the examination of corpses of people who have died naturally, violently, or accidentally to determine the cause of death. They then provide a report of their findings to an appropriate criminal justice official for use in criminal or civil matters. Imhotep, an Egyptian polymath, is believed to have been the first forensic pathologist around 2600 B.C. The forensic pathologist is an **expert witness** with about 12 years of education and specialty training such as a completed fellowship. *See also* CORONER.

FORENSIC PSYCHOLOGY. A specialization within the medical profession that bridges law enforcement and the field of psychology. Forensic psychology has been widely written about and researched since 1893 when James McKeen Cattell, a psychology professor, conducted his study at Columbia University. It became recognized as a specialty by the American Psychological Association in 2001 and was recertified in 2008. Forensic psychology has become key to understanding or supporting what is presented by the **expert witness**, especially with regard to decision making about child custody or competence to stand **trial**. There are other areas of specialty in which testimony from a forensic psychologist has become indispensable, such as supporting rulings of sanity. To testify competently, the forensic psychologist must be knowledgeable in rules of law.

FORENSICS. The work of forensics is not new to criminal justice. However, advances in medicine, academic disciplines, and enhancements in the work of practitioners has produced a proliferation of terms that describe and refine forensic science. Forensics is a field of study that combines subfields such as accounting, anthropometry, art, biology, botany, cartography, chemistry, engineering, entomology, geology, medicine, and **toxicology** and the work of technicians, nurses, and medical doctors. The objective is the examination of **evidence**, utilizing the appropriate methodology, to obtain the desired results in a criminal investigation to prove either guilt or innocence for a defendant. For example, in 1832, James Marsh, a chemist, became the first to introduce forensic science into a court of law by testing for arsenic (the test is referred to as the Marsh test) in a **murder** case. In another context, forensic accounting provided compelling evidence that led to the successful 2006 prosecution of Jeffrey Skilling in the Enron case. *See also* RAMSEY, JONBENÉT (1990–1996).

FORFEITURE. A penalty imposed against an entity or person whereby property is taken for an act of wrongdoing. The U.S. Congress enacted the Forfeiture Act in 1970, which authorized federal prosecutors to file civil forfeiture actions against individuals' property who were convicted of dealing drugs. Forfeiture laws have existed since the colonial period. Since 2009, the federal government seized more than $773 million following the **Bernard Madoff** prosecution for his financial Ponzi scheme. *See also* ASSET FORFEITURE.

FORGERY. The act of producing an illegal document to replicate an original to deceive someone or for monetary gain. Printing, handwriting, and typewriting are several means by which a forgery can be perpetrated. In 1983, a German reporter, Gerd Heidemann, sold a diary alleged to have been written by Adolpf Hitler in the early 1930s to mid-1940s. He purchased the documents from a memorabilia dealer, but the documents were later found to be fake. Other types of forgeries include signatures, stamps, and labels for wine bottles. Among famous forgeries by presidents was a letter purported to have been written by Abraham Lincoln to a grieving widow. The forged letter was the inspiration for the film *Saving Private Ryan*. *See also* VINTAGE FRAUD.

FORTAS, ABE (1910–1982). An attorney and **U.S. Supreme Court** justice who before being selected to sit on the U.S. Supreme Court represented a defendant, Clarence E. Gideon, before the Court. In 1961, Gideon had been convicted of burglary in the state of Florida and sentenced to **prison** for five years. The Florida court had denied Gideon the right to counsel stating that it only applied to those found guilty of **capital offenses**. In 1963, Gideon appealed, and attorney Fortas was assigned to represent him. The issue before the court was whether Gideon's Sixth Amendment rights were violated. Attorney Fortas, with the help of other attorneys, won the appeal in a 9–0 decision. Gideon was ultimately acquitted but subsequently died of cancer in 1971. President Lyndon B. Johnson would later appoint attorney Fortas to the U.S. Supreme Court as an associate justice from 1965 to 1969. Justice Fortas ultimately resigned due to allegations of corruption. *See also GIDEON V. WAINWRIGHT*, 372 U.S. 335 (1963).

FORT HOOD SHOOTING. The scene of a mass shooting in 2009 at the hands of **Major Nidal Hasan**, an army psychiatrist. Fort Hood is a military base located in Texas where Major Hasan was stationed, assigned to evaluate soldiers. Major Hasan, a practicing Muslim, was believed to have been radicalized via the internet. He was convicted of **murder** and attempted murder. In 2013, he was sentenced to **capital punishment** but has a pending appeal. He is currently confined in **USP Leavenworth**, Kansas. *See also* UNITED STATES DISCIPLINARY BARRACKS (USDB).

FOURTEENTH AMENDMENT. An amendment to the U.S. Constitution that addresses citizenship rights, **due process**, and equal protection. It was adopted and ratified by several states in 1868. The premise for the amendment pertained to issues regarding former slaves in the aftermath of the Civil War and specifically recognizing that anyone born in the United States was a citizen. Refer to appendix 1, "The Bill of Rights."

FOURTH AMENDMENT. A change to the U.S. Constitution that prohibits the unreasonable **search and seizure** of an individual's personal property without a **warrant** that is based upon **probable cause**. It was established based on the principles of the rule of law to protect citizens from the threatening powers of law enforcement and selective enforcement by government officials. Congress passed the Fourth Amendment in 1789 and ratified it in 1791. Refer to appendix 1, "The Bill of Rights."

FRAME-UP. The intentional incrimination of someone who is not guilty. Frame-ups are used for such reasons as getting rid of opponents or in law enforcement to subvert **due process**. One of the most precedent-setting cases was in 1931 when false accusations were levied against nine black teenagers (the **Scottsboro Boys**) for raping two white women on a train in Alabama. They were convicted and sentenced to death. The defendants appealed their case to the **U.S. Supreme Court** in 1932, which held that they were denied their **Fourteenth Amendment** rights. The case was remanded to a lower court, and they were found guilty and sentenced to various **prison** sentences. They were defended by Samuel Leibowitz. *See also NORRIS V. ALABAMA*, 294 U.S. 587 (1935).

***FRANK V. MAGNUM*, 237 U.S. 309 (1915).** A **U.S. Supreme Court** case that challenged whether the defendant, Leo M. Frank, a Jewish businessman, who was on **trial** for the **murder** of a 13-year-old girl, had his **Fourteenth Amendment** rights violated due to mob intimidation. The court ruled against Frank, and he was subsequently lynched after the governor of Georgia had commuted his sentenced to life in **prison**. *See also* LYNCHING.

FRATERNAL ORDER OF POLICE (FOP). An organization that represents hundreds of thousands of **police** officers and thousands of lodges across the United States. Pittsburgh, Pennsylvania, police officers Martin Toole and Delbert Nagle founded the organization in 1915 to address the working conditions of police officers. It became a national organization in 1918.

FREEDOM OF ASSEMBLY. The right of citizens who reside in the United States to come together collectively to express, promote, or defend actions they deem worthy of sharing such as political rights, **human rights**, or civil liberties. The **First Amendment**, which was adopted in 1791, prohibited the infringement of these rights. Some important **U.S. Supreme Court** cases include the following:

Dennis v. U.S, 341 U.S. 494 (1951)—government censorship.
Dejonge V. Oregon, 299 U.S. 353 (1937)—peaceable assembly may not be made a crime.

See also CIVIL RIGHTS.

FREEDOM OF INFORMATION ACT (FOIA). A federal law which mandates that the general public be provided access to public information, which is in the custody of state or federal government agencies. The only exception is if the information falls under one of the nine listed exemptions (such as national security or trade secrets) contained within FOIA. Congress passed the FOIA provision, which had been supported by Ralph Nader and was signed by President Lyndon B. Johnson in 1966.

FREEDOM OF PRESS. A provision under the **First Amendment** to the U.S. Constitution that protects the press from censorship. In 1976, the **U.S. Supreme Court** case ***Nebraska Press Association v. Stuart*, 427 U.S. 539 (1976)**, reviewed whether district court judge Hugh Stuart violated the petitioner's First Amendment rights by placing a "gag order" on information. The attempt was to publish a confession made to the **police** by a defendant who allegedly murdered six people. The rationale was that the defendant wouldn't receive a fair **trial** if the information had been published. The court ruled for the Nebraska Press Association, citing that the defendant's rights to a fair trial would not be jeopardized. *See also* FREEDOM OF INFORMATION ACT (FOIA); FREEDOM OF SPEECH; MURDER.

FREEDOM OF SPEECH. A right guaranteed by the **First Amendment** to the U.S. Constitution that prohibits government censorship or restraint. This right was challenged in *Dennis v. U.S.*, 341 U.S. 494 (1951), and the Court ruled that the defendant did not have the right under the First Amendment to free speech or assembly if it involved a conspiracy to overthrow the government. Refer to appendix 1, "The Bill of Rights." *See also* BILL OF RIGHTS.

FRONTIER JUSTICE. The exercise of **punishment** in the absence of substantive law and justice. It can also be referred to as street justice or vigilante justice. An early instance of this form of justice was recorded in 1882 when Wyatt Earp and Doc Holliday pursued and subsequently killed four men responsible for the death of Wyatt's brother, Morgan Earp. *See also* VIGILANTISM.

FRUIT OF THE POISONOUS TREE DOCTRINE. All **evidence** obtained by **police** officers through unreasonable searches, interrogations, or arrests that violate rights protected by the U.S. Constitution shall be considered "fruit of the poisonous tree" and may not be used in a **trial**. This was addressed in *Silverthorne Lumber Co. v. United States*, 251 U.S. 385 (1920), which held that information gathered through **interrogation** is a violation of the **Fourth Amendment** and would be excluded in a trial. *See also* EXCLUSIONARY RULE; SEARCH AND SEIZURE; WARRANT.

FRYE RULE. The benchmark to ascertain if scientific **evidence** would be admissible in court. Also referred to as the Frye standard, it was derived from *Frye v. United States*, 293 F. 1013 (1923), which involved the admissibility of a **polygraph** test. *Daubert v. Merrell Dow Pharmaceuticals*, 509 U.S. 579 (1994), has since superseded the Frye rule. *See also* DAUBERT RULE.

FURLOUGHS. The approved temporary absence of an **inmate** from a federal or state correctional facility. Furloughs provide inmates with opportunities to work, train, transfer to medical facilities, and be present during a family crisis. Many states have similar provisions. Furloughs were initiated in correctional facilities to assist a convict's transition from **prison** back into the community upon **parole** or the completion of their sentence. While releases from prison have a long history, programs of furloughs officially began after the 1960s.

***FURMAN V. GEORGIA*, 408 U.S. 238 (1972).** The **U.S. Supreme Court**, in a 5–4 decision, set the requirements to ensure uniformity in the implementation of the **death penalty** and held that the death penalty was a violation of the U.S. Constitution. This case started the ban on arbitrary **capital punishment** in the United States, which ultimately ended with the ***Gregg v. Georgia*, 428 U.S. 153 (1976)**, decision, which allowed the reinstatement of the death penalty.

G

GACY, JOHN WAYNE (1942–1994). An American **serial killer**, born in Chicago, Illinois. He was one of three children, and his alcoholic father ridiculed him for not doing boy activities and physically abused him and the rest of his family. He had problems growing up, including being ostracized by his classmates, and suffered from a congenital heart condition. Gacy had an attraction to men, which caused confliction about his sexuality. Gacy married Marylyn Myers in 1964 and later divorced. He then married Carole Hoff, and they too divorced. His first sexual offense was in 1967, and he was charged with oral sodomy. Gacy denied the charges and was ordered to undergo a psychological evaluation and was diagnosed with antisocial personality disorder. Gacy's bizarre behavior extended into the world of entertainment when he joined a clown club and took on the alter ego of "Pogo the Clown." He is alleged to have killed approximately 33 teenage boys and young men between 1972 and 1978. He confessed to and was convicted of several murders and was **executed** on 10 May 1994. He was known as the "Killer Clown" and is listed as one of the most vicious serial killers in U.S. history. *See also* EXECUTION; MURDER.

GAINESVILLE RIPPER. The name given to serial killer Daniel Harold "Danny" Rolling. Rolling was born in Shreveport, Louisiana, to an abusive father who was a **police** officer. Rolling was later arrested as a teenager for committing robberies in the state of Georgia. He couldn't embrace mainstream societal norms and found himself unable to maintain steady employment. In 1990, Rolling tried to kill his father during an argument. In the latter part of 1990, Rolling murdered four students from the University of Florida and one student from Santa Fe Community College, New Mexico. He utilized different techniques to desecrate the bodies of his victims. Some were mutilated, one was decapitated, and all were staged for shock value. Rolling was subsequently found guilty in 1992 and executed by **lethal injection** on 25 October 2006 in Florida State Prison. *See also* EXECUTION; MURDER.

GALLO, JOSEPH (1929–1972). A reputed member of the Profaci, aka the Colombo, crime family. Gallo was nicknamed "Crazy Joe" and "Joe the Blond" by associate **mobsters**. He was raised in the Red Hook section of Brooklyn, New York. He was diagnosed as schizophrenic and arrested numerous times. In 1961, he was convicted and sentenced to state **prison** for extortion and conspiracy. While in prison, Gallo is alleged to have befriended African American drug trafficker Nicky Barnes and recruited African Americans as soldiers into **La Cosa Nostra**. When Gallo was released from prison, he became involved in an ongoing dispute with **gang** members regarding monies owed to him. In 1971, Gallo was alleged to have been responsible for the shooting of crime boss Joseph Colombo. Gallo was consequently killed by Colombo gunmen in Umberto's Clam House while celebrating his 43rd birthday. *See also* DRUG TRAFFICKING; MAFIA.

GALLOWS. A device, usually made of wood, with two supporting crossbeams attached to a suspended rope, which was used to hang condemned persons. The earliest recorded history of the usage of gallows dates to 1630 when an angry mob hanged John Billington for suspicion of the **murder** of settler John Newcomen. The earliest history of a female **hanging** was in 1632 when Jane Champion was hanged for the murder of her unborn child. Hanging has fallen out of favor as a method of **execution** in the United States. The last hanging to occur in the United States was in Delaware on 25 January 1996. *See also* CAPITAL PUNISHMENT; DEATH PENALTY.

GAMBINO, CARLO (1902–1976). The "don" of the Gambino crime family, nicknamed the Godfather, Gambino was born in Palermo, Sicily, and immigrated to the United States in 1921. He formed a group of **mobsters** referred to as the "Young Turks" and became a "made man" in **La Cosa Nostra**. Gambino was instrumental in the killing of crime bosses Joe "the Boss" Masseria and Sal Maranzano, which precipitated his promotion to **underboss** to **Albert Anastasia**. In the mid-1960s, he was promoted to "boss of bosses." Gambino is alleged to have supported prominent music performers such as Frank Sinatra, Sammy Davis Jr., Dean Martin, Joey Bishop, and Peter Lawford, known as the "Rat Pack." He was indicted in 1972 for **hijacking**, but he was also involved in **gambling**, loan-sharking, and **narcotics** trafficking. His failing health led to the postponement of his **trial**, and he subsequently died of natural causes in 1976. *See also* CASTELLAMARESE WARS; DRUG TRAFFICKING; MAFIA.

GAMBLING. The act of engaging in a game of chance with the possibility of winning or losing either money or property. State-sponsored gambling is legal and takes place in a casino, online betting, or lotteries. Many societies have had a history of gambling. France had lotteries to support its war efforts in Italy dating back to 1539, and China's keno games have been documented in 2,300 B.C. American colonists utilized lotteries to fund military defense in 1776.

GANG. A group of three or more individuals who gather to commit a crime or engage in antisocial behavior. Gangs can be identified by specific colors, hand signs, **graffiti**, language, and initiations. The earliest record of a gang's presence in America came during the early 1780s around the end of the American Revolution. Immigrants of the 1800s formed gangs to fight against each other over turf and ethnic pride. Gang activity died down during the Great Depression and World War II but became more prominent beginning in the late 1950s. Gangs are involved in a wide range of criminal activity, especially **drug trafficking. Violence** is used to support criminal activity as well as gang membership and control of territories. *See also* CRIPS; GANGSTER DISCIPLES; LATIN KINGS.

GANGLAND KILLING. A term used to describe an **execution**-style **murder** in which the perpetrator kills their victim at close range, typically with a knife or gun. Members of **organized crime** mainly perpetrate this type of killing. One of the most infamous gangland killings happened in 1929 and was called the **Saint Valentine's Day massacre**, where the assailants posed as **police** officers and killed seven North Side Irish **gang** members during **Prohibition**. *See also* MURDER INC.

GANG RESISTANCE EDUCATION AND TRAINING (GREAT). A program initiated by the Bureau of Alcohol, Tobacco, and Firearms (ATF) and the Phoenix **Police** Department in Arizona in 1991 to provide instruction to middle school students to prevent **violence** and dissuade them from engaging in **gang** activity. The program is taught by police officers, and since its inception, more than six million students have graduated.

GANGSTER. Someone who is a member of a violent criminal organization that may be described as a street **gang** or a part of **organized crime**. The term was initially assigned to members of organized crime in the 1920s and 1930s. *See also* MAFIA; MOBSTER.

GANGSTER DISCIPLES. A street **gang** started on the South Side of the city of Chicago in the latter part of the 1960s. Larry Hoover, High Supreme Gangsters, and David Barksdale, Black Disciples, founded the gang and formed the Black Gangster Disciple Nation, which has approximately 30,000 members, who wear the colors blue and black as its representation.

***GANNETT CO. V. DEPASQUALE*, 443 U.S. 368 (1979).** A **U.S. Supreme Court** case which decided that members of the public do not have the right to access judicial proceedings when the involved parties—the prosecutor, the defendant, and **trial** judge—have previously agreed to a closed proceeding to ensure a fair trial. *See also* DUE PROCESS.

***GARCETTI V. CEBALLOS*, 547 U.S. 410 (2006).** A **U.S. Supreme Court** case held in a 5–4 decision that a government official had no protection under the **First Amendment** when he criticized the validity of a **warrant**. The plaintiff, Richard Ceballos, alleged that he was subsequently denied a promotion for his believed whistle-blowing actions. The outcry from this decision had advocates for the **First Amendment** calling this decision a setback for future whistle-blowers protection. *See also* SERPICO, FRANK (1936–); WHISTLE-BLOWER.

GARDNER, RONNIE LEE (1961–2010). A **death row inmate** executed in 2010 by a **firing squad** for the 1984 **murder** of a bartender in Salt Lake City, Utah. Gardner was convicted in 1985 and sat on death row for approximately 25 years before his **execution**. His case was the impetus for the Utah House of Representatives restricting the number of **capital punishment** appeals. Gardner is the last person in the United States to be executed by firing squad. *See also* WRIT OF HABEAS CORPUS.

GAROFALO, RAFFAELE (1851–1934). A criminologist born in Naples, Italy. He studied under **Cesare Lombroso**, father of **criminology**, but later went on to reject Lombroso's **classical school**'s belief in the "free will" doctrine and posited that crime could only be studied scientifically. He later formulated his theory of "natural crime," which is comprised of crimes of **violence** and property crime. *See also* BENTHAM, JEREMY (1748–1832).

GAS CHAMBER. An airtight enclosed room filled with a poisonous gas used for executions. In the United States, the gas chamber has been used to execute **inmates** who were on **death row**. The first person executed in a U.S. gas chamber was **Gee Jon**. In 1924, the state of Nevada attempted unsuccessfully to pump **lethal gas** into a room where Jon had been secured for **execution**. The execution was unsuccessful due to gas leaking out of the room. A gas chamber was subsequently constructed and provided the necessary means to facilitate a proper execution. Walter LaGrand was the last person to be executed in a gas chamber, in Arizona on 3 March 1999. *See also* CAPITAL PUNISHMENT.

GAULT, GERALD (1949–). As a 14-year-old, Gault was convicted of making a prank telephone call and then sentenced to a juvenile center for seven years. Gault's parents appealed the verdict before the **U.S. Supreme Court**. In an 8–1 decision, the court held that Gault's Sixth Amendment rights were violated for denial of the right to counsel, the right to be formally notified of charges filed against him, the right against **self-incrimination**, and being denied the opportunity to face his accuser. *See also IN RE WINSHIP*, 397 U.S. 358 (1970); *IN RE GAULT*, 387 U.S. 1 (1967).

GAY BASHING. Physical or verbal abuse of an individual who is believed to be gay, bisexual, lesbian, or living another alternate lifestyle that is offensive to a perpetrator. The most infamous case of gay bashing occurred in New York City in 1969 when members of the New York **Police** Department raided the Stonewall Inn, a gay bar, and a riot occurred. Later referred to as the Stonewall riots, the aftermath led to the gay liberation movement. *See also* POLICE MISCONDUCT.

GEIN, ED (1906–1984). A murderer and grave robber who became infamous in the late 1950s for exhuming bodies from graveyards in his hometown of Plainfield, Wisconsin. It was after his arrest that it was revealed that Gein had killed two women in 1957. Afterward, he was sentenced to life in **prison** but was later found not guilty due to reasons of insanity and acquitted. He was committed to a mental hospital where he eventually passed away. *See also* GUILTY BUT MENTALLY ILL; HINCKLEY, JOHN (1955–); HUGHES, FRANCINE (1947–); INSANITY DEFENSE; MURDER; NOT GUILTY BY REASON OF INSANITY.

GENDER SPECIFIC SERVICES. A program developed to advocate social competence, healthy attitudes, and positive lifestyles for young girls as a method of prevention from **juvenile delinquency**. The primary focus is to address issues about family, relationships, community, and school. The focus toward gender equity began in 1992 with the reauthorization of the **Juvenile Justice and Delinquency Prevention Act**.

GENERAL DETERRENCE. *See* DETERRENCE; SPECIFIC DETERRENCE.

GENERAL STRAIN THEORY. A theory developed by **Robert Agnew** in 1992, which states that criminal and deviant acts are a response to stress. Agnew identified three major types of deviance-producing strain, including the inability to achieve positively valued goals, the removal of or threat to remove positively valued stimuli, and confrontation with negatively valued stimuli.

GENOCIDE. The intentional mass killing of individuals, usually from a distinct nation, religion, or racial or ethnic group. Raphael Lemkin conceived this term in 1944. The Nazi concentration camps during World War II have been documented as being one of the worst cases of genocide in modern history. The United States has been accused of similar policies and actions against Native Americans, such as occurred in 1838 during the infamous "Trail of Tears," which resulted in the deaths of more than 4,000 members of the Cherokee Nation. The Indian Removal Act of 1830 legitimized the action. *See also* DEATH SQUAD; MASS MURDER; WOUNDED KNEE MASSACRE.

GENOVESE, KITTY (1935–1964). Kitty Genovese was viciously attacked in 1964 while going home from her job as a bartender. She was in proximity to her apartment in Queens, New York, when a stranger, Winston Mosley, ran up to her and stabbed her twice in the back and ran away. Genovese screamed out, and even though some of her neighbors later admitted to hearing her screams, no one came to her rescue. She made it to the rear of her building, but Mosley returned and stabbed her again, stole her money, and raped her. A neighbor witnessed the subsequent attack when he opened his door, but slammed it shut instead of helping. Genovese died afterward. Mosley was eventually captured and sentenced to life in **prison**. Following Genovese's death, social psychologists Bibb Latané and John Darley coined the "bystander effect" in 1968, which posits that there is a greater likelihood that people will intervene in an encounter if there are fewer spectators.

GEOGRAPHIC PROFILING. A method used during a criminal investigation that examines a series of locations to establish a probable neighborhood where the offender may reside. This investigative method originated in 1989 in British Columbia, Canada, at the Simon Fraser University School of **Criminology**. *See also* CRIME MAPPING.

***GEORGIA V. RANDOLPH*, 547 U.S. 103 (2006).** A **U.S. Supreme Court** case in which the court held in a 5–3 decision that the **police** had no right to search a resident without a **search warrant**, even if one resident consents to a search and another resident does not. *See also* FOURTH AMENDMENT; *MAPP V. OHIO*, 367 U.S. 643 (1961); WARRANTLESS SEARCHES.

GET TOUGH ON CRIME. A campaign slogan that can be traced back to the 1960s and 1970s during the administrations of Presidents Nixon and Reagan, which proposed policies that focused on **punishment** as the reaction to crime. Since this time there has been a shift from the **due process model** to the crime control model. Some of the penalties under the policies in later years were the **three-strikes law**, **zero tolerance**, and **truth in sentencing**. The shift in policy has resulted in **mass incarceration**, relying on the **plea bargain**, which diminishes an individual's rights (such as the right to a **trial**), as the mechanism to move defendants through the court system. *See also* MARTINSON, ROBERT (1927–1979).

GHENT. A correctional facility built in 1772 that was the first to feature an architectural design to aid in the rehabilitation of the convict. Ghent followed the model proposed by **Jeremy Bentham**—a blueprint for a proposed circular **prison**, the **panopticon**, whereby every prisoner could be observed. The panopticon was utilized as the model for future prisons such as Statesville Prison in Illinois. It was also the original design for Western Pennsylvania in the mid-1800s, but that was converted into what would become the more accepted design referred to as the warehouse model.

***GIDEON V. WAINWRIGHT*, 372 U.S. 335 (1963).** A 1963 **U.S. Supreme Court** case which unanimously ruled that defendants are required to be provided with the right to counsel under the Sixth Amendment even if they are incapable of paying their attorneys. The Court's ruling allowed approximately 2,000 Florida prisoners to be freed. *See also* FORTAS, ABE (1910–1982).

GILLIS, LESTER JOSEPH (1908–1934). A notorious American bank robber in the early 1930s, also known as "Baby Face" Nelson because of his adolescent appearance and undersized stature. He was culpable for the deaths of three **FBI** agents killed in the line of duty. After committing numerous bank robberies, he joined a criminal **gang** headed by **John Dillinger**, an American **gangster**. He was another gangster who received the title Public Enemy No. 1 and was killed in a gun battle with the FBI. *See also* PURVIS, MELVIN (1903–1960).

GILMORE, GARY (1940–1977). The first person to be executed (1978) in the United States, in Utah, following the reinstatement of the **death penalty**. His final statement has been recorded as "Let's do it," which was followed up by "Dominus vobiscum" (The Lord be with you), to which the Catholic priest, Reverend Thomas Meersman, responded, "Et cum spiritu tuo" (and with your spirit). "Let's do it" is often incorrectly associated with the Nike slogan "Just do it." *See also* EXECUTION; FIRING SQUAD.

GITEAU, CHARLES JULIUS (1841–1882). Giteau was convicted of assassinating the 20th president of the United States, James A. Garfield. Giteau had been upset that President Garfield rejected his job applications and subsequently shot and killed him in 1881. He pled not guilty to the charge of **murder** but was found guilty and **hanged** in 1882. *See also* CAPITAL OFFENSE.

GLUECK (ELEANOR, 1898–1972, AND SHELDON, 1896–1980). A husband and wife research team who focused on the field of delinquency and **criminology**. Their seminal work was a **longitudinal study** of prisoners sentenced between 1911 and 1922 to the Massachusetts Reformatory. Their study sought to discover the variables that contributed to continuation in crime and those that factored into the abstention from crime.

GOOD-FAITH DOCTRINE. Evidence obtained illegally becomes admissible if it can be shown by the **police** that they were not aware of a violation of **Fourth Amendment** rights. *See also MAPP V. OHIO*, 367 U.S. 643 (1961); SEARCH AND SEIZURE; WARRANTLESS SEARCHES.

GOTTI, JOHN (1940–2002). The former crime boss for the Gambino crime family, referred to as the "Teflon Don." Gotti was reared in the South Bronx, New York, and was involved in **gang** activity when he was about 12 years old. He ran errands for **mobsters** and was later arrested by the **FBI** in 1968 for **hijacking** stolen goods. Gotti was initiated into the Gambino crime family under the control of then crime boss Paul Castellano. Gotti became disgruntled with Castellano's leadership and had him killed in 1985. Gotti rose to prominence and took control of the Gambino crime family in 1986. Gotti was later convicted of **murder** and racketeering and sentenced to life imprisonment in 1992. In 1998, while incarcerated in ADX Florence (the Federal **supermax prison**), he was diagnosed with throat cancer and died in 2002. *See also* GAMBINO, CARLO (1902–1976); MAFIA.

GRAFFITI. Graffiti are illegal markings that are drawn, painted, or written on walls or canvases by individuals and exposed to the general public. Similar type markings were found in Italy circa A.D. 54–68. However, it became an artistic form during the 1970s and was popularized by the "hip-hop" generation. Street **gangs** mark their turf using this artistic form. Law enforcement utilizes graffiti to identify gang territory and changes in gangs in a region.

GRAFT. A form of corruption used by politicians to exert their power for personal gain or an unfair advantage. **William Magear Tweed**, aka Boss Tweed, popularized the term during his reign over Tammy Hall, the New York City Democratic Party machine in the 19th century. He was subsequently convicted of stealing millions of dollars from taxpayers in 1877. Graft is aggressively prosecuted by the Office of the **United States Attorney**.

***GRAHAM V. FLORIDA*, 560 U.S. 48 (2010).** A **U.S. Supreme Court** case which held that a juvenile couldn't be sentenced to life without **parole** for any crime excluding **homicide** because the **punishment** is tantamount to a **death sentence**. The Court ruled in a 6–3 decision that the defendant's **Eighth Amendment** rights were violated. *See also* PROPORTIONALITY.

GRAND THEFT AUTO. The intentional stealing of or attempt to steal a motor vehicle. With the 1912 advent of Henry Ford's Model T touring cars, the creation of the car thief began. The theft of three motor vehicles led to the formation of the Automobile Protective and Information Bureau to assist insurance companies in dealing with the growing problems of car theft.

GRASS EATER. A term used in the 1972 Knapp Report to describe one of the two types of corrupt cops. The other type is called a **meat eater**. Grass eaters are involved in lower-level forms of corruption. The report was a by-product of the 1970 creation of the **Knapp Commission**, which was formed to investigate corruption within the New York City **Police** Department. Grass eaters are alleged to be involved in passive forms of corruption by accepting bribes. *See also* POLICE CORRUPTION; POLICE MISCONDUCT; SERPICO, FRANK (1936–).

GREEN RIVER KILLER. A **serial killer**, Gary Leon Ridgeway (1949–) was convicted of murdering 49 people during the 1980s and 1990s, and based on his accounts that number may be upward of 70 or more. Many of his victims were **prostitutes** and young girls. Ridgeway grew up having both sexual and violent fantasies about his mother. He had an IQ of 82, which placed him in the below-average intelligence range. At age 16 he stabbed a young boy whom he coaxed into following him into a wooded area. Ridgeway was subsequently convicted of 49 counts of first-degree **murder** and sentenced to life imprisonment without **parole**. *See also* MURDER.

***GREGG V. GEORGIA*, 428 U.S. 153 (1976).** The **U.S. Supreme Court** holding that led to the reinstatement of the **death penalty** in the United States and resulted in **Gary Gilmore** becoming the first person to be executed after the reinstatement in 1977. *See also* FIRING SQUAD; *FURMAN V. GEORGIA*, 408 U.S. 238 (1972).

GRIEVOUS BODILY HARM. Intentional, serious bodily injury inflicted upon another person. This term was first used in the 1803 English Lord Ellenborough's Act statute, which found it illegal to perform or cause an **abortion**. The term entered the U.S. legal lexicon in the Offenses against Persons Act of 1861.

***GRIFFIN V. CALIFORNIA*, 380 U.S. 609 (1965).** A **U.S. Supreme Court** case which held in a 6–2 decision that the defendant's **Fifth Amendment** rights to avoid **self-incrimination** were violated due to a prosecutor's comments to a **jury** that the defendant's silence was proof that he was guilty.

GROSS, HANS (1847–1915). An Austrian judge and professor of criminal law. He is believed to be one of the founders of criminal investigation, **forensics**, and criminal profiling based on his research and book, *Criminal Investigations: A Practical Textbook*, published in 1893, which helped establish the field of forensics.

GROUND-PENETRATING RADAR. An instrument utilizing radar pulses reflected into the ground which produces an image of a subsurface. Christian Hulsmeyer created the concept of radar systems in 1904. In 1921, Gotthelf Leimbach and Heinrich Lowy patented a radar design system that sought to unearth buried objects, including bodies. An improved version, which led to greater depth discovery, was subsequently invented and patented by Dr. Hulsenbeck in 1926. Law enforcement utilizes this device for both specific sites and larger area inspections.

GROUP CONFERENCING. A formalized meeting between family members and public officials who may represent social services or law enforcement that is mediated to safeguard a child. This process originated in New Zealand via their Children, Young Persons, and Their Families Act in 1989. It is a form of **Balanced and Restorative Justice**.

GUANTANAMO BAY. A naval base located in Guantanamo Bay, Cuba, which is also referred to as "Gitmo." President George W. Bush established a **prison** on the site in 2002 to indefinitely house prisoners who were suspected members of terrorist organizations such as **Al-Qaeda** and soldiers from the

Taliban, an Islamic fundamentalist group. The base was controversial because numerous complaints were lodged against the United States due to allegations of **human rights** violations. *See also* TERRORISM.

GUARDIAN ANGELS. A volunteer organization of unarmed crime prevention patrollers founded in February 1979 by **Curtis Sliwa**, a radio talk show host and media personality. The organization was created to combat **violent crime** that had been occurring on the New York City subways. It has approximately 130 chapters in the United States and other parts of the world. The Guardian Angels are often resisted by law enforcement because they are a volunteer organization and not sworn law enforcement. Their white T-shirts and red berets identify its multiracial volunteers, who were primarily drawn from McDonald's restaurants. *See also* PEEL, SIR ROBERT (1788–1850); VIGILANTISM.

GUILLOTINE. A device used to execute those sentenced to death. Dr. Joseph-Ignace Guillotin proposed the utilization of the guillotine to the French government as a more civil way of executing individuals in 1789. The guillotine's last official usage was in France in 1977, when Hamida Djandoubi was executed after having been convicted of **murder**. The guillotine has never been a sanctioned method of **execution** in the United States. *See also* CAPITAL PUNISHMENT; DEATH PENALTY.

GUILTY BUT MENTALLY ILL. A defense used by a defendant who claims to be innocent due to a mental health issue or guilty because of insanity. The **insanity defense** is only inserted in about 1 percent of all criminal cases. The **U.S. Supreme Court** in ***Ford v. Wainwright*, 477 U.S. 399 (1986)**, held that an insane person could not be executed. *See also* EXECUTION; GEIN, ED (1906–1984); M'NAGHTEN RULE.

GUILTY PLEA. The acceptance of formal charges against someone alleged to have committed a crime. The admission may also be part of an agreement made between a defendant and the prosecutor. A direct impact of a guilty plea is reducing the burden of the court system with the **trial** and the ancillary costs. In 1970, the **U.S. Supreme Court** established the guidelines for guilty pleas in *Brady v. United States*, 397 U.S. 742 (1970). *See also* DUE PROCESS; PLEA BARGAIN.

GULAG. A Russian acronym that translates to Chief Directorate of Camps. A network of labor camps, particularly for political prisoners who were sentenced between 1930 and 1955 under the former Soviet Union. Millions of prisoners died due to maltreatment and starvation. *See also* TRANSPORTATION.

GUN BUYBACK PROGRAM. A program instituted by law enforcement to purchase firearms to decrease the number of weapons owned by private citizens and for the citizens to sell their weapons without any likelihood of prosecution. The first gun buyback program was thought to have been initiated in Baltimore in 1974. *See also* COMMUNITY-ORIENTED POLICING.

GUN CONTROL. Gun control refers to the guidelines and policies that monitor the sale, manufacture, ownership, possession, and alteration of any weapon by civilians. Gun control legislation was codified under the National Firearms Act of 1934, and all sales of firearms were documented in a national registry. The many recent school shootings and other mass shootings, such as the Las Vegas, Nevada, and the Sutherland Springs, Texas, church shootings in 2017, have seen an increased call for gun control to keep weapons out of the hands of those convicted of criminal offenses or who suffer from mental illness. *See also* COLUMBINE MASSACRE; SANDY HOOK MASSACRE.

GUN COURT. An established branch of the Jamaican judicial system that was implemented in 1974 under the Suppression of Crime Act and the Gun Court Act to tackle the increase in gun violence and to adjudicate defendants without the use of a **jury**. Gun court is also a special, **problem-solving** or **community court** in the United States, which followed the model of **drug court** to provide more efficient and pragmatic solutions for persons who illegally carry or possess firearms. *See also* VIOLENCE.

GUN LOBBY. An organized advocacy group that tries to persuade politicians to promote public policy and laws that are favorable to the rights of citizens who are gun owners. The most recognized gun lobby organization is the National Rifle Association (NRA), a nonprofit organization founded by William C. Church and George W. Wingate in 1871.

GUN PERMIT. A gun permit is also known as a firearm permit and is a license, typically issued by a **police** agency, which gives a person the right to possess, purchase, or conceal a weapon on their person. In 1791, the Second Amendment became the first legal document to give rights to citizens to own a firearm. *See also* GUN CONTROL; MAY ISSUE.

GUNRUNNING. The unlawful buying and selling of arms or munitions. One of the most infamous U.S. gunrunning operations was called Fast and Furious, which between 2009 and 2011 was guided by the Bureau of Alcohol, Tobacco, Firearms and Explosives, Phoenix Field Division. The operation allowed approximately 2,000 firearms to be lost or misplaced. Some wound up in Mexico at several killing scenes and were found at the **murder** scene of U.S. Border Patrol agent Brian Terry.

GUN SHOW LOOPHOLE. A legal provision that allows private gun dealers, including those at gun shows, to sell firearms without having the prospective buyer submit to a firearms **background check**. While the 1993 Brady **Handgun** Violence Prevention Act made it mandatory for background checks for anyone purchasing a gun from dealers who are federally licensed, this loophole exempts private party sellers. *See also* GUN CONTROL.

GUZIK, JAKE (1886–1956). A Polish émigré, who in the 1920s became a legal and financial advisor for an **organized crime syndicate** called the Chicago Outfit and close friend to the **mobster Alphonse Capone**. Guzik's primary responsibility was to pay off the local **police** and politicians. As a result, he was given the nickname "Greasy Thumb." He later served time for **tax evasion** but returned to his old ways once released. He died of a heart condition years later.

H

HABEAS CORPUS, WRIT OF. *See* WRIT OF HABEAS CORPUS.

HABITUAL OFFENDER. Someone who has previously committed a crime and subsequently commits another crime. Habitual offender statutes were used by the United States in the 17th century and were promoted through get-tough rhetoric during the 1970s, which resulted in more severe penalties such as **three-strikes laws** in 22 states and a **two-strikes law** in Georgia by the end of the 1990s. Habitual offender statutes have contributed to **mass incarceration** because they require lengthy and often life sentences. The intention of these laws is to prevent **recidivism**. Some laws include a life without **parole** sanction. *See also* PUNISHMENT.

HAIR TRIGGER. The trigger of a gun that requires minimal pressure to engage. It was invented in Germany in 1540. In 1804, Secretary of State Alexander Hamilton, in a duel with Vice President Aaron Burr, used a **pistol** with a hair trigger. At the time, **dueling** was legal. Hamilton had an unfair advantage but was fatally wounded and died. A federal law was passed in 1839 prohibiting dueling in the United States.

HALFWAY HOUSE. A building used to assist recovering drug addicts, mental health patients, ex-convicts, and others to readjust to mainstream society. The establishment of halfway houses in the United States began in Chicago, Illinois, in 1843. However, the term is believed to have originated in England in the 1800s.

HAMAS. A Palestinian organization, which supports a Sunni-Islamist ideology. It was founded in 1987, shortly after the initial intifada, when it became a subsidiary of the Egyptian Muslim Brotherhood with the intent of forming an Islamic state in Palestine. Its military wing, the Izz al-Din al-Qassam brigades, has attacked Israeli and Palestinian areas starting in the 1990s. In 2006, Hamas won legislative elections by defeating the secular Fatah party.

Since 2003, Hamas has been considered a terrorist organization and remains on the U.S. watch list of the **FBI**'s Terrorist Screening Center. *See also* TERRORISM.

HANDGUN. A firearm used with one hand that can discharge a bullet from a chamber. The first use of a handgun was recorded in China in 1364 and the weapon spread quickly to Europe by 1375. The Colt Manufacturing Company produced a revolver referred to as the "Peacemaker," which was reputed to be the "gun that won the West." Handguns have advanced in style from single-shot revolvers to automatic weapons capable of firing many rounds in succession without repeatedly pulling the trigger. Handguns are carried by law enforcement as both a sidearm and as concealed weapons.

HANDSCHU GUIDELINES. A set of provisions resulting from a class action lawsuit that was forced on the New York City **Police** Department (NYPD) due to their actions regarding surveillance of politically active groups. The plaintiffs in the 1985 lawsuit, Barbara Handschu and codefendants, alleged that informants and infiltrators provoked groups to engage in criminal acts. They also claimed that the NYPD violated their **Fourth Amendment** right against unreasonable **searches and seizure**. The guidelines were modified in 2003 and directed the NYPD to provide copies of their videorecordings of political demonstrations.

HANDS-OFF DOCTRINE. A reference to the federal courts' position in the 19th and 20th centuries, which dissuaded them from interfering with or extending the rights of prisoners. The judges believed that prisoners gave up their rights by breaking the law, and the courts were not to provide them with protections. The official doctrine was established in 1866 in ***Pervear v. Massachusetts*, 72 U.S. 475 (1866)**, and reaffirmed in *Ruffin v. Commonwealth*, 62 Va. 790 (1871), whereby both courts rejected the notion that prisoners had rights. The doctrine was officially ended in 1974.

HANDWRITING ANALYSIS. An examination of someone's style of writing to determine their personality and possible behavior. The Chinese developed this technique approximately 3,000 years ago. However, in the 1870s, French clerics made advancements toward the practice and formed modern-day procedures for analysis. Handwriting analysis was primarily responsible for helping to solve two modern **murder** cases: Robert Durst in 2000 and **Dennis Rader**, or the BTK (bind, **torture**, kill) **serial killer**, in 2005. Both cases had been "cold cases," Rader for more than 15 years. *See also* FORENSICS.

HANGING. A form of **capital punishment** (also referred to as a **death sentence**) and the act of killing someone by attaching a rope to their neck. The person to be executed (or lynched) is suspended in air, without support, allowing them to strangle until they are dead. Prior to the 1890s, it was primarily used in the United States as a means of **execution** or illegally as a **lynching**. The procedure for a hanging has been prescribed by the U.S. Army Corps of Engineers. The last execution by hanging in the United States occurred on 25 January 1996 in Delaware. *See also* GALLOWS.

HANSEN, ROBERT CHRISTIAN (1944–2014). Hansen, a **serial killer**, was the son of a Danish immigrant who followed in his father's footsteps and became a baker. Hansen's childhood was not ideal because his father compelled him to work long hours. In high school, Hansen suffered from a bad case of facial acne, a stuttering problem, and was bullied, which led him to become a loner. Shortly after graduating from high school, Hansen enlisted in the U.S. Army Reserves and was discharged after one year. Afterward, he opened and operated his own bakery in the 1970s and 1980s. Hansen confessed to killing 17 women ranging in age from 16 to 41 between 1971 and 1983, many of whom were strippers and **prostitutes**. He was eventually charged with murdering four women, but as part of a plea agreement he led authorities to more bodies. Hansen was sentenced to 461 years plus life without the possibility of **parole**. He died while in **prison** at the age of 75. *See also* MURDER.

HARM PRINCIPLE. A person should be able to live their life as they choose as long as their actions don't harm others. English thinker John Stuart Mill (1806–1873) articulated this principle in his essay *On Liberty*. The harm principle is fundamental to U.S. criminal law.

HARRIS, ERIC (1981–1999). *See* COLUMBINE MASSACRE.

HARRISON NARCOTICS TAX ACT (1915). A federal law proposed by Representative Francis Harrison of New York, which regulated and taxed the distribution, production, and importation of coca products and opiates. Its goal was to regulate the medical use of opiates and to criminalize the nonmedical use.

***HARRIS V. NEW YORK*, 401 U.S. 222 (1971).** The defendant Harris was charged with selling **heroin** to an **undercover police** officer. The defendant alleged that the bags sold to the officer contained baking powder. The defendant testified and was cross-examined by the prosecution. During cross-examination, the prosecution used the defendant's statements given to law enforcement against him even though the defendant had not been properly Mirandized. The **U.S. Supreme Court** held, in a 5–4 decision, that the **evidence** was admissible and the defendant's rights were not violated. *See also MIRANDA V. ARIZONA*, 384 U.S. 436 (1966).

HARVEY, DONALD (1952–2017). A convicted **serial killer**, characterized as an **angel of death**, who worked in the medical field and claimed to have murdered 87 patients and civilians. Harvey said that the reason he killed was due to compassion for the patients and that he tried to ease their pain. While growing up, a family member and a neighbor sexually abused Harvey. In later years, he had a consensual relationship with a man, which lasted approximately 15 years. He got a job at a hospital and was subsequently raped by a roommate. He suffered from mental health issues and attempted to kill himself on several occasions. He'd later commence his killing spree, which he was able to conceal for more than 17 years. Harvey was eventually indicted and confessed to several murders beginning in 1987. He was sentenced to 28 consecutive life sentences. *See also* KEVORKIAN, JACK (1928–2011); MURDER.

HASAN, NIDAL (1970–). *See* FORT HOOD SHOOTING.

HATE CRIME. A crime committed against a person or structure based on race, sexual orientation, disability, nationality, religion, or gender identity. The **Civil Rights** Act of 1968 outlined the differences between ordinary crimes and those motivated by any form of bias. In the 1990s, enhancements to hate crime legislation were enacted, which included the Hate Crimes Statistics Act of 1990, modified to become the **Matthew Shepard** and James Byrd, Jr., Hate Prevention Act of 2009. This act required the U.S. Justice Department to gather data from law enforcement departments about crimes based on racial **discrimination**, religion, ethnic background, or sexual orientation. The findings of the data are published annually.

HATFIELD AND MCCOY FEUD. *See* FEUDING.

HAVILAND, JOHN (1792–1852). An English-born architect whose work was instrumental in the architecture of the first penitentiaries, jails, and other prominent buildings in the United States. He was commissioned to design **Eastern State Penitentiary**, Philadelphia, Pennsylvania (1821); New Jersey State Penitentiary (1833); and the Essex County Courthouse and County Jail, Newark, New Jersey (1836).

HAYES, RUTHERFORD B. (1822–1893). The 19th president of the Unites States, he was the governor of Ohio and elected as the first president of the National Prison Association, which later became the **American Correctional Association (ACA).** The ACA was founded in 1870 to assist correctional practitioners who work in juvenile facilities, jails, adult **prisons**, and **halfway houses**. The association also spearheaded the establishment of worldwide correctional policies and standards.

HAZELWOOD, ROBERT ROY (1938–2016). An **FBI** profiler who specialized in sex crimes and is regarded as the innovator of sexual predators profiling, establishing six categories of rapists. Hazelwood also distinguished between organized and disorganized murderers in 1980. He is among the earliest to propose that there is no cure for sexual offenders, especially those categorized as pedophiles or sadists. He was the founder of the **Violent Criminal Apprehension Program (ViCAP)** in 1985, which contains the largest fact-finding database of **violent crimes**, including **murder**, missing persons, sexual **assault**, and human remains, in the United States. *See also* DISORGANIZED OFFENDER; ORGANIZED OFFENDER; PROFILING.

HEARSAY. A statement received from another person and offered in a court proceeding to prove the accuracy of a circumstance, which cannot be confirmed or denied and may, or may not, be allowed by a judge. The statements may be presented verbally or in written form. The hearsay rule was first introduced in *Wright v. Doe D. Tatham* (Exchequer Chamber 1837) and hinged upon three letters submitted to the court concerning an heir attempting to establish the competency of a testator. At the federal level, there are 24 exceptions for hearsay **evidence** that may be presented before the court.

HEARST, PATTY (1954–). An American citizen related to the prominent publisher William Randolph Hearst. In 1974, while 19 years old, Patty Hearst was **kidnapped** by the **Symbionese Liberation Army (SLA)**. While in their custody, she became sympathetic to their cause and participated in criminal acts on their behalf. She later announced that she had joined the group. The **FBI** and San Francisco **Police** Department subsequently arrested her in 1975. Court-appointed doctors concluded that she was brainwashed into committing crimes on behalf of the SLA. However, in 1976 she was convicted of using a weapon in the commission of a felony and for bank robbery. Hearst had her sentence commuted in 1979 by President Jimmy Carter and was pardoned in 2001 by President Bill Clinton. *See also* HOSTAGE; PARDON; STOCKHOLM SYNDROME; TERRORISM.

HEBEPHILE. An adult who has a strong sexual penchant for individuals in the age range of 11–14. Hebephiles have been studied since the early 1970s and have been discussed in the psychiatry practice dating back to the early 1900s. The diagnosis for hebephiles appears in the *Diagnostic and Statistical Manual of Mental Disorders* (*DSM-IV-TR*) and provides a coded mental disorder for offenders who target pubescent youth.

HELLS ANGELS. An international motorcycle **gang** with chapters in Canada, Australia, Europe, and the United States. Considered an **organized crime** entity by American law enforcement officials, the Hells Angels were incorporated in the late 1940s in Fontana, California. The name Hells Angels became popular during World Wars I and II. Many of its members can be observed wearing denim or leather jackets, with membership in an exclusive club signified by patches and lettering that represent the 1 percenters of motorcycle clubs. One of its infamous members was Ralph "Sonny" Barger, the founding member of its Oakland, California, chapter.

HELTER SKELTER. The title of a Beatles song, which was made infamous by **Charles Manson** in 1969. The literal meaning of *Helter Skelter* describes confusion or a disorderly haste. However, Manson, a cult leader, convinced his followers that it meant the world would end in an inevitable race war whereby the blacks would kill all the whites. His supporters, a band of young hippies, would commit nine murders at four different locations. *See also* MURDER.

HEMP. A cannabis plant that has a small amount of THC, the active drug ingredient of **marijuana**, used to produce hashish and can also be used for making clothing, shoes, and baggage. The first laws for the production of hemp came in 1619. In the 1700s, a person could be jailed for not growing hemp. Hemp's affiliation with marijuana came to fruition in the 1930s and was regulated under the Marihuana Tax Act of 1937.

HEROIN. A white and odorless narcotic, often referred to as horse or smack, which is derived from morphine and is highly addictive. It is generally prescribed as a painkiller but has turned into a recreational drug. Charles Romley Adler Wright, an English chemistry and physics researcher, created it in 1874. It was widely used during and after the Civil War to help wounded soldiers end their **addiction** to morphine. Possession of heroin is illegal as stipulated by the Controlled Substances Act of 1970. Possession of more than 100 grams of heroin carries a mandatory minimum federal **prison** sentence of five years. *See also* NARCOTICS.

***HERRERA V. COLLINS*, 506 U.S. 390 (1993).** A **U.S. Supreme Court** case which held in a 6–3 decision that the innocence of a defendant does not qualify for federal relief via **habeas corpus** under the **cruel and unusual punishment** provision of the **Eighth Amendment**. The defendant, Herrera, had been convicted of shooting and murdering **police** officer David Rucker. The dying declaration of the police officer was that Herrera shot him while fleeing from the shooting. Rucker died later. Herrera filed his motion claiming that new **evidence** would exonerate him. Herrera was executed several months after the court rejected his claim of cruel and unusual punishment. *See also* EXECUTION; EXONERATION; MURDER.

HIDDEN CRIME. Hidden crime refers to the "**dark figure of crime**" and is used by sociologists and criminologists to describe crimes that are either unreported or undiscovered. The term came into use following the uniform collection of crime data which first occurred in England in 1856. The United States began collecting crime data under the **FBI's Uniform Crime Report** starting in 1930. The **National Crime Victimization Survey** (and other surveys) later augmented the data collection in 1973, which helped to provide a measurement of hidden crime when one report is compared to another.

HIERARCHY RULE. A requirement when counting numerous crimes that only the most egregious crime will be documented when multiple crimes have been committed during a single incident. This rule is in accordance with the **FBI**'s **Uniform Crime Report**, begun in 1930.

HIGH-SPEED PURSUIT. The chase in a vehicle by a law enforcement officer of a suspected or confirmed violator who has committed a serious crime when their capture is paramount to prevent other crimes from occurring. The **U.S. Supreme Court** in *Scott v. Harris*, 550 U.S. 372 (2007), held in an 8–1 decision for a local **police** officer's actions in a high-speed chase, which had been determined to endanger the lives of innocent bystanders.

HIGH-VELOCITY BLOOD SPATTER. The bloodstain pattern left at a crime scene caused by a gunshot or high-speed machinery. Dr. Eduard Piotrowski, a Polish academician, first studied blood spatter analysis and published his findings, which influenced other investigators from Germany and France. The seminal moment for the usage of blood spatter patterns in the United States was highly publicized in the 1954 **murder** case *State of Ohio v. Samuel Sheppard*, 100 Ohio App. 399 (1955). *See also* FORENSICS; SHEPPARD, SAM (1923–1970).

HIGHWAY PATROL. A term used to define a law enforcement entity that was created to **patrol** and enforce traffic safety laws on state highways and may also be assigned to assist local **police** agencies with enforcing similar functions. Stephen F. Austin unofficially created the **Texas Rangers** in 1823, which was the first state agency of law enforcement in the United States. The highway patrol is a unit of law enforcement synonymous with **state police** in a few states, while in other states it may be a unit of the state police.

HIJACKING. To illegally force a person to give up control of their mode of transportation. The term derived its meaning from law enforcement's seizure of liquor trucks during **Prohibition**. The first recorded car hijacking, also referred to as **carjacking**, occurred in 1912 in France. The first recorded hijacking of an aircraft took place in 1931 in Peru. The most infamous hijackings of airliners occurred in 2001 in connection with an act of **terrorism** that killed more than 3,000 people. *See also* WORLD TRADE CENTER (WTC) BOMBINGS.

HILLSIDE STRANGLER(S). *See* BIANCHI, KENNETH (1951–); SERIAL KILLER.

HINCKLEY, JOHN (1955–). An American who tried to assassinate President Ronald Reagan in 1981. During the commission of the attempted **assassination**, Hinckley shot and injured two law enforcement officers and critically injured James Brady, President Reagan's press secretary. Hinckley was subsequently arrested and was later found **not guilty by reason of insanity**. However, he was confined to a psychiatric hospital until his release in 2016. *See also* GUILTY BUT MENTALLY ILL; INSANITY DEFENSE.

HIRSCHI, TRAVIS W. (1935–2017). An American criminologist who received his Ph.D. in sociology from the University of California, Berkeley. Hirschi's seminal work discussed his perspective that crime can be explained by the absence of social bonds or what he coined as "social bond theory." In 1969, he identified four types of social bonds—attachment, commitment, involvement, and belief—which connect individuals to society. Later in his career, he departed from his bonding theory, and in 1990, Hirschi, along with criminologist Michael R. Gottfredson, developed self-control theory, which hypothesized that an individual's lack of self-control is the predominant factor in their criminal behavior. In 1981, he became a member of the Department of Sociology at the University of Arizona. He retired in 1997. *See also* ATTACHMENT THEORY.

HISTORICAL VIOLENCE DATABASE. A collaborative research project developed to assist scholars in better understanding **violent crime**, serious **assault**, and politically contentious acts that may lead to **violence**. The database allows social scientists to experiment with their theories and help historians get their research expounded upon, and it serves as a repository for historical research. The researchers have investigated violent incidents as far back as 1630.

HOBBS ACT. A federal law named after Alabama senator Sam Hobbs enacted in 1946 to combat racketeering. The act was an amendment to the 1934 Anti-Racketeering Act. It was later used to criminalize acts of robbery and extortion as it pertained to public and labor union corruption, which affected interstate and foreign commerce. *See also* RACKETEER INFLUENCED CORRUPT ORGANIZATION (RICO).

HOLLYWOOD MADAM. The designation given to **Heidi Fleiss**, a former owner of a high-class **prostitution** ring in the 1990s, whose clients included actors, athletes, politicians, and musicians. Her story was made into a documentary in 1996.

***HOLMES V. JENNISON*, 14 PET. (39 U.S.) 540 (1840).** A **U.S. Supreme Court** case which held that jurisdiction over foreign affairs lies in the federal government. The defendant Holmes was ordered extradited to Quebec, Canada, to be tried for **murder** by Vermont governor Silas Jennison even though the United States didn't have an **extradition** treaty with Canada. Governor Holmes appealed to the Vermont Supreme Court and was denied. The U.S. Supreme Court held, in a 5–4 decision, that the federal government is the sole entity to have jurisdiction of extradition to another country and ordered that the state of Vermont release Holmes.

HOME CONFINEMENT. An alternative to housing someone in jail or **prison**, which is also referred to as home detention or house arrest. It requires that an individual's confinement be restricted to their home and is normally monitored using an electronic device. Judges have used home confinement since the 1900s.

HOME INVASION. The unauthorized and sometimes forceful entry into a person's home with the intention to commit a heinous crime against the occupants of the home. Perpetrators are not charged with the crime of home invasion but are accused of accompanying offenses, such as robbery, **murder**, **assault**, or **kidnapping**. One of the most infamous American home invasions occurred in 1959 in Holcomb, Kansas, where four people were killed. Truman Capote wrote about this case in his nonfiction book *In Cold Blood* (1965).

HOMELAND SECURITY ACT. The 2002 Homeland Security Act reorganized federal agencies to better coordinate efforts that would effectively combat threats of **terrorism** (such as the 9/11 attacks) and other circumstances that jeopardize national security, including natural disasters (such as Hurricane Irma). The practices of U.S. Homeland Security have been disapproved of by other nations, especially the signers of the Geneva Conventions, because the United States regards some prisoners as unlawful combatants who when brought into custody by military forces are not considered as opposing military forces covered by the Geneva Conventions.

HOMICIDE. The intentional and illegal killing of someone by another person. There are different degrees of homicide, which are usually based on the intent of the perpetrator. Scientists believe the first known homicide occurred in Spain approximately 430,000 years ago. **Evidence** suggests that a Neanderthal victim suffered from blunt-force trauma before death. *See also GRAHAM V. FLORIDA*, 560 U.S. 48 (2010); JUSTIFIABLE HOMICIDE; MANSLAUGHTER; MURDER; VICTIM PRECIPITATED CRIME (THEORY); WOLFGANG, MARVIN EUGENE (1924–1998).

HOMOSEXUAL. A person who is sexually interested in someone of the same sex. In many cultures, the act of homosexuality is contradictory to established religious norms. In the late 1940s and early 1950s members of the military who were suspected of being homosexual were discharged. The mental health profession listed homosexuality in its *Diagnostic and Statistical Manual* (*DSM IV*) in the early 1950s, and it remained a mental disorder until the early 1970s. Homosexual establishments were targeted by members of the New York **Police** Department in the late 1960s, which sparked the Stonewall riots, which lasted six days. *See also* SHEPARD, MATTHEW (1976–1998).

HONOR KILLING. The deliberate killing of a person, in particular a woman, who has been thought of as bringing dishonor to a family. The means of death include beheading, stoning, **hanging**, and strangulation and are committed in public. The act of honor killing was codified in the Napoleonic Code, Article 324, in 1810. Honor killing is also an aspect of the **Mafia**'s code of honor. *See also* OMERTÀ.

HOOLIGANISM. A term used to describe the actions of violent youth **gangs** (the members are called hooligans) associated with lawlessness in the South East London area in the late 1890s and at sporting events in London, England, beginning in the 1970s. Similar effects of hooliganism surfaced in the United States starting in the mid-1970s when hooligans attacked a Texas Rangers baseball player at the Cleveland Municipal Stadium in Cleveland, Ohio. *See also* JUVENILE DELINQUENCY.

HOOVER, J. EDGAR (1895–1972). The former director of the **FBI**. Hoover began his employment with the federal government in 1917 and became the director of the Department of the Bureau of Investigation in 1924. The bureau was reorganized and officially became the FBI in 1935. Hoover was renowned for his investigation techniques and for covertly monitoring alleged subversive groups. His tenure in the FBI lasted until his death. *See also* FEDERAL BUREAU OF INVESTIGATION (FBI).

***HORTON V. CALIFORNIA*, 496 U.S. 128 (1990).** This holding by the **U.S. Supreme Court** resulted in the **plain view doctrine**. **Evidence** or contraband that is in "plain view" may be acquired by law enforcement without a **warrant**. The **Transportation Security Administration (TSA)** since its creation in 1991 has used the plain view doctrine during airport screenings of passengers. *See also* WARRANTLESS SEARCHES.

HOSTAGE. An individual who has been taken and held against their will for either monetary gain or to satisfy a condition of demand. The status of hostages has been studied as far back as the Middle Ages, with a noted widespread evolution into a judicial practice that surfaced in the 13th century. During this period, hostages were used as pawns in international affairs as terms of an agreement between nations. Hostage taking is a popular theme in television and movies when capture by law enforcement is imminent and the hostage is used to prevent it. *See also* HEARST, PATTY (1954–); STOCKHOLM SYNDROME.

HOSTAGE NEGOTIATION. A technique that is utilized by trained law enforcement personnel to connect with a person who either has conveyed that they want to violently harm someone else or who has taken another person **hostage**. The New York **Police** Department was credited with developing the principles of hostage negotiations in 1972 under the tutelage of former NYPD **detective** and psychologist Harvey Schlossberg.

HOSTILE WITNESS. A person who has been summoned to appear in court and has an adverse attitude toward helping the party who made the request. As such, the **witness** may not tell the truth even though they have taken an oath. The witness may then be cross-examined, and if found to be antagonistic, the opposing attorney can petition the judge whether the witness can be deemed a hostile witness and asked leading questions to get to the truth. During the 1995 **O. J. Simpson murder trial**, Brian "Kato" Kaelin was considered a hostile witness by the prosecution because it appeared he was changing his testimony to benefit O. J. Simpson, the defendant. The prosecutor, Marcia Clark, requested that the presiding judge declare him to be a hostile witness and compel him to testify. *See also* SUMMON(S).

HOWARD, JOHN (1726–1790). A high **sheriff** of Bedfordshire, England, during the early 1770s. An inspection of one of his **prisons** led to his concern about the treatment of prisoners who were unable to pay their **fines**. He continued his inspection of jail conditions and published his research (*The State of the Prisons in England and Wales*, 1777) detailing conditions in prisons, which were praised as establishing the usage of the single cell in both the United Kingdom and the United States. During his inspection of Russian prisons, he contracted what was described as gaol fever (probably tuberculosis), died, and was buried there. Among the outcomes of Howard's labors was the foundation of the Howard League for **Penal Reform**, a nonprofit organization, founded in 1866 initially as the John Howard Association. It is the oldest penal reform agency and is based in London, England. The organization merged with the prisoner-centered Penal Reform League in 1921 and is voluntarily funded with donations even though it receives some funding from outside sources. Similarly, the John Howard Society, a nonprofit, Canadian-based and church group–centered organization, was created in 1867. Other associations, similarly influenced by Howard's writing, have been created in the United States. These organizations advanced an improved understanding of crime and prison problems and promoted reform and prisoner- and victim-centered initiatives.

***HUDSON V. MICHIGAN*, 547 U.S. 586 (2006).** A **U.S. Supreme Court** case which held, in a 5–4 decision, that **evidence** obtained by a **police** officer while executing a **warrant** and violating the **Fourth Amendment** "knock-and-announce" rule need not be suppressed. The defendant, Hudson, challenged his conviction since the police officers did not wait for the required 20–30 seconds before entering his residence. *See also* SEARCH AND SEIZURE; WARRANTLESS SEARCHES.

HUGHES, FRANCINE (1947–). A woman who, in 1977, after being the victim of **domestic violence** for approximately 13 years, killed her ex-husband by setting fire to the bed where he lay drunk. Hughes had packed her four children into her car before returning to the house and setting it ablaze. She then drove to the county jail to admit her guilt to law enforcement officials. A **jury** of 10 women and 2 men subsequently found Hughes not guilty because of insanity. Her acquittal set a legal precedent for future domestic violence cases. Her case was turned into a nonfiction book, *The Burning Bed*, written by author Faith McNulty, which became a made-for-television movie starring Farrah Fawcett in 1984. The case promoted better responses for women who have been victims of domestic violence. *See also* GUILTY BUT MENTALLY ILL; INSANITY DEFENSE; NOT GUILTY BY REASON OF INSANITY; VIOLENCE.

HULKS. Decommissioned ships that were used by **prison** officials as floating prisons. Popular in England in the 18th and 19th centuries, hulks were useful because they were incapable of making trips and sat at anchor in a harbor. Initially, in 1776, members of the British Parliament authorized the use of hulks for a period of two years. However, they were kept in service until the final expiry of the act in 1857. Decommissioned naval ships were considered for use to house prisoners in the United States, specifically for New York and New Jersey, in the 1990s because of overcrowding.

HUMAN RIGHTS. The underlying rights, such as life, equality, and freedom from slavery and **torture**, that are presumed to apply to everyone. This concept was codified in the Universal Declaration of Human Rights and agreed upon in 1948 by the United Nations General Assembly due to heinous acts of extreme cruelty that occurred during World War II. Human rights were conveyed in legal terms within the U.S. Declaration of Independence in 1776 and the U.S. **Bill of Rights**, which was added to the U.S. Constitution in 1789. Convicts have been determined to retain these rights. Refer to appendix 1, "The Bill of Rights."

HUNG JURY. The name given to a **jury** that is deadlocked and cannot render a verdict in a criminal matter after extensive deliberation. Once the judge has granted a hung jury, the prosecutor in the presence of a different jury can retry the case. The **U.S. Supreme Court** held, in *United States v. Perez*, 22 U.S. 9 Wheat. 579 (1824), that a retrial is permitted in the event of a hung jury. *See also* TRIAL.

I

IDENTITY THEFT. The unlawful and fraudulent assumption of another person's identity, usually for financial gain. Identity theft dates to the 1950s and was initially a physical crime when criminals murdered their victims and stole their identity. It thrived with the distribution of credit cards in the 1960s. The means of acquisition have changed since the advent of the internet. There are two forms of identity theft: true name and account takeover. True name is when a victim's personal information is unknowingly used to open new accounts. An account takeover occurs when an imposter accesses an unsuspecting victim's existing accounts and changes the mailing address to facilitate the fraud unbeknownst to the victim. In early U.S. history, identity theft was also used for voter fraud, that is, casting a vote under the name of someone else. *See also* CYBERCRIME; CYBERSECURITY; MURDER.

ILLEGAL SEARCH AND SEIZURE. Illegal **search and seizure** is when any law enforcement officer intentionally circumvents the **Fourth Amendment** and conducts a **warrantless search** (a search that lacks the sanction of the court through the issuance of a **warrant**) of a person, home, vehicle, or any other property and retrieves **evidence**. ***Mapp v. Ohio*, 367 U.S. 643 (1961)**, is a landmark case that disallows evidence seized without proper consent or warrant from a state or federal court. The issue of what constitutes an allowable search has been addressed in several cases before the **U.S. Supreme Court**. Evidence obtained through illegal searches is referred to as the "**fruit of the poisonous tree**," first used in the *Silverthorne Lumber Co. v. United States*, 251 U.S. 385 (1920). *See also KATZ V. U.S.*, 389 U.S. 347 (1967); *KER V. CALIFORNIA*, 374 U.S. 23 (1967); *KYLLO V. U.S.*, 533 U.S. 27 (2001).

IMPRESSION EVIDENCE. A process of compacting numerous objects together, which allows the transference of characteristics of one object onto another. Examples of impression **evidence** are tire tracks, bite marks, shoe prints, and tool markings. The impression is created to produce evidence used by crime scene investigators to connect suspects to a crime scene. In

1910, the theory of impression evidence, called the Edmond Locard theory, was first presented by criminologist Edmond Locard, who found that "every contact leaves its trace." *See also* EVIDENCE; FORENSICS; LOCARD'S EXCHANGE PRINCIPLE.

INCEST. Incest is sexual activity that occurs between individuals of the same family. It is legal in some societies and cultures and frowned upon and considered taboo in others. The act of incest was made punishable by death in England in 1605. In other cultures, it has been encouraged and even insisted upon. The prohibited acts and relationships of incest in the United States vary from state to state. Some infractions are punishable with a **fine** and/or imprisonment. Rhode Island is the only state where incest has not been ascribed any **punishment**.

INCITEMENT TO IMMINENT LAWLESS ACTION. A standard of law that was based on the **U.S. Supreme Court** case ***Brandenburg v. Ohio*, 395 U.S. 444 (1969)**. This case established the limits of free speech under the **First Amendment**. Accordingly, no protection is provided if the speaker intends to advocate or incite an imminent or likely violation of the law. Speech that directs another to commit **violence** loses First Amendment protection as described in ***Feiner v. New York*, 340 U.S. 315 (1915)**. *See also* BAD TENDENCY TEST; KU KLUX KLAN (KKK).

INCOME TAX EVASION. The intentional and illegal act of a person, corporation, or organization to fail to pay their official tax liability or misrepresenting the facts of their financial affairs. Laws pertaining to the regulation of taxes were codified under the *Revised Statutes of the United States* in 1874. After a few revisions to the Internal Revenue Code of 1939 and the Internal Revenue Code of 1954, the tax codes were recodified under the Tax Reform Act of 1986. Violations for tax evasion are punishable by up to five years' imprisonment and a **fine** of up to $250,000 for individuals and up to $500 million for a corporation. **Alphonse Capone** was sentenced to **Alcatraz** for **income tax evasion**.

INCOMPETENT. Having the inability to perform a skill or complete a task. This term is often used to describe someone who is incapable of taking care of his or her personal affairs based on a mental deficiency. The **U.S. Supreme Court** addressed the issue of incompetence in defendants in ***Ford v. Wainwright*, 477 U.S. 399 (1986)**, and held that mentally incompetent people can avoid prosecution if found to be incapable of standing **trial**.

INCOMPLETE CRIMES. Inchoate crimes are another expression for incomplete crimes. These crimes are those that have been attempted, but the necessary goals of the crimes were never achieved. The **U.S. Supreme Court**'s first case regarding incomplete crimes was *Rex v. Scofield*, Cald. 397 (1784). In this case, the defendant was charged with a misdemeanor for attempting to burn down a house. The holding is that while the crime may be incomplete, the intention may be criminal.

INCRIMINATING EVIDENCE. Evidence which suggests or can prove that an individual is guilty of committing a crime or may have been involved in the commission of a crime. The most incriminating types of evidence are **DNA**, **fingerprints**, hair, blood, skin, written documents, semen, **witness** testimony, **ballistics**, photographs, and videotapes. The **U.S. Supreme Court** in ***Mapp v. Ohio*, 367 U.S. 643 (1961)**, held that incriminating evidence seized illegally is inadmissible in a criminal **trial** and is a violation of the **Fourteenth Amendment**. *See also* FORENSICS.

INDEFINITE SENTENCE. A term of incarceration that has no definite set period but instead has a range of time. The rationale for **indeterminate sentencing** is an expectation that a prisoner is rehabilitated while incarcerated. An initial application of the usage of this form of imprisonment occurred in New York in 1817 and was central to **Zebulon Brockway**'s process at **Elmira Reformatory**. *See also* DETERMINATE SENTENCING.

INDETERMINATE SENTENCING. An unspecified time of incarceration that a prisoner will serve for carrying out a crime, which has no specific end date. A **parole** board resolves the specific date of release for prisoners. The premise for indeterminate sentencing was founded in 1870 under a program sponsored by the National Congress of the American **Prison** Association.

INDEX CRIMES. Distinct classifications of offenses that are outlined by the **FBI** in the **Uniform Crime Report**. Those offenses include **motor vehicle theft**, burglary, larceny, robbery, aggravated **assault**, forcible rape, **murder**, **arson**, and nonnegligent **manslaughter**. Arson was added to the crime index with the passage of the Anti-Arson Act of 1982. Also referred to as Part I Offenses, index crimes were first used in 1960.

INDICTABLE OFFENSE. A higher-order violation (crime) of a federal or state law, usually a felony, which requires a grand **jury** to determine that the **evidence** is sufficient to warrant charging and thus prosecuting. Indictable offenses are legislated at the state and federal levels and often require a term in jail, imprisonment, or prosecution as a **capital offense**. *See also* OBSTRUCTION OF JUSTICE.

INDIGENT. An indigent is a poor person who needs assistance. In 1881, New York state law approved the use of lawyers, appointed by the courts, to assist indigent criminals. The **U.S. Supreme Court**, in ***Gideon v. Wainwright*, 372 U.S. 335 (1963)**, unanimously held that the Sixth Amendment stipulates that indigent defendants are required to be provided counsel even though they are incapable of paying. The defense of indigents is further grounded in the **Fourteenth Amendment** for equal protection. The Gideon case resulted in his representation by **Abe Fortas** before the U.S. Supreme Court. *See also BETTS V. BRADY*, 316 U.S. 455 (1942); *FURMAN V. GEORGIA*, 408 U.S. 238 (1972).

INDIVIDUAL DETERRENCE. Punishment directed toward the individual offender, which attempts to discourage them from further criminal behavior. Theories concerning **deterrence** and punishment are attributed to classical philosophers **Jeremy Bentham**, Thomas Hobbes, and **Cesare Beccaria** during the early 1700s and 1800s. The concept of deterrence remains a goal of sentencing. *See also* RECIDIVISM; SPECIFIC DETERRENCE.

INDUSTRIAL ESPIONAGE. Intentional spying is conducted to obtain secrets regarding business practices, industrial secrets such as formulas, or other information from a rival company to gain an economic advantage. One of the earliest documented occurrences of industrial espionage happened in China in 1712 when secrets about the manufacturing of Chinese porcelain were exposed by the French Jesuit priest Father Francis Xavier d'Entrecolles. The U.S. Industrial Espionage Act of 1996 criminalizes acts of industrial espionage. *See also* ECONOMIC ESPIONAGE.

INEBRIATE. The intoxicated nature of a person who has consumed an excessive amount of an alcoholic beverage. In the late 19th century, the courts, believing that alcoholism was a medical condition, committed alcoholics to mental health facilities. The first inebriate **asylum** was opened in 1868 in New York State to treat alcoholics but closed in 1875. *Powell v. Texas*, 392 U.S. 514 (1968), held that the criminalization of public intoxication did not represent **cruel and unusual punishment** and thus was not a violation of the **Eighth Amendment**.

INEFFECTIVE ASSISTANCE OF COUNSEL. An accusation against an attorney that their performance on behalf of a client in a criminal matter violates the Sixth Amendment guarantee for assistance of counsel. The **U.S. Supreme Court** in *Strickland v. Washington*, 466 U.S. 668 (1984), upheld this U.S. constitutional right, and in this case the defendant's representation by counsel was ineffective for failure to inform him about the direct consequence of a criminal conviction. This is known as the Strickland standard. *See also* COLLATERAL CONSEQUENCES.

IN FORMA PAUPERIS. Someone who doesn't have the funds to pursue a lawsuit or pay for their defense in a criminal case may file to proceed in forma pauperis. When the courts afford a defendant this status, they are appointed counsel without monetary cost. The ability to proceed in a criminal case has a foundation in the Criminal Justice Act of 1964, 18 U.S.C. § 3006A. Most of the awardees are prisoners. In forma pauperis was granted in ***Gideon v. Wainwright*, 372 U.S. 335 (1963)**, which enabled Gideon to be represented by **Abe Fortas** before the **U.S. Supreme Court**. *See also* INDIGENT.

INFORMED CONSENT. A person alleged to have committed a crime cannot give up their right to **Fifth Amendment** protection unless they have been properly informed by Miranda warnings and are capable of understanding the meaning of informed consent. The **U.S. Supreme Court** in ***Brown v. Mississippi*, 297 U.S. 278 (1936)**, held that an involuntary confession taken by the **police** violates the **Fourteenth Amendment**. *See also MIRANDA V. ARIZONA*, 384 U.S. 436 (1966).

INITIAL APPEARANCE. This is the first appearance of a defendant before a judge shortly after an arrest. The appearance determines whether there is **probable cause** for the arrest. Defendants are afforded the right to counsel in furtherance of their Sixth Amendment right, ratified in 1791. The **U.S. Supreme Court** held in *Rothgery v. Gillespie County, Texas*, 554 U.S. 191 (2008), that a defendant had a right to counsel at the initial appearance.

INMATE. Someone who has been incarcerated and confined to a correctional institution. The term was first used in the 1500s to mean someone who lived in a rented home, but the meaning changed in the 1830s and carried the connotation of someone housed or confined with others against their will. The term *inmate* has been challenged by Ross and Richards (2003) who urge that the term *convict* be used. *Inmate* has broader usage. *See also* RICHARDS, DR. STEPHEN.

INMATE CLASSIFICATION. A system to assess the risks and dangerousness of individuals confined to a **prison** to balance the security needs of the facility. Classification designates which custody status (such as maximum, medium, or minimum) is appropriate for the **inmate** based on factors such as the length of sentence and offense and assigns the inmate to a correctional facility appropriate to the custody status. Initial inmate classification began in the 1870s and was focused on the types of offenses committed and assigned the appropriate **punishment**. However, during the 19th century, reform and rehabilitation became the model for prisons, and inmate classification changed to include treatment categories based on results from risk assessment instruments such as the Level of Service Inventory–Revised (LSI-R) regarding offender pathologies, the likelihood of reoffense, and the risk to themselves and others. *See also* EVIDENCE-BASED PRACTICES; MARTINSON, ROBERT (1927–1979).

INMATE SUBCULTURE. The behavior of prisoners that is acquired while incarcerated. It is the unwritten code and norms expected of inmates by other inmates in prison. Often referred to as an **inmate** code, this belief system ties prisoners together in developing their internal system of inmate regulations. In 1818, Sir Walter Scott first wrote about the inmate subculture in his book *The Heart of Midlothian*. Gresham Sykes (1958) elaborated on the subculture as it develops through enforcement of the rules by correctional officers. **John Irwin** (1970) emphasized that the **prison** process ensures the development and maintenance of a subculture that juxtaposes the convict and the guard through a distinct identification of patterns to be maintained. *See also* PRISONIZATION; RICHARDS, DR. STEPHEN.

INNOCENCE PROJECT. A nonprofit organization founded in 1992 at the Cardozo School of Law by famed criminal defense attorneys Barry Scheck and Peter Neufeld, who also played a prominent role in the 1994 **O. J. Simpson murder trial**, for which he was found not guilty. The Innocence Project's mission is to exonerate wrongly convicted individuals through **DNA** testing. In some cases, the investigations of the Innocence Project have affirmed the guilt of the offender. There is an Innocence Project in each state. Approximately 400 wrongly convicted persons have been exonerated after serving an average of 14 years in **prison** or on death row. *See also* EXONERATION.

INNOCENT UNTIL PROVEN GUILTY. A principle in the criminal justice system which posits that a defendant is innocent until the prosecution can prove **beyond a reasonable doubt** that the accused committed the alleged crime. The **U.S. Supreme Court** held in *Taylor v. Kentucky*, 436 U.S.

478, 98 S. Ct. 1930, 56 L. Ed. 2d 468 (1978), that judges must charge the **jury**, upon request of the defendant, with remarks made by the defendant for the jury which is in keeping with their **Fourteenth Amendment** right to a fair **trial**. In this case the victim was the only **witness** to the crime.

***IN RE GAULT*, 387 U.S. 1 (1967).** A **U.S. Supreme Court** case which held that juveniles are entitled to procedural **due process** rights under the **Fourteenth Amendment**. In this case, the defendant, at the age of 15, was charged with making lewd telephone calls and sentenced to a juvenile facility until he reached the age of majority. The court found that the defendant had been denied his due process rights, which were afforded to adults. *See also* *IN RE WINSHIP*, 397 U.S. 358 (1970).

***IN RE WINSHIP*, 397 U.S. 358 (1970).** A **U.S. Supreme Court** case which held that juveniles must be afforded **due process** rights if charged with an act that would be considered a crime if committed by an adult. This defendant was found guilty of illegally entering a locker and stealing money and found guilty due to a preponderance of the **evidence**. The **U.S. Supreme Court** justices ruled that the **Fourteenth Amendment** protects defendants against conviction unless there is proof **beyond a reasonable doubt**. With this holding, **juvenile rights** were further expanded from the ***in re Gault*, 387 U.S. 1 (1967)**, holding. *See also* JUVENILE COURT; JUVENILE DELINQUENCY.

INSANITY DEFENSE. A legal defense used by attorneys for a defendant in a criminal court case. The defendant is said to suffer from a mental health disorder and so should not be held culpable for their actions based on a preexisting mental health disease. England was the first country to address an insanity defense in 1843, when they acquitted a defendant, Daniel M'Naghten, of **murder** by reason of insanity. The M'Naghten ruling was recognized in the United States in the 1850s, and the insanity defense, referred to as the M'Naghten rule, was ultimately affirmed in *Durham v. United States*, 214 F. 2d 862 (D.C. Cir 1954). *See also* DURHAM RULE; GUILTY BUT MENTALLY ILL; HINCKLEY, JOHN (1955–); HUGHES, FRANCINE (1947–); NOT GUILTY BY REASON OF INSANITY.

INSTITUTIONALIZATION. *See* PRISONIZATION.

INTEGRATED AUTOMATED FINGERPRINT IDENTIFICATION SYSTEM FOR THE CLASSIFICATION OF FINGERPRINTS (IAFIS). A U.S. national **fingerprint** and criminal history system begun in 1999 and operated by the **FBI**. All state, local, and federal agencies voluntarily submit records. The system allows all law enforcement agencies to match fingerprints from crime scenes to names and backgrounds of those fingerprinted. Currently, it is the largest database in the world, holding approximately 55 million fingerprint records.

INTENSIVE SUPERVISION PROGRAM (ISP). A program that originated in 1983 and is widely used as an alternative to incarceration or after incarceration for offenders viewed as a risk. Offenders assigned to this program are strictly monitored (by **parole** or **probation**) in the community as a substitute for placing or keeping the offender in **prison**. ISP is a cost-saving measure for states because it eliminates the necessity of housing and feeding prisoners physically.

INTENT. Intent is the willingness to commit an action. In criminal law, it is defined as a decisive element in ascertaining if a person's acts were criminal in nature. The term, as it pertains to criminal law, is also referred to as **mens rea**. The **U.S. Supreme Court** in *Morissette v. United States*, 342 U.S. 246 (1952), addressed the concept of criminal intent. As it pertains to laws of tort, intent determines civil liability on the part of the person committing harm.

INTERMEDIATE SANCTIONS. Sanctions imposed on offenders that monitor their behavior to make them responsible for their actions. The concept of intermediate sanctions became popular in the 1980s as an alternative to incarceration and is usually a function of **probation** once imposed by the court. The courts can impose intermediate sanctions, which vary from probation to incarceration. *See also* COMMUNITY CORRECTIONS.

INTERNATIONAL ASSOCIATION OF CHIEFS OF POLICE (IACP). A nonprofit law enforcement association created in 1893 by 47 chiefs of **police** to advance the art and science of policing and to develop improved administrative techniques to assist police professionals.

INTERNET CRIME. An intentional illegal action taken by someone via the internet to deceive someone or an entity for personal gain. Internet crimes include, but are not limited to, **cyber-bullying**, bomb threats, copyright violations, credit card fraud, virus spreading, and financial extortion. One of the first notable internet crimes occurred in 1989 when the First National Bank was the victim of a $70 million computer theft crime. *See also* COPYRIGHT INFRINGEMENT; CYBERCRIME.

INTERNET PREDATOR. An individual who utilizes the internet to lure unsuspecting children for personal sexual pleasure. Internet predators search for vulnerable children on sites frequented by children to gain their trust in an attempt to meet and exploit them. News reports of internet predators surfaced in the 1990s as the internet began to be used on a large scale. The holding of *Doe v. Shurtleff*, 628 F.3d 1217 (10th Cir. 2010), was that internet predators must register their internet identifiers. In addition, the holding also concluded that this registration was neither a **First** nor a **Fourth Amendment** violation. *See also* CYBERSTALKING.

INTERRACIAL CRIME. A crime that occurs between individuals from different races. In 1958, an interracial couple was married, violating Virginia's 1924 Racial Integrity Act, which referred to interracial marriage as miscegenation. The **U.S. Supreme Court** case *Loving v. Virginia*, 388 U.S. 1 (1967), held that laws prohibiting interracial marriage were unconstitutional. Historically, interracial crime dates back to the 16th century and the Middle Passage with the forced **transportation** of Africans to the New World where they were beaten, enslaved, and murdered.

INTERROGATION. The act of questioning a suspect to gain information. Interrogations are often conducted by law enforcement or military personnel officials. The **U.S. Supreme Court** held in *Frazier v. Cupp*, 394 U.S. 731 (1969), that a **police** officer may use deceptive practices when interrogating suspects. Prior to the interrogation of a suspect, they must be read their Miranda rights. *See also MIRANDA V. ARIZONA*, 384 U.S. 436 (1966).

INTERSTATE COMPACT. An agreement between states and U.S. territories that promotes the successful transportation of supervised offenders across state lines. The authority recognizing the interstate compact was established in *Virginia v. Tennessee*, 148 U.S. 503 (1893).

INVOLUNTARY MANSLAUGHTER. The unintentional killing of someone which was a result of criminal negligence or recklessness was first described in *Commonwealth v. Welansky*, 55 N.E. 2d 902 (Mass. 1944). **Sentencing guidelines** for involuntary **manslaughter** vary from state to federal. *See also* MURDER.

IRISH SYSTEM. *See* CROFTON, SIR WALTER (1815–1897); MACONOCHIE, CAPTAIN ALEXANDER (1787–1860).

IRWIN, DR. JOHN (1929–2010). An internationally renowned criminologist whose expertise was in the field of the American **prison** system. He was a former convict who finished a semester of college while incarcerated and after being released went on to attain a bachelor's degree and doctorate. In 1967, he founded Project Rebound, a program that assists former convicts in going to college. He is the author of several books, including *The Felon* (1970) and *Prisons in Turmoil* (1980). Irwin is also a founding member of **Convict Criminology** (2003) and is considered, by that organization, to be the original convict criminologist because his work focused on convicts, their experiences inside prison, and their difficulties reemerging from prison to assume responsible positions in society. *See also* RICHARDS, DR. STEPHEN.

ISLAMIC STATE IN IRAQ AND SYRIA (ISIS). A militant extremist group that was designated a terrorist organization by the United Nations. The group formed as **Al-Qaeda** in Iraq (ISI) in 2004. They then merged with other insurgent groups in 2006. In 2013, the group changed its name to ISIS. It is also referred to as Islamic State (IS) and Islamic State in Iraq and the Levant (ISIL). ISIS's intention is to create an Islamic state by implementing sharia law. ISIS has been responsible for many terroristic attacks on the United States and involving U.S. citizens abroad. *See also* TERRORISM.

IVINS, BRUCE EDWARDS (1946–2008). A former researcher at the U.S. Army Medical Research Institute of Infectious Disease, Fort Detrick, Maryland. He was a principal suspect in the 2001 anthrax attacks due to suspicious letters sent to news agencies and elected officials. During a 2002 investigation at Fort Detrick, anthrax spores escaped highly guarded rooms and seeped into unprotected areas at the facility. In 2006, Ivins became the dominant suspect in the investigation. In 2008, he was involuntarily committed to a mental hospital for treatment of depression and suicidal ideations and later committed suicide by taking an overdose of Tylenol with codeine.

J

JACK ROLLER. A term used in the 19th and 20th centuries to describe an individual who frequented the poorer sections of metropolitan cities and intentionally preyed upon persons who were asleep or appeared under the influence of an alcoholic beverage. The assailant normally assaulted the victims and robbed them of their valuable possessions. The term is still used on the waterfronts in San Francisco, California, and Seattle, Washington. A modern crime description is of someone who commits strong-arm robbery. *See also* ASSAULT; AUTO-ETHNOGRAPHY.

JAILBREAK. The deliberate fleeing from **prison**. Among the techniques to enable escape include trickery, such as dressing as a prison guard or employee; tunneling, which is digging under the walls of the prison; and **use of force**, such as overpowering the guards through **violence**. There have been numerous documented jailbreaks. One that remains unsolved is the **Alcatraz** prison break in 1962. Three prisoners, Clarence Anglin, John Anglin, and Frank Morris, utilized trickery and concocted life-size body dummies and placed them in their bunks to make it appear that they were in them. They then used a utility cord to escape and fled on an improvised raft. Rumors have placed two of the escapees in Brazil, but there is no **evidence** of their successful escape and the investigation remains open. *See also* SUTTON, WILLIE (1901–1980).

JAILHOUSE LAWYER. A term that refers to and/or describes an **inmate** who has generally never attended law school but assists other inmates with their legal issues. The **U.S. Supreme Court** held that while they are not lawyers, they are permitted to assist other inmates in filing petitions for postconviction relief and other legal writs providing that the state hasn't provided an adequate alternative. The *Jailhouse Lawyers Handbook* (now in its fifth edition) was prepared by the National Lawyers Guild to assist inmates with court filings to overcome mistreatment and poor conditions in jails and prisons. One of the most infamous jailhouse lawyers was Jerome Rosenberg. Rosenberg, while serving life in **prison** for killing two **police**

officers, amassed three law degrees and was referred to as "Jerry the Jew." He went on to argue a case in a New York courtroom without being a member of the **American Bar Association**.

***J.D.B. V. NORTH CAROLINA*, 564 U.S. 261 (2011).** A **U.S. Supreme Court** case that challenged the age of consent for individuals who are questioned by the **police**. The defendant, in this instance, was a 13-year-old male who was interviewed by the police regarding his involvement in two robberies. The defendant confessed and was later convicted. An attorney representing the defendant attempted to have the confession suppressed, based on the age of the accused and that he had neither been given his Miranda warning nor had an opportunity to speak to his legal guardian. The defendant's case was appealed and heard by the U.S. Supreme Court, who held that the police should have considered his age. They remanded the case back to a lower court with specific instructions to consider the age of the accused. *See also MIRANDA V. ARIZONA*, 384 U.S. 436 (1966).

JEFFREY, C. RAY (?–2007). A professor emeritus at Florida State University and criminologist who in 1971 coined the term *crime prevention through environmental design* (CPTED). CPTED was created to discourage criminal offenders by altering the physical design of a structure. Its effectiveness is meant to address a variety of communities and utilizes bushes and barriers to dissuade criminal activity.

JFK ASSASSINATION. John F. Kennedy, the 35th president of the United States, was assassinated while riding in a motorcade in downtown Dallas, Texas. His wife, Jacqueline; Texas governor John Connolly; and his wife, Nellie, accompanied President Kennedy, who had plans to campaign for his 1964 presidential reelection. The alleged shooter, **Lee Harvey Oswald** (1939–1963), was arrested after shooting and killing a **police** officer who spotted him walking a couple of miles away from the scene of the presidential **assassination**. Oswald was later charged with both **murders**. However, two days later, while being transported to the county jail, he was shot and killed on live television by Jack Ruby, a nightclub owner.

The assassination was the subject of conspiracy theories that divided the governmental groups that investigated it. The **Warren Commission** determined that Oswald was a lone shooter. The U.S. House Select Committee on Assassinations determined that there may have been a conspiracy and that there may have been a second shooter (that was based on an interpretation of an audio recording); however, subsequent investigation denied the reliability of the audio recordings to substantiate a second shooter. Declassified documents released in 2017 have confirmed no conspiracy and no second shooter.

JOHN ADAMS PROJECT. The project was formed in 2009 by the **American Civil Liberties Union** and the **National Association of Criminal Defense Lawyers** to assist military lawyers assigned to prisoners being detained at the **Guantanamo Bay** detention camp, which housed hundreds of men following the 9/11 tragedy and the Afghanistan War. An issue of concern was the gathering of open-sourced photos by the attorneys on behalf of their clients that were deemed classified by the U.S. government. The lawyers were ultimately cleared of any wrongdoing in 2012. Detention at Guantanamo Bay remains a contentious political issue. *See also* STANFORD PRISON EXPERIMENT.

***JOHNSON V. LOUISIANA*, 406 U.S. 356, 404 (1972).** A **U.S. Supreme Court** case that challenged whether or not a **jury** needed to reach a unanimous verdict for a conviction. The defendant was arrested in his home in 1968 for an armed robbery and subsequent second robbery without an arrest **warrant**. He pled not guilty but was convicted by a jury with a 9–3 verdict and sentenced to 35 years. The defendant appealed the decision, which was overruled by the U.S. Supreme Court in a 5–4 holding. The Court held that Louisiana's varying of the size of a jury does not violate the **Fourteenth Amendment**'s equal protection clause.

***JOHNSON V. ZERBST*, 304 U.S. 458 (1938).** A **U.S. Supreme Court** case in which the defendant, an ex-marine who was on military leave in 1934, was charged with feloniously possessing **counterfeit** money, passing it, and uttering (the placement of counterfeit money into circulation). He appeared before the court without the assistance of an attorney and was convicted. He was sent to a federal **penitentiary** and subsequently filed a **writ of habeas corpus** but was denied by the district court and the court of appeals. The U.S. Supreme Court in a 6–2 holding held that the federal courts had no right to deprive the defendant of his Sixth Amendment right to an attorney unless he legitimately and intelligently waived his rights. *See also GIDEON V. WAINWRIGHT*, 372 U.S. 335 (1963).

JOINT RESPONSIBILITY RULE. The rule is based on the premise that every person involved in a crime is legally liable even if they didn't commit the offense. The most famous instance of this rule pertains to **Charles Manson**. In 1971, the state of California convicted Manson of first-degree **murder**. While he didn't physically kill anyone, he told his coconspirators what to do and planned the crime. He was sentenced to death but had his sentence commuted to life in **prison** in 1972.

JON, GEE (1895–1924). The first person to be executed in the United States in a **gas chamber** in the state of Nevada in 1924. Gee had shot to death an elderly man as he answered his door. The first attempt to execute Gee failed, as the state tried to pump gas into his cell. The next attempt succeeded in a first-of-its-kind gas chamber, which was built in the **prison**'s butcher shop. The controversial nature of the gas (designed to kill rodents) raised issues of liability, the resignation of guards, and the evacuation of the viewing area when the gas leaked in. Gee continued to move for approximately six minutes after the gas entered the chamber. *See also* CAPITAL PUNISHMENT; EXECUTION.

JONES, JIM (1931–1978). An American, born in Crete, Indiana. In 1956, he founded and became the cult leader of the Peoples Temple, an evangelist group headquartered in Indiana, which helped needy people. During the 1950s and 1960s, his charismatic reputation garnered him a large following, and he moved his organization to California. In 1971, he was accused by a news journalist and former cult members of illegally transferring funds to his personal accounts. Jones, along with hundreds of followers, moved to Jonestown, Guyana. He set up a commune and confiscated passports and money from his supporters. He blackmailed, beat, and threatened to kill his followers to control them. In 1978, relatives of the commune members along with Representative Leo Ryan of California traveled to Guyana to look into allegations of abuse at the hands of Jones. As Ryan attempted to leave with 14 defectors, Jones ordered his assassination. Ryan and three newsmen were killed, while others escaped. Four days later, concerned that the escapees would bring law enforcement authorities, Jones orchestrated the mass suicide and murder of 913 followers, of which 276 were children. This would become known as the Jonestown massacre, the second-greatest mass killing prior to the 11 September 2001 terrorist attack. The victims drank a grape-flavored drink filled with cyanide and valium from which they died within five minutes. Afterward, Jones died of head trauma from a gunshot wound. There is no definitive answer to determine whether the wound was self-inflicted. *See also* MASS MURDER.

JUDD, WINNIE RUTH (1905–1998). Born in Oxford, Indiana, in 1931, she was employed as a medical secretary when she was accused of killing two friends who had been in love with Jack Halloran, a prominent businessman. Judd was captured when she attempted to transfer the dismembered bodies of her friends, in luggage and trunks, on a train from Phoenix, Arizona, to Los Angeles, California. In 1932, she was found guilty of first-degree **murder** and sentenced to death but was later found to be mentally **incompetent**. In 1933, after a repeal of her **capital punishment**, she was committed to Arizona State Hospital. Between 1933 and 1963, she escaped on six different occasions. During her last escape, she remained at large for six years before being recaptured in 1969. She was paroled in 1971 and died in 1998. The Judd case has raised issues about the use of the **death penalty**. *See also* PAROLE.

JUDICIAL DISCRETION. A feature within the judiciary that allows judges to make legal decisions based on their discretion and provides them freedom from having to base decisions solely on precedent. John Winthrop, an English Puritan lawyer, wrote the first documented discourse regarding judicial discretion in the early 1600s. Since the 1970s, there has been an effort to limit discretion through mandatory sentencing and to provide more balanced sentencing through the use of **sentencing guidelines**.

JUDICIAL IMMUNITY. A protection afforded to judges and other court officers to absolve them from civil action based on acts they committed under the scope of their professional title. In *Stump v. Sparkman*, 435 U.S. 349 (1978), the courts reinforced a similar position taken in *Bradley v. Fisher*, 80 U.S. 335 (1871). In the case of *Stump v. Sparkman*, the judge allowed the sterilization of a minor. While the decision is controversial, the judge remains protected from civil action.

JUKES FAMILY. A pseudonym for a family studied to determine if genetics played any role in criminality. In the late 19th century and early 20th century, several studies were conducted on families that were known to have family members who were criminals, paupers, and vagrants. The researchers wanted to better understand feeblemindedness and low intelligence to support the advocacy of the eugenics movement. The case was reported by Richard Dugdale (1877).

JURY. A group of individuals called jurors (normally 12) chosen and sworn to provide a verdict of guilty or not guilty in either a civil or criminal case. The right to a **trial** by jury is incorporated in the **Fifth**, Sixth, and Seventh **Amendments** to the U.S. Constitution. The first grand jury in the United States took place in Massachusetts in 1635 and decided cases of **wife beating**, **murder**, and robbery. The establishment of the jury system in the United States was influenced by English common law. *See also JOHNSON V. LOUISIANA*, 406 U.S. 356, 404 (1972).

JURY DUTY. A civic responsibility performed by citizens of the United States, which involves participating in the criminal justice system by appearing before the court to be on a panel to assess the deeds of another citizen.

Juries derived their structure from the Assize of Clarendon in 1166, which established the model for modern-day juries. In 1787, the U.S. Constitution's Sixth Amendment protected the rights to a **jury** trial in a criminal matter. Jury duty is regarded as a condition of citizenship and has been upheld by the **U.S. Supreme Court** (*Butler v. Perry*, 240 U.S. 328 (1916). However, exclusion or excusal from jury duty may be granted when an individual asserts a conscientious objection such as for religious purposes.

JURY INSTRUCTIONS. The set of rules given to jurors to use as a guide for determining the outcome of a civil or criminal **trial**. They are presented at the conclusion of closing arguments to assist jurors in their deliberations. **Jury** instructions are thought to have originated in the 13th century because juries began to hear cases, and it is believed that they had been instructed by judges. However, in 1938, the **American Bar Association**, after expressing concerns regarding trial practice, adopted a standard for jury instruction.

JURY NULLIFICATION. The right of a **jury** to acquit a defendant who is technically guilty of a crime when, contrary to a judge's instructions, they do not believe that the defendant should be punished. The history of jury nullification is rooted in the British legal system dating back to 1670 whereby a jury acquitted Quakers for violating laws regarding religious assembly. The **Fourteenth Amendment** protects the rights of citizens to assemble for peaceable purposes.

JURY SELECTION. The process of picking a **jury** for a **trial** to reach a verdict based on the **evidence** presented. The selection starts with a pool of individuals chosen to be part of the process. The jurors are then questioned by a judge to determine if they are suitable candidates. At this point, the defense and prosecution utilize a process called **voir dire** and take turns attempting to weed out prospects who may be detrimental to their case. Each side uses peremptory challenges to complete this task. Jury selection began sometime in the 8th century and has played a central role in U.S. courtrooms starting in the colonial era. The U.S. Constitution, under a Sixth Amendment guarantee, requires that jurors be selected from a list of subjects from the community. Refer to appendix 1, "The Bill of Rights."

JURY TAMPERING. The act of intentionally attempting to influence, disrupt, or sway a **jury** through any method other than the **evidence** provided to the jury to decide the fate of a **trial**. It is a crime if anyone tries to speak with, bribe, or coerce a juror with the intent of persuading him or her to accept a position when rendering a verdict. A federal conviction of jury tampering is punishable by 10 years of incarceration and a **fine** of $25,000 on each count.

Jury tampering was attempted in cases involving both John Gotti and Jimmy Hoffa. In the 1987 Gotti case, the jury foreman contacted associates of Gotti to solicit a bribe for obtaining a not-guilty verdict. The foreman was sentenced to three years in **prison**. Hoffa was convicted of jury tampering in 1964 and sentenced to 13 years in prison. He received a **pardon** in 1971 from President Nixon in return for his resignation from the union presidency and his agreement to avoid union activities until 1980.

JUST DESERTS. *See* LOMBROSO, CESARE (1835–1909).

JUSTIFIABLE HOMICIDE. The killing of someone under conditions that are not viewed in the eyes of the criminal justice system to be criminal. It applies when a killing occurs to prevent more harm to innocent civilians and is deemed justified if it can be shown that the perpetrator posed an impending threat. The 13th century had been a time when an occasional acquittal was provided for those executing captured outlaws and other felons. However, in the 14th century judges provided more latitude for victims of heinous crimes. Justifiable **homicide** is also considered to be a condition of self-defense. The **U.S. Supreme Court** in ***District of Columbia v. Heller*, 554 U.S. 570 (2008)**, held that the possession of firearms for self-defense was a right protected by the Constitution.

JUVENILE BIND OVER. A term that describes the transfer of a juvenile from the **juvenile court** to the jurisdiction of an adult court for prosecution. The process of bind over had been utilized prior to the 1920s and is also referred to as a waiver and has become more prominent in the juvenile court system since the 1970s. The bind over is the recognition that the offense has a sufficiently serious nature and that more severe consequences are warranted than would be handed down in the juvenile court. There are three states—New York, Nebraska, and New Mexico—that don't provide the judicial waiver. Illinois in 1903 was the first state that began transferring juveniles to adult courts in limited cases.

JUVENILE COURT. A court created to address issues specifically for youth under the age of 18 years. The court was first established in 1890 in Illinois. Unlike adult courts, juvenile courts do not utilize the adversarial system. The goal is to involve parents or other entities of the juvenile justice system to rehabilitate the juvenile. The juvenile court does not retain jurisdiction if the minor has been charged as an adult. *See also* JUVENILE BIND OVER; *PARENS PATRIAE*.

JUVENILE DELINQUENCY. The participation of youth, under the age of 18, in illegal behavior that is deemed antisocial and a violation of law or **status offenses**. Several theorists, dating back to the 1940s, have tried to explain why juvenile delinquency occurs. Their main focus centers on external social control and internalized social values. *See also* FOCAL CONCERNS THEORY; GAULT, GERALD (1949–); GLUECK (ELEANOR, 1898–1972, AND SHELDON, 1896–1980).

JUVENILE DELINQUENCY AND YOUTH OFFENSES CONTROL ACT OF 1961. Federal legislation signed into law by President John F. Kennedy that allowed the federal government to become active partners assisting local and state authorities in combating **juvenile delinquency**. The law established federal grants totaling $10 million to be administered by the secretary of health, education, and welfare over a three-year period for training and developing techniques for the prevention of youth offenses.

JUVENILE DELINQUENT. A minor between the ages of 10 and 18 who has committed an infraction of the law, commonly referred to as a delinquent act. In 1961, the **Juvenile Delinquency and Youth Offenses Control Act** was enacted to specifically address the needs of juvenile delinquents. This act was subsequently replaced by the **Juvenile Justice and Delinquency Prevention Act of 1974**. *See also* YOUTHFUL OFFENDER.

JUVENILE DETENTION. A short-term secured center solely utilized to house youth 18 years old and younger while they await either a court hearing or being placed in a facility or program. Many centers provide rehabilitation for the juveniles while they are in custody. The United States began using juvenile detention centers in the 19th century.

JUVENILE HOMICIDE. A legal category that applies solely to juveniles who have committed **murder**. Documented **evidence** of youths who have committed **homicide** in the United States dates back to 1874 with Jesse Pomeroy, age 14, who killed a 4-year-old boy and a 10-year-old girl in Boston, Massachusetts.

JUVENILE JUSTICE AND DELINQUENCY PREVENTION ACT OF 1974. The act was created to help prevent juveniles from committing delinquent acts and to deinstitutionalize status offenders (offenses such as drinking under age, which do not apply to adults) by forbidding them to be detained in detention centers or adult jails. Among the initiatives funded by the act was the Juvenile Mentoring Program for disadvantaged youth. Grants were for a three-year period. *See also* STATUS OFFENSES.

JUVENILE OFFENDER. A juvenile offender, also referred to as a **juvenile delinquent**, is under the age of 18 and has committed a crime that is not punishable by death or life incarceration. The first laws concerning juvenile offenders were documented in the 14th century. A juvenile offender is further defined by the creation of the **juvenile court** by the Illinois Juvenile Court Act of 1899 in Chicago. The distinction between juvenile and adult offenders requires that juveniles be maintained separately from adult offenders. The act recognized that juveniles should not be treated as criminals or as adults and led to the establishment of the juvenile justice system as separate from adult criminal justice. *See also* JUVENILE DELINQUENCY; STATUS OFFENSES.

JUVENILE RIGHTS. The rights afforded to juveniles via the judicial system. The change in how juveniles were adjudicated within the courts began in the early 1900s, with Progressive Reformers establishing the **juvenile court** with the Illinois Juvenile Court Act of 1899 in Cook County, Chicago. Juveniles were given more rights ***in re Gault*, 387 U.S. 1 (1967)**. *See also* JUVENILE OFFENDER.

JUVENILE (WAIVER) TRANSFER. *See* JUVENILE BIND OVER.

K

K-9. A common expression for a **police** dog. Dogs have been associated with law enforcement since the Middle Ages, when they accompanied night watchmen. A variety of breeds have been selected for specialized tasks, including a bloodhound to track down **Jack the Ripper** in the 1880s. Many modern police departments have developed K-9 units to assist in the search for drugs and explosives, **evidence** from crime scenes, protection of police, riot control, and searching for lost persons or **cadavers**. Causing harm to a police dog is a felony. Many modern police departments have developed K-9 units. The use of K-9s has been reviewed by the **U.S. Supreme Court**, including the following: in *United States v. Place*, 462 U.S. 696 (1983), the court held that a dog sniffing was not considered a search or a violation of the **Fourth Amendment**. This was further refined in *United States v. Sharp*, No. 10-6127 (6th Cir. 2012), which held that if a K-9 enters a car, then it is a search and must abide by the circumstances that make a search appropriate according to the Fourth Amendment. *See also* PROBABLE CAUSE; SEARCH AND SEIZURE; WARRANT.

KACZYNSKI, THEODORE (1942–). A **serial killer** referred to as the **Unabomber** because of what has been called the Unabomber Manifesto, *Industrial Society and Its Future*. The publication of the manifesto by the **FBI** resulted in his brother and sister-in-law identifying him to the FBI. He is serving a life-without-**parole** sentence at the federal **supermax prison**, ADX Florence, Colorado. He committed acts of **domestic terrorism** employing a variety of homemade mail bombs. He killed three people and injured 23 more between 1978 and 1995. Later, it was discovered that Kaczynski, while an undergraduate at Harvard University, had been a subject in ethically questionable experiments conducted by prominent psychologist Henry A. Murray. He holds a Ph.D. in mathematics from the University of Michigan.

KANKA, MEGAN (1986–1994). *See* MEGAN'S LAW.

KANSAS CITY MASSACRE. Sometimes referred to as the Union Station massacre of 17 June 1933. This was a **gang murder** of two **FBI** agents and two **police** officers during their effort to return **gangster** Frank "Jelly" Nash to **USP Leavenworth** after an escape. The resulting FBI investigation implicated Charles "Pretty Boy" Floyd in the planning and shooting. There are disputed accounts of whether Floyd was or was not involved. *See also* GANG; MURDER INC.

KANSAS CITY PREVENTIVE PATROL EXPERIMENT. The experiment was conducted between 1972 and 1973 and was the first to test the validity of **patrol** as it affects crime and feelings of safety by the community. The findings concluded that citizens did not notice increases or decreases in patrol, and they noted little or no effect on rates and types of crimes. The result was that patrol resources could be deployed differently without risk to public safety.

***KANSAS V. HENDRICKS*, 521 U.S. 346 (1997).** The **U.S. Supreme Court** upheld a state court decision (the 1994 Kansas Sexually Violent Predator Act) in a civil **trial**, which allowed confinement (a **civil commitment**) after a **prison** sentence is served when there is a likelihood that the offender will recommit crime. This is not confinement that is a sentence or part of a sentence. In this case, the court is upholding the right of a state to protect society from someone already convicted as an offender from offending again. The offender in this case had committed an act of sexual violence (pedophilia). An appeal of this decision by Hendricks challenged the decision under the following constitutional provisions: **double jeopardy**, **due process**, and **ex post facto**. The appeal was denied, affirming the right of states to protect themselves from those deemed to pose a threat to public health and safety. Similar statutes exist in most states. *See also* FIFTH AMENDMENT.

***KANSAS V. MARSH*, 548 U.S. 163 (2006).** The **U.S. Supreme Court** held that when **aggravating** and mitigating circumstances have equal value, the **death sentence** is permissible. Justice Clarence Thomas wrote the majority opinion saying that this is not a circumstance of a tie, or to put it another way, that this did not represent indecision. The minority opinion wrote differently, suggesting that equal circumstances do represent a tie and that a sentence of death is not warranted since the **Eighth Amendment** prohibits death sentences when there is doubt. The importance of this holding is that the use of aggravating and mitigating circumstances in the penalty phase of a capital case is different in individual state statutes, meaning that each state by statute specifies how aggravating and mitigating circumstances impact on the finding of death or other sentence for a defendant.

KARPIS, ALVIN (CREEPY) (1907–1979). Karpis was nicknamed Creepy or Creepy Karpis because of his evil smile. He was infamous for bank robbery and had the distinction of being the last of the four persons listed as **Public Enemy** No. 1 by the **FBI**. Director **J. Edgar Hoover** made a personal point of being present at his capture. Karpis served more time (26 years) at **Alcatraz** than any other convict sent to the island **prison**. Following the closure of Alcatraz, he was transferred to McNeil Island Prison, Washington, and was paroled after 33 years. Karpis was deported to Canada and died in Spain. He was a leader of the **Barker-Karpis gang**. He was a career criminal in and out of jails and prisons from 19 years of age. *See also* PAROLE.

KATZ, JACK (1927–). A sociologist best known for his second book, *Seductions of Crime: Moral and Sensual Attractions in Doing Evil* (1988), now regarded as a seminal work on the role of emotions in crime and in cultural **criminology**. Katz's book approached the nature of crime as a phenomenological teasing out ethnographically the personal and political in the visceral lived experiences of offenders themselves. Scholars look to this work as part of a wave in criminology that returned theory to symbolic interactionism. Memorable chapters include "Doing Stickup" and "Ways of the Badass."

***KATZ V. U.S.*, 389 U.S. 347 (1967).** The **U.S. Supreme Court** holding that expanded the interpretation of the **Fourth Amendment** clause of unreasonable **search and seizure**. The issue in this case was privacy when making a phone call from a phone booth. Paying the toll and shutting the door should ensure privacy and thus protection from electronic eavesdropping when there is no **warrant** and such eavesdropping would therefore be a violation of the Fourth Amendment. The Fourth Amendment was originally intended to protect privacy in the home. However, the many reviews by the U.S. Supreme Court have both refined this meaning and expanded protections beyond the home.

KEATING, CHARLES (1923–2014). The primary figure in the Savings and Loan scandal of the 1980s, Keating was sentenced to a four-year **prison** term for conspiracy, fraud, and racketeering. The sentence was overturned, and he pled guilty to lesser charges of bankruptcy and wire fraud and was sentenced to time served. The scandal cost the federal government more than $3 billion and left bank customers holding worthless bonds. Bank fraud occurs frequently, and other scandals have included such practices as the

2008 **Bernard Madoff** Ponzi scheme in which he paid investors with money from new investors; the 2009 Galleon Group hedge fund, which relied on insider trading for its massive gains; 2010, when several banks engaged in robo-signing to force foreclosures; the 2009 Wells Fargo Bank settlement for discriminating against black and Hispanic borrowers; and the 2013 JPMorgan Chase settlement of $970 million in what was called the "London Whale" trading scandal. *See also* RACKETEER INFLUENCED CORRUPT ORGANIZATION (RICO).

KEFAUVER COMMITTEE. A special committee of the U.S. Senate created to investigate **organized crime** and its influence across state borders, especially as it affected interstate commerce. The committee operated between 1950 and 1951 and was named after its chair senator Estes Kefauver.

KELLY, GEORGE (1895–1954). Nicknamed "Machine Gun" because of his favorite weapon—a Thompson submachine gun—Kelly was born George Barnes and changed his name to avoid contact with the **police** and achieved notoriety as a bootlegger and armed robber but was captured and sentenced to life in **prison** for **kidnapping**. He died at **USP Leavenworth** in 1954. Some notable historical features include that Kelly was the first major arrest and crime solved by the **FBI** as revamped by (then FBI director) **J. Edgar Hoover**. Kelly's 1933 **trial** for kidnapping was the first in which cameras were permitted in the courtroom, and it was the first application of the "Little" Lindbergh Law because the victim had been taken across state lines. *See also* BOOTLEGGING; LINDBERGH KIDNAPPING, "THE CRIME OF THE CENTURY".

KEMMLER, WILLIAM (1860–1890). Convicted of murdering Matilda Ziegler with an axe, he was the first person to be executed by electrocution on 6 August 1890 at **Auburn Prison**. The first application of 700 volts of electricity was unsuccessful, and a second charge of 1,030 volts was applied for two minutes to complete the **execution**. *See also* CAPITAL PUNISHMENT; DEATH PENALTY; MURDER.

***KENNEDY V. LOUISIANA*, 554 U.S. 407 (2008).** A **U.S. Supreme Court** holding that **cruel and unusual punishment**, as described in the **Eighth Amendment**, was insufficient for prohibiting the **death penalty** for child rape that did not involve the death of the child. The Court examined national consensus in this matter and found that it was lacking; only six states advocated for death sentences for rape. The last **execution** for rape was carried out in 1964 due to disproportionality (Tenth Amendment); that is, rape by itself is not equal to death. However, the court did not rule against, that is, left open the idea of, a death sentence for drug lords. Drug lords were viewed as committing crimes against the state, which include the crimes of **terrorism**, **treason**, and **espionage**. *See also* CAPITAL PUNISHMENT; PROPORTIONALITY.

***KENT V. UNITED STATES*, 383 U.S. 541 (1966).** The **U.S. Supreme Court** holding was that a waiver to adult court was a violation of the **Juvenile Court** Act because the defendant was denied a hearing, an investigation, counsel, or access to his records. In addition, the juvenile court did not specify a reason for the waiver. At the time of the holding, Kent was 21 years of age, and the juvenile court would lose jurisdiction; thus the conviction was vacated. *See also* JUVENILE JUSTICE AND DELINQUENCY PREVENTION ACT OF 1974.

***KER V. CALIFORNIA*, 374 U.S. 23 (1967).** A case of criminal procedure in which the **U.S. Supreme Court** held that the prosecution could not use **evidence** obtained during an illegal search in state and federal courts. This decision provided further clarification of the standards of reasonableness for **warrantless searches**. The ***Mapp v. Ohio*, 367 U.S. 643 (1961)**, decision two years earlier had established that evidence obtained during an illegal search would be inadmissible. This is a protection guaranteed by the **Fourth Amendment** and the **Fourteenth Amendment** of the U.S. Constitution. *See also* SEARCH AND SEIZURE; WARRANT.

KERNER COMMISSION. Also referred to as the National Advisory Commission on Civil Disorders, it was created by President Lyndon Johnson on 28 July 1967 to investigate the race riots of 1967. Illinois governor Otto Kerner chaired the 11-member commission, which was expected to provide recommendations based on answers to three questions: What happened? Why did it happen? What can be done to prevent it from happening again? Ironically, the 1964 **Civil Rights** Act had been passed with support from President Johnson and without input from the Kerner Commission. The Kerner Report was made public in 1968, and one month later Martin Luther King Jr. was assassinated, which was the impetus for riots across the United States.

KEVORKIAN, JACK (1928–2011). Kevorkian was a public advocate for **euthanasia** and was popularized in the media as "Dr. Death" for his more than 100 physician-assisted suicides. He was convicted in 1999 of second-degree **murder** for his participation in euthanasia and received an 11–25-year **prison** sentence. He stated, "Dying is not a crime." His 2007 release from prison was contingent on his agreement not to participate in, provide guidance for, or endorse euthanasia. Euthanasia is only legal in California, Colorado, Oregon, Vermont, Washington State, and Washington, D.C. Legislation is pending in other states for its approval.

KIDNAPPING. The illegal taking of a person against their will. Kidnapping occurs in cases of child abductions during custody disputes, holding someone for **ransom**, or as a factor in another crime. The Federal Kidnapping Act was passed after the infamous 1932 New Jersey Lindbergh kidnapping case and authorized the **FBI** to investigate kidnappings that cross state lines. *See also* KELLY, GEORGE (1895–1954); LINDBERGH KIDNAPPING, "THE CRIME OF THE CENTURY".

KING, RODNEY (1965–2012). The infamous 1992 case of the videotaped beating of King by the Los Angeles **Police** while other police stood by and watched. Four officers were charged with **excessive force** and **assault** with a deadly weapon and acquitted. A federal **civil rights** case resulted in the indictment of the same four police officers. Two were again acquitted, and two were sentenced to **prison**. The case became the focal point of riots in Los Angeles requiring the National Guard to restore order. Fifty-three deaths were associated with the riots and more than 2,000 were injured. *See also* DEADLY FORCE; USE OF FORCE.

KLAAS, POLLY HANNAH (1981–1993). A 12-year-old **kidnapping/murder** victim who was the subject of a massive search involving more than 4,000 persons and was the subject of *20/20* and ***America's Most Wanted*** TV shows. An outcome of the case was the creation of the Polly Klaas Foundation (a 501[c][3] charity) in 1993 to prevent crimes against children, recover missing children, and lobby Congress for legislation to sustain these efforts. Amber Alerts and training to prevent abductions were created from these efforts. *See also* AMERICA'S MISSING: BROADCAST EMERGENCY RESPONSE (AMBER) ALERT.

KLANWATCH PROJECT. The project was begun in 1981 by the **Southern Poverty Law Center (SPLC)**, Montgomery, Alabama, to monitor the Klan, hate groups, independent militias, the Patriot Movement, and other extremist groups. The Klanwatch Project was renamed the SPLC Intelligence Project in 1998 as its efforts expanded to cover the radical right. *See also* KU KLUX KLAN (KKK).

KLEBOLD, DYLAN (1981–1999). *See* COLUMBINE MASSACRE.

***KLOPFER V. NORTH CAROLINA*, 386 U.S. 213 (1967).** After a mistrial, the prosecution sought **nolle prosequi**, which would allow prosecution at the discretion of the prosecutor, although the defendant would not be held in custody. The court held that this was a violation of the Sixth and **Fourteenth Amendments**, specifically the denial of a **speedy trial**.

KNAPP COMMISSION. *See* POLICE CORRUPTION; SERPICO, FRANK (1936–); WHISTLE-BLOWER.

KNOX, AMANDA (1987–). An American student studying in Italy who was sentenced for the 2007 **murder** of a roommate. She was acquitted and returned to the United States. The prosecution attempted an unsuccessful appeal. Controversy in the case surrounded the method of **interrogation** of her boyfriend, the investigation of others who may or may not have been involved, and the analysis of **forensic evidence**, which U.S. forensic experts have suggested was not congruent with claims of her involvement. There was also the issue of **police** striking her during interrogation. In 2015, Knox was exonerated by the Italian court.

KORNHAUSER, RUTH (1926–1995). A sociologist who pioneered work on **juvenile delinquency** and advanced interest in **social disorganization theory** rather than **anomie theory**, **strain theory**, and **differential association**. Kornhauser's influence is largely responsible for a shift in perspective that focuses on crime and delinquency as it is affected by institutional controls, community groups, schools, churches, and family.

KU KLUX KLAN (KKK). The KKK was originally a social club begun in 1866 in Pulaski, Tennessee. Its intentions were to provide resistance through intimidation and **violence** to counter Reconstruction efforts to institute economic and political opportunities for blacks and to restore **white supremacy**. Many original Klan members had been Confederate soldiers, and its first "grand wizard" was former Confederate general Nathan Bedford Forrest. The KKK operates in secrecy and its members are depicted wearing white robes and hoods or masks. There have been declines in KKK activity. KKK activities include staging rallies, burning crosses, and marching in parades in protest not only against backs but also Jews, Catholics, and immigrants. The KKK is notorious for acts of violence against schools and churches and **lynchings**, often carried out in the darkness of night. While the KKK predominantly operates in the South, KKK gatherings have also taken place in northern states. The number of KKK members is unknown, but estimated total membership is near 10,000. *See also* KLANWATCH PROJECT.

***KYLLO V. U.S.*, 533 U.S. 27 (2001).** The **U.S. Supreme Court** held that the use of thermal imaging of a home was an unreasonable search without a **warrant** and was a violation of the **Fourth Amendment**. This decision has influenced reviews of the use of new technologies and their implications for constitutional rights to privacy. *See also* WARRANTLESS SEARCHES.

L

LABELING THEORY. A sociological theory that explains labeling (the description of someone or a group) as the means of controlling and identifying behavior that is deviant. The theory also proposes that it contributes to a self-fulfilling prophecy/stereotyping which, once applied, contributes to individuals living up to a label such as delinquent, and the person then acts in a delinquent or non-law-abiding manner. The influence of labels has led to attempts to change the way both juvenile and adult offenders are addressed. For example, ***Convict Criminology*** (2003) emphasizes that the label ***inmate*** or *prisoner* not be used and suggests referring to individuals as *convicts* or *nonconvicts*. *See also* IRWIN, DR. JOHN (1929–2010); RICHARDS, DR. STEPHEN.

LA COSA NOSTRA. Also known by other names, including the Sicilian **Mafia**, Cosa Nostra, Italian Mafia, and Italian mob. Cosa Nostra translates as "Our Thing" and refers to criminal organizations (**organized crime** or crime **syndicates**) in Italy and the United States. The origins date back to the late 1800s in Italy. Membership is limited to Sicilian men. Forms of crime are called rackets and include **gambling**, protection, **prostitution**, loan-sharking, bid rigging, and drugs. Characteristics of La Cosa Nostra include an organizational structure that specifies activities at each level and codes of honor, such as "**omertà**," which is the **rule of silence**. *See also* GAMBINO, CARLO (1902–1976); GALLO, JOSEPH (1929–1972); GOTTI, JOHN (1940–2002); LUCIANO, CHARLES (1897–1962).

LANSKY, MEYER (1902–1983). Lansky is an example of incomplete information regarding **organized crime**. He was born Meier Suchowlanski in Grodno, Russia. Recognized as a member of the Jewish mob, his relationship with **Charles "Lucky" Luciano** resulted in his acknowledgment as the "mob's accountant" and as a principal architect of the "**National Crime Syndicate**." Lansky is reputed to have had an extensive **gambling** territory both in and outside the United States. While Lansky was never convicted of anything other than gambling, he has the reputation of having financed organized crime figures. He also made his money in **narcotics** smuggling, extortion, **prostitution**, and labor racketeering. With this reputation comes the suspicion of personal wealth in the multimillions of dollars that has never been substantiated. Lansky had been on the **FBI**'s radar and faced several indictments. However, acquittals, overturned appeals, and declining health kept him from serving any **prison** time. He ultimately died of cancer in 1983.

LANZA, ADAM (1992–2012). *See* NEWTOWN MASSACRE.

LATENT FUNCTIONS. Latent functions were first explained by **Robert Merton** as unintended, unconscious, unforeseen, and beneficial for society. They are contrasted to both manifest functions and dysfunctions. Manifest functions are conscious, intended, and beneficial, while dysfunctions are harmful or disruptive for society. An example of latent functions was the rise of criminal activity in the 1920s because of **Prohibition**. Latent functions in schools are other than education and would include social networking, dating, teamwork, and political activism.

LATIN KINGS. The largest Hispanic criminal street **gang** (predominantly Mexican and Puerto Rican), formed in Chicago, Illinois, in 1954 with about 50,000 members in all factions. Formally referred to as the Almighty Latin King and Queen Nation, it is known by the acronyms ALKQN, ALKN, and LKN. Initially, their main desire was to protect their neighborhoods; however, they soon developed into a violent street gang. Latin Kings engage in extortion, **murder**, robbery, drug sales and distribution, and other criminal activity. The Latin Kings currently have chapters across the United States and are a primary force in the barrios in New York City. Black and gold are the colors worn by the Latin Kings. The black symbolizes death, and gold symbolizes life. *See also* CRIPS.

LAW ENFORCEMENT ASSISTANCE ADMINISTRATION (LEAA). A federal agency responsible for providing state and local law enforcement agencies with funding for research, planning, crime initiatives, and educational programs. LEAA was established in 1968 by the **Omnibus Crime Control and Safe Streets Act of 1968** and was abolished 21 April 1982. LEAA, in 1973, used federal funding to leverage **police** departments to remove the minimum height restriction, which had prevented many women from entering law enforcement.

LEAD FEDERAL AGENCY. Any agency designated by public law or precedent which prescribes that agency to proceed in an unfettered manner. This is not always clear cut, as has been seen during the **Waco siege** and the events that followed the 9/11 terrorist attacks when agencies vied for control or did not cooperate to share intelligence. There have been efforts since the 9/11 events to consolidate and more clearly specify the duties and responsibilities of state and federal agencies. The most notable change was the creation of the Department of Homeland Security. *See also* PATRIOT ACT; TERRORISM; WORLD TRADE CENTER (WTC) BOMBINGS.

LEARNING THEORY. Learning theory is also referred to as **differential association** as defined by **Edwin Sutherland** in the late 1930s. It had been proposed to explain how we acquire criminal behavior. **Social learning theory** suggests that criminal conduct is learned from peer groups by observing, modeling, and then replicating.

LEAVENWORTH, USP. USP Leavenworth, located in Leavenworth, Kansas, is the oldest federal **prison**, built in 1895 as a maximum-security prison in the **Auburn** style of construction and downgraded to medium security in 2005. It is a prison for males. Leavenworth was the "Death House" for the federal government until 1993 and utilized **hangings** until that function was transferred to USP Terre Haute (also referred to as "The Last Word"), which utilizes **lethal Injection**. Federal executions were also conducted at state prison/jail facilities in the state in which the federal crime occurred. In these cases, the method of **execution** was that designated by the state (i.e., **electrocution**, **gas chamber**, etc.). Leavenworth has been nicknamed "The Hothouse" because of the intense heat in the cellblocks. *See also* CAPITAL PUNISHMENT; FEDERAL BUREAU OF PRISONS (BOP).

LEFT REALISM. Left realism comes from the school of **critical criminology**. Carlsen (1992) describes the working class or poor as exceedingly affected by crime. That is, the solutions for crime offered by right realism emphasize law and order through the passage of repressive laws and sentences that additionally disenfranchise the affected poor, which increases the crime problem. Left realism argues that crime should be controlled through prevention and the reduction of deprivation in the working class.

LEGAL AID SOCIETY. Legal aid societies such as the one in New York City (founded in 1876 to defend German immigrants) provide legal representation for civil, criminal, and juvenile matters for **indigents**, including the homeless, welfare recipients, foster children, the elderly, and prisoners held in detention centers. They also conduct class action suits on their behalf.

LEGIS HENRICI PRIMI. These are six manuscripts written around 1115 that comprise the first legal discourse of English legal history. The treatise included laws prescribed by previous monarchs and were referred to as the laws of Henry I. It was not an official document but was a written record of medieval customs with explanations of their interpretation of such crimes as **murder**, theft, and **treason** and the penalties for them. Many of the ideas contained in these manuscripts were later codified in English law and became fundamental principles for the development of U.S. law.

LEMERT, EDWARD (1912–1996). Lemert researched drug **addiction** and its influence on individuals. Significantly, he introduced **labeling theory**. He was a symbolic interactionist. His specific contribution was the idea of secondary deviance as a coping mechanism (a social act) for society's reaction to the individual's primary deviance. That is, negative labels produce undesired consequences. Lemert's research would later influence **Howard Becker**, who would research the circumstances of labels and would write about them in *The Outsiders* (1963).

LESS-THAN-LETHAL FORCE. A term that is usually associated with less-than-lethal weapons or those that cause pain and compliance. Less-than-lethal force is to be used when lethal force is forbidden or detrimental to the achievement of other objectives. Examples of circumstances when less than lethal force would be desired include crowd/riot control and self-defense. Less-than-lethal weapons were developed for use by the military in the mid-1990s. Examples of less-than-lethal implements include rubber, salt, and beanbag rounds; batons; tear gas; water hoses; pepper spray; and Tasers. *See also* DEADLY FORCE; USE OF FORCE.

LETHAL GAS. Convicts to be executed for **capital offenses** are placed into sealed chambers, called **gas chambers**, into which a gas is released for the **execution**. A variety of gases have been used for this purpose, including hydrogen cyanide, carbon monoxide, and carbon dioxide. **Gee Jon** was the first person subjected to death in a gas chamber in 1924 in Nevada. *See also* DEATH PENALTY.

LETHAL INJECTION. Lethal injection is the predominant form of **capital punishment** in the United States. Currently, the federal government and 34 states allow capital punishment. Dr. Julius Mount Bleyer proposed its use in 1888 with the claim that it was cheaper than **hanging**. The Chapman protocol was proposed and adopted by Oklahoma in 1977. Texas was the first state to utilize lethal injection in 1982, successfully executing Charles Brooks Jr. Lethal injection is the process of injecting a condemned person (someone convicted of a **capital offense**, i.e., **murder** or several offenses in the federal system, including **treason**) with a lethal (fatal) drug or combination of drugs to induce a painless death. The common combination of drugs includes a barbiturate for pain and to induce sleep, a paralytic agent to stop breathing, and potassium chloride to stop the heart. A few states use a one-drug administration for lethal injection. Some states are seeking alternative methods of **execution** because of the difficulty of obtaining drugs. Pharmaceutical companies have begun to refuse to supply the drugs, stating their opposition to capital punishment. States are reconsidering authorizing the use of the **electric chair**, hangings, and the **firing squad**, which had been the primary means of performing executions. Refer to http://www.deathpenaltyinfo.org. *See also* DEATH PENALTY; LETHAL INJECTION.

LETOURNEAU, MARY KAY (1962–). A former sixth-grade teacher who became pregnant by her student. She served six months of an 89-month sentence for second-degree rape. Letourneau's plea agreement also specified no contact with the student. Following release from **prison**, she continued the affair with the student, which resulted in the birth of a second child and her return to prison for violating the "no contact" agreement. Judge Linda Lau resentenced her to seven years in prison. The no contact order was rescinded by the judge after her release from prison in 2004 because the student was then over 18 years of age. Letourneau and the student married in 2005 and separated in 2017. She is a registered sex offender.

***LEX TALIONIS*.** Translated from Latin, *lex talionis* means the law of **retaliation**. The law of retaliation, revenge, or **retribution** has a history that dates at least as far back as the **Code of Hammurabi**. The principle or law is mentioned by the Apostle Paul and has guided criminal justice pursuits through the Middle Ages, providing us with such phrases as *a tooth for a tooth* or *an eye for an eye*. The point was that the response to crime should be commensurate with the offense. Modern criminal law reflects that point of view. The **U.S. Supreme Court** has held in several cases, including *Edmund v. Florida*, 458 U.S. 782 (1982), and *Tison v. Arizona*, 481 U.S. 137 (1987), that there should be **proportionality**. These holdings are generally founded in the **Eighth Amendment** prohibition against **cruel and unusual punishment**.

LIE DETECTOR. The lie detector is also called a **polygraph** and was invented by John Larson in 1921 while he was a **police** officer and a medical student at the University of California, Berkeley. The lie detector is a machine that records changes in blood pressure, pulse rate, and perspiration as well as other bodily responses that may be indicative of not telling the truth.

The lie detector is a popular tool of law enforcement and for entertainment in TV and movies, but challenges to its effectiveness and reliability have rendered it inadmissible in court. Some scientific reviews have also referred to it as pseudoscience.

LIFE COURSE THEORY. Life course theory examines changes in crime patterns and how offenders and potential offenders are influenced by events or other circumstances over time. That is, when there is a consistency of social factors in a person's life, such as a single-parent household, there is a greater inclination to be involved in crime. However, when an adult is actively involved in home, family, and job, there is less likelihood to be involved in crime. Rolf Loeber and Marc LeBlanc proposed the theory in 1990 and investigated why some people will act in an antisocial manner or why their criminal behavior begins to intensify.

LINDBERGH KIDNAPPING, "THE CRIME OF THE CENTURY". On 1 March 1932, 20-month-old Charles Morrow Lindbergh was kidnapped from the Lindbergh summer home in East Amwell, New Jersey. Bruno Richard Hauptmann, 33, was charged with and found guilty of the crimes of **kidnapping** and **murder**, sentenced to death, and executed in the **electric chair** in Trenton State **Prison** on 3 April 1936. The attention given to the crime resulted in the passage of the 1932 Federal Kidnapping Act (also referred to as the Little Lindbergh Law), making it a federal crime to transport a kidnapped victim across state lines. Also implicated (by Hauptmann) was Isidor Fisch. Fisch, however, had returned to Germany and purportedly died there on 29 March 1934. The New Jersey **State Police** Museum maintains an elaborate, well-presented display of the case, which includes **evidence** with explanations of it and of the investigation. *See also* BARKER-KARPIS GANG (1931–1935); CHESSMAN, CARYL (1921–EXECUTED 1960); EXECUTION; KELLY, GEORGE (1895–1954).

LINEAR STYLE OF PRISON CONSTRUCTION. This style is also called the intermittent surveillance design and was the more familiar style of **prison** construction until 1983. The linear style consists of long rows of cells, which did not allow direct supervision. The guard providing supervision must walk down the tier (or cellblock) and look into each cell to ensure custody. Since 1983, correctional experts have suggested that the linear style be avoided. The POD or direct style of supervision is now favored. *See also* EASTERN STATE PENITENTIARY (PENNSYLVANIA).

LINEUP. A law enforcement process of assembling a number of persons (or pictures of persons) so that a victim or **witness** can (if possible) pick out the potentially guilty person. Lineups have been falling out of favor since the mid-1970s and are becoming a less prominent feature in **police** investigations. Research conducted since 1975 has shown that eyewitnesses/victims do poorly when trying to identify a suspect of a crime. Dr. Gary Wells provided some of the earliest research to this effect. The **U.S. Supreme Court** has held that the **Fifth Amendment** privilege against **self-incrimination** is inapplicable for the lineup. One reason law enforcement is utilizing the lineup less frequently is because of its unreliability. In the United Kingdom, a lineup is referred to as an identity parade. *See also* INNOCENCE PROJECT; SCOTTSBORO BOYS.

LIST, JOHN (1925–2008). List was convicted of killing five family members (mother, wife, and three children) on 9 November 1971 in Westfield, New Jersey. He was a longtime fugitive (17 years) before his capture in Virginia. ***America's Most Wanted*** broadcast an episode in 1989 about List which included a bust of List as he was suspected to have aged. He was identified from the bust and was reported to the **police**, which resulted in his apprehension. He had lived as a fugitive under the name Bob Clark and eventually remarried. He died in Trenton State **Prison** of pneumonia while serving five consecutive life sentences.

LOCARD'S EXCHANGE PRINCIPLE. In 1934, Dr. Edmund Locard (1877–1966) proposed that contact with persons, places, and things leaves what has become commonly referred to as "**trace evidence**." That is, no crime may be committed without leaving behind or taking away something that will provide documentation of or connection to the crime. This refers to physical substances such as blood and other bodily fluids, clothing, **DNA**, hair, and more. He considered this to be factual **evidence** in criminal investigations. The modern crime scene investigator has the responsibility of collecting such evidence and documenting it to tell the story of the crime. *See also* FORENSICS.

LOCKDOWN. The term *lockdown* describes a **prison** circumstance of confining convicts to their cells for security reasons. During times of emergency, disturbance, escapes, or for other reasons, a prison utilizes lockdown to ensure that all movement in a prison is halted to protect persons and the facility. A lockdown helps to ensure an accurate accounting of the prison population. Lockdown is also applied to nonprison situations to ensure that any ongoing problem does not escalate. A lockdown is essentially a hold in place until normal operations may be resumed. Lockdown has become a more common expression since 9/11 when the U.S. airspace was locked down. The Boston authorities locked down all transportation following the bombing during the 2013 marathon. School shootings have caused schools to run drills to lock-down in place.

***LOCKHART V. MCCREE*, 476 U.S. 162 (1986).** Ardia McCree was accused of capital **murder**. Jurors were removed by the judge because they stated they could not impose the **death penalty**. The decision of the judge was found to be a violation of both the Sixth and **Fourteenth Amendments** by the Eighth Circuit Court of Appeals. The **U.S. Supreme Court**, however, concluded that this was not a violation of either the Sixth or Fourteenth Amendments, finding that a **jury** must be impartial, represent a cross section of the community, and properly apply the law to protect the rights of the defendant. *See also* CAPITAL PUNISHMENT; *WITHERSPOON V. ILLINOIS*, 391 U.S. 510 (1968).

LOGIC MODEL. A methodology for evaluating criminal justice programs developed in the 1970s by Carol Weiss and Joseph Wholey. The model components help to distinguish between direct and indirect results of a program as well as short-term effects. The logic model helps criminal justice officials determine the effectiveness and efficiency of programming. However, a criticism of programs utilizing the logic model is that they tend to oversimplify and are projected as successful programs, and they continue to be used despite unforeseen variables that appear and inhibit their success.

LOITERING. Staying in a general location, usually public, without a defined reason. Depending on the situation, loitering may be illegal. Loitering laws are created to prevent criminal activity such as thievery, drug sales, **prostitution**, or begging. Legislation in England (the **Vagrancy** Act of 1824) outlined the legal definition of loitering. State laws and municipal ordinances of the United States address prostitution, sex offenders, and **gangs**. Loitering legislation has been successfully challenged in the appellate courts for failure to adequately define acceptable conduct.

LOMBROSO, CESARE (1835–1909). One of the early fathers of **criminology** and the founder of the Italian school of positivist criminology. His belief was that the cause of crime was an inheritance or that someone was a "born criminal" with congenital defects associated with features described as atavistic; that is, the criminal was an evolutionary throwback. His theories have been discredited, but he may be remembered for his efforts to establish criminological theory and criminalistics. *See also* ATAVISM; CLASSICAL SCHOOL OF CRIMINOLOGY.

LONGITUDINAL STUDY. A criminological, psychological, or sociological study (continuous observation) of a variable (such as a cohort—the same group) over a period of time to observe changes. An example is the famous cohort study by **Dr. Marvin Wolfgang** (1924–1998) (conducted during the 1960s and early 1970s) which determined when youth "age out" of crime.

LONG LINE RIDER. An armed **prison** guard or a convict trustee in the Arkansas prison system who rode horseback to guard convicts working in the fields. Ironically, the convict trustee was often serving a long sentence for **homicide** or other serious offense. Both the prison guard and the convict trustee were authorized to shoot escaping convicts. The practice of using convict trustees in this capacity was ended by *Gates v. Collier*, 501 F.2d 1291 (5th Cir. 1974). *Gates* held that the practice was **inmate** abuse, a violation of the **cruel and unusual punishment** clause of the **Eighth Amendment**. Long line riders are discussed in Murton's book, *Accomplices to the Crime* (1970), which discusses abuses in the Arkansas prison system. *See also* STATE USE SYSTEM.

***LOUISIANA EX REL. FRANCIS V. RESWEBER*, 329 U.S. 459 (1947).** The issue before the court was whether the **death penalty** could be imposed a second time when the first attempt fails. In this case it was an **electric chair** malfunction. The challenge to the court concerned **double jeopardy**, **due process**, and **cruel and unusual punishment** (**Fifth, Eighth**, and **Fourteenth Amendments**). The Court held that none of the challenges constituted constitutional conflict. Willie Francis was executed on the second attempt in 1946. *See also* CAPITAL PUNISHMENT; EXECUTION.

LUCAS, HENRY LEE (1936–2001). A **serial killer** called "the confession killer" because of his admission to more than 3,000 murders. He died in **prison** of heart failure. Initially convicted of killing 11, he was sentenced to death. A case review suggests he falsely confessed, and his sentence was commuted to life without **parole**. He had previously served a prison sentence for the **murder** of his mother. *See also* MASS MURDER.

LUCIANO, CHARLES (1897–1962). Luciano, nicknamed Lucky, was the father of **organized crime** and the Genovese crime family. He created the first crime commission in 1936, which became the **National Crime Syndicate**. He was prosecuted by Thomas Dewey for **prostitution** and received a 30-year sentence. The U.S. government made a deal with Luciano (brokered by **Meyer Lansky**) during World War II that allowed him to leave the United States prior to the completion of his sentence. *See also* MURDER INC.

LUSH WORKER. A typology of criminal more common to the 1800s and early 1900s. Lush workers were usually men, although there were some women who would use a sharp blade such as a straight razor to cut open a pocket and remove the wallet or other contents. A place frequented by them was the subway. In England they were characterized as "cutpurses."

LYNCHING. Unsanctioned **executions** that were used against African Americans in the south and Chinese, Mexicans, and whites in the old west. Lynchings were most active from the late 1700s through the mid-1900s. The outcry against lynching resulted in more than 200 bills presented to Congress, with three passed by the House and none by the Senate. An early origin for the term is from "Lynch's law" named for Charles Lynch of Virginia (1736–1796) who prescribed lynching for British loyalists.

LYSERGIC ACID DIETHYLAMIDE (LSD). Commonly referred to as acid, it is a recreational drug widely used in the counterculture movement of the 1960s. LSD is a psychedelic drug that alters the thinking process, causing hallucinations, paranoia, and anxiety. Albert Hoffman synthesized the drug in 1938. LSD was experimented with on convicts in Massachusetts and other states during the 1960s.

M

MACDONALD, JEFFREY (1943–). Jeffrey MacDonald's wife and two daughters were murdered in 1970. In 1978 a charge of **murder** was brought against MacDonald, and in 1979 he was convicted on one count of first-degree murder and two counts of second-degree murder for which he received three consecutive life sentences. All appeals were unsuccessful, and **parole** was denied. The case was the subject of the book *Fatal Vision*, which ironically MacDonald asked Joe McGinniss to write. McGinniss portrayed MacDonald as a sociopath. At the time of the murders, MacDonald was a medical doctor and a U.S. Army Special Forces Green Beret.

MACE. A chemical aerosol spray invented in 1965 by Alan Litman (following the **assault** of his wife) for self-defense and used by law enforcement to disable or incapacitate individuals or to disperse hostile crowds. The use of Mace has been discontinued because of the danger of the chemical and has been replaced by pepper spray.

MACONOCHIE, CAPTAIN ALEXANDER (1787–1860). The father of **parole**, Maconochie was a British naval captain assigned to Norfolk Island to institute correctional reforms. Following a visit to Van Diemen's Land in 1836, he wrote of the abuses and forms of discipline with commentary on appropriate actions that should be used during incarceration. Among the comments that stand out include that cruelty was not effective and that the goals should be for the convict to accept social norms. He also believed in tasks for release and that they should be based on achievements of labor. Those points would later be incorporated into the work of **Walter Crofton** in Ireland and **Zebulon Brockway** of **Elmira Reformatory**, New York. Maconochie's writings resulted in his assignment as governor to Norfolk Island, where he would initiate wide-sweeping reforms that were unusual for their time. His success treating prisoners resulting in dismantling the harsh treatment of convicts and returning them to Australia. Maconochie's work also resulted in his transfer back to England. Unfortunately, Maconochie's methods received a less favorable response in England, where the release of convicts into the community was frowned upon and this time led to his removal from his post as governor of the prison. Many of the initiatives he began on Norfolk Island remain fundamental to modern parole practices. *See also* PRISON REFORM; TRANSPORTATION.

MADOFF, BERNARD (1938–). In 2009, Madoff, a former NASDAQ chairman and investment advisor, was convicted on 11 federal felonies (securities fraud) and sentenced to 150 years in **prison**, the maximum allowed by law, for committing the largest Ponzi scheme in history, which defrauded investors of billions of dollars. The Madoff Ponzi scheme is believed by federal authorities to have been operating since the 1980s.

MAFIA. The term was originally applied to Sicilian and American/Italian **organized crime** groups that began in the 1920s. Italian Americans refer to themselves as **La Cosa Nostra**, whereas the term *Mafia* is used by the media and the public. The criminal activities associated with the Mafia include **gambling**, drug trafficking, protection, loan-sharking, and fraud. These events are also referred to as rackets. While the name Mafia is more likely to be applied to Italian organized crime, other ethnic groups engaged in organized crime have been given the name, such as the **Russian mafia**, the Mexican mafia, the Chinese mafia, and the Japanese mafia. However, they are also recognized by more formal names, such as the Japanese or Chinese **Triads**. The "Mafie" or private army began in the early to mid-19th century in Italy to protect against invaders and was noncriminal. In time, it became criminal, extorting money from landowners. *See also* LA COSA NOSTRA; VALACHI, JOSEPH (1903–1971).

MAGNA CARTA. (Latin for the Great Charter.) An English document of 1215 that established legal rights, including habeas corpus, protection against false imprisonment, and arbitrary actions by the English Crown. Since its original composition, the Magna Carta has undergone many revisions that eventually helped shape English medieval law and later **common law**. The Magna Carta influenced early colonial law (the charters of Massachusetts, Virginia, and Maryland) and later the U.S. Constitution and its amendments. Of special note is the **Fifth Amendment** phrase "no person shall be deprived of life, liberty, or property, without **due process** of law" proposed in 1789. The passage was a direct quote from the Magna Carta. *See also* BILL OF RIGHTS; WRIT OF HABEAS CORPUS.

MALA IN SE. *Mala in se* translates to "evil in itself." For most human beings and in most cultures, such crimes as **murder**, rape, or theft are considered to be wrong, and there are regulations/statutes that prohibit such acts.

This is distinct from ***mala*** (or *malum*) ***prohibita***, in which something is wrong (but not necessarily evil in itself) because it is legislated as such. An example would be statutes that only allow parking on one side of the road on specified days.

MALA PROHIBITA. *Mala prohibita* refers to acts that are wrong because they are legislated as such and are not generally considered to be morally offensive. The intention of such statutes was affirmed in the case of *State v. Horton*, 139 N.C. 588, 51 S.E. 945, 946 (1905). Examples of such offenses include jaywalking, hitchhiking, illegal hunting, and **copyright infringement**. *See also MALA IN SE.*

***MALLORY V. U.S.*, 354 U.S. 449 (1957).** The holding established what is sometimes referred to as the McNabb-Mallory rule. This is a rule of **evidence** which finds that a confession is inadmissible if there is an unreasonably long period of time after an arrest during which the defendant is held in detention before an initial court appearance.

***MALLOY V. HOGAN*, 378 U.S. 1 (1964). U.S. Supreme Court** holding that **Fifth Amendment** rights were applicable in state and federal courts—a defendant cannot be forced to be a **witness** against themselves. *See also* TAKING THE FIFTH.

MALVO, LEE (1985–). *See* MUHAMMAD, JOHN ALLEN (1960–2009); SERIAL KILLER.

MANACLES. One of several types of restraint devices, also referred to as handcuffs, that secure a person's wrists together with a locking device that requires a key. Three of the more common types of manacles use a short piece of chain, a hinge, or a rigid bar to separate the cuffs by a few centimeters and to minimize the degree of motion possible. Among the earliest origins of manacles was by Richard Topcliffe, remembered as a tyrant who worked in service of the queen and devised manacles in the mid-1500s to painfully hang up offenders by their wrists. Manacles were also used in early U.S. **prisons** as **punishment** to hang an offender in such a way that their feet would barely touch the floor. The most recent evolution in wrist restraints are zip ties made of plastic, which are popular because of the ease and swiftness with which they can secure the wrists of a suspect.

MANDATORY DEATH PENALTY. The **death penalty** is not mandatory following conviction for specified crimes. While many countries authorize a mandatory death penalty for certain crimes, the **U.S. Supreme Court** decision in *Woodson v. North Carolina*, 428 U.S. 280 (1976), struck down the mandatory death penalty, stating, "The fundamental respect for humanity underlying the **Eighth Amendment** requires consideration of the character and record of the individual offender and the circumstances of the particular offense." In cases that are death penalty eligible, the United States requires a **bifurcated process**. This process requires two phases: phase one determines guilt, and phase two determines **punishment**. The bifurcated process was established in Gregg v. Georgia, 428 U.S. 153 (1976), and does not violate the Eighth Amendment. *See also* PROPORTIONALITY.

MANDATORY MINIMUM SENTENCING. These sentences are created by the legislature for specific crimes that a judge may not change. Examples include drug laws that specify incarceration for **drug possession** over a certain amount and **three-** and **two-strikes laws** in which an offender with two or three criminal convictions receives a mandatory sentence. These sentences vary from state to state and have specifications for the commission of a violent offense. A variation on mandatory sentencing is **sentencing guidelines**—a range of sentences that are matched to the degree of the crime. Mitigating and **aggravating circumstances** of a crime may be considered for a sentence in the sentencing guideline, but these are usually not considered with a strict mandatory **minimum sentence**, referred to as a mandatory sentence. A frequent use of mandatory sentencing is for crimes with morality applications such as drugs, alcohol, and sexual offenses. An early example of legislation by the U.S. Congress is the 1951 Boggs Act, which established a 2 to 10-year minimum sentence for possession of **marijuana** with a **fine** of up to $20,000, which was repealed in 1970. States have passed similar legislation with applications to drugs. The legislation was in keeping with President Nixon's 1971 declaration of a **War on Drugs**.

MANHATTAN BAIL PROJECT. The 1961 Manhattan Bail Project was established to aid defendants who could not post **bail**. It was the first pretrial program in the United States and operated in New York City. The program established the risk level of defendants. Those defendants considered low risk, that is, who would appear in court, were released on their own recognizance (ROR). Research has demonstrated that whether a defendant can make bail or is released on ROR has little influence on court appearance, and this has influenced initiatives of similar projects around the country. The Manhattan Bail Project was funded by the **Vera Institute of Justice**.

MANN ACT. The Mann Act is also referred to as the White-Slave Traffic Act. The act was passed 25 June 1910. The Mann Act specifies that it is a felony for someone to participate in interstate or foreign transportation of women or girls for **prostitution**, debauchery, or other immoral acts. A flaw of the act is that it also criminalizes consensual sexual acts between adults when they cross state lines.

MANNER OF DEATH. A **police** investigation conducted by a **medical examiner** to determine the cause and manner of death. Five official terms describe the manner of death: natural, accident, **homicide**, undetermined, and suicide. Among the earliest autopsies conducted to determine cause and manner of death was that of Julius Caesar in 44 B.C. In the case of Caesar, he was stabbed 23 times, but the fatal blow was the second one. The modern legal system seeks satisfactory answers, such as whether the death is to be classified a homicide or of natural causes. The manner of death is determined through the forensic autopsy. *See also* FORENSICS.

MANO NERA. The origins of the "Black Hand" predate the **Mafia** and stem from a Serbian secret military sect (circa 1911) devoted to freeing Serbia from Austro-Hungarian rule. Modern use of the term refers to groups who use extortion and other forms of serious crime (some organized and individualized criminal activity). Other notable applications of the term involve Italian immigrants in the 1880s who spoke regional dialects as opposed to standard Italian language. Those purporting to be members of the Black Hand embellished their letters for **ransom** with daggers dripping blood, a black hand held in various positions, and skulls and crossbones to symbolize that the threats and demands should be taken seriously. **Police** sometimes refer to acts of **kidnapping**, extortion, and **violence** as the work of the Black Hand. The term is also popular in works of crime fiction. The Black Hand became a functional **organized crime** element that extended from New York to San Francisco by the early 1900s. There are noted victims of the Black Hand, including the singer Enrico Caruso, from whom a sum of $2,000 was demanded. When the extortionists raised the sum to $15,000, Caruso engaged the police and they were captured. *See also* MAFIA.

MANSLAUGHTER. A legal term that differentiates a killing from **murder** with conflicting definitions in varying jurisdictions. This expression dates back to the 7th century B.C. when Draco, an Athenian lawmaker, articulated that the commission of manslaughter was less blameworthy than murder. There are two classifications of manslaughter. **Involuntary manslaughter** occurs when there has been no previous intention of killing. Voluntary manslaughter often occurs in the "heat of passion," which suggests the person committing the offense is temporarily disturbed and perhaps picks up an object and strikes the victim. *See also* HOMICIDE.

MANSON, CHARLES. (1934–2017). The cult leader of the "Manson Family" sentenced to death in 1971 for conspiracy to commit the **murder** of seven people, including actress Sharon Tate. California has a "**joint responsibility rule**," which makes any person conspiring to commit murder guilty of murder. His death sentence was commuted to a life sentence in 1972 when the California Supreme Court eliminated the **death penalty**. He was imprisoned at Corcoran State **Prison**, Corcoran, California, until his death in 2017 from cardiac arrest complicated by colon cancer. Manson's notoriety was advanced when he carved a swastika in his forehead and his followers carved an "X" in their foreheads during the **trial**. Manson adopted the phrase "**Helter Skelter**" from a Beatles song and applied the lyrics to his belief in a forthcoming race war. He believed the murders would start the race war. Prosecutor Vincent Bugliosi wrote the book *Helter Skelter* about the Manson case.

***MAPP V. OHIO*, 367 U.S. 643 (1961).** A landmark case that established protection against unreasonable **search and seizure**. This was a case of criminal procedure in which the **U.S. Supreme Court** held that **evidence** which was acquired in a manner that violated the **Fourth Amendment** could not be used by the prosecution in either state or federal prosecutions. *See also* DUE PROCESS; EXCLUSIONARY RULE; WARRANTLESS SEARCHES.

MARIJUANA. A psychoactive drug, also known as cannabis, that when taken recreationally, religiously, or medically by smoking, as a vapor, with food, or as an extract results in mental and physical effects commonly referred to as getting "high" or "stoned." The history of cannabis or marijuana dates to the 3rd century B.C. in China where it was used for its medical benefits. In the 1930s, the U.S. Federal Bureau of Narcotics described it as powerfully addictive and as a gateway drug to **narcotics addiction**. It became a Schedule 1 drug in the Controlled Substances Act of 1970. This act also denied its medical use. The **War on Drugs** of the 1970s and 1980s saw the emergence of mandatory sentences for possession of marijuana. Currently, there are efforts to decriminalize the possession and use of marijuana. Marijuana has many nicknames; the current one is "weed." *See also* DECRIMINALIZATION; ROCKEFELLER DRUG LAWS.

MARION, USP. Marion **Penitentiary**, located in Illinois, is currently a federal medium-security **prison** that houses male convicts. It began operations in 1963 as a replacement for **Alcatraz** and was expected to eliminate the abuses of Alcatraz. A feature of significance is that it became the first **supermax prison**, using long-term **solitary confinement** following a violent episode in 1983. The cellblocks for this use were built in 1973 as a control unit. This model would later influence the design of ADX Florence located in Colorado as perhaps the most supermax prison in the world. In 2006, Marion was officially reclassified to medium security with major renovations. *See also* ADMAX; FEDERAL BUREAU OF PRISONS (BOP).

MARITAL RAPE. Also referred to as spousal rape, partner rape, or rape in marriage, there was little acknowledgment of marital rape in society or by criminal justice until the latter half of the 20th century when greater attention was paid to **violence** against women. All states would not adopt legislation criminalizing marital rape until 1993 because there was too little knowledge about forced intercourse when the couple was in a relation or were married, or agreement about its legality. Many states had statutes that provided marital immunity. These have now been generally overturned. While marital rape is now criminalized, there remains confusion about whether it is covered under existing rape legislation or whether it should be covered by legislation for **assault** and battery or other forms of violence legislation. Marital rape has seen an increase in law enforcement involvement since the 1980s. *See also* DOMESTIC VIOLENCE.

MARSHAL. Marshals operate at the federal, state, and local levels of government. Their tasks range from court bailiffs and process servers to fully sworn law enforcement officers transporting **inmates** from one **prison** to another. Historically, as in the American old west of the late 1800s, they functioned as town marshals (elected or appointed) who were responsible for public safety. The position is still in use in some southwestern states. The brothers (Morgan, Virgil, Warren, and Wyatt) Earp were all marshals in the Arizona Territory. Federal marshals perform a variety of law enforcement services such as an assignment to each of the 94 federal judicial districts. There is a marshal of the **U.S. Supreme Court**, which provides the security of the Court and the justices and assumes responsibility for many court assignments. A U.S. marshal oversees federal court security, **asset forfeiture**, fugitive recovery, and prisoner transportation and serves arrest warrants. The Federal Air Marshal Service provides armed protection against **hijacking** to commercial airlines. *See also* WARRANT.

MARSHALL HYPOTHESIS. Thurgood Marshall (1908–1993) was an associate justice of the **U.S. Supreme Court** from 1967 to 1991 and developed what has been called the Marshall hypothesis, that the **death penalty** is unconstitutional and immoral. Marshall believed that if the public were informed about it and its effects, it would lose its popular support. Marshall argued that it was racist and resulted in the **execution** of innocent persons.

He emphasized the following: that life imprisonment deterred crime, not the death penalty; that persons who committed **murder** infrequently received the death penalty and that after incarceration they did not return to a life of crime; and that executions are more expensive than **life sentences**, which has recently resulted in some states eliminating the death penalty following cost analysis of executions. *See also FURMAN V. GEORGIA*, 408 U.S. 238 (1972).

MARTIN, TRAYVON (1995–2012). A 17-year-old African American killed on 5 February 2012 by **George Zimmerman**, a **neighborhood watch** member in Sanford, Florida. The shooting resulted in national controversy and protesting over **racial profiling** and the rights of armed neighborhood watch. Charged with second-degree **murder** on 11 April 2012, Zimmerman was tried by an all-female **jury** and was subsequently acquitted. His defense was based on Florida's "Stand Your Ground" law, which permits defense, including the use of **deadly force**, when threat of harm is imminent.

MARTINSON, ROBERT (1927–1979). Robert Martinson is remembered for having said "***nothing works***." In 1974, he published "What Works: Questions and Answers about **Prison Reform**." What he actually said was, "Of those things we have studied we have not found anything to work," and then he introduced an exception. He was misquoted and taken out of context. The result affected all aspects of criminal justice operations, especially the courts, legislation, **parole**, and corrections. The belief that nothing works added increased fire to the **War on Crime** rhetoric and tough sentencing, leading to **mass incarceration**. *See also* EVIDENCE-BASED PRACTICES.

MARXIST CRIMINOLOGY. Also known as conflict criminology, it is focused on the division of wealth, prestige, and power as they shape the legal system and the causal relationships between crime and society. The examination of the relationship between those elements provides an understanding of crime and **criminogenic factors**. Marxian criminology has its origins in the 1850s in socialist criminology, which originally emphasized economic determinism. *See also* SELLIN, THORSTEN (1896–1994).

MASSAGE PARLOR. The massage parlor can be a place of legitimate enterprise. In criminal justice it is a place that serves as a front for **prostitution**. This is a common practice in many countries. The massage scandals of 1894 in the United Kingdom exposed the illegal practice for its massage abuses, high fees, false claims, poor training of the masseuse, and forged credentials. This led to regulation of the legitimate industry. Legitimate massage parlors do exist in the United States and generally require a licensed massage therapist.

MASS INCARCERATION. Mass incarceration was achieved in the United States as a consequence of a series of ill-conceived policies supported by legislation and operations that resulted in the greatest incarceration of any country. Incarceration was viewed as the solution to crime and threats to public safety. The United States has had a steadily rising **prison** population since prisons were first built. In 1964, the slow increase began to change with the **War on Crime**. This was followed by the **War on Drugs** and mandatory incarceration for drug offenses. Mass incarceration was further advanced following the poorly reported Martinson article. In 1975, the total prison population in the United States was approximately 250,000 convicts. By 2017, the United States confined more than 2.3 million persons in its criminal justice system. *See also* MARTINSON, ROBERT (1927–1979); NOTHING WORKS; TOUGH ON CRIME.

MASS MURDER. The act of killing four or more persons (**FBI** definition). A mass murderer frequently dies from suicide or "**death by cop**." It is differentiated from serial **murder** because it generally happens in one location or without a long separation of time referred to as a "cooling off period." It is differentiated from a spree killing, which typically involves one or two persons with a short break between killings. Genocide is a form of mass murder with additional qualifiers such as being a **crime against humanity**. Uniquely, mass murder is also an event (crime) carried out by government agents (frequently military or others such as doctors) with a political agenda who attempt the extermination of a culture. There are few convictions for these crimes. *See also* GENOCIDE; SANDY HOOK MASSACRE; SERIAL KILLER.

MATERIAL WITNESS. An individual with information about a crime. The First Judiciary Act of 1789 is the earliest statute to allow the detention of a material **witness**. Amended in the 1984 **Bail** Reform Act, detention was allowed to ensure testimony before a grand **jury** and for other criminal proceedings. The statutes allow an **arrest warrant** without criminal charging to be issued. Controversy with the statutes somewhat limits their application. For example, **Attorney General** John Ashcroft was sued for his use of a material witness. The federal Ninth Circuit Court of Appeals held Ashcroft immune from the suit due to the official capacity of the office he held. The statutes have not been tested in the **U.S. Supreme Court**. *See also* WARRANT.

MAY ISSUE. The term refers to obtaining a permit to carry a concealed weapon. The permit may be issued by a **sheriff**'s department, a **police** department, or in accordance with state legislation. Each jurisdiction with may-issue establishes its own requirements (or there must be good cause) to carry a concealed weapon. The earliest may-issue laws were a result of laws banning concealed weapons (deemed the custom of criminals) which originated in 1813 in Louisiana and Kentucky and were followed by other southern states. However, in the early to mid-19th century many northern states quickly followed by other southern states began passing shall-issue or may-issue laws that permitted the carrying of concealed weapons. The may-issue laws consistently became less rigorous until present times. Such laws are currently under attack because of the advocacy to limit weapons surrounding mass shootings in the past decade. *See also* GUN CONTROL; GUN PERMIT.

McCLELLAN COMMITTEE. The 1963 McClellan Committee Hearings (also known as the Valachi Hearings) looked into **organized crime** (especially the American **Mafia** and the Giancana crime family of Chicago, Illinois) and featured **Joseph Valachi**, an organized crime figure of the Genovese crime family of New York who turned government **witness**. Valachi provided the committee with a first-ever look into the day-to-day activities of organized crime. Two important pieces of legislation (the **Omnibus Crime Control and Safe Streets Act of 1968** and the **Racketeer Influenced Corrupt Organizations [RICO]** statute of 1970) were passed to control organized criminal enterprise and carried severe penalties.

***McCLESKEY V. KEMP*, 481 U.S. 279 (1987).** A **U.S. Supreme Court** finding that upheld the **death penalty**—that is, would not overturn a guilty verdict—when a study indicated that there was no racially disproportionate impact on a **jury** unless it could also be shown that there was a racially discriminatory purpose. The court decision has been considered an influential challenge to the death penalty and is described as one of the worst decisions of the U.S. Supreme Court because it allows for an expression of racism in an important aspect of law.

McCORD, JOAN (1930–2004). American criminologist. The first woman president of the **American Society of Criminology**. Her areas of study included **juvenile delinquency**, alcoholism, and psychopathy. McCord's study of mentoring suggested that it was counterproductive. Her findings were often the result of longitudinal studies. *See also* CRIMINOLOGY.

McKAY, HENRY D. (1899–1980). McKay and Clifford Shaw turned the Sociology Department at the University of Chicago into the most prominent sociology program in the United States. **Social disorganization theory** brought about a significantly improved understanding of **juvenile delinquency** especially as it occurs in urban areas, delinquency occurrences or frequency, and the characteristics of delinquency in cities and communities. The work of McKay and Shaw emphasize that the location of the juvenile affects the likelihood of delinquency. Social disorganization theory expanded on the work of Park and Burgess in concentric **zone theory**.

***McKEIVER V. PENNSYLVANIA*, 403 U.S. 528 (1971).** Two juveniles, Joseph McKeiver and Terry Edwards, had been charged with **assault**, escape, and robbery while they were teenagers. The **U.S. Supreme Court** held that juveniles were not entitled to a **trial** by **jury**. The Sixth and **Fourteenth Amendments** did not apply. *See also IN RE GAULT*, 387 U.S. 1 (1967).

***McNABB V. U.S.*, 318 U.S. 332 (1943).** McNabb had been imprisoned for 45 years for **murder**. He was not represented by an attorney when **evidence** (the confession) was obtained. The court held that procedural safeguards were not adhered to. An outcome was the McNabb-Mallory rule, which establishes the inadmissibility of a confession when it is given after an excessive time in custody between the events of arrest and the first court appearance. *See also GIDEON V. WAINWRIGHT*, 372 U.S. 335 (1963).

McVEIGH, TIMOTHY (1968–2001). An American terrorist executed by **lethal injection** at USP Terre Haute (also known as "The Last Word"). His offense is commonly referred to as the **Oklahoma City bombing** because he detonated a truck bomb at the Alfred P. Murrah Federal Building in Oklahoma, which killed 168 people while injuring more than 600 others. McVeigh acted for revenge against the **Waco siege** of 1993 and the Ruby Ridge incident of 1992. The Oklahoma City bombing is the worst incident of **domestic terrorism** in the United States. *See also* EXECUTION.

MEAT EATER. One of two groupings of **police corruption** used by the **Knapp Commission** formed in April 1970 by New York mayor John Lindsay. *Meat eater* refers to police officers who engage in such activities as shakedowns and theft for personal gain of **evidence** such as drugs for resale and other activities that they can manipulate for financial gain. *See also* GRASS EATER; POLICE; SERPICO, FRANK (1936–).

MECHANICAL THEORY OF CRIME AND INCARCERATION. The theory proposes that changes in rates of crime have a direct correlation with increases or decreases in incarceration. Similarly, it also proposes that increases in incarceration relate to reductions in crime. This theory helps explain the rise in incarceration since 1970; however, there is little data to illustrate that increases in incarceration do reduce crime. *See also* UNIFORM CRIME REPORT (UCR).

MEDELLÍN CARTEL. The Medellín Cartel was formed in Medellín, Colombia, and operated in the 1970s and 1980s in South American countries, the United States, Canada, and Europe. The cartel engaged in smuggling and drug sales, often collaborating with other **drug cartels**, and at its height was grossing almost half a billion dollars per week. The cartel engaged in **murder**, **bribery**, and **kidnapping** of **police**, judges, politicians, and government officials to maintain its enterprise. In 1991 and 1992 more than 50,000 people met violent deaths to ensure the dominance of the cartel. The United States took an aggressive lead role dismantling and shutting down the Medellín Cartel. The Medellín Cartel officially collapsed following the killing on 2 December 1993 of Pablo Escobar (one of the founding members of the cartel) by the Colombian National Police.

MEDIA VIOLENCE. The depiction of aggressive acts by one or more characters against one or more other characters in a media format. Research has been conducted since the 1950s and has demonstrated a correlation between viewing aggression and the commission of **violence**. There have been attempts to regulate portrayals of violence, including the 1996 Computer Decency Act, which was intended to control the distribution of violent materials to minors. The act was challenged in *Reno v. ACLU*, 521 U.S. 844 (1997), and the **U.S. Supreme Court** held that the act was unconstitutional, a violation of the **First Amendment** protection of free speech. Other efforts at regulation included the Child Online Protection Act, and again in *Ashcroft v.* ***American Civil Liberties Union***, 535 U.S. 564 (2002), the attempt was held to be unconstitutional, a violation of the First Amendment's free speech protection.

MEDICAL EXAMINER. The medical examiner has origins as far back as the 12th century in England. The medical examiner investigates deaths and related injuries to determine the cause of death (suicide, **homicide**, overdose of drugs, etc.). The precise duties of the medical examiner often overlap with those of the **coroner** and are determined by jurisdiction. Among the functions of a medical examiner are to issue a death certificate, identify the deceased, and examine the liver, stomach, brain, and other organs to establish a **manner of death**. The medical examiner is an officer who is generally medically qualified (this is not a requirement in all jurisdictions in the United States) and a trained pathologist to conduct investigations and report to the district attorney when there is suspicion of death by other than natural causes. The position of medical examiner has proven to be a popular topic for television and movies (*Quincy, M.E.*, *Crossing Jordan*, and *Body of Proof*). These portrayals often present an exaggerated position of the medical examiner. *See also* FORENSICS.

MEDICAL MODEL. After World War II, the medical model was adopted by **prisons** to facilitate rehabilitation. The model followed the practice of medical doctors investigating an illness. The convict would be examined, diagnosed, and prescribed a treatment regimen for their criminal offense, expecting a cure. The problems with the medical model were that prisons lacked sufficient resources to individualize treatment, and many methodologies were not **evidence-based practices**. The "What Works" article by **Robert Martinson** in 1974 devastated any confidence in the medical model and in effect was its death knell.

MEDICOLEGAL. The concept of medicolegal has roots in the history of the establishment of the role of **coroner** dating back to 925 A.D., before the Norman Conquest. An attending physician is obligated to report to law enforcement any medical case (injuries or illnesses) with legal implications, that is, with some existing possibility of criminality in the case. *See also* MEDICAL EXAMINER.

MEESE COMMISSION. The Meese Commission is more formally known as the **Attorney General**'s Commission on **Pornography** ordered by President Ronald Reagan in 1986. The report from the Meese Commission addressed **First Amendment** rights, the history of pornography, and its existence as an industry. The commission claimed a link to **organized crime**. The report had critics within and outside of the pornography industry who claimed it to be, among other things, inaccurate. Prior to Meese, the 1970 report from the President's Commission on **Obscenity** and Pornography found that pornography was not a critical social issue and that legal solutions might cause more problems than they would solve.

MEGAN'S LAW. California was the first state to initiate a sex offender registry in 1947. Megan's Law is a reference to federal and state legislation that mandated registration of sex offenders. The law was a direct response to the 1994 New Jersey rape and **murder** of seven-year-old **Megan Kanka** by convicted sex offender Jesse Timmendequas. All 50 states and the federal government now maintain sex offender registries.

MEMPHIS MODEL. The Memphis model was promulgated in 1988 following the killing of a Memphis **police** officer in 1987 by a mentally ill person. The Memphis model was a pioneering effort to create a crisis intervention team (CIT) or first responders for a mental illness circumstance as a prearrest jail **diversion** method. The model recognized that law enforcement officers were the first responders to such situations and had not been trained and should be trained. Officers desiring to participate are volunteers. Studies show that after the model had been initiated, police officer injuries declined when responding to the mentally ill. *See also* MENTAL HEALTH COURT; MENTALLY ILL OFFENDER.

MENÉNDEZ BROTHERS (JOSEPH, 1968–, AND ERIC, 1970–). The brothers were convicted in the sensational 1994 **murders** of their parents and sentenced to life incarceration without **parole**. They are incarcerated in separate California **prisons** and have not been in contact with each other. The event has resulted in books, documentaries, and dramas about the killings and the brothers.

MENS REA. The need to prove that someone intended to commit a crime. The term roughly translates to "guilty mind." Demonstrating that someone intended to commit a crime proved a slippery slope for the prosecution, and in 1957 the **Model Penal Code (MPC)** was published and classifications of mens rea were clarified in Section 2.02(2) of the MPC. Those classifications include negligence—the awareness of "substantial and unjustifiable risk" resulting in prohibited acts; recklessness—indifference to "substantial and unjustifiable risk" resulting in prohibited acts; knowledge—the individual knows that the conduct will result in prohibited acts; and purpose—the individual intends or hopes that their action will result in the prohibited act. *See also ACTUS REUS*.

MENTAL HEALTH COURT. A specialized court or **problem-solving court** created to address underlying criminal justice issues that result in offenders with mental health issues being sentenced to **prison**. Mental health court seeks to provide solutions and services that ensure public safety while acting as a **diversion** to jail or prison. The significance of the mental health court is that the court provides ongoing monitoring (by a judge) of the offender's needs and treatment to ensure public safety. These courts are modeled after **drug courts**. The first mental health court was created in Indianapolis, Indiana, in the early 1980s. They have been replicated in several states. *See also* COMMUNITY COURT.

MENTALLY ILL OFFENDER. Historically, mentally ill offenders were more likely to be housed in hospital-like settings than **prisons** because of their mental status. Beginning in the 1980s and increasing through the 1990s, hospitals and other settings for the mentally ill began to close, and the mentally ill were transferred into community settings. As facilities for the mentally ill closed, prison populations began to increase, and proportionally with the mentally ill. To be more specific, the criminalization of the mentally ill has increased. Estimates of the mentally ill in prisons are that about one-quarter of the female population and about 70 percent of the male population in prison suffer from some form of mental illness. *See also* MEMPHIS MODEL.

MERCY. The legal context of mercy refers to forgiveness, benevolence, compassion, and kindness toward an offender. Mercy may be shown by a judge or a **jury** toward someone convicted of a crime, for example, a **capital offense** for which a death sentence will not be assigned. The concept of mercy has a long history in the judicial system, although compared to modern standards, it too might be considered merciless. For example, in medieval times, mercy being shown to someone scheduled to be **hanged** might mean being blinded and castrated instead.

MERCY KILLING. Mercy killing is also referred to as **euthanasia**, physician-assisted suicide, or the intentional termination of a life. Mercy killing may be either voluntary or involuntary. Mercy killing is causing death to prevent the suffering of a person who endures, for example, a terminal or painful illness such as cancer or dementia. Mercy killing is also viewed as a necessary preventive measure—that is, the death (not a sanctioned **execution**) of someone who may seek to harm others. The permissibility and procedure of mercy killing varies by jurisdiction, from being illegal to doctor enabled. Many **serial killers** claim to perform mercy killing. The contentious issues surrounding mercy killing are legal, ethical, and moral. Francis Bacon in the 17th century is among the earliest to implement mercy killing, seeing it as a physician's duty. More recently, **Jack Kevorkian** (also called "Dr. Death") helped his terminally ill patients to achieve death with dignity (euthanasia). He was charged with and convicted of second-degree **murder** and sentenced to 10–25 years in **prison**. Some states have now legalized mercy killing. Oregon passed a Death with Dignity Act in 1994, which allows physician-assisted suicide. While physicians in large numbers support physician-assisted suicide for terminal illnesses, it remains a contentious issue with the Catholic Church and other religious groups. *See also* ANGEL OF DEATH/MERCY; HARVEY, DONALD (1952–2017).

MERTON, ROBERT (1910–2003). A leading figure developing the direction of American sociology, considered the father of modern sociology. He was a professor at Columbia University. Among his contributions to **criminology** are terms such as *role models* and *self-fulfilling prophecy* as they affect criminal conduct. Merton stressed that deviance is influenced when anomie results in an individual's break with the dominant culture.

MESCALINE. A psychedelic alkaloid that produces hallucinogenic effects. Mescaline is found in the **peyote** cactus and has been in use by Native Americans for at least 5,700 years. The Comprehensive Drug Abuse Prevention and Control Act of 1970 made its use illegal in the United States. A series of **U.S. Supreme Court** holdings have arrived at the following—the federal government may not restrict the use of mescaline in religious ceremonies. However, the states have a right to restrict its use. Many states do have legislation permitting its use in religious ceremonies.

META-ANALYSIS. A research methodology that identifies patterns from which to derive a common truth. The significance in criminal justice of meta-analyses became evident in the research of the 1970s and 1980s, which produced the expression ***evidence-based practices***. Previously many practices in criminal justice were "feel good" approaches that failed to produce success. One of the foremost results of meta-analyses has been the development of risk-needs assessment tools. *See also* MARTINSON, ROBERT (1927–1979); RISK ASSESSMENT.

METHADONE. Methadone is also known as Dolophie and is a relatively inexpensive opioid used for detoxification and maintenance (also referred to as methadone **diversion**) for those dependent on opioids. Methadone was produced in Germany in the late 1930s and was in use in the United States by 1947 as a diversion for opioid **addiction**. Previously, and used extensively following the Civil War, **heroin** was used similarly for morphine addiction.

METHAMPHETAMINE. A stimulant discovered in 1893 that affects the central nervous system, causing experiences of euphoria, mood elevation, improved concentration, and increased energy, and it is used as an aphrodisiac for prolonged sexual activity. It is a Schedule 2 (illegal) drug because it is highly addictive, with serious side effects such as **addiction**, reduced appetite, and increased energy.

***MICHIGAN, DEPARTMENT OF STATE POLICE V. SITZ*, 496 U.S. 444 (1990).** A **U.S. Supreme Court** holding that **police** sobriety checkpoints did not represent unreasonable **search and seizure** and did not violate the **Fourth Amendment**. The Court applied a balancing test and found that sobriety checkpoints (searches) were on the side of government. *See also* BALANCING TEST AND BRIGHT LINE RULE; WARRANTLESS SEARCHES.

MIDDLE ATLANTIC–GREAT LAKES ORGANIZED CRIME LAW ENFORCEMENT NETWORK (MAGLOCEN). A federal government agency founded in 1981 and comprised of eight states, the District of Columbia, and two Canadian provinces. Previously it was the **Regional Information Sharing Systems (RISS)** founded in 1974. The purpose is to share information and to conduct criminal investigations into satanic cults, outlaw motorcycle **gangs**, domestic threat groups, Russian and Jamaican **organized crime**, and cybercrime.

MIDNIGHT BASKETBALL. A 1990s initiative to curtail inner-city crime. It was viewed as an alternative to drugs and street crime. Property and **violent crimes** did decrease in cities where it functioned, although caution is encouraged with these results due to other factors such as the implied association of crime with African Americans.

MILGRAM STUDY. Stanley Milgram's 1960s research focused on compliance to authority figures when following directives that would harm people or result in other criminal behavior. Milgram's work was a reaction to the acts of people in Nazi Germany and specifically asked the question, "Could millions of people simply be following orders?" His experiments have been replicated with consistent results; that is, people will comply with authority even when it does harm and they know it. *See also* STANFORD PRISON EXPERIMENT.

MILITARY JUSTICE. Authorized by the U.S. Constitution, Article I, Section 8, the **Uniform Code of Military Justice** (1951), as it is currently called, is found in the U.S. Code, Title 10, Chapter 47, and was first promulgated in the Articles of War of 1806. The Lieber Code of 1863 further refined them. Military justice regulates the behavior of those in the armed forces as well as to preserve the peace and discipline and to oversee the legality of orders.

MILITARY POLICE. Each branch of the armed services has both enlisted and civilian **police** units. These units have federal law enforcement powers and are restricted from civilian enforcement unless martial law exists. However, state laws are enforceable on federal installations. The limitations on military police are defined in the **Posse Comitatus** Act of 1878.

MILITARY PRISON. Also referred to as a stockade, brig, or guardhouse, they are operated by the branch of the military in which they are situated. Military **prisons** confine prisoners of war, combatants, those who violate the **Uniform Code of Military Justice** or other laws (federal or state), and/or those who represent a threat to national security. The first military prison, created by an act of Congress in 1874, was called the United States Military Prison, now known as **USP Leavenworth**. *See also* UNITED STATES DISCIPLINARY BARRACKS (USDB).

MILKEN, MICHAEL (1946–). Milken, nicknamed the "junk-bond king," pled guilty to a 1989 indictment for violations of security laws. He was not convicted of either insider trading or racketeering violations. He received a 10-year sentence that was later reduced to two years for his cooperation against others in the offense and his good behavior in **prison**. Milken, after prison, has been a philanthropist, which includes a charitable trust and significant funding for medicine and education. He has been called the man who changed medicine. *See also* BOESKY, IVAN (1937–).

MILLER, JEROME (1931–2015). An advocate for juvenile and adult correctional reform, he was criticized for closing Massachusetts reformatories in the 1970s, which included the Lyman School for Boys, the first **reformatory** for delinquent boys in the United States. Miller believed that the **institutionalization** of delinquents was traumatizing and detrimental to youth. He went on to be the cofounder of the National Center on Institutions and Alternatives. The National Center advocated for sentencing reform, **reentry**, and alternatives to incarceration. He was a believer in community-based alternatives. *See also* JUVENILE DELINQUENCY.

***MILLER V. ALABAMA*, 567 U.S. __ (2012).** A **U.S. Supreme Court** case which held that life sentences for **juvenile offenders** were unconstitutional. The significance is that at the time of the ruling more than 2,000 juveniles were serving time in the United States for crimes committed before the age of 18. The United States is one of the few countries that allows life without **parole** for juveniles. *See also* JUVENILE DELINQUENCY.

MINIMUM SENTENCE. Also referred to as mandatory minimum sentences, they were the result of criticism and misunderstanding of judicial sentencing practices and were intended to create greater transparency through "**truth in sentencing**." Mandatory minimum sentences are sentences prescribed by legislation that judges cannot lower. Sentencing takes into account mitigating and **aggravating circumstances**. Judges may assign longer terms because of aggravating circumstances but may not assign lower than the minimum sentence for mitigating factors. The dilemma of appropriate sentencing, including minimum sentencing, was believed to have been made more equitable by the development of **sentencing guidelines** that prescribe sentences according to offense, degree of offense, and repeat offending. The first legislation restricting sentencing was the Boggs Act of 1951, which prescribed a 2- to 10-year sentence for a first-time possession of cannabis. This law was repealed in 1986 by the Anti-Drug Abuse Act. Other extreme examples of mandatory sentencing include **three-strikes laws** enacted by many states, Georgia's **two-strikes law** enacted in 1996, and California's one-strike law for sex offenders in 1994. There are current court challenges to many of these laws.

MINORITY OVERREPRESENTATION. A concern with the deprivation of basic **civil rights** for people of color, the adverse effects of it on individuals and communities, and as it forms barriers to participation in the democratic process and community reintegration. The issue of minority overrepresentation began in 1988 with an examination of the juvenile justice system and soon expanded to consider the adult system.

***MIRANDA V. ARIZONA*, 384 U.S. 436 (1966).** In 1963, Ernesto Miranda was accused of the **kidnapping** and rape of an 18-year-old retarded woman. He confessed to the crime during questioning. Miranda was not informed that he could have a lawyer present or that he did not have to speak. A motion to have the confession thrown out was denied during the **trial**. **Police** were initially concerned that the Miranda warning would interfere with their ability to question suspects and obtain a confession. In 1966, the **U.S. Supreme Court** held that statements Miranda made to police could not be used. Police must provide suspects with a warning. Warnings come in two forms: one that is short and another that seeks to ensure that the suspect understands what is being said. The simple warning reads as follows: "You have the right to remain silent. Anything you say can and will be used against you in a court of law. You have the right to speak to an attorney, and to have an attorney present during any questioning. If you cannot afford a lawyer, one will be provided for you at government expense." The more thorough warning asks the suspect at the end of each part of the statement if he/she understands. This may be made more comprehensive by having the suspect sign that they understand. The result was that police work became more effective and led to an increase in convictions and a decrease in successful appeals. The terms Miranda rights and Miranda warning are commonly associated with the apprehension of a suspect and precede questioning of the suspect. *See also* FOURTH AMENDMENT.

M'NAGHTEN RULE. The M'Naghten rule (often spelled McNaughton) is more commonly referred to by the expressions "**not guilty by reason of insanity**" and "guilty but insane." In 1843 Daniel M'Naghten was acquitted of the **murder** of Edward Drummond, whom he had mistaken for British prime minister **Robert Peel**. Since that time, rules or tests for sanity have been developed to determine whether the defendant is mentally disordered. The establishment of the mental incapacity of the defendant relieves the defendant of liability for the offense. While M'Naghten is not common to the United States, the intention is often popularized in book and other media, though it is seldom utilized as an actual defense. *See also* GUILTY BUT MENTALLY ILL; INSANITY DEFENSE.

MOBILIZATION FOR YOUTH. The concept originated in 1957 in the Lower East Side of New York during the board of directors meeting for the Henry Street Settlement House as a means of combating delinquency. The program did not officially begin until 1962 and focused on **gangs**, drugs, and **violence**. Mobilization for Youth emphasized the need for education, job training, counseling, and services to families. The program also emphasized the development of community. The program has not been viewed as successful because of an overfocus on youth and not the community and ignoring other variables in the community that affect youth.

MOBSTER. A mobster is someone who belongs to a **gang** or has an association with **organized crime**. The term became popularized with law enforcement and the public with the rise of gangs in the 1920s and newspaper and film coverage of such persons as **Alphonse Capone** and those who associated with him and other gangs. *See also* MAFIA; RACKETEER INFLUENCED CORRUPT ORGANIZATION (RICO).

MOCK PRISON. *See* STANFORD PRISON EXPERIMENT.

MODEL PENAL CODE (MPC). The Model Penal Code was developed in 1962 by criminal law scholars led by the American Law Institute. The Model Penal Code was updated again in 1981. The purpose for developing the

Model Penal Code was to encourage consistency in the penal systems of the United States, given that each state codifies its own sets of laws. *See also* PENAL CODE.

MODUS OPERANDI (MO). A term used by law enforcement to refer to the method used in the commission of a crime. MO is an element of criminal **profiling** with origins that date back to the 1956 case of George "Mad Bomber" Metesky, when psychiatrist James Brussel was asked by the New York City **police** to examine the case. Metesky's process was correct as he utilized such features as an analysis of the personality, habits, age, and reason for committing the crimes of a would-be suspect. Metesky helped pave the way for the development of criminal profiling. *See also* BEHAVIORAL ANALYSIS UNIT (BAU); RESSLER, ROBERT (1937–2013).

MONEY LAUNDERING. Money laundering is the hiding of funds for such reasons as not paying taxes or taking money gained from crime and making it legal, that is, converting it into legitimate business to generate legal income. The history is ancient and includes hiding money so that the Chinese government (ca. 2000 B.C.) would not know of it and then confiscate the money. A recent popular activity is hiding money in offshore banks. Seizing money became a tool against money laundering during **Prohibition** in the 1930s and drug sales in the 1980s. These cases turned the rules of **evidence** around because in order to recover seized money (deemed dirty because of illegal gain), there had to be proof that it had been legally earned. *See also* ORGANIZED CRIME.

MORAL PANIC. Moral panic is the fear that some evil jeopardizes the welfare of society and that crime will increase. The fear is applied to such legislation and offenses as **prohibition**, drug **addiction**, sex offenses, and especially pedophilia, child **pornography**, human trafficking, **prostitution**, and child abduction. The problems are compounded when the issue of moral panic is associated with something else such as AIDS with drugs and prostitution or **violence** with video games. Of course, even the associated concerns gain more momentum when they are tied into real events such as the shootings at Columbine High School in 1999. The fear is counteracted with the passage of laws criminalizing the behavior or that seek to regulate the actions. Attempts to regulate have not met with success, such as the 2011 **U.S. Supreme Court** holding that regulating video game sales to minors was unconstitutional and that research was not convincing.

MORES. Mores, or social norms, are society's way of expressing its approval or disapproval of habits, customs, or taboos. Norms are not universal and are guided by cultural and religious customs. Some mores are more broadly applied than others, such as regarding acts of **incest**, which result in legislation criminalizing that behavior. Another broad application was the passage of the Eighteenth Amendment in 1919, which banned alcohol. A consequence was that **bootlegging** became a crime throughout the 1920s until the Twenty-First Amendment repealed the Eighteenth Amendment in 1933. *See also* FOLKWAYS; PROHIBITION.

MORRIS, NORVAL (1923–2004). Norval Morris was a criminologist, law professor, consultant, author of 15 books, frequent contributor to academic journals, and a reformer advocating for the rights of convicts. Among his more outstanding books are *Maconochie's Gentlemen: The Story of Norfolk Island* (2003), *The Roots of Modern* ***Prison Reform*** (2003), and *The Oxford History of the Prison* (1995). *See also* MACONOCHIE, CAPTAIN ALEXANDER (1787–1860).

MOTHERS AGAINST DRUNK DRIVING (MADD). A nonprofit group, represented in every U.S. state and Canada, founded to stop drunk driving, prevent underage drinking, and advocate for stricter policy. MADD was founded in 1980 by Candace Lightner following the death of her 13-year-old daughter caused by a drunk driver. MADD provides support for victims and advocates the safe use of alcohol. Drunk driving has declined by approximately 50 percent since the formation of MADD. Since 2000, MADD has proposed several plans and new legislation to impact drunk driving, such as implementation of the alcohol ignition interlock device in 2006.

MOTION FOR A BILL OF PARTICULARS. A formal request for a detailed written statement of charges from the prosecuting attorney. The motion for a bill of particulars, as a tool of the judicial process, was abolished in court systems during the 1930s and 1940s because **discovery** would provide the same information. *See also* EXCULPATORY EVIDENCE.

MOTION FOR A CHANGE OF VENUE. The legal process to move a **trial** to a new location to ensure a fair and impartial process. The earliest example seems to be Central Court Act of 1865, which governed England and Wales, in the case of William Palmer because of excessive publicity about the case. Recent U.S. examples include the 1991 Rodney King case—moved from Los Angeles to Ventura County; the 1995 **Timothy McVeigh** case—moved from Oklahoma to Denver, Colorado; and the 2002 cases of **John Muhammad** and **Lee Malvo**—moved from Northern Virginia to the

Chesapeake and Virginia Bay areas. A different perspective was taken in the 1996 **murder** case of Bernhardt Tiede, moved from Carthage to Henderson, Texas, because of fear that a **jury** would not convict. The victim was portrayed as an evil woman. *See also* BELTWAY SNIPER; OKLAHOMA CITY BOMBING.

MOTION FOR CONTINUANCE. A motion for continuance is a postponement of a judicial proceeding. A motion for continuance may be granted for many reasons, including illness (or to establish mental illness) or to secure **evidence**, witnesses, or other **trial** preparation, when through no fault the defendant has not been able to obtain them. *Barker v. Wingo*, 407 U.S. 514 (1972), established a four-part test to ensure that postponement would not violate the Sixth Amendment. Those factors are the cause for the delay, the length of the delay, an assertion of rights for a **speedy trial**, and prejudice that might result from a delay. *Sheppard v. Maxwell*, 384 U.S. 333 (1966), is often cited as the most famous case because of the news coverage which caused excessive speculation about his guilt. *See also* WITNESS.

MOTIVATED OFFENDER. A motivated offender is the focal point of crime opportunity theory as discussed by theorists Gottfredson and **Garofalo** (1978) and Cohen and Felson (1979). They suggest that motivated offenders focus on high reward, make rational choices, are ready to commit a crime, have the right environmental conditions, and there is little effort or risk. Crime opportunity theory provides a foundation for **community-oriented policing**, problem-solving policing, and environmental design for crime prevention. *See also* RATIONAL CHOICE THEORY.

MOTOR VEHICLE CHECKPOINTS. The creation of a roadblock for highway safety and to perform other law enforcement functions, including to inspect for valid identification and safety of vehicles; to search for fugitives, weapons, and contraband; and to assess for DUI. Three important **U.S. Supreme Court** cases include:

United States v. Martinez-Fuerte, 428 U.S. 543 (1976), which allowed discretionless immigration checkpoints.

Michigan Department of ***State Police*** *v. Sitz*, 496 U.S. 444 (1990), which allowed focused informational checkpoints.

City of Indianapolis v. Edmond, 496 U.S. 444 (2000), which held that general crime fighting and discretionary checkpoints were not allowed.

MOTOR VEHICLE THEFT. The term refers to the theft or attempted theft of a motor vehicle. There are more than 721,000 such thefts each year with losses totaling more than $4 billion. The first car theft occurred in Paris in June 1896 of a Peugeot by the manufacturer's mechanic during repairs. All-time car theft highs were reached in 1991 when they surpassed 1.6 million. The first federal legislation intended to assist states combating vehicle theft was the Dyer Act of 1919, which addressed the transportation of cars across state lines. The penalties included incarceration up to 10 years and **fines**. Theft of motor vehicles has a variety of descriptions depending upon the jurisdiction and includes **carjacking**, theft of motor vehicles without keys, opportunistic theft, fraudulent theft, theft with access to keys, and taken without owners' consent.

MOULAGE. A wax model of persons and injuries to assist in criminal investigations. The practice began in the 16th century probably by Andreas Vesalius (1514–1564) at the University of Paris to aid physicians and scientists in the study of anatomy and injuries. Previous knowledge of human anatomy was based on animal dissections and descriptions, which contained many errors. Moulage has evolved into several skilled forensic activities, which include composite and postmortem drawing and forensic sculpture that enable investigators to attain an image of the victim with which to achieve an identification. The field of forensic artistic skills also includes crime scene sketching. *See also* FORENSICS.

MUFFLER. A muffler is also known as a silencer or sound suppressor that is attached to the barrel of a firearm to reduce muzzle flash and noise at the time of firing. Hiram Maxim invented the Maxim silencers in 1902. Civilian use of silencers is banned.

MUG SHOT. A mug shot is a photograph taken by the **police** after an arrest. It is used to assist **witnesses** and victims in ascertaining the identity of a perpetrator. Mug shots began to be taken in the 1840s (the earliest are probably from Belgium in 1843), but **Alfred Bertillon**, a French police officer, standardized the process by utilizing a full face and profile. Among the earliest uses of the mug shot was by the Pinkerton **detective** agency by placing them on **wanted posters** and later by the **FBI** when it created its 10 Most Wanted list. The frontal and side or profile mug shots were probably first used to help capture those involved in the Lincoln assassination. Following John Anglin's June 1962 escape from **Alcatraz**, a mug shot wanted poster was circulated to assist in his unsuccessful capture.

MUHAMMAD, JOHN ALLEN (1960–2009). The "**Beltway Sniper**" who along with Lee Malvo (1985–) killed 10 persons and wounded three others in the Washington metropolitan area. These were spree killings that occurred in 2002. Lee Malvo was a 17-year-old juvenile who along with Muhammad stood **trial** on one count of **murder** in Virginia and was also convicted of six murders in Maryland. Muhammad has been linked to murders in Alabama, Arizona, Louisiana, Washington, California, and Texas. Muhammad was sentenced to death in 2004 and was subsequently **executed** on 10 November 2009. *See also* MASS MURDER.

MULTIPLE HOMICIDE. Multiple **homicide** is also referred to as **mass murder**. This type of **murder** includes intentional and indiscriminate killing. In addition, it is usually associated with government agents such as soldiers who would shoot protesters or use other weapons to kill civilians. Such killings have often come under the heading of **crimes against humanity**. The qualifications for multiple homicide have changed. In the 1960s and 1970s the more defining feature was a high body count. The definition became more refined in the late 20th century to include the variables of time, place, and methodology of the killings.

MULTIPLE PERSONALITY DISORDER (MPD). MPD is also referred to as dissociative identity disorder (DID) and had previously been diagnosed as hysterical neurosis. MPD is described as a mental disorder differentiated by two or more separate states of personality that are interchangeably confirmed in an individual's behavior, states of consciousness, or identity. The more dominant opinion is that these are not separate and distinct entities of personality but rather the manifestation of a failure to possess a single unified identity. MPD is a controversial topic regarding the cause. One of the suspected primary causes is trauma. DID is the defense in less than 1 percent of criminal accusations and is seldom successful. The *State v. Milligan* (1978), a state of Ohio Supreme Court case, was the first use of the defense. Milligan was judged to be insane (not a psychiatric diagnosis) and not blameworthy of the offense. An immense public furor followed, and the defense has been unsuccessful following this case. However, there has been controversy over its acceptance until *State v. Green*, 03C01–9610-CR-00379 (Tenn. Crim. App. 1998), which found that reliable standards of scientific **evidence** were not met and that expert testimony was not admissible in court because of unreliability. *See also* INSANITY DEFENSE.

MULTISYSTEMIC THERAPY (MST). Multisystemic therapy is a crime prevention program that teaches parenting skills/family therapy to prevent **juvenile delinquency**. The program better enables youth and family to manage problems encountered in the home, at school, with peers, and in the neighborhood. The multisystemic therapy approach was developed in the late 1970s by the Family Services Research Center of the Department of Psychiatry and Behavioral Sciences Medical Center, South Carolina.

MURDER. *See* FELONY MURDER DOCTRINE.

MURDER CASTLE. The "Murder Castle" was located a few miles from the site of the 1893 Chicago World's Fair. Specially built by H. H. Holmes (1861–1896), the structure was a city block and three stories high and nicknamed the Castle. Holmes has been described as one of the more prolific **serial killers** with confirmed deaths of 27 and a suspected total of 200 or more. A large number of gruesome human remains were found in the basement of the building. The killings and the means of death are largely conjecture, inasmuch as no one ever admitted to the specifics of the deaths. Holmes was **hanged** in Philadelphia for another crime. *See also* EXECUTION; MASS MURDER.

MURDER INC. Murder Inc. is also called Murder Incorporated and is believed to be responsible for up to 1,000 **organized crime** murders or **contract killings**. The name probably originated in the press after its founding in the late 1920s following the establishment of the **National Crime Syndicate**. Murder Inc. reportedly carried out murders for several organized crime groups in the 1930s and 1940s. Dutch Schultz, one of the more well-known **gangsters** of the 1920s, was killed by Murder Inc. for his disobedience to the Commission when he attempted to kill New York City prosecutor Thomas Dewey. Many reputed members of Murder Inc. were convicted and executed for **murder**. *See also* MAFIA.

MURPHY, JACK ROLAND "MURPH THE SURF" (1938–). A colorful surfing champion, author (*Jewels for the Journey*, 1989), artist, and musician who became infamous for his criminal acts. His infamy and popularity began with the 1964 burglary of the J. P. Morgan collection of jewels, which included the Eagle Diamond (never recovered) and the Star of India, for which he received a three-year sentence. He was convicted of **murder** in 1968 and received a life without **parole** sentence. A jailhouse conversion occurred in 1974. His ministry inside the **prison** resulted in his parole in 1986. He continued his ministry, and in 2000 his lifetime parole was terminated. The 1975 movie *Murf the Surf* chronicled his criminal acts.

MUSIC PIRACY. Copying and circulating the work of a recording artist or a composer without the consent of the artist or the holder of a copyright. While widespread piracy developed with the internet and the creation of digital media, the history is extensive. Beethoven in the mid-1700s experienced lost income from unauthorized copies of his music. The internet company Napster found itself at the center of the controversy over what may be copied and distributed. A lawsuit filed in 2000 by Metallica resulted in Napster's being shut down. Copying and distributing are not illegal in all countries. *See also* COPYRIGHT INFRINGEMENT.

MUTILATION. Mutilation has been an accepted and at times a common form of **punishment** for those committing criminal acts. Mutilations were also meant to send a message to other would-be wrongdoers because the punishment was visible. Famous examples include *The Scarlet Letter* (the **branding** or the wearing of a placard that bore the letter of the offense, e.g., *A* for adultery or *B* for blasphemy) and the removal of hands (for thievery) or severing of the nose (for adultery). One of the more macabre descriptions is provided by Foucault for the crime of regicide and included the tearing of flesh, being drawn and quartered by four horses, and finally being placed on a burning pyre. Mutilation is no longer permitted as punishment. *See also* CRUEL AND UNUSUAL PUNISHMENT; EIGHTH AMENDMENT.

N

NAÏVE CHECK FORGER. Edward Lemert's research has divided check forgers into two groups: naïve and systematic. Naïve check forgers are those who have no prior criminal record and are passing a bad check for the first time. The forger is motivated by circumstance and situation, for example, other deviant behavior such as **gambling** or alcoholism. The systematic check forger is the professional and is also called a "paper hanger."

NARCOTERRORISM. In 1983, former president Fernando Belaúnde Terry of Peru coined the term to describe attacks against the antinarcotics **police**. Threats, intimidation, and **violence** were used to manipulate legislation, law enforcement, and policies related to drug traffickers. An example of an individual and an organization is Pablo Escobar and the Colombian **drug cartel**. A more recent example is **Al-Qaeda**. The merger of the drug trade and terrorism has created new difficulties for the United States. Drugs help to finance terrorism. *See also* DRUG TRAFFICKING; NARCOTICS; TERRORISM.

NARCOTICS. The Greek physician Galen is one of the earliest recorded users of the term to mean something that numbs or causes paralysis. Narcotics are referred to as depressants. Opioids such as morphine and **heroin** as well as derivatives such as hydrocodone and oxycodone reduce pain and induce sleep or can induce coma. Other examples include amphetamines and cocaine. These are referred to as stimulants. Narcotics have a legitimate use in medicine and must be prescribed by a medical doctor for use. When obtained by means other than a prescription, they are illegal, and possession, use, and distribution have legal consequences.

NARRATIVE CRIMINOLOGY. A criminological approach to understanding relationships between patterns of life events and crime and **desistance from crime**. These are stories that help explain offending, its moralization and motivations. The narrative has been suggested as a means through which individuals become predisposed to conduct that which is unacceptable in society (Toch 1993). On the other hand, it is also a conduit through which to reinforce desistance from the criminal lifestyle (Maruna 2001).

NATIONAL ARCHIVE OF CRIMINAL JUSTICE DATA (NACJD). The archive assists criminal justice research by archiving, maintaining, improving, distributing, and making available research data. NACJD, founded in 1978, provides workshops in quantitative analysis of data.

NATIONAL ASSOCIATION OF CRIMINAL DEFENSE LAWYERS (NACDL). The mission statement for NACDL defines the purpose of the organization as being to ensure justice and **due process** for persons accused of crime; foster the integrity, independence, and expertise of the criminal defense profession; and promote the proper and fair administration of criminal justice.

NATIONAL BULLYING PREVENTION CENTER. The center was created in 2006 to focus on the **bullying** of children with disabilities and has expanded its concerns to being an agency of social change, providing resources for schools, parents, and others to address bullying in any form with children, emphasizing that it is not a childhood phase and that it affects the developmental process of youth. *See also* OLWEUS BULLYING PREVENTION PROGRAM.

NATIONAL CENTER FOR EXPLOSIVES TRAINING AND RESEARCH (NCETR). A function of the Bureau of Alcohol, Tobacco, Firearms and Explosives that provides research and training for crime with explosives and other related activities, including improvised explosive devices (IEDs).

NATIONAL CRIME INFORMATION CENTER (NCIC). The database created by **FBI** director **J. Edgar Hoover** in 1967, which shares crime-related information between branches of law enforcement. Among the many crime-related subjects maintained in the database are foreign fugitives, **gang** files, **identity theft**, immigration violators, missing persons, the National Instant Criminal **Background Check** System, the Sex Offense Registry, **terrorism**, unidentified persons, and wanted persons.

NATIONAL CRIME SYNDICATE. An association with uncertain origins of a criminal organization comprised of Italian **Mafia** and Jewish **mobsters** in the United States. There is some agreement that the syndicate was the creation of **Meyer Lansky**, who proposed it to crime bosses in Atlantic City in 1929. The rationale for the syndicate was to have the various mob groups work together for a more profitable enterprise. One of the more infamous outgrowths was **Murder Inc.**, supposedly the enforcement subdivision for the syndicate. The syndicate and Murder Inc. lost their significance by 1940 due to the incarceration, **execution**, and deportation of the leaders.

NATIONAL CRIME VICTIMIZATION SURVEY (NCVS). Data for the NCVS was first collected in 1972 to gather information about victimization. The NCVS is a self-report study that asks respondents about crime and the frequency of crime during the preceding six months. The survey helps fill gaps between the **Uniform Crime Report** and the "**dark figure of crime**." Current samples surveyed are approximately 90,000 households and approximately 160,000 individuals.

NATIONAL GANG CENTER (NGC). A federal project sponsored by the Department of Justice. It has collected data annually between 1996 and 2012 from law enforcement agencies, which created a series of databases from which to assess information about gangs in the United States. The information was used to develop a registry of gangs, their characteristics, activities and other issues associated with gangs. *See also* CRIPS; GANG; LATIN KINGS.

NATIONAL INCIDENT-BASED REPORTING SYSTEM (NIBRS). The National Incident-Based Reporting System is maintained by the **FBI** as a nationwide effort to compile statistical reports from more than 18,000 federal, state, county, city, college, and tribal law enforcement agencies. The data collected are incident based and arrest reports from category A, which specifies 49 crimes that fall into 23 categories. The NIBRS system is more comprehensive than the **Uniform Crime Report (UCR)** because it includes specific facts about each of the crimes. NIBRS began operations in 1989 following a study in 1982 as a more inclusive collection of data than had been previously gathered for the UCR and which would better meet the needs of law enforcement for research and planning. In time, NIBRS will replace the UCR, begun in the 1920s by the **International Association of Chiefs of Police**. Inadequacies in the UCR were noted in 1970, which led to recognition of the need for a new way to document and compile crime statistics. The FBI anticipates that NIBRS will replace the UCR by 2021.

NATIONAL NIGHT OUT. A crime prevention program created in 1984 by the Bureau of Justice Assistance. The strategy is to build trust and improve relationships with **police** and community around local events. Research has validated that the program improves feelings of public safety while enhancing policing programs by having individuals know their neighbors and their neighborhoods. Sponsored events include cookouts and demonstrations during which a variety of crime prevention and law enforcement awareness opportunities are presented with the purpose of enhancing town watches, **neighborhood watches**, and drug prevention.

NATIONAL ORGANIZATION FOR THE REFORM OF MARIJUANA LAWS (NORML). The Playboy Foundation provided an initial $5,000, which created the private nonprofit foundation in 1970. NORML seeks to improve public opinion about cannabis, allow cultivation for personal consumption, and decriminalize it. It is a grassroots organization in the United States and has since spread to other countries, including Canada, the U.K., and France. *See also* DECRIMINALIZATION.

NATIONAL ORGANIZATION OF BLACK LAW ENFORCEMENT EXECUTIVES (NOBLE). NOBLE was founded in 1970 to address concerns about urban crime, equity for black **police** officers (including hiring and promotion), police-community relationships, and other issues facing minorities in the law enforcement profession.

NATIONAL SECURITY AGENCY (NSA). The NSA began as the Cipher Bureau in 1917 three weeks after the United States entered World War I. The NSA has at other times been called the Black Chamber and MI-8 in 1919. To mask its high-security work, it was known as the New York Commercial Code Company in 1918 when it was relocated to New City. The NSA is responsible for many intelligence activities designed to protect the United States. For example, in 1986 the NSA obtained information that implicated Libya in the Berlin discotheque bombing, which led to the U.S. bombing of Libya. The NSA has also been an agency of controversial activities (since the events of 9/11 and the passage of the **Patriot Act**), particularly for "data mining" the personal information of U.S. citizens, including personal information from phone records and social media interactions. Such actions have been suggested to be illegal and violations of the **Fourth Amendment**.

NATURE-NURTURE DEBATE. The debate whether innate (inherited) qualities or experience (interactions with the environment) is the primary foundation or source of human behavior. Among the earliest considerations is the work of John Locke in the late 1600s who proposed that the human mind is a tabula rasa or blank slate. His proposition was that individuals acquire all or almost all behavior from their experiences. In the 1920s and 1930s, John Watson pursued the significance of cultural influence, which has gained greater acceptance. Meanwhile, heritability studies since the 1930s, especially those involving twins, have shifted the argument from emphasis on nurture to the influence of nature and to the identification of which factors from nurture or from nature may influence criminal behavior. The argument has influenced criminal justice in terms of the culpability of individuals who commit crime. A resurgence in interest in the debate has occurred over the past few decades with investigations into the brain and genetics. Notable efforts have been the Human Genome Project begun in 1990 and twin studies. A determination that has changed our perspective is that perhaps the balance is 50/50 in terms of nature-nurture shaping behavior.

NEAR REPEAT ANALYSIS. A tool for law enforcement agencies developed in the early 1990s utilizing Near Repeat Analysis Calculator software to analyze patterns of victimization for specific types of crimes within geographic areas and time frames, such as the phenomenon of near repeat or repeat crime, that is, crime that is repeated at the same crime scene because of the comfort of the offender after a few days or because of a specified distance from a previous crime. This analysis is used in conjunction with **crime mapping**, which identifies mapped zones of crimes for initiating crime prevention efforts across communities. *See also* VICTIMOLOGY.

***NEBRASKA PRESS ASSOCIATION V. STUART*, 427 U.S. 539 (1976).** A landmark **U.S. Supreme Court** holding which held that media presence during criminal trials was not unconstitutional. Chief Justice Warren Burger affirmed the **First Amendment** right for freedom of the press unless a "clear and present danger" existed that would jeopardize a fair **trial**.

NECROPHILIA. Necrophilia is also called thanatophilia and is the attraction to or a sexual act with a corpse. The term was coined by Joseph Guislain in 1850. **Jeffrey Dahmer** was a convicted **serial killer** who first murdered his victims and then performed sexual acts upon them. Another example was Jeffrey Nilsen (1945–), who is serving a life term in a British **prison**. There are no federal statutes against necrophilia. About 30 states prohibit it. *See also* MURDER.

NEIGHBORHOOD WATCH. A group of civilians sometimes referred to as a crime watch that is organized and provided with some security training to prevent crime and **vandalism** and to report suspicious actions to law enforcement. The earliest forms of neighborhood watch were the "hue and cry" developed in England in 1285. This was adapted to become the town watch in Colonial America. Interest in neighborhood watch increased after the 1964 **Kitty Genovese murder** in New York, which was marked by no one coming to her aid while she screamed for her life. However, controversy developed after the 2012 **Trayvon Martin** shooting by **George Zimmerman** in Florida. Zimmerman was a civilian, and the shooting led to his **trial** for second-degree murder. Zimmerman claimed self-defense and was acquitted.

NEOCLASSICIAL SCHOOL OF CRIMINOLOGY. The neoclassical school of criminology furthers the conventions of the classical school of thought that begins with **Cesare Beccaria** and **Jeremy Bentham**. A resurgence of neoclassical theory development began in the 1970s and continued into the 1990s because of renewed emphasis on harsher **punishments** due to the collapse of rehabilitation. The major difference between the two schools is recognition of individual differences of offenders and that punishment should reflect that recognition. Among the factors to be taken into consideration were age, social class, and gender. The primary differences are the disavowal of inflexible punishment and the use of discretion. The **plea bargain** and the **jury** system may be viewed as outgrowths of this school of thought. *See also* DUE PROCESS MODEL; TOUGH ON CRIME.

NESS, ELLIOT (1903–1957). A law enforcement official in Cleveland and Chicago. In Cleveland, he weeded out corruption that involved more than 200 **police** officers and 15 politicians. **Ness** began his law enforcement career as a federal treasury agent and later as a Justice Department agent. He headed up a **Prohibition** squad that became known as the "untouchables." His mission was to select special agents (there would be nine) who would seek to shut down the **Alphonse Capone** crime empire in the Chicago, Illinois, area. *See also* MAFIA; MOBSTER; ORGANIZED CRIME.

NET WIDENING. The **War on Crime** initiated in the 1960s resulted in social control measures that increased the number of juveniles under the influence of the juvenile justice system, programs were created to divert juveniles from entry points into the system. However, there were unintended consequences to this action. Research revealed that **diversion** programs became a gateway into the system, or what was also referred to as widening the net, destabilizing the intention of the programs. Diversion was also initiated in the adult correctional systems and had a similar effect. Net widening is used to describe entry into both juvenile and adult correctional systems as a consequence of diversion programs. *See also* MASS INCARCERATION.

NEUTRALIZATION THEORY. Proposed by David Matza and Gresham Sykes in 1964 to suggest that those who commit crime or acts of delinquency drift from traditional values using neutralization techniques—shifting off the mechanisms used by individuals to maintain a moral balance so that illegal/

immoral acts may occur. The theory proposes that moral codes are not replaced but are provisionally supplanted by other codes that permit acts of crime and delinquency. Matza and Sykes were influenced by **Edwin Sutherland**'s research in the 1950s on **differential association**.

NEWGATE PRISON, CONNECTICUT (1773–1827). Newgate **Prison** has the distinction of being the first official **penitentiary** in the United States. The prison was converted from tunnels built to mine copper. It mirrored the philosophy of **Eastern State Penitentiary**, which sought a more humane environment to the **whipping** post and other **corporal punishments**. It confined political prisoners as well as those convicted of criminal offenses and later women. Despite its original humane intentions, the treatment of prisoners became cruel. They were used to mine copper until it was no longer profitable. For that reason and for its deplorable conditions, it was closed in 1827. *See also* CRUEL AND UNUSUAL PUNISHMENT.

NEW GENERATION JAIL. New generation jails were introduced by the National Institute of Corrections in the 1980s and are comprised of two types: indirect supervision and direct supervision—both designs improve effectiveness and allow ongoing supervision of **inmates**. They are a response to older architectural styles that date back to the original **prisons** of the early 1800s, which limited observation and provided spaces in which jail occupants could violate the rules of the jail. Indirect supervision places a secure officer's station within a POD and uses microphones and speakers for communication. Direct supervision is structured with a cluster of cells around a living area (POD), which contains tables, chairs, games, books, television, etc. The officer is inside the POD, which allows direct contact and interaction with the inmates. There is a raised station outside the POD, which allows other officers to supervise activity in all PODS surrounding that station. Both indirect and direct supervision designs are intended to improve monitoring while decreasing disturbances and other unwanted behavior.

NEWSMAKING CRIMINOLOGY. Criminologist Gregg Barak advocated that criminologists involve the media to reframe popular and misconceived notions of crime and justice. Barak began his work in the 1980s, and it has since spread to other countries, influencing the manner in which events such as **domestic violence** and gender issues are perceived.

NEWTOWN MASSACRE. The Newtown massacre is also referred to as the Sandy Hook Elementary School shooting. It was the worst school shooting and the second-worst mass shooting in U.S. history. In 2012, 20-year-old **Adam Lanza** first killed his mother and then shot and killed 20 children and six adults before committing suicide. The shooting fueled the ongoing debate about **gun control**, emphasizing the types of guns and ammunition owned by citizens as well as urging stricter **background checks**. No motives have been determined for the shootings. *See also* COLUMBINE MASSACRE; MASS MURDER; SANDY HOOK MASSACRE.

NEW YORK HOUSE OF REFUGE. Built in Manhattan in 1825 in the congregate style of **prison** construction, the New York House of Refuge would initiate the **reformatory** system (and youth detention centers) in the United States. The idea was put forth by the Society for the Prevention of Pauperism to remove delinquents deemed poor, incorrigible, or abandoned from the streets. Significantly, the idea would be the first effort to separate youth from adults. The movement would rapidly spread nationally.

***NEW YORK V. FERBER*, 458 U.S. 747 (1982).** The **U.S. Supreme Court** holding which clarified that the **First Amendment** free speech guarantee did not prohibit states from forbidding the sale of pictures and other media that portrayed children involved in sexual activity. *See also* FREEDOM OF SPEECH; PORNOGRAPHY.

***NEW YORK V. QUARLES*, 467 U.S. 649 (1984).** *See* QUARLES DECISION, *NEW YORK V. QUARLES*, 467 U.S. 649 (1984).

NICHOLS, TERRY L. (1953–). One of three coconspirators in the truck bombing of the Alfred P. Murrah Federal Building in Oklahoma City, Oklahoma, on 19 April 1995. He was convicted of 161 counts of first-degree **murder** involving federal law enforcement officials, conspiracy to use a **weapon of mass destruction**, and **involuntary manslaughter**. The **jury** was deadlocked over the **capital murder** charge, and he was given 161 consecutive life sentences without the possibility of **parole**. He is serving his sentence at ADX Florence, Colorado, the federal **supermax prison**.

***NIX V. WILLIAMS*, 467 U.S. 431 (1984).** The **U.S. Supreme Court** holding which determined that **evidence** that would inevitably be discovered would be admissible and not a violation of the **Fourth Amendment**. *See also* EXCLUSIONARY RULE; *MAPP V. OHIO*, 367 U.S. 643 (1961); SEARCH AND SEIZURE; WARRANTLESS SEARCHES.

NO-FLY LIST. The Terrorist Screening Center of the United States maintains a list of those not allowed to fly on domestic and foreign commercial aircraft either inside or outside of U.S. airspace. The list is also used to divert commercial aircraft away from U.S. airspace. The list was created following the attacks of 11 September 2001. While the list increases each year, it has been broadly criticized for reasons such as privacy, establishing false positives, **discrimination**, cost, **due process**, and civil liberties violations. *See also* TERRORISM; WORLD TRADE CENTER (WTC) BOMBINGS.

NO FRILLS PRISONS AND JAILS. No frills **prisons** and jails refer to the elimination of "amenities" for prisoners. Among the amenities eliminated include weightlifting, hot meals, and personal clothing. The "no frills" movement began in the early 1990s as a response to frustration with prison success and as a favorite vehicle for politicians to promote themselves as **tough on crime**. Many states have passed legislation limiting what convicts may have. Notably, many states and the **Federal Bureau of Prisons** have developed "no frills" policies.

NOGUCHI, THOMAS (1927–). The chief **medical examiner** of Los Angeles County, California, from 1967 to 1982. He either autopsied or supervised the autopsies of high-profile public figures such as Robert Kennedy, Sharon Tate, and Natalie Wood as criminal cases or potential criminal cases.

NOIR CRIME NOVEL. The noir crime novel followed the "hard-boiled" **detective** novel of the 1920s. Edgar Allen Poe is credited with originating the detective story. The "noir" crime novel is comprised of one of two themes. Either it is based on true-life crime, or it addresses a variety of social issues such as racism or sexual equality. The noir crime novel also includes **police** procedure. *See also* CRIME NOVEL; TRUE CRIME.

NO-KNOCK WARRANT. Law enforcement officers are allowed to enter premises without alerting the occupants. The purpose is to avoid the destruction of **evidence** before seizure or to avoid increasing the risk to law enforcement. No-knock warrants have increased from about 3,000 a year in the early 1980s to more than 50,000 a year since 2000. The **Fourth Amendment** prohibits unreasonable searches and seizures. The **warrant** is issued in cases where there is reasonable suspicion of crime or other illegal circumstances. The constitutional protection raises controversial issues of **probable cause** due to the severe increase in no-knock warrants being issued. Additional controversy has surrounded the number of innocent victims resulting from the warrants as well as instances of no findings following the search. *See also* *MAPP V. OHIO*, 367 U.S. 643 (1961); SEARCH AND SEIZURE; WARRANTLESS SEARCHES.

NOLLE PROSEQUI. A legal term that refers to a prosecutor abandoning further prosecution against a defendant. The declaration may come before legal proceedings begin, during the proceedings, or at any time prior to a verdict. Judges generally do not challenge these decisions and sign a **dismissal** order. The rationale for the declaration varies and includes lack of **evidence**, tainted evidence, or other circumstances in which a **burden of proof** is not possible or is in question. The earliest use of nolle prosequi may be a 1902 case in Peasenhall, England, in which a 16-year-old unmarried pregnant girl was murdered. A local minister was twice tried, and each time the **jury** could not reach a verdict. The jury in the second trial voted 11–1 in favor of the defendant. The prosecutor then declared nolle prosequi. A more recent example is the case of **Osama bin Laden**. The U.S. Department of Justice filed for nolle prosequi following his death.

NOMADIC KILLER. A **serial killer** who does not remain in a single location but often moves from one place to another after completing their crime. Angel Maturing Resendiz (called the Railroad Killer) is an example. He committed at least 15 murders in five states. *See also* MURDER; TERRITORIAL KILLERS.

NONINSTITUTIONAL CORRECTIONS. Correctional practices that are carried out in the community, such as residential treatment, **halfway houses**, day reporting, and other interventions by both governmental and private providers.

***NORRIS V. ALABAMA*, 294 U.S. 587 (1935).** A **U.S. Supreme Court** case which held that African Americans being systematically excluded from **jury duty** was **discrimination** and a violation of the **Eighth Amendment**. Clarence Norris was one of the black men of the infamous **Scottsboro boys** case. *See also POWELL V. ALABAMA*, 287 U.S. 45 (1932).

NORTHWESTERN UNIVERSITY CENTER FOR PUBLIC SAFETY. The center was founded in 1936 and given its present name in 2000 as a response to traffic fatalities. It provides training to both law enforcement and private business in matters of traffic safety, crash scene analysis, **police** operations, transportation engineering, and other management courses.

NOT GUILTY BY REASON OF INSANITY. A plea entered by a defense attorney on behalf of the defendant or a disposition by the court that the mental state of the defendant is such that they cannot be held legally accountable for the crime for which they have been charged. The defendant cannot distinguish that their actions are right or wrong, or they cannot determine the legality of their actions. While the concept has historical precedent dating back to the **Code of Hammurabi**, it is an infrequent defense since the Criminal Procedure Act of 1991 (described as the Insanity or Unfitness to Plead Act), which replaced the Criminal Procedure Act of 1964 or Insanity Act. *See also* DURHAM RULE; GUILTY BUT MENTALLY ILL; INSANITY DEFENSE; M'NAGHTEN RULE.

NOTHING WORKS. A phrase erroneously attributed **Dr. Robert Martinson** in his article "What Works: Questions and Answers about **Prison Reform**," published in 1979. The phrase suggests and was interpreted to mean that programs in correctional facilities to rehabilitate offenders will not work. Martinson was misquoted and taken out of context, which helped contribute to the most massive changes in criminal legislation, correctional policy, and operations in correctional history. *See also* EVIDENCE-BASED PRACTICES; MASS INCARCERATION.

NO TRUE BILL. No true bill is a grand **jury** decision not to indict an offender. A prosecutor may or may not accept the determination and present the indictment again to the same grand jury or another grand jury. The decision of no true bill does not prevent a prosecutor from proceeding with a federal prosecution. No true bill does not prevent a civil action. The use of "true bill" and "no true bill" dates to the reign of Edward I of England, approximately 1827, and was adopted by the American colonies. *See also* CIVIL LAW.

NUMBERS RACKET. The numbers racket (an illegal lottery) is also referred to as the numbers game, policy racket, and Italian lottery. The numbers racket dates back to colonial times and was very popular during the Depression as participants hoped for a win and their salvation from poverty. Bets would be placed at small businesses such as mom-and-pop grocery stores and taverns, referred to as betting parlors. The operations generally are found in poor neighborhoods wherein the participant selects three numbers. The winning lottery number(s) is selected the following day. One of the more popular means for selecting the number is to use the published account in a newspaper of the amount bet at the racetrack. The final three numbers of that amount would be the winning numbers. It has been common for **organized crime** to take over small numbers rackets because of their profitability as a cash business.

NUREMBURG WAR CRIMES TRIALS. Nazi **war criminals** (important leaders of Nazi Germany) were tried before military tribunals after World War II. Most of the **trials** were conducted during 1945 and 1946. Some were imprisoned while others committed suicide before **execution** by **hanging**. The most notable offenses were those related to the Holocaust. The precedent for the Nuremburg **War Crimes** Trials were the Leipzig Trials of 1921 following World War I. The Nuremburg Accords were developed at this time to regulate the treatment of prisoners in all countries including the United States. *See also* GENOCIDE; MASS MURDER.

O

OBSCENITY. A statement, explanation, expression, or action that is offensive or that affronts public moral values. Obscenity, for example, is often associated with **pornography**, **murder**, and sex. A variety of laws seek to regulate and/or punish obscenity on the state and federal levels. That which is considered obscene comes under review as it infringes on personal (or civil) liberty. An example of **punishment** for obscenity was the case of in re Gault, **387 U.S. 1, 20 (1967)**. **Gerald Gault** received a six-year **custodial sentence** for an obscene phone call.

OBSTRUCTION OF JUSTICE. An **indictable offense** which may be committed by a suspect, **witness**, judge, prosecutor, defense attorney, or other government official such as an **attorney general**. Obstructions of justice may come in the form of lying, destruction of **evidence**, providing a false alibi, or concealment of their own involvement in a specific crime under investigation or some other crime for which they are not as yet implicated. Such persons may invoke their **Fifth Amendment** rights. A case of obstruction of justice includes former president Richard Nixon, who influenced his staff to remain silent about their involvement in the Watergate break-in. Baseball player Barry Bonds was accused and convicted of providing false testimony with regard to the steroid scandal. His conviction was overturned in the appellate court. There may soon be a new related term, "anticipatory obstruction of justice," in which acts are committed in the event that there might be an investigation—such an act would be the destruction of records before the fact.

OCCUPATIONAL CRIME. Crime that occurs during the course of a standard occupation. An employee who takes advantage of a job to do something illegal. This type of crime has been referred to as workplace crime and occupational deviance. Generally, occupational crime falls into four categories: professional, individual, state-based authority, and organizational. Professionals violate the trust of clients and patients, such as overbilling the client. Individuals take advantage of opportunities such as submitting falsified expense reports. State-based authorities abuse the exercise of power such as accepting bribes and kickbacks. And organizational professionals take advantage of circumstances to benefit the company, such as price fixing or falsifying records. *See also* WHITE-COLLAR CRIME.

OFFENSES KNOWN TO POLICE. Offenses known to **police** is a phrase commonly associated with the **Uniform Crime Report**, which gathers crime statistics from about 18,000 law enforcement agencies. Crimes known to police include crimes discovered by law enforcement and others that are reported to the police from sources such as the general public. This phrase does not encompass all crimes committed, since some crimes remain unknown. Efforts to gather information about crimes and unknown crimes is done independently through other research such as the **National Crime Victimization Survey**. *See also* DARK FIGURE OF CRIME; NATIONAL INCIDENT-BASED REPORTING SYSTEM (NIBRS).

OFFICE FOR VICTIMS OF CRIME (OVC). The 1984 Victims of Crime Act (VOCA) created the office to administer the Crime Victims Fund. OVC provides funding for a wide variety of programs that are centered on the needs of victims affected by crime so that their lives may be restored. All states have access to victim compensation, technical assistance, training, and other programs from OVC. *See also* VICTIM ASSISTANCE PROGRAM; VICTIMIZATION RATE.

OFFICE OF COMMUNITY ORIENTED POLICING SERVICES (COPS). COPS was created in 1994 with the mission of improving the relationship of communities and law enforcement through improved community policing practices. COPS provides reports on serious incidents such as the 2016 shooting in Orlando, Florida, at the Pulse Nightclub, which reviewed the police response and cited examples to be learned from the incident.

OFFICE OF JUSTICE PROGRAMS (OJP). OJP was preceded by the Office of Law Enforcement Assistance (1965–1968) and then by the **Law Enforcement Assistance Administration** (1968–1984). OJP continues and expands the work of its predecessors by building local, state, and federal partnerships through which to distribute information about best practices, encourage new approaches to managing crime through grants, and identify the most recent challenges to law enforcement and the justice system.

OFFICE OF JUVENILE JUSTICE AND DELINQUENCY PREVENTION (OJJDP). OJJDP was created by the Juvenile Justice and Delinquency Prevention (JJDP) Act (Pub. L. No. 93-415, 42 U.S.C. § 5601 et seq.) in 1974. OJJDP has had a broad influence on the improvement of the juvenile justice system through the development and implementation of effective programs. OJJDP has a multifaceted mission that seeks to improve public safety through the treatment and accountability of offenders and research at the state and local levels. The work of OJJDP that affects both juveniles and their families is accomplished through grants of aid to local and state agencies to implement new programs (that are generally based on **evidence-based practices**) or to improve their operations. The leadership role of OJJDP was enhanced by the reauthorization of the act on 2 November 2002.

OFFICE OF SEX OFFENDER SENTENCING, MONITORING, APPREHENDING, REGISTERING, AND TRACKING (SMART). The 2006 **Adam Walsh** Child Protection and Safety Act created SMART. SMART monitors and follows legislation and other legal circumstances regarding sex offenders. Of special interest to SMART are the registration, monitoring, and apprehension of sex offenders. SMART also supports efforts by states, public and private organizations, local governments, and others through grants, guidance, and technical assistance. *See also* WALSH, JOHN EDWARD, JR. (1945–).

OHLIN, LLOYD (1918–2008). An early expert in **juvenile delinquency** beginning in the 1950s who sought to identify the conditions of poverty and other impediments to upward mobility. He made strong points regarding the establishment of goals and the failure to achieve them as primary circumstances of risk for juveniles and the resulting delinquency. He is noted for his work with the Illinois **Parole** and **Pardon** Board and the Manhattan **Mobilization for Youth** in the 1960s. He was unique in his academic studies clarifying the harmful effects of the criminal justice system. He was a prolific writer and the recipient of numerous academic awards, including the 1992 **Academy of Criminal Justice Sciences** Bruce Smith Award. *See also* JUVENILE DELINQUENCY; JUVENILE OFFENDER.

OKLAHOMA CITY BOMBING. *See* McVEIGH, TIMOTHY (1968–2001); NICHOLS, TERRY L. (1953–).

OLWEUS BULLYING PREVENTION PROGRAM. Dan Olweus began programs to prevent **bullying** in the 1970s. The program addresses bullying issues with elementary, middle, and high school students. The emphasis of the program is to diminish or prevent bullying in common environments for school-age children, including schools, communities, and classrooms, by groups or by individuals. Research suggests the program helps to eliminate or mitigate bullying in schools. *See also* CYBERSTALKING; NATIONAL BULLYING PREVENTION CENTER.

OMERTÀ. Omertà or ***code of honor*** is common with the **Mafia** and **organized crime**. The origins of omertà date back to the mid-19th century and the creation of the Mafia in Sicily as small private armies that would become criminal organizations. Among the common definitions for omertà are that members of the crime organization will not interfere with the criminal operations of other crime families and will maintain their silence to authorities whether or not they are guilty of the crime for which they are accused. The meaning is extended to noncooperation with law enforcement. The penalty for violating omertà is death. *See also* LA COSA NOSTRA.

OMNIBUS CRIME CONTROL AND SAFE STREETS ACT OF 1968, PUB. L. NO. 90-351, 82 STAT. 197. The writing of the law was begun after the **assassination** of President John F. Kennedy and was signed into law by President Lyndon Johnson. The introduction to the act specifies its purpose: "(1) encourage States and units of general local government to prepare and adopt comprehensive plans based upon their evaluation of state and local problems of law enforcement; (2) authorize grants to states and units of local government in order to improve and strengthen law enforcement; and (3) encourage research and development directed toward the improvement of law enforcement and the development of new methods for the prevention and reduction of crime and the detection and apprehension of criminals." The act affected several law enforcement functions and sought to improve law enforcement performance. For example, the **FBI** received a 10 percent increase in its budget for training. The act established rules for **wiretaps**, prohibited interstate trade in **handguns**, and raised the age to 18 for the purchase of a handgun. The **Gun Control** Act of 1968 was influenced by this legislation seeking to control the sale and possession of firearms in the United States.

ONSET. Onset refers to the initiation of crime and delinquency. Developmental and life course **criminology** research suggests two influencing linkages for the onset to occur. Moffitt's research report of 1993 puts forward that the onset of crime may be either "adolescent limited" or "**life course** persistent." The first begins late in adolescence and ends in adolescence, whereas the latter group starts earlier in adolescence and continues into adulthood. *See also* JUVENILE DELINQUENCY.

OPERATION BORDERLINE. The U.S. Customs Bureau used a dummy mail-order house as a sting in 1988 to arrest pedophiles who would order child **pornography**. *See also* MEESE COMMISSION.

OPERATION CEASEFIRE. Operation Ceasefire began in Boston in 1996 to address gun violence and **murders** associated with youth. It was a problem-oriented policing program sponsored by the National Institute of Justice (NIJ). *See also* OPERATION NIGHT LIGHT; VIOLENCE.

OPERATION MONGOOSE. A 1961 Kennedy administration plan of the Central Intelligence Agency (CIA) to enlist the aid of **organized crime** for an **assassination** attempt against Fidel Castro, the prime minister of Cuba. The plan was to overthrow the Castro regime and return power to the Cuban people. The plan failed, and to date the Castro family, under the auspices of Prime Minister Raúl Castro, brother of Fidel, is still in control of the Cuban people.

OPERATION NIGHT LIGHT. Operation Night Light (1992) in Dorchester, Massachusetts, utilized **probation** and **police** officers to confront **gang** and juvenile violence and the increasing **murder** rate of youth under 17 years of age. Operation Night Light officers identified high-risk offenders and would make surprise visits to work sites, homes, and schools. This was a component of Boston's crime reduction strategy, and success was noted in decreased arrests and **violence** during a time when similar events were increasing. The program was replicated in other states including New Jersey.

OPERATION UNDERWORLD. Organized crime figures were recruited by the U.S. Navy during World War II to assist the navy with protection of docks.

OPERATION UNIRAC. The **FBI** conducted a sting operation in the 1970s to determine the involvement of **organized crime** on the waterfront involving shipping and longshoremen.

OPPORTUNITY THEORY. The theory proposes that crime is the consequence of opportunities with high rewards when combined with low risk and little effort. This is a rational decision for the **motivated offender** willing to commit crime. The theory was proposed in 1978 by Hindelang, Gottfredson, and **Raffaele Garofalo**.

ORCHID CELLMARK. The company was established in 1987. The company became the first to license the technology of **DNA** fingerprinting. In 2007, the company was the target of a letter bomb campaign that resulted in the injury of a receptionist. In 2004, Orchid Cellmark became the first company to be accused of tampering with DNA analysis electronically, thus introducing the idea that DNA data could be manipulated. *See also* BERTILLION, ALPHONSE (1853–1914); DACTYLOGRAPHY; FINGERPRINT; FORENSICS.

ORDER MAINTENANCE POLICING. George Kelling (1996) defined order maintenance policing as "the intervention and suppression of behavior that threatens to be offensive, that threatens to disturb the public peace, or that emanates from conflicts among individuals that are public in nature. Order maintenance situations tend to be ambiguous, and the **police** have broad discretion in what their response should be." This is also referred to as **broken windows**.

ORGANIZED CRIME. The **FBI** defines organized crime as any group having some manner of a formalized structure and whose primary objective is to obtain money through illegal activities. Such groups maintain their position through the use of actual or threatened **violence**, corrupt public officials, **graft**, or extortion, and generally have a significant impact on the people in their locales, region, or the country as a whole. The origins of organized crime can be traced to the street **gangs** of the 1800s. These early street gangs formed from the groups of immigrants who arrived in America, for the purposes of both protection and illicit enterprise. An example of an organized crime group would be the **Mafia**. Organized crime can be a local organization, a transnational group, or other structured initiative that engages in illegal activity. *See also* COSA NOSTRA; DRUG CARTELS; RACKETEER INFLUENCED CORRUPT ORGANIZATION (RICO).

ORGANIZED OFFENDER. A classification of **serial killer** describing someone who often possesses above-average intelligence, exercises control, knows what they are doing, utilizes careful planning for their crime, is specific about the type of victim, learns/improves with each crime, tends to hide victims, and may collect items of victims as trophies. **FBI** profiler **Robert Roy Hazelwood** distinguished between organized and disorganized offenders. *See also* DISORGANIZED OFFENDER.

OSWALD, LEE HARVEY (1939–1963). The assassin of President John F. Kennedy in Dallas, Texas, on 22 November 1963. The shooting was investigated by no less than five government agencies, including the **Warren Com-**

mission, who in 1964 agreed with the **FBI**, the Dallas **Police** Department, and the Secret Service that there was no second shooter and that Oswald had acted alone. Oswald had been a U.S. Marine and defected to the Soviet Union in 1959. Jack Ruby shot and killed Oswald two days later while he was being transferred to the county jail. This **assassination** and the events that followed have been the subject of controversy and conspiracy theories.

P

PACKER, HERBERT L. (1925–1972). An American criminologist and legal scholar best known for his model of the criminal justice system that proposed either a crime control or a **due process** vision (Packer 1968). Packer coined the phrase "**assembly line justice**" used to describe the conveyer belt–like process through which defendants are funneled through the American criminal justice system. Despite the influence of Packer, the United States has steadily moved toward the crime control model and the use of **plea bargains** to streamline the judicial process. The result has been **mass incarceration** reflected in a huge increase in the U.S. **prison** population (now the largest prison population in the world) and the necessary increase in prison facilities. Packer was born in Jersey City, New Jersey, and graduated from Yale Law School in 1944. After clerking for one year and then working in private practice, Packer became a law professor at Stanford in 1956. He published two books, *Ex-Communist Witnesses: Four Studies in Fact Finding* (1962) and *The Limits of the Criminal Sanction* (1968), before his untimely death by suicide at the age of 46 following a debilitating stroke three year earlier. *See also* DUE PROCESS MODEL.

PAGANS MOTORCYCLE CLUB. Commonly referred to as the Pagans, they are considered to be an organized crime syndicate which operates with a national president under a constitution. The Pagans are one of the four largest of the outlaw motorcycle clubs (the **Hells Angels** is the largest and a rival club) with at least 13 chapters ranging over the East Coast and as far south as Florida. They are referenced as a 1 percenter motorcycle club with membership restrictions, such as you must be 21 years of age and own a Harley-Davidson motorcycle that is 900 CCs or larger. The origin of the club dates to 1959 in Prince George County, Maryland, under the leadership of Lou Dobkin. They became known for criminal activity (drugs) and violence in the mid-1960s. Law enforcement has targeted them for their illegal activities, and as the Hells Angels group has grown, Pagan membership has declined.

PAINS OF IMPRISONMENT. The seminal work describing the pains of imprisonment experienced by convicts was *The Society of Captives* (1958) by Gresham Sykes. His dissertation studied the interactions between guards and prisoners at Trenton State **Prison** (currently the oldest operating prison in the United States). Irving Goffman (*Asylums*, 1961) would later describe the prison as a **total institution** and emphasized the deprivations of liberty, heterosexual relationships, security, goods and services, and more which are experienced by convicts and are detrimental to their welfare. This early work by Sykes helped pave the way to search for the answer to **recidivism** and, more specifically, "what works" to successfully reclaim convicts once their prison time is served. Martinson, Lipton, and Wilkes began doing **meta-analyses** in the 1970s. Their work has been followed up by others who have developed today's **risk assessment** instruments, such as the Level of Service Inventory–Revised (LSI-R), to help identify static and dynamic risk factors that influence the development of individualized treatment plans. *See also* MARTINSON, ROBERT (1927–1979).

***PALKO V. CONNECTICUT*, 302 U.S. 319 (1937).** Palko, in 1935, shot and killed a **police** officer while escaping from a robbery. In his first **trial**, he was found guilty of second-degree **murder** and sentenced to life in **prison**. Connecticut successfully appealed the sentence, and Palko was given a new trial and this time was convicted of first-degree murder and sentenced to death. The appeal was an argument that the second trial represented **double jeopardy**, which is protected against by the **Fifth Amendment**. However, at this time, the states had not yet incorporated the **Bill of Rights**, which meant that the **Fourteenth Amendment due process** clause guaranteeing protection at the state level was not in effect. Justice Benjamin Cardozo in his opinion, which impacted on the Bill of Rights, held that incorporation should be considered on a case-by-case basis, thus setting the stage for selective incorporation to occur. However, the **U.S. Supreme Court** in an 8–1 decision upheld the conviction and held that an appeal which argued double jeopardy was not essential to a fundamental scheme of ordered liberty. Palko was executed in the **electric chair** on 12 April 1938. In ***Benton v. Maryland*, 395 U.S. 784 (1969)**, the Palko decision was overruled and protection against double jeopardy in the states was incorporated. *See also* CAPITAL PUNISHMENT; EXECUTION; FIFTH AMENDMENT.

PALMER RAIDS. Raids that were executed between 1919 and 1920 by the U.S. Department of Justice to arrest suspects identified as anarchists. The raids resulted in the deportation of more than 500 foreign nationals. This tactic was the first of the "Red Scare" fears of radical leftism and communism prompted by bombings, worker strikes, and race riots. **Attorney Gen-**

eral A. Mitchell Palmer was the organizing force behind the raids and was often discouraged in his deportation efforts by the Department of Labor, who disagreed with Palmer and regulated control over deportations. **J. Edgar Hoover** was selected in 1919 as the director of the Department of Justice's Bureau of Investigations (which would become the **FBI** in 1935). The first raid was unsuccessful following a federal judge's ruling against Palmer because the suspects advocated for nonviolent methods (free speech) to reform government. Palmer then used immigration statutes to pursue those who violated them. The second raid of 1919 saw the arrest of 650 people. However, only 43 were deported. Hoover now pursued the Communist Labor Party and in 1920 arrested more than 3,000 in 23 states and more than 20 cities. There were no bombs recovered in any of the raids. Additional raids resulted in other large-scale arrests totaling more than 10,000 persons. The Department of Labor again took a different stance from Palmer and Hoover and canceled over 200 warrants and through the 1918 Immigration Act deported only 556 foreign nationals. U.S. district court judge George Anderson criticized the actions of the Department of Justice and released 17 foreign nationals, an action that effectively ended the raids. Since the attacks of 9/11, there is a current fear of **terrorism** from foreign nationals located in the United States. President Trump has campaigned for a border wall as a barrier between Mexico and the United States. Former **sheriff Joe Arpaio** defied a federal court order and continued to arrest undocumented immigrants, for which he was charged and convicted of criminal contempt. *See also* WARRANT.

PAN AM 103 LOCKERBIE BOMBING. A 21 December 1988 flight from London to New York crashed in Lockerbie, Scotland, killing all 243 passengers (many of whom were U.S. citizens returning home) and the crew (16) and 11 persons on the ground. The cause was a suitcase bomb planted by Libyan terrorists. The Dumfries and Galloway Constabulary led what has been referred to as the greatest criminal inquiry in the United Kingdom. Abdelbaset al-Megrahi was found guilty (a suspected coconspirator was acquitted) and sentenced to life imprisonment in 2001. He was granted a compassionate release in 2009 following a diagnosis of prostate cancer, and he died in 2012. Muammar Gaddafi admitted Libyan responsibility (but not guilt), and compensation was paid to the families. Pan Am was found guilty of negligent airport security screening and for failure to obtain Libyan compensation, and the resulting lawsuits led to Pan Am's bankruptcy. *See also* TERRORISM.

PANOPTICON. The ill-conceived **prison** idea of utilitarian philosopher **Jeremy Bentham** in the late 18th century intended to be cost efficient and operationally effective. The panopticon featured cells on the outer walls of a conical-shaped structure, spiral staircases, and a center tower from which the guards could observe the cells. Central to the guards maintaining security were lights shined at the cells, which prevented the convicts from seeing out while allowing the guards to see into the cell. Bentham, as far as is known, had never visited a jail or prison. While the conception of the panopticon appeared practical in its design and administration, it has proved to be more problematic than effective or efficient. Pennsylvania began construction of **Western Penitentiary** in Pittsburgh, Pennsylvania, in the early 1800s. The construction had just begun when there was a realization that it was operationally problematic. Pennsylvania changed its construction in favor of the warehouse design of New York. Statesville Prison, Illinois, was also built in this style. *See also* EASTERN STATE PENITENTIARY (PENNSYLVANIA).

PANZRAM, CARL (1891–1930). A **serial killer**, rapist, arsonist, and murderer who claimed to have committed 21 murders and over 1,000 rapes and sodomies. He had been arrested in six states and was finally committed to **USP Leavenworth**, where he was executed in 1930. During his final incarceration, he confessed to his murders as reported in the "Panzram Papers." His life was reported in a book (1970) and movie titled *A Journal of Murder* (1995). *See also* ARSON; EXECUTION; MURDER.

PARDON. Pardon has meanings that vary from state to state and the federal government. A pardon may mean to free a person from jail or **prison** because it excuses the person of guilt, forgives them of the crime of which they have been convicted, or is a means of resolving a conviction as though it never happened. Pardon is often used interchangeably with the idea of clemency, which also has multiple meanings, such as absolving a person of guilt, reducing a sentence, or restoring rights such as suffrage. Historically, the granting of pardons has been the right of a monarch or ruling figure of a country, and today it is often a function of a **parole** board. Some other examples of the granting of pardons include France, which requires that pardons be signed off on by the prime minister, the president, and other ministers, including the minister of justice. In Russia, there is a pardon committee who, after review, directs the pardon request to the president for signature. U.S presidential pardons date back to George Washington, who granted several, and a pardon of former president Richard M. Nixon by President Gerald Ford. Pardons are frequently granted by state governors and presidents near the end of their term in office. President Obama pardoned 1,927 persons convicted of federal offenses.

PARENS PATRIAE. Latin for "parent of the country," it is the power of the state to act as the guardian for those who are unable to care for themselves, such as children or disabled individuals. For example, under this doctrine a judge may change custody, child support, or other rulings affecting a child's well-being, regardless of what the parents may have agreed to. The concept of *parens patriae* dates to the 16th century and became the safeguard for children with the creation of the **juvenile court** in Chicago in 1899. Use of the term is the foundation of the authority for today's **family court**. *See also* JUVENILE JUSTICE AND DELINQUENCY PREVENTION ACT OF 1974.

PARENTAL ABUSE. A form of **violence**, including parental battery, researched in the late 1970s which found that it may include the following characteristics: the use of a weapon, verbal abuse, physical abuse, and throwing items. The research suggests that most parental abuse is against mothers, the primary caregiver who spends the majority of parental time with the abusive child, and that abusers generally exceeded the age of 11. These cases are normally adjudicated by the **family court** when the abuser is recognized as a **juvenile offender**, or if the abuser is an adult, then the case may be heard by a criminal court.

PARKER, BONNIE (1910–1934). An outlaw of the 1930s who robbed banks with **Clyde Barrow** and his **gang** during a two-year crime spree. Parker and Barrow were reportedly responsible for several **murders** which included law enforcement officials. In 1934, Parker and Barrow were caught in a **police** ambush and during the ensuing gun battle were shot to death. There is uncertainty whether Bonnie Parker ever engaged in a gun battle or murdered anyone. The Bonnie and Clyde ambush was the first of several fatal shootouts that would eliminate **John Dillinger**, Charles "Baby Face" Nelson, and **Lester "Pretty Boy Floyd" Gillis**, and it concluded the **FBI**'s 1930s era of the **public enemy**. *See also* PURVIS, MELVIN (1903–1960).

PAROLE. Originally from the French, meaning to give your "word of honor," it is a system of supervision of those who have been confined in correctional institutions and are now released into the community to complete their sentence under the supervision of the state department of corrections. Parole is conditional release, which originated with **Captain Alexander Maconochie**, was improved on by **Sir Walter Crofton** and the Irish system, and was adapted in the mid-1870s by **Zebulon Brockway** at **Elmira Reformatory** in New York. In order to structure the release of convicts, the U.S. Congress created the federal parole board in 1930. Parole boards may be independent of other governmental agencies or perhaps be located within the department of corrections for a specific state. Accusations of patronage and other corruption have led to the appointment of multiple persons to serve on a parole board after World War II.

PATRIOT ACT. On 11 September 2001, the United States experienced the most grievous act of foreign **terrorism** on U.S. soil, and in reaction to the attack, the U.S. Congress passed legislation titled "Uniting and Strengthening America by Providing Appropriate Tools Required to Intercept and Obstruct Terrorism Act of 2001," or PATRIOT Act, which was signed into law by President George Bush on 26 May 2001. The broad legislation enabled the **FBI** (and other agencies of law enforcement) to investigate email, financial records, telephone records, and business and library records of suspected foreign terrorists without a **search warrant** with the intention of preventing acts of terrorism. *See also* WARRANTLESS SEARCHES; WORLD TRADE CENTER (WTC) BOMBINGS.

PATROL. Patrol is the performance of duty by **police** officers to watch/observe specified areas and to maintain public order through their presence, make arrests, file crime reports, or engage in other activities that improve public safety. Patrol, a primary function of policing, dates back to the origins of police as organized by **Sir Robert Peel** in the early 1800s. While patrol was conducted originally on foot or horseback, today patrolmen use a variety of methods to cover their assigned areas, including dogsleds, automobiles, bicycles, boats, or other means of conveyance. Patrol areas have been expanded by the use of cameras and drones. The more effective use of patrol methods is credited with reducing contemporary crime in cities. Police patrol continues to undergo review and research to determine effectiveness. The Philadelphia foot patrol research (Ratcliffe et al. 2011) reaffirmed the effectiveness of patrol, specifically foot patrols, noting especially that there was a decrease in **violent crime** by 23 percent.

PATROLMEN'S (POLICEMEN'S) BENEVOLENT ASSOCIATION (PBA). Starting in 1892, the first **police** unions were established to provide a contract negotiating unit for law enforcement officers. Today all police departments have a designated representative group to represent police officers in labor negotiations. Law enforcement labor unions in the United States may use several different titles. (e.g., PBA of the City of New York, NJ State

PBA, Port Authority PBA). In 1978, the National Association of Police Organizations (NAPO), a coalition of police unions across the United States, was established.

***PAYNE V. TENNESSEE*, 501 U.S. 808 (1991).** A **U.S. Supreme Court** case which held that a **victim impact statement** was admissible during the sentencing phase of a capital **murder** case and is not an **Eighth Amendment** violation of the **cruel and unusual punishment** clause.

PAYOLA. A contraction of the words *pay* and *Victrola* (an LP record player), which entered the English language via the record business. Payola is accepting illegal payment for radio time to influence listeners to buy certain records. The first court case involving payola was in 1960. On 9 May 1962, Alan Freed (1921–1965) was indicted for accepting $2,500 that he claimed was a token of gratitude and did not affect airplay. He was found guilty and ordered to pay a small **fine** and was released. His radio career faltered, and in 1965 he drank himself to death.

***PAYTON V. NEW YORK*, 445 U.S. 573 (1980).** The **U.S. Supreme Court** held that **Fourth Amendment** protection applied to a search of Theodore Payton's home. New York state law permitted **warrantless searches** of suspects, and Payton's house was searched when he was not home, acquiring **evidence** against him. Payton had been suspected of murdering a gas station attendant, for which he was found guilty from the evidence obtained during the search. *See also* MURDER.

"PEACEABLE ASSEMBLY FOR LAWFUL DISCUSSION CANNOT BE MADE A CRIME". *See* FOURTEENTH AMENDMENT.

PEACEMAKING CRIMINOLOGY. *See* BALANCED AND RESTORATIVE JUSTICE (BARJ).

PEEL, SIR ROBERT (1788–1850). *See* PATROL; POLICE; PROACTIVE POLICING.

PENAL CODE. The penal code is also called the criminal code and has been legislated to detail and define the offenses and penalties within a particular jurisdiction. Penal codes are subject to revision and are influenced by political and social events. Penal codes are meant to regulate and provide safety for society and to avoid such actions as feuds and other disruptive events. The original penal code for the United States was legislated in 1873 and was called the Revised Statutes of the United States, which is now referred to as Title 18 of the U.S. Code. Each state's written statutes contain a penal code in its constitution. The **Code of Hammurabi**, comprised of 282 laws, was the earliest attempt to codify laws and was written in 1754 B.C. *See also* MODEL PENAL CODE (MPC).

PENAL COLONY. Penal colonies in foreign or faraway lands have been used to exile convicts who have been convicted of serious offenses or who are thought to be politically disruptive. Those sent to such colonies are in exile and are forbidden under penalty of **execution** to return to their native land. Penal colonies were often situations of hard and dangerous labor in unsettled areas. The North American Penal Colony was used to send British convicts to the Maryland and Virginia colonies where convicts were rented to farmers. When the American Revolution started, the decision was made to stop sending convicts to North America. Penal colonies were used extensively by Russia (Siberia, 1857), the United Kingdom (North America, Australia, New South Wales, early 18th century), and France (French Guiana, 1852). *See also* TRANSPORTATION.

PENAL PHILOSOPHY. Penal philosophies incorporate the ideas, attitudes, and beliefs that influence the manner in which **penal codes** and **punishments** are organized. The philosophy guiding the **Code of Hammurabi** (1754 B.C.) was a literal incorporation of the idea of "an eye for an eye." The **Pennsylvania system** gave birth to the modern **prison** system in the early 1800s, relying upon **solitary confinement** so that "man" could comprehend the evil of his ways. Fear of crime and the **War on Drugs** during the mid- to late 20th century resulted in **mass incarceration** as the means to solve both. Currently, philosophical shifts in the United States are being considered to decriminalize (such as changing drug laws that mandate incarceration and implementing **drug legalization**), make more efficient use of **community corrections** (such as **community courts**), and other alternative ways to address criminality (such as **bail** reform). *See also* DECRIMINALIZATION; WAR ON CRIME.

PENAL REFORM. Penal reform is the attempt to correct or improve conditions inside penitentiaries which would enable prisons to respond to the needs of convicts more effectively or bring prisons into compliance with other standards, such as those established by the **American Correctional Association (ACA)**, or into compliance with the U.S. Constitution. Among the earliest efforts to report on **prison** conditions and to emphasize the need for reform was the report by English high **sheriff John Howard** in 1777. The prison in its creation was a reform effort. Reform has been ongoing in both design and operations since that first prison. In October 1870, the National Prison Association (which would become the ACA in 1954) held the first congress, which drafted the Declaration of Principles to guide prisons.

PENAL SERVITUDE. Some, but not all, states and the **Federal Bureau of Prisons (BOP)** require that convicts work during their confinement. The Thirteenth Amendment (1934) forbids involuntary work except as **punishment**. Persons not convicted may not be compelled to work. Penal servitude has been mostly industrial in northern **prisons** and agrarian in southern institutions. In some cases, such as southern prisons, convicts were leased out to private farms to provide labor, and the prisons were compensated. Penal servitude was abolished in the 20th century due to abuses. Convicts today are paid for their labor. The Prison Industry Enhancement Certification passed by Congress in 1979 provided both employment for convicts and certifications that could be used in private industry upon release. *See also* CONVICT LEASE SYSTEM.

PENITENTIARY. A **prison** for those convicted of committing a crime. The first modern penitentiary was Pennsylvania's **Eastern State Penitentiary**. After 30 years of discussion, the prison was opened in 1829 using the Quaker principles of reflection, repentance, and reform. Prisoners were kept in **solitary confinement** to encourage reflection on their sin (crime) and to encourage repentance. Short, individual cell doors required the convict to bend to enter the cell. The cells were large enough to encourage work by the **inmate**. The original cells had no windows. Convicts were not allowed visitors except their pastors and no books except the Bible and religious tracts. It was known as the **Pennsylvania system** (abandoned by the United States in 1913) or the separate system. The Pennsylvania State Prison was closed in 1971. *See also* WALNUT STREET JAIL.

PENNSYLVANIA SYSTEM. *See* PENITENTIARY.

***PENRY V. LYNAUGH*, 492 U.S. 392 (1989).** Johnny Paul Penry was sentenced to death for **murder**. The **U.S. Supreme Court** held that the **execution** of the mentally retarded was not an **Eighth Amendment** violation and remanded the case for review because the **jury** had not considered his intellectual capacity. Penry was retried and again sentenced to death; however, in *Penry v. Johnson*, 532 U.S. 782 (2001), intellectual capacity was again not introduced during the sentencing phase of the **trial** as a mitigating factor. The subsequent ruling in ***Atkins v. Virginia*, 536 U.S. 304 (2002)**, did not look favorably on assigning the **death penalty** for the mentally retarded. However, Penry stood trial for the third time in 2002 and was again found guilty, but a plea agreement was reached for a sentence of life without **parole**. *See also* CRUEL AND UNUSUAL PUNISHMENT.

PEOPLE NATION. An alliance of approximately 50 gangs in the Chicago area. The People Nation was formed in the late 1970s in Joliet **Penitentiary**. The alliance was meant to control **gang** wars, the drug trade, and other illegal activity. They are often considered to be allied with the **Latin Kings**, the **Bloods**, and other national gangs. The alliance is currently active. *See also* CRIPS; FOLK NATION.

PERJURY. Perjury is lying or making false statements (verbally or in writing) after taking an official oath, such as being sworn to tell the truth prior to testimony in a formal proceeding. U.S. laws concerning perjury have taken their lead from English **common law**, which begins to be recognized in the late 1700s. While English common law depends on the ruling of a sitting judge, it is not codified as is U.S. law. In the United States, perjury is considered to be a felony and can result in indictment and conviction. An example is Mark Furman, who was convicted of perjury during the 1995 **O. J. Simpson trial**. While he bargained for a sentence that resulted in three years' **probation** and a $200 **fine**, Furman is considered a convicted felon.

***PERVEAR V. MASSACHUSETTS*, 72 U.S. (5 WALL) 475 (1866).** A landmark prisoners' rights case brought before the **U.S. Supreme Court**. The holding was that prisoners have no constitutional rights, including **Eighth Amendment** rights. In addition, the U.S. Constitution did not apply to the states, only the federal government. This early U.S. Supreme Court holding established the hands-off policy that dominated U.S. correctional practices until the middle of the 20th century. The court's rationale for this decision was (1) that they did not have the right to act because corrections lies in the executive branch of government, (2) that they lacked experience in corrections, and (3) that should they act, it might precipitate disciplinary problems in **prisons**. *See also* CIVIL RIGHTS.

PEYOTE. A psychoactive plant containing **mescaline**, native to Mexico and Texas and used by Native Americans for more than 5,000 years as a spiritual stimulant. During the late 1880s and the 1930s, the U.S. government attempted to ban the use of peyote by Native Americans. The Controlled Substances Act of 1965 once more banned the use of peyote. The *Native American Church of New York v. United States*, 468 F. Supp. 1247 (S.D.N.Y. 1979), court case affirmed the right of Native Americans to use the drug in their religious practices. *See also* ADDICTION; NARCOTICS.

PHENOMENOLOGY. The term *phenomenology* refers to the study of consciousness and was used by philosophers such as Kant, Hegel, and Marx in the mid-1700s. Edmund Husserl (1859–1938) and then Martin Heidegger (1889–1976) and Maunce Merleau-Ponty (1908–1961) revived interest in subjective experience with existential phenomenology. Other scholars of consciousness, such as George Herbert Mead (1863–1931), often cited as a founding father of social psychology, were criticized for failing to take into account the reciprocal relationship between the private and the public. Consciousness cannot exist separate of the social world. Modern criminologists using a phenomenological approach typically ascribe to a social interactionist theory of crime and focus on the lived experience of crime and the internal meanings it has for the subject.

PHRENOLOGY. In this pseudoscience of the 18th century, Franz Gall of Austria proposed that personality characteristics could be ascertained by examining the bumps and crevices of the skull as well as measuring the area of the head that covered an equivalent area of the brain. While it was influential at the time, the study of phrenology was short lived and was being called a pseudoscience by the middle of the 19th century. However, there remained an interest in it for psychiatry and neuroscience during the 19th century. *See also* ATAVISM; LOMBROSO, CESARE (1835–1909).

PIRACY. Traditionally, piracy has been viewed as attacks on ships to commit theft, commandeer the ship, and commit **violence** upon those on the ship. Piracy was recorded during the late Bronze Age or prior to 1400 B.C., with far-ranging attacks on civilizations such as Egypt and its ships of trade. Piracy sometimes refers to attacks on land or in the air and is like attacks on the sea. The attacks are intended to be instances of theft or commandeering a vehicle, such as a car, train, or aircraft. Modern piracy is very active in Somali and Indonesia, where pirates have hijacked boats, holding crew, passengers, and cargo for **ransom**. The U.S. Navy assigned three ships to join with the multinational counter**terrorism** group called the Combined Task Force 150 to **patrol** these waters to curtail piratical acts.

PISTOL. The earliest pistol, sometimes referred to as a hand cannon or **handgun**, was developed in Europe during the mid-16th century. In 1835, Samuel Colt mass-produced the first multishot handgun in Hartford, Connecticut. Automatic pistols were invented in 1892 by Joseph Laumann. Today, handguns are a worldwide problem for law enforcement agencies.

PISTONE, JOE (1939–). An **FBI** agent who for six years during the 1970s and early 1980s assumed the name Donnie Brasco (1989, and the alias "the Jewel Man") to go **undercover** to investigate mob activity. Pistone's undercover success led to the proposal by **mobster** Angelo Ruggiero (1940–1989) that Pistone receive full family membership (that he become a "made man"), an offer that resulted in the FBI ending his undercover task. *See also* MAFIA; ORGANIZED CRIME.

PLAIN VIEW DOCTRINE. In ***Horton v. California*, 496 U.S. 128 (1990)**, the **U.S. Supreme Court** held that a law enforcement officer may, without a **warrant**, take **evidence** when it is in plain view. There is a legal right to secure evidence and when there is an incriminating character associated with the evidence to place the person under arrest. The decision is the basis for Transportation Safety Administration (TSA) officers seizing contraband items at international airports. *See also* EXCLUSIONARY RULE; FOURTH AMENDMENT; FRUIT OF THE POISONOUS TREE DOCTRINE; *MAPP V. OHIO*, 367 U.S. 643 (1961); SEARCH AND SEIZURE; WARRANTLESS SEARCHES.

PLEA BARGAIN. Also referred to as a plea agreement, a plea in mitigation, and less formally as an arrangement, plea deal, or copping a plea, it is a negotiated arrangement between a prosecutor and a defense attorney and must be agreed to by the defendant to accept a consequence for a criminal offense. The plea bargain must be accepted by the judge. This is considered an advantageous arrangement for all parties. The defendant may plead guilty to a reduced charge and will receive a lesser sentence, which guarantees the prosecutor a conviction. The plea bargain avoids a lengthy criminal proceeding such as a **trial**, and once accepted by the courts there is no appeal. The plea bargain is essential to the **crime control model**, which has been emphasized since the late 1970s as critical to the criminal justice process to mitigate crime and is used in about 90 percent of the total number of criminal cases. There are concerns that many guilty pleas are made to avoid a greater sentence, even when the defendant is actually innocent. *See also* DUE PROCESS.

***PLESSY V. FERGUSON*, 163 U.S. 537 (1896).** A landmark **U.S. Supreme Court** case that sustained the state of Louisiana's racial segregation laws and maintained the doctrine of "separate but equal." Plessy purchased a ticket for a first-class seat and entered the "whites only" car. Plessey was charged, found guilty, and ordered to pay a $25 **fine**. His appeal challenged the Thirteenth and **Fourteenth Amendments**, which addressed the "separate but equal" doctrine and upheld the right of states to create institutions that are racially segregated. The "separate but equal" doctrine would remain in effect until it was challenged in *Brown v. Board of Education of Topeka*, 347 U.S. 483 (1954). The holding did not overturn *Plessy*, but it did specify that segregation was unconstitutional in public education. Other cases that affected segregation include the **Civil Rights** Act of 1964 and the Voting Rights Act of 1965. *See also* RACIAL DISPARITY.

***POINTER V. TEXAS*, 380 U.S. 400 (1965).** A landmark **U.S. Supreme Court** case that upheld the right of a defendant to confront an accuser, a Sixth Amendment guarantee resulting in the reversal of Pointer's conviction. Pointer was accused and convicted of the robbery of a convenience store and sentenced to life imprisonment. Texas conducts what are called "examining trials," which closely resemble grand **jury** hearings. The intent of the "examining **trial**" is to show **probable cause** through the presentation of **evidence**, which if successful results in the indictment of the defendant. Pointer did not have legal representation and had no opportunity to challenge the prosecution's **witness**. This witness was unavailable for Pointer's criminal trial, and the prosecution introduced the witness's statement. There was no cross-examination. This was one of several court cases that addressed the necessity of adequate counsel for defendants and the capacity of those counsels when representing defendants. *See also GIDEON V. WAINWRIGHT*, 372 U.S. 335 (1963).

POLICE. Modern policing is generally attributed to **Sir Robert Peel**. However, the first police force was founded by **Gabriel Nicolas de la Reynie** in Paris, France. Early police officers were called peace officers. In the United States, Boston developed the first established police force in 1838. Soon afterward, New York followed in 1844 and then Philadelphia in 1854. *See also* COMMUNITY-ORIENTED POLICING; PROACTIVE POLICING.

POLICE ACADEMY. Mandatory training of law enforcement officers began in 1908. In 1935, following the **Wickersham Commission** report, a National Academy was created by the **FBI** to reinforce the idea of centralized training. Every state has a training academy, but training requirements and time required for training are different from state to state. In New Jersey, for example, the training curriculum and its course content are authorized by the **Police** Training Commission. The 1967 **President's Commission on Law Enforcement and Administration of Justice** has had an influence on all training of law enforcement with its recommendations of a minimum of 400 hours of training, and trainees must have completed standard educational training. The Commission also recommended that each officer complete a 12- to 18-month probationary period.

POLICE BRUTALITY. A type of **police misconduct** which involves the excessive physical control of civilians in the process of an arrest or other confrontation during official duty. The origin of the term is likely to be associated with an 1872 incident at the Harrison Street Police Station in Chicago, Illinois. Since the earliest days of policing, officers have carried nightsticks or blackjacks, which they would regularly employ in the line of duty, whether or not they were making an arrest. Law enforcement officers are seldom sanctioned for inappropriate **use of force**, in part because of the code of silence. Incident such as the 1991 Los Angeles beating of Rodney King, for which two officers were tried and convicted, have increased awareness. Law enforcement officers receive training in a use-of-force continuum that helps to clarify which is appropriate force and which is police brutality. *See also* LESS-THAN-LETHAL FORCE; RULE OF SILENCE.

POLICE CHECKPOINT. The **police** checkpoint is sometimes referred to as a **police roadblock**. Prior to ***Michigan Dept. of State Police v. Sitz*, 496 U.S. 444 (1990)**, law enforcement was required to establish **probable cause** to set up a checkpoint. The earlier contention was that a checkpoint constituted a seizure and thus was prohibited by the **Fourth Amendment**. The **U.S. Supreme Court** holding was that a checkpoint represented only a slight inconvenience to motorists and not a Fourth Amendment violation as previously held by the Michigan courts in 1986. Related actions such as ticketing and car impounds have not been reviewed by the court as potential forfeiture of Fourth Amendment protections. *See also* MOTOR VEHICLE CHECKPOINTS.

POLICE CORRUPTION. Law enforcement officers who use their official position to engage in criminal or ethical violations for personal advantage is corruption. **Police** corruption has occurred since the formation of the first police departments in the 1800s and includes acts such as **prostitution**, **gambling**, bribes, and protection. Two widely publicized attempts to eradicate corruption were the 1972 **Knapp Commission**, formed after corruption was revealed by Patrolman **Frank Serpico**. Twenty years later in 1992, The Mollen Commission investigated drug-related crimes and other corruption in the New York City Police Department. In the Mollen instance, corruption was viewed as having a cyclical nature illustrating the difficulty to eliminate it. In each instance, recommendations included improved oversight. The Mollen Commission expanded the recommendations and included changes in penalties for corruption, regular reporting by Internal Affairs to the police commissioner, and investigations by state and federal agencies. *See also* POLICE MISCONDUCT; USE OF FORCE.

POLICE ETHICS. Ethical conduct for law enforcement has been expressed as doing what is right when no one is looking. The work of law enforcement is often performed when there is no one to observe and officers are expected to be principled and honest, not to lie, cheat, steal or engage in corruption. Ethical standards have been developed and, in some cases, dictated by the courts, professional organizations, and organizations of oversight. Landmark **U.S. Supreme Court** cases include ***Miranda v. Arizona*, 384 U.S. 436 (1966)**, and ***Carroll v. United States*, 267 U.S. 132 (1925)**. The first case addressed advising suspects of their rights and the second case addressed **probable cause** and searches. Guidelines with which to formalize **police** conduct began in 1957 with the Law Enforcement Code of Ethics promulgated by the **International Association of Chiefs of Police** and revised by them in 1989. This was then followed up by the formation of an Ethics Subcommittee in 1995 to recommend training. Today, all police departments have developed their own codes of ethics and specify necessary training in the subject of ethical conduct for police.

POLICE FOUNDATION. A nonprofit agency located in Washington, D.C., and created in 1970 with support from the Ford Foundation and currently by private donations and grants. The Foundation seeks to improve policing through research to overcome challenging issues which affect **police** performance and especially community policing, police safety, and management. Among the more notable experiments are the 1972–1973 **Kansas City Preventive Patrol Experiment**, which evaluated the use of marked cars and crime prevention. Other studies included the 1970s Newark Foot Patrol Experiment, which examined the effect of foot patrols on crime and public perceptions of police.

POLICE LINEUP. The **police** lineup consists of a suspect who stands along with several other individuals (also called fillers or foils), all of whom have the same basic characteristics. The intention is that the suspect should not stand out so as to encourage or lead the **witness** (or victim) to an identification. The witness/victim views the lineup from behind a one-way mirror or other position to minimize their recognition by the suspect. There is no available record of when lineups were first introduced to police work. However, there is a long history of their use in police procedures. Since the advent of the **Innocence Project**, the accuracy of **witness identification** has been called into question. While there is a substantial error in witness and victim identification in **lineups**, its use has been held up by the **U.S. Supreme Court**. (see *Schmerber v. California*, 384 U.S. 757, 86 S. Ct. 1826, 16 L. Ed. 2d 908 [1966]). However, police must exercise diligence to ensure that no actions are taken by police which would bias identification.

POLICE MISCONDUCT. Misconduct, associated with official **police** duties, can range from **discrimination** to **obstruction of justice** to common crime such as theft or **murder**. Explanations for police misconduct vary and range from lack of education to greed to a failure to trust the system. A New York City police officer of the late 1800s, Alexander "Clubber" Williams, is reputed to have remarked that the law is found at the end of a nightstick rather than in **U.S. Supreme Court** holdings. Record keeping for police misconduct is relatively scarce and poorly reported because police have exercised wide latitudes of discretion. Police officers operate with minimal direct supervision. **Police brutality**, one form of misconduct, was recorded during the labor movements of the late 1800s and early 1900s such as the 1884 Pullman Strike. A more modern example of police brutality was the 1991 beating by Los Angeles police of Rodney King (1965–2012). The King beating was videotaped and was part of the beginning of the trend of citizens recording such incidents to bring them into public focus. Studies of police misconduct suggest that one of the reasons for low reporting is that it is intimidating for citizens to go to police stations to report such an incident. These documented reports have resulted in the formation of independent oversight committees beginning in the late 1990s. *See also* KNAPP COMMISSION; POLICE CORRUPTION; SERPICO, FRANK (1936–); USE OF FORCE.

POLICE POWERS. Police powers represent the ability of the state to enforce laws not otherwise granted to the federal government. The Tenth Amendment (ratified in 1791) of the U.S. Constitution assures that the states have the authority to pass legislation that defines the means of the states to regulate behavior. Police are provided the authority to ensure compliance with the law. The right of the state to possess and to authorize the use of police powers has been upheld by the **U.S. Supreme Court** and is clearly stated in *Jacobson v. Massachusetts*, 197 U.S. 11 (1905).

POLICE PROTECTION. Police protection has multiple meanings in justice. The creation of police in the 1820s by **Sir Robert Peel** was an attempt to protect the public from crime. That has remained the primary form of protection by the police. Other types include the protection of witnesses and, at times, those who have committed a crime, such as **witness protection programs**. While police have a history of protecting those who provide assistance, the federal government formalized the service through the **Organized Crime** Control Act of 1970. Federal witnesses are protected through the U.S. Marshals Service. *See also* MARSHAL; WITNESS.

POLICE ROADBLOCKS. *See* POLICE CHECKPOINT.

POLICE TORTURE. *See* POLICE BRUTALITY; POLICE CORRUPTION; THIRD DEGREE; TORTURE; USE OF FORCE.

POLYGAMY. The practice of plural marriage, or of having more than one spouse, is currently illegal in all U.S. states. The earliest effort to establish polygamy as a practice in the United States was by Joseph Smith (in the 1820s and 1830s), the founder of the Church of Jesus Christ of Latter-day Saints (LDS). While LDS has officially renounced the practice of polygamy, some sects of the church have openly supported it. Polygamy was made illegal by the federal government through the Morrill Anti-Bigamy Act by the 1862 U.S. Congress, Sess. 2., ch. 126, 12 Stat. 501. Statutes rendering polygamy illegal exist in all 50 states to make it either a misdemeanor or a felony.

POLYGRAPH. The polygraph is more commonly known as a **lie detector**, which measures physiological reactions, including blood pressure, respiration, pulse, and skin conductivity during a question-and-answer session. John Larsen invented the device in 1921. The polygraph has been used for **interrogation** and as part of the screening process for both governmental and private sector employees. The polygraph is not considered to be a foolproof instrument from which to determine truth from untruth. Research since the 1990s suggests that when innocent persons are challenged with crime-related questions, there are increased physiological effects.

PONZI SCHEME. A fraudulent investment opportunity named after Charles Ponzi of Boston in the early 1900s. The Ponzi scheme is advertised as an investment opportunity that pays from the top down. That is, the original investors recruit new investors, who in turn continue to recruit. Eventually the scheme becomes top-heavy, with those at the top being rewarded while those newest to the scheme recoup progressively less of their original investment and never receive the promised rewards. Other Ponzi schemes perpetrators operated in the late 1800s and included Sarah Howe, who was sentenced to three years in prison. Novels employed the scheme as a plot prior to that time. The most notorious and longest running of Ponzi schemes was operated by **Bernard Madoff** (a former chairman of the NASDAQ stock market), who admitted to beginning it in the 1990s, although investigators believe the 1980s was more likely. The Ponzi scheme may have defrauded almost 5,000 individuals for about $70 million by the end of 2008. Madoff received the maximum sentence allowed of 150 years in prison.

PORNOGRAPHY. Pornography is any depiction of sexually explicit material that is intended to stimulate sexual arousal. This material may be printed, pictorial, film, or other contextual matter. Sexually explicit material has been recovered from such ancient sites as Pompeii and the Roman Empire. The development of sex products and films becoming available on the internet has raised concerns about pornography becoming more readily available, especially to children. The effect of pornography **addiction** is now being seriously debated by marriage counselors. There have been many attempts to pass statutes that would argue that pornography does not enjoy **First Amendment** protection and would render pornography illegal, including films that center on **prostitution**. In each case, the statutes were overruled by state and federal appellate courts. Examples of cases that overruled pornography as illegal include *1973 American Booksellers v. Hudnut*, *1988 California v. Freeman*, and *2005 People v. Paulino*. *See also* CIVIL RIGHTS.

POSSE COMITATUS. The drafting of citizens under the authority of sheriffs or other law enforcement agents to assist in the capture or detainment of a person suspected of breaking the law. The term *posse* (a shortened version) enjoyed popularity in the United States during the 19th century. It was originally part of English **common law**. It is now out of date in the United Kingdom. However, there are some states—for example, Georgia—in the United States that have not repealed its use.

***POWELL V. ALABAMA*, 287 U.S. 45 (1932).** In 1931, nine young black men, including Ozzie Powell, were convicted of raping two white women on a train. The **trial**, conducted in Scottsboro, Alabama, denied them many fundamental rights, including attorney representation and being informed of their rights. The **U.S. Supreme Court** held that the **Bill of Rights** applied to state courts and reversed the conviction and ordered a new trial. The precedent of this case ensured that any capital defendant in either state or federal court be granted attorney representation. It should be noted that subsequent court decisions, such as ***Gideon v. Wainwright*, 372 U.S. 335 (1963)**, ensured that this right also pertained to misdemeanors. Refer to appendix 1, "The Bill of Rights." *See also* DUE PROCESS; SCOTTSBORO BOYS.

PREMEDITATION. The act of planning or deliberating a criminal act. The amount of time needed for premeditation depends on the person and the circumstances. The time must be long enough, after forming the intent to act, for the person to have been fully conscious of the intent of the act and to have considered the outcome of the act.

PRESIDENT'S COMMISSION ON LAW ENFORCEMENT AND ADMINISTRATION OF JUSTICE. The commission was formed in 1967 by President Lyndon B. Johnson to address problems with the criminal justice system, including what were recognized as unfairness, rising crime rates, and unjust **police** practices. The commission in 1967 produced a report titled *The Challenge of Crime in a Free Society*, which would be recognized as the most comprehensive criminal justice review of its time. The report proposed a systemized approach to criminal justice that would coordinate the functions of the three branches of criminal justice—the courts, police, and corrections. The influence of the report resulted in many recommendations being undertaken through the **Omnibus Crime Control and Safe Streets Act of 1968, Pub. L. No. 90-351, 82 Stat. 197 (1968).**

PRESUMPTION OF INNOCENCE. The legal right of a person accused of crime. It places the **burden of proof** on the agency/person making the accusation and not on the defendant. In other words, the state or accusing party must make their case. The origins of presumption of innocence date back to the 6th century and Roman law. In *Taylor V. Kentucky*, 436 U.S. 478 95 S. Ct. (1930), the **U.S. Supreme Court** held that there is an assumption of innocence in the absence of contrary **evidence**. In the United Kingdom there is a slight difference for determining the burden of proof, which is that the **jury** must be convinced.

PRETRIAL DIVERSION. The attempt to selectively redirect those accused of criminal offenses from traditional courts and other criminal justice practices including incarceration. This may begin before the suspected offender has been charged and in other cases after charges have been filed. The idea is to have the offender complete a program from which there will be some assurance that they will not reoffend. In the first case, successful completion means that charges will not be filed and in the second case that charges will be dismissed. Those who fail **diversion** programs can be charged or processed through the traditional court system. Pretrial diversion programs operate on both the state and federal level. The earliest example is the Brooklyn Plan for juveniles, which operated from 1946 to 1974. Other plans developed for both juveniles and adults were driven by the **mass incarceration** movement. The second wave of diversion programs, initiated in 1989 with the creation of the first drug court, led the way in the 1990s to the founding of special or problem-solving courts such as **gun courts**, **domestic violence courts**, homeless courts, and others. Not all special courts exist in all states. *See also* PROBLEM-SOLVING COURT.

PRISON. *See* PENITENTIARY.

PRISON ARGOT. *See* ARGOT.

PRISON CODE. The **prison** code is also referred to as the convict code. These are the informal rules and behavioral expectations that each convict anticipates will be adhered to by another convict. Adherence to the prison code helps to assure that a convict will not run afoul of another convict and thus offers some assurance of survival in the prison environment. This code also assures agreement between convicts with regard to associations and relationships with guards who enforce the formal rules of the prison. The idea of a code was first explored by Gresham Sykes (1958) in his study (*The Society of Captives*) of Trenton State Prison, followed by **John Irwin** (1970) in his study *The Felon*; Matthew Sheridan (1991) in his dissertation, *An Exploration of the Personal Experience of "**Prisonization**": Utilizing the **Concept** of Environmental Press and the Introduction of a Concept of Minor Press to Account for Exceptional Circumstances in the Environment*; and Jeffrey Ross and **Stephen Richards** (2003) in ***Convict Criminology***. Each study affirmed the existence, necessity, and importance of the code for convict survival.

PRISON EXPERIMENTS. Human-subject **prison** research (scientific, medical, and social) has been conducted on convicts within U.S. prisons since their beginning in the early 19th century. Social research has been reported in journals and other scholarly publications. However, other scientific and medical experimentation has been hidden from public view because of the exploitive and harmful nature to the convicts, although sanctioned by major pharmaceutical companies and state and federal government. For example, *Acres of Skin* (1991) details the medical experiments conducted by Dr. Kligman at Holmsburg Prison, from which many convicts never recovered. The same is also true of the vivisection experiments (implanting animal parts and the parts of executed convicts into human convicts) conducted at **San Quentin** Prison by Dr. Leo Stanley for more than 30 years in the mid-1900s.

PRISON FARM. Prison farms emerged shortly after the invention of the prison. The time of greatest growth for the farms was from the end of the Civil War until the middle of the 20th century. The establishment of prison farms coincided with the use of convict or penal labor in other categories such as logging, road clearance, mining, and quarrying. A challenge to convict labor through the Thirteenth Amendment was denied. Farms have been viewed as a means for prisons to cut costs and keep convicts busy. Among the more famous farms are Parchman Farm in Mississippi (20,000 acres) and Angola in Louisiana (18,000 acres). Prison farms have a long history of abuse of convicts, such as that noted by sociologist and prison warden Tom Murton (*Accomplices to the Crime)* from his time at Tucker Farm in Arkansas. *See also* CONVICT LEASE SYSTEM.

PRISON GANGS. Groups of convicts who organize within a **prison**. Prison **gangs** have organization, a hierarchy, membership limited by characteristics such as race or ethnicity, and lifelong commitment. Prisons monitor gangs through their designated "security threat group." Prison gangs, first **identified** in California, emerged with the advent of **mass incarceration** in the mid-1960s and serve as a means of protection, enforcement against those who would snitch, and other illegal activities in the prison. Camp and Camp (1985) conducted a national survey and at that time recognized 13,000 gang members. A later study, also by Camp and Camp (2001), published data that confirmed a significant increase in the prison gang population to 65,183.

PRISONIZATION. Donald Clemmer (1940) coined the term *prisonization* in his seminal work *The **Prison** Community*. He defined it as "the taking on, in greater or lesser degree, of the **folkways**, **mores**, customs, and general culture of the **penitentiary**." The theory has been challenged by other theories such as "importation theory," but these have failed to explain the culture with the efficacy of prisonization. In the late 1980s and the 1990s, prisonization was understudied until **convict criminology** encouraged that it be a focal point for understanding the effect of prison on convicts and for influencing their failure upon returning to society.

PRISON RAPE ELIMINATION ACT (PREA). PREA was passed unanimously by Congress in 2003 to investigate and prevent rape in **prison**. The results of PREA included for the first time that the existence of rape was officially acknowledged as an occurrence in prisons committed by both convicts and prison staff. **Zero-tolerance** policies were enacted. A National Resource Center was created in 2010 to help states comply with PREA standards. By 2012, federal standards became operational for the elimination of prison rape. A national survey of prison rape and other forms of molestation is conducted every two years.

PRISON REFORM. Prison reform is almost as old as the prison itself. Shortly after operations began at **Eastern State Penitentiary** in the early 1800s, reforms to prison practices began, and work was included. In prisons, which followed Eastern, there were reforms in architectural style (**Auburn**, **panopticon**). Work was provided or mandated, along with the addition of **chain gangs** in the late 1800s in Southern prisons. In addition, other types of **punishments** were allowed (including **executions**). Also, provisions for medical practices, experiments on convicts, rehabilitation and education, living arrangements and more were allowed. Some reforms were the consequence of **U.S. Supreme Court** holdings such as *Estelle v. Gamble*, 429 U.S. 97 (1976), and others because of public outcry (*I Am a Fugitive from a Georgia Chain Gang*, 1932). Prison reform has been a constant component of prison operations. *See also* AUGUSTUS, JOHN (1785–1859).

PRISON TENDER. Referred to as a "**trusty**" and in some instances as "building tenders," the trusty is common to most **prison** systems. The prison tender was more common to southern prisons as a means to control the prisons and working convicts. The prison tenders would report on other convicts who violated rules, supervise convicts on work sites, and manage entrance and egress from prisons. Prison tenders were often armed on work sites and served as the guard force for the prison. They would administer discipline, including physical **punishments** such as **whippings**. The prison tender system began after the Civil War and was abolished in the 1980s (*Ruiz v. Estelle*, 503 F. Supp. 1265 [S.D. Tex. 1980]) after abuses became evident. *See also* PRISON FARM.

PRIVATE PRISON. Private **prisons** are also referred to as for-profit prisons. State and federal prisons contract with private providers, such as Correctional Corporation of America (CCA), which obtained the first contract to incarcerate in Tennessee 1984, to provide for convict custody and care. **Mass incarceration** vastly increased the cost of prisons, and privatization was seen as a cost-saving measure. Private prisons are mostly located in southern and western states. There has been controversy about the legitimacy of private prisons. In 2016, the U.S. Department of Justice announced that it would be discontinuing the use of such prisons because of issues with abuse, safety, security, and excessive **punishment**. *See also* PRISON FARM.

PRIVATE SECURITY. Private security has origins in ancient Rome, Europe, and England prior to the creation of formal law enforcement. During earlier times, it may have functioned as night watchmen or town criers. Private security was not replaced by the creation of law enforcement. They are also referred to as security guards or have a position as an agent, and they act in both armed and unarmed capacities to protect property, persons, or tangible assets. One of the earliest agencies was the Pinkerton Agency, founded by Alan Pinkerton in 1843. Private firms developed a reputation for pursuing and bringing to justice outlaws of the old west. Modern private security officers outnumber law enforcement officers and are required to be licensed, and in the case of being armed must have a weapons permit. The earliest attempt to regulate and license private security officers was in California in 1915.

PROACTIVE POLICING. A component of community policing directed toward partnering with the community to prevent crime rather than react to crime. Law enforcement engages the community and works with citizens to understand community needs and as a problem-solving initiative, which when successful is prevention, control, and reduction in community fear of crime. This is among the earliest concepts of the role of **police** and was a foundation of **Sir Robert Peel**'s formation of police in 1829 as an alternative to military forces. The concept became a driving force in the 1980s with renewed interest in community policing and was seen as a means to restore community faith in policing. *See also* COMMUNITY-ORIENTED POLICING; GUARDIAN ANGELS.

PROBABLE CAUSE. Probable cause denotes that there is reasonable suspicion and that the facts presented are probably true. The language allows **warrants** to be served but does not assert that the **evidence**/facts are sufficient for a conviction. The concept of probable cause and its meaning as used in the **Fourth Amendment** has been upheld by the **U.S. Supreme Court** in *Brinegar v. United States*, 338 U.S. 160 (1949), and *Illinois v. Gates*, 462 U.S. 213 (1983). The emphasis is that what had been called general warrants or **writs** of assistance lacked specificity, which had been challenged in the courts since the mid-1700s. The writ of assistance, founded in British **common law**, allowed entrance into a home without probable cause. Probable cause must be demonstrated for the issuance of a warrant. Probable cause is also essential to the preliminary hearing before a case goes to **trial**. Unless probable cause, that is, reasonable suspicion that facts are probably true, is supported, then a defendant must go free. *See also* DUE PROCESS.

PROBATION. A criminal court sanction that allows an offender (called a probationer) to remain in the community under supervision. Probation is usually used for first-time offenders and minor offenses and was first developed by **John Augustus** during the 1850s in Boston, Massachusetts. Probation is the most frequent sanction applied by U.S. courts. More than 50 percent of adult offenders serve probation sentences under correctional supervision. Probation is a conditional sentence mandated with conditions (a contract) that the probationer must adhere to. Any failure to adhere to the conditions results in a violation of probation and the potential for resentencing to a term of incarceration. *See also* ALTERNATIVE SENTENCING; COMMUNITY CORRECTIONS; PAROLE; SHOCK PROBATION.

PROBLEM-SOLVING COURT. Problem-solving courts are also referred to as **community courts** or special courts. The earliest courts in America were community courts that addressed the needs of their communities, solving problems as they occurred. The modern problem-solving courts have their origin with the creation of the **drug court** in 1989 in Miami. The success of drug court to address the needs of offenders and communities that were not resolved in traditional courts led to the application of the concept to other community problems. The newer courts include **gun court**, **reentry court**, **domestic violence court**, and more. These courts do not replace traditional courts but attempt to address themselves to lower-level and nonviolent offenders receptive to treatment and the services the courts offer. Drug court now has a long history of research which has demonstrated that the court is more efficient and cost effective than traditional courts.

PROFILING. The earliest efforts to develop a criminal profile involved the unsuccessful and unsolved case of Jack the Ripper in London. Modern efforts were established by Howard Teten of the FBI in 1960, and by 1970 he produced his first profile. His belief was that the evidence at a crime scene would detail the kind of person who would commit such a crime. The 1970 case was a murder, and the female victim had been stabbed. The success of the case resulted in requests for his assistance in other cases. Even though a case might be more problematic, Teten continued to be successful, thus beginning the technique of criminal profiling. The FBI has since established the **Behavioral Science Unit (BAU)** in 1970, which was headed up by Jack Kirsch and continued to produce very positive results solving cases. Profiling next became more specialized, profiling serial killers through the work of **Robert Ressler** and **Roy Hazelwood**, and the FBI would go on to create the Behavioral Analysis Unit and later the **Violent Criminal Apprehension Program (ViCAP)** in 1985. *See also* GEOGRAPHIC PROFILING; RACIAL PROFILING.

PROHIBITION. A period from 1920 to 1933 in the United States. The Eighteenth Amendment to the U.S. Constitution was ratified in 1919 and repealed in December 1933 with the ratification of the Twenty-First Amendment to the U.S. Constitution. There have been many efforts to enforce prohibition for either religious or political reasons. The earliest codified effort was the **Code of Hammurabi** in approximately 1733 B.C. The 20th century saw many countries attempt to prohibit the sale and consumption of alcohol. While bans have lasted for as long as eight decades, they have all failed and resulted in the repeal of prohibition. In addition to alcohol being a desired commodity, prohibition became an opportunity for a variety of criminal enterprises such as speakeasies and "**bootlegging.**" Notably, **Alphonse Capone** fashioned a criminal enterprise in Chicago during Prohibition with alcohol as the primary product.

PROMOTIONS IN CUSTODY (PIC). In the early days of the **prison**, convicts who demonstrated that they could be trusted were advanced in custody status to "trustees," or what has been called in other states "**prison tenders**." Promotions in custody meant that the convict received more liberties in the prison system and could be trusted to work outside of the locked-in circumstances of prison. Following the institution of the **medical model** in prisons in the late 1930s, **inmate classification** systems used psychosocial evaluations, behavior, observations, and performance in prison to evaluate the convict for a reduction in custody status. Instruments of **risk assessment** (such as the LIS-R) that were developed in the 1980s have become primary tools for assessing a convict's readiness for promotions in custody. Promotions in custody also permit a convict to participate in community release programs outside the prison, such as school and **work release** as well as **furloughs** or temporary release from custody. *See also* CLASSIFICATION; COMMUNITY CORRECTIONS; INMATE.

PROPORTIONALITY. Proportionality has been addressed in several **U.S. Supreme Court** cases, including *Edmund v. Florida*, 458 U.S. 782 (1982), and *Tison v. Arizona*, 481 U.S. 137 (1987). The issue of proportionality was treated as an **Eighth Amendment cruel and unusual punishment** clause issue and focused on the principle that the punishment should be proportional to the crime. This is an old principle in criminal law generally understood to mean an eye for an eye. *See also* CODE OF HAMMURABI.

PROSECUTORIAL MISCONDUCT. The action of a prosecutor to wrongly convict a defendant through such tactics as withholding information, producing false **evidence** as though it is accurate, or **witnesses** who provide false testimony. Examples of prosecutorial misconduct include the 2006 Duke lacrosse case. The defendant's conviction was overturned because there was no **DNA** evidence to link the defendants to the case, two defendants had alibis, and there were inconsistencies in the complainant's testimony. In this case, the prosecutor was disbarred. In the 1987 case of Michael Morton, evidence was withheld, and Morton was convicted and spent 25 years in **prison**. The prosecutor was charged, spent 10 days in jail, and was disbarred.

PROSTITUTION. Prostitution has been a practice in most cultures throughout history. There are three main types: street worker, brothel worker, and escort service. A prostitute may be male or female and agrees to commit a sex act for payment. Prostitution may be illegal or legal (Nevada is the exception where it has been legal and regulated since 1970). Prostitution is often referred to as a **victimless crime**; however, "**white slavery**," so called in the 1910 **Mann Act**, banned women from being transported for "immoral purposes." Telephones, and later cell phones, changed the management of prostitution, and prostitutes became known as "call girls." The availability of the internet for the general public in the early 1990s saw advertising for brothels, escorts, and agencies for prostitution shift because of its wide reach. *See also* SEX TRADE.

PROTECTIVE CUSTODY (PC). The placement of persons in some restricted setting to prevent them from being harmed or causing harm to others. Protective custody was sparsely utilized prior to the middle of the 20th century. The primary uses of it include **witness protection** (which developed into the **federal witness protection program**) and is used for **police** informants and witnesses to crime who will testify on behalf of the prosecution. There are separate sections of the **prison** to safeguard persons who are at risk from others, represent a risk to others, or are a risk to themselves. Examples include those who are mentally ill, corrupt politicians and police officers who are sentenced to prison, and **gang** members.

PSYCHOSURGERY. A controversial treatment for mental disorders that originated in the late 1800s and gained prominence in the early 1900s despite mixed results. The procedures are called a leucotomy and later advanced to become a lobotomy. The effectiveness of psychosurgery as a technique to control unwanted and criminal behaviors was steadily undermined both by the medical profession and by others such Ken Kesey (1963), who included it in his novel *One Flew over the Cuckoo's Nest* about **total institutions**. Psychosurgery has largely been discontinued since the late 1970s.

PUBLIC DEFENDER. *See* COURT-APPOINTED ATTORNEY.

PUBLIC ENEMY. A term popularized in the 1930s and probably first used by the Chicago Crime Commission, quickly followed by its use in the media, political speeches, books, and film, such as *Public Enemy* which stared Jimmy Cagney. Although associated with the **FBI**, which did declare some **gangsters** as Public Enemy No. 1, no federal agency used the appellation to advertise or campaign its efforts to fight crime. Among the more infamous gangsters of the 1930s to bear the title of Public Enemy No. 1 were Chicago crime boss **Alphonse "Scarface" Capone**, **John Dillinger**, Charles "Pretty Boy" Floyd, George "Baby Face" Nelson, and **Alvin "Creepy" Karpis**. The use of the term *public enemy* ended during the early 1940s, although it was adopted by a California street **gang** in the 1980s. *See also* HOOVER, J. EDGAR (1895–1972).

PUNISHMENT. Criminal punishment is the assignment of a consequence for violating a criminal statute. Sanctioned punishments range from minor consequences such as **fines** to the **death penalty** for **murder** and other serious crimes. Punishments must be proportional to the crime, although they are affected by mitigating and **aggravating circumstances**. The written history of sanctioned punishments dates to the **Code of Hammurabi**. Modern punishments, while governed by both federal and state criminal codes, may be altered when challenged in the appellate courts and especially the **U.S. Supreme Court** through its interpretation of the U.S. Constitution. There are generally four justifications that influence not only the creation of law but also the imposition of the punishment: **deterrence**, rehabilitation, **retribution**, and incapacitation. The intent of punishment, therefore, is to ensure the discontinuance of criminal behavior. Punishment represents the public disapproval of a criminal action and as such intends to educate regarding what is correct and what is incorrect behavior. Also, official sanctions serve to deter society from becoming vigilantes or engaging in **blood feuds**. *See also* FEUDING; VIGILANTISM.

PURVIS, MELVIN (1903–1960). An **FBI** agent from 1927 to 1935. He practiced law after resigning from the FBI in 1935. He was acknowledged for apprehending more of the FBI's public enemies than any other agent, including **John Dillinger**, Charles "Pretty Boy" Floyd, and George "Baby Face" Nelson. **J. Edgar Hoover** demoted him because the attention he gained detracted from Hoover. Purvis's death is questionable whether it was an accident or a suicide from his weapon. *See also* PUBLIC ENEMY.

PYRAMID SCHEME. An illegal form of marketing often associated with legitimate multilevel marketing. The pyramid scheme, in many cases, implies that it is selling a product when in reality it is marketing distributorships for a commission, and the item(s) for sale (if available) is the by-product. Each recruit is supposed to assure that the next up-line person receives a share of whatever they market. The problem is that those at the top reap the rewards, and as the pyramid extends down, there is less likelihood of the promised return on the commission (investment), or there may be a loss. Pyramid-scheme models do have some variance in design. However, all operate similarly. Some examples include the eight-ball model, matrix scheme, gifting scheme, airplane model, and affinity schemes, which are religious based. The **Ponzi scheme** (named after Charles Ponzi who began his scheme in 1920, which lasted until the 1940s) is similar except that it purports to sell financial products. The **FBI** classifies pyramid schemes as franchise fraud. Two early schemes were John Law's 1719 "Mississippi Bubble" scheme in France and William Franklin Miller's short-lived Franklin Syndicate of March–November 1899. Pyramid schemes have expanded during the past 15 years. *See also* MADOFF, BERNARD (1938–).

PYROMANIA. Deliberate fire setting, classified as an impulse-control disorder, is often associated with past criminal, antisocial, or traumatic events such as **truancy**, abuse, and possibly may include revenge as a motivation. Pyromania should not be mistaken for **arson**. Arson is fire setting for profit or another type of gain. Investigations into pyromania began in the early 1880s, and it was associated with insanity and moral imperfections. *See also* INSANITY DEFENSE.

Q

QUANTICO, VIRGINIA. A small town in Prince William County completely surrounded by the Marine Corps Base Quantico. Quantico is one of the largest Marine Corps bases in the world. The base was established in 1917. Today, Quantico is also the home of the **FBI** and the Drug Enforcement Administration training academies.

QUARLES DECISION, *NEW YORK V. QUARLES*, 467 U.S. 649 (1984). The **U.S. Supreme Court** decision which held that overriding considerations of public safety (called the public safety exception) justified an officer's failure to provide Miranda warnings before he asks questions about locating an abandoned weapon. *See also MIRANDA V. ARIZONA*, 384 U.S. 436 (1966); WARRANTLESS SEARCHES.

QUETELET, ADOLPHE (1796–1874). Belgian mathematician whose 1831 publication *Recherches sur le penchant au crime aux differens ages* (1831, see "Age Crime Curve") used statistics to analyze crime and age-specific crime rates by gender, country, and social group. His work has been extremely influential in the development of sociological criminology. He set the pattern for criminal analytical research, which is used today. He is also known for his work in the arts (poetry, painting, and opera).

R

RACIAL DEMOCRACY, CRIME & JUSTICE NETWORK. The network was founded in 2003 as a consortium of college professors and graduate students who research criminal justice issues. Their specific objectives are to (1) advance the study of the intersections among democracy, crime and justice, and actions of citizenship, and (2) support junior scholars from underrepresented groups in pursuing career advancement. The network is supported by the National Science Foundation's Sociology and Law and Social Sciences programs. Membership consists of 140 scholars of diverse backgrounds. The network is located at the Criminal Justice Research Center at Ohio State University.

RACIAL DISPARITY. The proportion of a racial or ethnic group in the control of the criminal justice system or agency which is greater than the proportion of the same group in the general population. Reasons for **disparity** include differing levels of criminal activity, law enforcement emphases on particular neighborhoods or communities, legislative policies, or decisions by criminal justice practitioners. Unwarranted racial disparity in the criminal justice system is caused by dissimilar treatment of people based on race. Historically, racial disparity has a long history in the American justice system. It was not until the **civil rights** movement in the 1960s–1970s that studies identified the problem and research projects were undertaken to understand the problems that contributed to disparity and to seek remedies. There were national and state efforts to reform the situation. While progress has been made to reduce racial disparity, there remains more to be done.

RACIAL PROFILING. Actions of criminal justice agencies taken against a minority or racial community based on perceived notions concerning race, ethnicity, national origin, or religious affiliation. Racial profiling violates the **Fourteenth Amendment** of the U.S. Constitution, which guarantees equal protection under the law and freedom from unreasonable searches and seizures. Early laws in the United States, especially those referred to as "**Black Codes**" and later referred to as "Jim Crow laws," targeted blacks without cause. The mid-1960s saw increased awareness of racial injustice, and efforts were begun to mitigate such egregious actions. Among the first actions taken were the elimination of what have been referred to as "Terry stops." *See also* DRIVING WHILE BLACK (DWB); *TERRY V. OHIO*, 392 U.S. 1 (1968).

RACKETEER INFLUENCED CORRUPT ORGANIZATION (RICO). Federal legislation developed to counter criminal activity to gain control of business organizations. RICO was enacted in 1970 after investigations led by Senator Robert Kennedy into the criminal activities of the **Mafia**. Congress passed legislation that enabled federal prosecutors to bring additional criminal/civil charges against people or groups whose multiple criminal acts constitute a conspiracy, which is also referred to as racketeering. RICO allows federal prosecutors to use monetary penalties to confiscate all profits from criminal activities, thus bankrupting criminal organizations. *See also* GANG; ORGANIZED CRIME.

RADER, DENNIS (1945–). Born in Pittsburg, Kansas, he was known as the BTK (bind, **torture**, kill) killer or the BTK strangler. Starting with his first murders in 1974 until 1991, he terrorized the Wichita, Kansas, area. He was responsible for 10 murders. Looking for more publicity, he inadvertently helped the local **police** to his discovery and arrest. Dennis Rader pled guilty and was ordered to serve 10 life sentences in **prison**. *See also* MURDER; SERIAL KILLER.

RADZINOWICZ, SIR LEON (1906–1999). A Polish-born criminologist who became a naturalized British citizen in 1947. A scholar, author, and professor, he made **criminology** an intellectually respected discipline in the United Kingdom. He served as a member of the law faculty at Cambridge for many years. Radzinowicz served on many commissions to study Britain's **prisons**, criminal procedures, and education. Radzinowicz founded the faculty of criminology at Cambridge University. He is recognized as an international authority in criminology and lauded for his work; he was knighted in 1970.

RAMSEY, JONBENÉT (1990–1996). A six-year-old victim of sexual abuse and **homicide**. The victim was found dead in the basement of the family home in Boulder, Colorado, on Christmas Day 1996. The Boulder Colorado **Police** Department, despite an in-depth investigation, could not solve the crime. Using **DNA evidence**, the parents and brother were cleared of any involvement. While the case was closed in 2008 because of lack of evidence, it was reopened by the authorities in 2010. The case remains unsolved. *See also* FORENSICS.

RAND CORPORATION. A nonprofit, nonpartisan organization committed to public interest research. Originally part of the Douglas Aircraft Company, it separated from Douglas in 1948 and became a separate organization. Since its founding, Rand has become an internationally known and respected research firm. Rand helps organizations internationally in areas of security, health, education, sustainability, justice, growth, and development. Rand has been a major contributor to criminal justice research with various projects, including **Bail** Bond Reform, **Juvenile Courts**, the Volunteer in **Probation** project, and presentence reports. Rand has over 1,800 employees and works in 53 different countries. The corporation relies on philanthropic support to reach beyond its client-sponsored work to tackle questions too large or complicated for some clients to address.

RANSOM. An ancient process that has been used by warring factions since written history began. Known to the Greeks, Romans, Persians, and ancient Chinese, ransom was demanded by what is referred to as the ransom note. Upon receipt of money or other form of compensation, release from captivity would be promised. Ransom was heavily used during the Middle Ages, especially during the Hundred Years' War. The first known ransom note recorded in U.S. history was the 1874 Ross brothers **kidnapping** in Philadelphia. The case was never solved, and the victim Charley Ross was never returned.

RAPE KIT. Medical equipment/procedure used by medical staff to gather forensic **evidence** (**DNA**, hair, and skin samples) from the rape victim's body to identity the rapist. The official name is Sexual **Assault** Evidence Kit. Rebecca Clark was the first victim to be given an exam using the rape kit on 12 January 1999 at Magee-Women's Hospital in Pittsburgh. *See also* FORENSICS.

RATIONAL CHOICE THEORY. Rational choice theory argues that an individual makes choices from available preferences that are practical, in their best interest, and achieve the more productive or satisfying economic gain. The foundation for the theory lies in the work of **Cesare Beccaria** in the 18th century and was later advanced to incorporate the theories of **deterrence**, **routine activity theory**, and **situational crime theory**.

RAY, JAMES EARL (1928–1998). A known racist who was convicted of the **murder** of **civil rights** leader Dr. Martin Luther King Jr. in 1968. Ray pleaded guilty to avoid the **electric chair** and was sentenced to 99 years of incarceration. He denied any involvement in the **assassination** of Dr. King. He subsequently died from liver disease and kidney failure while a prisoner at the Tennessee Department of Correction.

RAZOR RIBBON. Also known as razor wire, it is made of metal with sporadic blades that are used on fences to create a barrier and to discourage either entrance or egress. It is the improved version of barbed wire used in the 1870s American West. During World War I, Germany developed razor wire to better contain enemy soldiers. In the United States, razor ribbon is used in **prisons** as perimeter barriers.

REASONABLE DOUBT. In criminal court, the defendant may be convicted when the standard of proof exists that guilt is established **beyond a reasonable doubt**. This was a standard in English **common law** practice dating to the 1800s. ***In re Winship*****, 397 U.S. 358.S.Ct. 1068, 25 L.Ed. 2d 368 (1970)**, was the **U.S. Supreme Court** decision which held that the **Fifth Amendment due process** protections included that reasonable doubt must be established for a guilty conviction. Justice Brennan, writing the majority opinion, stated that the decision reflected "a fundamental value determination of our society that it is far worse to convict an innocent man than to let a guilty man go free."

RECIDIVISM. Recidivism is difficult to define inasmuch as different researchers have used different definitions for their research. For example, some researchers might include arrests. Arrests do not automatically become a charging, a charging does not automatically become a conviction, and a conviction does not automatically become a statistic of reincarceration. A general definition would include any involvement with law enforcement for suspected or real criminal activity that may or may not have been previously exhibited by the suspect and for which there are legal consequences that may range from time served to **prison** commitment. A review of some descriptions (and taking into consideration the descriptive language for recidivism) reveals the following information. The **Bureau of Justice Statistics (BJS)** claim that of 405,000 prisoners released during 2005 from both prisons and jails in 30 states, 58 percent reoffended (in this case were arrested for a new crime) within the first three years after their incarceration. The Urban Institute review of released prisoners conducted in 2003 produced a similar conclusion, with 70 percent of males being rearrested. In keeping with the introductory caution about recidivism definitions, the Urban Institute also noted that of that number, 50 percent would return to prison. Other studies such as that conducted by the U.S. Department of Justice in 1994 reveal through their use of different definitions of recidivism that persons convicted of different crimes have different rates of recidivism. In addition, when the variable of race is included, the rates of recidivism also change. *See also* REENTRY.

RECKLESS, WALTER CADE (1899–1988). A graduate of the University of Chicago School of Sociology who became a noted criminologist and researcher, he developed **containment theory**, part of the social control theories in criminal justice. He wrote that **juvenile delinquency** could affect anyone, that all humans are deviant in their behavior, but not all become delinquent. There are noncausal explanations for those who become delinquent and those who don't. People have inner and outer containment that controls behavior. If young people are properly socialized during their development (by family or social institutions), they have a sense of belonging and an identity, which assists them in their desire to remain nondelinquent. Containment theory was one of the primary reasons for the development of the Head Start Programs for underprivileged children that were begun in 1965. Reckless's theory became the foundation for future **social control theorists**, including **Edwin Sutherland**, Larry Siegel, and **Travis Hirschi**.

RECORD PIRACY. *See* PAYOLA.

RED-LIGHT DISTRICT. A section of a city in which brothels, strip clubs, stores specializing in objects used for sexual gratification, or theaters specializing in adult sex films (such as **pornography**) are located. At different times in U.S. history, such enterprises could be found in many cities throughout the United States. The origin of the term dates to the middle 19th century when a red lantern was hung outside the establishment to designate that its contents were of a sexual nature. Red-light districts have at different times during the 19th and 20th centuries been legally designated and referred to as "sporting districts" in attempts to regulate the contents and **prostitution**. The unpopularity of the districts with citizens and politicians led to their demise in the United States by the 1950s.

REENTRY. *See* BROCKWAY, ZEBULON (1827–1920); MACONOCHIE, CAPTAIN ALEXANDER (1787–1860); PAROLE.

REENTRY COURT. Modeled after **drug court**, reentry courts began as an initiative by the **Office of Justice Programs** in 2000 to facilitate offender **reentry** into the community. Initially there were nine states in which the special courts focused on job development, housing, and personal accountability for ex-offenders. The court applies graduated sanctions for violations of release conditions and positive reinforcement to encourage appropriate reintegration. A judge, generally, maintains active oversight of the cases, meeting with offenders and case managers. Offenders are on supervised release. Offenders are provided with counseling, drug and mental health treatment, and other services. *See also* PROBLEM-SOLVING COURT.

REFORMATORY. After the establishment of **prisons**, the reform movement started the campaign for housing for younger offenders separate from adults. **Zebulon Brockway** founded **Elmira Reformatory** in 1876. It differed from many prisons of the day as it focused on reforming the convict using psychological and training methods rather than physical ones. *See also* REFORM SCHOOL.

REFORM SCHOOL. An institution, sometimes referred to as a **training school**, to which young offenders are sent as an alternative to adult institutions. Reform schools focus on education and training rather than **punishment**. Jamesburg, the New Jersey State Home for Boys, was created in 1867 and is one of the first reform schools in the country. In 1848, the first reform school was opened using state funding in Westborough, Massachusetts. *See also* REFORMATORY.

REGIONAL INFORMATION SHARING SYSTEMS (RISS) PROGRAM. The RISS program is comprised of six regional centers, with the first created in 1973, to handle the growing need for criminal justice information, technological changes, and to help ensure officer safety. RISS is federally funded and administered by the U.S. Department of Justice, Bureau of Justice Assistance, which provides oversight and program management. RISS membership has grown to over 9,000 law enforcement agencies, including more than 117,000 access officers. RISS offers many websites to handle information provided by and for use by many federal, state, and local agencies. *See also* MIDDLE ATLANTIC–GREAT LAKES ORGANIZED CRIME LAW ENFORCEMENT NETWORK (MAGLOCEN).

REINTEGRATIVE SHAMING. A theory developed in 1989 by John Braithwaite as a response to **Howard Becker**'s 1963 **labeling theory**. Braithwaite proposed that by shaming the offender, ties are broken with society. His theory seeks to bring the offender back into society as a law-abiding citizen. In some historically black churches, a sinner, as long as he confesses to his misbehavior, is forgiven and returned to his place in the community. The model is used in some **juvenile offender** programs to avoid the development of a juvenile record.

REISS, ALBERT J. (1922–2006). An author and **police** reformer born in Cascade, Washington. He studied **police misconduct** and found that police behavior was determined by whether the police officer was proactive or reactive to the situation. The more proactive the officer, the more accepted the outcome was by the offender. Reiss became an expert in measuring crime. The Carter administration funded Reiss's work, which was later ended by the Reagan administration. His theory was used by Police Commissioner William Bratton and Mayor Rudy Giuliani in New York City in their quest to lower crime during the 1990s. Reiss finished his career teaching at Yale University from 1970 to 1993. *Police and the Public* (1973) was the result of his research. *See also* POLICE CORRUPTION.

RESSLER, ROBERT (1937–2013). A **profiler** and behavior specialist for the **FBI**. He started his career while in the U.S. Army and divided his time between the **military police** and the Reserve Officer Training Corps (ROTC) program. He completed his education at Michigan State University and joined the FBI in 1970, becoming a member of the Behavior Science Unit. He specialized in violent offenders and is credited with coining the term ***serial killer***. Ressler worked on the **Ted Bundy**, **Jeffrey Dahmer**, and **John Wayne Gacy** cases. Ressler wrote, *Whoever Fights Monsters: My 20 Years in Tracking Serial Killers for the FBI* (1992). *See also* BEHAVIORAL ANALYSIS UNIT (BAU); HAZELWOOD, ROBERT ROY (1938–2016).

RESTITUTION. The concept which specifies that part of the **punishment** for an offender should be to repair or make repayment for damages done. Restitution has roots in both the **Code of Hammurabi** in the 18th century B.C. and from the Old Testament. In the early 20th century, the condition of restitution in the modern judicial system is critical to the imposition of suspended sentences and the determination of **probation**. The latter part of the 20th century envisioned probation as an enhancement to the new emphasis on **victims' rights**, which is to relieve the financial pain and suffering and other losses borne by the victims which were caused by the crime(s). The imposition of restitution is in keeping with the current importance placed on **community corrections** as an alternative to institutional corrections. The U.S. federal government has reinforced the use of restitution as a tool of sentencing reform through the findings of the 1982 President's Task Force on Victims of Crime, after which almost all states have passed legislation requiring restitution. *See also* BALANCED AND RESTORATIVE JUSTICE (BARJ).

RESTORATIVE JUSTICE. Restorative justice emphasizes repairing the harm done to people and relationships rather than only punishing offenders. Restorative justice originated in the 1970s as mediation and reconciliation between victims and offenders with a focus on the needs of victims, offenders, and society, as opposed to the sole punishment of the offender. The view of restorative justice is that victims, society, and (with the exception of the unyielding need to punish offenders) offenders are neglected when it comes to repairing the damage. Restorative justice is portrayed as a triangle with victims, society, and offenders at each of the points, indicating the need for justice to be a complete process. According to John Braithwaite, "No person has done more to inspire the restorative imaginations of citizens of this planet than Howard Zehr." He is the author of *Changing Lenses: A New Focus for Crime and Justice* (1960), which proposed a theory of restorative justice—an alternative framework for thinking about crime and justice. Retributive justice sees crime as an offense against the state, while restorative justice sees it as a violation of people and relationships. By the 1990s restorative justice had achieved popularity with many segments of society, law enforcement, judges, politicians, correctional practitioners, and others. While restorative justice remains popular in some circles and was supported by positive research, by the end of the 20th century it has become less frequently utilized because the original funding sources have been discontinued. *See also* BALANCED AND RESTORATIVE JUSTICE (BARJ).

RETALIATION. *See* BLOOD FEUDS; FEUDING; *LEX TALIONIS*.

RETRIBUTION. Retribution is one of the goals of a criminal sentence. The sentence for a criminal offense is supposed to qualify as an appropriate punishment, neither too excessive nor too lenient. *See also* PUNISHMENT.

REYNIE, GABRIEL NICOLAS DE LA (1625–1709). De La Reynie is regarded as the founder of the first modern **police** force in Paris. As the lieutenant general of police (a position established in 1667 and which he held for 30 years), he created an independent police force for reducing crime. Crime control, at this time, was overseen by at least four separate units of policing, which would be reorganized into one consolidated force with jurisdiction broken down into 17 districts, each with its own commanding officer who would report daily to De La Reynie. Modern police concepts attributed to him include the creation of the first **detective** bureau, the use of informants, the arrangement of streetlights, mandates that controlled the movement of horse-drawn vehicles, parking arrangements, and provisions for assisting the homeless. De La Reynie summed up his work as follows: "Policing consists in ensuring the safety of the public and of private individuals, by protecting the city from that which causes disorder." De La Reynie's use of departmental units for policing is considered the basis for modern police organizations and has been replicated throughout the United States.

***RHODE ISLAND V. INNIS*, 446 U.S. 291 (1980).** The **police** questioned Innis about his role in a **murder**, and he requested an attorney. Before the attorney arrived, the police in conversation questioned each other about the location of the gun and how it would be a shame if a kid found the gun and the gun later hurt someone. Innis led them to the site of the gun, and this information helped to convict him of the crime. Innis appealed, citing failure to follow proper criminal procedure (**interrogation**) under Miranda. The Court held that the police were correct in their behavior since Innis had willingly shared the information. *See also HARRIS V. NEW YORK*, 401 U.S. 222 (1971); INFORMED CONSENT; *MIRANDA V. ARIZONA*, 384 U.S. 436 (1966); POLICE ETHICS.

RICHARDS, DR. STEPHEN. *See* CONVICT CRIMINOLOGY.

***RIDDICK V. NEW YORK*, 445 U.S. 573 (1980).** A **U.S. Supreme Court** holding, in cases of criminal prosecution, which provides for the defendant to have qualified "assistance of counsel" of their choosing, whether or not the defendant can afford to pay counsel. The U.S. court process is in large part modeled after the British court, however. While many states did authorize counsel in criminal cases, some states, such as Florida, had limited the right of representation. In Florida, counsel was only authorized for capital cases. This was challenged in the U.S. Supreme Court by **Clarence Earl Gideon** who had been arrested in 1961 for breaking into a Panama City (Florida) pool hall. He was sentenced to five years' imprisonment. The U.S. Supreme Court held in its 1963 review of Gideon that his conviction was unconstitutional. Gideon, with an attorney of his choosing, was retried in 1963 and found not guilty. *See also* FORTAS, ABE (1910–1982); *GIDEON V. WAINWRIGHT*, 372 U.S. 335 (1963).

RIGHT TO COUNSEL. Prior to 1963, a defendant in a criminal case could be defended by an attorney of his/her choosing, so long as they could afford that attorney. What was also the case was that a defendant could choose to represent themselves and in some cases would be tried without the benefit of counsel. In 1963, the **U.S. Supreme Court**, in ***Gideon v. Wainwright*, 372 U.S. 335 (1963)**, recognized that the judicial system was an adversarial system and that few untrained persons were either qualified or capable of putting up an adequate defense. Gideon overturned the ***Betts v. Brady*, 316 U.S. 455 (1942)**, holding that indigent and other defendants were not entitled to an attorney. The Betts decision may be seen as somewhat unusual since in ***Johnson v. Zerbst*, 304 U.S. 458 (1938)**, the court had previously held that defendants were entitled to counsel in the federal court. The court in the Gideon case held that the Sixth Amendment guaranteed that an individual when faced with the potential loss of their liberty, even if indigent, must be afforded an attorney who is trained to stand before the bar. Other cases would follow Gideon's landmark decision, further clarifying the right to counsel position in other court matters such as appeals that would challenge a sentence and further extending it to **juvenile court** proceedings and cases of misdemeanors. *See also POWELL V. ALABAMA*, 287 U.S. 45 (1932).

***RING V. ARIZONA*, 536 U.S. 584 (2002).** A criminal case against Timothy Ring. When the **jury** found Ring guilty of felony **murder** and not premeditated murder, the judge decided that the **punishment** would be **execution**. The case was appealed to the **U.S. Supreme Court**. On 24 June 2002, the Court decided 7–2 that this was a Sixth Amendment case and the punishment could only be determined by the jury. *See also* DEATH PENALTY.

RISK ASSESSMENT. *See* EVIDENCE-BASED PRACTICES.

***ROBINSON V. CALIFORNIA*, 370 U.S. 660 (1962).** An **Eighth Amendment** interpretation protecting personal conduct from being criminalized. This case involved a person addicted to drugs. An **addiction** may not be criminalized. In this case, a **police** officer noticed that Robinson's arms were scarred from injections, and he admitted to using **narcotics**. He was arrested and charged with a misdemeanor, for which he received a sentence of 90 days. The **U.S. Supreme Court** held the California law to be unconstitutional.

***ROCHIN V. CALIFORNIA*, 342 U.S. 179 (1973).** A **due process** case of deputy **sheriffs** entering a residence without a **warrant**, placing their fingers into Rochin's mouth, and then with hands around his neck retrieving capsules. Rochin was then taken to a hospital, given an emetic, and vomited the capsules into a bucket. The capsules were found to be morphine, and Rochin was charged with **drug possession**. The **U.S. Supreme Court** held that the conduct of the deputies "shocks the conscience" and that the **evidence** was inadmissible. *See also* FIFTH AMENDMENT; FOURTEENTH AMENDMENT; POLICE POWERS; SEARCH AND SEIZURE; WARRANTLESS SEARCHES.

ROCKEFELLER DRUG LAWS. Governor Nelson Rockefeller in 1973 successfully had the New York state legislature pass what are known as the Rockefeller drug laws—statutes regarding the sale and possession of "narcotic" drugs in New York State. The penalty for selling two ounces or more of narcotic drugs or possessing four ounces or more of narcotic drugs had a mandatory minimum of 15 years to life in **prison** and a maximum of 25 to life. These laws and similar statutes passed in other states contributed to the great rise in the prison population referred to as **mass incarceration**. *See also* NARCOTICS.

ROLLING, DANNY HAROLD (1954–2006). *See* GAINESVILLE RIPPER; SERIAL KILLER.

ROME STATUTE. The Rome Statute established the International Criminal Court in 1998 and was enacted in 2002 to prosecute such offenses as **crimes against humanity**, crimes of aggression (added in 2010), **genocide**, and **war crimes**, which are referred to as core international crimes. The Rome Statute was the result of a United Nations conference held in 1998. The International Court may assume jurisdiction through a tribunal of judges when a nation-state is unable to or will not prosecute.

***ROPER V. SIMMONS*, 543 U.S. 551 (2005).** A **U.S. Supreme Court** case that affected numerous previous decisions, holding that defendants under the age of 18 at the time of the offense could not be subject to the **death penalty**. This decision voided the **death sentences** of 72 others who were currently on **death rows** across the country for crimes committed prior to their 18th birthday. Prior to this decision and since 1976, there had been 22 **executions** carried out on individuals younger than 18 at the time of their offenses. *See also* EIGHTH AMENDMENT; JUVENILE JUSTICE AND DELINQUENCY PREVENTION ACT OF 1974; JUVENILE RIGHTS.

ROSENBERG, JULIUS (1918–1953) AND ETHEL (1915–1953). On 29 March 1951, Julius and Ethel Rosenberg were sentenced to death for violating the Espionage Act of 1917 and executed in **Sing Sing Correctional Facility** by **electrocution** on 19 June 1953. They have the distinction of being the only civilians to be executed for the crime of **espionage** during the Cold War. The significance of the crime is that the information provided by them enabled Russia to develop the atomic bomb many years earlier than it would have achieved otherwise. While the Rosenbergs never acknowledged their guilt, substantial **evidence** exists to the contrary. *See also* EXECUTION.

ROUTINE ACTIVITY THEORIES. Routine activity theories suggest that three circumstances are present for crime: a **motivated offender**, an available target, and the absence of prevention. An issue of importance for the theory is the argument that inequality, poverty, and unemployment are not always the motivation for committing crime. The principal theorists have been Marcus Felson and Lawrence E. Cohen, who examined crime after World War II. Their 1979 research paper argues for an expanded **opportunity theory** suggesting that after the war there was a good economy, which expanded opportunities for crime to include **employee theft**, **copyright violations**, and other criminal activity in the corporate sphere.

RULE OF SILENCE. *See* AUBURN PRISON; EASTERN STATE PENITENTIARY (PENNSYLVANIA).

RUSSIAN MAFIA. The Russian **mafia** is also referred to as Bratva, which loosely translated means Brotherhood. The Russian mafia emerged during the Soviet era as a loose collection of **organized crime** groups, preceded by **prison gangs**, which emerged under the harsh conditions of the Russian **gulags** prior to World War II. The collapse of the former Soviet Union allowed for the spread of the Russian mafia beyond its borders, including entrance into the world of crime in the United States. It has established a strong base of illegal operations in New York State, New Jersey, California, and Florida. Some of the significance of the Russian mafia is that it has been perceived as the largest organized crime group in the world. At one time it was projected that they controlled approximately two-thirds of the Soviet economy. In addition, it has also been alleged that their cocaine sales in the United States have surpassed $34 billion annually. The Russian mafia maintains a triangle of criminal operations between Russia, Israel, and the United States.

S

SABOTAGE. The deliberate effort to destroy or hamper some element of a workplace to harm profits or output to achieve better wages or workplace conditions or to further a political agenda. The person who engages in such activity is referred to as a saboteur. As the name suggests, the origin is probably French, dating to the 19th century. Some groups that have engaged in sabotage include the Luddites, English textile workers who engaged in sabotage as a tool for wage negotiations. It was part of the philosophy of "Big" Bill Haywood while forming the Industrial Workers of the World in the early 1900s. The Irish Republican Army used sabotage as a tactic of **terrorism**.

SACCO, NICOLA (1891–1927). *See* FEDERAL BUREAU OF INVESTIGATION (FBI); VANZETTI, BARTOLOMEO (1888–1927).

SAFE HOUSE. Originally a hideaway for criminals to avoid arrest in colonial days. Prior to the Civil War, a safe house was a stop on the Underground Railroad for runaway slaves. The idea later developed into a place to hold **witnesses** or victims of crime where they were free from danger or harm. More recently, it is a place where federal agents stow witnesses awaiting **trial** for racketeering and/or drug cases. Currently, it is a term for places of refuge for victims of **domestic violence**. *See also* VICTIM WITNESS PROGRAM.

SAINT VALENTINE'S DAY MASSACRE. Seven **gangsters** believed to be confederates of George "Bugs" Moran were gunned down on 14 February 1929, allegedly at the order of **Alphonse Capone**. These seven **murders** were part of 64 gangland murders that occurred between 1924 and 1929. The "massacre" is presumed to have been an effort by Capone to consolidate control by eliminating his rivals. Capone supposedly was at his Florida home, and no one was ever brought to **trial**. This event is recognized as the beginning of the end for Capone, who had been dubbed **Public Enemy** No. 1 by the newspapers. *See also* MURDER INC.

SALEM WITCH TRIALS. The only known American witch **trials** occurred between 1692 and 1693. More than 200 people were accused, by four young girls, of being witches. This is an example of mass hysteria overtaking a small colonial community, which resulted in 20 people being executed. The incident was made famous by Arthur Miller's 1953 play *The Crucible*. The earliest documented case of **execution** of a witch was that of Alse Young in 1647 in Hartford, Connecticut. *See also* LYNCHING.

SANDY HOOK MASSACRE. The deadliest mass school shooting in U.S. history occurred on 14 December 2012 at Sandy Hook Elementary School, Newtown, Connecticut. Six teachers and 20 children (aged six and seven) were murdered by 20-year-old **Adam Lanza**, who had also murdered his mother. Lanza shot himself in the head, committing suicide, before **police** could apprehend him. Lanza suffered from developmental disorders and mental illness. The reason for the shooting is unresolved. The high-powered weapons and the large quantity of ammunition in Lanza's possession caused renewed calls for gun control and **background checks** prior to the purchase of weapons and ammunition at both the state and federal levels. President Obama signed 23 executive orders to address these issues, but Wayne LaPierre, executive vice president of the National Rifle Association, protested against it. Three states (New York, Maryland, and Connecticut) did pass some gun control measures, but the U.S. Senate, in 2013, defeated measures for improved gun control. *See also* GUN CONTROL; MASS MURDER; MURDER; NEWTOWN MASSACRE.

SAN QUENTIN. San Quentin is California's oldest and best known maximum-security **prison**. Founded in 1852, the institution is operated by the California Department of Corrections and Rehabilitation. Today it houses 6,000 prisoners who are supervised by 1,700 staff members. The prison is home to California's **death row**, where **executions** had previously occurred in the **gas chamber**. **Lethal injection** became the accepted method of execution in 1994, and on 23 February 1996 William Bonin became the first person to be executed in California by lethal injection.

SCARED STRAIGHT. Scared Straight programs began in U.S. prisons in the 1970s. Youth are taken to a **prison** to experience prison living conditions and to undergo a hard-line introduction to prison life delivered by convicts. In East Jersey Prison, New Jersey (formerly Rahway **Reformatory**), the presentation to at-risk youth is delivered by the Lifers Program. Scared Straight programs were popularized by the well-known Arnold Shapiro film by the same title in 1978, which won an Academy Award and an Emmy that same year. The program has had its critics. Notably, Dr. James Finkenauer, a

Rutgers professor, conducted research on the program in 1978 and found that youth were more likely to commit crime after attending such a program. A larger study of Scared Straight programs in 2002 had similar findings and that there were greater reoffense rates. *See also* JUVENILE DELINQUENCY.

***SCHALL V. MARTIN*, 467 U.S. 253 (1984).** The New York **Family Court** Act authorizes the detention of juveniles deemed to be a "serious risk," specifically with the potential to commit a new crime. The federal district court held that such a determination violated **due process**, that is, **punishment** without **adjudication**. The determination affirmed that juveniles are entitled to due process to protect them from nonadjudicated punishment. *See also* JUVENILE DELINQUENCY; JUVENILE RIGHTS; JUVENILE (WAIVER) TRANSFER.

SCHOOL-TO-PRISON PIPELINE. The school-to-**prison** pipeline is a euphemism for describing youth who are suspended, expelled, or have minor involvement with law enforcement, which ultimately results in their entrance into the criminal justice/correctional system. The concept was identified in the 1950s by social scientists and others as they struggled to explain the causes of delinquency and rising levels of juvenile incarceration. Focus on this concept has resulted in a stream of intermediary measures intended to improve school focus on youth who required interventions that would have an impact on their future involvement with the criminal justice system. The results of recognizing the school-to-prison pipeline include the formation of the **Office of Juvenile Justice and Delinquency Prevention** (1974), a greater role for **community corrections**, and the recognition that poverty and race need to be addressed to mitigate the failures associated with schools that result in the school-to-prison pipeline. *See also* JUVENILE DELINQUENCY; JUVENILE JUSTICE AND DELINQUENCY PREVENTION ACT OF 1974.

SCOTLAND YARD. The **detective** arm of the Metropolitan **Police** (formed after passage of the Metropolitan Police Act of 1829) that provides law enforcement services for the greater London area. Scotland Yard is named for the street (Great Scotland Yard) on which it was originally located. Scotland Yard maintains the records for the United Kingdom's criminals and serves as the communications link between the United Kingdom's police forces and Interpol. Among the infamous cases examined by Scotland Yard include "**Jack the Ripper**" and the famous headless torso of a female—both remain unsolved crimes. The modern Scotland Yard provides protective service for visiting dignitaries and other important persons and conducts investigations such as into the 2005 terrorist bombing in London. Charles Dickens during the 1830s observed Scotland Yard officers to study their police methods. The officers have retained the nickname "Bobbies," for **Sir Robert Peel**, the founder of the Metropolitan Police and a major influence on the establishment of police and police procedures in the United States.

SCOTTSBORO BOYS. In 1931, nine African American teenagers were charged in Alabama with the rape of two white women. The case was widely publicized, and there was international criticism for its handling and the accompanying racism. With one exception, a 12-year-old, all were sentenced to death. They were accused unjustly, and the case was inflamed with racism and handled with improper law enforcement and judicial proceedings intended to obtain a guilty verdict despite what the **evidence** suggested. For example, there was no medical evidence to suggest a rape had occurred, and the defendants were not afforded competent counsel or an impartial **jury**. Appeals began immediately, sentences were overturned, new **trials** were granted, and judges were replaced. Two **U.S. Supreme Court** appeals resulted in landmark case decisions affirming the right to counsel and nondiscrimination in juror roles. The teenagers would suffer abuses in **prison**, including the shooting of one by a prison guard. The cases and various rulings would linger, with one defendant remaining behind bars for twenty years (released in 1950) and until the governor, George Wallace, in 1976 granted the remaining defendant a **pardon** after his recapture from escape. The cases have been widely accepted as miscarriages of justice. *See also* DISCRIMINATION; *NORRIS V. ALABAMA*, 294 U.S. 587 (1935); *POWELL V. ALABAMA*, 287 U.S. 45 (1932).

SEARCH AND SEIZURE. A law enforcement process of searching property or a person when crime is suspected and confiscating what may be considered as **evidence** relevant to a case under review. There are constitutional provisions that protect citizens from unreasonable search and seizure; that is, there must be reasonable suspicion, which is **probable cause**, to conduct a search followed by seizure of what is found. There is a fundamental right to privacy that protects citizens from unreasonable search and seizure. Generally, law enforcement must obtain a **warrant** to conduct a search. There are very specific exceptions (such as items in "plain view") when officers do not need a warrant. The **exclusionary rule**, which has a foundation in English law, has been formulated from interpretations of **Fourth Amendment** protections. The landmark case ***Mapp v. Ohio*, 367 U.S. 643 (1961)** established that evidence may not be seized without first obtaining a **search warrant**.

Evidence illegally obtained without a warrant is referred to as the "**fruit of the poisonous tree**." *See also* PLAIN VIEW DOCTRINE; WARRANTLESS SEARCHES.

SEARCH WARRANT. *See* WARRANT.

SELF-INCRIMINATION. The act of exposing oneself to an accusation of committing a crime by a public statement. In many legal systems, accused individuals cannot be compelled to incriminate themselves. People may speak to law enforcement authorities, but they cannot be punished for refusing to do so. In the United States, the right against self-incrimination is spelled out in the **Fifth Amendment** to the U.S. Constitution and is commonly known as "**taking the Fifth**." The right against self-incrimination has its roots in 16th-century English law. *See also* DUE PROCESS.

SELLIN, THORSTEN (1896–1994). Thorsten Sellin, a University of Pennsylvania sociologist from 1922 until his retirement in 1967, was a prolific author of academic books and papers on **criminology** and criminal justice. He wrote *Culture, Conflict and Crime* in 1938, followed by articles in the Social Science Research Council and the American Institute *Journal of Criminal Law and Criminology*. Sellin became a leader in his field with his article "Youth and Crime" in the journal *Law and Contemporary Problems* in 1942. He pioneered scientific criminology, utilizing law, psychology, history, and sociology for the analysis of crime. He explored cultural diversity through **critical** and **Marxist criminology**. His reputation was largely based on the use of criminal statistics to understand crime and deviance. He was one of the authors of the United States Uniform Criminal Statistics Act of 1944.

SENTENCING DISPARITY. A term for unequal treatment in sentencing by a court for different individuals for committing similar criminal acts. Sentencing **disparity** arises when the differences in the sentencing have little or nothing to do with the legal issues of the matter. Disparity has its roots in both gender and racial **discrimination**. Once sentencing disparity was identified, both the federal and state courts established **sentencing guidelines** to assist judges and magistrates in deciding appropriate sentences for use in criminal sentences. All sentencing guidelines are published to allow public review. Sentencing guidelines are often placed in a grid that denotes the degree of the crime and the number of offenses, which assists a judge with consistent sentencing patterns. Among the actions taken to reduce disparity include the passage of the Fair Sentencing Act of 2010. This act reduced the sentencing disparity between offenses involving crack and powder cocaine. The act reduced the ratio of disparity from 100:1 to 18:1. Crack cocaine laws have been viewed as primarily affecting minorities.

SENTENCING GUIDELINES. *See* DISPARITY; SENTENCING DISPARITY.

SENTENCING PROJECT, THE. Malcolm Young, attorney, became the first director in 1981. Marc Mauer, the current executive director, took over in 2005. The project is managed by attorneys, practitioners, and academics. It conducts research and performs advocacy directed at having an impact on **racial disparity** and the overuse of incarceration. *See also* DISPARITY; MASS INCARCERATION.

SEPARATE SYSTEM. *See* PENNSYLVANIA SYSTEM.

SERIAL ARSONIST. A person who sets three or more fires. The arsonist is usually a young white male with a tenth-grade education and poor ability to establish emotional relationships. Historically, the serial arsonist sets fires for revenge or excitement. Until the development of modern technology, fire was a perfect weapon because it left little or no **evidence**. Some American arsonists include John "Pillow Pyro" Orr (1949–), who was sentenced to life imprisonment for setting as many as 2,000 fires which killed four people; Raymond Lee Oyler (1971–), sentenced to death for setting 24 fires which killed five people; Peter Dinsdale (1960–), who confessed to 11 fires, was convicted of 26 counts of **manslaughter**, and was sentenced to life in **prison**; and Thomas Sweatt (1955–), who set more than 300 fires over a 20-year time frame which killed five people and is serving a mandatory life sentence. *See also* SENTENCING DISPARITY.

SERIAL KILLER. A serial murderer is a person who commits three or more **murders** taking place over more than a month. It also includes a "cooling-off period" between murders. The **FBI** definition is a series or two or more murders committed at separate events by one offender acting alone. *See also* BERKOWITZ, DAVID (1953–); BUNDY, THEODORE (1946–1989); DAHMER, JEFFREY (1959–1994); GACY, JOHN WAYNE (1942–1994); MASS MURDER; MUHAMMAD, JOHN ALLEN (1960–2009); RADER, DENNIS (1945–); ROLLING, DANNY HAROLD (1954–2006); SHAWCROSS, ARTHUR (1945–2008); ZODIAC KILLER.

SERPICO, FRANK (1936–). Police officer Frank Serpico was a **witness** to corruption in the New York City Police Department and would later describe his role as a **whistle-blower** or lamplighter. New York City mayor John Lindsay created the **Knapp Commission** in April 1970 to investigate **police corruption**. The findings of the commission led to major reforms within the New York City Police Department. Serpico resigned his position and moved to Europe for almost a decade. He is the author of *Serpico* (1973), his story of the corruption and of being a whistle-blower. *See also* POLICE MISCONDUCT.

SEX TRADE. *See* PROSTITUTION; WHITE SLAVERY.

SHAWCROSS, ARTHUR (1945–2008). A **serial killer** known as the **Genessee River Killer** and the Rochester Strangler, who had been paroled after serving a sentence for **manslaughter** and then went on to be responsible for approximately 11 more deaths (predominantly prostitutes) in the Rochester, New York, area. Shawcross had a troubled life, which possibly included bedwetting and **incest** and later progressed to include **arson** and burglary. He would be diagnosed as a "schizoid psychopath" during his second **prison** term for **murder**. The first **trial** for the murders resulted in a sentence of 250 years to life, and in a second trial for the final murder charge, he received life in prison. Shawcross died in prison of cardiac arrest. *See also* PAROLE; SERIAL ARSONIST.

SHEPARD, MATTHEW (1976–1998). The victim of abduction, robbery, and a brutal beating. This was a **hate crime** attack that raised the national and international consciousness about homophobia and resulted in the Matthew Shepard and James Byrd, Jr., Hate Crimes Prevention Act (2009) signed into law by President Obama. There had been previous efforts to pass similar legislation that failed to gain support, and in one instance the **murder** was called a "hoax" by North Carolina representative Virginia Foxx (who later referred to her remark as a poor choice of words). The perpetrators, Aaron McKinney and Russell Henderson, were convicted of **kidnapping** and felony murder but not for a hate crime. Each received two consecutive life sentences.

SHEPPARD, SAM (1923–1970). A controversial sensationalized 1954 case that resulted in Sheppard being convicted of murdering his wife. He received life in **prison** for second-degree **murder**. After six years of failed appeals, Sheppard in 1961 enlisted the counsel of **F. Lee Bailey**, and in 1965 the **U.S. Supreme Court** heard the case and in an 8–1 vote overturned the murder conviction because the **jury** was aware of the media input and had not been sequestered. The **trial** judge had also spoken to the media. Sheppard was tried a second time, and the jury found him not guilty. The U.S. Supreme Court held that the trial was tainted by the "carnival atmosphere." The "not guilty" verdict did not restore Sheppard's reputation. A **civil trial** also failed to clear his name. Controversy continued to surround the case with a mysterious assailant who Sheppard said committed the murder, and it would later be the foundation for the hit TV show *The Fugitive*. The suspect was Richard Eberling, a convicted burglar and suspect in two other murders, who died in prison in 1998. Sheppard attempted to provide his side of the story in his book *Endure and Conquer* (1966). Sheppard did return to medical practice for a short time and remarried twice. However, alcohol consumption contributed to his death on 6 April 1970. *See also* DUE PROCESS.

SHERIFF. The sheriff, originally an early law enforcement officer in England, first referred to as the shire reeve, was responsible for maintaining law and order in a shire. In Scotland, the person holding the position would act as a judge. The position of sheriff would be adopted in the American colonies and become an elected position. George Washington's father, Augustine Washington, and grandfather, Lawrence Washington, would both hold the position of high sheriff of Virginia in the late 1600s and the mid-1700s prior to the establishment of the United States as a country. The sheriff is usually the highest level of law enforcement officer at the county law enforcement level. The duties of sheriff vary from state to state and generally include guarding and maintaining the local courthouses and running the local jails.

SHOCK PROBATION. A short period of incarceration followed by a change of sentence that allows the offender to remain in the community under **probation** supervision. Shock probation is assigned at the discretion of a judge and is considered a privilege, not a right. Shock probation is intended to reduce **recidivism**. Shock probation had its origins in the 1960s as a solution for **prison** overcrowding. *See also* BOOT CAMP.

SIEGAL, BENJAMIN "BUGSY" (1906–1947). Bugsy Siegel began his **criminal career** by extorting money from New York City's pushcart peddlers. Siegel, in 1918, joined Meyer Lansky to form the Bugs-Meyer **gang**. He gained his nickname because of his explosive nature. In the 1920s, along with **Charles "Lucky" Luciano**, he created the **National Crime Syndicate**, a union of crime families. In the 1930s, he began, with eastern crime family money, to develop what would become Las Vegas and in 1947 opened the Flamingo Hotel and Casino. Allegedly **organized crime** was unhappy with the profits from Siegel, and he was gunned down in 1947 and the casino was taken over by organized crime. *See also* MAFIA.

SIGHT AND SOUND SEPARATION. Under the core requirements of the **Juvenile Justice Delinquency Prevention Administration (JJDPA)**, which was established in 1974 and reauthorized in 2002, all **juvenile detention**, correctional facilities, and jails or other lockup facilities must have provisions that provide facilities with sight and sound separation of juveniles from adults. Rule 115.14 states for youthful inmates, (a) a youthful **inmate** shall not be placed in a housing unit in which the youthful inmate will have sight, sound, or physical contact with an adult inmate through use of a shared dayroom or common space, shower area, or sleeping quarters; (b) in areas outside of housing units, agencies shall either (1) maintain sight and sound separation between youthful inmates and adult inmates or (2) provide direct staff supervision when youthful inmates and adult inmates have sight, sound, or physical contact; and (c) agencies shall make the best efforts to avoid placing youthful inmates in isolation to comply with this provision. Absent exigent circumstances, agencies shall not deny youthful inmates daily large-muscle exercise and any legally required special educational services to comply with this provision. *See also* JUVENILE DELINQUENCY.

SILENT SYSTEM. The silent system was conceived of by New York **prison** officials in the mid-19th century. Convicts would be placed in enforced silence as a means of prison control. This was a variation on the theme of the **separate system** devised at **Eastern State Penitentiary**, where convicts were kept in solitary and silence from influences that would impede redemption. Elements of the silent system remain in prison today for the purpose of prison control.

SIMPSON, O. J. (1947–). A pro football star (a Heisman Trophy winner in college) and actor, he was released in 2017 after serving a 33-year sentence with a nine-year minimum term for armed robbery and **kidnapping**. Simpson was previously tried and acquitted for the **murder** of his ex-wife and her friend. The **trial** has been referred to as the trial of the century because of the team of attorneys who defended him. The closing line of the summation, delivered by lead attorney **Johnnie Cochran** before the **jury**, has become famous: "If it doesn't fit, you must acquit." Simpson was later found culpable in a **civil trial**, and $33.5 million in damages was awarded.

SING SING CORRECTIONAL FACILITY. A maximum-security **prison**, located in Ossining, New York, that was built by convict labor in 1826 to replace **Newgate Prison** and originally known as Mount Pleasant Prison. It is known for its harsh conditions in the 19th and 20th centuries. The early convicts traveled by boat to Sing Sing, and the phrase "up the river" came into existence. Sing Sing became one of the New York prison sites for the

electric chair in 1891, and 614 men and women were executed, the last in 1963. The first psychological work with **inmates** began there. Sing Sing Prison currently houses more than 2,000 inmates. *See also* EXECUTION.

SITUATIONAL CRIME THEORY. The concept of situational crime was formed by **Edwin Sutherland** in 1947. Sutherland argued that crime was either "historical," that is, influenced by previous personal history, or "situational," caused by the environmental factors encompassing the crime scene. The concept gained additional acceptance in the 1980s when Michael Gottfredson and **Travis Hirschi** asserted that although criminality is a necessary condition, it alone is not sufficient for a crime to be committed. Crime requires situational incentives found in the form of motivation and opportunity. The central concepts of situational crime prevention theory are found in and influenced by other theories, including **rational choice theory**, routine activity theory, and **crime pattern theory**.

***SKINNER V. OKLAHOMA*, 316 U.S. 535 (1942).** Skinner had two previous convictions for offenses that were considered to have involved "moral turpitude." His third conviction made him eligible under Oklahoma's 1935 Habitual Criminal Sterilization Act to be subject to compulsory involuntary sterilization. His crimes had been chicken stealing and twice for armed robbery. These crimes were held to be treated differently from other law violations and thus were violations of the **Fourteenth Amendment**'s equal protection clause, and his sentence was overturned. *See also* PROPORTIONALITY.

SLIWA, CURTIS (1954–). The founder of the New York City–based **Guardian Angels**, a group of citizen volunteers organized in the late 1970s to fight crime and **violence** in the city's subway system. The Guardian Angels received both positive and negative reactions from the public and the New York City **Police** Department. Currently the organization claims to operate in nine countries and 82 cities around the world. *See also* VIGILANTISM.

SOCIAL CONTROL THEORY. A subtheory of **social process theories** developed in the 1930s by **Edwin Sutherland**. **Travis Hirschi**, during the 1960s, based his social bond theory on the foundation of social control theory. The theory is based on ways in which a society encourages conformity to its norms and rules of behavior through interaction with community institutions and individuals. The goal is to establish and/or develop crime prevention through interaction with family, friends, and social institutions.

SOCIAL DISORGANIZATION THEORY. A theory that explains the growth of **juvenile delinquency** in minority neighborhoods. The change in moral values tied to a lack of social control and few community organizations that assist young people in their development of social coping skills leads to more extensive delinquency by a neighborhood's young people. This theory was developed by Shaw and McKay as they studied Chicago's neighborhoods in the early 1900s. The concentric **zone theory** is often noted as the base of social disorganization theory. *See also* CRIME MAPPING; McKAY, HENRY D. (1899–1980).

SOCIAL LEARNING THEORY. Edwin Sutherland developed the theory of learning and social behavior which stated that new behaviors can be learned by observation and imitating others. He stated that learning is a cognitive process, which happens in a social setting. Clark Lewis Hull, Neil Miller, and John Dollard wrote in their book *Social Learning Theory* (1941) that personality consisted of learned habits. Social learning theory has been used to explain the emergence and maintenance of criminal behavior. *See also* DIFFERENTIAL ASSOCIATION; LEARNING THEORY.

SOCIAL PROCESS THEORY. A group of three theories (**social control**, **social learning**, and **labeling theory**) that perceive crime as the relationship between a person and the environment—that harmful interactions will result in criminal behavior when the benefits seem to outweigh the costs. The theory recognizes that persons can commit crime in these situations. Social bonds that are positive help prevent criminal behavior. Labeling theory adds the additional dimensions of having someone labeled as criminal and thus encourages criminal interactions. *See also* SUTHERLAND, EDWIN (1880–1951).

SODERMAN, HARRY (1902–1956). Soderman was born in Stockholm, Sweden, and became a policeman and later a criminologist, having earned a Ph.D. in **forensic science** from the University of Lyon (1928). In 1930, he became a lecturer at Stockholm's Hogskola University. In 1934, he contributed to the organization of the New York City **Police** Department's forensic laboratories. In 1939, he was appointed to head the National Laboratory of Forensic Science in Sweden and held this position until 1953. After World War II, he became famous for his role in liberating political prisoners, including detainees in German concentrations camps in Norway. After the war, Soderman helped revive the International Police Commission and served the commission until his death in 1953. He was a pioneer of modern **criminology** in Scandinavia.

SOLITARY CONFINEMENT. Solitary confinement is the most severe **punishment** allowed in U.S. **prisons**, with the exception of **capital punishment**. Solitary confinement began with **Eastern State Penitentiary** in Philadelphia in 1829. The Quakers and other religious groups believed someone could be reformed by placement in solitary confinement to allow the prisoner to reflect on misdeeds and restore a relationship with God and the community. Solitary confinement requires that the **inmate** be isolated from any human contact for 22–24 hours a day, the only exception being necessary contact with prison staff. Today, solitary confinement is used as a punishment beyond incarceration; it is also used to separate unruly inmates and to provide safe **protective custody** for mentally ill inmates and for vulnerable inmates. Inmates held in solitary confinement especially for long periods of time have a history of mental health problems. *See also* ADMAX; SUPERMAX PRISON.

SON OF SAM. A nickname for **David Berkowitz**, a **serial killer**, who drove New York City to hysteria and fear in 1976 and 1977. After speculation that various publishers were offering Berkowitz a large amount of money for his story, New York State passed the first "Son of Sam laws" that prevented convicted criminals and their relatives from benefiting financially from the sale of their stories. Originally, it was struck down by the **U.S. Supreme Court** for violating the **First Amendment**'s right of free expression. New York State later produced a revised statute that was acceptable to the Court. Many states and the federal government have since enacted Son of Sam laws.

SOUTHERN POVERTY LAW CENTER (SPLC). Founded in 1971 by Morris Dees and Joseph J. Levin Jr., the center is dedicated to fighting hate and bigotry while it seeks justice for the most vulnerable members of southern society. Located in Montgomery, Alabama, it is a nonprofit organization that argues cases against white supremacist groups and **discrimination** in criminal cases. During the **civil rights** movement of the 1970s, the SPLC was an advocate for the poor and a leader in the civil rights movement. *See also* RACIAL DISPARITY.

SPECIFIC DETERRENCE. Cesare Beccaria developed the theory in his original *Essay on Crimes and Punishments* (1764). The general belief was that criminal action could be deterred by **police** enforcement and severe **punishment**. Specific **deterrence** seeks to inhibit the offender from repeat criminal behavior by unpleasant punishment for the original behavior. Specific deterrence involves reducing **recidivism** (repeated offenses committed by convicted, punished offenders). *See also* GENERAL DETERRENCE; RATIONAL CHOICE THEORY.

SPECK, RICHARD BENJAMIN (1941–1991). Speck was the seventh child of eight children born to Benjamin and Mary Speck. He grew up in a poor family where he was psychologically abused by his stepfather. Speck started drinking alcohol at age 12 and by age 15 was getting drunk every day. His first arrest occurred at the age of 13 for trespassing, which began a long arrest record. At 20 years of age he dated a 15-year-old girl, Shirley Annette Malone, who became pregnant. They married in 1962 and divorced in 1966. His arrest record soon included disorderly charges, **assault** with a knife, and rape. On 13 July 1966 Speck broke into a townhouse serving as a dormitory for student nurses. He held nine student nurses **hostage** for hours, eventually leading them out one by one, stabbing or strangling each to death. One student survived by hiding under a bed. Speck was charged with **murder** and sentenced to death. On 28 June 1971, the **U.S. Supreme Court** upheld his conviction and reversed his **death sentence** because of **jury selection**. Speck's case was remanded back to the Illinois Supreme Court for resentencing, and on 21 November 1972 he was sentenced to 400 to 1,200 years in **prison**. Speck died of a heart attack on 5 December 1991. *See also* MASS MURDER.

SPEEDY TRIAL. A Sixth Amendment provision that prohibits the prosecution from arbitrary and capricious delays of **trial**. The point is that delays may require lengthy periods of incarceration that should be reserved as a response to convictions. Prosecutors therefore must be diligent in their efforts to accumulate **evidence** or otherwise prepare their case. The Virginia Declaration of Rights (1776) provided an early precedent. The **U.S. Supreme Court** emphasized the importance of the "speedy trial" by creating a four-part test for determining the appropriateness of delays in *Barker v. Wingo*, 407 U.S. 514 (1972). Violating the provision of a speedy trial is cause for **dismissal** with prejudice. Refer to appendix 1, "The Bill of Rights." *See also* BILL OF RIGHTS; *KLOPFER V. NORTH CAROLINA*, 386 U.S. 213 (1967).

STAND YOUR GROUND LAW. Twenty-three states have adopted this statute, where citizens have the right to use force to defend themselves without first trying to flee. In these states, a claim of self-defense provides immunity from prosecution. The general purpose of the law is to reduce crime by allowing individuals protection from **assault**. Eighteen states require that there is a duty to retreat before using force to protect themselves. *See also* MARTIN, TRAYVON (1995–2012); ZIMMERMAN, GEORGE (1983–).

STANFORD PRISON EXPERIMENT. A 1971 study of the psychological effects of university students becoming a **prison** guard or a prisoner. The study, led by Dr. **Philip Zimbardo** at Stanford University, was designed to better understand the conflict that exists between guards and prisoners. Student participants adapted to their roles more quickly than the study anticipated. As the guards enforced their rules, the prisoners reacted with hostility, and the guards began to use psychological **torture** to enforce their rules. The study became a matter of who was in control. Two prisoners quit the study because of the level of hostility. The study was curtailed halfway through because of the amount of anger and hostility generated. It has become a classic study of role conflict. The results of the study were later revisited in Zimbardo's book *The Lucifer Effect: Understanding How Good People Turn Evil*. The book was prompted by the actions of guards at Abu Ghraib prison, who between 2003 and 2004 tortured, sodomized, and abused captured combatants.

***STANFORD V. KENTUCKY*, 492 U.S. 361 (1989).** Kevin Stanford, a 17-year-old juvenile, was convicted in a Kentucky court for the rape, sodomy, and **murder** of Barbel Poore. When he was sentenced to death, his case was appealed first to the Kentucky Supreme Court and later to the **U.S. Supreme Court**. The case drew public debate and strong feelings in the legal community over the issue of executing a minor. The U.S. Supreme Court upheld the findings of the Kentucky Court, saying that there was no national or historical consensus against executing someone over the age of 16, and the decision to do such had to be made by the states. ***Roper v. Simmons*, 543 U.S. 551 (2005)**, was a landmark case in which the U.S. Supreme Court overturned the *Stanford v. Kentucky*, 492 U.S. 361 (1989), decision holding that it was unconstitutional to execute someone under the age of 18. *See also* EXECUTION.

STARKWEATHER, CHARLES RAYMOND (1938–1959). Born in Lincoln, Nebraska, the third of seven children to working-class parents, Starkweather developed a James Dean fixation after seeing the film *Rebel without a Cause* and began to comb his hair and dress to look like Dean. He related to Dean's character, believing they were similar people sharing similar type problems. Starkweather developed a severe inferiority complex and became self-loathing. He became involved with Karil Ann Fugate, age 13. He dropped out of school and then was employed in minimum-wage jobs. The first killing in a long spree of murders occurred when Starkweather killed a gas station attendant. He was angry because the clerk turned him down for a credit sale. He then went looking for his girlfriend, and when he came to her house, he killed her parents because they wanted him to stay away from their daughter. This was followed by eight other senseless murders. Later, the two young people were arrested in Wyoming. Starkweather was found guilty and sentenced to death. He was executed in the **electric chair** in 1959. This would be the last **execution** in Nebraska until 1999. This was the first of several similar **murder** sprees by antisocial young men. Since Starkweather was the first spree murderer of this type, criminologists have called this the Starkweather syndrome.

STATE POLICE. In the United States, state **police** units are a function of state government that provide law enforcement services, primarily supervising traffic on state and interstate highways. The first state police unit to be established was the **Texas Rangers** in 1836 when Texas was a new republic. The development of the automobile and the need to **patrol** the new highways being built to accommodate automobiles at the beginning of the 20th century required a different operation of patrol. Pennsylvania was the first state to call such a unit the state police in 1906. Many state police units are named the state **highway patrol**. All states have a state police organization with the exception of Hawaii.

STATE USE SYSTEM. One of six systems that were developed between 1865 and the early 1930s to utilize convict labor to support or defray the cost of prisons. The economic depression of the late 1920s and 1930s resulted in the passage of the Hawes-Cooper Convict Labor Act of 1929 and the **Ashurst-Sumners Act**, Pub. L. No. 74-215, 49 Stat. 494 (1935). These acts effectively ended the selling of **prison**-made goods to the public and the transportation of prison-made goods across state lines for public consumption. The state use system primarily made goods that could be sold to other prisons and to state and federal governments, making it the primary prison work system. *See also* CONVICT LEASE SYSTEM.

STATIONARY KILLERS. While the least prolific of the different types of multiple murderer, they encompass several subsets of serial killers, such as those who commit murder at home or at work. Stationary killers usually do not move around, and if they do it is for reasons other than killing. Examples would be those called "black widows." John Wayne Gacy is an example of a home killer. *See also* NOMADIC KILLER; TERRITORIAL KILLERS.

STATUS OFFENSES. Delinquent, not criminal, offenses committed by young people under the age of 18. In 1974, the U.S. Congress enacted the **Juvenile Justice and Delinquency Prevention Act (JJDPA)**, which provided federal funds to ensure that the prohibition of contact between juvenile and criminal offenders is maintained and that **juvenile offenders** are not placed in physically secure adult institutions. Status offenses are acts that can only be committed by juveniles, such as **truancy**, **curfew** violations, underage possession and consumption of alcohol, underage possession and use of tobacco, and running away and being unmanageable (beyond the control of parents or guardians). Different states have classified these offenses differently, but generally young people who commit these offenses are called juveniles in need of supervision (JINS). The emphasis on status offenders has encouraged the courts to divert status offenders from **juvenile court** and toward other governmental social agencies. *See also* JUVENILE DELINQUENCY.

STOCKHOLM SYNDROME. A term, synonymous with traumatic bonding and capture bonding, that describes the attachment of victims of abduction, **hostage**, and **kidnappings** to the perpetrators. The term derives from a 1973 failed bank robbery in Stockholm, Sweden. Jan-Erik Olsson took three women and a man as hostages for six days. After the incident, the hostages expressed a fear of **police**; were critical of them, claiming that they did not like the police attitude during the incident and negotiations; and refused to testify against Olsson, requested his release, and raised money for his legal defense. The syndrome is attributed to trauma experienced by victims. **Patty Hearst** has been suspected of acquiring Stockholm syndrome following her abduction by the **Symbionese Liberation Army**. The syndrome is currently classified under posttraumatic stress disorder (PTSD) in the *DSM-V* (2013).

STOP AND FRISK. Originally from English **common law**, a **police** officer is allowed to stop, question, and frisk suspects given reasonable circumstances and then to act without **probable cause**. William Bratton adopted it as a **zero-tolerance** policy, first as head of the New York City Transit Police Department and later for New York City when he was appointed as police commissioner. The usual policy was that an officer could only search people after arrests. The **U.S. Supreme Court** in ***Terry v. Ohio*, 392 U.S. 1 (1968)**; *Sibron v. New York*, 392 U.S. 40 (1968); and *Peters vs. New York*, 392 U.S. 40 (1968), gave permission to search for weapons without probable cause when the officer felt the person was dangerous. The policy was dropped after minorities claimed racial **discrimination**.

STOP TURNING OUT PRISONERS ACT (STOP). A federal law that revised the **Violent Crime** Control and Law Enforcement Act of 1994 by prohibiting the courts from actions that would release convicts from serving their time in correctional institutions before the appointed release time. That is, no early **parole** is allowed to offset problems or conditions within institutions, with the exception of **prison** overcrowding.

STRAIN THEORY. Developed by **Robert Merton** to explain that society places strains on individuals to achieve socially accepted goals, but when they fail to meet these goals, frustration causes them to commit crimes. **Robert Agnew** developed his "**general strain theory**" (GST) in 1992, which became the leading strain theory and one of the major theories of crime.

STROUD, ROBERT FRANKLIN (1890–1963). In 1909, he was convicted of **murder** and sentenced to the McNeil Island federal **penitentiary** at Puget Sound. Stroud, because of **assaults** against convicts and guards, was transferred to **USP Leavenworth**. He was sentenced to life imprisonment after he murdered a guard and was ordered to be held in **solitary confinement**. While in solitary confinement, he found three sick sparrows and nursed the sick birds back to health. A reform-minded warden allowed him to keep birds in his cell and to purchase equipment. He eventually became a known ornithologist who wrote several books about the subject. However, he violated **prison** rules and was transferred to the federal prison at **Alcatraz**. Though he was not allowed to keep birds at Alcatraz, he continued to write and became known as the "Birdman of Alcatraz." A movie was made about his experience, and he earned worldwide fame. He died in 1963 while still in federal prison custody.

SUICIDE BY COP. *See* DEATH BY COP.

SUMMON(S). *See* WARRANT.

SUPERMAX PRISON. An expanded security concept in corrections. **Mass incarceration**, begun in the late 1970s, has promoted an increase in the number of enhanced-security facilities for convicts identified for their potential to cause trouble through **assault**, **violence**, escape, threats, or their likelihood of promoting disturbances in the general **prison** population or other disturbances to the orderly operation of a prison. They are also referred to as super-maximum and administrative segregation (ADMAX). Convicts housed in a supermax are generally maintained in **solitary confinement**, which eliminates contact with other **inmates** and minimizes contact with staff. **Al-**

catraz (which was operated by the **Federal Bureau of Prisons** between 1934 and 1963) is deemed the first supermax prison, and its operational process to maintain control has been replicated in other supermax prisons. *See also* MARION, USP.

SUTHERLAND, EDWIN (1880–1951). An American sociologist and criminologist who taught sociology at the University of Chicago during the 1930s and the 1940s. Sutherland developed the theories of **differential association**, **social learning**, and **white-collar crime**. He also coined the terms *white-collar crime* and ***organized crime*** in 1949. He was the 29th president of the American Sociological Association.

SUTTON, WILLIE (1901–1980). A noted American criminal and bank robber, active in the 1920s and 1930s as a **bank robber**, convicted several times and sentenced to **prison**. He escaped from custody on three occasions, including once from **Eastern State Penitentiary**. Sutton often used disguises in the commission of his crimes, which earned him the nickname "Willie the Actor." Final **parole** was granted in 1969 from **Attica** Correctional Facility, New York, in part because of his ill health. His most famous quote was "I robbed banks because that where the money was."

SWANGO, JOSEPH MICHAEL (1954–). An American **serial killer** and medical physician. After finishing a tour of duty in the U.S. Marine Corps, Swango graduated from Quincy University (Illinois), summa cum laude, and went on to the Southern Illinois University School of Medicine. He was noted to have had more interest in dying people than in trying to help sick patients. He had a poor reputation and had problems getting along with other medical personnel. He was given a surgical internship at the Wexner Medical Center at Ohio State University. Healthy patients began to die when he was on duty. Swango was arrested and convicted for aggravated battery for poisoning coworkers. He was sentenced to five years' imprisonment. Lying about his criminal background, he was hired as a career counselor in Newport News, Virginia. Later, he was fired from several jobs for lying on job applications. Swango fled to Africa to work in the medical field, and authorities pursued him for his involvement in several poison cases. When caught, he pled guilty to **murder** and fraud charges to avoid being sent back to Zimbabwe and a possible **death penalty**. He is currently incarnated at ADX Florence (a **supermax prison**). Swango used a variety of methods for murder; with nonpatients he used both poison and an overdose of drugs. Circumstantial **evidence** linked him to 35 suspicious deaths and perhaps as many as 60 other murders during his career. His life was the subject of several books and television shows.

SYMBIONESE LIBERATION ARMY. *See* HEARST, PATTY (1954–); STOCKHOLM SYNDROME.

SYNANON. A California rehabilitation program founded in 1958 by Charles Dederich (1913–1997). Initially, Synanon developed a reputation as a successful treatment facility for **addiction**, including having clients who were court ordered to attend. However, it evolved into what has been called a cult and a terroristic organization, which relied upon its incorporation as the Church of Synanon to operate as a tax-free entity. Dederich and other members of Synanon have been charged and convicted of a variety of criminal offenses including **assault**, tax code violations, destruction of **evidence**, conspiracy to commit **murder**, and suspicion of murder. Some of its members went to **prison**, and its property was confiscated by the Internal Revenue Service for back taxes. Synanon officially disbanded in 1991.

SYNDICATE. *See* ORGANIZED CRIME.

T

TAKING THE FIFTH. The **Fifth Amendment** of the U.S. Constitution protects individuals from incriminating themselves. "Taking the Fifth" has become the recognized phrase used by persons who refuse to answer questions about themselves or others in a criminal prosecution, such as **witnesses** and defendants involving the **Mafia**. The historical relevance is the 17th-century English practice of the Star Chamber oath. Anyone refusing to take the oath was considered guilty. "Taking the Fifth" does not render the individual exempt from penalties. During the House Committee on Un-American Activities, individuals "taking the Fifth" would be denied unemployment benefits or blacklisted from employment opportunities. Some examples include Hillary Clinton and her staff taking the Fifth in 2018 to avoid discussion of her private emails and Michael Cohen in 2016 to avoid discussion about "hush payments" to Stormy Daniels. *See also* SELF-INCRIMINATION.

TARASOFF DECISION. The *Tarasoff* decision is also called the "duty to warn." Prosenjit Poddar had informed his therapist of his desire to kill Tatiana Tarasoff. The clinician did not warn of the threat, and the argument revolves around patient-client confidentiality. The holding was that public safety is of greater importance than patient-client confidentiality. The Tarasoff decision has paved the way for other legislation that emphasizes a duty to warn, such as the 1990 Clery Act, 20 U.S.C. 1092 (amended in 1994), which specifies that there is a duty to warn, in this case of an existing criminal record for the client preceding the threat. The effort to protect was expanded in the Violence against Women Reauthorization Act of 2013.

TARDE, GABRIEL (1843–1904). Tarde was a pioneer in **criminology** who challenged **Lombroso**'s idea of **atavism**. While acknowledging that physical characteristics may contribute to criminal activity, he argued that environmental factors were more persuasive. Among his more influential ideas was that there is a relationship between the exchanges of individuals, criminal repetition by returns to the crime scene, and the impulse to commit a crime. The research of modern criminologists has demonstrated the credibility of Tarde's theories. *See also* BIOLOGICAL CRIMINOLOGY.

TAX EVASION. Avoidance or nonpayment of taxes is an illegal act that may be committed by individuals, businesses, corporations, or other entities required by law to report income, profits, capital gains, or other financial benefits (including exaggerated deductions) specified in tax codes. The 1968, *Crime and Punishment: An Economic Approach* by Gary Becker was the foundation for Allingham and Sandmo's 1972 model of tax evasion in which they theorized that tax evasion was prompted by the degree of unlikely **discovery** and the amount of **punishment**. Tax evasion has become less common, although not infrequent, as a consequence of the U.S. Tax Reform Act of 1986, which revised the penalties for evasion to include **fines** and imprisonment. The Internal Revenue Service is responsible for investigating tax evasion estimated in the hundreds of billions of dollars. *See also* CAPONE, ALPHONSE (1899–1947).

***TAYLOR V. LOUISIANA*, 419 U.S. 522 (1975).** A **U.S. Supreme Court** holding that overturned *Hoyt v. Florida*, 368 U.S. 57 (1961), which had allowed the exclusion of women from **jury** pools because of registration for **jury duty**. Hoyt, a female, was convicted of **murder** by an all-male jury. *See also WITHERSPOON V. ILLINOIS*, 391 U.S. 510 (1968).

TEAM ADAM. An American quick-response team developed in 2003 by former law enforcement officials and officers in the aftermath of the brutal child abduction and **murder** of **Adam Walsh** in 1981. The program is coordinated by the National Center for Missing and Exploited Children. Team Adam is sent to assist law enforcement agencies and families in cases of suspected stranger child abduction. *See also* CODE ADAM; AMERICA'S MISSING: BROADCAST EMERGENCY RESPONSE (AMBER) ALERT.

TEEN COURT. Teen court is one of what are known as special courts, **community courts**, or **problem-solving courts**. Teen court is also referred to as a peer court. The objectives of teen court include streamlining the judicial process to divert youth from entering the juvenile justice system. Among the earliest mentions of such a process was in Maine in 1940. However, the first courts to appear were in the 1970s in Illinois, Indiana, New York, and Texas. The courts expanded during the 1980s, received additional support from the **Office of Juvenile Justice and Delinquency Prevention** in the 1990s, and continued their development during the 2000s under the idea of Global Youth Justice. The idea gained additional support because of the increasing incarceration of youth, and some courts began to adopt the process from **restorative justice** of avoiding the word *verdict* in favor of *restorative plan*. *See also* JUVENILE COURT; JUVENILE DELINQUENCY.

***TENNESSEE V. GARNER*, 471 U.S. 1 (1985).** A **Fourth Amendment** case determined by the **U.S. Supreme Court** which held that **deadly force** may not be used by a **police** officer to prevent escape. The holding of the Court emphasized that in instances of **deadly force**, there must be **probable cause** that the suspect represents a threat of physical danger to others. The Court examined this as a **civil rights** violation. This case prompted a reexamination of **use of force** policies by law enforcement agencies.

TERRITORIAL KILLERS. Serial killers who conduct their activity in one geographic area. Some examples include **David Berkowitz** (in New York City during 1976), also referred to as the **Son of Sam**; **John Allen Muhammad** (during 2002) of the D.C. Beltway killings; **Gary Ridgeway** (during the 1980s and 1990s), also referred to as the **Green River Killer**; and **Jack the Ripper** (during 1888) of London (which was never solved). A distinguishing feature of territorial killers is that they can elude detection for long periods of time. *See also* MASS MURDER; MURDER; NOMADIC KILLER.

TERRORISM. Definitions of terrorism are somewhat inconsistent and thus contain different elements. Generally terrorism consists of illegal acts of **violence** sponsored by a government or another powerful body that initiate fear, are disruptive, and are intended to support a sociopolitical or religious agenda. Attacks of terrorism do not differentiate victims or the resultant damage. Acts of terrorism date back to ancient civilizations such as Macedonia in the 6th century B.C. and were usually **assassinations**. The tools of terrorists have progressed with technology to include bombings and cyberterrorism. Concerns about terrorism in the United States have steadily increased since the occurrence of tragic events such as the 1988 bombing of the plane over Lockerbie, Scotland, which killed 190 U.S. citizens. However, the attacks of 9/11, which shut down all air travel and resulted in the deaths of almost 3,000 people and injured more than 6,000 others, resulted in dramatic responses. Those responses are highlighted by the 2001 **Patriot Act** and the consolidation of U.S. law enforcement and intelligence agencies, which signaled the need for greater vigilance against future attacks from without and within the United States. Events since that time, including the Boston (Massachusetts) Marathon bombing and the disruption of planned attacks, have justified the need for greater protective measures. *See also* BIN LADEN, OSAMA (1957–2011); WORLD TRADE CENTER (WTC) BOMBINGS.

***TERRY V. OHIO*, 392 U.S. 1 (1968).** A landmark **U.S. Supreme Court** case in which Terry and others were observed and believed to be acting suspiciously. The **police** officer decided this was adequate motivation to conduct a search, during which a **handgun** was located and Terry was convicted. The Court held that the Terry **stop and frisk** search because of suspicion was unreasonable and unconstitutional. Such stops have come to be known as "Terry stops." *See also* FOURTH AMENDMENT.

TEXAS RANGERS. The Texas Rangers were founded by Stephen Austin (known as both the founder of Texas and the father of Texas) in 1823 when he called for a force of 10 men, whom he referred to as "Rangers," to defend against attacks by Native Americans. The Rangers operated as a paramilitary force from 1835 to 1845. The Rangers were disbanded following the Civil War and then reestablished in 1873 after state rule was returned. Legislation was enacted to prevent future actions that would disband them. Currently, the Texas Rangers are a division within the Texas Department of Public Safety and are the investigatory arm of state law enforcement. The Rangers are the United States' longest-standing law enforcement agency. *See also* STATE POLICE.

THERAPEUTIC COMMUNITY. The concept of a therapeutic community originates in 1946 as a hospital setting. It evolved to become a long-term residential setting for persons with mental illness and chemical dependency. The therapeutic community relies on both the peer group and professionals to assist persons in managing their illnesses and in developing a healthy perspective about them. The residents share responsibility for managing the community. In the 1960s, the idea of therapeutic communities became popular in **prison** settings beginning with **USP Marion** and utilized a variety of milieu therapies including transactional analysis and 12-step programs. Initial results illustrated a reduction in **recidivism**. Through the 1970s and 1980s, therapeutic communities further expanded to include day treatment and other self-help programs. *See also* SYNANON.

THIRD DEGREE. The third degree has been associated with **police** procedure to acquire information and confessions from suspects. The term is also synonymous with **torture**, or the infliction of fear, pain, and physical abuse through which to achieve the desired end. Precedents for the third degree include the Inquisition of the middle ages and the witch **trials** of Europe and North America, which utilized the progressive infliction of pain and fear to elicit confessions. The **Wickersham Commission** made note in its findings of 1931 that the use of the third degree was widespread in the United States. Following this finding, it was considered illegal. This led to the development of the Reid technique for **interrogation** by law enforcement. Similar to the third degree, the Reid technique has also been criticized for eliciting false confessions. *See also* POLICE BRUTALITY.

THOMPSON SUBMACHINE GUN. The Thompson submachine gun goes by many names, including the Thompson, the tommy gun, the chopper, and the Chicago organ grinder. John T. Thompson invented the American submachine gun in 1918. During the era of **Prohibition**, it would be used by **gangsters**, other criminals (**Willie Sutton** to rob banks), and law enforcement. The Thompson was also popularized in gangster films, including the depiction of the **Saint Valentine's Day massacre**. They were adopted by the **FBI** in 1933 after the Kansas City massacre. The use of the weapon by gangsters and its lethal capacity was a primary influence for the National Firearms Act of 1934, which included a provision that the weapon and variations of it would be registered with the ATF.

***THOMPSON V. OKLAHOMA*, 487 U.S. 815 (1988).** The first challenge to the **death penalty** since the cessation of its use following the **U.S. Supreme Court** holding in ***Furman v. Georgia*, 408 U.S. 238 (1972)**. *Thompson v. Oklahoma* overturned Thompson's death sentence and was a case of **cruel and unusual punishment** because it involved a minor. *See also* CAPITAL PUNISHMENT; EIGHTH AMENDMENT.

THREAT ASSESSMENT. Threat assessments are the determination of whether there is a credible potential for **violence** and harm. Threat assessments are carried out by military and law enforcement to help protect in a variety of environments, including communities, workplaces, schools, cybertechnology, and other civilian and governmental infrastructures. Threat assessment is a violence-prevention strategy that seeks to identify the source, underlying motivation or goals, and seriousness of the threat and the development of strategies for intervention. The earliest efforts to perform assessments occurred during the Cold War to address the Soviet threat. The more recent efforts at assessment have followed school shootings and have produced responses such as the Virginia Model for Student Threat Assessment. Though threat assessments began with physical attacks, they now include cyberattacks against technology and the concept of international **terrorism** as demonstrated by the attacks of 9/11. *See also* TERRORISM; WORLD TRADE CENTER (WTC) BOMBINGS.

THREE-STRIKES LAW. *See* HABITUAL OFFENDER; TWO-STRIKES LAW.

TICKET OF LEAVE. The ticket of leave is the forerunner of **parole**, which was first established in the United Kingdom in 1853 and afterward by the United States, Canada, and Ireland. The idea was that part of the sentence was completed in some form of confinement and finalized through conditional release. A ticket of leave could be issued to convicts who through good behavior demonstrated their intention to reform. The ticket of leave, like parole, listed provisions thought to be essential to continued good behavior. Convicts were expected to maintain employment. **Alexander Maconochie** had developed a similar system at Norfolk Island in 1840 which predates the United Kingdom's system. Maconochie's work reached **Sir Walter Crofton** of Ireland, who further revised the idea. Finally, **Zebulon Brockway** of **Elmira Reformatory** in New York became the father of parole in the United States, which incorporated many of the principles of the ticket of leave. The ticket of leave and later parole could be revoked for either minor or major transgressions, returning the offender to confinement.

TOOLE, OTTIS (1947–1996). Police named **Ottis Toole** as the murderer of **Adam Walsh** (there is no **DNA evidence**; **Jeffrey Dahmer** has also been a suspect of the killing). He confessed, later recanting the confession, and because of lost evidence was never brought to **trial** to be convicted of the offense. He made a deathbed confession to his niece. Several other murders are attributed to him, by confession or attributed by others. Some confessions by him or others have been described as compliant and thus raise issues of reliability. The compliant interviews were used to clear unsolved **murder** cases. Toole did receive two death sentences which were later commuted to life sentences. Toole died at age 49 of cirrhosis. *See also* MURDER.

TORTURE. The deliberate infliction of pain has been used as a process of coercion, **interrogation**, and **punishment** in the administration of justice. Torture has been considered instrumental for ensuring **deterrence**, that is, for providing examples that would compel others to follow the law and as a step toward saving the soul of the offender. "**Third degree**" interrogation tactics by law enforcement were considered essential to obtaining a confession from a suspect. The Inquisition in Europe from the 13th through 16th centuries used torture both for confession and punishment. Torture, for punishment, coercion, or interrogation, is forbidden by the **Eighth Amendment**. *See also* CRUEL AND UNUSUAL PUNISHMENT.

TOUGH ON CRIME. "Tough on crime" was one of several conservative political slogans that originated with Presidents Nixon and Reagan that expressed dissatisfaction with the effects of the criminal justice system. The slogan is commonly associated with the Republican Party; however, the

Democratic Party has not neglected its usefulness as a strategy to attract voters. The use of the slogan "tough on crime" suggested that the criminal justice system had failed to impact crime and that harsher penalties would serve as a more effective **deterrence**. It is frequently used in conjunction with the slogan "law and order." The slogan remains a popular tool of rhetoric in political campaigns.

TOWER OF LONDON. The Tower of London was officially constructed as a fortress and castle with the initial foundations set in 1078. The significance of the Tower of London is its extended use as a **prison**, which began in 1100 and lasted until 1952. The Tower of London initially served as a prison for royalty, while those of lesser status would suffer other **punishments** until imprisonment as punishment was accepted for all violators of British law.

TOXICOLOGY. A component of a forensic analysis that examines a crime scene for chemical, biological, or pharmacological **evidence**. The examination seeks to establish the origins of toxicological evidence, including the amounts and relationships or effects to victims. Toxicological examinations for poisons date to the 9th century and the **murder** case of Count Bocarme in the 1800s which helped lead to his conviction. *See also* FORENSICS.

TRACE EVIDENCE. Trace **evidence** is what is left behind when one object comes into contact with another object. **Locard's exchange principle** (Dr. Edmund Locard) emphasizes that every contact leaves a trace. Trace evidence is used for the descriptive development in forensic analysis of crime scenes and the relationship between people, places, and things. Trace evidence includes hair, fibers, soil, dust, debris, and body fluids. *See also* FORENSICS.

TRAINING SCHOOL. *See* REFORM SCHOOL.

TRANSNATIONAL CRIME. Transnational crime is a recent term that describes the illegal activities of **organized crime** that crosses the borders of one country to another. The types of transnational crimes that are more common include human trafficking, drug smuggling, arms trafficking, and the introduction of plants and animals into countries that forbid them. The United Nations Convention against Transnational Organized Crime, which was authorized during the 200th session of the General Assembly in 2016, is the only international agreement enacted with the intent to deter and gain international cooperation to combat these crimes. *See also* CAMORRA; SEX TRADE.

TRANSPORTATION. Transportation was a **punishment** utilized by many nations, including Russia (Siberia, from the 17th to the mid-20th century), France (French Guiana, 1852–1939), and the United Kingdom (New South Wales, 1788–1868; North America, 1610–1776; and Australia, 1787–1868) to send convicted persons from civilized areas to distant locations or foreign lands. The sentence of transportation carried with it a provision that the convict would be exiled and could never return to their homeland. The policy behind transportation included that the convicts would settle these lands and recover natural resources which would be shipped back to the sending country. Transportation became controversial because of the hardships and brutality encountered by the convicts. For example, 50 percent of each year's shipment of convicts to French Guiana perished. Siberia was a cold and forbidding environment. The hardships and reported inhumanity of the **penal colonies** led to their discontinuance.

TRANSPORTATION SECURITY ADMINISTRATION (TSA). The Transportation Security Administration was established as part of the U.S. Department of Transportation after the tragic events of 11 September 2001 and relocated shortly afterward into the Department of Homeland Security in 2003. The Transportation Security Administration is responsible for providing airport security, the prevention of **hijacking**, port security, and some highway and railroad security utilizing armed federal air **marshals** and dog handlers to secure vulnerable points of transportation. *See also* HOMELAND SECURITY ACT; WORLD TRADE CENTER (WTC) BOMBINGS.

TREASON. Treason refers to acts that threaten a country or its leaders and are considered traitorous. Treason originally was broken down into two categories. The lesser involved acts such as the **murder** of a husband or a master by a servant. High treason would be any attack against the sovereign (king). Acts of treason are treated harshly, with **punishments** such as long periods of imprisonment or **execution**. Among the more infamous acts of treason in the United States was committed by Benedict Arnold, who was a general in the Continental Army and attempted to surrender West Point to the British. He was never captured and died in London. **Julius and Ethel Rosenberg** were convicted of spying for the Soviet Union and were executed by **electrocution** in **Sing Sing Prison** in 1953. Jonathan Pollard was convicted of spying for Israel in 1987 and received a life sentence. He was released from federal **prison** in 2015.

TREATMENT ALTERNATIVES TO STREET CRIME (TASC). The Special Action Office for Drug Abuse Prevention was created in 1971. TASC was part of this initiative intended as **pretrial diversion** for drug offenders. The program developed from the realization that after drug offenders received **bail**, they would continue their **addiction** and commit crime to support it. The program had a three-part focus of reducing drug use, diverting offenders from a **punishment**-based system, and eliminating the stigma attached to addiction. *See also* NARCOTICS.

TRIAD. The term Triad was coined by the British during their colonial rule of Hong Kong in the late 1840s. The criminal organizations date back to the 1700s. The Triads use numbers to designate rank within the organization and to identify others such as law enforcement. An **undercover** agent may receive the designation "25." Similar to other **organized crime** groups, they rely upon secrecy, members take oaths, and they engage in induction ceremonies. The criminal enterprises extend throughout Southeast Asia and the Americas. They are now recognized as a **transnational criminal organization** with activities that include drug smuggling, human trafficking, **counterfeiting** (currency and goods), and **money laundering**.

TRIAL. The trial is the process of examining **evidence** presented by a prosecutor and a defense attorney. A judge oversees the judicial proceeding. In the case of a **jury** trial, the jury determines guilt or innocence following the presentation of evidence. A jury after deliberation may also determine that they cannot come to an agreement of guilt or innocence. This is referred to as a "**hung jury**." Prior to the modern trial process, other methods, such as tests or **torture**, were used to obtain confessions from the suspect. Some modern **police** tactics with suspects have been derived from these tests and have been referred to as the **third degree** until **U.S. Supreme Court** decisions held them to be violations of the Eighth and other amendments. Among the earlier types of trials were the trial by fire—a test of individual resolve—and the trial by ordeal, generally associated with the **Inquisition**. These were often overseen by clergy, and the accused was subjected to a variety of increasingly atrocious and threatening incidents designed to elicit fear and thus to encourage admissions of guilt. Survival, while unlikely, would mean innocence. Trials of hot and cold water, dating back to the 6th century, also have religious connotations. The trial by water subjected the accused to being bound and immersed in water. Those who sank were considered innocent, and those who floated were guilty. This method was used in Europe and adopted in the United States during the **Salem witch trials**. Hot-water trials caused the defendant to dip a hand into scalding water to retrieve a stone, with the depth and number of stones increasing as the offenses increased. If the hand healed within three days, the defendant was presumed innocent. This practice began in the 6th century and continued until the 12th century. Cold-water trials began in about the 800s and continued until the 1300s. This was a variation on the water trial during which the defendant was tossed into a stream or submerged in a barrel of cold water. *See also* EIGHTH AMENDMENT.

TRIAL COURT. The United States utilizes both **jury** and bench **trial** courts in which a jury or a judge makes decisions of fact in criminal matters. Federal trial courts originated in 1789 with 13 judicial districts. The use of a trial has its origins in ancient Athens in which juries were comprised of between 500 and 1,500 citizens. The U.S. Constitution, Article 3, guarantees any person accused of criminal acts a trial by jury. This in turn was advanced to the states through the **Fourteenth Amendment**. However, in cases for which there may be imprisonment of six months or less, there may not be a jury trial or the jury trial may be waived in favor of a bench trial. There are some states that require a jury trial for all criminal matters. *See also* PLEA BARGAIN.

TROJANOWICZ, ROBERT (1941–1994). A criminologist and researcher who studied **police** departments and their role in the community. Tranjanowicz developed the concept of "community policing." He taught at Michigan State University, where he was also the chair of the criminal justice program. He founded the National Center for **Community Policing** and wrote *Community Policing: A Contemporary Perspective*. *See also* COMMUNITY-ORIENTED POLICING.

TRUANCY. Truancy is absence from school without a legitimate reason. Prior to the 19th century, mandatory school attendance did not exist. After this time, truants might be picked up or arrested by a school officer or a **sheriff**. Truancy is a **status offense** and may be addressed in **juvenile court**. Parents are notified when a child is truant and may be assessed **fines**, and a student may have a driver's license revoked. *See also* JUVENILE DELINQUENCY.

TRUE CRIME. The depiction (in book or film) of real crime, victims, perpetrators, **police** detectives, private detectives, **witnesses**, and others purported to have been involved in the before, during, and after events of a crime. These are generally the more serious or sensational crime exploits such as ***Helter Skelter*** (1974) and *In Cold Blood* (1966). True crime became popular in the early 1920s, although the exploits of lawmen and bad men were popular as inexpensive dime novels in the 1800s. True crime has been the public's source of explanations of crime, detection, and **punishment**. *See also* CRIME NOVEL; DETECTIVE; NOIR CRIME NOVEL.

TRUSTY. A trusty was part of what has been called the trusty system, predominantly used in the southern states and in the New York State **prison** system. Prisons relied on trusty convicts to both control the prison and to produce goods for the prison as a means to reduce costs. The use of the trusty began in the 1800s and was effectively ended by *Gates v. Collier*, 501 F.2d 1291 (5th Cir. 1974). The **U.S. Supreme Court** holding was that the trusty system in use at Parchman **Penitentiary** in Mississippi was responsible for **inmate** abuse and was a violation of the **Eighth Amendment**. Soon after Mississippi ended its trusty system, all other states followed. What is likely the most extensive description of the abusive use of trusties or prison tenders can be found in Murton and Hyams's *Accomplices to the Crime* (1970). *See also* PRISON FARM; PRISON TENDER.

TRUTH IN SENTENCING. Truth-in-sentencing legislation followed the law-and-order and **War on Crime** politicization of crime. Truth in sentencing contends that the public has a right to know the terms of a sentence. This has been a result of the **disparity** between the sentence and the actual amount of time served. **Prison** sentences are complicated by such processes as good time, work time, and **parole**. The result is that the sentence or eligibility of parole may be shortened or appear to the uninformed that the sentence served is less than the sentence handed down by the judge. These have historically been management practices of prisons as authorized or permitted by legislation, which rewards good behavior and work performed in prison—practices little understood by correctional outsiders. The truth-in-sentencing legislation has considerably increased the amount of time served by convicts by instituting new practices that set minimum standards for parole eligibility and mandatory sentencing, minimized the effect of earned time credits for good behavior and work performed by convicts, or denied or abolished parole entirely. The first laws regarded as truth-in-sentencing practices were passed in 1984. Truth in sentencing has contributed to the current rise in prison populations regarded as **mass incarceration**.

TSARNAEV BROTHERS (DZHOKAR, 1993–, AND TAMERLAN, 1986–2013). The Tsarnaev brothers were suspects in the Boston, Massachusetts, Marathon Bombing of 2013. Tamerlan Tsarnaev was shot and killed by law enforcement resisting arrest. Dzhokar Tsarnaev was wounded during his capture and charged with 30 counts, many of which were **capital offenses**, found guilty, and sentenced to death. He is currently awaiting **execution** at USP Terre Haute. *See also* DEATH PENALTY; TERRORISM.

TWEED, WILLIAM "BOSS" (1823–1878). William Tweed was a New York City politician infamously referred to as "Boss" Tweed because of his control of the Democratic Party through Tammany Hall. He was elected to the U.S. House of Representatives in 1852 and the Senate in 1867. His power and influence, such as control over political patronage, was reportedly the result of his control over the ballot box. Political cartoons by Thomas Nast, depicted in *Harper's Weekly* and the *New York Times*, unfavorably characterizing Tweed for his political influence and corruption (which netted him millions of dollars) became famous and helped to lead to his downfall. He was convicted twice and escaped jail once when he could not make **bail**. He contracted pneumonia and died in the Ludlow Street Jail (a federal **prison** in Manhattan, New York).

TWO-STRIKES LAW. A two-strikes law is one of several types of legislation that is usually directed at offenders with two or more felony convictions. These types of laws (which include one-strike and **three-strikes laws**) deliver harsher and certain **punishments** that range from 10 years to life imprisonment upon conviction of a third felony. Georgia passed its two-strikes law in 1994, which piggybacked on California's three-strikes law (the first of its kind in the United States). *See also* HABITUAL OFFENDER.

TYBURN TREE. The Tyburn Tree, located in London, England, has several distinctions that include its many names (Tyburn **Gallows**, The Elms, the King's Gallows, and the Deadly Never Green Tyburn Tree). It has also been called the Triple Gallows, which refers to both its form and function: a gallows that was designed in the shape of a triangle from which three persons could be hanged at any one time. The Tyburn Tree is also notable for its length of service (1196–1783), the many who were executed (criminals, traitors, and martyrs), and the method of **execution**. It was a location to which the condemned were drawn through the streets by cords attached to a horse. Upon arrival, the condemned was hanged and then quartered, perhaps beheaded, and disemboweled. These were public executions that attracted large crowds of spectators. One group of condemned, the martyrs, caused the tree to be renamed Tyburn's Tree of Life. There are estimates of more than 50,000 having been hanged at the site. In the United States, lynchings or "being strung up" was popular as both a legitimate practice following a sentence or an act of **vigilantism**. *See also* CAPITAL OFFENSE; HANGING; LYNCHING.

TYLENOL MURDERS. Unsolved murders that occurred in Chicago, Illinois, during 1982. The seven victims ingested Tylenol capsules tainted with potassium cyanide. Other deaths followed in copycat killings. James Lewis was a suspect (however, there was insufficient **evidence** to charge him with **murder**). He demanded $1 million from Johnson & Johnson, was convicted of extortion, and served 13 years of a 20-year sentence. In the aftermath, pharmaceutical companies changed packaging to make it more tamperproof and developed caplets. *See also* UNABOMBER.

U

UNABOMBER. *See* KACZYNSKI, THEODORE (1942–).

UNDERBOSS. The underboss is also referred as a capo or ***capo di tutti capi*** and is the second in command in Sicilian and **Mafia** crime families. Historically, the underboss has assumed great power or exists on the fringe of the powerful boss. Often the underboss is considered as the next in line to be the boss in the event that the boss is no longer in a position to control the crime family. *See also* McCLELLAN COMMITTEE; VALACHI, JOSEPH (1903–1971).

UNDERCOVER. An expression that describes law enforcement who disguise their identity to gain the trust of those who are assumed to commit criminal acts. The undercover officer observes and collects **evidence** that will later be used to charge someone with an offense. The French Sûreté, in 1811, was among the earliest of police agencies to engage in organized undercover work. A similar function was developed in England by **Sir Robert Peel** in 1829. Some "Peelers," as they were called, wore plainclothes to go undetected. This was formalized in 1869, which specified that undercover work required the approval of the **police** superintendent. The New York City police department may have created the first organized undercover work for a specific purpose with the establishment of the "Italian Squad" in 1906. This was soon followed by federal agencies including the **FBI** with its formation in 1908.

UNIFORM CODE OF MILITARY JUSTICE (UCMJ). The underpinnings for the Uniform Code of Military Justice are found in 64 Stat. 109, 10 U.S.C. §§ 801–946, and in the U.S. Constitution, Article I, Section 8. The forerunner to the Uniform Code of Military Justice was written in 1775 by the Second Continental Congress to regulate the behavior of the Continental Army. In 1788, the U.S. Constitution, in Article I, Section 8, specified that the U.S. Congress had the authority to enact codes of conduct for military forces. Other modifications and regulations addressed the individual needs of the armed services until 5 May 1950, when President Truman signed into law the UCMJ, which would apply to all branches of the U.S. Armed Services and replace all other codes of justice. Since the original passage of the UCMJ, there have been revisions that include important **U.S. Supreme Court** holdings such as ***Gideon v. Wainwright*, 372 U.S. 335 (1963)**, and ***Miranda v. Arizona*, 384 U.S. 436 (1966)**.

UNIFORM CRIME REPORT (UCR). A document prepared by the **FBI**, which is the voluntary and cooperative reporting of crime statistics by almost 18,000 law enforcement agencies. In the 1930s the **International Association of Chiefs of Police** began gathering the crime statistics that would later become the UCR. The UCR is published annually, and many states publish their own UCR based on the format used by the FBI.

UNIONE CORSE. The Unione Corse is a Corsican secret criminal society. The French Connection was formed by the unification of the Unione Corse and the American and Sicilian **Mafia**. This criminal enterprise controlled the trafficking of **heroin** between France and the United States beginning in the 1950s and continuing through the 1970s. The Unione Corse believes in a **code of silence** and, like the American Mafia, the organization consists of several crime families.

UNITED STATES ATTORNEY. United States attorneys are also known as United States district attorneys or federal prosecutors. The office of the U.S. attorney is in the Department of Justice and was created by the Judiciary Act of 1789. U.S. attorneys represent the U.S. government in the federal district courts and appellate courts. The duty of the U.S. attorney is to "prosecute in each district all delinquents for crimes and offenses cognizable under the authority of the United States, and all civil actions in which the United States shall be concerned." The office of U.S. attorney predates the Department of Justice, which was created in 1870. Until that time, the U.S. attorney functioned independently of the U.S. **attorney general**. *See also* DISTRICT ATTORNEY.

UNITED STATES BOMB DATA CENTER. The U.S. Bomb Data Center is the information repository of **arson** as well as other criminal events classified as explosives. The information is primarily but not exclusively gathered from other federal agencies that conduct investigations into criminal incidents. Legislation, passed in 1996, ordered the secretary of the Treasury to create the U.S. Bomb Data Center. Following the terrorist attacks of 9/11 and the passage of the 2002 Homeland Security Act, the U.S. Bomb Data Center was moved into the Department of Justice. In 2004, by order of the

U.S. attorney general, all offices of the Department of Justice would merge their databases into the Bomb Arson Tracking System. *See also* WORLD TRADE CENTER (WTC) BOMBINGS.

UNITED STATES DISCIPLINARY BARRACKS (USDB). A maximum-security military **prison**, referred to as **USP Leavenworth**, located in Kansas. It was authorized by the U.S. Congress in 1874 and houses about 1,500 convicts. Those convicted through the **Uniform Code of Military Justice** include soldiers with sentences of more than 10 years, officers, and those with offenses related to national security. The original design followed **John Haviland**'s design for **Eastern State Penitentiary** with individual cells, and later construction followed New York's **Auburn** plan. *See also* AUBURN PRISON.

UNITED STATES SENTENCING COMMISSION. The United Sates Sentencing Commission was established by the 1984 **Comprehensive Crime Control Act**. The commission created the federal **sentencing guidelines**, which limit judicial sentencing discretion and replaced indeterminate sentencing. The **U.S. Supreme Court** holding in *Mistretta v. United States*, 488 U.S. 361 (1989), affirmed the constitutionality of the commission. The U.S. Sentencing Commission is distinct from other commissions because it is a permanent agency comprised of seven members with six-year terms appointed by the president and confirmed by the Senate.

UNREPORTED CRIME. *See* DARK FIGURE OF CRIME.

USE OF FORCE. The concept of use of force addresses physical force (as opposed to **excessive force** or abuse of power) by law enforcement required to achieve compliance or direction from law enforcement. Use of force also addresses the degree of force necessary to ensure the safety of the officer or others who are placed in danger. Law enforcement recognizes a continuum of force that may be utilized in different instances. For example, the **U.S. Supreme Court** holding in ***Tennessee v. Garner*, 471 U.S. 1 (1985)**, affirmed that there must be **probable cause** of threat to others to use **deadly force** with a fleeing suspect.

U.S. SUPREME COURT. The U.S. Supreme Court, also referred to as the "court of last resort," is the highest appellate court in the United States and was established in 1789 in Article III of the U.S. Constitution. The court consists of a chief justice and eight associate justices (all of whom have life tenure), nominated by the president of the United States and confirmed by the U.S. Senate. A justice may only be removed from the court through resignation, retirement, or impeachment. No member of the court has ever been removed through impeachment. Initially the Court consisted of six justices. The court expanded in 1807 to seven justices and in 1837 to nine. However, in 1863, Congress increased the number of justices to 10 but in 1866 reduced the number to nine, the current number. The only other attempt to change the composition of the U.S. Supreme Court was President Roosevelt's infamous court-packing scheme of 1937, which was rebuked by Congress.

USURY. The illegal practice of creating loans with high rates of interest, practiced by an individual referred to as a "loan shark," and the interest is known as the "vig" or **vigorish**. Making loans with high profit has historically been frowned upon as immoral and corrupt. The Catholic Church banned loans for interest in medieval Europe. While the federal government has not created statutes to govern lending rates, under **Racketeer Influenced Corrupt Organization Act (RICO)** statutes (established in 1970), loans offered at more than twice the state-set limits qualify as usury and are federal offenses.

***U.S. V. RABINOWITZ*, 339 U.S. 56 (1950).** A **Fourth Amendment** case in which the **U.S. Supreme Court** held that after an arrest a **warrant** was not required for a search of the person. Previously, searches had been banned by *Trupiano v. United States*, 334 U.S. 699 (1948). *See also MAPP V. OHIO*, 367 U.S. 643 (1961); SEARCH AND SEIZURE.

***U.S. V. SALERNO*, 481 U.S. 279 (1987).** A holding of the **U.S. Supreme Court** that established the detainment of a person without **bail** prior to **trial** based on a determination of their dangerousness to the community. The decision revolved around the arrest and the detainment of Anthony Salerno, who was indicted in 1986 on **Racketeer Influenced Corrupt Organization Act (RICO)** violations. Salerno was an **underboss** for the Genovese crime family and subsequently died in **prison** in 1992. *See also* EIGHTH AMENDMENT.

V

VAGRANCY. A criminal violation originating from English **common law**, the Vagrancy Act, of the early 1800s. Although vagrancy is seldom prosecuted in free and democratic societies, vagrancy characterized persons as vagrants, also referred to as drifters, vagabonds, hobos, or tramps (and sometimes those who would loiter) who were often impoverished and drifted from place to place without the means to support themselves or their families. Vagrancy violations are utilized as a form of management, such as for slaves who had been freed. They would be charged and fined, and when they could not pay the **fine** they were then leased out to former plantation owners who, because of emancipation, no longer had a workforce. The term derives from the Latin word, *vagari*, meaning "wander," and has been historically linked to outlaws, mistrustful persons, or individuals with whom to sympathize and provide charitable giving. Vagrant conditions have been associated with religious life, and many of the world's religions teach their congregations to show vagrants compassion. Vagrancy laws differ from other criminal statutes because apart from making certain acts illegal, they also criminalize the status of being something, such as a panhandler, drug addict, gambler, prostitute, unemployed, or homeless. The **U.S. Supreme Court** has held that these laws are often violations of the **Fourteenth Amendment**, too vague in their **construction** and a violation of **due process**. *See also* BLACK CODES; LOITERING; PROSTITUTION.

VALACHI, JOSEPH (1903–1971). Joseph Valachi was also known as "Charles Charbano," "Anthony Sorge," and "Joe Cargo." He was a "soldier" in the New York City Genovese crime family. In October 1963, Valachi became the first **Mafia** member to publicly acknowledge the existence of such an organization when he testified before Arkansas senator John L. McClellan's congressional committee on **organized crime**. The testimony was broadcast on radio and television. Although his testimony as someone with low-ranking status within the organization did not directly lead to any arrests, Valachi's disclosures provided the government with many details into the history, operations, and organizational culture of the Mafia and was used to identify more than 300 members in the organized crime **syndicate**. A biography titled *The Valachi Papers*, based on Valachi's memoirs and interviews, was written by journalist Peter Maas. *See also* LA COSA NOSTRA.

VANDAL. The world *vandal* originated from an ancient Germanic tribe that invaded Western Europe, destroying Gaul and Spain, during the 5th century and who eventually settled in Africa. The Vandals were known in particular for sacking Rome during the reign of King Genseric in 455. The destruction inspired the British poet John Dryden to write, "Till Goths, and Vandals, a rude Northern race, Did all the matchless Monuments deface." While the Vandals were not any more destructive than other attackers of that ancient era, their name is linked to the term *vandalisme*, meaning the destruction of art, because they purposely destroyed the artistic and literary works, statues, and public buildings of Rome. The Vandal king, Gaiseric, and his son persecuted Catholic Christians brutally and have since been lumped with other barbarians responsible for the collapse of the Roman Empire. The term and the acts associated with it have common usage in the American criminal justice system. *See also* VANDALISM.

VANDALISM. Henri Grégoire, bishop of Blois, coined the term in 1794 in describing the destruction of art following the French Revolution. The term was thereafter widely used to illustrate the unique savagery of the Vandals to deliberately destroy artwork. The term has since been used to generally describe the actions of individuals who purposely destroy, damage, or deface public or private property. Vandalism can take on many different forms. Examples include the unauthorized spray painting of property also known as tagging or graffiti, slashing tires, scratching or "keying" vehicles, smashing windows, razing mailboxes, salting lawns, and creating crop circles. Graffiti, which is commonly found in inner cities, is used by gangs to demarcate territories of operation, but it can also be regarded as an expression of art. Although vandalism is generally considered to be on the lower end of the crime spectrum, the seriousness of the actions can quickly escalate when it is accompanied with violence and rioting. In the 2014 California case of *Luis M. v. Superior Court*, S207314, the defendant paid $3,800 in restitution.

VANZETTI, BARTOLOMEO (1888–1927). A fish peddler from Villafalletto, Italy, who immigrated to the United States in 1908 when he was 20 years old. He was later convicted with **Nicola Sacco** of murdering two men of the Slater and Morrill Shoe Company during a 1920 armed robbery in South Braintree, Massachusetts. He had become involved in left-wing politics after witnessing the conditions of working-class immigrants in America and attended anarchist meetings where he met Sacco. Both men were believed to have been followers of Luigi Galliano, an Italian anarchist who published *Cronaca Sovversiva* (*Subversive Chronicle*), a periodical that Sacco wrote for and which advocated revolutionary **violence**, including bombings and **assassinations**, against the government they perceived as violent and oppressive. Italian anarchists at the time were ranked high on the government's watch list of dangerous enemies. Following the crime, many eyewitnesses purported that the robbers looked Italian. Many Italian immigrants were questioned by the authorities, but the investigation eventually centered on Vanzetti and Sacco. The government claimed the robbery financed anarchist propaganda. After a controversial **trial** in which the **jury** deliberated for a few hours, the men were found guilty of first-degree **murder**. A private defense committee was established to fund a series of appeals, and as the details of the case were made known, it became clearer that the men were likely innocent. All appeals were denied by the trial judge and the Massachusetts Supreme Court. The case prompted worldwide protests favoring the innocence of Vanzetti and Sacco. Both men were executed on 23 August 1927 by the **electric chair** at Charlestown State **Prison**, Boston, Massachusetts. On 23 August 1977, Michael Dukakis, governor of Massachusetts, issued a proclamation absolving Vanzetti and Sacco of the crime. *See also* EXECUTION; TERRORISM; WITNESS.

VERA INSTITUTE OF JUSTICE. An independent, nonprofit national research and policy organization founded in 1961 by philanthropist Louis Schweitzer and magazine editor Herb Sturz. The organization explored the problems associated with the New York City **bail** system and its unfair treatment of those of lower-income brackets who could not afford the cash bails. They demonstrated that individuals too poor to afford bail could be granted release based on their community status without increasing the risk of failing to appear for **trial**. Initially termed the **Manhattan Bail Project**, the bail model that was devised was replicated in other major cities. The success of the program led to the landmark Bail Reform Act of 1966 signed by President Lyndon B. Johnson. More recently, the organization spearheaded projects examining the justice system, its impact on communities, and proposed solutions. The institute is based primarily in New York City with additional offices in Washington, D.C., and New Orleans, Louisiana. Its mission is to build and improve justice systems to "ensure fairness, promote safety, and strengthen communities," with strategic priorities focusing on **mass incarceration**; promoting safety, trust, and justice; and improving the conditions of confinement.

VETERANS COURT. A **problem-solving court** that involves military veterans or active-duty service members with the additional criteria that program applicants are members of the military, charges are related to their military service, and they have a clinical diagnosis of a mental health or substance abuse disorder. The applications are reviewed prior to acceptance into the program by an assigned judge. **Violent crimes** such as **murder**, rape, or robbery would preclude the applicant from acceptance into the program. Veterans court was founded in 2008 by the Honorable Robert Russell, associate judge of the Buffalo City Court, New York. A separate docket for veterans occurred when Judge Russell noticed an increase in the number of defendants appearing in his **drug court** and a mental health caseload that required specific services. The Buffalo Veteran Court incorporated a mentoring program comprised of veterans who partnered with the court to support and assist in treatment. The Buffalo court has been used as a model in establishing other veterans courts throughout the United States. In 2009, the Veterans Justice Outreach was launched by the Veterans Administration to collaborate with veteran courts in addressing the homelessness, mental health, and substance abuse issues of veterans. By 2014, more than 220 veteran courts had been established around the country, and scores of others that were being piloted. *See also* COMMUNITY COURT.

VICE LORDS. Another name for the Almighty Vice Lord Nation, Vice Lord Nation, Conservative Vice Lords, Imperial Vice Lords, Insane Vice Lords, and Four Corner Hustlers. It is the oldest and one of the largest and most influential criminal organizations based in Chicago, Illinois. The **gang** was formed during the late 1950s by a group of African American juveniles at the Illinois **Training School** for Boys in St. Charles, Illinois, as protection against rival gangs. Originally formed in the **prison** as a club, the group was led by Edward Perry, who decided on the term *vice* after looking the word up and found the meaning as "having a tight hold." The club's notoriety as a gang occurred as some of the original members were released and returned to their North Lawndale neighborhood of Chicago. As membership increased, the criminal enterprise expanded and included robbery, theft, **assault**, and extortion. By 1964, the gang, notorious for its **violence**, became a primary target of law enforcement. Today, they are known for their **drug trafficking** and weapons smuggling, as well as violence and **murder** used to protect these enterprises. Since the 1990s, the gang has grown more sophisticated and expanded into financial crimes, including mortgage and credit card fraud and **money laundering**.

VICTIM ASSISTANCE PROGRAM. A government program developed during the early 1970s and influenced by the victims' rights movement. **Victim assistance programs** have been established in each of the 50 states to provide government-funded services to crime victims. In 1984, the Justice Department created the **Office for Victims of Crime**, which notifies victims of their rights and provides them with support. Programs provide information and aid to individuals who have endured a physical, emotional, or economic injury or other harm resulting from a crime. Some of the services include crisis counseling, group and individual support networks, general information and referrals, criminal justice system advocacy, and other types of assistance. Other programs for victims include the Victims Compensation Program, which provides funds to compensate crime victims. By 2003, each of the 50 states had established a victim-dedicated fund. Monies assist victims with medical and counseling expenses, burial and funeral costs, and lost wages. Victims are required to cooperate with the **police** and prosecutors and cannot have been involved in the commission of the crime. The pool of funds is sometimes subsidized with taxpayer money; however, many programs draw from a general pool funded by fees paid by all defendants convicted of crimes. *See also* VICTIMS' RIGHTS.

VICTIM IMPACT STATEMENT. A statement made as part of the decision-making process which allows crime victims to address or be represented at the defendant's **probation**, sentencing, or **parole** hearing. Such statements are viewed as personifying the crime and are purported to assist victims in their emotional recovery from the experience. The first victim impact statement in the United States was presented in 1976 by Doris Tate, the mother of Sharon Tate, who was murdered by the **Manson** family cult, because of her concern that the assailants would be released on parole. California subsequently made victim impact statements a lawful part of the judicial legal process in 1982. In 1991, the **U.S. Supreme Court** held that such statements were constitutional and were admissible in **death penalty** cases. A 1992 report by the U.S. **attorney general** enumerating a series of recommendations centering on the treatment of victims included an endorsement of allowing impact statements as part of the process and suggested that judges and others consider those perspectives in their decisions. They are not limited to direct victims in that friends and family members of the victim can also be provided the opportunity to address the court or agency. Victim impact statements provide victims the opportunity to present how their state of being was altered and affected, including the physical, emotional, or financial harm or trauma, as well as the associated medical, psychological, and economic costs that were caused by the crime. Some jurisdictions allow victim impact information to be addressed during other disposition stages of the case, such as at the **bail**, pretrial release, or **plea bargain** hearings, and permit victims to express their views of the crime, the offender, and the appropriate sentence. In some states, child victims are allowed to submit a drawing to depict the impact that the crime has had on them. Currently, all 50 states allow victim impact statements at some stage of the criminal justice process. *See also* MANSON, CHARLES. (1934–2017); TRIAL; UNITED STATES ATTORNEY; VICTIMIZATION RATE.

VICTIMIZATION RATE. The rate is the number of victimizations per 1,000 persons or households as measured by the **National Crime Victimization Survey**, which is administered by the **Bureau of Justice Statistics**. The survey work demonstrated that several categories of crime are underreported because in many instances victims did not report the crime to **police** and began in 1972 to follow work conducted by the National Opinion Research Center and the **President's Commission on Law Enforcement and the Administration of Justice**. *See also* DARK FIGURE OF CRIME.

VICTIMLESS CRIME. A term used to describe an offense that while illegal has no identifiable victim. The crime ordinarily implicates individuals in which the act is consensual or involves a sole person where there is no direct victim or complaining participant and **police** are often not contacted. These offenses are sometimes referred to as public order offenses and considered crimes against society and community standards. In some countries, victimless crimes are not illegal and are instead restricted. During the 1960s and 1970s, these crimes were beginning to be **decriminalized** in the United States, but as the **broken windows theory** emerged, policing efforts became more aggressive in their enforcement of these offenses because of the purported connection with more serious crimes and the adverse impact they had on the economic stability and quality of life of communities. Examples of victimless crimes include **prostitution**, **gambling**, **pornography**, and recreational drug use.

VICTIMOLOGY. An area of study that researches and analyzes the process, rates, incidence, and prevalence of **victimization**, including the relationships between victims and offenders or perpetrators, as well as the interactions between victims and the criminal justice system. Victimology examines the correlations between victims and other groups and institutions impacting individuals and broad **human rights** violations including media outlets, corporations and business enterprises, and cultures. Research is used by various criminal justice organizations to determine the causal relationship between the individual and their vulnerability to victimization. Victimology examines the totality of the victimization experience, including antecedents, events, and responses to that experience. The scientific study of the discipline began during the early 1970s following the **civil rights** movement when the **FBI** established a **Behavioral Analysis Unit (BAU)** to examine the connections between victims and offenders. Through the trainings, law enforcement eventually discerned differences and patterns between victims and perpetrators. These analyses guided research about these relationships. The BAU was the precursor to other victim support organizations, including **Mothers against Drunk Drivers (MADD)**, founded on 5 September 1980, and Parents of Murdered Children (POMC), which were established to study criminal victimization, albeit specific to their affected families.

VICTIM PRECIPITATED CRIME (THEORY). A criminological theory sometimes referred to as the victim precipitation approach, which is most commonly associated with the crimes of **homicide**, robbery, rape, and **assault**. The theory seeks to understand the interaction between the offender and victim in examining how the victim's behavior may have initiated (precipitated) or contributed to the crime being committed. The application of the theory posits that victims are active participants in their own victimization and make themselves more vulnerable to crime when they engage in risky behavior by acting first and then provoking or emboldening the offender. The theory has been criticized for blaming victims for their own victimization, particularly as applied to sexual assault. Victim precipitation was coined by the criminologist **Dr. Marvin Wolfgang**, who examined homicide rates and discussed the findings of victim-initiating behavior in his article "Victim Precipitated Criminal Homicide" (1957). Earlier attempts to identify the impact of victim behavior on victimization were codified along typologies that assessed the relative culpability of the victim in the commission of the crime. *See also* VICTIMOLOGY.

VICTIMS' RIGHTS. A movement that brought the rights as well as equal and fair treatment of crime victims to the forefront of social consciousness. The movement began during the 1970s following the **U.S. Supreme Court** holding in *Linda R. S. v. Richard D.*, 410 U.S. 614 (1973), which determined that the victim had "no formal legal status beyond that of a **witness** or piece of **evidence**." The court's holding advanced a shift in the system's focus from being victim-centric to societal-centric and excluded the victim's role in decision making. The ruling stated that Congress could create legislation in support of victims' rights. The decision sparked the modern victims' rights movement, which grew from a prevalent belief about the emphasis of the criminal justice system on the constitutional rights of defendants, resources provided to **inmates**, and **prison** conditions over the interests of those victimized by crimes. The cause was further bolstered by media accounts of offenders who would seek out victims and their families in **retaliation** for having reported the crime in which they were convicted. Victims bemoaned the system's failure to keep them apprised of investigations and important events in the prosecutorial process. It challenged the way the system considered victims and served as the impetus in developing the nation's resources and support network for victims, including shelters and hotlines. The movement has lobbied government to provide victims with a more meaningful role in the criminal justice process. Federal and state laws generally require that victims, family members, or legal guardians be kept informed during all stages of the criminal investigation and prosecution, including postconviction events. Laws also grant victims other rights noted in the Victims' Bill of Rights, including **restitution**. *See also* VICTIM ASSISTANCE PROGRAM.

VICTIM WITNESS PROGRAM. A program designed to provide victim witnesses with information, services, and support during the criminal justice process to safeguard **victims' rights** and protection, while not compromising the constitutional rights of defendants. Some of the available services include explanation of court procedures, notifications, and testimonial assistance. The program was put into practice following the enactment of the 1982 Victim and Witness Protection Act (VWPA), which was conceived by the United States President's Task Force on **Violent Crime** the prior year. Since then, the U.S. Department of Justice together with the Offices of the **United States Attorneys** oversees the implementation of the law and related guidelines and serves as a model by which state governments develop local programs. *See also* VICTIM ASSISTANCE PROGRAM; WITNESS; WITNESS PROTECTION PROGRAM.

VIDEO PIRACY. The illegal reproduction, distribution, or unauthorized sale or prohibited use of copyrighted audiovisual work without the permission or prior consent of the copyright owner. Video piracy has evolved with technological changes and advancements in how audiovisual works are stored and distributed and is frequently identified as being the most detrimental factor to the entertainment industry economy. Video piracy is generally classified into two categories—digital and physical. Digital piracy involves the illegal duplication and distribution of copyrighted content through electronic means. Exchanges of digital content occur online through peer-to-peer (P2P) networks, and copyrighted media is uploaded through video sharing sites and the like. Physical piracy is the unauthorized physical duplication and dissemination of audiovisual work. This form of piracy involves illegally burning media onto CDs and DVDs and then selling the product for a fraction of the retail price. Pirated videos are primarily released by "warez" groups or organized piracy groups that distribute videos in a variety of formats and versions. When the pirated video is initially distributed, it is generally a relatively low-grade-quality film. As sources multiply, better-quality videos become available to a wider viewership. The earliest attempts at video piracy were known as cam releases, whereby individuals would record the on-screen projection of a movie playing in a theater not yet released on video for personal entertainment. Video piracy crimes proliferated with the inception of the internet in 1998, and warez groups began releasing feature films onto the web prior to their theatrical release. The reproduction, distribution, and sale of pirated videos over the internet has become more widespread as its popularity increased and the service became faster and more accessible. Prosecutions have not impeded its growth, particularly in countries without copyright laws. *See also* COPYRIGHT INFRINGEMENT.

VIDOCQ SOCIETY. A crime-solving association based in Philadelphia, Pennsylvania, that is exclusive to members only. The society is named after the 19th-century French **detective** Eugene Francois Vidocq. Vidocq had a criminal history and would use his understanding of the criminal's psychology to assist law enforcement in solving **homicide** cases that had gone cold. The society was formed in 1990 by William Fleisher, a special agent with the U.S. Customs Service; Richard Walter, a forensic psychologist; and Frank Bender, a sculptor and forensic reconstructionist. The following year, the group solved its first case when it assisted in exonerating an innocent man in the **murder** of Huey Cox in Little Rock, Arkansas. The original bylaws of the society set a limit of 82 members (one for each year of Vidocq's life), but the organization's membership has grown to more than 150 men and women working in diverse professions including **forensics**, profilers, investigators, scientists, psychologists, prosecutors, and **coroners**. During the meetings, law enforcement officials from various jurisdictions present their cold case homicides for members to review. The society's service is gratis and will pay for the travel expenses of law enforcement who come to the meetings to present their cold cases. Cases that are presented must meet the following criteria: the case must be an unsolved death that is at least two years old, the victim cannot have been involved in illegal activity, and the appropriate law enforcement agency must present the case. Since its founding, the society has been the subject of popular culture, including the final episode of the 2007–2008 season of *Law and Order: Special Victims Unit* and the book *The Murder Room* (2011) by Michael Capuzzo. *See also* DETECTIVE; EXONERATION.

VIGILANTISM. The unlawful practice of civilians carrying out duties assigned to **police**, prosecutors, judges, and other government officials who have authorized roles in the criminal justice system to pursue and punish criminals without offering them the benefit of **due process** or other legal recourse. Vigilantism, as it is formally defined, evolved during the mid-18th century when citizens personally carried out justice in protecting the interests of colonists and early settlers before towns had any established form of government. Although few vigilante names and groups were widely known and recorded, there were newspaper accounts of vigilantism, most notably in the southern and western parts of the United States. Vigilantism arose in these areas as the criminal justice system did not safeguard the early settlers of the new frontier. Given the absence of any organized and structured legal system to address the injustices of victims, they were more inclined to personally pursue those who had wronged them. Voluntary associations were sometimes organized into "vigilance committees," comprised almost always of men who cooperated in fighting and preventing genuine and imagined risks to the community. Vigilantes targeted individuals and groups by harassment, expulsion, beatings, and sometimes **murder**. In many instances, the vigilantism involved an excessive **use of force** not commensurate with reasonable actions. In contemporary society, vigilantism can be more broadly applied to warring **gang** and **organized crime** factions who resolve conflicts through revenge killings. These groups involved in illicit activity resort to methods of **retaliation** because they cannot present their injury through legal channels without incriminating themselves. *See also* MURDER INC.

VIGORISH. Also known as the "vig" and sometimes referred to as the "juice," *vigorish* is Yiddish slang originating from the Russian word meaning "winnings." The term refers to a charge that is taken on bets by a casino or gaming establishment or the interest paid to a bookmaker, or **bookie**, for taking a bet from a gambler. The rate can vary, but it is often 10 percent of the amount wagered. The term can also be used to describe the specific ways casinos integrate a company advantage into games or the interest owed to a usurer or loan shark. The term initially appeared in print during the early 20th century in the book *The Apaches of New York*, which was a compendium of stories describing the corruption of New York politics. The modern use of the term, as in the interest on a loan, appeared during the 1930s. Bookmakers incorporate the vigorish into wagers so that they make money irrespective of the outcome and will minimize their risk by setting the odds or adjusting the line so that losing bets pay off winning bets. The **gambling** book will make money by collecting the small commission on the total amount wagered. *See also* USURY.

VINTAGE FRAUD. Wine fraud involves the adulteration of wine and the fraudulent use of labels to deceitfully represent the product in order to profit from vintage wine collectors and the general public. In some cases, vintage fraud is perpetrated by unregulated wine investment firms, who dupe investors by selling them something other than the genuine product, or never providing the product at all. Fraudulent practices include affixing labels from a premium, rare, or expensive wine onto an inferior bottle or by adding or blending adulterants. Label fraud, which sometimes involves manipulating the entire packaging of the wine including the bottles and corks, was originally done to deceive buyers with respect to the region where the wine was produced. During ancient Rome and the Middle Ages, the supply and sale of fraudulent wine was prevalent among all classes, including the nobility, which led to the creation of strict laws by local authorities and severe penalties for producers who were caught, including death by **hanging**. Beginning in the early 19th century, concern over fraudulent wine production became widespread and eventually led to the Adulteration of Food and Drink Act of 1860 enacted by the British Parliament. France became the first country in 1889 to legally define wine as the product of fermented grape juice. In an effort to curtail wine fraud, some producers have developed technology that authenticates the winery's lot of bottles. These measures include unique seals, engraved serial numbers, scannable codes and labels, encrypted **DNA** tags, isotope analysis, and tamperproof capsules that change color once the bottle is opened. *See also* COPYRIGHT INFRINGEMENT; COUNTERFEITING.

VIOLENCE. Any kind of force used by one person or group against themselves, another individual, or community that results in or has the propensity to cause death, injury, or some other form of destruction to persons or property. Violence can be categorized into three broad groupings, including self-inflicted (suicide and self-abuse), interpersonal (family members, acquaintances, or members of the community), or collective (structural with political, social, or economic ends). Violent acts can take on many different forms but are generally characterized as physical, psychological, sexual, or deprivation. The genesis of violence among humans is unsettled, with different schools of thought. Conventionally defined violence among human beings is believed to have started during the Holocene epoch dating back to approximately 9,700 B.C. This period in human history encompassed the advent of higher population densities and the growth and expansion of civilizations throughout the world. While some contend that warfare is linked to the very first humans and ancestral primates, others argue that violence was an outgrowth of material conditions beginning with the development of agriculture approximately 10,000 years ago. Violence is viewed as a public health issue by the Centers for Disease Control and Prevention because it affects and impacts all groups and ages in society. Part of the mission is to prevent violence before it occurs. *See also* ASSAULT; MURDER.

VIOLENCE AGAINST WOMEN ACT (VAWA). A U.S. federal law passed in 1994 and signed by President Bill Clinton. The act was drafted by the office of Senator Joe Biden of Delaware following the grassroots efforts of advocates and professionals in a variety of fields that manage and provide services to women victimized by domestic and sexual violence. It was the first federal legislation that recognized **domestic violence** and sexual **assault** as crimes. The primary objective of the act is to counteract violence against women, including domestic violence, stalking, dating violence, and sexual assault by providing federal resources and assistance to communities and to facilitate the development of policies, programs, services, and best practices. VAWA funds are administered by the Office on Violence against Women (OVW) established within the Department of Justice in 2002 with a presidentially appointed, Senate-confirmed director. The act was reauthorized in 2000, 2005, and again in 2013. A key provision of the act was struck down in *United States v. Morrison*, 529 U.S. 598 (2000), when the **U.S. Supreme Court** held that the **civil rights** remedy of allowing victims of gender-based violence to sue their assailants in federal court was unconstitutional because it exceeded the federal government's powers under the commerce clause and Section 5 of the **Fourteenth Amendment** to the U.S. Constitution. *See also* VIOLENCE.

VIOLENT CRIME. A violation of the law characterized by offenders including robbers, burglars, terrorists, rapists, **kidnappers**, **gangsters**, **drug cartels**, and murderers, among others, who use or threaten to use force with or without a weapon on a victim. The classification of violent crimes varies by jurisdiction, but ordinarily they comprise **murder**, nonnegligent **manslaughter**, forcible rape, robbery, and aggravated **assault** as denoted by the **FBI's Uniform Crime Report**. The **Bureau of Justice Statistics** maintains the **National Crime Victimization Survey**, which tracks nonfatal violent crimes classified as rape, sexual assault, robbery, aggravated assault, and simple assault. Violent crime in the United States has varied since the collection of records began during colonization and has shown a steady decline since that period. Following World War II, violent crime rates began increasing and then peaked between the 1970s and the early 1990s. During the past 25 years, violent crime rates have declined, which has been attributed to a variety of theoretical perspectives. *See also* TERRORISM.

VIOLENT CRIME IMPACT TEAM (VCIT). A 2004 federal initiative that was an outgrowth of the Project Safe Neighborhoods program and began as a pilot program under **Attorney General** John Ashcroft and the director of the ATF, Carl J. Truscott. The nationwide strategy uses an integrative law enforcement approach of local, state, and federal personnel and resources, including the latest technology and investigative methods, to identify, interrupt, arrest, and prosecute the most violent criminals in selected cities around the country. The initiative originally targeted 15 U.S. cities including Los Angeles, California; Las Vegas, Nevada; Miami, Florida; Philadelphia, Pennsylvania; Columbus, Ohio; and Tulsa, Oklahoma. Cities are selected on the basis of their local crime statistics, which differ from national rates that have shown a steady decline, and the extent to which a law enforcement team can reduce the number of **violent crimes** over a six-month period. Currently, the VCIT program encompasses 31 cities. The law enforcement team assigned to each city includes federal agents from the ATF, DEA, and U.S. **Marshals** Service as well as a federal prosecutor from the Department of Justice who oversees the prosecutions of those arrested under the program. The team partners with state and local prosecutors, law enforcement officers, and **parole** officers in addition to actively working with community leaders, faith-based groups, nonprofit organizations, educational establishments, corporations and small businesses, media affiliates, and social service agencies to forge relationships, thwart **gang** domination, and improve prevention within at-risk communities.

VIOLENT CRIMINAL APPREHENSION PROGRAM (ViCAP). A department within the **FBI**'s National Center for the Analysis of Violent Crime that assists law enforcement agencies throughout the United States and the world in identifying and apprehending violent offenders. The program was initially established by the FBI in 1985 and centered in **Quantico**, Virginia, to study the behavior of **serial killers** and rapists. The program has since been expanded to analyze **homicides**, **kidnappings**, missing person reports, sexual **assault**, and cases of unidentified persons. Pierce Brooks, a former homicide **detective** in Los Angeles, proposed the idea after learning that serial homicides could be linked by the unique or "signature" aspects of the crime. He was appointed the program's first director. The ViCAP Web National Crime Database is operated by ViCAP and cannot be accessed by the media or general public. In 2008, the FBI provided law enforcement agencies with the access to track and correlate information on **violent crime**, including sexual assaults, solved and unsolved homicides, and cases of missing persons or unidentified human remains where authorities suspect foul play. The database is the nation's largest repository of violent criminal cases. Authorized personnel access the system to enter data specific to their case such as victim details, type of trauma, weapons used, suspect information, composite images, crime scene features, vehicle descriptions, and **modus operandi** . The data helps facilitate the comparison of cases and psychological profiles of offenders to establish connections with potential leads. The system allows different jurisdictions to collaborate on the details of similar cases and has been particularly effective in identifying and apprehending serial killers, where separate victims might not otherwise be linked. *See also* MASS MURDER; PROFILING; RESSLER, ROBERT (1937–2013).

VIOLENTIZATION. A theory developed by the criminologist Lonnie Athens and subject of his book, *The Creation of Dangerous Violent Criminals* (1989). Violentization developed over the course of several years of research in which Athens extensively interviewed scores of **prison inmates** in Iowa and California correctional facilities who had engaged in violent behavior. Violentization is grounded in symbolic interactionism, one of the foundational theories in sociology that examines small-scale patterns within society in which social interaction, the self, role taking, and the meanings ascribed to symbols are the main foci and proposes that behaviors are dependent on meanings individuals derive and interpret from their interaction with others. In accordance with these principles, individuals who behave violently learned to be violent from their primary group in which **violence** was fundamental to their social norms and cultural context and are thus prone to interpret and then respond to situations violently. Violentization is a gradual, developmental process encompassing four sequential stages: (1) brutalization, in which the person is exposed, normally during childhood, to the teaching and demonstration of violent behavior and is taught to respond violently to conflict; (2) belligerency, the stage where in response to their violent treatment, the individual resolves to use serious violence when provoked, if they believe the outcome will be successful; (3) violent performances, the transitional stage from resolution to actual use of violence; and (4) virulency, the final stage in which the actor is prepared to use extreme violence on another with little or no provocation. In this stage, they are defined by others and themselves as being dangerous following successful violent performances.

VIOLENT OFFENDER RECONCILIATION PROGRAM (VORP). A reference to the initial victim-offender mediation programs that were developed during the 1970s and 1980s. This program paved the way for the more generic mediation programs that exist today and was used as part of the conflict-resolution process that permits the victim to be an active participant in the criminal justice process as opposed to an observer. While the focus is generally on **juvenile offenders** and low-level, property-related crimes, an increasing number of programs include adult offenders involved in serious, **violent crimes**. The first program of this kind began in 1976 in Kitchener, Ontario, when a **probation** officer overseeing a juvenile caseload persuaded the judge to require two juveniles convicted of **vandalism** to meet the victims. Following the conference, the judge ordered them to pay **restitution** as a condition of their probation. In 1978, this probation-based model was used to launch a similar program in the United States in Elkhart, Indiana. *See also* BALANCED AND RESTORATIVE JUSTICE (BARJ).

VIOLENT VIDEO GAMES. Video games are electronic, interactive diversions that entertain players with lively colors, sound effects, and intricate graphics. They provide users with a variety of simulated violent options that permit players to kill, maim, dismember, or sexually **assault** an image of a human being within the game. Defining a video game as violent since the industry emerged in the 1970s has been an imprecise process. The first major controversy occurred in 1976 when the arcade game *Death Race* allowed players to drive a crudely designed car over black-and-white stick figures, turning them into tombstones. The game was a predecessor to the more recent development of the ***Grand Theft Auto*** series of games. During the 1980s, the advent of more sophisticated systems created more realistic graphics. Video games that were particularly violent appeared in the marketplace in the early 1990s. In 1992, two games, *Mortal Kombat* and *Night Trap*, were launched. This series of games showed an intense level of graphic **violence** animating actual photographs rather than the more cartoonish images of the past. The public's alarm that ensued prompted the then senator Joe Lieberman to propose federal guidelines to regulate the sale of video games. In response, the gaming industry established the Entertainment Software Rating Board, which instituted a grading system to assess the sexual and violent content of games, which could result in a game being removed from most major retailers because of explicit content. In *Brown v. Entertainment Merchants Association*, 564 U.S. 786 (2011), the **U.S. Supreme Court** held that the California law that barred the sale and distribution of violent video games to minors was unconstitutional and that, akin to literature, video games are protected under the **First Amendment**. *See also* CIVIL RIGHTS.

VITAL STATISTICS. Annual reports or statistics concerning principal events or conditions affecting human life that provide detailed data including the rates of birth, mortality, marriages, and divorces within a given population or locale. Vital statistics data are ordinarily collected through a civil or vital registration system, which is organized and managed by a governing body to record the rate of these events in their jurisdiction or territory. The National Center for Health Statistics, which functions under the auspices of the Centers for Disease Control and Prevention, is the agency that administers the registration system in the United States. The accuracy of vital statistics is correlated with the country's civil registration process and its relative state of economic development. Vital statistics are used in the formation of public policy, in measuring population shifts and making projections, and in identifying, assessing, and monitoring the occurrence and prevalence of health issues, in addition to the design and effect of prevention strategies. Parochial registration preceded vital registration, but they were often inaccurate, particularly as it related to the number of births because all children were not always baptized. Historically, the study of mortality data prompted the collection of vital statistics. The prevailing interest in accurately recording the nature and number of deaths was further bolstered in the 18th and 19th centuries because of life insurance, which required an account of variables such as age, sex, health, and occupation and the extent to which each of these factors contribute to mortality rate. The Scandinavian nation-states were the first to have vital registration systems, with Finland starting in 1628. In the United States, the first law mandating the registration of births, deaths, and marriages was enacted in Massachusetts in 1639. The vital registration system in America, however, developed gradually and remained incomplete until the early 1900s, when the Census Bureau was established and federal law mandated registration.

VOICE STRESS ANALYSIS. Also referred to as voice risk analysis, which evaluates changes in an individual's voice patterns that are caused by the psychological stress of being untruthful or deceptive in response to a question or other stimulus. The technology is grounded in the idea that the stress an individual undergoes while attempting to obscure the truth has a physiological and psychological impact on their voice. The technology has been compared to **polygraph** testing, which analyzes variations in a person's respiration, heart rate, and skin secretions. During the late 1960s, the U.S. Army conducted studies to determine the viability of distinguishing whether someone was being deceitful by measuring changes in their voice. In 1970, three military officers associated with the research, Alan Bell, who specialized in counterintelligence; Bill Ford, an expert in electronics; and Charles McQuiston, specializing in polygraphy, retired and formed the Dektor Counterintelligence and Security Company, based in Virginia. They developed a device that would record the human voice and then slow it down to a fraction of its normal rate. The recording subsequently passed through a filter and then was depicted onto charts showing the variations. The device was initially called the Psychological Stress Evaluator and was the first voice stress analyzer available to the public. Research measuring the reliability and validity of the PSE instrument has varied, with many studies concluding that the ability to detect deception is equivalent to chance. Other similarly based technologies have since been developed, including the Computerized Voice Stress Analyzer and the Diogenes Lantern. Research conclusions into the merits of the results have been mixed and they are limited as an investigative tool if and when they are used in questioning individuals.

VOID FOR VAGUENESS. A constitutional law doctrine that is based on the **due process** clauses of the **Fifth** and **Fourteenth Amendments** of the U.S. Constitution, which requires that a law be void on constitutional grounds if it is too vague for the average citizen to comprehend what elements constitute a crime. The doctrine requires laws to provide fair notice to all persons by stating explicitly what it mandates and what conduct is punishable or prohibited. A statute can also be ruled void for vagueness if the authority, delegated to the other branches of government by the legislature, is so broad that it would bring about the arbitrary and discriminatory enforcement and prosecution of the law. In order to safeguard the public from subjective enforcement, the doctrine reinforces due process rights by entitling individuals to understand what the government requires and prohibits vis-à-vis the scope and nature of statutes, including the definitions of terms that could be potentially vague, in which criminal penalties could be imposed. In *Connally v. General Construction Co.*, 269 U.S. 385 (1926), the **U.S. Supreme Court** established the key constructs of the void for vagueness doctrine, ruling that laws which fail to have the fundamental requirements so that they can be appropriately enforced are deemed to be void. The case originated from an Oklahoma statute deemed unconstitutional because it required businesses to compensate workers in accordance with a vaguely set standard.

VOIR DIRE. A legal term derived from Old French and the Latin phrase *verum dicere*, meaning "to speak the truth," which denotes the process of questioning and assessing prospective jurors by the judge, prosecutor, or defense attorney in determining whether the juror is qualified and appropriate to serve on a **jury**. The practice of using voir dire emerged in the United States as population shifts caused communities to become more diversified and disconnected from one another. Parties in court matters utilized voir dire to gather specific information about **jurors** because they could no longer rely on those details from the at-large community. In 1911, New Jersey was the first state to pass a statute allowing voir dire. In the United States, the term can also be used in reference to the questioning of witnesses, expert and otherwise, in determining their capacity and competency to provide testimony on the matter at hand. The right to a jury is incorporated in the Sixth and Seventh Amendments to the U.S. Constitution. The process includes an oral examination of prospective jurors which may include a questionnaire to which they take an oath to answer truthfully. The jurors' responses assist the court, prosecutor, and defense attorney in selecting or excusing members of the juror pool from serving on the jury for a **trial**. Some questions may include whether the juror is acquainted with any of the trial participants, if they have any prior knowledge of or involvement in the case, or if they have had any dealings with the defendant or other persons associated with the defendant. The attorneys are provided an opportunity to inquire with each juror about their background, experiences, attitudes, and other relevant aspects of their person in determining potential bias for or against the defendant. During the process, attorneys may exercise one of two types of challenges—challenges for cause and peremptory challenges. Challenges for cause are exercised to excuse jurors in instances when there is a clear conflict or indication of prejudice. Attorneys have a limited number of peremptory challenges that can be used to remove those jurors they suspect will not be supportive of their intended arguments. Trial judges generally have a great deal of autonomy in establishing the parameters of voir dire, including the substance and appropriateness of questions. The length and nature of voir dire, including whether potential jurors are sequestered or questioned individually, varies depending, among other things, on the circumstances of the case, the seriousness of the charges, the notoriety of the defendant, and the publicity surrounding the matter. *See also* JURY SELECTION; *WITHERSPOON V. ILLINOIS*, 391 U.S. 510 (1968); WITNESS.

VOLD, GEORGE (1896–1967). A conflict theorist from Platte, South Dakota, who is considered the primary contributor to the conflict perspective, which links societal class to crime. He earned his Ph.D. in 1930 from the University of Minnesota, where he also served as a professor from 1927 until his retirement in 1964 and was a subject matter expert in criminal sociology. In 1934, he assisted in drafting the psychopathic personality law in Minnesota. He was also an advisor to the state's crime commission, where his work in drafting a prominent report served as the basis for the state's **prison** reform. Vold viewed crime as a problem stemming from social control and political structures and conflict. The view holds a Marxist philosophy that distinguishes society along different classes who are vying for competing and disparate vested interests. Crime occurs as a result of these class conflicts, which are central, perpetual, and prevalent to their existence. Those groups that hold the greatest control in the political process exercise the authority to pass laws to maintain the shared interests and needs of their group while limiting outside groups' ability to control and access resources including money, education, and employment. This maintenance and expansion of power causes a perpetual struggle and conflict between groups within the same culture. Vold wrote *Theoretical Criminology* (1958), which chronicled the history of the **criminology** field through the classical and positivist schools to the then-contemporary period, expounded upon his group conflict theory of crime, and distinguished the issues surrounding the legal and sociological meanings of crime and **punishment**. He served as the coeditor of the *American Sociological Review* (1944–1946), was elected president of the

Midwest Sociology Society (1949–1950), and in 1966 received the **Edwin H. Sutherland** award for his work in criminology from the American Criminological Society. *See also* MARXIST CRIMINOLOGY.

VOLSTEAD ACT. Legislation that is more formally known as the National **Prohibition** Act, attributed to Andrew J. Volstead, a Republican representative from Minnesota and chairman of the House Judiciary Committee. With the support of Wayne Wheeler, a prohibitionist and affiliate of the Anti-Saloon League, Volstead championed the bill that prohibited the manufacture, sale, and transportation of intoxicating liquors. The bill did not regulate the consumption or use of alcohol but left it to the federal and state governments to devise legislation in enforcing the ban. Violations were punishable by **fines** of up to $1,000 (considerable at the time given the median annual income), imprisonment up to six months, and **forfeiture** of vehicles used in the commission of the crime. Intoxicating liquors were defined as any beverage that exceeded 0.5 percent by volume, exempting wine used for religious ceremonies and medicinal liquor prescribed by a physician. The bill was introduced to the 66th Congress in 1919 but was vetoed by President Woodrow Wilson, who regarded the threshold as too severe, but in particular he objected to the wartime prohibition that the bill also included. President Wilson's veto was overridden by Congress, and the act became law on 28 October 1919. Public adherence continued notwithstanding Volstead's failed reelection bid in 1922, but support waned and opposition grew as crime rates rose and alcohol consumption became more socially acceptable. In 1933, Congress passed the Blaine Act, sponsored by Wisconsin senator John J. Blaine, which initiated the repeal of the Eighteenth Amendment. The repeal was formally adopted after Utah became the 36th state to ratify the Twenty-First Amendment to the U.S. Constitution.

VOYEURISM. Originates from the French word *voir*, meaning "to see," and is the furtive observation or practice of spying on an exposed body or people engaged in an intimate act such as sexual activity, undressing, or other private activity. Voyeurism is a form of paraphilia and a psychosexual disorder in which the person doing the observing draws sexual pleasure and gratification from viewing the subject, who is often unaware that they are being observed. The voyeur is usually hidden from the view of others, and the person being observed is ordinarily a stranger to the observer. Voyeurism may also involve taking an unauthorized photograph or video of the person while engaged in the private activity. Since the 1880s, spy cameras have been small enough to fit inside a pocket watch. Advances since the 1950s, however, have greatly reduced the size of these electronics and at the same time enhanced their quality and affordability. The purpose of the voyeur is to achieve sexual excitement from the observation, and if an orgasm is sought, it is typically attained through masturbation because the observer does not normally interact with or seek out the person for sexual contact. Voyeurism is classified as a sexual abuse crime in many states, which prohibits recording the image of anyone without their consent in their home or other private place. When the interest in a particular person is obsessive, the individual may be charged with stalking. There is no scientific consensus on the causes of voyeurism, but some experts believe that repeated acts can potentially reinforce and perpetuate the voyeuristic conduct. Male voyeurs, who are generally more voyeuristic than women, are sometimes characterized as "jags" or "Peeping Toms." The term "Peeping Tom" is derived from the legend of Lady Godiva, in which a voyeur named Tom was struck blind or dead from watching Godiva, Countess of Mercia, ride a horse through the streets of Coventry covered only in her long hair.

W

WACO SIEGE. *See* BRANCH DAVIDIANS.

WAINWRIGHT, LOUIS L. (1923–). The secretary of the Florida Division of Corrections appointed by Governor Cecil Farris Bryant on 16 July 1962. Wainwright would remain in the position over the course of four agency name changes and six governors until 31 December 1986. He was preceded by H. G. Cochran and succeeded by Richard L. Dugger. He also served as president of the Florida Peace Officers Association and as president of the Corrections Foundation of Florida. Prior to entering the private sector in 1987, he was acknowledged as the dean of American correctional administrators in recognition of his service to the field of corrections. During his tenure as secretary of corrections, he was most notable for being named the respondent in two **U.S. Supreme Court** cases—***Gideon v. Wainwright*, 372 U.S. 335 (1963)**, and ***Ford v. Wainwright*, 477 U.S. 399 (1986)**—and several **habeas corpus** petitions. In the *Gideon* case, the U.S. Supreme Court confirmed that state courts are required to provide defendants with legal counsel in all criminal cases. In the *Ford* matter, the Court upheld the **common law** rule, which prohibited the **execution** of defendants determined to be insane. The Court ruled that petitioners are entitled to a competency assessment and evidentiary hearing in ascertaining whether they are competent to be executed.

WALKER SPY RING. An **espionage** ring led by John A. Walker Jr., an American citizen and U.S. Navy communications specialist, who over the course of 18 years between 1967 and 1985 sold classified documents including military communication ciphers, blueprints of naval vessels and weapons, and secret reports on the movements of submarines and surface ships to the Soviet Union. The Walker spy ring has been described as the gravest espionage breach of the Cold War. Walker began his espionage in October 1967 when he smuggled classified information from a facility in Norfolk, Virginia, and brought it to the Soviet embassy in Washington, D.C., and persuaded the Soviets that he was not attempting to dupe them as an **under-**

cover American operative. He was reportedly honest with them, stating that he was only doing it in the interest of money. Walker continued distributing classified documents while on active duty and then following his retirement in 1976 recruited his brother, Arthur, a retired lieutenant commander who worked for a defense contractor, his son, Michael, who was serving as a petty officer stationed aboard the USS *Nimitz*, and a friend and fellow naval communications specialist, Jerry Whitworth. Whitworth originally thought the information was being given to Israel, a U.S. ally, but when he discovered that it was instead going to the Soviet Union, he continued supplying Walker with classified material. Walker was arrested in May 1985 after leaving classified material at "dead drop" locations in Norfolk. The 129 documents that were seized by the **FBI** at the location were determined to have been stolen by his son. Walker agreed to cooperate with authorities, including a detailed account of the material that was breached; plead to a conviction; and testify against Whitworth, who supplied him with most of the code information that was provided to his Soviet handlers, in exchange for his son's maximum sentence of 25 years' imprisonment. Jerry Whitworth received 365 years in **prison** and was **fined** $410,000. Arthur Walker was sentenced to three life sentences plus an additional 40 years and later died in prison on 5 July 2014. John Walker received a life sentence and died in a federal **penitentiary** on 28 August 2014 at the age of 77. He would have been eligible for **parole** in 2015. Michael Walker was sentenced to 25 years and released on parole in 2000.

WALNUT STREET JAIL. A jail in Philadelphia, Pennsylvania, that took its name from the street on which it was located and is regarded as the first modern **penitentiary**. The construction of the facility began in 1773 and was completed in 1776 when the first prisoners were admitted. The jail was closed in 1838 following a series of disciplinary problems. The jail was designed by Robert Smith, a prominent Philadelphia architect at the time, with the intent to accept prisoners from the overcrowded High Street Jail. The original U-shaped structure of the facility had been designed to house large groups of **inmates** in open rooms with little regard for prisoners' welfare or rehabilitation. In 1790, following the insistence of Quaker reformers, the jail began to be converted into a penitentiary, but the transformation was not completed until 1795 because of certain political factions who were against the change. As a penitentiary, it was modeled after a monastic chamber and was the first **prison** to use individual cells. The arrangement of the cells prevented inmates from communicating with each other or viewing the outside world. **Solitary confinement**, as the system came to be known, enforced repentance through silence, and despite its ill effects, it was through this contemplation that the reformers believed transformation could be achieved. *See also* EASTERN STATE PENITENTIARY (PENNSYLVANIA).

WALSH, ADAM (1974–1981). An American boy born 14 November 1974 who was **kidnapped** from a department store in Hollywood, Florida, and was later believed to have been murdered by **Ottis Toole**, a drifter and convicted **serial killer**. The boy disappeared on 27 July 1981 after his mother left him in an electronics toy department where several boys were playing video games while she went to inquire about a lamp in a different department. Upon returning to the toy department, she was informed that security directed the unaccompanied boys to leave the store following a dispute they had among themselves over the arcade game. The security guard, who was unaware that Adam was not in the company of the older boys, made them all leave the store together from the same exit. Alone and unfamiliar with his surroundings, the boy was abducted by Toole, who later killed him. The boy's severed head was found two weeks later on 10 August 1981 by fishermen 120 miles away from the site of his abduction in a canal in Vero Beach, Florida. The body was never recovered. The **coroner** determined that the cause of death was asphyxiation and that the decapitation occurred after the boy had already died. Toole confessed to having killed the boy but was never convicted in Adam's death because of law enforcement's investigative errors and loss of **evidence**. Toole recanted his confession, which he admitted twice. Toole's niece told **John Walsh**, the boy's father, that he confessed to killing Adam on his deathbed. He died in **prison** at the age of 49 of liver failure on 15 September 1996 while serving five life sentences for other crimes. The case was closed on 16 December 2008 after Chief Chadwick E. Wagner of the Hollywood **Police** Department stated that accumulation of circumstantial evidence convinced them that Toole had murdered the boy. The death was the catalyst to a host of changes in law enforcement responses to missing children cases. After being lobbied, Congress enacted the Missing Children's Act of 1982, which required the entry of missing children data into the **FBI**'s **National Crime Information Center (NCIC)** database, and the Missing Children's Assistance Act of 1984. On the 25th anniversary of Adam's disappearance in 2006, President Bush signed into law the Adam Walsh Child Protection and Safety Act, which enhanced the penalties for crimes committed against children, expanded the National Sex Offender Registry, and created a new registry for child abuse offenders. Beginning in the late 1980s, many department stores, retail stores, supermarkets, and other businesses have adopted the practice known as "**Code Adam**," which prompts employees to a protocol to secure the store and locate the child while a description of the child is broadcasted over the intercom to alert patrons. *See also* AMERICA'S MISSING: BROADCAST EMERGENCY RESPONSE (AMBER) ALERT; MURDER; TEAM ADAM.

WALSH, JOHN EDWARD, JR. (1945–). A television host, producer, author, and victims' rights advocate who became nationally known for his anticrime activism following the abduction and **murder** of his six-year-old son, **Adam Walsh**, in 1981. The devastating loss of his son led him to dedicate his life to law-and-order efforts to apprehend fugitives and to advocate for victims. In 1984, the nonprofit organization, the Adam Walsh Resource Center, which was founded by the Walsh family with various locations, merged with the National Center for Missing and Exploited Children, where Walsh serves on the board of directors. Since its inception, the center has assisted law enforcement in locating almost 200,000 missing children. In 1988, Walsh became the host of the television program ***America's Most Wanted***, a Fox-produced show that depicted fugitive profiles. *See also* LIST, JOHN (1925–2008); TOOLE, OTTIS (1947–1996).

WANTED POSTER. A poster or wanted sign is a public notice depicting a photograph or facial composite of a fugitive. Composite images are created using a variety of technological methods, including the Electronic Facial Identification Technique and PhotoFit (photographic identification technique). The posters are issued by law enforcement agencies, most commonly the **FBI**, which promulgates the "FBI Most Wanted List" as a medium to advise the public about an alleged criminal whom they are seeking to apprehend. Reward posters of the 1870s and 1880s that are associated with the old west were handbills or postcards provided to law enforcement officials and were limited to a description of the wanted person. The notices were not originally made for public consumption, but a reward or wanted poster would occasionally be printed in the newspaper. With the exception of John Wilkes Booth, who assassinated President Abraham Lincoln, photos were not included with descriptions until the turn of the century, when photo reproduction technology was enhanced. The 10 Most Wanted poster that is most commonly known and used by the FBI was not formalized until 14 March 1950 by the bureau's late director, **J. Edgar Hoover**, following the publicity generated from an International News Service story about the "toughest guys" they sought to capture. The first fugitive to be placed on this list was Thomas James Holden, who was wanted for the **murder** of his wife, her brother, and her stepbrother. Prior to that and beginning around 1919, the FBI issued fliers that were known as "IOs" or identification orders. William N. Bishop, who was wanted for deserting the military, is believed to be the first IO issued in 1919. In the early 1930s, the agency published a fugitive bulletin of who were wanted by law enforcement from across the nation. The FBI's most wanted posters were issued in black and white until 1998 when the color scheme was changed to blue and white with the addition of Harry Joseph Bowman. Color pictures were incorporated into the list in 2009 with the addition of Joe Luis Saenz. Since its inception in 1950, there have been 512 fugitives listed, and 481 of them have been captured or located.

WAR CRIMES. Acts in violation of established laws of war or international humanitarian law that contravene the rules of battle or treaties for which individual criminal responsibility is incurred. Violations deemed serious in nature can occur in both domestic and international armed conflicts. Prohibited acts constituting a war crime include **mutilation** or **torture**; hostage taking; conscripting children into armed conflict roles; rape or other forms of sexual violence; perfidy; pillaging; unlawful deportation, confinement, or transfer; directing attacks against buildings dedicated to religion, education, art, science, charity, hospital care, or those structures of historical significance; and the purposeful targeting of attacks against protected persons such as sick or incapacitated combatants, prisoners of war, humanitarian workers, UN peacekeepers, combat medics, or civilians, and using weapons that cause excessive injury or unnecessary suffering. Limitations on armed conflict date back to the ancient Greeks, who are considered the first to have instituted laws to govern wartime actions. Defining particular actions as a war crime became more fully constituted in the Hindu Code of Manu in 200 B.C. before becoming adopted into Roman law. Peter von Hagenbach is considered to be the first **war criminal** convicted and then beheaded in 1474 by the Holy Roman Empire. He had command responsibility as a knight over crimes that he had a duty to prevent. In the United States, the earliest example of a war criminal was Henry Wirz, a Confederate officer, who was convicted and hanged in 1865 by a military tribunal because of the grave conditions of Andersonville **Prison** where many U.S. prisoners of war died during the American Civil War. International law regarding the concept of war crimes has evolved over time, but it was largely codified between the latter part of the 19th century and the beginning of the 20th century. The first system to codify a broad set of war crimes, known as the Lieber Code and named after its principal author, Francis Lieber, was instituted by President Abraham Lincoln during the Civil War. The Leipzig War Crimes **trial** of 1921 following World War I, in which the Allied powers attempted to hold German officials accountable for crimes committed during the war, represented the first efforts in developing a comprehensive approach and system for prosecuting international law violations. Since 2002, the definitions of war crimes have been codified in international statutes and are heard by the International Criminal Court, a treaty-based court located in The Hague. The court is authorized to try civilians or military personnel of state parties who have been accused of committing atrocities or those who commit crimes in the territory of a member state. *See also* HANGING; VIOLENCE.

WAR CRIMINAL. An individual, military or civilian, who has been found guilty of conduct in violation of the rules of warfare in accordance with international law and conventions intended to safeguard civilians and prisoners of war. The actions that constitute **war crimes** have evolved over time to include traditional war crimes (acts in violation of customary wartime practices), crimes against peace (hostile military actions against a sovereign nation that are not carried out in self-defense), and **crimes against humanity** (acts of unwarranted **violence** and brutality that involve the enslavement, persecution, or **murder** of civilians, prisoners of war, or other noncombatant people.

WAR ON CRIME. A national policy agenda established in 1965 by President Lyndon Johnson with the **President's Commission on Law Enforcement and Administration of Justice**. The intention was a "thorough, intelligent, and effective war against crime" through a three-prong strategy: the Immediate Attack, a Comprehensive Agenda, and Attacking Crime at the Roots. The agenda sought to bring together the policing efforts of local, state, and federal governments and agencies. The agenda reflected a bipartisan effort to respond to the **violent crime** rate, bolstered by the country's racial tensions and the **assassination** of leaders that had been steadily increasing. The "fight against crime" platform led to stiffer legislation such as mandatory **minimum sentences** while supplying local **police** forces with additional resources and personnel through the Law Enforcement Assistance Act, and the slogan was used by subsequent campaigns to gain public support for their political candidacy. The 1965 legislation created a grant-making agency in the Department of Justice (DOJ) that supplied local **police** departments with millions of dollars to purchase bulletproof vests and military-grade vehicles and equipment. The **Omnibus Crime Control and Safe Streets Act of 1968, Pub. L. No. 90-351, 82 Stat. 197 (1968)**, provided the Department of Justice with greater influence through the **Law Enforcement Assistance Administration (LEAA)**, which expanded the grant-making agency of the initial legislation. *See also* TOUGH ON CRIME; WAR ON DRUGS.

WAR ON DRUGS. A policy agenda term used by the U.S. government in its national campaign to restrict the use, manufacture, and distribution of drugs by using **police** agencies at the local, state, and federal levels, as well as the military, to intervene in the illegal drug trade. The campaign includes the development and implementation of policy that aims to preclude the production and abuse of specifically targeted drugs. The term was initially used by President Richard Nixon as a part of the *Comprehensive Drug Abuse Prevention and Control Act* of 1970, a wide-scale policy initiative to address the drug abuse problem that had steeply risen during the 1960s. The term, however, was only popularized by the media following the 18 June 1971 press conference in which he declared illicit drug use as "**Public Enemy** No. 1." The policy stance of the Nixon administration was a continuation of the national perspective in restricting drug use, which dated back to the early part of the 20th century and remained unchanged in subsequent administrations, except that the Obama administration avoided using the "War on Drugs" term as a part of their discourse.

WARRANT. A **writ** issued by a qualified magistrate that specifically authorizes a law enforcement officer to make an arrest, seize property, conduct a search, or execute some other judgment or order. There are generally three types of warrants related to criminal procedure, including arrest, **search and seizure**, and **execution**. An arrest warrant authorizes an officer to take a named individual into custody. A search and seizure warrant permits an authorized official to search a specific person, vehicle, dwelling, or other location and to confiscate items that can potentially serve as **evidence** in the case. An **execution warrant** is a court order that authorizes the execution of a person who has been sentenced to death in a **capital punishment** matter. Prior to the colonists declaring independence from British rule, agents of the English government used lifelong writs or general warrants that enabled them to search their property and to seize whatever these officials believed to be illegal. These blank **search warrants** placed little to no limitation on the search and arresting power of the agent and for many years were used as the means to enforce British law. When the **Fourth Amendment** to the U.S. Constitution was ratified in 1791, it guaranteed Americans that officials could no longer search their quarters without a warrant and **probable cause**. The Fourth Amendment was later augmented by the **Fourteenth Amendment**, wherein the **U.S. Supreme Court** held that the federal constitutional rights of a person's life, liberty, and property cannot be deprived without **due process** and that this applies to all states. A search and seizure warrant must specify the precise nature of the search and have proper cause. Individuals being arrested or having their property seized are provided a copy of the court order, which affords the individual authorized to execute the action protection from what ordinarily would be a violation of the subject's rights. In order for an arrest to be effectuated, the officer must have either probable cause or a valid arrest warrant that denotes the probable cause, the magistrate's authorization (signature), a **police** affidavit, and a description of the person identified for arrest. *See also* PLAIN VIEW DOCTRINE; WARRANTLESS SEARCHES.

WARRANTLESS SEARCHES. A warrantless search is conducted on persons or property without a **search warrant**. A warrantless **search and seizure** is restricted by the **Fourth Amendment** of the U.S. Constitution, which stems from the abuse of power carried out by British officials during the early settlement of the American colonies when they would search the dwellings and businesses of colonists without a warrant. The ratification of the Fourth Amendment prohibited warrantless searches and safeguarded people in their persons and effects, but over the course of time these protections have been subject to interpretation and limitation, in particular as it relates to times of war. Searches without a warrant have been allowed given certain exceptions when it is deemed reasonable by the court. These instances include searches that are voluntarily consented to by the subject or an authorized third party; when exigent circumstances are present so as to prevent harm, escape, or the destruction of **evidence**; when law enforcement is in hot pursuit of a suspect; or when a search is conducted on property that is abandoned or as part of a protective sweep, on particular businesses that are highly regulated such as gun shops, by law enforcement in the course of a **stop and frisk** (a pat down) or arrest of a suspect, or on vehicles as long as the policing agency has **probable cause**. Evidence can also be seized without a warrant if it is determined that it was in plain view or would have been inevitably discovered through legitimate means. *See also CHIMEL V. CALIFORNIA*, 395 U.S. 752 (1969); *U.S. V. RABINOWITZ*, 339 U.S. 56 (1950).

WARREN COMMISSION. More formally known as the President's Commission on the **Assassination** of President Kennedy, which became more commonly referred to by the name of the commission's chairman, Chief Justice Earl Warren. The commission was formed by President Lyndon B. Johnson through an executive order on 29 November 1963 to investigate the assassination of President John F. Kennedy, which occurred seven days earlier on 22 November 1963. President Johnson hoped that by assembling the commission the country would avoid having to decipher the facts of the assassination from multiple contradictory reports. Deputy **Attorney General** Nicholas Katzenbach has been credited with providing the advisement to White House aide Bill Moyers to investigate the assassination through a presidential commission in a memo dated 28 November 1963. The seven members appointed to the commission included the chairman, Earl Warren; U.S. senators Richard Russell Jr. and John Sherman Cooper; U.S. representatives Hale Boggs and Gerald Ford; the head of the Central Intelligence Agency, Allen Welsh Dulles; and the former president of the World Bank, John J. McCloy. The initial meeting of the commission occurred on 5 December 1963 in the National Archives Building in Washington, D.C., and most of the hearings were conducted as sessions closed to the public. During one point in the investigation, it later became known that the Cuban dictator Fidel Castro met with one of the commission's attorneys, William Coleman, and denied having been involved in the assassination. The 888-page report concluded that there was no conspiracy and that **Lee Harvey Oswald** acted alone with no specific motive to assassinate America's 35th president.

WARREN COURT. The term used to describe the **U.S. Supreme Court** under the leadership of Chief Justice Earl Warren between 1953 and 1969. He was succeeded by Warren E. Burger. Chief Justice Warren was appointed by President Dwight D. Eisenhower as a recess appointment on 11 January 1954 following the death of Chief Justice Fred M. Vinson. The U.S. Senate confirmed his appointment six weeks later. Warren had previously served as a three-term governor of California and was the Republican nominee for vice president in 1948. The Warren Court is characterized by its unwillingness to allow constitutional rights to vary among the states, its attention to ethical principles over narrow interpretive structures and strict precedent, as well as its general consensus established by the controversial and groundbreaking cases deliberated by it. Some of the court's most significant decisions included *Brown v. Board of Education*, 347 U.S. 483 (1954), racial segregation in public schools; *Reynolds v. Sims*, 377 U.S. 533 (1964), one person, one vote; *Griswold v. Connecticut*, 381 U.S. 479 (1965), general right to privacy; *Engel v. Vitale*, 370 U.S. 421 (1962), official prayer in public schools; and ***Miranda v. Arizona*, 384 U.S. 436 (1966)**, criminal procedure.

WARTIME TRADE VIOLATIONS. The prohibited sale or exchange of specific goods or resources reserved for a war effort or intended military use. These violations can be instituted through a variety of means by businesses, including rationing, price-ceiling offenses, tie-in sales, or failing to assure quality controls. Government policies barring particular lines of trade during wartime are based on economic and noneconomic variables, viability of monitoring and enforcement, and overall costs to impacted industries. There have been instances throughout history when countries have continued to trade with one another during active hostilities, such as the supply of binoculars and rubber which Britain and Germany traded during World War II.

WASHINGTON NAVY YARD SHOOTING. A mass shooting perpetrated on 16 September 2013 by the 34-year-old civilian contractor and lone gunman Aaron Alexis in which he killed 12 people and injured eight others (three by gunfire) at the Washington Navy Yard located in Washington, D.C. The ages of those killed in the attack ranged from 46 to 73. The shooting was the second-deadliest **mass murder** incident on a U.S. military base. *See also* SERIAL KILLER.

WATCHMAN STYLE. A style of policing emphasizing an informal means of resolving petty or relatively minor disputes. The term originated in England during the 13th century when a group of citizens were appointed to observe their neighborhoods for criminal activity at night. The social and political scientist **James Q. Wilson** conducted a study of eight different communities in 1968 and identified three distinct policing styles (methods, routines, and processes in carrying out **police** work): watchman, legalistic, and service. Wilson found that a police department's style was associated with the characteristics of their community, including its size, government organization, and socioeconomic composition. Police departments employing a watchman style allow officers to use discretion by assessing the seriousness of the infraction and its immediate consequence in determining which offenses can be ignored or otherwise resolved informally on-site. The overall goal of the watchman style is to maintain peace and order and is not preoccupied with deterring crime or as being a method to prevent disputes.

WATCH SYSTEM. The first organized system of protection and early policing of the masses devised during the Middle Ages in England was comprised of citizens arranged by church parish to guard against disturbances and breaches of the peace during the hours of night. These men served under the direction of a local constable, who was the chief peacekeeper appointed to guard the city and pursue criminals. The system was later adopted and instituted by those settling in the English colonies. The system is known to have been initially established in Boston, Massachusetts, in 1631 when the city formed a watch comprised of six watchmen, a constable, and several volunteers who patrolled the streets at night on a rotating schedule. In areas that were less populated, the governor appointed a **sheriff** (derived from the British term *shire reeves*), who was responsible for serving legal documents and collecting taxes. Generally, the watch was reactionary law enforcement responsible for reporting fires, pursuing and arresting criminals, and maintaining the order and public health conditions of the jurisdiction. During this early period, watchmen would use a wooden rattle that generated a distinct noise to alert citizens of danger and that served as a distress signal. The Dutch colony New Amsterdam (present-day New York) established a similar watch system several years later in 1652. As the population of the colonies grew and social problems affecting law enforcement became more common, the work of watchmen became more time consuming and as result attracted fewer volunteers and those willing to adhere to service mandates. In 1749, Philadelphia restructured the watch by appointing a warden, who was given the authority to hire watchmen as he deemed appropriate and necessary. This system transitioned the watch from a volunteer, **summons**-based system to a paid structure, with similar reforms made in other jurisdictions. *See also* PATROL.

WEAPON OF MASS DESTRUCTION (WMD). A weapon that is a nuclear, radiological, chemical, biological, or other destructive device designed to massacre or cause extensive harm to a significant number of persons and devastate both natural and human-made structures with a single strike. The weapons can also be used to adversely disrupt the biosphere, affecting both types of structures and indigenous populations. The term was first coined by Cosmo Gordon Lang, archbishop of Canterbury, in 1937 to describe the aerial **assault** designed with chemical explosives on Guernica, Spain. The WMD phrase was adopted by the United Nations General Assembly in 1946 in London as part of a resolution to eliminate atomic bombs from national armaments, from which the Atomic Energy Commission was established. The phrase was used in a lecture titled "Atomic Energy as an Atomic Problem" given by J. Robert Oppenheimer on 17 September 1947 to the State Department and Foreign Service. Since World War II, the term has been used to describe those weapons that have the capacity through their chemical, biological, radiological, or nuclear components to destroy persons, property, and their habitats on a wide scale. The WMD term has evolved over time, defined in part by its technical use and in part by its political implications.

WEATHER UNDERGROUND ORGANIZATION (WUO). A group formed in 1969 on the Ann Arbor campus of the University of Michigan which was comprised of radical, left-wing American militants. The group sought to inspire and lead a revolution based on a communist ideology in protest of the Vietnam War, racism, and American imperialism, among other claims, against the U.S. government using **terrorism**, violent strategies, and other aggressive tactics. The WUO emerged as a violent offshoot faction of the Students for a Democratic Society, who believed that peaceful protesting, community organizing, and elections were ineffective as a means to stimulate social and political change. The organization's name originated from the lyric "You don't need a weatherman to know which way the wind blows" from the Bob Dylan song "Subterranean Homesick Blues." The organization's first public demonstration, known as the Days of Rage, occurred on 8 October 1969, which was timed with the **trial** of the Chicago Seven—a group of seven men (originally eight) charged by the federal government with conspiracy and inciting to riot, among other charges, in opposition to the Vietnam War during the 1968 Democratic National Convention in Chicago, Illinois. Following the **murder** of Black Panthers Fred Hampton and Mark Clark in a December 1969 Chicago **police** raid, Bernardine Dohrn publicly declared war on behalf of the WUO in March 1970 against the U.S. government. Days later, three of its members were killed when a bomb they constructed inadvertently exploded in the basement of their Greenwich Village, Manhattan, New York, townhouse. The device was intended for a noncommissioned officers' dance at the Fort Dix, New Jersey, army base. Following the accidental detonation, the central figures and leadership, including Dohrn, Bill Ayers, and Kathy Boudin, went into hiding, and the organization became more commonly known as the Weather Underground. The years that followed included a bombing campaign targeting government buildings and bank institutions. In 1974, the manifesto *Prairie Fire* was released by the group, citing their extreme left position on issues. The group claimed responsibility for 25 bombings, which were preceded by evacuation warnings, including the 1970 bombings of a New York City police station and the Harvard Center for International Affairs, the 1971 bombing of the U.S. Capitol, the 1972 bombing of the Pentagon, and the 1975 bombing of the U.S. Department of State. The WUO also assisted with the escape of Timothy Leary from the California Men's Colony **prison**. The peace accord that the United States struck with Vietnam in 1973 resulted in a diminishing influence by the New Left, which the WUO sought to represent, and by the late 1970s and early 1980s, many of its radicals began to turn themselves over to authorities. Dohrn and Ayers pleaded guilty in 1980 to a **bail** offense stemming from a 1969 antiwar protest. The WUO was officially declared defunct in 1981 when Boudin and others were arrested for the shooting deaths of three men, including two police officers, during an armed robbery in Nanuet, New York. Boudin was released from prison in 2003 after she served a 22-year sentence.

WEED AND SEED. A 1991 U.S. Department of Justice program instituted in three pilot communities to prevent, control, and reduce **violent crime**, drug abuse, and **gang** activity. It is guided by four fundamental principles, including collaboration, coordination, community participation, and leveraging resources. The program employs a comprehensive strategy along a two-prong approach to "weed" out the detrimental elements in targeted neighborhoods, namely gang activity, **drug trafficking**, and violent crime, while "seeding" those same communities with economic revitalization and rebuilding. The program is a multiagency initiative that integrates the resources and expertise of federal, state, and local governments, private enterprise, social services, and community and other public sector groups to restore high-crime areas into safe and economically vibrant neighborhoods. The multilevel strategy revitalizes neighborhoods through enhancement of four components: (1) law enforcement; (2) community policing; (3) prevention, intervention, and treatment of crimes; and 4) neighborhood restoration.

WELFARE FRAUD. The illegal use of the government's welfare system by knowingly withholding or providing information to obtain the designated funding or a greater amount than what would otherwise be allocated. Prior to the 1900s, local governments together with charitable organizations took on the responsibility of providing the **indigent** with public assistance relief.

Programs and benefits varied considerably by state; however by the mid-1920s, 40 states had some type of public relief system in place for mothers with dependent children. As the economy expanded and urban areas became more concentrated, the need for public assistance exceeded the capacity of local governments and philanthropic efforts to manage, which was further exacerbated during the Great Depression of the 1930s. Unemployment overwhelmed local public assistance systems, and the federal government's involvement became a necessity. The welfare system in the United States was established by President Franklin D. Roosevelt with the 1935 Social Security Act (SSA). The SSA established the national welfare system and was designed to provide aid to various segments of the population, including the poor, the elderly, the disabled, and dependent children, by guaranteeing one-third of the total amount spent by states for assistance. Since the Great Depression, the coverage and regulations governing public assistance have been expanded through a variety of methods at the state and federal levels. In 1996, a Republican Congress passed, and President Bill Clinton signed, the Personal Responsibility and Work Opportunity Reconciliation Act, which decentralized the control and management of welfare back to the states. The Office of Management and Budget, the General Accounting Office, and other federal agencies monitored welfare payments that were improperly allocated, including cases of fraud accounting for approximately 10 percent of all disbursements. Some notable welfare fraud cases include a 1977 claim by Linda Taylor of Chicago, who used 14 aliases to unlawfully obtain $150,000 for medical assistance, cash assistance, and food stamps; a 1979 claim by Esther Johnson of California, who collected more than $240,000 for 60 nonexistent children; and the 1978 fraudulent claim by Arlene Otis of Cook County, Illinois, in which she received more than $150,000.

WESTERN PENITENTIARY. A low- to medium-risk correctional institution that most recently specialized in treating **inmates** with substance abuse issues. The **prison** was located on the bank of the Ohio River, comprising 21 acres of land, and was renamed the State Correctional Institution of Pittsburgh when the Pennsylvania legislature created the Bureau of Corrections in 1953 to administer the state prison system. The prison was originally constructed in 1826 when the commonwealth was being pressured by the Philadelphia Society of Alleviating the Miseries of Public Prisoners. The facility was called Western Penitentiary because the **Eastern Penitentiary** was being built in Philadelphia during the same time period. It was the first correctional facility located west of the Atlantic Plain, and its backdrop is believed to be the inspiration of Charles Dickens's *A Christmas Carol*, from when he visited the prison in 1842. It served as a major Civil War prison between 1863 and 1864, when it detained 118 Confederate soldiers of Morgan's Cavalry who were captured in Ohio. During this time, the prison was generally a self-sufficient facility, which manufactured a variety of goods including footwear, brooms, cigars, and knit items. The prison was also the primary facility that housed the rioters and demonstrators in protest of the G-20 Pittsburgh Summit in 2009. The facility was scheduled to close in 2017. *See also* BENTHAM, JEREMY (1748–1832); GHENT; PANOPTICON.

WETTERLING ACT. A U.S. law also known as the Jacob Wetterling Crimes against Children and Sexually Violent Offender Registration Act as part of the Federal **Violent Crime** Control and Law Enforcement Act of 1994, which required states to institute a registry of offenders convicted of sex crimes against children. The law is named after Jacob Erwin Wetterling, an 11-year-old boy who was abducted on 22 October 1989 in his hometown of St. Joseph, Minnesota, by Danny Heinrich while biking home from a convenience store with his younger brother and a friend. Wetterling's remains were found and his death confirmed almost 27 years later on 1 September 2016 in a pasture in close proximity to Paynesville, Minnesota. Authorities were led to the location by Heinrich, who was a suspect in an **assault** of another boy and confessed to **kidnapping** and killing Wetterling. The confession was part of a plea agreement in which prosecutors agreed not to charge him with the **murder**, and he was instead convicted on charges of child **pornography** and sentenced to 20 years in **prison**. As part of the plea deal, the state may also seek his **civil commitment** as a sexual predator when his prison term culminates. The Wetterling Act was amended by **Megan's Law** in 1996, which required law enforcement to release information about registered sex offenders for the purposes of protecting the public. The law was amended in 1998 when states were provided greater discretion in their protocols for contacting registered sex offenders to update their addresses and was amended again in 2006 with the **Adam Walsh** Child Protection and Safety Act.

WHIPPING POST. A post to which a person is fastened and whipped, flogged, or lashed as a form of **punishment** or discipline for having violated a law or code. **Corporal punishment** is one of the oldest and most prevalently used sanctions dating back to the late 1500s. The posts held criminals convicted of specified offenses, and the whipping was administered in a public setting to humiliate the subject and at the same time to entertain and serve as a deterrent to onlookers. The whipping post method was brought over to the United States during the early settlement days and was used as a preliminary penalty for lesser crimes over harsher punishments for more serious or repeated offenses, including **banishment**, cutting one's nose or ears, **branding**, or boring one's tongue. Among the offenses in which the offender was sentenced to the whipping post included **forgery**, **counterfeit-**

ing, Sabbath breaking, blasphemy, and witchcraft. Whipping posts were widely used by slave owners and **prison** guards in the United States during the period of slavery, on slaves who failed to satisfactorily perform assigned tasks or for breaching slave codes. The individual was tied by the wrists with a rope or cord facing the post so that the person's bare back was exposed. A beam, tree limb, or other makeshift column was used as the post, and the person was stretched along its surface area without raising the person's feet from the ground. An implement such as the whip, lash, switch, cat-o'-nine-tails, *sjambok*, or birch rod (legal terminology sometimes distinguished the type of beating instrument) was then used to lash the individual across their back, arms, head, and ears for a specified number of lashes. The subject was often whipped 39 times because the law allowed for no more than 40 lashes, but there are instances in which slaves were whipped 70 and 100 times for offenses. In most states, the punishment was repealed from statutes in lieu of imprisonment, but the criminal codes in a couple of states, namely Maryland and Delaware, allowed judges to sentence offenders of larceny, breaking and entering, and wife beating, among other crimes, to the whipping post into the 20th century. In Maryland, the punishment was last used by Cecil County in 1940 on a man who was convicted of beating his wife and sentenced to 60 days in jail and 10 lashes. Delaware last used the punishment in 1952 for a man convicted of wife beating. In 1963 another man was sentenced to the whipping post, but the sentence was commuted by the then governor of the state, Bert Carvel. The statute remained a part of the Delaware criminal code until 1972, when it became the last state in the nation to repeal the law. *See also* CRUEL AND UNUSUAL PUNISHMENT; EIGHTH AMENDMENT.

WHISTLE-BLOWER. A reference to an individual who reports a violation of a law, regulation, or organizational policy, or information on activity that is unethical or poses a threat to the public's interest, security, or welfare, to the authorities. The individual reporting the violation or activity is usually employed by the organization purportedly engaged in the wrongdoing. The alleged wrongdoing can be reported against a specific individual, such as sexual harassment, or the organization in general, such as unlawful pollution. Allegations can be reported internally to individual superiors within the organization or externally to third parties, including government authorities, media, or other interest groups. There are laws that protect whistle-blowers from **retaliation**; however, stipulations in the laws can leave the individual vulnerable to reprisals. The term dates to the 19th century describing **police** officers but was popularized by the U.S. civic activist Ralph Nader during the 1970s in an effort to supplant colloquial terms, such as "snitch," that had a negative connotation of reporting wrongdoing. The earliest known usage of the word was in 1883 in the *Janesville Gazette* when a story referred to a policeman blowing on his whistle to warn the public about a riot and other officers about an imminent danger or threat. Samuel Shaw, a naval officer in the U.S. Continental Navy in 1777, was instrumental in the passage of the first whistle-blower law enacted on 30 July 1778 by the Continental Congress when he and another officer, Richard Marven, reported Commodore Esek Hopkins for torturing British POWs. The law also stipulated that the United States would defend the two officers against a libel suit that was filed against them by Hopkins. Since the 1970s, numerous federal and state whistle-blower laws and protections have been passed, including statutes specific to violations of various guidelines regarding workplace safety and health, airlines, commercial motor carriers, consumer products, environmental issues, financial reforms, food safety, health insurance reforms, motor vehicle safety, nuclear facilities, pipelines, public transportation agencies, railroads, maritime concerns, and securities. These laws safeguard whistle-blowers from **retaliation** for filing a claim, refusing to participate in the violation, or assisting in the investigation, provided that the individual believes in good faith that the organization or its employees are violating a law or regulation or are involved in illicit activity, irrespective of whether wrongdoing is ultimately determined. *See also* SERPICO, FRANK (1936–).

WHITE ARYAN RESISTANCE (WAR). A **white supremacist**, neo-Nazi organization formerly known as the White American Resistance based in Warsaw, Indiana, founded in 1983 by a former **Ku Klux Klan** member, Thomas Linton Metzger. Metzger was initially associated with the White Brotherhood, which he headed through the mid-1970s. He later joined the Knights of the Ku Klux Klan in 1975, led by David Duke, where he rose to become the Grand Dragon of the California Realm. Between 1980 and 1982, he pursued a variety of electoral positions, but after losing the California Senate primary in 1982 he reorganized the White American Political Association—a group he founded that same year and dedicated to promoting "pro-white" candidates—as the WAR. The organization, which uses the slogan "White Revolution is the Only Solution," was generally developed from a loose-knit group of skinheads who gained notoriety from their appearances in the media, including talk shows and its local-access cable television show, *Race and Reason*. In 1990, Metzger declared bankruptcy from a **Southern Poverty Law Center** civil suit involving the **murder** of a black graduate student. On 13 November 1988, three white supremacists associated with WAR beat to death an Ethiopian man, Mulugeta Seraw, during a street confrontation. The **jury** found Metzger, among others, and WAR culpable in Seraw's death and awarded Seraw's family $12.5 million in damages. Since Metzger's bankruptcy, WAR has been used as a hate symbol, promulgating its propaganda through Metzger's website, broadcasts, hotline, and publication, *The Insurgent*. Metzger now advocates a "lone wolf" strategy for white supremacists as opposed to an organized resistance effort built around a membership structure. Some **prison inmates**, particularly those housed in western states, have been known to use the name, for Warskins, but not necessarily with knowledge of Metzger's affiliation or founding of the original group. *See also* WHITE SUPREMACY.

WHITE-COLLAR CRIME. A category of crime coined in 1939 by **Edwin Sutherland** to describe violations of law committed by persons of respectability and high socioeconomic status in the course of their employment, business, or profession. Sutherland sought to integrate the disciplines of economics and sociology, illustrating the relationship between business methods and crime. The earliest documented white-collar crime law dates to the 15th century in England. The law was known as the Carrier's Case and was enacted in response to an individual who was entrusted to transport wool and attempted to pilfer some of it for himself. The crimes are characterized by deception, concealment, and a violation of trust that does not necessarily rely on the intimidation, threat, or **use of force** that is more commonly experienced in **violent crime**. There are, however, types of white-collar crime that can incorporate **violence**, such as blackmail wherein money or other consideration is demanded under the threat that the person will be harmed. Offenders are typically business and government professionals whose primary motivation in committing the crime is monetary gain through such means as to gain or circumvent the payment of monies, property, or service or to procure a financial advantage. Following the Industrial Revolution when companies in Western societies became more prominent and powerful and monopolistic practices had a greater impact on the public, the government began to intervene. In 1890, the U.S. Congress enacted the Sherman Antitrust Act, which made monopolies illegal. The Sherman Act was later strengthened in 1914 by the Clayton Antitrust Act, which specified monopolistic activity as unlawful. White-collar crime has come to encompass a wide spectrum of crimes, but it most commonly includes various types of fraud and **identity theft**, **copyright infringement**, insider trading, **bribery**, embezzlement, **tax evasion**, and **money laundering**. The **FBI** classifies the array of offenses into four categories, including fraud, **counterfeiting/forgery**, embezzlement, and miscellaneous. Although the crimes are not violent in nature, scams and frauds can be detrimental to the economy, can bankrupt a company, and can cost investors and other affected persons considerable sums of money—in some cases billions of dollars or entire life savings accounts. Among the agencies responsible for investigating and prosecuting white-collar crimes are the FBI, the Internal Revenue Service, the U.S. Postal Inspection Service, the Securities and Exchange Commission, the Commodity Futures Trading Commission, and the Treasury Department's Financial Crimes Enforcement Network. **Punishment** for those convicted of white-collar crimes in the United States include a range of sanctions, such as imprisonment, **fines**, **restitu-**

tion, community service, and **probation**, but since the turn of the century as new scandals and fraudulent activities have emerged, legislation has been enacted to increase penalties. The Sarbanes-Oxley Act of 2002, signed by President George W. Bush, was in response to the corporate and accounting scandals enacted by several corporations including Enron, Tyco International, Peregrine Systems, and WorldCom.

WHITE SLAVERY. Referred to as the white slave traffic or trade, it historically referred to the enslavement of Europeans, but the denotation of the term has changed over time. The term originally emerged during the 17th and 18th centuries as a pejorative reference to Irish laborers. **Evidence** shows that Irish laborers did not endure the kind of hereditary slavery, that was based on race in colonial America. Large bands of Irish persons immigrated to the British colonies of North America as indentured servants, but the servitude was not hereditary, was typically subject to a contracted period, and, along with other stipulations, they were not treated as chattel slavery. Over the past century, white slavery has come to signify the **kidnapping** and human trafficking of women who are exploited and compelled into lives of **prostitution**. In 1910, the U.S. Congress enacted the White-Slave Traffic Act, also known as the **Mann Act**, named after Illinois representative James R. Mann, who sponsored the law. The law made it a felony to transport women across state borders for any immoral purpose to impede prostitution and sexual trafficking. The legislation was in large part a response to the urbanization and technological advancements at the turn of the century, which for the first time in American history provided women with independence from the control of their fathers and brothers.

WHITE SUPREMACY. Referred to as white supremacism and based on the actions, values, and beliefs of a racist and political ideology dating back to the 17th century in which white Europeans are believed to be superior and therefore should politically, economically, and socially rule nonwhite people. White supremacist ideology opposes all persons of color and Jews and is grounded on pseudoscience from which a philosophical, ethical, economic, scientific, religious, and political system of thinking is used to perpetuate the domination of those identified as nonwhite. The goal is the transfer of wealth and power and the securing of resources, opportunities, and privileges to the white in-group at the expense of the nonwhite out-group. White supremacist activism has included the elimination of nonwhite populations, particularly through violent means, preventing cross-racial marriage, and maintaining racial segregation. Many U.S. states banned interracial marriage until 1967, when these laws were invalidated by the **U.S. Supreme Court**'s holding in *Loving v. Virginia*, 388 U.S. 1 (1987). The term is also used in critical race theory, which is used to delineate the structural advantages that white people have over other ethnic groups. In modern usage, the phrase is used to describe individuals and groups who espouse ultranationalist, racist, or fascist doctrines. The transatlantic slave trade set the course for what would be a critical event in distinguishing the biological differences between white Europeans and Africans. White supremacy achieved the height of its popularity during the period of European colonial expansion to the Western Hemisphere, Africa, and Asia beginning in the late 1800s through the first half of the 20th century. During the 17th century, white and black indentured servants in Virginia came together to revolt against white elitists. The elitists eventually defeated the rebellion and instituted a racial classification system in which white servants were freed upon the completion of their service, while blacks were made into a permanent slave class. The Naturalization Act of 1790 limited U.S. citizenship to whites only, and it was not until the Immigration and Nationality Act of 1965 that the demographic mix of persons in the United States was altered by opening up immigration to persons from areas of the world other than Northern Europe. During the era of slavery in the United States, followed by Jim Crow segregation laws, white supremacism had broad political support, particularly in the South; consequently, white supremacist ideology persisted through the end of the American Civil War and the Reconstruction era. Ethnic groups that were considered white had expanded considerably in the United States, and it was not until well into the 20th century that Italians and Arabs were included among the group identified as white. The Statement by Experts on Problems of Race, sponsored and published by the United Nations in the early 1950s, together with desegregation, decolonization, and the mapping of the human genome, which demonstrated that there are few genetic differences between races, aided counterarguments to white supremacy. Several laws, including the **Civil Rights** Act of 1964, the Voting Rights Act of 1965, and the U.S. Supreme Court's holding in *Brown v. Board of Education of Topeka*, 347 U.S. 483 (1954), were subsequently enacted to eliminate the racial divide. The prevalence of white supremacy declined during the second half of the 20th century, but there was a white supremacist "white power" movement in response to the "black power" movement and U.S. government policy on affirmative action, school busing, and measures against housing **discrimination**. White supremacists in the United States were unable to defend the laws that ensured white domination, and they eventually lost most of their support. The internet in its facility to exchange documents and enable supporters over vast geographic territories is now used as a vehicle by hate groups and citizen militias to invoke religious and nationalist mythology to rally their adherents against the increased power of groups identified as nonwhite. *See also* KU KLUX KLAN (KKK); WHITE ARYAN RESISTANCE (WAR).

WHITE WIDOW. A reference to Samantha Louise Lewthwaite, born 5 December 1983, who is considered to be among the most wanted persons linked to **terrorism** in the Western world. She is an alleged member of the Somalia-based Islamic militant group **Al-Shabaab**. Originally from Aylesbury, England, she was pursuing a degree in politics and religion at the School of Oriental and African Studies, University of London, before dropping out in 2002 and marrying Abdullah Shaheed Jamal, also known as Germaine Lindsay. The media nicknamed Lewthwaite the "white widow" because of her race, the death of her first husband, and to juxtapose her to Chechen female suicide bombers, who are dubbed "black widows." She had two children with Lindsay. Lindsay was determined to be one of four suicide bombers who killed more than 400 people in the 7 July 2005 London bombings. Soon after the attack, Lewthwaite fled her home in Aylesbury, Buckinghamshire, eventually making her way to South Africa, where she married her second husband, Fahmi Jamal Salim, with whom she had two more children. Lewthwaite, who has used the alias Natalie Faye Webb, is currently being sought by British and U.S. intelligence agencies and has been a fugitive of Kenya since 2011 on charges of possession of explosives and conspiring to bomb tourist resorts. She is also the subject of an Interpol "red notice," meaning that they seek the location and arrest of Lewthwaite because she is wanted by a judicial jurisdiction or an international tribunal with a view to her **extradition**. She has been implicated in several terror attacks, including the 2012 Mombasa bar attack and the 2015 Garissa University College massacre. In 2014, she was rumored to have been killed; however those accounts were later rejected. Lewthwaite is believed to be an **Al-Qaeda** recruiter and has been sheltered in the Arabian Peninsula and Lower Shebelle in southern Somalia where she trains contingents of female jihadists to carry out suicide attacks.

WHITMAN, CHARLES JOSEPH (1941–1966). Known as the "Texas Tower Sniper," Whitman was a former U.S. Marine marksman who randomly targeted and killed 14 people while wounding another 31 from the clock tower at the University of Texas at Austin on 1 August 1966. A 15th person would die in 2001 due to injuries sustained in the shooting. The rampage was ended by Allen Crum, a university co-op employee, and Austin policemen, Ramiro Martinez, Houston McCoy, and Jerry Day, who responded to the tower where Whitman was subsequently shot and killed by Martinez and McCoy. Whitman was born in Lake Worth, Florida, and as a child was known to be remarkably intelligent. He was an accomplished pianist and Eagle Scout at 12 years of age. He enlisted in the marines after graduating from high school in 1959 and completed an 18-month tour of duty before being approved to enroll in the University of Texas to major in mechanical engineering. While at the university he met his wife, Kathryn Leissner, who was studying education, and they were married in 1962. In 1963, Whitman was required to go back onto active duty in the marines to complete his five-year enlistment because of his poor academic performance, and he was honorably discharged in 1965. He returned to the University of Texas and changed his major to architecture. In 1966, Whitman consulted a university therapist to complain about severe headaches he was experiencing and concerns he had regarding his mental health and violent impulses. The psychiatrist's notes following Whitman's visit revealed that he spoke to him about going to the tower with a rifle to shoot people. That same year, Whitman's mother eventually left his father following years of **domestic violence** and relocated to Austin. On the evening of 31 July 1966, Whitman went to his mother's apartment, where he stabbed and shot her. He then returned home and stabbed his wife to death while she slept. The next day he proceeded to the 307-foot tower at the university armed with assorted weapons, ammunition, and supplies. He initially killed the receptionist and two tourists in the tower and then made his way up to the 28th-floor observation deck, where, over the course of 93 minutes, he indiscriminately shot people on the ground. Prior to committing the massacre, he left a series of writings, and in one of his notes, he requested that his brain be examined following his death to determine if there was a physical cause to his mental illness. A **police** autopsy revealed that he had a brain tumor, but there was disagreement among medical experts whether this affected Whitman's behavior. The tower was subsequently closed to the public in 1975 following a string of suicides at the site and was reopened in a 1999 ceremony after iron barriers were installed to deter suicides. *See also* MASS MURDER; VIOLENCE.

WHORL. Circle-like or spiral pattern segment of a human **fingerprint** shaped as tiny whirlpools. There are four groups of whorl patterns, including plain (a series of concentric circles), central pocket loop (a loop with a whorl at the end), double loop (two loops that create an S-like pattern), and accidental loop (an irregular-shaped whorl). The whorl, loop, and arch are the three basic fingerprint patterns that make up the Henry Classification System. Whorls constitute approximately 35 percent of all fingerprints, loops comprise an estimated 60 percent, and arches make up 5 percent. The Henry system, which uses the physiological characteristics of fingerprints to sort them, was developed between 1896 and 1925 by Sir Edward Henry, an inspector general of the Bengal **Police** in India, and his two assistants, Hem Chandra Bose and Azizul Haque. Sir Henry devised the system after corresponding with Sir Francis Galton, the author of *Finger Prints*, published in 1892, which outlined three primary fingerprint patterns—whorls, loops, and arches. The Henry system expanded upon Sir Galton's patterns and was subsequently used to investigate and identify criminal suspects in British India. The system assigns a numerical value to fingers that contain a whorl pattern and is tabulated as a fraction ranging between 1/1 (indicating no whorl patterns) to 32/32 (meaning all fingers have whorl patterns). The Henry system was later implemented in most English-speaking countries, but it has more recently been replaced by ridge flow classification methods. *See also* BERTILLION, ALPHONSE (1853–1914).

WICKERSHAM COMMISSION. A federal commission established on 20 May 1929 by U.S. president Herbert Hoover to assess the criminal justice system. The committee was charged with reviewing several aspects of criminal justice, but the most notable task was to evaluate **Prohibition**, as it existed under the Eighteenth Amendment and the **Volstead Act**, including the knowledge, training, and investigation of **police** agencies and to make public policy recommendations. The commission was formally known as the National Commission on Law Observance and Enforcement and was established in recognition of the unintended consequences that Prohibition was having in advancing the growth of **bootlegging** and **organized crime** in the country, particularly as the Chicago gang wars were coming to a head in 1929. It was comprised of an 11-member group including Henry W. Anderson, Newton D. Baker, Ada Comstock, William Irwin Grubb, William S. Kenyon, Monte M. Lemann, Frank J. Loesch, Kenneth Mackintosh, Paul John McCormick, and Roscoe Pound, dean of Harvard Law School. George W. Wickersham, the former **attorney general** of President Taft's administration, chaired the group. The prominent criminologist August Vollmer was responsible for authoring portions of the final report. The commission's report, published in 14 volumes during 1930 and 1931, is considered the first federal study of the U.S. criminal justice system. Its conclusions were generally critical of policing organizations, operational methods, and **interrogation** tactics.

WIFE BEATING. A term formerly used to describe the physical violence committed by a husband on his wife. Other terms, including *wife abuse* and *wife battering*, were also used to define **domestic violence**. With the exception of the Body of Liberties of the Massachusetts Bay of 1641, wife beating was not a crime under most legal systems until the mid-1800s. The shift in public opinion during the latter part of the 19th century prompted legislative change. In 1850, Tennessee became the first state that prohibited wife beating, and by 1870, most U.S. courts ruled against a husband's authority and right to physically **assault** his wife. At the turn of the 20th century, arrests were still rare, but it was not uncommon for **police** to intervene in domestic violence incidents. By 1920, wife beating was illegal throughout the nation. The terms are no longer used to denote domestic violence because it did not encompass all types of offenders, including unmarried partners, female perpetrators, and same-sex relationships, as well as other aspects of the abuse that are not physical in nature. The data, however, continues to show that the majority of domestic violence victims are female, who are often economically or socially dependent upon an abusive partner. Domestic violence has been more broadly defined to include physical, sexual, emotional, and economic acts of **violence** that are committed by an intimate partner or family member. Since the 1980s, there has been more public awareness in addressing domestic violence, and criminal justice systems have instituted measures to adjudicate offenders quickly and severely while at the same time affording victims with support services. *See also* VIOLENCE AGAINST WOMEN ACT (VAWA).

WILDLIFE CRIME. Referred to as illegal wildlife trade or poaching that involves the illicit hunting, capturing, trading, exploitation, or consumption of nondomesticated, wild animals that are extracted from their natural habitats or bred in a controlled environment for the primary purpose of commercial enterprise. Violations include hunting and fishing without a license; baiting; use of explosives or other devices, tactics, or weapons to kill or capture animals; or taking wildlife from land that is protected or tagged for research. In some instances, the species may be listed as endangered by the International Union for Conservation of Nature, a body established in 1948 that assesses the worldwide conservation status of species. It can also relate to the illegal extraction or development of wild plants from their natural environment. The crimes involve the trafficking of wildlife, which can be dead or alive and are sought after for a variety of purposes. Research indicates that while wildlife crime is frequently committed for commercial intentions, such as the trading of skin and bone products, individuals also poach for consumption, sport, medicinal, religious, or ceremonial reasons, or because they generally disagree with the legal authority that prohibits their right to hunt. The earliest instances of poaching were recorded during the 1700s in Europe when impoverished groups consumed the meat as a means of survival. Almost two centuries later, peasant farmers of the continent were permitted to hunt small game exclusive to their property. In some instances, the illegal hunting of wildlife has resulted in armed conflicts, as was the case during the joint U.S.-British Bering Sea Anti-Poaching Operations of 1891, which was fought over the hunting of seals. In 1900, U.S. president William McKinley signed the Lacey Act, a conservation law that prohibited the sale, possession, or transportation of wildlife, fish, and plants and instituted civil and criminal penalties for violations of the act.

WILLIAMS, WAYNE BERTRAM (1958–). An American **serial killer** convicted in 1981 of killing two adult men, 27-year-old Nathaniel Cater and 29-year-old Jimmy Ray Payne, and who is the suspected killer in the "Atlanta Child Murders," which included the **murder** of 29 African American children and youth in the Atlanta, Georgia, area. On 22 May 1981, **police** were staking out 14 bridges traversing the Chattahoochee River, a site where several bodies of victims had been discovered. During the stakeout at one of the crossings, officers heard a loud splash at approximately 3:00 a.m. suggesting that something had been thrown from the bridge into the river. Williams's vehicle was the first automobile to exit the bridge following the splash, and when police stopped to question him, he stated that he was on his way to a music audition for a singer named Cheryl Johnson. The name and contact information he provided of the singer were later proven to be fictitious. Two days later, Cater's body was discovered in the river with the cause of death determined to be asphyxia and that he had not been in the river for more than 36 to 48 hours. Williams was subsequently arrested on 21 June 1981 and failed multiple **polygraph** tests when police conjectured that the splash was that of Cater's body being thrown from the bridge by Williams. Hairs and fibers obtained from another victim were found to be consistent with those retrieved from Williams's vehicle, residence, and dog. The **jury** convicted Williams on 27 February 1982 in the murder of Cater and Payne based on matching fibers and eyewitness accounts linking him to the crimes. He was sentenced to two consecutive life terms and is currently housed at the Hancock State **Prison** in Georgia. *See also* EYEWITNESS TESTIMONY; FORENSICS.

WILSON, JAMES QUINN (1931–2012). A political scientist, criminologist, and public administration expert who served as a professor at the University of California, Los Angeles; Harvard University; Pepperdine University; and Boston College and is credited with making significant contributions to the understanding of urban politics, policing and crime, political organizations, bureaucracy, and culture. From 1961 to 1987, he was the Shattuck Professor of Government at Harvard University. From 1987 to 1997, he was the James Collins Professor of Management and Public Policy at the UCLA Anderson School of Management. Between 1998 and 2009, he was the Ronald Reagan Professor of Public Policy at Pepperdine University's School of Public Policy. From 2009 until his death in 2012, he served as distinguished scholar in the Department of Political Science and senior fellow at the Clough Center for the Study of Constitutional Democracy at Boston College. He was born in Denver, Colorado, and raised in Long Beach, California. In 1952, he received a B.A. in political science from the University of Redlands and was the national debate champion in 1951 and 1952. Following graduation, he served in the U.S. Navy between 1952 and

1955. He subsequently earned an M.A. and Ph.D. in political science from the University of Chicago (Illinois) in 1957 and 1959, respectively. His dissertation analyzed the political behavior of African Americans in Chicago, which was later the basis of his first book, *Negro Politics: The Search for Leadership* (1960). Wilson authored, coauthored, or edited more than two dozen books, including *Thinking about Crime* (1975), *Crime and Human Nature* (1985), *Bureaucracy* (1989), *The Moral Sense* (1993), and *American Government: Institutions and Policies*, which had more than a dozen editions published and is a widely used textbook on American government and politics. In 1982, he coauthored an article with George L. Kelling in the *Atlantic Monthly* introducing the **"broken windows" theory**. The theory's policing strategy gained national attention and was applied by **police** departments in many cities, including New York and Los Angeles, California. The theory proposed that when police departments focus their efforts on the maintenance of order and quality-of-life crimes, such as drug dealing in the open public, **vandalism**, and turnstile jumping, rather than the periodic and random pursuit of more serious criminals such as rapists, murderers, and carjackers, the rate of more serious crime decreases. The crime reduction program was a cornerstone strategy during the 1990s, particularly in New York and Los Angeles, which saw a significant reduction in felonies following its application. Wilson was critical of positivist thought, believing instead that crime could be more effectively controlled by reducing criminal opportunities and selectively incapacitating recidivists. He was a former president of the American Political Science Association and served as a former chairman of the White House Task Force on Crime (1966) and the National Advisory Commission on Drug Abuse Prevention (1972–1973). Wilson also served as the chairman of the Council of Academic Advisors of the American Enterprise Institute. In 2003, President George W. Bush awarded him the nation's highest civilian award, the Presidential Medal of Freedom.

WIRETAP. A reference to the act of intercepting and recording telephone or telegraph transmissions for the purposes of gathering information or **evidence** to criminally prosecute a party. Wiretapping initially became a concern following the invention of the telegraph in 1837. Wiretapping had become more widespread by the end of the 19th century when the telephone was invented in 1876. As corporate **espionage** and private wiretapping became more prevalent, many state courts in the United States began enacting legislation prohibiting the unauthorized listening of communications made through these devices. Since that time, it is generally illegal for unauthorized individuals to record telephone conversations including personal phone calls if the other person is unaware that they are being recorded. U.S. law enforcement began using wiretapping as an investigative tool during the 1890s. In 1928, during the height of the **Prohibition** era, the **U.S. Supreme Court**

held to allow government officials and law enforcement to wiretap to enforce the law pursuant to the National Prohibition Act. Despite its allowance, the practice of obtaining evidence through wiretapping during criminal investigations was banned by federal law enforcement and the Justice Department. In the case of a Seattle **bootlegger**, Roy Olmstead, who was convicted on wiretap evidence drawn from his home, the court upheld his conviction, stating that eavesdropping was not a physical invasion of his privacy and therefore did not violate his **Fourth Amendment** rights. In 1934, Congress passed the Communications Act, the first federal wiretapping law, and over the course of the next 34 years, wiretapping remained illegal. Other aspects of law limited wiretapping to other circumstances including the length of time the conversation could be recorded. Law enforcement's authority was further mitigated during the 1960s and 1970s when **police** agencies were required to obtain a court order to intercept and listen in on private conversations. In another landmark case, ***Katz v. United States*, 389 U.S. 347 (1967)**, the court ruled that devices intercepting private conversations violated an individual's Fourth Amendment rights irrespective of where the wiretapping occurs if the person had a reasonable expectation of privacy. In 1968, Congress used the court's decision in the Katz case and its ruling in *Berger v. New York*, 388 U.S. 41 (1967), to ensure the constitutionality of the overarching federal laws regarding wiretapping to enact the **Omnibus Crime Control and Safe Streets Act of 1968, Pub. L. No. 90-351, 82 Stat. 197**. In 1986, the United States enacted the Electronic Communications Privacy Act, which protects emails, pagers, and mobile phone calls from being wiretapped because those devices were not shielded by the same laws as traditional telephones. As technologies and data encryption capabilities have advanced, wiretapping has kept pace with these latest developments, and therefore laws have continued to evolve along these measures.

***WITHERSPOON V. ILLINOIS*, 391 U.S. 510 (1968).** A **U.S. Supreme Court** case where the Court ruled that an Illinois law that provided the state with an unlimited number of challenges for cause for jurors who expressed an objection against the **death penalty** was unconstitutional because it violated the defendant's rights guaranteed by the Sixth and **Fourteenth Amendments**. The court reasoned that the statute allowed the state to assemble a panel that was biased in favor of the prosecution, thereby affecting the impartiality of the **jury** to which the defendant is entitled. The petitioner in the case, William C. Witherspoon, was convicted by an Illinois jury of **murder** in 1960 and sentenced to death. During the 1960s and 1970s, the U.S. Supreme Court was reviewing many issues involving the constitutionality of the death penalty, and the Witherspoon case was but one of them. Witherspoon contested the constitutionality of his conviction and sentence when the state dismissed all prospective jurors ahead of the **trial** who expressed not only a conscientious and religious objection toward **capital punishment** but also all those who opposed the death penalty in principle. The wide latitude in which the statute provided for the prosecution enabled them to eliminate half of the venire and, according to the court, allowed them to structure a jury panel that was exceptionally more willing to condemn the defendant to death. The petitioner's appeals were rejected by the Illinois courts before the U.S. Supreme Court decided to hear the case. The issue in the case was whether the U.S. Constitution allowed the state to execute a person if that person was sentenced to death by a jury that was assembled in a manner that was more likely to find the defendant guilty of the crime and sentence him to death. The Court ultimately reversed the lower courts' decisions and ruled that the state breached the neutrality divide by allowing the prosecution to intentionally structure a panel to impose a death sentence by dismissing all jurors who generally objected to capital **punishment**. The court found that unless the juror unequivocally affirms that he would vote against capital punishment, notwithstanding the facts of the case, the state cannot assume that this will be the juror's position at the time of sentencing. *See also* DEATH-QUALIFIED JURY.

WITNESS. An individual who has or is believed to have inculpatory or exculpatory **evidence** through documentation, observation or other sensory input, experience, specialized knowledge, or other information regarding the commission of a crime that may incriminate or exonerate a person through their testimony of the event or matter of interest. Witnesses may testify voluntarily or can be compelled to provide testimony in a proceeding by a subpoena issued by a judge or attorney. Witnesses are required to take an oath to tell the truth under penalty of **perjury** and can be requested to testify by the prosecution or defense. The Judiciary Act of 1789 established the responsibility of material witnesses to appear and testify in U.S. courts and regulated their examination in proceedings. Until 1948, when the U.S. Congress repealed the provisions granting the authority to arrest **material witnesses**, the act codified the authorization to imprison those witnesses who failed to adhere to their duty. The confrontation clause of the Sixth Amendment of the U.S. Constitution guarantees the accused the right to confront and cross-examine witnesses brought against them in a criminal matter. In the **U.S. Supreme Court** case *Mattox v. United States*, 156 U.S. 237 (1895), the court articulated three purposes of the confrontation clause regarding witnesses, including (1) to ensure that witnesses would testify under oath and by this process understand and appreciate the serious nature of the criminal justice process, (2) to allow the defendants to cross-examine those who testify against them; and (3) to allow jurors to assess the credibility of the witness's testimony. There are three general types of witnesses, including lay witnesses (those who have or are believed to have a personal account of the matter), **expert witnesses** (those with specialized knowledge or experience in a particular topic relevant to the matter), and character witnesses (those who know or were familiar with the victim, defendant, or other people implicated in the matter and can attest to their reputation and qualities).

WITNESS IDENTIFICATION. A legal term referring to the testimonial **evidence** provided by an individual who has or is believed to have witnessed the crime under investigation. **Witness** identification has traditionally been used in court as the most significant and reliable form in establishing the guilt of a defendant. Recent studies, however, have shown that individual memories and perceptions can be manipulated and subject to bias, leading to inaccurate identification and wrong convictions. In 1907, Hugo Munsterberg's book *On the Witness Stand* was one of the first texts in which the reliability of witness identification was called into question. This was followed by the 1932 book *Convicting the Innocent*, authored by Edwin Borchard, who found that misidentification was the leading cause of **wrongful convictions**. Since the 1967 case *United States v. Wade*, 388 U.S. 218 (1967), the court has recognized and addressed the inherent flaws with **eyewitness testimony**, which often represents the most compelling **evidence** to jurors when determining guilt. Several factors have been identified to affect the accuracy of eyewitness identifications, including witness stress at the time of the incident or during the process of identifying the suspect; the presence or use of a weapon during the commission of the crime; perpetrator disguise or lack of distinguishing marks, characteristics, or tattoos; environmental factors; the health and physical condition of a witness; cross-**racial disparity** between the witness and suspect; witness confidence level in identifying the suspect; number of perpetrators present at the scene of the crime; transference; the influence of other eyewitness testimony; and identification practices and processes employed by law enforcement. *See also* DISPARITY; INNOCENCE PROJECT; TRIAL.

WITNESS PROTECTION PROGRAM. A U.S. federal government program referred to as the **Witness** Security Program (WITSEC) established in 1970 as a part of the **Organized Crime** Control Act. The Title V section of the law, Protected Facilities for Housing Government Witnesses, outlines the fundamental practices of the program and provides the **attorney general** with the autonomy to protect witnesses in accordance with the issues and circumstances of individual cases. WITSEC is administered by the U.S. Department of Justice and is operated by the U.S. **Marshals** Service to protect the health, safety, and welfare of witnesses who testify against criminals in federal cases before, during, and after a **trial**. Grants are also provided by the federal government to individual states to enable them to develop similar programs and services. Witnesses and their families are provided new identities and are relocated to distant communities where they can commence a new and different life without the fear of being killed as a result of their testimony against drug traffickers, terrorists, **organized crime** members, and other major criminals. Historically, criminal justice agencies have used four approaches to protect witnesses, including requesting that defendants' **bail** be denied or set considerably high so that they are detained during criminal proceedings, aggressively prosecuting those who attempt to intimidate witnesses, instituting a detailed process in managing witnesses, and enhancing the basic services provided to witnesses. WITSEC evolved during the early 1960s when Attorney General Robert F. Kennedy led the U.S. Department of Justice efforts to prosecute organized crime cases. Gerald Shur, the **United States attorney** in charge of the Intelligence and Special Services Unit of the Organized Crime and Racketeering Section of the Department of Justice, was the principal creator of the **Witness Protection Program** as a result of his intention to protect witnesses. The program was later incorporated into a crime bill drafted by Senator John L. McClellan of Arkansas in 1969. Shur would go on to conceive of the program being administered by the U.S. Marshals Service, which would oversee the operational logistics and expenses of protecting witnesses, with the **Federal Bureau of Prisons** having responsibility of safeguarding incarcerated witnesses. The act was later amended in 1984 as part of the **Comprehensive Crime Control Act of 1984** to include the protection of persons associated with the witness including relatives and dependents and to provide the framework for which government attorneys could apply for witness protection services. WITSEC provides 24-hour witness protection while in high-risk environments, such as during court and testimonial proceedings; financial assistance for housing; living expenses; and health care, job training, and employment. *See also* MARSHAL; RACKETEER INFLUENCED CORRUPT ORGANIZATION (RICO); TERRORISM.

WOLFGANG, MARVIN EUGENE (1924–1998). An American sociologist and pioneer in the field of **criminology**, who explored criminal behavior from an interdisciplinary perspective. His breakthroughs and approach to studying crime led the *British Journal of Criminology* to acknowledge him as "the most influential criminologist in the English-speaking world." Following his service in World War II, where he fought in the Battle of Monte Casino, he earned his bachelor's degree from Dickinson College (Pennsylvania) and went on to complete his graduate studies at the University of Pennsylvania, where he earned an M.A. (1950) and Ph.D. (1955) in sociology/criminology. He began teaching at the University of Pennsylvania in 1950 and remained a professor there until his death in 1998. During his career, he was a past president of the American Academy of Political and Social Science and was conferred numerous awards including the Hans Von Hentig Award, the **Edwin Sutherland** Award, and the **Beccaria** Gold Medal. Wolfgang was appointed to many national commissions, including the presidential Commission on the Causes and Prevention of **Violence**, where he served as research director in 1968. In the 1972 **U.S. Supreme Court** landmark case ***Furman v. Georgia*, 408 U.S. 238 (1972)**, his finding that **capital punishment** was disproportionately applied to African American, young, or **indigent** offenders was cited in the court's ruling that the **death penalty** was unconstitutional. He authored more than 30 books and 150 articles. His major works included *Patterns in Criminal Homicide* (1958), a landmark analysis of **homicide** and the relation between offenders and their victims; *The Subculture of Violence: Towards an Integrated Theory in Criminology* (1967), coauthored with **Franco Ferracuti**, which portrayed how the theme of violence is central and more highly valued than conventional behavior among some subcultures and thus precipitates a higher rate of crime among these circles; and *Delinquency in a Birth Cohort* (1972), a collaboration with **Thorsten Sellin** and Robert Figlio, which examined two male birth cohorts from Philadelphia in 1945 and 1963. In this study, the researchers found that 6 percent of the cohort, who were later known as the "chronic 6 percent," accounted for 54 percent of all delinquency and criminal activity. At the time of his death, Wolfgang was conducting a 10-year **longitudinal study** examining **juvenile delinquency** in China.

WOOTTON, BARBARA (1897–1988). A social scientist, criminologist, and professor who featured widely in the public life of Britain, having campaigned for the parliamentary vote for women, equal pay, **abortion** rights, abolition of **capital punishment**, criminal justice reform, and offender rehabilitation, among other social equality and policy issues. She was one of the first four life peers appointed under the 1958 Life Peerages Act and honored with the title Baroness Wootton of Abinger. Wootton was born Barbara Frances Adam in Cambridge, changing her name in 1917 when she married an army officer, John Wootton, who was killed while serving in World War I only weeks following their nuptials. The premature deaths of her father, brother, and then husband would change the course of her life and alter her decision from studying the classics to social problems. She graduated from Girton College and in 1919, after refusing to accept a war widow's pension, was awarded a research scholarship at the London School of Economics. She was named director of studies in economics at Girton College where she served between 1920 and 1922. She was a past president of the British Sociological Association and was one of the first women to sit in the House of Lords. In 1944, she was appointed reader in social studies at Bedford College and in 1948 was promoted to professor at the University of London. Between 1952 and 1957, she was named Nuffield Research Fellow of Bedford College at the University of London. Wootton authored several books, including *Lament for Economics* (1938); *End Social Inequality* (1941); *Social Science and Social Pathology* (1959), which was an exploration into what she termed "the criminal personality"; *In a World I Never Made: Autobiographical Reflections* (1967); and *Crime and Penal Policy: Reflections on Fifty Years' Experience* (1978). One of her more controversial books, *Crime and the Criminal Law* (1964), was based on the premise that crime be regarded as a strict liability action so that the state need not demonstrate the intent or recklessness of the defendant. *See also* CRIMINOLOGY.

WORKHOUSE. Referred to as a poorhouse, which was originally maintained by local parishes in England, Wales, and Ireland housing the **indigent**, who were required to work on modest-size farms or assigned other parish jobs within the community. With the passage of the Poor Law, county and municipal governments would eventually oversee the administration of the facilities. During the mid-16th century, while being indigent was not a crime, it was considered dishonorable, and workhouses were built to resemble penal camps, where **inmates** were assigned manual labor and were subjected to physical **punishment**. In some instances, entire families were housed in the facilities, with males and females separated and prohibited from communicating with each other. In the United States, workhouses boarding the poor were common during the 19th century and early part of the 20th century and sometimes adjoined **prison** farms. The purpose of penal labor was punitive and at times productive, such as to secure labor or in providing convicts with an occupation during their prison term. Prison labor was used extensively throughout the South after the Civil War when state governments unable to afford the penitentiaries would lease convicts to private organizations. The practice of leasing convicts to private enterprises was ended during the Progressive era of the 20th century. Poorhouses declined substantially after 1935, when Social Security took effect, and many closed entirely by 1950. In 1934, following the burgeoning instability in prisons, officials petitioned the government to create work programs for inmates. The lobbying efforts led to the creation of the government-owned corporation Federal Prison Industries, which would use penal labor from the **Federal Bureau of Prisons** to produce goods and provide services. At the time, the goods and services were limited to federal government agencies and could not be used for commercial purposes. In 1979 when Congress approved the Prison Industry Enhancement Certification Program, private firms were again authorized to provide employment opportunities for inmates under specified circumstances. Penal labor is permitted pursuant to the Thirteenth Amendment of the U.S. Constitution ratified in 1865 for all convicted detainees. Since then, the courts have ruled that inmates can be required to work and are not protected by the constitutional prohibition against involuntary servitude. Work requirements for inmates vary by state; however provisions by the **American Correctional Association** mandate that sentenced inmates be required to work and be compensated for their labor. *See also* CONVICT LEASE SYSTEM; PRISON.

WORK RELEASE. A community-based correctional program in which eligible prisoners are released into the community so that they can work a regular job at a privately owned business and earn a reasonable wage for their labor. Prisoners who are qualified to participate in the program are generally nearing the end of their sentence and are classified in the lowest custody status. The structure, process, and eligibility of work-release programs vary in accordance with the correctional facilities in each state. Some programs obligate **inmates** to return to the facility where they remain under limited supervision until they are required to return to work. Other programs allow prisoners to follow a traditional Monday–Friday schedule where they live at home during the workweek but must return to a facility on the weekends. The terms of some programs allow work-release inmates to complete their sentence in home confinement or at a **halfway house** when they are not at work. The primary objective and common aspect of the program is to transition inmates so that they can reintegrate back into the community by securing and maintaining employment while managing their income. Inmate salaries are deducted for obligations such as child support and victim **restitution**, as well as other payments required by the state. The program was originally introduced in 1913 in Wisconsin and was commonly known as the Huber Law, written by state senator Henry Huber. The first contemporary work-release program was instituted in 1957 in North Carolina. Prior to the passage of the Federal Prisoners Rehabilitation Act in 1965, work-release programs were slow to expand to individual states. By 1973, 42 states had instituted some form of work-release program, whereas prior to the law's passage, only three states had work-release programs.

WORLD COURT. Referred to as the International Court of Justice or The Hague, it was formed in 1945 following the end of World War II as the principal judicial organ of the United Nations (UN). The court serves to resolve disputes and provide advisory opinions involving international law. The court is governed by the Statute of the International Court of Justice and is headquartered at the Peace Palace in The Hague, Netherlands. The court is composed of 15 judges, who are elected to nine-year terms by the UN General Assembly and Security Council. Elections are staggered, with special elections held when unexpected vacancies occur to ensure continuity within the court. The seats are distributed by geographic region, with no two judges being elected from the same nation. Permanent members of the Security

Council, including the United States, Russia, China, the United Kingdom, and France, always have a judge on the court. Resolutions made by the court may not be accepted by countries in which those rulings are implicated, notwithstanding the sanction and approval made by the UN. The court was preceded by the Permanent Court of International Justice (PCIJ), which was established in 1920 pursuant to Article 14 of the Covenant of the League of Nations, which ceased to function following Germany's occupation of the Netherlands in 1940 and was formally dissolved in April 1946. Following the war and a series of exchanges, a joint declaration was issued in October 1944 by the United States, the United Kingdom, the Soviet Union, and China acknowledging the importance of forming a general international organization that incorporated an international court of peace. A committee of jurists representing 44 nations and chaired by G. H. Hackworth of the United States was established in April 1945 to draft a statute for the formation of an international judicial body. The statute was finalized in June 1945 during the UN Conference on International Organization held in San Francisco, which 50 member states attended. It was decided at the conference that the new court would be formed as one of the principal organs of the UN, together with the General Assembly, Security Council, Economic and Social Council, Trusteeship Council, and Secretariat. Membership in the UN began with 51 states and has since grown to 193 nations. The first election of the court occurred on 6 February 1946 during the first session of the United Nations General Assembly and Security Council. In April 1946, the court met for the first time and elected its first president judge, José Gustavo Guerrero of El Salvador and the most recent president judge of the PCIJ. The first case submitted to the court occurred in May 1947 in a matter concerning the Corfu Channel filed by the United Kingdom against Albania. *See also* WAR CRIMES; WAR CRIMINAL.

WORLD TRADE CENTER (WTC) BOMBINGS. The 110-story twin towers located in New York City were the target of a terrorist attack on 26 February 1993 and again on 11 September 2001. The buildings were officially dedicated and opened on 4 April 1973, and at the time of their completion they were the tallest buildings in the world. The 1993 attack was carried out using a truck bomb, which was driven beneath the North Tower of the World Trade Center (WTC) and parked in a public parking garage. At a few minutes past noon, the bomb was detonated, with the intent being to have the North Tower collapse into the South Tower so that both towers would be destroyed and kill the thousands of people occupying them. The blast did not result in a collapse, but it created a massive explosion in the facility, which killed six people and injured more than a thousand others as they sought to evacuate the tower. The investigation determined that a group of seven terrorists were responsible for the bombing, including the uncle and financier of Ramzi

Yousef, the main organizer of the attack. In 2001, two Boeing 767 jets were used to destroy the WTC as part of a coordinated strike that included an attack on the Pentagon and another failed attempt on an unknown target. The attack was carried out by a group of 19 **Al-Qaeda** terrorists and resulted in the deaths of 2,996 people and injury to more than 6,000 others, as well as more than $10 billion in property damage and approximately $3 trillion in total costs. On the morning of the attack, American Airlines flight 11 and United Airlines flight 175 bound for California were hijacked by 10 terrorists and flown into the North and South Towers, respectively. The flights were selected because of the high volume of fuel that the aircrafts contained for the transcontinental commute. The hijackers took control of the planes using box cutters and knives, and having taken commercial flight lessons in the United States over the prior year, they were able to commandeer the planes into the towers. The American Airlines flight departed Logan Airport at 7:59 a.m. and struck the North Tower near the 80th floor at 8:46 a.m. The United Airlines flight departed Logan Airport at 8:11 a.m. and struck the South Tower near the 60th floor at 9:03 a.m. More than 90 percent of the victims who perished in the WTC towers were located above the point of the planes' impact into the building. A total of 1,462 persons died in the North Tower, and 630 persons died in the South Tower. Estimates by the Port Authority indicated that there were more than 14,000 persons in the WTC towers at the time of the initial strike on the North Tower. The point of impact on the South Tower was lower than that of the North Tower, but there were fewer victims because some of the occupants decided to evacuate the tower after the North Tower was struck. Cantor Fitzgerald L.P., an investment bank located on the 101st through 105th floors of the North Tower, lost the greatest number of employees with a total of 658 causalities. The heat generated from the jet fuel caused the South Tower to collapse at 9:59 a.m. and the North Tower to collapse at 10:28 a.m. At the time of the attack, the North and South Towers were the fifth- and sixth-tallest buildings in the world, standing at 1,368 and 1,362 feet, respectively. The resulting debris and fires from the towers' collapse caused the subsequent collapse of 7 World Trade Center—a 47-story tower—at 5:21 p.m. The attack was the deadliest incident in U.S. history involving firefighters, 343 of whom died, and law enforcement officers, 72 of whom were killed. The attack prompted the United States to declare the War on Terror and invade Afghanistan, the country ruled by the Taliban regime and known to be harboring Al-Qaeda. The leader of Al-Qaeda, **Osama bin Laden**, who declared a holy war against the United States in 1998, called for the **execution** of all Americans and claimed responsibility for the attack in a 2004 message aired on an Arabic news station. The motive for the attack included the United States' support of Israel, support for countries in their ostensible **assault** against Muslims, the existence of pro-American governments and its continued military presence in the Middle

East, and its involvement in the Persian Gulf War and sanctions levied against Iraq. The terror leader evaded capture until he was located and killed in Abbottabad, Pakistan, in May 2011 by the U.S. Navy's SEAL Team Six. The cleanup of the WTC site was completed in May 2002 and is currently the location of the National September 11 Memorial and Museum. The memorial features two reflecting pools that are the largest manmade waterfalls in the world and are built on the footprints of the towers in remembrance of those who perished in the 1993 and 2001 attacks. *See also* PATRIOT ACT; TERRORISM.

WOUNDED KNEE MASSACRE. Referred to as the Battle of Wounded Knee, it was the site of a massacre between Native Indians and federal officials on 29 December 1890. The site is located on the Lakota Pine Ridge Indian Reservation near Wounded Knee Creek in the southwest region of South Dakota. During the winter of 1890, the Sioux living on the South Dakota prairies were in despair because of their living conditions on the confined government reservations but began to take hope in a spiritual movement known as the Ghost Dance. Sioux leaders preached that their plight was the result of angering the gods for having abandoned their way of life and that if they practiced this ritual, the gods would destroy the white man and all nonbelievers and create a new world of peace and prosperity for them. The emerging movement created increasing alarm among white settlers, and on 15 November 1890 a request for protection against what was believed to be an imminent uprising was sent to the commissioner of Indian affairs. The U.S. 7th Cavalry was deployed to the prairie, led by General Nelson Miles, who ordered the arrest of several Sioux leaders. On 15 December, reservation **police** attempted to arrest Sitting Bull and killed the Sioux chief in the process, after mistakenly identifying him as a Ghost Dancer. A result of the noted leader's killing was that tensions escalated, and on 28 December troops caught up and arrested Chief Big Foot, who was in charge of leading scores of others to join Chief Red Cloud, located near the bank of Wounded Creek in the Lakota camp. The following day, the cavalry mounted their horses, surrounded the encampment, and began confiscating weapons. As the weapons were being seized, a deaf tribesman, Black Coyote, was unable to hear the troops' order to surrender their arms. While confiscating his rifle, a dispute ensued and a gunshot was fired, but it was unclear as to which side discharged the weapon. The American soldiers surrounding the camp immediately responded to the initial shot by indiscriminately firing their weapons, including the rapid-fire Hotchkiss guns, into the teepees. It marked the final major confrontation between the Sioux and federal troops, which ended with at least 150 Native American men, women, and children killed (some historians purport that the number killed was considerably higher), along with 25 soldiers of the Cavalry. The site was the scene of another violent confrontation in 1973. Between 27 February and 8 May 1973, 200 Native Americans led by leaders of the American Indian Movement (AIM) occupied Wounded Knee to protest the conditions on the reservation. Sioux traditionalists engaged in a demonstration against the elected tribal council head, Richard Wilson, who was allegedly corrupt and used intimidation tactics to suppress his adversaries. When the local authorities were unable to peacefully disband the protest, approximately 2,000 Native Americans, together with the **FBI** and other law enforcement personnel, were drawn to the site. The congregation was surrounded by armed officers, and the siege eventually ended when the two sides began shooting at one another. Frank Clearwater and Buddy Lamont, two Native Americans, were killed during the melee before a negotiated settlement was reached. The site has been designated a National Historic Landmark, and in 1990 a resolution was passed by the U.S. Congress that formally expressed deep regret over the massacre.

WRIT. A written order issued by a judicial officer or court ordering or forbidding the person to whom it is directed to perform or abstain from performing a specific act. The etymology of the word comes from Old English meaning a document, deed, treatise, or letter. Writs in English law can be traced to the 13th century, when Anglo-Saxon kings used them as charters to transfer land grants, patent letters for commissions to royal officials, and letters to convey information to an individual or group. Norman kings were the first to use writs for judicial purposes and most commonly as original writs, which were similar to how contemporary **summons** are used—that is, served upon a defendant requiring appearance in court for failing to recompense on a stated matter. The writ was ordinarily written in Latin and sealed. During the early stages of English **common law**, a writ was required to have a matter brought before one of the royal courts. Writs were not necessary for those plaintiffs who sought to have their matter heard before a local court. A command by the king in the form of a writ was required for any plaintiff who had the ability to pay and the desire to seek recourse from one of the king's courts. Writs were generally atypical actions when common law was first instituted. The use of writs eventually became a more regular part of England's justice system, however technical and restrictive their development. The English writ system was inherited by the United States. The All Writs Act was incorporated into the Judiciary Act of 1789 and authorized U.S. federal courts to issue all necessary writs deemed appropriate in overseeing their jurisdictions. The act was amended several times, with only a few writs remaining in use among the federal courts.

WRIT OF CERTIORARI. A superior court order derived from Latin, meaning "we wish to be informed," which seeks to review a lower-court decision. The usage of the term dates back to ancient Rome and British law. The order was used on a discretionary basis by a superior court and was under no requirement to provide the lower court with an explanation for requiring the review. It is most commonly issued by the **U.S. Supreme Court** to an inferior court to review a matter for an error in the court's ruling or to review as a matter of appeal. The terminology varies among the states, such as California, which uses "writ of review" in lieu of "writ of certiorari" as a means to purge Latin from law language. Prior to the Judiciary Act of 1891, cases would reach the U.S. Supreme Court on appeal as a matter of right. As the nation expanded through the 19th century, the backlog of cases in the U.S. Supreme Court increased considerably until the act transferred the cases on appeal to the newly created Circuit Courts of Appeals. Thereafter, the U.S. Supreme Court used its discretion in determining which of the cases from the circuit courts it would review through a **writ** of certiorari. Since the Judiciary Act of 1925 and the U.S. Supreme Court Case Selections Act of 1988, cases cannot be appealed to the high court as a matter of right. A party who seeks a review of a lower-court decision by the U.S. Supreme Court must file a petition for writ of certiorari.

WRIT OF HABEAS CORPUS. A legal pleading, meaning "to produce the body," that requires an official detaining an individual to produce that individual before a court of law to review the legality of their custody. Habeas corpus is derived from the 39th clause of the **Magna Carta** signed by King John in 1215, which specified that individuals could not be taken into custody and detained without lawful judgment. By the 17th century, courts in England were more regularly considering habeas corpus petitions wherein judges sought an account of the king's subjects whose liberties were actively being denied. The safeguard to individual liberty was the subject of debate between the Crown and Parliament, but Parliament prevailed when the Habeas Corpus Act of 1679 was enacted and required habeas relief under given conditions and coupled it with substantial penalties for noncompliance. The United States adopted the habeas corpus concept from English **common law**. The **writ** is one of only two federal constitutional provisions that is explicitly referenced and is protected by a specified remedy noting that it cannot be suspended except under conditions when the public's safety requires it, such as during times of war. The writ is most commonly used to challenge the legality of criminal convictions and sentences, but it has also been filed to challenge a defendant's custody during pretrial events or deportation proceedings. A writ of habeas corpus may challenge the legal basis of detention including the conditions and duration of confinement. The court may hold an evidentiary hearing and review the facts of the application before ruling.

Relief may be granted in a variety of forms, including releasing the defendant from custody, reducing the sentence, or issuing an order prohibiting the illegal conditions of confinement or declaration of rights. *See also* TRIAL.

WRONGFUL CONVICTION. A finding of guilt or conviction of a person accused of committing a crime who is subsequently proven to be innocent of the charges and not having committed the crime. Conviction reversals are based on **evidence** brought to bear in the criminal justice process. Edwin Borchard is credited with being the first to study erroneous convictions when in 1932 he identified 65 persons he believed were wrongfully convicted. Between 1987 and 1992, **Hugo Bedau**, Constance Putnam, and Michael Radelet identified more than 400 **death penalty** cases in which the defendants were wrongfully convicted. The emergence of forensic analysis of **DNA** evidence during the 1980s provided wrongfully convicted persons with more persuasive means in overturning verdicts due to erroneous findings. The first DNA **exoneration** in the United States occurred in 1989. Since then, evidence has been employed by authorities both to facilitate the veracity of guilt and to exonerate the wrongfully convicted. In the past, subsequent evidence that would support overturning the conviction, however true, was often discounted and was not as influential as the scientific proof of error. DNA evidence has been commonly used by the **Innocence Project**, an organization founded in 1992 by Peter Neufeld and Barry Scheck at the **Cardozo** School of Law. It is dedicated to identifying innocent persons who are incarcerated for crimes they did not commit.

WRONGFUL EXECUTION. An individual who is falsely convicted of a **capital crime** and is subsequently put to death. Opponents of the **death penalty** use instances of wrongful **execution** and that the cost is greater than life without parole as the primary basis of their argument. The problem of wrongful execution is not a recent concern. During the 17th and 18th centuries, leading Anglo-American scholars of law were the first to address the issue. Prominent writers such as Matthew Hale and William Blackstone urged the courts to implement and enforce strict evidentiary policy and process to safeguard innocent persons from being wrongfully executed. During the 19th century the criminal justice system in America preserved the sanction by repudiating that wrongful executions occur and by instituting what were believed to be practices that safeguarded against the risk. Legal reform to abolish the death penalty on this basis since the **U.S. Supreme Court** reinstituted the sanction in ***Gregg v. Georgia*, 428 U.S. 153 (1976)**, has been protracted because of the difficulty in identifying cases wherein wrongful execution was irrefutable. Since 1992, **DNA evidence** has been used to exonerate more than 20 death row **inmates**, while other sentences have been commuted because of other factors, including inadequate evidence and wrongful prosecution. The Death Penalty Information Center is a national nonprofit organization founded in 1990 to provide information about **capital punishment**. *See also* INNOCENCE PROJECT.

WUORNOS, AILEEN CAROL (1956–2002). An American **serial killer** who killed seven men in Florida between 1989 and 1990 and was convicted of six of the murders. She was sentenced to death and was the 10th woman in the United States to be executed since ***Gregg v. Georgia*, 428 U.S. 153 (1976)**, when the **U.S. Supreme Court** reinstituted the **death penalty**. Wuornos was executed on 9 October 2002 by **lethal injection** after 10 years on **death row** and being deemed mentally competent. Wuornos was a sexually abused child and gave birth to her only child when she was 14 after being impregnated by an adult friend of her grandfather. At around the same age, she was forced to leave home and began working as a prostitute along Florida's highways. In 1986, she began a romantic relationship with Tyria Moore and partnered with her selling stolen items to pawnshops. She was working as a prostitute when she killed her first victim, Richard Mallory, in 1989, followed by at least an additional five men. She would shoot her victims and then rob and steal their vehicles. In 1992, a **jury** convicted her of first-degree **murder** in the death of Mallory. She would later plead guilty to the other five murders and received a **death sentence** in each of those cases. She claimed responsibility but was never tried for the murder of Siems, whose remains were never recovered. Her life and crimes have been depicted in two documentaries, *Aileen Wuornos: The Selling of a Serial Killer* (1993) and *Aileen: Life and Death of a Serial Killer* (2003); a television movie, *Overkill: The Aileen Wuornos Story* (1992); and the feature film *Monster*, starring Charlize Theron as Wuornos.

X

XENOPHOBIA. A term used to describe hatred and prejudice toward foreigners. The word originated from Greek meaning "foreigner" (*xenos*) and "fear" (*phobos*). Xenophobia is a distinct phenomenon specifically leveled against foreign cultures and has been associated with a fear of losing cultural identity, influence, and power. Throughout American history, as new groups of foreigners migrated to the United States, incidents of xenophobia appeared. In the 1840s, Chinese Americans were suspect, then the Italian Americans toward the end of the turn of the century, German Americans around the First and Second World Wars, and the Japanese Americans during the Second World War (e.g., internment camps in California). Following the 2001 attacks on America, Middle Easterners became targets for xenophobic fear and bias, and today Mexican Americans are broadly the targets of xenophobia. *See also* HATE CRIME.

XYY CHROMOSOME. *See* EXTRA Y CHROMOSOME.

Y

YOUTHFUL OFFENDER. A **juvenile delinquent** is an offender who is a minor, defined as an individual younger than the statutory age of majority, and who has committed a crime or violated a status offense. In most states, persons under 18 years of age are considered minors. Acts that would otherwise be a felony or misdemeanor if committed by an adult would constitute a crime. **Status offenses** such as **truancy**, **curfew** violations, underage drinking or smoking, and running away from home are illegal due to their underage status and are administered by **juvenile courts**. For serious crimes including **murder**, robbery, aggravated **assault**, and rape, or for offenders who recidivate, a court can try the minor as an adult. Minors who are not waived up to adult courts are processed through juvenile courts and serve out sentences in **juvenile detention** or **prison** (**reformatory**) facilities. Youthful offenders are more likely than adults to get sentenced to **probation** or other special programs targeting juveniles, such as community-based programming, **home confinement**, or detention shelter and ordinarily have limitations to their sentences. They are often given opportunities to have criminal convictions converted to noncriminal outcomes, and youthful offender determinations including all proceedings are not open to the public. *See also* JUVENILE DELINQUENCY; REFORM SCHOOL.

YUMA PENITENTIARY. A former **prison** located in Yuma, Arizona, when the state was a U.S. territory. The Arizona state parks maintain the prison as a historic museum. The prison opened in 1876 with seven convicts. During its 33 years as a prison, it confined a total of 3,069 convicts; 29 were women. While incarcerated, 112 convicts died of various ailments such as tuberculosis and 22 because of **violence**. The prison ceased operation in 1909. **Inmates** who caused the prison officials problems, including escape, would be secured with a ball and chain.

Z

ZAPRUDER FILM. A silent, color motion picture film shot by the private citizen Abraham Zapruder, who unexpectedly captured the **assassination** of U.S. president John F. Kennedy as his motorcade passed through Dealey Plaza in Dallas, Texas, on 22 November 1963, linking his name with the national tragedy. Zapruder, a Russian immigrant, was the co-owner of a women's clothing manufacturer, Jennifer Juniors, and an avid home movie hobbyist. The film was shot on a 414PD Director Series Bell and Howell 8 mm camera. The footage spans a total of 26.6 seconds—486 frames. The fatal shot hitting President Kennedy's head appears on frame 313. The leading publication *Life* agreed to pay Zapruder $150,000 for the film and copyright, of which he donated $5,000 to the widow of the Dallas **police** officer, J. D. Tippit, who was killed by **Lee Harvey Oswald** shortly after the assassination. *See also* JFK ASSASSINATION.

ZEBRA KILLINGS. A series of racially motivated murders that took place in San Francisco, California, between October 1973 and April 1974. The first victims were Richard Hague and his wife, Quita, who were **kidnapped** and forced into a van at gunpoint while taking an evening stroll around Coit Tower. Once in the van, Quita was sexually **assaulted** and then nearly decapitated with a machete. Hague was beaten and hacked with the machete and survived the attack. Manuel Moore, Larry Green, Jessie Lee Cooks, and J. C. X. Simon, four black men, were arrested and convicted of **murder** and conspiracy and sentenced to life in **prison**. During the crime spree, the group of black Muslims, who referred to themselves as the "Death Angels," are believed to have murdered at least 16 victims because they were white. One of the members of the Death Angels, Anthony Harris, saw himself in a composite sketch and contacted **police**. Harris was placed into the **witness protection program**. The murders were referenced as "Zebra" because of the police radio band that had been assigned to the investigation.

ZERO TOLERANCE. A concept that was subsequently developed into policy and implemented into practice by **police** organizations, the **Food and Drug Administration (FDA)**, and educational institutions. Zero tolerance imposes a fixed sanction irrespective of the mitigating factors or specific circumstances, history, or background of the individual in an attempt to divert or otherwise eradicate violations of rules of conduct or law. The practice also precludes individuals in positions of power or authority from exercising their discretion to more aptly impose a **punishment** for the crime, infraction, or misconduct given distinct circumstances. Examples include a workplace lateness policy that makes no distinction in amount such that two minutes is handled the same as 60 minutes, or a "drug-free zone" that makes no difference between a perpetrator who is apprehended with small amounts of **marijuana** and one who has large amounts of **heroin**. The etymology of the term originated in U.S. political discourse beginning with the 1973 New Jersey Safe and Clean Neighborhoods Act and was also used in food and drug regulations to compel manufacturers to eliminate compounds from their products because they were deemed to be hazardous however slight the concentration. The term was later popularized following an article by **James Q. Wilson** and George L. Kelling in the *Atlantic Monthly* in which they proposed "broken windows"—a theory centered on policing even nominal offenses such as panhandling and littering as a strategy to inhibit the commission of more serious crimes they believed these smaller class of offenses heralded. *See also* BROKEN WINDOWS THEORY.

ZETAS. A Mexican crime **syndicate** referred to as Los Zetas, Spanish for "the Zs." The name originated from the group's first commander, Arturo Guzman Decena, whose radio code as a high-ranking officer was "Z1." They are known for their military-like operations in their use of weapons, technology, and gathering intelligence. At one point, the group was considered one of the most feared and advanced **drug trafficking** cartels with a vast transnational network. Apart from drugs, the enterprise also directed sex trafficking rings, schemes to smuggle contraband weapons and ammunition, and DVD/CD piracy. The group originated in the late 1990s as a group of Mexican Army Special Forces deserters who defected to serve as the hired paramilitary enforcement arm of the Gulf Cartel and their leader Osiel Cárdenas Guillén. Decena was killed in 2002. In 2010 under the leadership of Heriberto Lazcano, "Z3," the Zetas seceded from the Gulf Cartel to form their own criminal enterprise and began to solidify their presence throughout Mexico in more than 400 municipalities and expanded their reach into Guatemala and the United States. Since 2012, the organization's splintering has been hastened by a lack of coordination and loss of leadership, who have been arrested or killed. The group has more recently been fragmented into more local factions with no central organization. *See also* TRANSNATIONAL CRIME.

ZIMBARDO, DR. PHILIP. *See* STANFORD PRISON EXPERIMENT.

ZIMMERMAN, GEORGE (1983–). An American known for fatally shooting **Trayvon Martin**, a 17-year-old African American male, on 26 February 2012 in the Retreat at Twin Lakes gated community in Sanford, Florida. Zimmerman was the coordinator for the **neighborhood watch** program, which was administered by the local **police** department. On the day he was killed, Martin and his father were visiting his father's fiancée and her son, who were residents in the community. In the year prior to Martin's shooting, Twin Lakes had experienced a rash of burglaries and thefts while home values continued to plummet from the recession. On the evening of 26 February 2012, at approximately 7:09 p.m., Zimmerman contacted Sanford police while driving through the neighborhood and observing Martin. Zimmerman stated to the dispatcher that the neighborhood had had break-ins, and he described Martin as behaving suspiciously. Zimmerman began pursuing Martin and eventually lost sight of him while on the phone with the dispatcher. An altercation between Zimmerman and Martin ensued at some point after the phone call ended at 7:15. The altercation ended when Zimmerman, who had been licensed to carry a firearm, shot Martin in the chest. When police arrived, they took Zimmerman into custody and treated him for injuries sustained to his head. Zimmerman claimed that he had acted in self-defense under Florida's **Stand Your Ground** statute, but he was subsequently charged with **murder** by a special prosecutor who was appointed to the case by the governor. On 13 July 2013, Zimmerman was acquitted of second-degree murder in *Florida v. George Zimmerman*, 592012CF001083A. The U.S. Department of Justice investigated Zimmerman on **civil rights** violations for the next three years and in February 2015 concluded that there was not sufficient **evidence** that Zimmerman intentionally violated Martin's civil rights.

ZIONIST MOVEMENT. A Jewish national movement that originated in eastern and central Europe during the latter part of the 19th century. Central to the movement was the objective of creating and supporting a Jewish national state in the historical region of Palestine, having maintained a connection to the area for hundreds of years. The sentiment was first introduced by Moses Hess and Myer Waxman in their book *Rome and Jerusalem*, which was later adopted by parts of Europe and the United States. The movement took its name from one of the hills named Zion in the region, meaning "marker" or "commemoration," and was precipitated by a Jewish ideology that Jews return to what was considered their ancient homeland and a groundswell of anti-Semitism that was being experienced in Europe at the outset of the 20th century. Early Zionists believed Jews to be a "people," but a people without a country, who as such would remain politically ineffective so long as they were without a national home. Zionism is not a monolithic ideology, and it varies depending on a variety of circumstances, including time period, geography, philosophy, etc., with the contemporary formulation of the movement being separated from religious aspirations. Consequently, there is no recognized authority of the movement's ideology. The initial groups of Jews who immigrated to the area were known as the "Aliya," meaning "going up" (as in coming to the Holy Land). The first Aliya occurred in the 1870s when an estimated 25,000 Jews began purchasing land and settling in Palestine. Beginning in 1904, the second Aliya, due primarily to emerging anti-Semitism in Russia, increased the Jewish population in Palestine to almost 100,000. The third Aliya occurred around 1919 when an additional 40,000 Jews mostly from Eastern Europe and Russia left or were expelled by the Turks following World War I. The fourth Aliya occurred between 1924 and 1932 when an estimated 70,000 Jews immigrated because of the anti-Zionist regime in Poland, immigration quotas imposed in the United States, and the rise of Nazi Germany. The fifth Aliya occurred between 1933 and 1939 when approximately 250,000 Jews arrived in Palestine, most of whom are said to have been German Jews fleeing Nazi persecution.

ZODIAC KILLER. A **serial killer** who stalked areas in Northern California during the late 1960s and early 1970s. He claimed responsibility for the **murder** of 37 people, but **police** linked him to only seven victims (four men and three women), of whom five died between 1968 and 1969. In a series of letters to the San Francisco Bay Area press in which he taunted police, he adopted the name "Zodiac Killer." The handwritten letters, the first of which was sent in triplicate on 1 August 1969 to the *San Francisco Examiner*, *San Francisco Chronicle*, and *Vallejo Times-Herald*, claimed responsibility for the murder of two teenagers the prior Christmas at Lake Herman and contained information that was not released to the public. The killer threatened future attacks if the letters were not printed on the front page of the newspapers. A series of letters followed between 1969 and 1974 in which the killer disclosed his insanity and included cryptograms offering clues to future murders. Each of the letters closed with a symbol depicted as a circle with a cross through it and was attached to one part of a three-part cipher, which allegedly contained his identity. In 1974, communication by the killer suddenly ended. The case remains open with the California Department of Justice as well as other police agencies in the state, and while suspects have been named, no person has ever been arrested for the crimes. The case has been the subject of a myriad of books, movies, news stories, and theories. *See also* INSANITY DEFENSE.

ZONE THEORY. A theory also referred to as concentric zone theory developed in the 1920s by Ernest Burgess and Robert Park of the University of Chicago and one of the earliest theoretical models to explain the distribution of urban social structures. The theory explained the socioeconomic divides of Chicago separating the areas on the basis of land usage using concentric zones or rings encircling the central area of the city. The social structures are defined by residential components and extend outward from Zone 1, Central Business District, known as the nonresidential center for business and commerce. Zone 2 is the Zone of Transition, a mixed area of residential housing and commercial infrastructure and has the highest crime rate and percentage of people moving in and out of the area. Zone 3, the Working Class of Independent Workers Zone, are the "inner suburbs" comprised of stable working-class families with the means to afford a modest home. Zone 4, the Middle Class or Better Residences Zone, encompasses the "outer suburbs" and more well-educated population living in newer, less dense residential areas. The outer ring, Zone 5, is the Commuters Zone, made up of mostly the upper class with the resources to commute into and out of the central business district for employment and entertainment purposes. The theory posits that crime varies on the basis of these zones, with crime rates increasing toward the central business district as density, mobility, poverty, and unemployment increases and community cohesion diminishes. Some of the criticisms and problems with the theory include that it is not applicable to more contemporary urban areas or cities outside of the United States. There are many instances where gentrification has made central business districts more expensive and desirable and the outer suburbs are comprised of impoverished communities. It also assumes a relatively flat, isotropic landscape, which can have varying impacts on the growth and desirability of geographic sectors. The theory also does not take into account changes influenced by information technology and the global economy, which have decentralized industries and more widely distributed employment. *See also* CHICAGO SCHOOL.

ZOOPHILIA. A condition characterized by a person's erotic fixation or sexual attraction toward animals. The sexual **fantasy** of the real or imagined contact with a nonhuman animal can result in sexual arousal. Although the terms are sometimes used interchangeably, distinctions are made between bestiality (the sexual act with an animal) and zoophilia (the sexual interest in or attraction toward animals). In most countries, bestiality is outlawed on the grounds of animal abuse and mistreatment or under laws governing crimes against nature. Zoophilic acts can also be prohibited on religious, ethical, psychological, legal, philosophical, or medical grounds.

Appendix 1

The Bill of Rights: Full Text

Amendment I

Congress shall make no law respecting an establishment of religion, or prohibiting the free exercise thereof; or abridging the freedom of speech, or of the press; or the right of the people peaceably to assemble, and to petition the government for a redress of grievances.

Amendment II

A well-regulated militia, being necessary to the security of a free state, the right of the people to keep and bear arms, shall not be infringed.

Amendment III

No soldier shall, in time of peace be quartered in any house, without the consent of the owner, nor in time of war, but in a manner to be prescribed by law.

Amendment IV

The right of the people to be secure in their persons, houses, papers, and effects, against unreasonable searches and seizures, shall not be violated, and no warrants shall issue, but upon probable cause, supported by oath or affirmation, and particularly describing the place to be searched, and the persons or things to be seized.

Amendment V

No person shall be held to answer for a capital, or otherwise infamous crime, unless on a presentment or indictment of a grand jury, except in cases arising in the land or naval forces, or in the militia, when in actual service in time of war or public danger; nor shall any person be subject for the same offense to be twice put in jeopardy of life or limb; nor shall be compelled in any criminal case to be a witness against himself, nor be deprived of life, liberty, or property, without due process of law; nor shall private property be taken for public use, without just compensation.

Amendment VI

In all criminal prosecutions, the accused shall enjoy the right to a speedy and public trial, by an impartial jury of the state and district wherein the crime shall have been committed, which district shall have been previously ascertained by law, and to be informed of the nature and cause of the accusation; to be confronted with the witnesses against him; to have compulsory process for obtaining witnesses in his favor, and to have the assistance of counsel for his defense.

Amendment VII

In suits at common law, where the value in controversy shall exceed twenty dollars, the right of trial by jury shall be preserved, and no fact tried by a jury, shall be otherwise reexamined in any court of the United States, than according to the rules of the common law.

Amendment VIII

Excessive bail shall not be required, nor excessive fines imposed, nor cruel and unusual punishments inflicted.

Amendment IX

The enumeration in the Constitution, of certain rights, shall not be construed to deny or disparage others retained by the people.

Amendment X

The powers not delegated to the United States by the Constitution, nor prohibited by it to the states, are reserved to the states respectively, or to the people.

Appendix 2

U.S. Supreme Court Cases

These cases establish criminal procedure as interpreted by the Court as allowable by the U.S. Constitution. The reader should note the date of the Supreme Court holding and not rely upon any one case listed as the definitive response for a rule of criminal procedure. Future holdings handed down by the Court may affirm, amend, or substantially change a previous holding. Supreme Court cases and the justices represent the living embodiment of the Constitution. Supreme Court cases are critical to criminal justice definitions. They affirm or deny what, how, where, and by whom criminal justice activity may be done. Furthermore, the holdings of the court specify the constitutional dictate of interactions between government and individuals to achieve what we refer to as justice and the maintenance or order of law.

The court holdings provide a sense of when and what the court regards as timely and critical, which is to say, what is best for the country and the operation of criminal justice. These are words, and the holdings, the review of the Constitution, and the determinations of what it means by the justices affect people, including those who are the least powerful or lacking in influence.

***ABRAMS V. U.S.*, 250 U.S. 616 (1919).** The Court addressed the issues of free speech, clear and present danger, as found in the Sedition Act of 1918. The First Amendment did not protect the defendants in this case.

***ADAMSON V. CALIFORNIA*, 332 U.S. 46 (1947).** The Court did not affirm Fifth Amendment protection against self-incrimination in state and local government. The Fourteenth Amendment due process clause did not incorporate all provisions of the Bill of Rights.

***AKE V. OKLAHOMA*, 470 U.S. 68 (1985).** The Court held that indigents must be provided with a psychiatrist, as part of the due process protection.

***ALBERTSON V. SUBVERSIVE ACTIVITIES CONTROL BOARD*, 382 U.S. 70 (1965).** The protection of the Fifth Amendment against self-incrimination was upheld by the Court.

***APPRENDI V. NEW JERSEY*, 530 U.S. 466 (2000).** The Court held that sentences higher than the maximum required must be determined by a jury.

***ARGERSINGER V. HAMLIN*, 407 U.S. 25 (1972).** The right to counsel for all cases that may be given jail time was upheld by the Court.

***ARIZONA V. FULMINANTE*, 499 U.S. 279 (1991).** The Court allowed conviction on other evidence even when the confession was coerced.

***ARTHUR ANDERSON, LLP V. U.S.*, 544 U.S. 696 (2005).** The Court reversed the lower court's decision of Arthur Anderson LLP's being guilty of obstruction of justice in the Enron case.

***ATWATER V. CITY OF LAGO VISTA*, 532 U.S. 318 (2001).** The protections of the Fourth Amendment are not abused when a defendant is arrested without warrant for a minor offense.

***AUSTIN V. U.S.*, 509 U.S. 390 (1993).** The Court allowed the seizure of property for monetary punishment.

***BALLEW V. GEORGIA*, 435 U.S. 223 (1978).** The Court threw out a criminal conviction because the jury did not meet the standards of the Sixth and Fourteenth Amendments.

***BATSON V. KENTUCKY*, 476 U.S. 79 (1986).** The Court determined that a prosecutor under the Sixth Amendment could not use peremptory challenges simply for racial reasons in jury selection.

***BENNIS V. MICHIGAN*, 516 U.S. 442 (1996).** The Court determined that the forfeiture process of Michigan law did not fail to meet the standard of the due process clause of the Fifth and Fourteenth Amendments.

***BENTON V. MARYLAND*, 395 U.S. 784 (1969).** The Court ruled that the state can be held liable for double jeopardy. Other cases affected by decision: *Louisiana ex rel. Francis v. Resweber*, 329 U.S. 459 (1947), *U.S. v. Ursery*, 518 U.S. 267 (1996).

***BETTS V. BRADY*, 316 U.S. 455 (1942).** The decision stated that all defenders did not have a right to counsel when prosecuted by the state. The decision was later overturned in *Gideon v. Wainwright* (1963). The Sixth and Fourteenth Amendments guarantee the right to counsel.

***BIGELOW V. VIRGINIA*, 421 U.S. 809 (1975).** The Court established First Amendment rights that protected advertising.

***BLAKELY V. WASHINGTON*, 542 U.S. 296 (2004).** Under the Sixth Amendment, only juries may enhance sentences beyond the state's sentencing guidelines.

***BOYD V. U.S.*, 116 U.S. 616 (1886).** Under the Fourth and Fifth Amendments, search and seizure of a man's private papers was not permitted.

***BRANDENBURG V. OHIO*, 395 U.S. 444 (1969).** Ohio's law regarding public speech was overturned by First Amendment rights unless the speech was a clear and present danger to public safety.

***BRAZENBURG V. HAYES*, 408 U.S. 665 (1972).** The Court overruled a reporter's protection under the First Amendment when called to testify in a grand jury action.

***BROWN V. MISSISSIPPI*, 297 U.S. 278 (1936).** A defendant's admission of guilt is not acceptable when torture was used. This was a violation of the due process protection of the Fourteenth Amendment.

***BURCH V. LOUISIANA*, 441 U.S. 130 (1979).** The Court's decision overturned Louisiana's permission of a nonunanimous jury conviction.

***BUTZ V. ECONOMOU*, 438 U.S. 478 (1978).** The Court allowed immunity from prosecution under governmental powers.

***CALDER V. BULL*, 3 DALL. (3 U.S.) 386 (1798).** The Court decided several constitutional issues. One regarded ex post facto laws, and the other was that the Court has no power to decide if the state is not following the state constitution.

***CARROLL V. U.S.*, 267 U.S. 132 (1925).** Known as the Carroll decision or Carroll doctrine, the "automobile exception" allowed warrantless searches of automobiles. It increased the use of warrantless searches.

***CHIMEL V. CALIFORNIA*, 395 U.S. 752 (1969).** The Court overthrew the conviction of Chimel, stating that arrest warrants only allowed searches of the area immediately under the control of the suspect. Warrantless searches are questioned under the Fourth Amendment.

***COUNSELMAN V. HITCHCOCK*, 142 U.S. 547 (1982).** The Court held that a Fifth Amendment protection from self-incrimination did not protect against conviction when there was compelling evidence.

***CUTTER V. WILKINSON*, 544 U.S. 709 (2005).** The Court held that the Religious Land Use and Institutionalized Persons Act (RLUIPA) protected the practice of religious beliefs in those institutions, specifically in the Ohio Prison, which received federal funding.

***DEMORE V. KIM*, 538 U.S. 510 (2003).** Legal permanent immigrants are entitled to due process, bail, habeas corpus, and other constitutional protections.

***DICKERSON V. U.S.*, 530 U.S. 428 (2000).** The Court held that all defendants in a case must be read their Miranda rights. The Court overruled a claim that the reading of Miranda rights had been disallowed in the Omnibus Crime Control and Safe Streets Acts of 1968

***DISTRICT OF COLUMBIA V. HELLER*, 554 U.S. 570 (2008).** The first U.S. Supreme Court holding to clarify that an individual had the right to possess firearms for self-defense under the Second Amendment.

***DUNCAN V. LOUISIANA*, 391 U.S. 145 (1968).** The Court held that everyone is entitled to a trial by jury and incorporated the Sixth Amendment, making it applicable to the states.

***ESCOBEDO V. ILLINOIS*, 378 U.S. 478 (1964).** The Court held that suspects have a right to counsel during interrogations.

***FAY V. NEW YORK*, 332 U.S. 261 (1947).** The Court held that the use of a blue-ribbon panel, that is, a specification of who may or may not serve on a jury, was permitted under due process in the Fourteenth Amendment.

***FAY V. NOIA*, 372 U.S. 391 (1963).** The Court held that due process had been afforded to the defendants and that there was no disparity in the jury selection at the time of the trial.

***FEINER V. NEW YORK*, 340 U.S. 315 (1915).** A First Amendment right does not provide protection from a riot that develops from a public disturbance.

***FERGUSON V. CITY OF CHARLESTON*, 532 U.S. 356 (2001).** The Court held that the University of South Carolina Medical School policy of involuntary drug testing of pregnant women was unconstitutional—that is, the search was unreasonable—and a violation of the Fourteenth Amendment.

***FLORIDA V. HARRIS*, 568 U.S. __ (2013).** If a sniffing dog is certified by a state agency, the dog's alert is enough for probable cause and thus a reason to search.

***FLORIDA V. JARDINES*, 569 U.S. __ (2013).** Even when a detection dog sniffs drugs within a home, police still must establish probable cause and get a search warrant to enter the premises.

***FRANK V. MAGNUM*, 237 U.S. 309 (1915).** The Court denied Frank's appeal stating that Frank failed to make an appeal in a timely fashion despite recognizing that his due process rights had probably been denied.

***GANNETT CO. V. DEPASQUALE*, 443 U.S. 368 (1979).** The Court upheld that the public does not have an independent right to be present at pretrial hearings.

***GARCETTI V. CEBALLOS*, 547 U.S. 410 (2006).** The Court held that a government official had no protection under the First Amendment when he criticized the validity of a warrant.

***GEORGIA V. RANDOLPH*, 547 U.S. 103 (2006).** The Court held that police must have a search warrant even when one resident has agreed to a search but the other has not agreed.

***GIDEON V. WAINWRIGHT*, 372 U.S. 335 (1963).** The Court determined that states are required to provide legal counsel to defendants even when they cannot afford an attorney.

***GRAHAM V. FLORIDA*, 560 U.S. 48 (2010).** The Court invalidated mandatory life sentences for juveniles in nonhomicide cases.

***GRIFFIN V. CALIFORNIA*, 380 U.S. 609 (1965).** The Court held that under the Fifth Amendment, defendants have a right to not testify to avoid self-incrimination.

***HARRIS V. NEW YORK*, 401 U.S. 222 (1971).** The Court held that an inadmissible statement may be used to show untrustworthiness of a defendant.

***HERRERA V. COLLINS*, 506 U.S. 390 (1993).** The Court held that evidence after conviction was not sufficient to grant habeas corpus even when it would exonerate the convicted.

***HOLMES V. JENNISON*, 14 PET. (39 U.S.) 540 (1840).** The Court held that jurisdiction over foreign affairs is to be retained by the federal government.

***HORTON V. CALIFORNIA*, 496 U.S. 128 (1990).** The Court held that a warrant is not necessary when the evidence is in plain view.

***HUDSON V. MICHIGAN*, 547 U.S. 586 (2006).** The Court held that a violation of the search and knock rule does not require suppression of evidence found on the property.

***IN RE GAULT*, 387 U.S. 1 (1967).** The Court held that juveniles in delinquency cases have the same rights as adults under the law, specifically due process.

***IN RE WINSHIP*, 397 U.S. 358 (1970).** The Court expanded juvenile rights after the Gault decision.

***J.D.B. V. NORTH CAROLINA*, 564 U.S. __ (2011).** The Court held that a defendant's age must be considered when he is to be held and interrogated.

***JOHNSON V. LOUISIANA*, 406 U.S. 356, 404 (1972).** The Court held that state juries are not required to have unanimity for a guilty verdict.

***JOHNSON V. ZERBST*, 304 U.S. 458 (1938).** The Court held that an attorney is required for indigent cases.

***KANSAS V. HENDRICKS*, 521 U.S. 346 (1997).** The Court set procedures for civilly detaining someone convicted of a sexual assault when there is a likelihood of recommitting the crime.

***KATZ V. U.S.*, 389 U.S. 347 (1967).** The Court extended protection for reasonable right to privacy under the Fourth Amendment.

***KENT V. UNITED STATES*, 383 U.S. 541 (1966).** The Court held that a waiver to adult court was a violation of the Juvenile Court Act. The defendant was denied a hearing, an investigation, counsel, or access to his records.

***KER V. CALIFORNIA*, 374 U.S. 23 (1967).** The Court held that evidence seized in a warrantless search was inadmissible.

***KLOPFER V. NORTH CAROLINA*, 386 U.S. 213 (1967).** The Court held that under the Sixth Amendment, the right to a speedy trial is a fundamental right of an American.

***KYLLO V. U.S.*, 533 U.S. 27 (2001).** The Court held that the use of thermal imaging required a warrant to conduct a search.

***MALLOY V. HOGAN*, 378 U.S. 1 (1964).** The Court held that defendants are protected by the Fifth and Fourteenth Amendments from self-incrimination.

***MALLORY V. U.S.*, 354 U.S. 449 (1957).** The Court held that suspects must be brought in front of a magistrate as quickly as possible.

***MAPP V. OHIO*, 367 U.S. 643 (1981).** The Court held that evidence found in violation of the Fourth Amendment is not admissible in court.

***McKEIVER V. PENNSYLVANIA*, 403 U.S. 528 (1971).** The Court held that juveniles do not have the right of jury trials.

***McNABB V. U.S.*, 318 U.S. 332. (1943).** The Court held that police cannot hold or interrogate a defendant without an attorney present.

***MICHIGAN, DEPARTMENT OF STATE POLICE V. SITZ*, 496 U.S. 444 (1990).** The Court held that police sobriety stops meet the standard for search and seizure.

***MILLER V. ALABAMA*, 567 U.S. __ (2012).** The Court held that mandatory life sentences for juveniles are unconstitutional.

***MIRANDA V. ARIZONA*, 384 U.S. 436 (1966).** A landmark case in which the Court held that the defendant must be told that he has the right to an attorney during questioning.

***NEW YORK V. FERBER*, 458 U.S. 747 (1982).** The Court clarified that First Amendment free speech guarantees did not prohibit states from forbidding the sale of pictures and other media that portrayed children involved in sexual activity.

***NEW YORK V. QUARLES*, 467 U.S. 649 (1984).** The Court clarified the limits or extensions of the Miranda case decision.

***NIX V. WILLIAMS*, 467 U.S. 431 (1984).** The Court held that evidence that would be inevitably discovered is admissible.

***NORRIS V. ALABAMA*, 294 U.S. 587 (1935).** The Scottsboro Boys case where the Court found that Negroes being systematically excluded from serving on juries is unconstitutional.

***PAYTON V. NEW YORK, RIDDICK V. NEW YORK*, 445 U.S. 573 (1980).** The Court held that warrantless and consensual entrance into a home is unconstitutional.

***PERVEAR V. MASSACHUSETTS*, 72 U.S. (5 Wall.) 475 (1866).** The Court held that prisoners have no constitutional rights; this decision was later overturned by the Warren Court.

***PLESSY V. FERGUSON*, 163 U.S. 537 (1896).** The Court held that racial segregation was permitted under the doctrine of "separate but equal." This was overturned in 1953.

***POINTER V. TEXAS*, 380 U.S. 400 (1965).** The Court held that the Sixth and Fourteenth Amendments provided defendants with the right to cross-examine and confront their accusers.

***POWELL V. ALABAMA*, 287 U.S. 45 (1932).** The Scottsboro Boys case was overturned by the Court because they were denied due process.

***RHODE ISLAND V. INNIS*, 446 U.S. 291 (1980).** The Court held that interrogation is not just direct questioning but any actions police take to elicit information.

***RIDDICK V. NEW YORK*, 445 U.S. 573 (1980).** The Court held that search warrants are required to enter a home under the Fourth Amendment.

***RING V. ARIZONA*, 536 U.S. 584 (2002).** The Court held that a jury must obtain the aggravating circumstances in order to make a determination of death sentences.

***ROBINSON V. CALIFORNIA*, 370 U.S. 660 (1962).** The Court held that particular behaviors or deeds are prohibited from criminalization.

***ROCHIN V. CALIFORNIA*, 342 U.S. 179 (1973).** The Court held that evidence gathered by a procedure that shocks the conscience tests the limits of due process.

***SCHALL V. MARTIN*, 467 U.S. 253 (1984).** The Court held that juveniles are afforded due process, which protects them from punishment without adjudication.

***SKINNER V. OKLAHOMA*, 316 U.S. 535 (1942).** The Court held that sterilization of criminals is not permitted under the equal protection section of the law.

***TAYLOR V. LOUISIANA*, 419 U.S. 522 (1975).** The Court held that Louisiana laws that restricted women from serving on juries were unconstitutional.

***TENNESSEE V. GARNER*, 471 U.S. 1 (1985).** The Court found that the use of force was unreasonable unless the police officer saw that there was a chance of harm to the officer or others.

***TERRY V. OHIO*, 392 U.S. 1 (1968).** A landmark case in which the Court held that the stopping and searching of Terry because of suspicion was unreasonable. Such stops have come to be known as "Terry stops."

***U.S. V. RABINOWITZ*, 339 U.S. 56 (1950).** The Court held that the search of a person and an area following an arrest is permissible.

***U.S. V. SALERNO*, 481 U.S. 279 (1987).** The Court held that judges may deny bail to persons deemed a risk to the community.

Appendix 3

U.S. Supreme Court Cases That Review Death Penalty Issues

Death penalty cases are particularly interesting because they may or may not protect a life. Supreme Court justices review constitutional amendments to determine applications of the amendments to protect rights, thus guiding criminal procedure. The rights of citizens and even those sentenced to be executed are critical not just because of the conviction but because they often have applications for all citizens and especially for the concept of justice.

***ATKINS V. VIRGINIA*, 536 U.S. 304 (2002).** The Court held that under the Eighth Amendment capital punishment is cruel and unusual punishment if the person is mentally disabled. The state sets the conditions as to who is mentally disabled.

***BAZE V. REES*, 553 U.S. 35 (2008).** The Court held that capital punishment by lethal injection is constitutionally permitted.

***COKER V. GEORGIA*, 433 U.S. 584 (1977).** The Court held that capital punishment is disproportionate punishment for rape of an adult woman under the Constitution.

***ENMUND V. FLORIDA*, 458 U.S. 782 (1982).** The Court held that accomplices to murder and aiding and abetting would be overturned as specified in the proportionality clause in capital offenses.

***FORD V. WAINWRIGHT*, 477 U.S. 399 (1986).** The Court held that under the Eighth Amendment the insane cannot be executed. There must be a test of mental competency.

***FURMAN V. GEORGIA*, 408 U.S. 238 (1972).** One of a series of cases that led to the discontinuance of the death penalty in the United States.

***GREGG V. GEORGIA*, 428 U.S. 153 (1976).** A capital punishment case that led to the reinstatement of the death penalty in the United States.

***HERRERA V. COLLINS*, 506 U.S. 390 (1993).** The Court held that criminal evidence presented after conviction is not sufficient to grant habeas corpus even when it would exonerate the convicted individual.

***KANSAS V. MARSH*, 548 U.S. 163 (2006).** The Court held that when aggravating and mitigating circumstances have equal value, the death sentence is permissible.

***KENNEDY V. LOUISIANA*, 554 U.S. 407 (2008).** The Court held that cruel and unusual punishment, as described in the Eighth Amendment, was insufficient for prohibiting the death penalty for child rape that did not involve the death of the child.

***LOCKHART V. MCCREE*, 476 U.S. 162 (1986).** Ardia McCree was accused of capital murder. The jurors were removed by the judge because they stated they could not impose the death penalty. The Court held that the removal of jurors did not violate either the Sixth or Fourteen Amendment protection for a fair trial.

***LOUISIANA EX REL. FRANCIS V. RESWEBER*, 329 U.S. 459 (1947).** The issue before the Court was whether the death penalty could be imposed a second time when the first attempt fails. The Court held that this was not a case of double jeopardy and that the execution could be imposed.

***McCLESKEY V. KEMP*, 481 U.S. 279 (1987).** The Court holding that upheld the death penalty—that is, it would not overturn a guilty verdict—when a study indicated that there was no racially disproportionate impact.

***PALKO V. CONNECTICUT*, 302 U.S. 319 (1937).** A decision that double jeopardy did not apply in Palko's case, that due process and the Fifth and Fourteenth Amendments did not apply. The matter was later overturned in *Benton v. Maryland* (1969).

***PENRY V. LYNAUGH*, 492 U.S. 392 (1989).** Johnny Paul Penry was sentenced to death for murder. The Court held that the execution of the mentally retarded was not an Eighth Amendment violation but did remand the case for review because the jury had not considered his intellectual capacity.

***RING V. ARIZONA*, 536 U.S. 584. A (2002).** The jury found Ring guilty of felony murder, not premeditated murder. The judge decided that the punishment would be execution.

***WITHERSPOON V. ILLINOIS*, 391 U.S. 510 (1968).** The idea of Witherspooning a jury came from this case. The Court addressed jury selection based on jurors' opinion of the death penalty.

Bibliography

CONTENTS

INTRODUCTION

Literature on the history of the American criminal justice system has at its fulcrum three intersecting literatures: one that pertains to the nature of crime and two that demonstrate the evolution of the science of crime and the system that seeks to control it. While the bibliography that follows is thus organized into discrete sections—crime, criminology, and the criminal justice system—in reality the boundaries of these interrelated areas are far less clear.

Publications from Western Europe throughout the 17th and 18th centuries form both the structural and intellectual foundations of modern criminal justice in the United States. For instance, *Leviathan* (1651), by English philosopher Thomas Hobbes, established the social contract theory, the basis for American police power. In 1775, Founding Father John Adams referenced *On Crimes and Punishments* (1764), a brief but widely read monograph by Italian legal philosopher Cesare Beccaria (McCullough 2001). This work helped to solidify the notion that the American system be based on the human capacity for free choice and not on religious forces. Beccaria's discussions of deterrence, penology, and torture continue to inform contemporary discussions in American sentencing. Not long after the founding of the country, another English philosopher, Jeremy Bentham, published *Introduction to the Principles of Morals and Legislation* (1789). The utilitarian theory of ethics articulated in this work has contributed to the shaping of correctional punishment and substantive criminal law in the United States since its publication.

Through the 1800s, what we now refer to as separate sciences in the academy, previously labeled philosophies, came into their own disciplinary monikers, as did sociology (e.g., Spencer 1874; Ward 1883). Within this context, Charles Darwin's *On the Origin of Species* (1859) was published, as was the work of other empiricists such as *The Criminal Man (1876)* by Italian physicist Cesare Lombroso. The observations Lombroso made on the physical characteristics of prisoners marked the movement of criminology from a legalistic and philosophical pursuit to a scientific one. For this reason, many criminologists consider Lombroso the father of criminology as a social science. Following the initial classical era in which crime was believed to be the result of reason, this positivist era dominated (e.g., Dugdale 1877). However, as other empiricists, such as Goring in his *The English Convict* (1913), failed to support Lombrosian hypotheses, positivism waned in popularity, and other causes of crime began to receive attention. From this point forward, the literature related to explanations of crime developed along at least three paths, from conflict, and sociological, to integrated theories.

Alcohol prohibition, corruption, and the Great Depression characterized the early 1900s in the United States. In this context, it made sense for emergent American sociologists to utilize the work of a French sociologist, Émile Durkheim, whose work explored the effects of rapid industrialization on social norms. Durkheim's *The Division of Labour in Society* (1893) and *Suicide* (1897) would become central to the American approach to crime advocated by the influential Chicago School. American urban sociologists captured growing interest in social disorganization in publications such as *The Gang: A Study of 1313 Gangs in Chicago* (Thrasher 1927) and *The City* (Parks, Burgess, and McKenzie 1925). It was around this same time that the Chicago Crime Commission, a professional association funded by private donations from local businesses, formed to oversee the activities of local criminal justice agencies. Not long afterward, in a report commissioned by President Hoover to address the same disorganization being researched by the Chicago School and the corruption being targeted by the Crime Commission, American agencies that respond to crime were framed as a "system" for the first time.

August Vollmer, who is often referred to as the father of modern American policing, was the lead author on this 1931 report known as the Wickersham Commission Reports. Vollmer advocated strongly for the professionalization of law enforcement through education and better funding. Vollmer, a police chief turned faculty at the University of California, Berkeley, led the development of degree programs there. The first were summer sessions from 1916 to 1927, then a full-session program in 1931, and eventually the School of Criminology in 1947. Prior to this, not long after the Wickersham Commission Reports, Michigan State University founded the country's first school of criminal justice (1935). Despite the differences in names (criminology v. criminal justice), both programs were built with the needs of current and future police officers in mind. Learning objectives pertained to the administration of justice, law, and practical knowledge (Brandsetter 1989). As part of the goals articulated there, Vollmer created the National Association of College Police Training Officials in 1941, which is today the American Society of Criminology, the largest professional organization of criminologists in the United States. As these structures—intended to bridge the administration of justice—to the science of justice were forming, American sociology continued to dominate thinking on crime. American sociologists, such as Sutherland and Cressey in their *Principles of Criminology* (1934) and Sellin in his *Culture Conflict and Crime: A Report of the Subcommittee on Delinquency of the Committee on Personality and Culture* (1938) began to incorporate concepts of social learning (e.g., differential associations) in social disorganization explanations of crime. Since this time, the American criminal justice system has grown exponentially, and so has the literature that seeks to explain it.

During the different civil unrest of the 1960s, American confidence in the ability of all branches of the criminal justice system to uphold constitutional rights again came into question. In response, like Hoover almost 40 years earlier, President Lyndon B. Johnson commissioned a report on challenges facing the criminal justice process in the United States in 1967. This report formed the basis for the Law Enforcement Assistance Administration (LEAA), which passed with the Safe Streets Act in 1968. This act delivered federal funding for research and education in criminal justice. This funding contributed greatly to increased education for criminal justice practitioners and for new scholars and scientists, as well as to various research grants that made the study of crime and the criminal justice system more possible than ever before. Around the same time, in *Delinquents and Nondelinquents in Perspective* (1968), Eleanor Glueck and Sheldon Glueck were successfully putting forth an empirical argument for a multidisciplinary approach to understanding crime. Recognizing the value of insights from fields such as anthropology, psychology, and biology, their work marked the expansion of the field from sociology.

Compared to the early American research into crime described above (e.g., out of the Chicago School), which can be characterized as qualitative, specific, and descriptive, the evolution of empirical studies in criminal justice and criminology in the United States over the past 50 years has been in the direction of quantification. The trend in the majority of governmental funding agencies has been to solicit research proposals that can answer causal and broad questions related especially to issues such as crime prevention, police response, legislative effects, and other concrete issues related to the discretion of criminal justice professionals and criminal justice policy. Studies that utilize large samples and/or experimental methods have gained prominence in the modern research literature on American criminal justice.

ORGANIZATION OF THE BIBLIOGRAPHY

The bibliography that follows is structured to reflect the multidisciplinary nature of the field. Headings are organized into crime, criminology, and the three branches of the criminal justice system: law enforcement, courts, and corrections. The selected works encompass a wide range of subjects related to the criminal justice profession, which like the dictionary as a whole focuses primarily on those works that are historically relevant and center on the American system and related scholarship. To present the largest, most complete, and factual development of the criminal justice system in the United States, the selection is large and diverse, coming from a wide range of sources. Some sources represent standardized texts, others a lifetime of contemplation, and some the thorough analysis of what has been and what currently is the practice, and what the path to a stable and just system might look like. Practitioners, scholars, students, and the general reader can thus access a broader understanding of the scope of the text here and identify historical and contemporary readings pertinent to their interests.

Behaviors that are deemed criminal and the methods of committing those crimes (e.g., firearms, computers) organize the system. As history bears witness to technological, cultural, and economic developments, authors from diverse perspectives (e.g., academia, politics, and popular culture) present their take on crime. These publications are reflected in the first section of the bibliography, where readers can find sections such as animal abuse, domestic violence and intimate partner violence, drugs and alcohol, firearms, gangs, gender and crime, hate crimes and genocide, piracy, race and crime, sex crimes, serial killers, terrorism, victims and victimology, violence, and white-collar crime.

Theories and methods that have evolved to explain crime are highlighted in the second section on criminology. This section contains three subsections: general criminology and history, research methods, and a large section on theoretical perspectives that have developed throughout the history of criminology. These subsections cover the following perspectives on crime: biological and biosocial, classical (deterrence, rational choice), conflict theories, cultural, feminist, labeling and reintegrative shaming, integrated (life course, developmental), psychological, social structure and disorganization (anomie, strain), social learning, and social bonding and control.

The next three sections of the bibliography represent works specific to the three branches of the criminal justice system: law enforcement, courts, and corrections. The law enforcement section covers areas such as criminal investigations, disaster management, federal police, forfeiture, police culture, private police, race and policing, security/school security, policing strategies (specifically, broken windows, community policing, and problem-oriented policing), and the use of force. The section on courts includes the following areas: capital punishment, constitutional law, criminal procedure, the defense, expert and eyewitness testimony, evidence, juries, law, trials, lawyers, specialized courts, substantive criminal law, Supreme Court cases, and wrongful conviction. The last section, on corrections, groups related literature into subgroups such as correctional administration, life on the inside, mass incarceration, reform, probation and parole, rehabilitation and other modes of correctional intervention, reentry, sentencing and punishment, and transportation of convicts.

CRIME

Animal Abuse

Arluke, Arnold. *Brute Force: Animal Police and the Challenge of Cruelty*. West Lafayette, Ind.: Purdue University Press. 2004.

Lockwood, Randall, and Robert Hoadge. "The Tangled Web of Animal Abuse: The Links between Cruelty to Animals and Human Violence." In *Cruelty to Animals and Interpersonal Violence: Readings in Research and Application*, ed. Frank Ascione and Randall Lockwood, 69–76. West Lafayette, Ind.: Purdue University Press, 1998.

Bootlegging

Allsop, Kenneth. *The Bootleggers and Their Era*. New York: Doubleday, 1961.

Butts, Edward. *Outlaws of the Lakes: Bootlegging and Smuggling from Colonial Times to Prohibition*. Holt, Mich.: Thunder Bay, 2004.

Hallwas, John. *The Bootlegger: A Story of Small-Town America*. Chicago: University of Illinois Press, 1999.

Crime Novels (true crime, autobiographies)

Alexander, Shana. *Anyone's Daughter: The Times and Trials of Patty Hearst*. London: Weidenfeld & Nicolson, 1979.

Block, Lawrence. *Gangsters, Swindlers, Killers, and Thieves: The Lives and Crimes of Fifty American Villains*. New York: Oxford University Press, 2004.

Blum, Howard. *American Lightning: Terror, Mystery, the Birth of Hollywood, and the Crime of the Century*. New York: Three Rivers, 2008.

Bugliosi, Vincent. *Helter Skelter*. London: Norton, 1974.

Burgess, Anthony. *A Clockwork Orange*. New York: Norton, 1986.

Burns, Robert. *I Am a Fugitive from a Georgia Chain Gang*. New York: Vanguard, 1932.

Capote, Truman. *In Cold Blood*. New York: Random House, 1965.

Capuzzo, Michael. *The Murder Room*. New York: Gotham, 2010.

Cochran, Johnnie *A Lawyer's Life*. New York: Macmillan, 2003.

Early, Pete. *The Hot House: Life inside Leavenworth Prison*. New York: Bantam, 1992.

Fisher, Jim. *The Lindbergh Case*. New Brunswick, N.J.: Rutgers University Press, 1987.

Frank, Gerald. *The Boston Strangler*. New York: New American Library, 1966.

Gaddis, Thomas, and James O. Long, eds. *Panzram: A Journal of Murder*. New York: Macmillan, 1970.

Geis, Gilbert, and Leigh B. Bienen. *Crimes of the Century: From Leopold and Loeb to O. J. Simpson*. Boston, Mass.: Northeastern University Press, 1998.

Goffman, Irving. *Asylums*. Garden City, N.Y.: Doubleday, 1961.

Gordon, R. Michael. *The American Murders of Jack the Ripper*. Santa Barbara, Calif.: Praeger, 2003.

Gorn, Elliot. *Dillinger's Wild Ride: The Year That Made America's Public Enemy Number One*. New York: Oxford University Press, 2009.

Guinn, Jeff. *Go Down Together: The True Story of Bonnie and Clyde*. New York: Simon and Schuster, 2009.

———. *The Last Gunfight: The Real Story of the Shootout at the O.K. Corral—And How It Changed the American West*. New York: Simon & Schuster, 2011.

Harris, Thomas. *Hannibal*. New York: Random House, 1999.

———. *Red Dragon*. New York. Random House, 1981.

———. *The Silence of the Lambs*. New York: St. Martin's, 1988.

Hollander, Xaviera, Robin Moore, and Yvonne Dunleavy. *Happy Hooker: My Own Story*. New York: HarperCollins, 2002.

Jennings, Dean. *We Only Kill Each Other: The Life and Times of Bugsy Siegel*. Englewood Cliffs, N.J.: Prentice Hall, 1967.

Klausner, Lawrence D. *The Son of Sam*. New York: McGraw-Hill, 1981.

Kobler, John. *Capone: The Life and World of Al Capone*. New York: Putnam, 1971.

Lane, Mark. *Murder in Memphis: The FBI and the Assassination of Martin Luther King*. Fair Lawn, N.J.: Lane, 1993.

Lewis, Alfred. *The Apaches of New York*. New York: Dillingham, 1912.

Linsey, Robert. *The Falcon and the Snowman*. New York: Simon & Schuster, 1984.

McGinniss, Joe. *Fatal Vision: A True Crime Classic*. New York: New American Library, 1983.

McNulty, Faith. *The Burning Bed: The True Story of Francine Hughes—A Beaten Wife Who Rebelled*. New York: Harcourt, 1980.

Murphy, Jack Roland. *Jewels for the Journey: Murph the Surf*. Costa Mesa, Calif.: International Prison Ministry, 1989.

Pistone, Joseph. *Donnie Brasco: My Undercover Life in the Mafia—A True Story by FBI Agent Joseph D. Pistone*. New York: Penguin Putnam, 1989.

Royce, Kenneth. *The XYY Man*. New York: Stein and Day, 1970.

Rudinsky, Red, and Don Riley. *The Gonif*. Blue Earth, Minn.: Piper, 1970.

Sheppard, Sam. *Endure and Conquer*. Cleveland, Ohio: World, 1966.

Smith, J. E. *Trillion Dollar Insurance Crook*. Blooming Grove, Tex.: Smith Engineering and Consulting, 2003.

Stewart, James. *Blind Eye: How the Medical Establishment Let a Doctor Get Away with Murder*. New York: Simon & Schuster, 1999.

Stone, Michael. *The Anatomy of Evil*. New York: Prometheus, 2009.

Walker, Keith, ed. *John Dryden: The Major Works*. New York: Oxford University Press, 1987.

Watson, Bruce. *Sacco and Vanzetti: The Men, the Murders, and the Judgment of Mankind*. New York: Penguin, 2008.

Domestic Violence/Intimate Partner Violence

Dowd, Michael. "Battered Women: A Perspective on Injustice." *Urban Law Journal* 19 (1991).

Rothenberg, Bess. "'We Don't Have Time for Social Change': Cultural Compromise and the Battered Woman Syndrome." *Gender and Society* 17, no. 5 (2003): 771–87.

Rule, Ann. *The Stranger Beside Me*. New York: Pocket Books, 2009.

Walker, Lenore. *The Battered Woman*. New York: Harper and Row, 1979.

Drugs/Alcohol and Crime

Alcoholics Anonymous. *Alcoholics Anonymous: The Story of How Many Thousands of Men and Women Have Recovered from Alcoholism*. Alcoholics Anonymous World Service, 1 December 1976.

American Medical Association and American Bar Association. *Drug Addiction, Crime or Disease? Interim and Final Reports of the Joint Committee of the American Bar Association and the American Medical Association on Narcotic Drugs*. Bloomington: Indiana University Press, 1961.

American Psychiatric Association. *Diagnostic and Statistical Manual of Mental Disorders*. 5th ed. Arlington, Va.: American Psychiatric Press, 2015.

Benezet, Anthony. *The Mighty Destroyer Displayed, in Some Account of the Dreadful Havock Made by the Mistaken Use as Well as Abuse of Distilled Spirituous Liquors*. Philadelphia: Joseph Crukshank, 1774.

Domestic Council (U.S.), Drug Abuse Task Force. *White Paper on Drug Abuse, September 1975: A Report to the President from the Domestic Council Drug Abuse Task Force*. Washington, D.C.: Supt. of Docs., U.S. Government Printing Office, 1975.

Huizinga, David, Rolf Loeber, and Terrence Thornberry, eds. *Urban Delinquency and Substance Abuse: Technical Report*. Washington, D.C.: U.S. Department of Justice, Office of Justice Programs, Office of Juvenile Justice and Delinquency Prevention, 1993. Retrieved 14 December 2016, https://www.ncjrs.gov/html/ojjdp/jjbul9712-2/jjb1297.html#contents.

Jonnes, Jill. *Hep-Cats, Narcs, and Pipe Dreams: A History of America's Romance with Illegal Drugs*. Baltimore, Md.: Johns Hopkins University Press, 1996.

White, William. *Slaying the Dragon: The History of Addiction Treatment and Recovery in America*. Bloomington, Ill.: Chestnut Health Systems, 1998.

Employee Theft

Kennedy, Jay P. "Shedding Light on Employee Theft's Dark Figure: A Typology of Employee Theft Nonreporting Rationalizations." *Organizational Management Theory* 13, no. 1 (2016): 49–60.

Firearms

Carroll, Water F. "National Instant Criminal Background Check System." In *Guns in American Society: An Encyclopedia of History, Politics, Culture and the Law*, ed. Gregg Lee Carter, 431–32. Santa Barbara, Calif.: ABC-CLIO, 2002.

Chase, Kenneth. *Firearms: A Global History to 1700*. Cambridge: Cambridge University Press, 2003.

Dixon, Jo, and Alan J. Lizotte. "Gun Ownership and the Southern Subculture of Violence." *American Journal of Sociology* 93, no. 2 (1987): 383–405.

Guilmartin, John Francis. *Gunpowder and Galleys: Changing Technology and Mediterranean Warfare at Sea in the 16th Century*. New York: Cambridge University Press, 1974.

Kennett, Lee, and James LaVerne Anderson. *The Gun in America: The Origins of a National Dilemma*. Santa Barbara, Calif.: Praeger, 1975.

Gangs

Asbury, Herbert. *The Gangs of New York: An Informal History of the New York Underworld*. New York: Knopf, 1928.

Becker, Howard. *The Outsiders: Studies in the Sociology of Deviance*. New York: Free Press, 1963.

Blum, Howard. *Gangland: How the FBI Broke the Mob*. New York: Pocket Books, 1993.
Fried, Albert. *The Rise and Fall of the Jewish Gangster in America*. New York: Columbia University Press, 1993.
Miller, Jody. *One of the Guys: Girls, Gangs, and Gender*. New York: Oxford University Press, 2001.
Nickel, Steven, and William Helmer. *Baby Face Nelson: Portrait of a Public Enemy*. Nashville, Tenn.: Cumberland House, 2002.
Simpson, Colton. *Inside the Crips: Life inside L.A.'s Most Notorious Gang*. New York: St. Martin's, 2005.
Thompson, Hunter S. *Hell's Angels: A Strange and Terrible Saga*. New York: Random House, 1966.
Thrasher, Frederick, *The Gang*. Chicago, Ill.: New Chicago School Press, 2000 (originally published 1927).
Venkatesh, Sudhir. *Gang Leader for a Day: A Rogue Sociologist Takes to the Streets*. New York: Penguin, 2008.

Gender and Crime

Branson, Susan. *Dangerous to Know: Women, Crime and Notoriety in the Early Republic*. Philadelphia: University of Pennsylvania Press, 2008.
Brownmiller, Susan. *Against Our Will: Men, Women, and Rape*. New York: Simon & Schuster, 1993.
Caputo, Gail A., and Anna King. "Shoplifting: Work, Agency, and Gender." *Feminist Criminology* 6, no. 3 (2011): 159–77.
Carlsen, Pat. "Criminal Women and Criminal Justice: The Limits to, and Potential of, Feminist and Left Realist Perspectives." In *Issues in Realist Criminology*, ed. Roger Matthews and Jock Young, 51–69. London: Sage, 1992.
Cass, Vivienne C. "Homosexual Identity Formation: A Theoretical Model." *Journal of Homosexuality* 4, no. 3 (1979): 219–35.
Chesney-Lind, Meda, and Randall G. Shelden. *Girls: Delinquency and Juvenile Justice*. 2nd ed. Belmont, Calif.: West/Wadsworth, 1998.
Cory, Donald. *The Homosexual in America: A Subjective Approach*. New York: Greenberg, 1951.
Datesman, Susan, and Frank Scarpitti. *Women, Crime, and Justice*. New York: Oxford University Press, 1980.
Flexner, Eleanor, and Ellen Fitzpatrick. *Century of Struggle: The Women's Rights Movement in the United States*. Cambridge, Mass.: Belknap, 1996.
Gill, Aisha K., Carolyn Strange, and Karl Roberts. *"Honour" Killing and Violence: Theory, Policy and Practice*. London: Palgrave Macmillan 2014.

Huebner, Beth M., Christina DeJong, and Jennifer Cobbina. "Women Coming Home: Long-Term Patterns of Recidivism." *Justice Quarterly* 27, no. 2 (2010): 225–54.

Huebner, Beth M., and Regan Gustafson. "The Effect of Maternal Incarceration on Adult Offspring Involvement in the Criminal Justice System." *Journal of Criminal Justice* 35, no. 3 (2007): 283–96.

Jimenez, Stephen. *The Book of Matt: Hidden Truths about the Murder of Matthew Shepard*. Hanover, N.H.: Steerforth, 2013.

Lootens, Tricia. "Women Who Kill: The Burning Bed." *Off Our Backs*, 31 December 1983, 16.

Miller, Jody. *One of the Guys: Girls, Gangs, and Gender*. New York: Oxford University Press, 2001.

Shepard, Judy. *The Meaning of Matthew: My Son's Murder in Laramie, and a World Transformed*. New York: Penguin, 2009.

Walker, Lenore. *The Battered Woman Syndrome*. New York: Springer, 1979.

Woolston, Howard Brown. *Prostitution in the United States*. New York: Century, 1921.

Zoglin, Richard. "The Burning Bed." *Time*, 8 October 1984, 85.

Hate Crime and Genocide

Alshuler, David A. *Hitler's War against the Jews: A Young Reader's Version of Lucy Dawidowicz's* The War against the Jews, 1943–1945. New York: Behrman, 1978.

Perry, Barbara. *In the Name of Hate: Understanding Hate Crimes*. New York: Routledge, 2001.

Sherwin, Byron L. "Teaching about the Holocaust: Some Guidelines." *Ped Rep* 33 (March 1982): 4–6.

Homicide/Suicide

Kasserman, David. *Fall River Outrage: Life, Murder, and Justice in Early Industrial New England*. Philadelphia: University of Pennsylvania Press, 1986.

Moses, Norton H. *Lynching and Vigilantism in the United States: An Annotated Bibliography*. Santa Barbara, Calif.: ABC-CLIO, 1997.

Nash, Jay Robert. *Murder America: Homicide in the United States from the Revolution to the Present*. New York: M. Evans, 1980.

Wolfgang, Marvin. *Patterns in Criminal Homicide*. Houston: Science Editions, 1966.

———. "Victim Precipitated Criminal Homicide." *Journal of Law and Criminology* 48, no. 1 (1957): 1–11.

Immigration

Gutierrez, David G., ed. *Between Two Worlds*. Lanham, Md.: Rowman & Littlefield, 1996.

Skerry, Peter. "Many Borders to Cross: Is Immigration the Exclusive Responsibility of the Federal Government?" *Publius* 25, no. 3 (Summer 1995): 71–85.

Identity Theft

United States Federal Advisory Committee on False Identification. *The Criminal Use of False Identification: A Summary Report*. Washington, D.C.: U.S. Department of Justice, 1976.

Missing Children

Lowery, Robert G. "Missing Children Division, National Center for Missing and Exploited Children." *Police Chief Magazine*, December 2010.

Platt, Anthony M. *Child Savers*. Chicago, Ill.: University of Chicago, 1977.

Walsh, John. *No Mercy*. New York: Simon & Schuster, 1998.

———. *Tears of Rage: From Grieving Father to Crusader for Justice; The Untold Story of the Adam Walsh Case*. New York: Simon & Schuster, 1997.

Waxman, Olivia B. "The U.S. Is Still Dealing with the Murder of Adam Walsh." *Time*, 10 August 2016.

Organized Crime

Abadinsky, Howard. *Organized Crime*. Boston: Cengage, 2017.

Albini, Joseph. *The American Mafia: Genesis of a Legend*. New York: Appleton-Century-Crofts, 1971.

Bonanno, Joe. *A Man of Honor: The Autobiography of Joe Bonanno*. New York: St. Martin's, 1983.

Cummings, John, and Ernest Volkman, *Goombata: The Improbable Rise and Fall of John Gotti and His Gang*. Boston: Little, Brown, 1990.

Downey, Patrick. *Gangster City: The History of the New York Underworld, 1900–1935*. Fort Lee, N.J.: Barricade, 2004.

Eghigian, Mars. *After Capone: The Life and World of Chicago Mob Boss Frank "The Enforcer" Nitti*. Nashville, Tenn.: Cumberland House, 2006.

English, T. J. *Havana Nocturne: How the Mob Owned Cuba and then Lost It to the Revolution*. New York: William Morrow, 2007.

———. *Paddy Wacked: The Untold Story of the Irish-American Gangster*. New York: Regan, 2005.

Fox, Stephen. *Blood and Power: Organized Crime in Twentieth-Century America*. New York: William Morrow, 1989.

Gambetta, Diego. *The Sicilian Mafia: The Business of Private Protection*. Cambridge, Mass.: Harvard University Press, 1996.

Goldfarb, Ronald. *Perfect Villains, Imperfect Heroes: Robert Kennedy's War against Organized Crime*. Grand Junction, Colo.: Capital, 1995.

Gosch, Martin, and Richard Hammer. *Lucky Luciano: The Last Testament of Lucky Luciano*. New York: Little, Brown, 1975.

Grennan, Sean, and Marjie Britz. *Organized Crime: A Worldwide Perspective*. Upper Saddle River, N.J.: Pearson, 2006.

Hoffman, Dennis. *Scarface Al and the Crime Crusades: Chicago's Private War against Capone*. Carbondale: Southern Illinois University Press, 1993.

Ianni, Francis. *A Family Business: Kinship and Social Control in Organized Crime*. New York: Russell Sage Foundation, 1972.

Jacobs, James. *Mobsters, Unions and Feds: The Mafia and the American Labor Movement*. New York: New York University Press, 2006.

Lesy, Michael. *Murder City: The Bloody History of Chicago in the Twenties*. New York: Norton, 2007.

Maas, Peter. *The Valachi Papers*. New York: HarperCollins, 1968.

Raab, Selwyn. *Five Families: The Rise, Decline, and Resurgence of America's Most Powerful Mafia Empires*. New York: Thomas Dunne, 2005.

Serio, Joseph. *Investigating the Russian Mafia*. Durham, N.C.: Carolina Academic, 2008.

Piracy

Konstam, Angus. *The History of Pirates*. New York: Lyons, 2002.

Lucie-Smith, Edward. *Outcasts of the Sea: Pirates and Piracy*. New York: Paddington, 1978.

Pennell, Richard, ed. *Bandits at Sea: A Pirates Reader*. New York: New York University Press, 2001.

Race and Crime

Anderson, Elijah. *Code of the Street: Decency, Violence, and the Moral Life of the Inner City*. New York: Norton, 1999.

Gabbidon, Shaun, and Helen Greene. *Race and Crime*. Los Angeles, Calif.: Sage, 2016.

Glotzer, Paige. "Exclusion in Arcadia: How Suburban Developers Circulated Ideas about Discrimination, 1890–1950." *Journal of Urban History* 41, no. 3 (2015): 479–94.

Hartney, Christopher, and Linh Vuong. *Created Equal: Racial and Ethnic Disparities in the US Criminal Justice System*. Washington, D.C.: National Council on Crime and Delinquency, 2009.

Norris, Clarence, and Sybil D. Washington. *The Last of the Scottsboro Boys: An Autobiography*. New York: Putnam, 1979.

Patterson, Haywood, and Earl Conrad. *Scottsboro Boy*. New York: Bantam, 1950.

Tonry, Michael. *Malign Neglect: Race, Crime, and Punishment in America*. New York: Oxford University Press, 1995.

Serial Killers

Douglas, John, and Mark Olshaker. *Mindhunter: Inside the FBI's Elite Serial Crime Unit*. New York: Gallery, 1997.

Egger, Steven A. *The Killers among Us: An Examination of Serial Murder and Its Investigation*. Upper Saddle River, N.J.: Prentice Hall, 2002.

Guillen, Tomas. *Serial Killers: Issues Explored through the Green River Murders*. Upper Saddle River, N.J.: Pearson, 2007.

Hare, Robert. *Without Conscience: The Disturbing World of the Psychopaths among Us*. New York: Guilford, 1993.

Keppel, Robert, Joseph Weis, Katherine Brown, and Kristen Welch. "The Jack the Ripper Murders: A Modus Operandi and Signature Analysis of the 1888–1891 Whitechapel Murders." *Journal of Investigative Psychology and Offender Profiling* 2, no. 1 (2005): 1–21.

Lane, Bryan, and Wilfred Gregg. *The Encyclopedia of Serial Killers*. New York: Berkley, 1995.

Ressler, Robert. *Whoever Fights Monsters: My 20 Years in Tracking Serial Killers for the FBI*. New York: St. Martin's, 1992.

Schwartz, Ted. *The Hillside Strangler: A Murderer's Mind*. New York: New American Library, 1981.

Wenzl, Roy, Tim Potter, L. Kelly, and Hurst Lavinia. *Bind, Torture, Kill: The Inside Story of BTK, the Serial Killer Next Door*. New York: HarperCollins, 2007.

Woods, Paul. *Ed Gein—Psycho*. New York: St. Martin's, 1995.

Sexual Crimes

Armstrong, Louise. *Kiss Daddy Good-Night: A Speak-Out on Incest*. New York: Hawthorne, 1978.

Byard, Roger, David Eitzen, and Ross James. "Unusual Fatal Mechanisms in Nonasphyxial Autoerotic Death." *American Journal of Forensic Medicine and Pathology* 21 (2000): 65–68.

Champagne, Rosaria. *The Politics of Survivorship: Incest, Women's Literature, and Feminist Theory*. New York: New York University Press, 1996.

Easton, Susan. *The Problem of Pornography: Regulation and the Right to Free Speech*. New York: Routledge, 1994.

Ehrlich, Edwin, and Sergey Sheleg. *Autoerotic Asphyxiation: Forensic, Medical, and Social Aspects*. Tucson, Ariz.: Wheatmark, 2006.

Harrison, Maureen, and Steve Gilbert, ed. *Obscenity and Pornography Decisions of the United States Supreme Court*. Carlsbad, Calif.: Excellent Books, 2000.

Hawkins, Gordon, and Franklin Zimring. *Pornography in a Free Society*. New York: Cambridge University Press, 1991.

Hughes, Donna M., Janice Raymond, and Carol Gomez. *Sex Trafficking of Women in the United States: International and Domestic Trends*. North Amherst, Mass.: Coalition against Trafficking in Women, 2001.

Keire, Mara L. *For Business and Pleasure: Red Light Districts and the Regulation of Vice in the United States*. Baltimore, Md.: Johns Hopkins University Press, 2010.

Klintschar Michael, Peter Grabuschnigg, and Alred Beham. "Death from Electrocution during Autoerotic Practice: Case Report and Review of the Literature." *American Journal of Forensic Medicine and Pathology* 19 (1998): 190–93.

Mackey, Thomas. *Pornography on Trial*. Santa Barbara, Calif.: ABC-CLIO, 2002.

———. *Red Lights Out: A Legal History of Prostitution, Disorderly Houses and Vice Districts, 1870–1917*. New York: Garland, 1987.

O'Halloran, Ronald, and Park Dietz. "Autoerotic Fatalities with Power Hydraulics." *Journal of Forensic Science* 38, no. 2 (1993): 359–64.

Sauvageau, Anne, and Vernon Geberth. *Autoerotic Deaths: Practical Forensic and Investigative Perspectives*. New York: Taylor & Francis, 2003.

Terrorism/Extremist Groups

Abu-Amr, Ziad. "Hamas: A Historical and Political Background." *Journal of Palestine Studies* 22 (Summer 1993): 5–19.

Asthana, N. C. *Urban Terrorism: Myths and Realities*. Jaipur, India: Pointer, 2009.

Carus, W. Seth. "R.I.S.E." In *Toxic Terror: Assessing Terrorist Use of Chemical and Biological Weapons*, ed. Jonathan B. Tucker, Steven E. Miller, and Sean M. Lynn-Jones, 55–70. Cambridge, Mass.: MIT Press, 2000.

Chase, Alston. *Harvard and the Unabomber: The Making of an American Terrorist*. New York: Norton, 2003.

Freilich, Joshua D. *Reducing Terrorism through Situational Crime Prevention*, ed. Joshua D. Freilich and Graeme R. Newman. Monsey, New York: Criminal Justice, 2009.

Gage, Beverly. *The Day Wall Street Exploded: A Story of America in Its First Age of Terror*. New York: Oxford University Press, 2008.

Gregory, Bridgett, and David Waag. *Military Medicine: Medical Aspects of Biological Warfare*. Office of the Surgeon General, Department of the Army, Library of Congress, 1997.

Hamm, Mark S. "Prison Islam in the Age of Sacred Terror." *British Journal of Criminology* 49, no. 5 (2009): 667–85.

Johnson, David. *Lockerbie: The Real Story*. London: Bloomsbury, 1989.

Kruglanski, Arie W., Xiaoyan Chen, Mark Dechesne, Shira Fishman, and Edward Orehek. "Fully Committed: Suicide Bombers' Motivation and the Quest for Personal Significance." *Political Psychology* 30, no. 3 (2009): 331–57.

LaFree, Gary, and Laura Dugan. "Introducing the Global Terrorism Database." *Terrorism and Political Violence* 19, no. 2 (2007): 181–204.

Linedecker, Clifford. *Massacre at Waco*. New York: St. Martin's, 1993.

Morrow, Lance, Nancy Gibbs, Richard Lacayo, and Jill Smolowe. *Mad Genius: The Odyssey, Pursuit and Capture of the Unabomber Suspect*. New York: Warner, 1996.

Newport, Kenneth. *The Branch Davidians of Waco: The History and Beliefs of an Apocalyptic Sect*. New York: Oxford University Press, 2006.

Novak, Matt. "The Largest Bioterrorism Attack in US History was an Attempt to Swing an Election." Gizmodo, 2016.

Reavis, Dick. *The Ashes of Waco: An Investigation*. New York: Simon & Schuster, 1995.

Ross, Brian. "Osama Bin Laden Killed: U.S. Intelligence Probes Possible Pakistani Support System." ABC News, 3 May 2011.

Schreiber, Brad. *Revolution's End: The Patty Hearst Kidnapping, Mind Control, and the Secret History of Donald Defreeze and the SLA*. New York: Skyhorse, 2016.

Stern, Jessica. "Terror in the Name of God: Why Religious Militants Kill." New York: Ecco, 2003.

Tucker, Jonathan. *Toxic Terror: Assessing Terrorist Use of Chemical and Biological Weapons*. Cambridge, Mass.: Belfer Center for Science and International Affairs, 2000.

White, Jonathan. *Terrorism and Homeland Security*. Belmont, Calif.: Wadsworth, 2012.

Wright, Lawrence. *The Looming Tower: Al-Qaeda and the Road to 9/11*. New York: Knopf, 2006.

Victims and Victimology

Adorjan, Michael, Tony Christensen, Benjamin Kelly, and Dorothy Pawluch. "Stockholm Opportunity Syndrome as Vernacular Resource." *Sociological Quarterly* 53, no. 3 (2012): 454–74.

Bennett, Georgette. *Crimewarps: The Future of Crime in America*. Garden City, N.Y.: Anchor Doubleday, 1987.

Davis, Randy, Authur Lurigio, and Susan Herman, eds. *Victims of Crime*. 4th ed. Thousand Oaks, Calif.: Sage, 2013.

Elias, Robert. *The Politics of Victimization: Victims, Victimology, and Human Rights*. New York: Oxford University Press, 1986.

Finkelhor, David. *Childhood Victimization: Violence, Crime, and Abuse in the Lives of Young People*. New York: Oxford University Press, 2008.

Frank, Linda. "The Collection of Restitution: An Often Overlooked Service to Crime Victims." In *New Directions from the Field: Victim's Rights and Services for the 21st Century*. Office of Justice Programs, Office for Victims of Crime, U.S. Department of Justice, 1998.

Hickey, Eric. *Serial Murderers and Their Victims*. Belmont, Calif.: Wadsworth, 2010.

Karmen, Andrew. *Crime Victims: An Introduction to Victimology*. Boston: Cengage Learning, 2015.

Ochberg, Frank. "The Ties That Bind Captive to Captor." *Los Angeles Times*, 8 April 2005.

Parent, D. G., B. Auerbach, and K. E. Carlsen. *Compensating Crime Victims: A Summary of Policies and Practices*. Washington, D.C.: U.S. Department of Justice, 1992.

Peterson, Christopher, Steven Maier, and Martin Seligman. *Learned Helplessness: A Theory for the Age of Personal Control*. New York: Oxford University Press, 1995.

Rand, Michael R., and Callie M. Rennison. *Criminal Victimization, 2002: Bureau of Justice Statistics National Crime Victimization Survey*. Washington, D.C.: U.S. Department of Justice, Office of Justice Programs, 2003.

Roberts, Albert. *Helping Crime Victims: Research, Policy and Practice*. London: Sage, 1990.

Violence

Brown, Richard Maxwell. *Strain of Violence: Historical Studies of American Violence and Vigilantism*. New York: Oxford University Press, 1975.

Davis, Hugh, Ted Gurr, and Robert Graham. *The History of Violence in America*. New York: Bantam, 1969.

Ferracuti, Franco, and Marvin Wolfgang. *The Subculture of Violence: Towards an Integrated Theory in Criminology*. New York: Routledge, 2001.

Foote, Lorien. *The Gentlemen and Rogues: Violence, Honor, and Manhood in the Union Army*. New York: New York University Press, 2010.

Gilligan, James. *Violence: Our Deadly Epidemic and Its Causes*. New York: Putnam, 1996.

Gordon, Linda. *Heroes of Their Own Lives: The Politics and History of Family Violence, Boston, 1880–1960*. Champaign: University of Illinois Press, 1988.

Gordon, Michael A. *The Orange Riots: Irish Political Violence in New York City, 1870 and 1871*. Ithaca, N.Y.: Cornell University Press, 1993.

Graham, Hugh, and Ted Gurr. *Violence in America: Historical and Comparative Perspectives*. Beverly Hills, Calif.: Sage, 1979.

Hofstadter, Richard, and Michael Wallace. *American Violence: A Documentary History*. New York: Random House, 1970.

Mariani, Cliff. *Domestic Violence Survival Guide*. New York: Looseleaf Law, 1996.

Raine, Adrian. *The Anatomy of Violence: The Biological Roots of Crime*. New York: Random House, 2013.

Rhodes, Richard. *Why They Kill: The Discoveries of a Maverick Criminologist*. New York: Knopf, 1999.

Scully, Diana. *Understanding Sexual Violence: A Study of Convicted Rapists*. London: Routledge, 1994.

Silberman, Charles E. *Criminal Violence, Criminal Justice*. New York: Random House, 1978.

Wickersham Commission Reports. Montclair, N.J.: Patterson Smith, 1931.

Zimring, Franklin E., and Gordon Hawkins. *Crime Is Not the Problem: Lethal Violence in America*. New York: Oxford University Press, 1999.

White-Collar Crime

Fitzpatrick, Robert L., and Joyce K. Reynolds. *False Profits: Seeking Financial and Spiritual Deliverance in Multi-Level Marketing and Pyramid Schemes*. Charlotte, N.C.: Herald, 1997.

Haddock, David D., and Jonathan Macey. "Regulation on Demand: A Private Interest Model, with an Application to Insider Trading Regulation." *Journal of Law and Economics* 30, no. 2 (1987): 311–52.

Kesselman, Jonathan. "Income Tax Evasion: An Intersectional Analysis." *Journal of Public Economics* 38, no. 2 (1989): 137–82.

Klepper, Steven, and Daniel Nagin. "The Autonomy of Tax Evasion." *Journal of Law, Economics, and Organization* 5 (1989): 1–24.

Lorie, James H., and Victor Niederhoffer. "Predictive and Statistical Properties of Insider Trading on the Stock Market." *Journal of Political Economy* 98 (1968): 35–53.

O'Shea, James. *The Daisy Chain: How Borrowed Millions Sank a Texas S&L*. New York: Pocket Books, 1991.

Salinger, Lawrence. *Encyclopedia of White-Collar and Corporate Crime*. Thousand Oaks, Calif.: Sage, 2013.

Singdahlsen, Jeffrey P. "Note: Risk of Chill; A Cost of the Standards Governing the Regulation of False Advertising Under Section 43(a) of the Lanham Act." *Virginia Law Review* 77 (1991): 335–95.

Soltes, Eugene. *Why They Do It: Inside the Mind of the White-Collar Criminal*. New York: PublicAffairs, 2016.

Stewart, James. *Den of Thieves*. New York: New York: Simon & Schuster, 1991.

Sutherland, Edwin H. *White Collar Crime: The Uncut Version*. New Haven, Conn.: Yale University Press, 1990.

Zuckoff, Mitchell. *Ponzi's Scheme: The True Story of a Financial Legend*. New York: Random House, 2006.

CRIMINOLOGY

General Criminology/History

Ackerknecht, Erwin. *Franz Joseph Gall, Inventor of Phrenology and His Collection*. Madison: University of Wisconsin Medical School, 1956.

Bowling, Ben, and James Ross. "A Brief History of Criminology." *Criminal Justice Matters* 65, no. 1 (2006): 12–13.

Brandstetter, A. "Genesis and Early History of Criminal Justice Studies at Michigan State University" Paper presented at the Midwestern Criminal Justice Association Meeting, Chicago, October 1989. Retrieved 2 April 2018, http://cj.msu.edu/assets/Brandstatter.pdf.

Cullen, Francis T., and Robert Agnew, eds. *Criminological Theory: Past to Present*. Los Angeles, Calif.: Roxbury, 2006.

Delisa, Matthew, and Kevin M. Beaver. *Criminological Theory*. Boston: Jones and Bartlett, 2011.

Felson, Marcus. *Crime and Everyday Life*. 3rd ed. Thousand Oaks, Calif.: Sage, 2002.

Forrest, D. W. *Francis Galton: The Life and Work of a Victorian Genius*, London: Taplinger 1974.

Miller, J. Mitchell, Christopher J. Schreck, Richard Tewksbury, and J. C. Barnes. *Criminological Theory: A Brief Introduction*. Upper Saddle River, N.J.: Pearson, 2015.

Reynolds, L. D., M. T. Griffin, and E. Fantham. "Annaeus Seneca (2), Lucius." In *The Oxford Classical Dictionary*, ed. S. Hornblower, A. Spawforth, and E. Eidinow, 93. New York: Oxford University Press, 2012.

Schafer, Stephen. *Theories in Criminology: Past and Present Philosophies of the Crime Problem*. New York: Random House, 1969.

Seigel, Larry. *Criminology*. 10th ed. Belmont, Calif.: Thomson Learning, 2009.

———. *Criminology: Theories, Patterns, and Typologies*. Boston: Cengage Learning, 2015.

Sellin, Thorsten. *Culture Conflict and Crime*. New York: Social Science Research Council, 1938.

———. "Youth and Crime." *Law and Contemporary Problems* 9 (Fall 1942): 581–87.

Sutherland, Edwin H., Donald R. Cressey, and David F. Luckenbill. *Principles of Criminology*. Lanham, Md.: AltaMira Press, 1992. (Originally published 1947)

Tarde, Gabriel. *La Criminalite Comparee*. Paris: Alcan, 1886.

Tibbetts, Stephen, and Craig Hemmens. *Criminological Theory: A Text/Reader*. Thousand Oaks, Calif.: Sage, 2009.

Weitzer, Ronald. *Current Controversies in Criminology*. Upper Saddle River, N.J.: Prentice Hall, 2003.

Williams, Frank P., and Marilyn D. McShane. *Criminological Theory*. Upper Saddle River, N.J.: Prentice Hall, 1999.

Research Methods

Becker, Howard. *Tricks of the Trade: How to Think about Your Research While You're Doing It*. Chicago, Ill.: University of Chicago Press, 1998.

Dent, Borden D. "Brief History of Crime Mapping." In *Atlas of Crime: Mapping the Criminal Landscape*, ed. Linda S. Turnbull, Elaine Hallisey Hendrix, and Borden D. Dent, 4–21. Phoenix, Ariz.: Oryx, 2000.

Maxfield, Michael G., and Earl R. Babbie. *Research Methods for Criminal Justice and Criminology*. Scarborough, Ont.: Nelson Education, 2014.

Thornberry, Terence P., and Marvin D. Krohn. "The Self-Report Method for Measuring Delinquency and Crime." *Criminal Justice* 4, no. 1 (2000): 33–83.

Theoretical Perspectives

Biological and Biosocial Theories

Athens, Lonnie. *The Creation of Dangerous Violent Criminals*. New York: Routledge, 1989.

———. *Violent Criminal Acts and Actors Revisited*. Chicago: University of Illinois Press, 1997.

Beckwith, Jon, and Jonathan King. "The XYY Syndrome: A Dangerous Myth." *New Scientist* 64, no. 923 (November 1974): 474–76.

Bertillion, Alphonse. "Les empreintes digitales." In *Fingerprints and Other Ridge Skin Impressions*, ed. Christoph Champod, Chris J. Lennard, Pierre Margot, and Milutin Stoilovic, 2nd ed., 1–32. Boca Raton, La.: CRC, 2016.

Darwin, Charles. *On the Origin of Species by Means of Natural Selection, or the Preservation of Favoured Races in the Struggle for Life* . London: John Murray, 1859.

Dugdale, Richard. *The Jukes: A Study in Crime, Pauperism, Disease, and Heredity*. New York: Putnam, 1877.

Eysenck, Hans J. "Personality and the Biosocial Model of Anti-Social and Criminal Behaviour." In *Biosocial Bases of Violence*, ed. A. Raine, P. Brennan, D. P. Farrington, and S. A. Mednick, 21–37. New York: Springer, 1997.

Gibson, Mary. *Born to Crime: Cesare Lombroso and the Origins of Biological Criminology*. Santa Barbara, Calif.: Praeger, 2002.

Glueck, Sheldon, and Eleanor Glueck. *Delinquents and Nondelinquents in Perspective*. Cambridge, MA: Harvard University Press, 1968.

———. *500 Criminal Careers*. New York: Knopf, 1934.

Goddard, Henry. *The Kallikak Family: A Study in the Heredity of Feeble-Mindedness*. New York: Macmillan, 1912.

Goring, Charles. *The English Convict: A Statistical Study*. London: His Majesty's Publishing Office, 1913.

Hooton, Earnest Albert. *Crime and the Man*. Cambridge, Mass.: Harvard University Press, 1939.

Lombroso, Cesare. *Criminal Man*. Durham, N.C.: Duke University Press, 2006. (Originally published 1876)

———. *Criminal Man, According to the Classification of Cesare Lombroso*. Montclair, N.J.: Patterson Smith, 1972.

March, William. *The Bad Seed.* New York: HarperCollins, 1997.
Mednick, Sarnoff A., William F. Gabrielli Jr., and Barry Hutchings. "Genetic Influences in Criminal Convictions: Evidence from an Adoption Cohort." *Science* 224 (1984): 891–95.
Meichenbaum, D., and R. Cameron. "Stress Inoculation: A Skill Training Approach to Anxiety Management." Unpublished manuscript. Waterloo, Ont.: University of Waterloo, 1972.
Novaco, Raymond. *Anger Control: The Development and Evaluation of an Experimental Treatment* . Lanham, Md.: Rowman & Littlefield, 1975.
Rafter, Nicole Hahn. *Creating Born Criminals.* Champaign: University of Illinois Press, 1997.
Rennie, Ysabel. *The Search for Criminal Man: A Conceptual History of the Dangerous Offender.* Lanham, Md.: Lexington, 1978.
Royce, Kenneth. *The XYY Man.* London: Hodder and Stoughton, 1970.

Classical, Deterrence, and Rational Choice/Situational Theories

Beccaria, Cesare. *On Crimes and Punishments and Other Writings.* Toronto, Ont.: University of Toronto Press, 2009. (Originally published 1764)
Bentham, Jeremy. *The Collected Works of Jeremy Bentham: An Introduction to the Principles of Morals and Legislation.* London: Clarendon, 1996. (Originally published 1765/1789)
Birkbeck, Christopher, and Gary LaFree. "The Situational Analysis of Crime and Deviance." *Annual Review of Sociology* 19 (1993): 113–37.
Clarke, Ronald V. "Situational Crime Prevention." In *Building a Safer Society: Strategic Approaches to Crime Prevention,* ed. M. Tonry and D. P. Farrington, vol. 19, *Crime and Justice: A Review of Research,* 91–150. Chicago, Ill.: University of Chicago Press, 1995.
———. "Situational Crime Prevention: Its Theoretical Basis and Practical Scope." *Crime and Justice: An Annual Review of Research* 4 (1983): 225–56.
Clarke, Ronald V., and R. Homel. "A Revised Classification of Situational Crime Prevention Techniques." In *Crime Prevention at a Crossroads,* ed. Steven Lab, 17–27. New York: Routledge, 1997.
Cohen, Lawrence E., and Marcus Felson. "Social Change and Crime Rate Trends: A Routine Activity Approach." *American Sociological Review* 44, no. 4 (1979): 588–608.
Felson, Marcus. *Crime and Everyday Life: Insight and Implications for Society,* Thousand Oaks, Calif.: Pine Forge, 2002.
Nagin, Daniel S., and Greg Pogarsky. "Integrating Celerity, Impulsivity, and Extralegal Sanction Threats into a Model of General Deterrence: Theory and Evidence." *Criminology* 39, no. 4 (2001): 865–92.

Conflict Theory

Bonger, Willem Adriaan. *Criminality and Economic Conditions*. Boston, Mass.: Little, Brown, 1916.

Chambliss, William J., and Robert Seidman. *Law, Order and Power*. Reading, Mass: Addison-Westley, 1971.

Quinney, Richard. *Class, State, and Crime*. New York: Longman, 1980.

———. *The Social Reality of Crime*. Piscataway, N.J.: Transaction, 1970.

Rusche, Georg, and Otto Kirchheimer. *Punishment and Social Structure*. Piscataway, N.J.: Transaction, 2003.

Sumner, William Graham. *Folkways: A Study of the Sociological Importance of Usages Manners Customs Mores and Morals*. New York: Ginn, 1906.

Turk, Austin T. *Criminality and Legal Order*. Skokie, Ill.: Rand McNally, 1969.

Vold, George. *Theoretical Criminology: Crime in the World*. New York: Oxford University Press, 1958.

Cultural Criminology

Ferrell, Jeff. "Cultural Criminology." *Annual Review of Sociology* 25, no. 1 (1999): 395–418.

Ferrell, Jeff, Keith Hayward, Wayne Morrison, and Mike Presdee, eds. *Cultural Criminology Unleashed*. London: Glass House, 2004.

Ferrell, Jeff, Keith Hayward, and Jock Young. *Cultural Criminology: An Invitation*. Los Angeles, Calif.: Sage, 2008.

Hayward, Keith J., and Jock Young. *Cultural Criminology*. Thousand Oaks, Calif.: Sage, 2008.

———. "Cultural Criminology: Some Notes on the Script." *Theoretical Criminology* 8, no. 3 (2004): 259–73.

Katz, Jack. *Seductions of Crime: Moral and Sensual Attractions in Doing Evil*. New York: Basic Books, 1988.

Presdee, Mike. *Cultural Criminology and the Carnival of Crime*. London: Routledge, 2000.

Shaw, Clifford. *The Jack Roller: A Delinquent Boy's Own Story*. With a new introduction by Howard S. Becker. Chicago, Ill.: University of Chicago Press, 1966. (Originally published 1930)

Toch, Hans. "Good Violence and Bad Violence: Self-Presentations of Aggressors through Accounts and War Stories." In *Aggression and Violence: Social Interactionist Perspectives*, ed. Richard B. Felson and James T. Tedeschi, 193–206. Washington, D.C.: American Psychological Association, 1993.

Desistance

Giordano, Peggy C., Monica A. Longmore, Ryan D. Schroeder, and Patrick M. Seffrin. "A Life-Course Perspective on Spirituality and Desistance from Crime." *Criminology* 46, no. 1 (2008): 99–132.

Glueck, Sheldon, and Eleanor Glueck. *Unraveling Juvenile Delinquency*. New York: Commonwealth Fund, 1950.

Laub, John H., and Robert J. Sampson. *Shared Beginnings, Divergent Lives: Delinquent Boys to Age 70*. Cambridge, MA: Harvard University Press, 2003.

Maruna, Shadd. *Making Good: How Ex-convicts Reform and Rebuild Their Lives*. Washington, D.C.: American Psychological Association, 2001.

Matza, David. *Delinquency and Drift*. New York: Routledge, 1990.

Prochaska, James O., and Carlo C. DiClemente. "Toward a Comprehensive Model of Change." In *Treating Addictive Behaviors*, 3–27. Springer, Boston, MA, 1986.

Sampson, Robert J., and John H. Laub. *Crime in the Making: Pathways and Turning Points through Life*. Cambridge, MA: Harvard University Press,1993.

Uggen, Christopher, and Candace Kruttschnitt. "Crime in the Breaking: Gender Differences in Desistance." *Law and Society Review* 32 (1998): 339.

Wolfgang, Marvin E. "Transitions of Crime in the Aging Process." *Current Perspectives on Aging and the Life Cycle* 4 (1995): 141–53.

Wright, Kevin N., and Karen E. Wright. "Does Getting Married Reduce the Likelihood of Criminality—A Review of the Literature." *Federal Probation* 56 (1992): 50.

Feminist Theory

Adler, Freda. *Sisters in Crime: The Rise of the New Female Criminal*. New York: McGraw-Hill, 1975.

Belknap, Joanne. *The Invisible Woman: Gender, Crime, and Justice*. 3rd ed. Belmont, Calif.: Wadsworth, 2007.

Chesney-Lind, Meda, and Lisa Pasko. *The Female Offender: Girls, Women, and Crime*. Thousand Oaks, Calif.: Sage, 2013.

Daly, Kathleen, and Meda Chesney-Lind. "Feminism and Criminology." *Justice Quarterly* 5 (1988): 497–538.

Lombroso, Cesare, and Guglielmo Ferrero. *The Female Offender*. Vol. 1. New York: D. Appleton, 1895.

Messerschmidt, James. *Crime as Structured Action: Gender, Race, Class, and Crime in the Making*. Thousand Oaks, Calif.: Sage, 1997.

Simon, Rita James. *Women and Crime*. Lanham, Md.: Lexington, 1975.

Labeling and Reintegrative Shaming

Becker, Howard S. *Outsiders*. New York: Simon & Schuster, 2008. (Originally published 1963)

Braithwaite, John. *Restorative Justice and Responsive Regulation.* New York: Oxford University Press, 2002.

Cooley, Charles Horton. *On Self and Social Organization.* Chicago, Ill.: University of Chicago Press, 1998.

Lemert, Edwin M. *Human Deviance, Human Problems and Social Control.* Carbondale, Ill.: Southern University Press, 1967.

———. *Social Pathology: A Systematic Approach to the Theory of Sociopathic Behavior*. New York: McGraw-Hill, 1951.

Tannenbaum, Frank. "Crime and the Community (1938)." In *Jacques Faget, Sociologie de la Délinquance et de la Justice Pénale, Toulouse, Erès* (2002), 80–87.

Life Course/Developmental/Integrated Theories

Blumstein, Alfred, Jacqueline Cohen, Jeffrey A. Roth, and Christy A. Visher. *Criminal Careers and Career Criminals*. Vol. 2. Washington, D.C.: National Academy, 1986.

Horney, Julie D., Wayne Osgood, and Ineke Haen Marshall. "Criminal Careers in the Short-Term: Intra-Individual Variability in Crime and Its Relation to Local Life Circumstances." *American Sociological Review* 60, no. 5 (1995): 655–73.

Huizinga, David. "Developmental Sequences in Delinquency." In *Pathways through Adolescence: Individual Development in Context*, ed. Lisa Crockett and Anne Crowder, 15–34. Mahwah, N.J.: Lawrence Erlbaum Associates, 1995.

Kelly, Barbara, Rolf Loeber, Kate Keenan, and Mary DeLamatre. *Developmental Pathways in Boys' Disruptive Behavior*. Office of Juvenile Justice and Delinquency Prevention. Retrieved 5 April 2016, https://www.ncjrs.gov/html/ojjdp/jjbul9712-2/jjb1297.

Park, Robert, Ernest Burgess, and Roderick McKenzie. *The City*. Chicago, Ill.: University of Chicago Press, 1984 (originally published 1925).

Sampson, Robert J., and John H. Laub. *Crime in the Making: Pathways and Turning Points through Life*. Cambridge, Mass.: Harvard University Press, 1995.

Thornberry, Terence P., Alan J. Lizotte, Marvin D. Krohn, Margaret Farnworth, and Sung Joon Jang. "Delinquent Peers, Beliefs, and Delinquent Behavior: A Longitudinal Test of Interactional Theory." *Criminology* 32, no. 1 (1994): 47–83.

Tittle, Charles R. *Control Balance: Toward a General Theory of Deviance*. Boulder, Colo.: Westview, 1995.

Psychological Theories

Bowlby, John. "Forty-Four Juvenile Thieves: Their Characters and Home Life." *International Journal of Psycho-Analysis* 25 (1944): 107–27.
Freud, Anna. *The Ego and the Mechanisms of Defense*. New York: International Universities Press, 1966.
Freud, Sigmund. "Dostoevsky and Parricide." In *The Brothers Karamazov and the Critics* (1928), 41–55.
Friedlander, Kate. *A Psycho-Analytical Approach to Juvenile Delinquency: Theory, Case Studies Treatment*. Vol. 9. London: Routledge, 2013.
Lipsey, Mark, Gabrielle Chapman, and Nana Landenberger. "Cognitive–Behavioral Programs for Offenders." *Annals of the American Academy of Political and Social Science* 578 (2001): 144–57.
Mead, George Herbert. *George Herbert Mead on Social Psychology*. Ed. Anslem Strauss. Chicago, Ill.: University of Chicago Press, 1977.
———. *Mind, Self, and Society*. Chicago, Ill.: University of Chicago Press, 1934.

Social Disorganization, Anomie, Strain, and Social Structure

Agnew, Robert. "Foundation for a General Strain Theory of Crime and Delinquency." *Criminology* 30, no. 1 (1992): 47–87.
———. "A Revised Strain Theory of Delinquency." *Social Forces* 64, no. 1 (1985): 151–67.
Agnew, Robert, Francis Cullen, Velmer Burton, T. David Evans, and B. Gregory Dunaway. "A New Test of Classic Strain Theory." *Justice Quarterly* 13, no. 4 (1996): 681–704.
Anderson, Elijah. *Streetwise: Race, Class, and Change in an Urban Community*. Chicago, Ill.: University of Chicago Press, 1993.
Cloward, Richard A., and Lloyd E. Ohlin. *Delinquency and Opportunity: A Study of Delinquent Gangs*. New York: Free Press, 1960.
Cohen, Albert K. *Delinquent Boys: The Subculture of the Gang*. London: Colher-Macmillan, 1955.
Durkheim, Émile. *The Division of Labour in Society*. New York: Free Press, 2014. (Originally published 1893)
———. *Suicide: A Study in Sociology*. New York: Free Press, 1951 (Originally Published in French in 1897; translated and published in English in 1951)

Merton, Robert. "Social Structure and Crime." *American Sociological Review* 3, no. 5 (October 1938): 672–82.

Messner, Stephen, and Richard Rosenfeld. *Crime and the American Dream*. Belmont, Calif.: Wadsworth, 1994.

Park, Robert E., Ernest W. Burgess, and Roderick Duncan McKenzie. *The City*. Chicago, Ill.: University of Chicago Press, 1984.

Schneider, Jo Anne. *Social Capital and Welfare Reform: Organizations, Congregations, and Communities*. New York: Columbia University Press, 2006.

Shaw, Clifford Robe, and Henry Donald McKay. *Juvenile Delinquency and Urban Areas*. Chicago, Ill.: University of Chicago Press, 1942.

Shorris, Earl. *Latinos: A Biography of the People*. New York: Avon, 1992.

Skogan, Wesley G., and Michael G. Maxfield. *Coping with Crime: Individual and Neighborhood Reactions*. Belmont, Calif.: Sage, 1981.

Spencer, Herbert. *The Study of Sociology*. New York: D. Appleton, 1874.

Ward, Lester. *Dynamic Sociology*. New York: D. Appleton, 1883.

Social Learning Theory

Akers, Ronald L. *Deviant Behavior: A Social Learning Approach*. Belmont, Calif.: Wadsworth, 1977. (Originally published 1973)

Brooks-Gunn, Jeanne, Greg Duncan, and J. Lawrence Aber, eds. *Neighborhood Poverty: Context and Consequences for Children*. Vol. 1. New York: Russell Sage Foundation, 1997.

Burgess, Robert L., and Ronald L. Akers. "A Differential Association-Reinforcement Theory of Criminal Behavior." *Social Problems* 14, no. 2 (1966): 128–47.

Clark, Lewis Hull, Neil Miller, and John Dollard. *Social Learning Theory*. New Haven, Conn.: Yale University Press, 1941.

Elliott, Delbert S., David Huizinga, and Suzanne S. Ageton. *Explaining Delinquency and Drug Use*. Thousand Oaks, Calif.: Sage, 1985.

Miller, Neil, and John Dollard, J. *Social Learning and Imitation*. New Haven, Conn.: Yale University Press, 1941.

———. "Social Learning Theory and Imitation." *American Anthropologist* 45, no. 1 (1943): 144–46.

Odum, Howard W. "Edwin H. Sutherland—1883–1950." *Journal of Social Forces* 29 (1951): 348–49.

Skinner, Burrhus F. *Beyond Freedom and Dignity*. New York: Bantam, 1974.

Sutherland, Edwin H., and Donald R. Cressey. "The Professional Thief." *Journal of Criminal Law and Criminology (1931–1951)* (1937): 161–63.

———. "A Theory of Differential Association." (1960). In *Criminological Theory: Past to Present*, ed. Francis T. Cullen and Robert Agnew, 122–25. Los Angeles, Calif.: Roxbury, 2006.

Thorndike, Edward L. *Provisional Laws of Acquired Behavior or Learning: Animal Intelligence*. New York: Macmillan, 1911.

Social Bonding and Control

Gottfredson, Michael R., and Travis Hirschi. *A General Theory of Crime*. Palo Alto, Calif.: Stanford University Press, 1990.

Hirschi, Travis. *Causes of Delinquency*. Berkeley: University of California Press, 1969.

Matza, David. *Delinquency and Drift*. New York: Routledge, 1990.

Nye, Francis Ivan. *Family Relationships and Delinquent Behavior*. New York: Wiley, 1958.

Reckless, Walter C. "A New Theory of Delinquency and Crime." *Federal Probation* 25 (1961): 42.

Reiss, Albert J. "Delinquency as the Failure of Personal and Social Controls." *American Sociological Review* 16, no. 2 (1951): 196–207.

Sykes, Gresham M., and David Matza. "Techniques of Neutralization: A Theory of Delinquency." *American Sociological Review* 22, no. 6 (1957): 664–70.

LAW ENFORCEMENT

Broken Windows

Kelling, George L., and Catherine Coles. *Fixing Broken Windows: Restoring Order and Reducing Crime in Our Communities*. New York: Free Press, 1996.

Community Policing

Duffee, David E., Reginald Fluellen, and Brian C. Renauer. "Community Variables in Community Policing." *Police Quarterly* 2, no. 1 (1999): 5–35.

Oliver, Willard. *Community-Oriented Policing: A Systemic Approach to Policing*. Upper Saddle River, N.J.: Pearson, 2008.

Reiss, Albert J. *Police and the Public*. New Haven, Conn.: Yale University, 1973.

Skogan, Lesley G. *Community Policing, Chicago Style*. New York: Oxford University Press, 1997.

Skolnick, Jerome H., and David H. Bayley. "Theme and Variation in Community Policing." In *Crime and Justice: A Review of Research*, ed. M. Tonry and N. Morris, 10:179–99. Chicago, Ill.: University of Chicago Press, 1988.

Trojanowicz, Robert, and Bonnie Bucqueroux. *Community Policing: How to Get Started*. Cincinnati, Ohio: Anderson, 1998.

Criminal Investigations

Buckley, David, and Brian C. Jayne. *Electronic Recording of Interrogations*. Chicago, Ill.: John E. Reid, 2005.

Galton, Sir Francis. *Fingerprints*. London: Macmillan, 1892.

Gross, Hans. *Criminal Investigations: A Practical Textbook*. Eagan, Minn.: Sweet and Maxwell, 1934.

Miller, Charles. "Fingerprint Identification not Scientific nor Infallible and Based on Fraud." *Law Society Advocacy Section Newsletter*, 2013.

Swanson, Charles R., Neil Chamelin, Leonard Territo, and Robert Taylor. *Criminal Investigation*. 9th ed. Boston, Mass.: McGraw-Hill, 2006.

Weston, Paul B., and Kenneth Wells. *Criminal Investigation: Basic Perspectives*. 4th ed. Englewood Cliffs, N.J.: Prentice Hall, 1986.

Disaster Management

Federal Emergency Management Agency. *Getting Started: Building Support for Mitigation Planning, FEMA 386-1*. Washington, D.C.: Federal Emergency Management Agency, 2002.

Hoag, Phillip L. *No Such Thing as Doomsday*. Emigrant, Mont.: Yellow River, 2001.

Federal Police

Gentry, Curt. *J. Edgar Hoover: The Man and the Secrets*. New York: Norton, 1991.

Hazelwood, Roy, and Stephen Michaud. *Dark Dreams*. New York: St. Martin's, 2001.

Horn, William. "Stress Training for Federal Police." *Police Stress* 1 (1978): 18–20.

Purvis, Melvin. *American Agent*. Garden City, N.Y.: Doubleday, Doran, 1936.

Forfeiture

Hudetz, Mary. "Forfeiture Reform Aligns Likes of Billionaire Charles Koch, ACLU." *Topeka Capital Journal*, 15 October 2015.

History of Police

Wadman, Robert C. *To Protect and to Serve: A History of Police in America.* Upper Saddle River, N.J.: Prentice Hall, 2004.

Walker, Samuel. *A Critical History of Police Reform: The Emergence of Professionalism*. New York: Lexington, 1977.

Police Culture

Paoline, Eugene A. "Taking Stock: Toward a Richer Understanding of Police Culture." *Journal of Criminal Justice* 31, no. 3 (2003): 199–214.

Reiss, Albert J. *Police and the Public*. New Haven, Conn.: Yale University Press, 1973.

Terrill, William, Eugene A. Paoline, and Peter K. Manning. "Police Culture and Coercion." *Criminology* 41, no. 4 (2003): 1003–34.

Police—General

Barkham, Patrick. "How a Cop Can Turn a Teen into a Hoodlum." *Guardian*, 14 May 2006.

Lewis, Alfred. *The Apaches of New York*. Chicago, Ill.: M. A. Donohue, 1912.

Linedecker, Clifford. *Massacre at Waco, Texas*. New York: St. Martin's, 1993.

Maas, Peter. *Serpico*. New York: Viking, 1973.

Meichenbaum, Donald. *Stress Inoculation Training*. New York: Pergamon, 1975.

Thibodeau, David, and Leon Whiteson. *A Place Called Waco: A Survivor's Story*. New York: Perseus, 1999.

Wilson, James Q. *Varieties of Police Behavior: The Management of Law and Order in Eight Communities*. New York: Antheneum, 1973.

Policing Strategies

Kelling, George L., and Mark H. Moore. *The Evolving Strategy of Policing*. Washington, D.C.: U.S. Department of Justice, National Institute of Justice, 1988.

Ratcliffe, Jerry H., Travis Taniguchi, Elizabeth R. Groff, and Jennifer D. Wood. "The Philadelphia Foot Patrol Experiment: A Randomized Controlled Trial of Police Patrol Effectiveness in Violent Crime Hotspots." *Criminology* 49, no. 3 (2011): 795–831.

Private Police

Cunningham, William C., John Strauchs, and Clifford W. Van Meter. *The Hallcrest Report II: Private Security Trends, 1970–2000*. McLean, Va.: Hallcrest System, 1990.

Nemeth, Charles. *Private Security: An Introduction to Principles and Practices*. Boca Raton, Fla.: Taylor & Francis, 2018.

Pastor, James. *The Privatization of Police in America: An Analysis and Case Study*. Jefferson, N.C.: McFarland, 2002.

Poulan, K. C., and Charles Nemeth. *Private Security and Public Safety: A Community-Based Approach*. Upper Saddle River, N.J.: Prentice Hall, 2004.

Schmalleger, Frank, Larry Siegel, and Carter Smith. *Private Security Today*. Upper Saddle River, N.J.: Pearson, 2016.

Shearing, Clifford, and Philip Stenning. *Private Policing*. Newbury Park, Calif.: Sage, 1987.

Problem-Oriented Police

Goldstein, Herman. *Problem-Oriented Policing*. New York: McGraw-Hill, 1990.

Race and Policing

Gelman, Andrew, Jeffrey Fagin, and Alex Kiss. "An Analysis of the New York Police Department's 'Stop and Frisk' Policy in the Context of Claims of Racial Bias." *Journal of the American Statistical Association* 102, no. 479 (2007): 813–23.

Payne, B. Keith, Alan J. Lambert, and Larry L. Jacoby. "Best Laid Plans: Effects of Goals on Accessibility Bias and Cognitive Control in Race-Based Misperceptions of Weapons." *Journal of Experimental Social Psychology* 38, no. 4 (2002): 384–96.

Sun, Ivan Y., and Brian K. Payne. "Racial Differences in Resolving Conflicts: A Comparison between Black and White Police Officers." *NCCD News* 50, no. 4 (2004): 516–41.

Security/School Security

Fierke, Karin M. *Critical Approaches to International Security*. Cambridge Mass.: Polity Press, 2007.

Trump, Kenneth S. *Practical School Security: Basic Guidelines for Safe and Secure Schools*. Thousand Oaks, Calif.: Corwin Press, 1998.

Use of Force

Garner, Joel H., Christopher D. Maxwell, and Cedrick G. Heraux. "Characteristics Associated with the Prevalence and Severity of Force Used by the Police." *Justice Quarterly* 19, no. 4 (2002): 705–46.

———. "Patterns of Police Use of Force as a Measure of Police Integrity." *Police Integrity and Ethics* (2004): 109–25.

Payne, B. Keith. "Prejudice and Perception: The Role of Automatic and Controlled Processes in Misperceiving a Weapon." *Journal of Personality and Social Psychology* 81, no. 2 (2001): 181.

Skolnick, Jerome H., and James J. Fyfe. *Above the Law: Police and the Excessive Use of Force*. New York: Free Press, 1993.

Terrill, William, and Michael D. Reisig. "Neighborhood Context and Police Use of Force." *Journal of Research in Crime and Delinquency* 40, no. 3 (2003): 291–321.

Worden, Robert. *The Causes of Police Brutality: Theory and Evidence on Police Use of Force*. Evanston, Ill.: Northwestern University, 1995.

COURTS

Capital Punishment

Barnet, Sylvan, and Hugo Bedau. *Current Issues and Enduring Questions: A Guide to Critical Thinking and Argument, with Readings*. New York: St. Martin's, 1996.

Bedau, Hugo, and Paul Cassell. *The Courts, the Constitution, and Capital Punishment*. Lexington, Mass.: Lexington, 1977.

———. *Death Is Different: Studies in the Morality, Law, and Politics of Capital Punishment*. Lebanon, N.H.: Northeastern, 1987.

———. *The Death Penalty in America*. New York: Oxford University Press, 1997.

———. *Debating the Death Penalty: Should America Have Capital Punishment? The Experts on Both Sides Make Their Case*. New York: Oxford University Press, 2004.

Chessman, Caryl. *Cell 2455, Death Row: A Condemned Man's Story*. New York: Carrol and Graf, 1954.

Falk, Aaron, and Emiley Morgan. "Ronnie Lee Gardner Executed by Firing Squad." *Desert News*, 18 June 2010.

Garland, David. "Capital Punishment and American Culture." *Punishment and Society* 7, no. 4 (2005): 347–76.

Haas, Kenneth, and James Inciardi, eds. *Challenging Capital Punishment: Legal and Social Science Approaches*. Newbury Park, Calif.: Sage, 1988.

Hatch, Virginia, and Anthony Walsh. *Capital Punishment: Theory and Practice of the Ultimate Penalty*. New York: Oxford University Press, 2015.

Latzer, Barry, and David McCord. *Death Penalty Cases*. Burlington, Mass.: Elsevier, 2011.

Palmer, Louis. *Encyclopedia of Capital Punishment in the United States*. Jefferson, N.C.: McFarland, 2007.

Paternoster, Raymond, Robert Brame, and Sarah Bacon: *The Death Penalty: America's Experience with Capital Punishment*. New York: Oxford University Press, 2007.

Scott, Walter. *The Heart of Midlothian*. London: Aeterna, 2010.

Steiker, Carol, and Jordan Steiker. *Courting Death: The Supreme Court and Capital Punishment*. Cambridge, Mass.: Harvard University Press, 2016. http://www.deathpenaltyinfo.org/state-lethal-injection.

Constitutional Law

O'Brien, David M. *Constitutional Law and Politics*. New York: Norton, 2000.

Sutherland, Arthur E. *Constitutionalism in America: Origin and Evolution of Its Fundamental Ideas*. New York: Blaisdell, 1965.

Courts—General

Aikman, Alex. *The Art and Practice of Court Administration*. Boca Raton, Fla.: Taylor & Francis, 2007.

American University. "Sequestration—A Possible Solution to the Free Press–Fair Trial Dilemma." *American University Law Review* 23, no. 4 (1974): 923–57.

Bureau of Justice Assistance. *Trial Court Performance Standards with Commentary*. Washington, D.C.: U.S. Department of Justice, Office of Justice Programs, 1997.

Dubois, Philip L, and Keith O. Boyum. "Court Reform: The Politics of Institutional Change." In *Handbook of Court Administration and Management*, ed. Steven W. Hays and Cole B. Graham Jr., 27–51. New York: Marcel Dekker, 1993.

Fritzler, Randal B., and Leonore M. J. Simon. "Principles of an Effective Domestic Violence Court." *Court Review* 37, no. 1 (2000): 22–27.

Gallas, Geoff. "The Conventional Wisdom of State Court Administration: A Critical Assessment and an Alternative Approach." *Justice System Journal* 2, no. 1 (1976): 35–55.

———. "Local Legal Culture: More than Court Culture." *Court Manager* 20, no. 4 (2005): 23–28.

Glick, Henry R. "The Politics of State-Court Reforms." In *The Politics of Judicial Reform*, ed. Philip L. Dubois, 17–32. Lexington, MA: D.C. Heath, (1982).

Goerdt, John, Chris Lomvardias, Geoff Gallas, and Barry Mahoney. *Examining Court Delay: The Pace of Litigation in 26 Urban Trial Courts, 1987*. Williamsburg, Va.: National Center for State Courts, 1987.

Hartman, Gary, Roy Mersky, and Cindy Tate. *Landmark Supreme Court Cases: The Most Influential Decisions of the Supreme Court of the United States*. New York: Checkmark, 2008.

National Association for Court Management. *Court Security Guide*. Williamsburg, Va., 1995.

National Center for State Courts. *Future Trends in State Courts: Performance Measurement Gains Momentum through CourTools*. Williamsburg, Va.: National Center for State Courts, 2006.

Neubauer, David. *America's Courts and the Criminal Justice System*, New York: Wadsworth, 1999.

Ostrom, Brian J., and Roger A. Hanson. *Efficiency, Timeliness, and Quality: A New Perspective from Nine State Criminal Trial Courts*. Williamsburg, Va.: National Center for State Courts, 1999.

Rehnquist, William. *The Supreme Court Revised*. Updated ed. New York: Knopf, 1987.

Rottman, David. "Does Therapeutic Jurisprudence Require Specialized Courts (and Do Specialized Courts Imply Specialist Judges)?" *Court Review* 37, no. 1 (2000): 22–27.

Tobin, Robert W. *Creating the Judicial Branch: The Unfinished Reform*. Williamsburg, Va.: National Center for State Courts, 1999.

———. *The Nine: Inside the Secret World of the Supreme Court*. New York: Doubleday, 2007.

———. *An Overview of Court Administration in the United States*. Williamsburg, Va.: National Center for State Courts, 1997.

Criminal Procedure

Acker, James, and David Brody. *Criminal Procedure: A Contemporary Perspective*. Burlington, Mass.: Jones and Bartlett, 2012.

American Bar Association. *Defeating Delay: Developing and Implementing a Court Delay Reduction Program*. Chicago, Ill., 1986.

Ashworth, A. *Human Rights, Serious Crime and Criminal Procedure*. Eagan, Minn.: Sweet and Maxwell, 2002.

Fraenkel, Osmond K. *The Rights We Have*. New York: Thomas and Crowell, 1971.

Levy, Leonard W. *Origins of the Bill of Rights*. New Haven, Conn.: Yale University Press, 1999.

Neely, Mark E., Jr. *The Fate of Liberty: Abraham Lincoln and Civil Liberties*. New York: Oxford University Press, 1991.

Rehnquist, William H. *All the Laws but One: Civil Liberties in Wartime*. New York: Knopf, 1998.

Defense

Abramson, Leslie. *The Defense Is Ready: Life in the Trenches of Criminal Law*. New York: Simon & Schuster, 1997.

Bailey, F. Lee, and Harvey Aronson. *The Defense Never Rests*. New York: New American Library, 1972.

Goldstein, Abraham. *The Insanity Defense*. New Haven, Conn.: Yale University Press, 1973.

Schreiber, Brad. *Revolution's End: The Patty Hearst Kidnapping, Mind Control, and the Secret History of Donald Defreeze and the SLA*. New York: Skyhorse, 2016.

Simon, Rita James, and David E. Aaronson. *The Insanity Defense: A Critical Assessment of Law and Policy in the Post-Hinckley Era*. New York: Praeger, 1988.

Thomas, Kimberly A. "Beyond Mitigation: Towards a Theory of Allocution." *Fordham Law Review* 75, no. 5 (2007): 2641–83.

Expert/Eyewitness Testimony and Evidence

Frowd, Charlie D., Derek Carson, Hayley Ness, Jan Richardson, Lisa Morrison, and Sarah McLanaghan. "A Forensically Valid Comparison of Facial Composite Systems." *Psychology, Crime and Law* 11, no. 1 (2005): 33–52.

Huber, Peter. *Galileo's Revenge: Junk Science in the Courtroom*. New York: Basic Books, 1991.

Munsterberg, Hugo. *On the Witness Stand.* Garden City, N.Y.: Doubleday, 1917.

Peissig, Jessie, Tamara Goode, and Pamela Smith. "The Role of Eyebrows in Face Recognition: With, Without, and Different." *Journal of Vision* 9 no. 8 (2009): 554.

Rhine, Stanley. "Facial Reproductions in Court." In *Human Identification: Case Studies in Forensic Anthropology*, ed. Ted A. Rathbun and Jane E. Buikstra, 357–61. Springfield, Ill.: Charles C. Thomas, 1998.

Juries

Amandes, Richard B. "From Voir Dire to Verdict." *Missouri Bar Journal* 27 (1965): 52–54.

American Bar Association. *Dialogue on the American Jury: We the People in Action*. Washington, D.C., 2005.

———. *Standards for Criminal Justice: Discovery and Trial by Jury*. Washington, D.C., 1995.

———. *Standards Relating to Juror Use and Management.* Washington, D.C., 1993.

Clark, Charles E., and Harry Shulman. "Jury Trial in Civil Cases: A Study in Judicial Administration." *Yale Law Journal* 43 (1934): 867–85.

Daniels, Stephen, and Joanne Martin. *Civil Juries and the Politics of Reform*. Evanston, Ill.: Northwestern University Press, 1995.

Jonakait, Randolph N. *The American Jury System*. New Haven, Conn.: Yale University Press, 2003.

Munsterman, G. Thomas. *Jury System Management.* Williamsburg, Va.: National Center for State Courts, 1996.

Volz, M. M. "The Wisconsin Method for Submission of Fact Issues to Juries." *University of Kansas City Law Review* 1966 (Summer 1966): 80–830.

Law

Abadinsky, Howard. *Law and Justice: An Introduction to the American Legal System*. 6th ed. Upper Saddle River, N.J.: Pearson Education, 2008.

Abernathy, M. Glenn. *Civil Liberties under the Constitution*. New York: Dodd, Mead, 1968.

Abraham, Henry. *The Judicial Process: An Introductory Analysis of the Courts of the United States, England, and France*. New York: Oxford University Press, 1993.

Bessler, John D. *The Birth of American Law: An Italian Philosopher and the American Revolution*. Durham, N.C.: Carolina Academic Press, 2014.

Burns, J., and H. Hart, eds. *An Introduction to the Principles of Morals and Legislation*. New York: Oxford University Press, 1982. (Originally published 1789)

Casper, Dale E. *Freedom of Information Act: Legal Actions and Interpretations, 1980–1985*. Monticello, Ill.: Vance Bibliographies, 1986.

Cover, Robert M., and T. Alexander Aleinikoff. "Dialectical Federalism: Habeas Corpus and the Court." *Yale Law Journal* 86 (1977): 1035.

McCullough, David. *John Adams*. New York: Simon & Schuster, 2001.

Mill, John Stuart. *On Liberty*. London: J. W. Parker, 1859.

Law—Case Management

Allen, Jennifer M., and Rajeev Sawhney. *Administration and Management in Criminal Justice: A Service Quality Approach*. Los Angeles, Calif.: Sage, 2010.

Bakke, Holly C., and Maureen Solomon. "Case Differentiation: An Approach to Individualized Case Management." *Judicature* 73, no. 1 (1989): 17–21.

Bureau of Justice Assistance. *Differentiated Case Management: Program Brief*. Washington, D.C.: Author, 1993.

Cooper, Caroline, Holly C. Bakke, and Maureen Solomon. *Differentiated Case Management: Implementation Manual*. Washington, D.C.: Bureau of Justice Assistance, 1993.

Heise, Michael. "Criminal Case Complexity: An Empirical Perspective." *Journal of Empirical Legal Studies* 1, no. 2 (2004): 331–69.

The Jailhouse Lawyers Handbook. 5th ed. New York: Center for Constitutional Rights and the National Lawyers Guild, 2010.

Pfeffer, Jeffrey, and Robert I. Sutton. "Evidence-Based Management." *Harvard Business Review* 84, no. 1 (2006): 1–11.

Solomon, Maureen, and Douglas K. Somerlot. *Caseflow Management in the Trial Court: Now and for the Future*. Chicago, Ill.: American Bar Association, 1987.

Steelman, David C., John A. Goerdt, and James E. McMillan. *Caseflow Management: The Heart of Court Management in the New Millennium*. Williamsburg, Va.: National Center for State Courts, 2000.

Lawyers

Berk, B. "Preliminary Data on Race and Crack Charging Practices in Los Angeles." *Federal Sentencing Reporter* 6, no. 1 (1993): 36–38.

Dershowitz, Alan. *The Best Defense*. New York: Random House, 1983.

Garner, Bryan A. "Attorney–Client Privilege." In *Black's Law Dictionary*, 1391. New York: Thompson West, 2014.

Kalman, Laura. *Abe Fortas: A Biography*. New Haven, Conn.: Yale University Press, 1990.

Leibowitz, Robert. *The Defender: The Life and Career of Samuel S. Leibowitz, 1893–1933*. Englewood Cliffs, N.J.: Prentice Hall, 1981.

Specialized Courts

Berman, Gregg, and John Feinblatt. *Good Courts: The Case for Problem-Solving Justice*. New York: New Press, 2005.

Curtis, Richard, Brian Ostrom, David Rottman, and Michele Sviridoff. *Dispensing Justice Locally: The Implementation and Effects of the Mid-Town Court*. New York: Harwood Academic, 2000.

Lindquist, Christine, Jennifer Hardison, and Pamela Lattimore. *Reentry Courts Process Final Report*. Washington, D.C.: U.S. Department of Justice, National Institute of Justice, 2003.

Nolan, James. *Drug Courts: In Theory and in Practice*. Social Problems and Social Issues. New York: Routledge, 2002.

Rottman, David B. "Community Courts: Prospects and Limits." *National Institute of Justice Journal* 231 (1996): 46–51.

Substantive Criminal Law

Association of the Bar of the City of New York, Committee of Federal Legislation. *The Law of Presidential Impeachment*. New York: Harper, 1974.

Bagaric, Mirko, and John Morss. "In Search of Coherent Jurisprudence for International Criminal Law: Correlating Universal Human Responsibilities with Universal Human Rights." *Suffolk Transnational Law Review* 29 (2006): 157–206.

Brecher, Edward. "The Harrison Narcotic Act (1914)." In *The Consumers Union Report on Licit and Illicit Drugs, 1972*. Retrieved 5 March 2017, https://bazaarmodel.net/phorum/read.php?1,98.

Brody, David, and James Acker. *Criminal Law*. 3rd ed., Burlington, Mass.: Jones and Bartlett Learning, 2015.

Mohr, James C. *Abortion in America: The Origins and Evolution of National Policy*. New York: Oxford University Press, 1978.

Packer, Herbert. *Ex-Communist Witnesses: Four Studies in Fact Finding*. Stanford, Calif.: Stanford University Press, 1962.

———. *The Limits of the Criminal Sanction*. Stanford, Calif.: Stanford University Press, 1968.

Samaha, Joel. *Criminal Law*. Belmont, Calif.: West/Wadsworth, 1999.

Schmallenger, Frank, and Daniel Hall, with John Dolatowski. *Criminal Law Today*. 4th ed. Upper Saddle River, N.J.: Prentice Hall, 2010.

Supreme Court Cases

Feiner v. New York, 340 U.S. 315 (1951). Accessed 3 January 2017, www.oyez.org/cases/1940-1955/340us315.

Ferguson v. City of Charleston, 532 U.S. 67 (2001). Accessed 3 January 2017, www.oyez.org/cases/2009/99-936.

Florida v. Jardines, 569 U.S. __ (2013). Accessed 3 January 2017, www.oyez.org/cases/2012/11-564.

Ford v. Wainwright, 477 U.S. 399 (1986). Accessed 3 January 2017, https://www.oyez.org/cases/1985/85-5542.

Furman v. Georgia, 408 U.S. 238 (1972). Accessed 14 March 2017, https://supreme.justia.com/cases/federal/us/408/238/case.html.

Gannet Co. v. DePasquale, 443 U.S. 368 (1979). Accessed 4 June 2017, http://caselaw.findlaw.com/us-supreme-court/443/368.html.

Georgia v. Randolph, 547 U.S. 103 (2006). Accessed 17 December 2016, https://www.oyez.org/cases/2005/04-1067.

Gideon v. Wainwright, 372 U.S. 335 (1963). Accessed 12 November 2016, https://supreme.justia.com/cases/federal/us/372/335/case.html.

Trials

Anderson, David. "Gallo Trial, Barely Begun, Ends; 17 Plead Guilty, and 18th Is Freed." *New York Times*, 23 September 1964.

Baker, Peter. *The Breach: Inside the Impeachment and Trial of William Jefferson Clinton*. Englewood Cliffs, N.J.: Prentice Hall, 1972.

Caplan, Lincoln. *The Insanity Defense and the Trial of John W. Hinckley, Jr.* Boston, Mass.: D. R. Godine, 1984.

Cherry, Paul. *The Biker Trials: Bringing Down the Hells Angels*. Toronto, Ont.: ECW, 2005.

Rosenberg, Charles E. *The Trial of the Assassin Guiteau: Psychiatry and the Law in the Gilded Age*. Chicago, Ill.: University of Chicago Press, 1968.

Wrongful Convictions

Borchard, Edwin M. *Convicting the Innocent: Sixty-Five Actual Errors of Criminal Justice*. New Haven: Yale University Press, 1932.

Cortner, Richard C. *A "Scottsboro" Case in Mississippi: The Supreme Court and* Brown v. Mississippi. Jackson: University of Mississippi Press, 1986.

Dwyer, Jim, Peter Neufeld, and Barry Scheck. *Actual Innocence: When Justice Goes Wrong and How to Make It Right.* New York: Signet Book/Penguin Putnam, 2000.

Scheck, Barry, Jim Dwyer, Peter J. Neufeld, and Michael Boatman. *Actual Innocence: Five Days to Execution, and Other Dispatches from the Wrongly Convicted.* New York: Doubleday, 2000.

CORRECTIONS

Correctional Administration

Camp, George, and Camille Camp. *Prison Gangs and Their Extent, Nature, and Impact on the Prisons*. Washington, D.C.: U.S. Government Printing Office, 1985.

Carlson, Peter, and Judith Garrett. *Prison and Jail Administration: Practice and Theory*. Boston, Mass.: Jones & Bartlett, 2008.

Pizarro, Jesenia, and Vanja M. K. Stenus. "Supermax Prisons: Their Rise, Current Practices, and Effect on Inmates." *Prison Journal* 84, no. 2, (June 2004): 248–64.

Corrections—General

Allen, Harry, Edward Latessa, and Bruce Ponder. *Corrections in America: An Introduction.* Upper Saddle River, N.J.: Pearson Higher Education, 2010.

Bentham, Jeremy. *The Works, 4. Panopticon, Constitution, Colonies, Codification*. London: Simpkin, 1843.

Clear, Todd, George Cole, and Michael Reisig. *American Corrections*. Belmont, Calif.: Thomson Higher Education, 2009.

Elias, Norbert. "Norbert Elias and the Civilizing Process." *Theory and Society* 5, no. 2 (1978): 219–28.

Feeley, Malcolm M., and Jonathan Simon. "The New Penology: Notes on the Emerging Strategy of Corrections and Its Implications." *Criminology* 30, no. 4 (1992): 449–74.

Glaser, Daniel. *The Effectiveness of a Prison and Parole System*. Indianapolis, Ind.: Bobbs-Merrill, 1964.

Glaze, Lauren, and Danielle Glaze. *Correctional Populations in the United States*. Washington, D.C.: Bureau of Justice Statistics, 2015.

Jacobs, James. *Statesville: The Penitentiary in Mass Society*. Chicago, Ill.: University of Chicago Press, 1977.

Murton, Thomas, and Joe Hyams. *Accomplices to the Crime: The Arkansas Prison Scandal*. New York: Grove, 1970.

Sheridan, Matthew. "An Exploration of the Personal Experience of 'Prisonization': Utilizing the Concept of Environmental Press and the Introduction of a Concept of Minor Press to Account for Exceptional Circumstances in the Environment." Ed.D. diss., Rutgers University, 1991.

Silberman, Matthew. *A World of Violence: Corrections in America*. Belmont, Calif.: Wadsworth, 1995.

Stohr, Mary, Anthony Walsh, and Craig Hemmens. *Corrections: A Text/Reader*. Belmont, Calif.: Sage, 2008.

History of Corrections

Foucault, Michel. *Discipline and Punish: The Birth of the Prison*. New York: Random House, 1971.

Hinkle, William. *A History of Bridewell Prison, 1553–1700*. Lampeter, Wales: Edwin Mellen, 2006.

Hornblum, Allen. *Acres of Skin: Human Experiments at Holmesburg Prison*. New York: Routledge, 1998.

Inciardi, James A., Alan A. Block, and Lyle A. Hallowell. *Historical Approaches to Crime: Research Strategies and Issues*. Sage Library of Social Research 57. Beverly Hills, Calif.: Sage, 1977.

Lipstadt, Deborah. *Denying the Holocaust: The Growing Assault on Truth and Memory*. New York: Plume, 1993.

Morris, Norval, and David Rothman. *The Oxford History of the Prison*. New York: Oxford University Press, 1995.

Porter, Roy. *Madmen: A Social History of Madhouses, Mad-Doctors and Lunatics*. Stroud, UK: Tempus, 2006.
Sellin, Thorsten. *Slavery and the Penal System*. New York: Elsevier, 1976.
Sevdiren, Oznur. "Some Reflections on the History and Development of Alternatives to Prison." In *Alternatives to Imprisonment in England and Wales, Germany and Turkey, a Comparative Study*, 13–43. Berlin: Springer-Verlag, 2011.

Juvenile Justice

Dryfoos, Joy. *Adolescents at Risk: Prevalence and Prevention*. New York: Oxford University Press, 1990.
Gebo, Erika, and Carolyn Boyes-Watson. *Youth, Crime, and Justice: Learning through Cases*. Lanham, Md.: Rowman & Littlefield, 2018.
Hale, Robert. *A Review of Juvenile Executions in America*. Lewiston, N.Y.: Edwin Mellen, 1997.
Howell, James C. *Juvenile Justice and Youth Violence*. Thousand Oaks, Calif.: Sage, 1997.
Moffitt, Terrie E. "Adolescence-Limited and Life-Course-Persistent Antisocial Behavior: A Developmental Taxonomy." *Psychological Review* 100 (1993): 674–701.
O'Connor, Jennifer M., and Lucinda K. Treat. "Getting Smart about Getting Tough: Juvenile Justice and the Possibility of Progressive Reform." *American Criminal Law Review* 33, no. 12 (1996): 1299–345.
President's Commission on Law Enforcement and the Administration of Justice, *Task Force Report: Juvenile Delinquency and Youth Crime*. Washington, D.C.: U.S. Government Printing Office, 1967.
Prothrow-Stith, Deborah. *Deadly Consequences*. New York: HarperCollins, 1991.
Snyder, Howard N., and Melissa Sickmund. *Juvenile Offenders and Victims: 2006 National Report*. Washington, D.C.: U.S. Department of Justice, Office of Justice Programs, Office of Juvenile Justice and Delinquency Prevention, 2006.
Wolfgang, Marvin, Robert Figlio, and Thorsten Sellin. *Delinquency in a Birth Cohort*. Chicago, Ill.: University of Chicago Press, 1972.

Life on the Inside

Abbott, Jack Henry. *In the Belly of the Beast: Letters from Prison*. New York: Vintage, 1981.
———. *My Return*. Amherst, N.Y.: Prometheus, 1987.
Bennet, James V. *I Chose Prison*. New York: Knopf, 1970.

Clemmer, Donald. *The Prison Community*. Boston, Mass.: Christopher, 1940.

Conover, Ted. *Newjack: Guarding Sing-Sing*. New York: Random House, 2000.

Irwin, John. *The Felon*. Englewood Cliffs, N.J.: Prentice Hall, 1970.

———. *Prisons in Turmoil*. Boston, Mass.: Little, Brown, 1980.

———. *The Warehouse Prison: Disposal of the New Dangerous Class*. New York: Oxford University Press, 2004.

Johnson, Robert, and Hans Toch. *The Pains of Imprisonment*. Prospect Heights, Ill: Waveland, 1982.

Karpis, Alvin. *The Alvin Karpis Story*. New York: Ishi, 1971.

———. *On the Rock*. Oakville, Ont.: Little Brick Schoolhouse, 2008.

Mailer, Norman. *The Executioner's Song*. New York: Little, Brown, 1979.

Ross, Jeffrey, and Stephen Richards. *Convict Criminology*. Belmont, Calif.: Wadsworth, 2003.

Sykes, Gresham. *The Society of Captives*. Princeton, N.J.: Princeton University Press, 1958.

Toch, Hans, and John C. Gibbs. *Living in Prison: The Ecology of Survival*. Washington, D.C.: American Psychological Association, 1992.

Wicker, Tom. *A Time to Die*. New York: Times Books, 1975.

Williams, Stanley Tookie. *Blue Rage, Black Redemption: A Memoir*. New York: Simon & Schuster, 2004.

Zimbardo, Philip. *The Lucifer Effect: Understanding How Good People Turn Evil*. New York: Random House, 2008.

Mass Incarceration

Austin, James, and John Irwin. *It's about Time: America's Imprisonment Binge*. Belmont, Calif.: Wadsworth, 2001.

Garland, David, ed. *Mass Imprisonment: Social Causes and Consequences*. Thousand Oaks, Calif.: Sage, 2001.

Peláez, Vicky. "The Prison Industry in the United States: Big Business or a New Form of Slavery?" *Global Research*, 2016. Retrieved 28 August 2016, http://www.globalresearch.ca.

Simon, Jonathan. *Governing through Crime: How the War on Crime Transformed American Democracy and Created a Culture of Fear*. New York: Oxford University Press, 2007.

Prisoner Families

Christian, Johnna. "Riding the Bus: Barriers to Prison Visitation and Family Management Strategies." *Journal of Contemporary Criminal Justice* 21, no. 1 (2005): 31–48.

Christian, Johnna, and L. W. Kennedy. "Secondary Narratives in the Aftermath of Crime: Defining Family Members' Relationships with Prisoners." *Punishment & Society* 13, no. 4 (2011): 379–402.

Comfort, Megan. *Doing Time Together: Love and Family in the Shadow of the Prison*. Chicago, Ill.: University of Chicago Press, 2009.

Duwe, Grant, and Valerie Clark. "Blessed Be the Social Tie That Binds: The Effects of Prison Visitation on Offender Recidivism." *Criminal Justice Policy Review* 24, no. 3 (2013): 271–96.

Mears, Daniel P., Joshua C. Cochran, Sonja E. Siennick, and William D. Bales. "Prison Visitation and Recidivism." *Justice Quarterly* 29, no. 6 (2012): 888–918.

Probation and Parole

Abadinsky, Howard. *Probation and Parole*. Upper Saddle River, N.J.: Prentice Hall, 1997.

Carney, Louis P. *Probation and Parole: Legal and Social Dimensions*. New York: McGraw-Hill, 1977.

Farole, Donald. *The Harlem Parole Reentry Court Evaluation: Implementation and Preliminary Impacts*. Washington, D.C.: U.S. Department of Justice, Office of Justice Programs, Bureau of Justice Assistance, 2003.

Reform

Byrne, James, and Mary Brewster. "Choosing the Future of American Corrections: Punishment or Reform?" *Federal Probation* 57, no. 4 (1993): 3–11.

Hemmens, Craig, Barbara Belbot, and Katherine Bennett. *Significant Cases in Corrections*. New York: Oxford University Press, 2013.

Johnson, Robert. *Hard Time: Understanding and Reforming the Prison*. Belmont, Calif.: Wadsworth, 1987.

Rehabilitation/Correctional Interventions

Beck, Aaron, John Rush, Brian Shaw, and Gary Emery. *Cognitive Therapy of Depression*. New York: Guilford, 1979.

Boothe, Maude Ballington. *After Prison—What?* New York: Fleming H. Revell, 1905.

Braithwaite, John. *Crime, Shame, and Reintegration*. New York: Cambridge University Press, 1989.

Dishion, Thomas J., and David Andrews. "Preventing Escalation in Problem Behavior with High-Risk Young Adolescents: Immediate and 1-Year Outcomes." *Journal of Consulting and Clinical Psychology* 63, no. 4 (1995): 538–48.

Fakhourya, Walid, and Stefan Priebea. "Deinstitutionalization and Reinstitutionalization: Major Changes in the Provision of Mental Healthcare." *Psychiatry* 6, no. 8 (2007): 313–16.

Feld, Barry C. "A Comparative Analysis of Organisational Structure and Inmate Subcultures in Institutions for Juvenile Offenders." *Crime and Delinquency* 27, no. 2 (1981): 336–63.

Howell, James C. *Preventing and Reducing Juvenile Delinquency: A Comprehensive Framework*. Thousand Oaks, Calif.: Sage, 2003.

Huisinga, David, and Cynthia Jakob-Chien. "The Contemporaneous Co-occurrence of Serious and Violent Juvenile Offending and Other Problem Behaviors." In *Serious and Violent Juvenile Offenders: Risk Factors and Successful Interventions*, ed. R. Loeber and D. P. Farrington, 46–67. Thousand Oaks, Calif.: Sage, 1998.

Kesey, Ken. *One Flew over the Cuckoo's Nest*. New York: Penguin Putnam, 1962.

Mackenzie, Doris, et al. "Boot Camp Prisons and Recidivism in Eight States." *Canadian Journal of Criminology* 3, no. 3 (1995): 327–55.

Martinson, Robert. "What Works: Questions and Answers about Prison Reform." *Public Interest* 35 (1974): 22–54.

Maruna, Shadd. *Making Good: How Ex-Convicts Reform and Rebuild Their Lives*. Washington, D.C.: American Psychological Association, 2001.

Milkman, Harvey, and Kenneth Wanberg. *Cognitive-Behavioral Treatment: A Review and Discussion for Corrections Professionals*. Washington, D.C.: National Institute of Corrections, 2007.

Novaco, Raymond. *Anger Control: The Development and Evaluation of an Experimental Treatment*. Lexington, Mass.: D.C. Health, 1975.

Rush, Benjamin. *Inquiry into the Effects of Ardent Spirits on the Human Mind and Body: With an Account of the Means of Preventing, and of the Remedies for Curing Them*. Boston: James Loring, 1784/1883.

Van Ness, Daniel, and Karen Heetderks Strong. *Restoring Justice*. Cincinnati, Ohio: Anderson, 1997.

Reentry

Hughes, Timothy, and Doris Wilson. *Reentry Trends in the United States*. Washington, D.C.: U.S. Department of Justice, Bureau of Justice Assistance, 2002.

Knollenberg, Laura, and Valerie A. Martin. "Community Reentry following Prison: A Process Evaluation of the Accelerated Community Entry Program." *Federal Probation* 72, no. 2 (2008): 54–60.

Petersilia, Joan. *When Prisoners Come Home: Parole and Prisoner Reentry*. New York: Oxford University Press, 2003.

Tripoli, Stephen J., J. Kim, and B. Kimberly. "Is Employment Associated with Reduced Recidivism? The Complex Relationship between Employment and Crime." *International Journal of Offender Therapy and Comparative Criminology* 54, no. 5 (2010): 706–20.

Visher, Christy A. *Transitions from Prison to Community: Understanding Individual Pathways*. Washington, D.C.: Urban Institute, Justice Policy Center, 2003.

Sentencing and Punishment

Alexander, Michelle. *The New Jim Crow: Mass Incarceration in the Age of Colorblindness*. New York: New Press, 2010.

Andrews, William. *Old Time Punishments*. New York: Dorset, 1991.

Beccaria, Cesare. *An Essay on Crimes and Punishment*. Wellesley, Mass.: Brandon, 2008. (Originally published 1764)

Becker, Gary. "Crime and Punishment: An Economic Approach." *Journal of Political Economy* 76, no. 2 (March–April 1968): 169–217.

———. *The Principles of Morals and Legislation*. New York: Prometheus, 1988.

Beckett, Katherine, and Theodore Sasson. *The Politics of Injustice: Crime and Punishment in America*. Thousand Oaks, Calif.: Sage, 2003.

Blumstein, Alfred. "Sentencing Reforms: Impacts and Implications." *Judicature* 68 (1984): 129.

Brunon-Ernst, Anne. *Beyond Foucault: New Perspectives on Bentham's Panopticon*. New York: Routledge, 2012.

Clear, Todd R., and Natasha A. Frost. *The Punishment Imperative: The Rise and Failure of Mass Incarceration in America*. New York: New York University Press, 2015.

Cohen, Stan. *Folk Devils and Moral Panics: The Creation of the Mods and Rockers*. London: MacGibbon & Kee, 1972.

Crow, Matthew, and William Bales. "Sentencing Guidelines and Focal Concerns: The Effect of Sentencing Policy as a Practical Constraint on Sentencing Decisions." *American Journal of Criminal Justice* 30, no. 2 (2006): 285–304.

Currie, Elliott. *Crime and Punishment in America*. New York: Metropolitan, 1998.

Farley, Lara Geer. "The Adam Walsh Act: The Scarlet Letter of the Twenty-First Century." *Washburn Law Journal* 47 (2008): 471–503.

Foucault, Michel. *Discipline and Punish: The Birth of the Prison*. New York: Random House, 1979.

Friedman, Lawrence. *Crime and Punishment in American History*. New York: Basic Books, 1994.

Garland, David. *The Culture of Control*. Vol. 367. New York: Oxford University Press, 2001.

———. *Punishment and Modern Society: A Study in Social Theory*. Chicago, Ill.: University of Chicago Press, 2012.

Green, David A. *When Children Kill Children: Penal Populism and Political Culture*. New York: Oxford University Press, 2012.

Griffiths, J. Gwyn. *The Divine Verdict: A Study of Divine Judgement in the Ancient Religions*. New York: E. J. Brill, 1991.

Hawthorne, Nathanial. *The Scarlett Letter*. Piscataway, N.J.: Dover, 2009.

Homer. *The Odyssey*. New York: Penguin Putnam, 1996.

King, Anna. "Going inside Crime and Punishment: The Oranges of Anti-rehabilitative Justice." *Journal of Theoretical & Philosophical Criminology* 9, no. 2 (2017): 99.

King, Anna, and Shadd Maruna. "Is a Conservative Just a Liberal Who Has Been Mugged? Exploring the Origins of Punitive Views." *Punishment & Society* 11, no. 2 (2009): 147–69.

Miethe, Terance D., and Hong Lu. *Punishment: A Comparative Historical Perspective*. New York: Cambridge University Press, 2005.

Mitford, Jessica. *Kind and Usual Punishment*. New York: Random House, 1973.

Pratt, John. *Punishment and Civilization: Penal Tolerance and Intolerance in Modern Society*. Thousand Oaks, Calif.: Sage, 2002.

Prettyman, E. Barret. "The Indeterminate Sentence and the Right to Treatment." *American Criminal Law Review* 11 (1972): 7.

Simon, Jonathan. *Poor Discipline*. Chicago, Ill.: University of Chicago Press, 1993.

Tonry, Michael. *Sentencing Matters*. New York: Oxford University Press, 1998.

Von Hirsch, Andrew. *Doing Justice: The Choice of Punishments; Report of the Committee for the Study of Incarceration*. Boston, Mass.: Northeastern University Press, 1976.

Welch, Michael. *Punishment in America: Social Control and the Ironies of Imprisonment*. Thousand Oaks, Calif.: Sage, 1999.

Transportation

Beer, Daniel. *The House of the Dead: Siberian Exile under the Tsars*. New York: Knopf, 2016.
Hughes, Robert. *The Fatal Shores: The Epic of Australia's Founding*. New York: Knopf, 1987.
Kennan, George. *Siberia and the Exile System*. Vol. 2. London: James Osgood, McIlvane, 1891.
Morris, Norval. *Maconochie's Gentlemen: The Story of Norfolk Island and the Roots of Modern Prison Reform*. New York: Oxford University Press, 2002.
Shaw, Alan G. L. *Convicts and the Colonies*. London: Faber and Faber, 1977.

Women and Imprisonment

Bloom, Barbara, Barbara A. Owen, and Stephanie Covington. *Gender-Responsive Strategies: Research, Practice, and Guiding Principles for Women Offenders*. Washington, D.C.: U.S. Department of Justice, National Institute of Corrections, 2003.
Cabeldue, Mollimichelle, Ashley Blackburn, and Janet L. Mullings. "Mental Health among Incarcerated Women: An Examination of Factors Impacting Depression and PTSD Symptomology." *Women & Criminal Justice*, April 2018, 1–21.
Chesney-Lind, Meda. "In Search of Safety: Confronting Inequality in Women's Imprisonment." *Theory in Action* 10, no. 4 (2017): 128–35.
Frost, Natasha A., Judith Greene, and Kevin Pranis. "Hard Hit: The Growth in the Imprisonment of Women, 1977–2004." *New York: Women's Prison Association: Institute on Women and Criminal Justice* 14 (2006).
Morash, Merry, Timothy S. Bynum, and Barbara Koons-Witt. *Women Offenders: Programming Needs and Promising Approaches*. Washington, D.C.: U.S. Department of Justice, Office of Justice Programs, National Institute of Justice, 1998.
Rafter, Nicole. *Partial Justice: Women, Prisons and Social Control*. New York: Routledge, 2017.

About the Authors

Matthew J. Sheridan, Ed.D., has more than 35 years of progressively responsible experience in the criminal justice field as both practitioner and academic. A convict criminologist, he is a frequent presenter of papers on corrections and criminology issues and a lecturer at New Jersey colleges and universities, professional, and other interested organizations. He is a member of the Criminal Justice faculty at Georgian Court University and the coordinator of internships. His core areas of expertise include correctional and parole operations, correctional administration, juvenile justice, correctional education, and the courts. He is recognized for criminal justice management, including institutions, community residential, day treatment, and private organizations for effective responses to need. He is a private consultant for improving institutional operational proficiency and for compliance with state and federal standards. He conducts reviews of criminal justice training program curricula.

Raymond R. Rainville, Ph.D. (1943–2018), had 35 years of experience with government administration and higher education, including Saint Peter's University, the College of New Jersey, Kean University, Brookdale Community College, and St. John's University. His core areas included history and philosophy of corrections; criminology; community-based corrections; probation and parole; juvenile delinquency; child protection agencies and the law; drugs, society, and behavior; comparative criminal justice; judicial process; introduction to criminal justice; and others. He was a member of Alpha Phi Sigma, the Criminal Justice National Honor Society, and past president of the New Jersey Association of Criminal Justice Educators.

Anna King, Ph.D., began her career in criminal justice working in corrections. She holds degrees in psychology (Clark University), criminal justice (University of Albany), and criminology (University of Cambridge). She worked at Keele University and Rutgers University before taking on her current position as associate professor and chair at Georgian Court University. She has been an H. F. Guggenheim Fellow, a Gates Cambridge Scholar, and a Ruth L. Kirschstein National Research Service Award Fellow. Her research examines the relationship between empirical criminology and social reform, the subjective experience of punishment, issues related to gender and crime, and the psychology of punitiveness. Her current work explores the impact of supportive relationships and education on female criminality and innovative partnerships with mental health practitioners in American policing. Her work has appeared in various academic peer-reviewed publications, institutional research reports, and books.

Brian L. Royster, Ed.D., is a graduate of Essex County College, having obtained an associate in science (A.S.) in physical education in 1993 and an A.S. in social science in 1994. He went on to attend Montclair State University and obtained a B.A. in sociology in 1997. He also received a master of arts in education (M.Ed.) in 1998, an educational specialists degree (Ed.S.) in administration and supervision in 2000, and a doctoral degree (Ed.D.) in education leadership management and policy in 2007. He also received an M.S. in criminal justice in 2009 from New Jersey City University. He is a retired 25-year veteran of the New Jersey State Police and a graduate of the FBI National Academy, 214th session, and the FBI Law Enforcement Executive Development Association (LEEDA) Command Institute for Law Enforcement Executives. He served in the U.S. Army Reserves and was honorably discharged in 1987. He is a certified professional mediator and a certified crisis negotiator. He has been an adjunct professor at Essex County College since 1999, an adjunct professor at New Jersey City University from 2009 to 2011, and an adjunct/assistant professor at Saint Peter's College since 2001.

Giuseppe M. Fazari, Ph.D., is an instructor in the Criminal Justice Department at Seton Hall University, where he was also an assistant dean of continuing education and professional studies. He was a court executive and chief administrative officer for the Superior Court of New Jersey, is on the faculty for the National Center for State Courts, and was an international consultant for the Federal Judiciary and National Industrial Court of Nigeria. He was a lead developer for the National Association for Court Management's Core Competencies for Court Administrators and is published in a variety of professional journals. He was the writer and director of the award-winning feature documentary *Why They Kill*, distributed by the Films Media Group and based on the book by the Pulitzer Prize–winning author Richard Rhodes. He earned his Ph.D. in higher education administration from Seton Hall University, where he was also granted a master's in public administration and a B.A. in criminal justice. He is a fellow of the Institute for Court Management, received the Award of Merit for Applied Research, and is a past president of the New Jersey Association of Criminal Justice Educators.

www.ingramcontent.com/pod-product-compliance
Ingram Content Group UK Ltd.
Pitfield, Milton Keynes, MK11 3LW, UK
UKHW041129071026
15587UKWH00009B/298

9 781538 111406